Third Edition
AMERICAN POLITICS
CHANGING EXPECTATIONS

Third Edition

AMERICAN POLITICS
CHANGING EXPECTATIONS

RONALD E. PYNN
University of North Dakota

Brooks/Cole Publishing Company
Monterey, California

Brooks/Cole Publishing Company
A Division of Wadsworth, Inc.

Printed in the United States of America
10 9 8 7 6 5 4 3 2 1

Library of Congress Cataloging-in Publication Data

Pynn, Ronald E.
  American politics.

  Bibliography: p.
  Includes index.
  1. United States—Politics and government.
I. Title.
JK274.P76 1987   320.973   86-32662
ISBN 0-534-07590-8

Sponsoring Editor: *Cynthia C. Stormer*
Editorial Assistant: *Maria Rosillo Alsadi*
Production Editor: *Penelope Sky*
Production Assistant: *Dorothy Bell*
Manuscript Editor: *Charles Hibbard*
Permissions Editor: *Carline Haga*
Interior and Cover Design: *Katherine Minerva*
Cover Photo: *Bill Binzen/Fran Heyl Associates*
Art Coordinator: *Lisa Torri*
Interior Illustration: *Precision Graphics*
Photo Editor: *Judy K. Blamer*
Photo Researcher: *Roberta Guerette/Omni Photo Communications*
Typesetting: *Allservice Phototypesetting Company, Phoenix, Arizona*
Cover Printing: *Phoenix Color Corporation, Long Island City, New York*
Printing and Binding: *R.R. Donnelley & Sons Company, Harrisonburg, Virginia*

Preface

With the bicentennial of the Constitution in 1987 we celebrate two hundred years of continuous government under the same basic principles. We celebrate the Constitution not only for its impressive history but also because it established principles, behaviors, and institutions that for two hundred years have symbolized the United States and that are still at work.

The nation changed a great deal in the eleven years between the beginning of the American Revolution and the Constitutional Convention in the summer of 1787. Another eleven years have passed between my beginning work on the first edition of *American Politics: Changing Expectations* and the publication of this third edition, and during this time America has again changed greatly. In 1976 we were still struggling with the effects of the Vietnam War, Watergate, and scandals in Congress. In the years immediately following, an outsider from Georgia was elected president, the OPEC oil embargo and inflation played havoc with the U.S. economy, and 52 Americans were taken hostage in Iran. In 1980 Ronald Reagan became president, promising to reduce the government, restore prosperity, and act as a global peace-keeper. Still, bewildering events continued to occur, as the federal deficit reached $200 billion a year and Americans became victimized by international terrorism.

Now, at the bicentennial of our Constitution, our expectations of government are changing once again, with a resurgence of confidence and optimism. Congress is making serious efforts to control and even eliminate the annual deficit. Public opinion has shifted toward approving a leaner role for government. Like the founding fathers in 1787, Americans today sense the opportunity for renewing their faith in their government and for shaping the course of politics for decades to come.

The Text: An Overview

The first edition of *American Politics: Changing Expectations* was written while the country remained in the throes of Vietnam and Watergate, struggling to understand the changes in its political system. The second edition came out just after Ronald Reagan was elected president. Change was evident in the course of events, if not yet in their magnitude. Reagan proposed a new political agenda, promising less government and greater prosperity. Now in the third edition I examine the altered expectations generated by the Reagan administration in relation to the foregoing decades of turmoil. The text is thus thematic even as it follows a traditional topical outline.

Since this book is intended for an introductory course in American government, it provides basic information as well as analysis and interpretation. Chapter 1 introduces the theme of changing expectations. Chapters 2 and 3 describe the Constitution and the federal system, the historical foundations of American politics. Chapters 4 and 5 are about individual liberties and equality, the two principles that are central to understanding how ideals and reality combine to produce policy. Chapters 6 and 7 consider public opinion and interest groups as vital parts of the political process. Chapter 8 is about the political parties as systems in themselves; in Chapter 9 we consider their role in the electoral process and in changing voting patterns. Chapters 10, 11, 12, and 13 survey the basic institutions of government: the presidency, the bureaucracy, Congress, and the courts. In the final chapter we look ahead and anticipate what changing expectations mean for our system as a whole.

Special Features and Study Aids

To sharpen the focus on change, to make basic concepts and issues clear, and to help bring American government alive in familiar terms, each chapter contains a number of special elements. These include:

- a running glossary of key terms, placed in the margin for easy access
- biographical sketches of important political figures
- a summary of the main points covered in the chapter
- a list of research projects that would enhance the students' understanding
- an annotated bibliography

Throughout the book, additional special features emphasize various topics discussed in the text:

- *Fact files* contain basic tabular data.
- *Public policy essays* analyze such subjects as revenue sharing, social welfare, and national security.
- *Changing consensus* features highlight particular issues and events that show the impact of consensus on real policies.
- *Practicing politics* provide information for the active, involved citizen on such topics as how juries are selected, where information about members of Congress may be found, and how to obtain a passport.
- *Drawings, photographs, and cartoons* are used throughout to illustrate and clarify events, issues, and concepts.

At the end of the book are

- a *glossary* of all the key terms in the text, and
- annotated versions of the *Declaration of Independence* and the *Constitution*, the two major documents of American politics.

In addition to the book itself are other aids to teaching and learning, the *Instructor's Manual* and a student *Study Guide*, both by Murray Fishel of Kent State University. The instructor's manual contains chapter summaries, teaching objectives, discussion questions, quiz items, and sources for further reading. The study guide also provides chapter summaries and annotated reading lists, as well as learning objectives, definitions of key terms, review outlines, and self-review tests.

With Thanks

Writing a textbook is never a solitary endeavor. I am indebted to numerous individuals who contributed greatly to this revision, from the production people at Brooks/Cole who labored to put words into print to the classroom instructors who sought to interpret those words to their students.

Several reviewers, many of whom adopted the last edition, made valuable comments on the draft and suggested possible revisions. They are: Larry Gerston, San Jose State University; Lawrence E. Hough, East Carolina University; George Largent, Northeastern Oklahoma A & M College; Elliot E. Slotnick, Ohio State University.

Finally, my wife Scharlene, and my children, Suzanne, Stephen, and Karen, are more insistent than ever that they see their names in print. After all, it is they who bore the brunt of these revisions. Their care and understanding are acknowledged in ways unspoken.

Ronald E. Pynn

Contents

CHAPTER EIGHT
Political Parties   281

CHAPTER NINE
The Changing Voter and the Electoral Process   314

CHAPTER FOURTEEN
The Future of American Politics 573

The Anguish of Change

Political expectations in America are changing. Change is nothing new to American politics, and there always has been a dynamic excitement associated with it. The recent past, however, illustrates both the speed and depth of change within the American political system. It is a change that offers both hope and fear to our political expectations: hope that the future will be brighter and more secure than the past but also fear that we may be unable to control events with the present arrangements of our governing institutions.

The political world of New Deal era politics has crumbled. In the wake of the Great Depression of 1929, President Franklin D. Roosevelt's New Deal promoted industrial growth and economic recovery through government involvement. New economic programs were passed that drew upon tax dollars to stimulate business and provide personal protection for incomes. In 1935 the Social Security Act was passed to provide retirement income for the elderly. **Keynesian economics** became the theory of the day: government would do the spending to support the economy if private enterprise would not or could not.

Keynesian Economics: *the theory that government spending should be used to regulate the economy.*

1

As a result government grew. The federal budget tripled between 1930 and 1940 and then expanded by another factor of four in the following decade. The expanding budget paralleled economic expansion, new jobs, and World War II. The political process changed too. Party loyalties realigned into a new Democratic majority supporting the presidency of Franklin Roosevelt, and Democrats also controlled Congress. Roosevelt, elected to an unprecedented fourth term in 1944, became the model for a strong, activist president utilizing the resources of the federal government to propel America forward at home and abroad.

By the 1960s, however, American politics were in a state of disarray. The coalition fashioned by Roosevelt was disintegrating, and the power of the presidency was under attack. Keynesian economics was not working. Government had grown in size and cost, but Americans did not feel better for it. In fact, the people felt that they were worse off than at any time in their history.

Liberal attitudes on social issues were giving way to a new conservative respectability; cynicism and distrust of politics and political leaders were also on the rise. Three events from the 1960s and 1970s bring into focus the change that was taking place in our political process: the Great Society program, the Vietnam War, and Watergate.

By the mid-1980s the extent to which these occurrences had changed the political process became clear. A conservative Republican, Ronald Reagan, won the presidency with landslide victories over Democratic challengers, and the U.S. Senate had a Republican majority for the first time in thirty years. The Reagan movement rejected the New Deal approach to politics. Reagan has pressed for large reductions in appropriations for social welfare programs and dismantled part of the federal government, eliminating some of its regulatory authority and "privatizing" (selling to private enterprise) a number of other government functions. The people in the Reagan administration see the federal government and federal spending as major causes of our domestic problems. They believe that the keys to a healthy and prosperous economy are private industry and voluntary assistance, not increased government. With the Reagan years, a new mood of conservatism and faith in America has emerged.

Changing Expectations: The Recent Past

Decades of Turmoil

The tumultuous 1960s and 1970s precipitated the decline of post-World War II politics. The experience of these decades has helped us understand better the extent to which the political process has changed since World War II. As Theodore H. White observed, "The postwar world was dead and awaited burial." Let us make a brief survey of the three events that provide the transition to the politics of the present.

The memory of the Vietnam War continues to influence American politics and to touch the conscience of the people.

The Great Society began as a bold program in social engineering. President Johnson announced a war on poverty, and Congress passed the first major civil rights legislation in nearly a hundred years. Medicare was added to the social security system, and food stamps were provided for the unemployed and disadvantaged. Housing and urban mass transit were to be revitalized. In short, as President Johnson described the Great Society, it "rests on abundance and liberty for all. It demands an end to poverty and racial injustice—to which we are totally committed."

Whether because of the escalation of the Vietnam War or poor planning or simple shortsightedness, the Great Society failed to meet expectations. Programs were badly designed; frequently they were funded by federal grants-in-aid to states and local governments with specific proj-

During the Nixon administration the Watergate scandal was exposed through the efforts of the Senate Select Committee on Presidential Campaign Activities, chaired by Sam Ervin of North Carolina.

ects in mind (categorical grants) but were not coordinated with other programs. Legislative victory appeared to be more important than administrative implementation. More critically, the Great Society raised the hopes of millions of Americans with the pledge of racial justice, jobs for the unemployed, medical care for the elderly, housing for slum dwellers, and the eradication of poverty. It created a climate of rising expectations but left promises unfulfilled. It represented a departure from the New Deal, which distributed money and provided regulation—relatively easily achievable goals within the framework of governmental administrations. But the Great Society required the fundamental reallocation of resources and values. It asked for social change and required governmental social engineering to implement it.

The second transitional event was the Vietnam War. What began in the 1950s and early 1960s as technical assistance to the South Vietnamese government became, under Lyndon Johnson, full-scale combat by U.S. forces in support of the South Vietnamese. Vietnam became for America an unwanted, undeclared, and socially devastating war. The Cold War was fading, and the claim that containment of communism in Asia was critical seemed unconvincing. For many Americans, the Vietnam War was a civil war and not a conflict in which America's national interest was at stake.

The war was divisive. Students and other Americans demonstrated in opposition to it, and opinion polarized between "doves" and "hawks." The Cambodian bombing touched off a wave of new and violent social protest. At Kent State University, four students were killed by National Guardsmen attempting to quell the protests. The Democratic party split over the war.

The war in Vietnam took a terrible toll. It sapped the resources of the Great Society, leaving hopes and promises unfulfilled. It created a credibility gap between government and its citizens. Support for the war and for government was ebbing. It remained a presidential war: Congress was ignored, even lied to. Critics claimed that presidential power had been imperialized and that the personality and prestige of the president had become more important than national policy.

The third event was Watergate. Originally labeled a "third-rate burglary," the illegal break-ins, "dirty tricks," cover-up, and conspiracy to obstruct justice we call Watergate eventually touched America to the roots of its constitutional and democratic processes. As the revelations implicated the White House and finally the president himself, questions were raised about the unprecedented growth of presidential power and the constitutional mechanism for checking that power. The "dirty tricks," illegal campaign contributions, and abandonment of party politics raised questions regarding the future of political parties.

The American people's confidence in their public officials and political system was at an all-time low. The mood on August 9, 1974, when Richard Nixon stepped down from the presidency, was one of gloom. The president himself had participated in the cover-up and conspired to obstruct justice. The office of the presidency had been disgraced.

The Watergate affair severely tested the political system. With the resignation of Richard Nixon, Gerald Ford became president, pledging to "put Watergate behind us." The people heaved a sigh of relief. The nation seemed safe, but the costs had been high and the presidency was in disrepute. Americans had grown cynical toward their government. Political parties were crumbling, and the electoral process was facing the challenge of reform in the wake of "dirty tricks" and rising costs. For two years the nation had been in the grip of Watergate; now its political leaders would seek to govern again. Gerald Ford pardoned Richard Nixon for his part in Watergate. Jimmy Carter came to the presidency in 1976 pledging to restore faith in government and to get on with the business of governing the nation.

Recovery and Change

It may be too early to label the 1980 election a watershed in political experience, but in one dimension Ronald Reagan's victory in 1980 was more than a personal triumph over Jimmy Carter at the polls. With the Reagan victories in 1980 and 1984 have come a growing conservative mood in America and a restored sense of faith and trust in America's political future. The result of the three events discussed above was a general dissatisfaction with government and its programs. Ronald Reagan clearly seized on this issue, promising to "get government off the backs of the people." The American people have responded to that message. The conservatives' concern for the economy and national defense became central issues for the political agenda.

The Reagan Experiment   The Reagan experiment found clear expression in the budgets the president proposed to Congress. Here were detailed several radical changes in policy. President Reagan has spoken out often on the need to depart dramatically from the policies of the recent past. His budgetary priorities reflect the bases of the Reagan experiment: reduced federal spending and taxation, increased defense spending, and a greater reliance on the private sector to stimulate the economy.

The heart of the Reagan formula is a reduced role for the federal government. Reagan is convinced that the national government must limit its programs and tax liabilities. He has called for a great reduction in federal obligations for education, programs for the unemployed and underemployed, health care, and social welfare, and has asked states and localities to assume more of the funding for such programs. His 1982 budget called for cuts of $48 billion; the 1983 budget asked for another $43 billion in cuts in nondefense entitlement and social programs. States, communities, and volunteer agencies were directed to shoulder more of the burden in caring for society's nonproductive members, and herein is the basis for Reagan's **new federalism.** He asserts that the federal government cannot underwrite a safety net of social and economic security for its citizens, and that the primary mission of the federal government is to secure peace and security at home and abroad.

The second great basis of the Reagan experiment is a militarily strong America. Americans must commit to vast increases in defense spending if the country wishes to face the Soviets in world diplomacy. Reagan has stressed time and again that the United States is losing ground in the

New Federalism:
Ronald Reagan's proposal of returning social and economic programs from the federal government to the states to run.

arms race to the Soviets, who are intent on world domination. The peace and security of the free world, indeed the national security of the United States, he says, depend on an alert and militarily strong America. Reagan's 1982 budget called for a 30 percent increase in defense spending, whereas in 1981 Jimmy Carter had proposed a 13 percent increase. Reagan's 1984 request was for $63 billion more than in 1982, an increase of $100 billion in four years

The final basis of the Reagan experiment is an economic recovery program premised on **supply-side economics,** commonly called **Reaganomics.** By restricting the growth of the federal budget and limiting federal spending, the administration argues, the federal government could return taxes to businesses and taxpayers. The money once destined for the federal government would then be put into the hands of private persons—businesspeople and consumers. This shift would stimulate the private sector of the economy to work harder, save money, and invest. In this manner inflation would be curbed, jobs created, and productivity increased. Supply-side economics holds that incentives to the private sector of the economy such as tax cuts, savings incentives, investment credits, and deregulation of industry stimulate economic enterprise, thereby enlarging the national wealth for all to enjoy.

Changing Attitudes Evidence of changing expectations accompanying the Reagan years also has become clear. The cynicism and distrust of politics dating from the turmoil of the 1960s and 1970s have given way to renewed waves of hope and optimism. The Reagan years have also produced a growing conservative philosophy, especially with college-age citizens. Both of these trends in the 1980s reverse previous attitudes.

In response to the events of the 1960s and 1970s a sense of powerlessness and cynicism swept across the political system. The trend toward cynicism and mistrust continued to grow through the 1970s, due in large part to the unpopularity of America's continued involvement in Vietnam. The Watergate revelations and political scandals also contributed to the trend. By the late 1970s about two-thirds of the American people claimed not to be able to trust government. An equally dramatic rise on the question of tax waste was also evident, likely part of the broader issue of economic instability and rising inflation. The American citizen had come to question the political process and along with it the integrity of public officials and their concern for the public interest.

Figure 1.1 shows the remarkable turnaround in public trust that occurred in the 1980s with the Reagan administration. In each of the indicators identified there has been a decline in cynical or distrustful attitudes toward government. In response to questions such as whether government wastes a lot of the money we pay in taxes, how much of the time government can be trusted to do what is right, and whether government is run for a few big interests or the benefit of all, the decline is most dramatic, with a 25 percent drop in cynical attitudes.

Supply-side Economics: *the economic theory, adopted by Ronald Reagan, that holds that the best way to stimulate economic growth is by enhancing supply, not demand.*

Reaganomics: *the term applied to Reagan's economic philosophy of reduced federal spending and tax cuts to enhance private economic activity.*

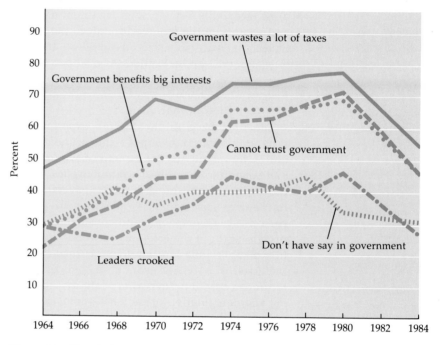

Figure 1.1   Trends in trust in government

However, a word of caution is in order. Despite the greater optimism of the American people in the 1980s, the fact is that nearly half of them remain distrustful or cynical of American politics. The levels of cynicism remain high—too high. The damage from the decades of turmoil cannot be undone in a few short years.

The other trend during the Reagan years is a growing conservatism in the population, especially among college-age youth, who will be involved in the political process for a long time to come. There have been remarkable increases in Republican party identifiers among voters aged 18 to 24—approximately a 15 percent increase over the twenty-year period from 1965 to 1985. Looking specifically at ideology, more college-age youth are willing to call themselves conservative. Figure 1.2 illustrates the change in political ideology among college students over a fifteen-year period of time.

The most dramatic evidence of conservative attitude changes, however, can be witnessed in college students' views on several issues during the period 1970–1985. Table 1.1 chronicles the changes in social attitudes among college students during this time. On almost every social issue reported, the frequency of conservative responses increased. While the conservative movement was more dramatic in some issues than in others, the march to the right is unmistakable across the spectrum of concerns.

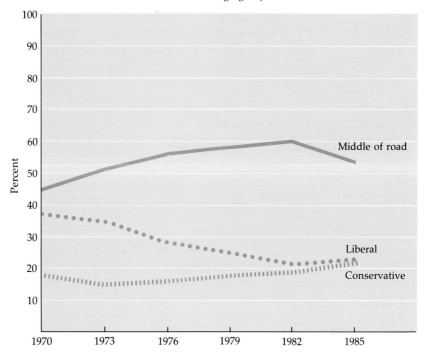

Figure 1.2   Political ideology of college students

Consequently, whether we look at social issues, political ideology, or partisanship, there is considerable evidence of change among college students. Add to this the new wave of optimism and trust in govern-

TABLE 1.1   Attitudes of college freshmen on selected social issues, 1970-1985 (%)

Agree strongly or somewhat	*1970*	*1976*	*1980*	*1985*
Abortions should be legal.	83	—	54	62
Marijuana should be legal.	38	49	39	23
Death penalty should be abolished.	56	—	35	24
There is too much concern in courts for rights of criminals.	52	60	66	—
Government is not doing enough to protect consumers.	—	74	75	57
Government should do more to discourage energy consumption.	—	80	83	72
Wealthy should pay larger share of taxes than they do now.	—	76	70	72
Women should receive the same salary and opportunities for advancement as men in comparable positions.	81	92	93	92

SOURCE: "What's Big on Campus," *Public Opinion Magazine,* August/September 1985, p. 52. Data for 1985 from American Council on Education and University of California, Los Angeles, 1985 Survey of College Freshmen.

ment and one must conclude that the environment and expectations of the present political era are much different from those of the 1960s and 1970s. The nature of the Reagan administration is itself good evidence of the change.

The Agenda for Change

As we have seen, expectations regarding politics were much changed as a result of the Great Society, the Vietnam War, Watergate, and most recently Reagan's election to the presidency. We must understand, however, that the agenda for these changed expectations was fashioned by the thrust of social policy in America over several decades and most recently since the New Deal.

We have witnessed throughout the twentieth century the increased activity of government in social and economic policies. The public sector of American life has added new responsibilities in response to demands as American life has changed.

Entitlement Programs: *programs that guarantee financial benefits to individuals by virtue of their age, income, or employment status.*

Much of the federal budget is designed to provide "guarantees" to citizens. These guarantees are **entitlement programs** that guarantee financial benefits to individuals by virtue of their age, income, or employment status. The most famous of such programs are social security, Medicare, and federal employment retirement. But they also include such social programs as food stamps, Aid to Families with Dependent Children (AFDC), and unemployment compensation. In the 1984 budget such

Population growth and mobility changed the American landscape.

TABLE 1.2   Population of the United States (in millions)

	1790	1820	1860	1900	1950	1960	1970	1980
Total population	4	9.5	31	76	151	180	204	226.5
Urban	0.2	0.7	6.2	30	97	126	149	167
Rural	3.7	9	25	46	54.5	54	54	59.5
White	3.2	8	27	67	135	159	179	188
Nonwhite	NA	2	4.5	9	16	20.5	25	38.5
Under 20			16	34	51	69	67.5	72
20–64			13.5	39	88	94.5	117.5	129
65–over		0.5	1.5	3	12	16.5	20	25.5
Male	NA	5	16	39	75	89	100	110
Female	NA	5	15	37	76	91	104	116.5
In school			65	17	28.5	42	51.5	58.5
In college			0.05	0.25	2	3.5	8	11.6

SOURCE: *Historical Statistics of the United States: Colonial Times to 1970*; 1980 data are from *Statistical Abstract*, 1981, Bureau of the Census.

guarantees amounted to over 40 percent of all expenditures—$362 billion. Government has become responsible for cushioning the impact of change—both intended and unintended. The net result is that governmental policy now affects every citizen in very real and personal ways.

Changes in Population

By 1900 America was no longer a rural nation. More citizens had come to live in metropolitan cities than on farms or in rural towns. This trend has continued, until today three out of four Americans live in an urban environment.

Not only has our population grown, but the composition of the population has changed internally (see Table 1.2). There have been four recent shifts in population that have great consequence in American politics. These are population changes according to age, race, ethnic background, and geography.

Age   In the years after World War II, half of America's population was under 30. The veterans had returned home and were settling down to jobs and families. The result was the well-noted post–World War II "baby boom" that produced an accelerated growth of population. A record number of children, 4.3 million, were born in 1957. Since that time, however, the number of births has declined annually. This has two important consequences.

Zero Population Growth: *the demographic situation in which the birth rate plus immigration equals the death rate plus emigration; thus there is no net gain in population.*

First, we are nearing **zero population growth,** the condition in which the birth rate plus immigration equals the death rate plus emigration. The nation continues to experience slight growth owing to increased longevity and immigration exceeding emigration.

Second, the population trend represents the "graying of America" as more and more of the population falls in the over-65 age category. These are citizens who are past their prime income-earning years and for whom

Fact File
A Population Profile of the States

	Population Total (millions)	Urban	Age 18-24	Age 65+	Median age	Racial composition White	Racial composition Black	Racial composition Hispanic	Employment White-collar	Employment Blue-collar
Alabama	3.9	60.0	13.2	11.3	29.2	73.8	25.6	.9	42.5	41.4
Alaska	.4	64.5	15.0	3.0	26.0	77.0	3.4	2.3	58.4	27.5
Arizona	2.7	83.8	13.6	11.3	29.2	82.4	2.8	16.2	57.8	27.6
Arkansas	2.3	51.6	12.2	13.6	30.6	82.7	16.3	.8	42.8	37.5
California	23.7	91.3	13.7	10.2	29.9	76.2	7.7	19.2	58.1	27.5
Colorado	2.9	80.6	14.5	8.5	28.6	89.0	3.5	11.7	57.9	26.9
Connecticut	3.1	78.8	12.4	11.7	32.0	90.1	7.0	4.0	58.4	29.6
Delaware	.6	70.7	14.1	9.9	29.7	82.0	16.1	1.7	54.2	29.6
D.C.	.6	100.0	15.2	11.6	31.0	27.0	70.3	2.8	66.6	16.1
Florida	9.7	84.3	11.7	17.3	34.7	84.0	13.8	8.8	52.5	29.8
Georgia	5.5	62.3	13.4	9.5	28.6	72.3	26.8	1.1	51.0	33.8
Hawaii	1.0	86.5	14.7	7.9	28.3	33.1	1.8	7.4	54.9	23.6
Idaho	.9	54.0	13.0	10.0	27.5	95.4	.3	3.9	47.8	31.9
Illinois	11.4	83.0	13.2	11.0	29.9	80.8	14.7	5.6	52.6	32.4
Indiana	5.5	64.2	13.4	10.7	29.2	91.1	7.6	1.6	43.6	38.6
Iowa	2.9	58.6	13.3	13.3	30.0	97.4	1.4	.9	45.6	30.3
Kansas	2.4	66.7	13.8	12.9	30.1	91.7	5.3	2.7	50.4	29.0
Kentucky	3.7	50.8	13.4	11.2	29.1	92.3	7.1	.7	44.0	35.4
Louisiana	4.2	68.6	14.2	9.6	27.3	69.3	29.4	2.4	50.2	33.7
Maine	1.1	47.5	12.5	12.5	30.4	98.7	.3	.4	44.7	39.6
Maryland	4.2	80.3	13.1	9.4	30.3	74.9	22.7	1.5	61.1	25.5
Massachusetts	5.7	83.8	13.7	12.7	31.1	93.5	3.9	2.5	55.1	30.6
Michigan	9.3	70.7	13.6	9.9	28.8	85.0	12.9	1.8	49.6	34.5
Minnesota	4.1	66.8	13.7	11.8	29.2	96.6	1.3	.8	50.6	26.3
Mississippi	2.5	47.3	13.4	11.5	27.6	64.1	35.2	1.0	44.1	39.1

| | Population | | Age | | Median age | Racial composition | | | Employment | |
	Total (millions)	Urban	18-24	65+		White	Black	Hispanic	White-collar	Blue-collar
Missouri	4.9	68.1	12.9	13.4	30.8	88.4	10.5	1.1	51.1	30.5
Montana	.8	52.9	13.2	10.8	29.0	94.0	.2	1.3	45.9	26.8
Nebraska	1.6	62.7	13.4	13.1	29.7	95.0	3.1	1.8	45.9	27.9
Nevada	.8	85.3	13.1	8.3	30.2	87.5	6.4	6.8	48.7	22.3
New Hampshire	.9	52.2	13.1	11.2	30.1	98.8	.4	.7	53.9	32.3
New Jersey	7.4	89.0	11.8	11.7	32.2	83.2	12.6	6.7	57.8	29.5
New Mexico	1.3	72.2	13.7	8.9	27.3	75.1	1.8	36.6	54.6	27.6
New York	17.6	84.6	12.3	12.3	31.8	79.5	13.7	9.5	57.6	26.8
North Carolina	5.9	48.0	14.0	10.2	29.6	75.8	22.4	1.0	45.8	39.5
North Dakota	.7	48.8	14.9	12.3	28.3	95.7	.4	.6	43.5	24.0
Ohio	10.8	73.3	13.1	10.8	29.9	88.9	10.0	1.1	50.1	34.5
Oklahoma	3.0	67.3	13.3	12.4	30.1	85.9	6.8	1.9	51.5	31.1
Oregon	2.6	67.9	12.5	11.5	30.2	94.6	1.4	2.5	54.1	30.5
Pennsylvania	11.9	69.3	12.7	12.9	32.1	89.8	8.8	1.3	50.0	35.7
Rhode Island	.9	87.0	13.6	13.4	31.7	94.6	2.9	2.1	48.7	38.0
South Carolina	3.1	54.1	14.3	9.2	28.0	68.8	30.4	1.0	45.4	39.0
South Dakota	.7	46.4	13.8	13.2	28.8	92.6	.3	.6	44.1	23.9
Tennessee	4.6	60.4	13.1	11.3	30.1	83.5	15.8	.7	45.4	39.2
Texas	14.2	79.6	14.0	9.6	28.0	78.7	12.0	21.0	51.7	33.0
Utah	1.5	84.4	14.8	7.5	24.2	94.7	.6	4.1	55.3	31.3
Vermont	.5	33.8	13.9	11.4	29.4	99.0	.2	.6	49.3	30.8
Virginia	5.3	66.0	13.9	9.4	29.8	79.1	18.9	1.5	55.3	30.7
Washington	4.1	73.6	13.4	10.4	29.8	91.5	2.6	2.9	54.8	29.9
West Virginia	2.0	36.2	12.5	12.2	30.4	96.2	3.3	.7	41.2	44.5
Wisconsin	4.7	64.2	13.7	12.0	29.4	94.4	3.9	1.3	46.4	33.4
Wyoming	.5	62.8	14.6	7.9	27.8	95.1	.7	5.1	46.4	33.7

SOURCE: U.S. Bureau of the Census, *Statistical Abstract*, Washington, D.C.: U.S. Government Printing Office, 1981; Bureau of Labor Statistics, *Geographic Profile of Employment and Unemployment*, 1980.

income maintenance is a major concern. In 1984 there were 28 million Americans over 65, all eligible for social security benefits.

The cost in 1984 for social security was $240 billion. Workers and employers are taxed to maintain that fund. There are three workers for every retired person. But by 2030 it has been predicted that 20 percent of the entire population will be 65 or older—65 million persons. That will give America a ratio of only two workers for every social security recipient. And with increased life expectancy, this will place an enormous burden on the solvency of the Social Security Trust Fund. Hence supporting the elderly into the twenty-first century is a critical issue at this juncture of American politics.

Black Americans   Black Americans constitute 12.1 percent of the total population. They constitute 30 percent or more of the seven largest cities in America. Sixty percent of the population of metropolitan central cities is black, often concentrated in ghettos.

Blacks have been the subject of historic discrimination in the United States. Because residence patterns have been tied to employment, blacks moved from the South to the North and Midwest in search of industrial employment. They were given the lowest-paying jobs, hence forced to live in the poorest areas of the city. This pattern, though diminished, continues. Inner cities are impoverished, crime-ridden, and predominately black.

A related problem for black Americans is the male-less household. In 1984, 43 percent of black households were headed by the female, almost double the number for whites. With worsening economic times, jobs and families become more difficult to support. Hence many black males abandon families in search of work elsewhere or to increase family income through welfare assistance. This is likely to be a significant problem for the remainder of the century, with half the black population being 25 years old or younger.

Political participation for blacks traditionally has been lower than for whites. Blacks hold the potential, however, for significant political power in several states and many cities. Continued efforts are being made by black leaders to register black people and get them to the polls. Approval for the extension of the 1965 Voting Rights Act is hailed as a victory for black groups in their continuing effort to increase the political influence of black Americans.

Hispanic Americans   The fastest growing ethnic group in America are Hispanic Americans. According to the 1980 census, the Hispanic population grew 61 percent during the 1970s; by 1985 it had reached 17 million persons. The rapid growth is attributed to a combination of immigration and a high fertility rate. The single largest group of Hispanics are of Mexican origin (60 percent), followed by Puerto Ricans (14 percent), and then Cubans (5.5 percent). If this rate of growth continues through the twentieth century, persons of Spanish origin (that is how the Census

In a democracy the most basic of rights is the right to vote.

Hispanic Americans belong to the fastest-growing minority in the United States. There are now large Hispanic neighborhoods in many cities.

Bureau defines Hispanic Americans) will be the nation's largest minority group by the end of the century.

The great bulk of Hispanics are concentrated in the Southwest section of the country, with New Mexico, Texas, and California having the highest percentages of Hispanic population. The 1980 census revealed, however, that for the first time, Hispanic people are beginning to leave the Southwest in significant numbers. Arizona, New Mexico, and Colorado all lost Hispanic population. Nonetheless there are regional patterns: Cuban Americans are highly concentrated in Florida (60 percent of Cuban Americans live there), Puerto Ricans are generally located in New York (50 percent), and Mexican Americans are generally in the Southwest. As more and more Hispanics establish themselves, we will see greater mobility among Spanish-origin persons throughout the country.

Electoral participation among Hispanic people generally has been low. Of course half the population is under 20, so a relatively small percentage are of voting age. Also an absence of Spanish-speaking registrars and political ads has contributed to a lack of interest. But voter participation is increasing. In Texas and throughout the Southwest voter turnout has increased. The 1982 Texas primary saw a greater percentage of Hispanic voters than of all other voters. Voter education and registration drives are making Hispanic Americans a potent political force.

Geography The 1980 census revealed another pattern: internal migration of people to southern and western states, which make up what is called the **Sun Belt.** The old cities of the urban Northeast and the factory regions of the industrial heartland of the Midwest, hard hit by worsening economic times, lost population between the 1970 and 1980 censuses. (This is the **Frost Belt** area of the country.) In turn, great growth occurred

Sun Belt: *the area of the nation comprising the South Atlantic and Gulf states, the Southwest, and the Far West, known for its defense and service opportunities as well as its political conservatism.*

Frost Belt: *the area of the nation comprising the urban Northeast, factory regions of the Midwest, and the Northwest, known for its depressed economic climate and its political liberalism.*

Industry has been affected by difficult economic conditions in America's Frost Belt.

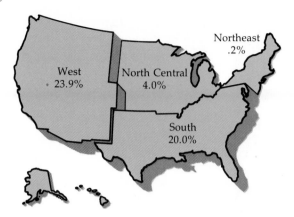

Figure 1.3 Population change: 1970–1980

all across the Sun Belt, which comprises the South Atlantic and Gulf states, the Southwest, and the Far West. The South's population grew 20 percent between 1970 and 1980, the West's by 24 percent (see Figure 1.3).

The lure of the sun plus high rates of employment due to defense and service industries located in the South and West brought new wealth and status to these areas. The divisions between Sun Belt and Frost Belt are frequently characterized as differences between eastern, liberal "yankees" and Sun Belt "cowboys." The differences transcend the Republican and Democratic distinctions or traditional group differences. Sun Belt cowboys derive their influence from new, post-World War II sources of wealth and the recent swelling of their numbers. Many see the Sun Belt as the base for a new Republican majority in America, for the Sun Belt is the strength of America's new conservatism.

Immigration   A land of immigrants, America has always beckoned the foreign-born to her shores. For much of our history, people of European and East European ancestry dominated settlement in our cities and countryside. Even as late as 1960, European immigrants dominated among persons entering the country.

Since then, however, things have changed dramatically as new waves of immigrants have come into the United States. As a result of the war in Southeast Asia in the 1960s and 1970s, the freedom flotilla of Cubans and Haitians in the late 1970s, and an influx of Mexican nationals—legal and illegal—the immigration pattern has shifted. Figure 1.4 illustrates this dramatic change.

The changed pattern of immigration has brought with it new problems. The shift to Asian immigration has created language problems in public schools. In the Los Angeles school system alone some 20 languages are needed to provide instruction. Furthermore, Asians are slower to assimilate than earlier immigrant groups have been, preserving Old World customs and cultural traits that make adjustment to America more difficult. They prefer to remain in groups by themselves.

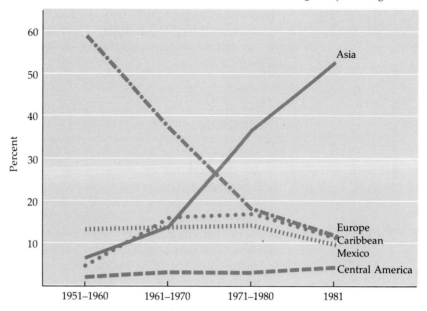

Figure 1.4   Immigration by location of birth

Asians are also noted for their perseverance and hard work. Their culture and drive to succeed mean they will work even for subminimal wages. Asian students are achieving at higher levels than their American counterparts and rank at the top of their classes in high school and college. The willingness of Asians to work, even at menial jobs, along with the larger percentage of unskilled immigrants coming from Latin nations—Central America, the Caribbean, and Mexico—has led to claims of reduced employment opportunities for Americans.

The tide of illegal immigrants, especially among Mexican nationals, is also often cited as a serious employment problem, especially in the Southwest, where migrant agricultural labor and sweatshops are dominated by illegal aliens. There are anywhere from three to twelve million illegal aliens in this country. The Immigration and Naturalization Service (INS) estimates that there are 8.1 million illegal aliens in America. The INS makes between 700,000 and 1.2 million arrests each year, 90 percent of them along the Mexican border. This figure is ten times larger than in 1965. The seriousness of the problem is a subject of dispute. Some argue that illegal aliens take jobs away from U.S. citizens; others counter that illegal aliens largely perform unskilled, low-paying jobs that Americans will not take.

The nation has had a difficult time agreeing on how to deal with illegal aliens. For several years, Congress debated but could not pass immigration legislation. Finally, in 1986, Congress passed a major immigration law. The law has two main features: amnesty and employer sanctions. The act gives legal status to aliens who arrived in the U.S. before January 1, 1982, and it provides temporary resident status for another 350,000

In the 1980s Asians have entered this country in large numbers, and their children are learning to share the American dream.

foreigners who could prove they worked in U.S. agriculture for at least 90 days between May 1985 and May 1986. The law further subjects employers to fines for first offenders ($250 to $2000), and jail sentences for repeat offenders if they knowingly hire illegal aliens.

Changes in Employment

Changing populations also means a changing labor force. The growth of technology has altered the nature and skills necessary for employment. Figure 1.5 shows that white-collar employees number nearly 50 percent of the labor market; the number of industrial blue-collar employees continues to decline as our economy and technology change. Sixteen percent of the work force is now employed by government. Today a **service economy** has relocated and dispersed employment. This means many Americans earn their living providing services (such as television repair, investment advice, or health care) to other Americans; these services often can be provided wherever people live.

Service Economy: *an economy in which persons are employed to provide services to other persons.*

The changing labor force has also demanded specialized skills and training. There has been a constant press for education. In 1940, 25 percent of the population had a high school education and 5 percent a college degree; by 1984, 73 percent of the population had a high school diploma and 19 percent were college educated.

A major problem associated with the rise of new technology and service employment as well as with the computer and electronics industries is that many blue-collar workers simply lack the education and training

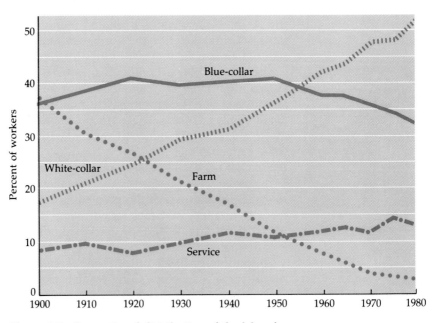

Figure 1.5 Occupational distribution of the labor force

necessary to obtain these more plentiful jobs. It is a sad fact that many blue-collar workers in industry, laid off by economic recession and high-technology modernization, may never reenter the labor force.

Another trend in employment is the continual rise in the number of women in the labor force: more than half of all women in America are now in the labor force. This compares with only a third two decades ago. The greatest influx of women into the labor market today are married—they now total 25 million—as the women's movement and a worsening economy continue to cause more and more women to seek employment.

Income   There has been a continual and constant increase in personal and family income over the years. As society and life-styles have changed, Americans' income has risen, although inflation during the 1970s took a heavy toll on increased earning power.

In 1984 the median family income was $26,433. In 1960 it stood at $5,620; in 1970 at $9,867. Yet the real growth occurred between 1960 and 1970 when family income rose by an average of $6,000. Between 1970 and 1980 inflation robbed families of real increases and median income actually declined slightly. The increases are the result of inflation and more husbands and wives both drawing an income.

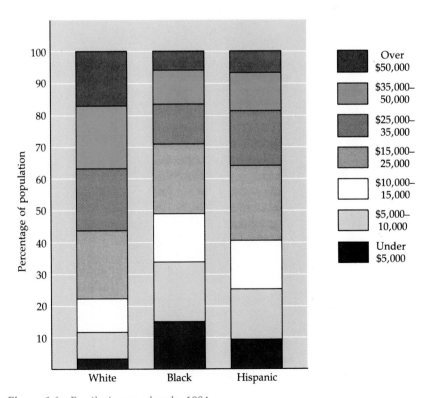

Figure 1.6   Family income levels, 1984

Without public benefits many people find it hard to maintain a decent standard of living.

The growth of median family incomes for both whites and blacks belies the fact that nonwhite families lost ground after 1970 (see Figure 1.6). The median income for nonwhite families in 1984 was $17,098. The distribution of incomes for families shows the increasing percentage of families with incomes over $25,000. However, nonwhite incomes over $25,000 continue to lag behind white incomes.

These figures do not reveal the full extent of income problems many Americans continue to face. Inflation erodes earning power. The purchasing power of the 1967 dollar was 67 cents in 1975. By 1980 the dollar was worth 40 cents; in 1984 it had slipped further to 32 cents. Inflation in 1974 and 1979 pushed the consumer price index up 11 and 13 percent, respectively. Particularly hard hit were the retired and others on fixed incomes.

Blacks and minorities continue to struggle for economic parity. There remain 34 million Americans with income levels below the officially defined level of poverty. Blacks make up 34 percent of the total, Hispanics 28 percent, 12 percent are elderly, and 42 percent are families with female heads of households.

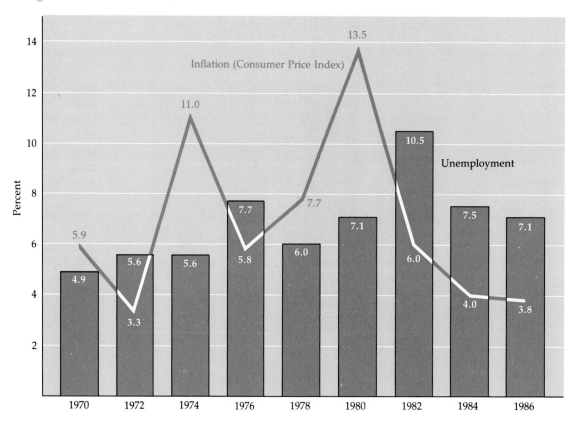

Figure 1.7   Unemployment and inflation, 1970–1986

Unemployment Unemployment is a major concern for Americans. A 1982 Gallup Poll reported 61 percent of Americans thought unemployment the most serious problem facing the nation. In the wake of the 1970s, we have had to live with an escalating unemployment rate, which reached 10.5 percent in 1982. Only a few years ago, 3 to 4 percent unemployment was considered permissible in times of economic growth and prosperity. As for the unemployed, one in five is under 20 years of age, one in five is nonwhite, two in five are female, and almost half are blue-collar employees (see Figure 1.7).

President Reagan made the economy and employment a major theme in his 1980 campaign. In fact, both parties campaigned on a platform to increase the number of jobs. Reagan inherited the presidency during a period of *stagflation*, with high inflation and no economic growth or no new jobs being created. The inflation rate in 1980 under President Carter reached 13 percent. President Reagan insisted that inflation had to be curbed before real economic recovery could occur. He embarked on policies designed to reduce inflation—slower federal spending, tight money policies, and high interest rates.

These measures did succeed in reducing inflation but at the cost of worsening unemployment. As Figure 1.7 illustrates, 1982 saw inflation halved, but unemployment soared to a post-Depression record of 10.5 percent. We are faced with a trade-off between high inflation and unemployment. We have either unemployment or a spiraling cost of living; we seem unable to get both under control at the same time.

ZIGGY, Copyright, 1983, Universal Press Syndicate. Reprinted with permission. All rights reserved.

It should be noted that, as an issue, inflation is felt by all Americans, whereas unemployment directly affects only about 7 to 10 percent of the population. Controlling inflation, therefore, provides relief for 100 percent of the population while 90 percent barely notice the effects of unemployment. No wonder, then, that public work programs to relieve unemployment find little sympathy with the American taxpayer. This is a classic example of majority versus minority rights.

Changes in Government

The changed agenda for government represents more than the growth of government: it represents a redefined goal for government policy. With the New Deal, government came to play growing roles in economic and social affairs.

Once established, New Deal programs became fixtures requiring future appropriations. Congress, eager to please its new clientele groups, committed future taxes to fund the programs. Thus, substantial amounts of money were increasingly dedicated to programs—such as Social Security and AFDC—committing future governments to spend. Government expenditure became a powerful incentive as a tool of public policy. Today all levels of government spending represent 36 percent of the GNP.

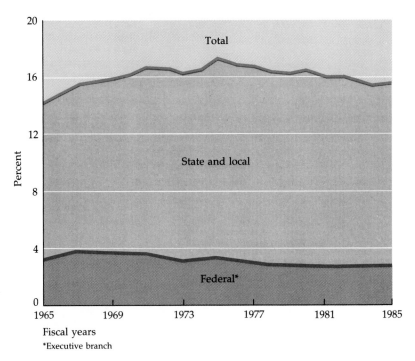

Figure 1.8 Growth in government civilian employment as a percent of total civilian employment

We can measure this change in government in three ways: first by the growth in public employment, second by the growth of the federal budget, and finally by the changing nature of expenditures.

Public Employment   One way to measure government's greater role is to note the growth in public employment. More government activity results inevitably in more hirings in the public sector. Public employment has grown approximately 40 percent in twenty years. But what is most clearly revealed by Figure 1.8 is the growth in public employment at the state and local levels. In fact, federal public employment has shown a slight decline in recent years. The real growth in federal employment came earlier, in the wake of the New Deal. The greater number of state and local public employees illustrates the growth of public services and the need for employment at the local and state levels to deliver those services.

The increased demand for public services, and hence for employment, is a direct response to the changing complexion of society. The changes

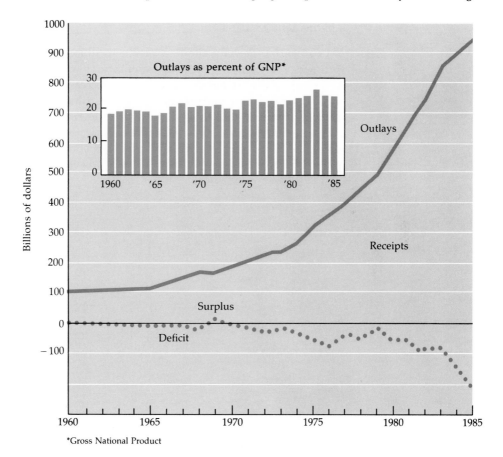

*Gross National Product

Figure 1.9   Federal budget and outlays: 1960–1985

in population and income have mandated personal and social protection policies as well as economic regulation. Public employees are needed to implement these increased and changed activities.

The Federal Budget   Public spending by the federal government surpassed half a trillion dollars in 1980. While government spending has been constantly on the rise, the dramatic growth in expenditures came in 1974. Throughout the 1960s and early 1970s, federal outlays as a percent of GNP remained constant, but in 1975 federal spending rose to 23 percent of the GNP. But these recent budget increases largely reflect the impact of inflation on the American dollar (see Figure 1.9).

The spiraling growth in the federal budget is principally caused by the nature of programs and spending, the so-called **uncontrollables.** Currently, 75 percent of the federal budget is uncontrollable. Uncontrollables are the dedicated and entitled programs such as social security, Medicare, interest payments on the debt, and so on, that are not subject to annual action by Congress. They are, in effect, permanent appropriations of Congress. Such programs and expenditures, therefore, become part of a permanent government.

Uncontrollables: *dedicated and entitled programs that are not subject to annual action by Congress. Presently, 75 percent of the federal budget is uncontrollable.*

Expenditures   Perhaps the best means to illustrate the changed agenda is to note the changing areas of expenditures within the federal budget. As a result of the changes in society—the increased social welfare policies and personal protection programs—the distribution of federal expenditures has changed and the federal deficit has risen.

Figure 1.10 shows that the major changes in expenditures have been in national defense and veterans' benefits, which during the late 1960s required 45 percent of the budget. In 1973, however, these functions were

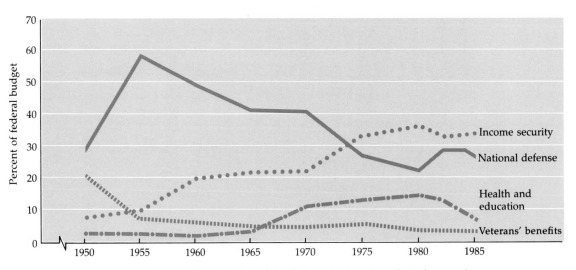

Figure 1.10   Portion of the federal budget by selected expenditures

Income Protection: *government payments that guarantee financial benefits to individuals by virtue of their age, income, or employment status.*

overtaken by welfare, health, and **income protection.** In 1980 defense and veterans' benefits were 25 percent of the budget; health, education, and income security rose to 50 percent of the budget. The effects of a changed environment were making themselves felt through the budget priorities of the national government.

President Reagan is committed to altering the trend in national defense. His budgets call for increased defense spending and reduced commitments for health, education, and social programs.

Changing Expectations and Government

The agenda for change produced a change in both the size and the scope of government. Not only the budget but also the range of governmental policy has grown. Two unmistakable trends stand out. First, government has become a major component of the nation's economy. Government is a major consumer of economic goods. The delivery of services and the size of increases in government spending do much to affect the state of economic health in America. Government is also a chief regulator of economic activity. The level of government spending stimulates or slows private business activity, and government regulation sets the boundaries for doing business as well as mandating standards and wages. Government policy now seeks to regulate economic activity as a means to control inflation and keep employment high.

The second trend is closely linked to the first. The achievement of the nation's economic goals is intertwined with the nation's social goals. We have seen increased government activity in response to shifting populations and income levels. Increasingly, government has sought to intervene on behalf of citizens to promote social values, frequently using its economic resources to achieve those social policies. Two examples are pollution abatement to protect the environment and affirmative action hiring practices to assist minority employment. Government has come to take prime responsibility for the maintenance of the democratic values of equality and justice. In many diverse areas such as housing, health, transportation, and prison reform, government policy seeks to promote equality and fairness for all citizens. More recently, government has intervened on behalf of its citizens to buffer the forces of change—often from the consequences of unintended changes, as in the case of high energy costs resulting from OPEC (Organization of Petroleum Exporting Countries) oil. Income security is the major budgetary consequence of such a policy.

Americans have been brought up to believe in their political system, that the democratic process benefits everyone, and that the values of a democracy make it the best form of government in the world. It comprises liberty and equality, a system of majority rule, and justice for all— along with a free enterprise economic system that seeks to harmonize individual initiative and mass efficiency. Americans long believed their society capable of infinite progress and prosperity.

It is because American democracy promises so much that uncertainty and changing expectations require us to reexamine and reassess the fundamental principles of democracy. First, let us examine briefly the changing expectations, the public's mood, and how the organs of government try to formulate public policy in such an environment.

Elections and Voting

The battle for the ballot has been one of the longest and most symbolic struggles in American history. The right to vote symbolizes the democratic nature of the political process, the opportunity for people of all races, occupations, and religions to meet on an equal plane and select the candidates of their choice. Yet today public officials are held in low esteem: they are viewed as captives of money and special interest groups. Many citizens consider the electoral process tainted by the high cost of campaigning, which makes elections seem bought and sold.

Increasingly over the past two decades, voter disaffection has been expressed in a decreased turnout at the polls. Throughout the twentieth century the proportion of the electorate going to the polls grew steadily until 1960. The tumultuous years between 1960 and 1980, however, produced a decline in voter turnout. Nineteen eighty saw a low turnout for the presidential contest—52.9 percent of eligible voters. The 1984 election produced a modest increase, to 53.2 percent. It remains to be seen whether the new optimism that is changing Americans' expectations can reverse this decline more permanently.

Party Disarray

Political parties are considered an indispensable ingredient of democracy because they provide the vehicle for competition and free choice at elections. Without parties, there would be no free elections. The great political vehicles of the New Deal era, however, are in a state of disarray. In 1968 George Wallace received a surprising 13.5 percent of the vote in his third-party presidential campaign. George McGovern challenged the Democratic party in 1972 and won the nomination for president. In that same election Richard Nixon, the Republican nominee, shunned the party by setting up his own reelection organization—The Committee to Re-Elect the President—and in 1976 Jimmy Carter campaigned on the slogan of restoring confidence in government by downplaying political parties and promising reform. In 1980 Ronald Reagan built upon the unfulfilled promises Carter made in 1976, as well as a large anti-Carter sentiment in the electorate, to capture the presidency.

Party identification continues to slip. Reagan's victories in 1980 and 1984 were achieved with the support of many traditional Democratic party identifiers. Split ticket voting, in which party identifiers vote for some candidates of the opposing party on the election ballot, has become

The Study of Public Policy

The study of public policy is the study of what government does. It involves a purposive course of action to be followed by government bodies and public officials in dealing with a problem, a matter of concern.* Public policy seeks to distinguish between what governments intend to do and what in fact they achieve. It is a process and not simply decision making, although decisions are frequently made among policy alternatives. The several components to the policy process that form a sequential pattern of activity follow:

1. *Agenda setting* How does an issue come before government? How does it become a public problem? How does an issue get placed on the government's agenda for recognition as a significant problem for society?

2. *Policy formulation* What are the alternatives being developed to solve the problem? Who participates in the proposal of solutions? What is the range of permissible alternatives?

3. *Policy adoption* What policy is finally adopted and what is the adoption process? What goals and participants gain legitimacy? How are adopted policies supported?

4. *Policy implementation* How is policy carried out? What resources are necessary to achieve the objectives? What impact, including changes in behavior, does the policy have?

5. *Policy evaluation* How effective was the policy? Who assesses policy impact and what happens as a result of that assessment?

There are several ways to examine public policy. It can be examined in terms of subject matter, such as education, tax, or welfare, or in terms of the institutions adopting policy—say, the legislature, bureaucracy, or judiciary. But the most useful typology is that developed by Theodore Lowi on the impact of public policy on society and the participants involved:**

1. *Distributive policy* The distribution of services and benefits to specific private groups and individuals in society. Governmental funds and benefits are provided to particular segments of society to subsidize their private activities. It is believed that such governmental support benefits all of society and that the policies produce benefits without direct costs to other specific groups. Hence there is no competition for public funds, and distributive policy normally has short-term consequences.

2. *Regulatory policy* Restricting or limiting the permissible range of activity for groups or individuals in society. Regulatory policy involves the competitive allocation of goods and services. One side wins, one side loses in the competition for the delivery of goods and services. Some activities and policies are deemed appropriate and permissible while others are declared illegitimate and not permissible. Regulatory policies determine, for example, which television stations can broadcast in a city or the amounts of pollution industries can discharge into the air or water.

3. *Self-regulatory policy* Like regulatory policy, this policy involves restrictions and controls. It seeks to establish general rules and policies; however, it does this by the regulated group's direct involvement and support in the formulation of policy as a means of protecting and promoting the group's interests and activities. A classic example of self-regulatory policy is professional licensure.

4. *Redistributive policy* The reallocation of wealth and benefits among broad classes of people in society. Such policies aim at a massive shift in wealth or rights enjoyed by groups so that significant changes in position in society are accomplished. Since groups are unwilling to give up their wealth or power, redistributive policies are difficult to achieve and involve the broadest range of issues.

*James E. Anderson, *Public Policy Making*, 2nd edition (New York: Holt, Rinehart & Winston, 1979), p. 3.

**Theodore J. Lowi, "American Business, Public Policy, Case Studies, and Political Theory," *World Politics* 16 (June 1964).

a significant trend. Some people see these changes as emerging realignment of the electorate into a new Republican majority; others suggest that the further decline of parties may eventually make them superfluous to the political system altogether.

The President

Traditionally, the president has enjoyed a high rating with the American people, but the Vietnam War, Watergate, and growing conflicts with Congress left people bewildered, skeptical, and shaken in their confidence. Popularity ratings for the president dramatically declined in the 1960s and 1970s from those of Franklin D. Roosevelt and John F. Kennedy. When Lyndon Johnson announced that he would not seek reelection in 1968, he was at his lowest popularity rating, 35 percent; on the eve of his resignation, Richard Nixon's approval rating was only 27 percent. Jimmy Carter, pledging to restore confidence and trust in government, had, in 1980, an approval rating of only 23 percent.

Ronald Reagan again provides the reversal of the trend (see Figure 1.11). He came to office with a higher public approval rating than his recent contemporaries (67 percent), and after a decline early in his first term, Reagan's popularity continued an upward surge. Only after he had been in office for 6 years did the American people seriously blame the president for his performance, with revelations of a secret Iranian arms deal.

Recent presidents have also had difficulty with Congress. The War Powers Act and Budget and Impoundment Control Act in 1974 significantly curbed the autonomy of the chief executive. Since then Congress

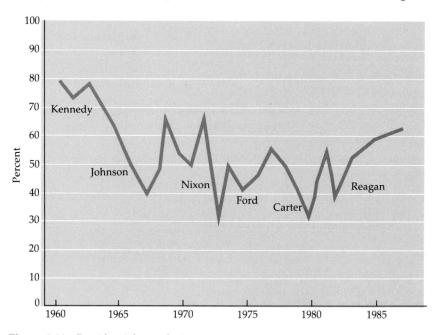

Figure 1.11 Presidential popularity

has more often refused to acquiesce to presidential wishes, as the debates over SALT (Strategic Arms Limitation Treaty) II and military aid to Nicaragua illustrate.

Critics have been frustrated at the imperialization of the presidency—that is, at the extension of the limits of executive power and accountability often at the expense of Congress and the courts. The chief complaint is that the array of laws and powers is more than any one person can exercise or control. We have continually expanded the presidency in order to facilitate presidential control, and Americans now wonder if it is wise to place such great power in only one person.

Congress

If Congress is enjoying a resurgence in the post-Watergate era, there remain lingering doubts regarding its ability or resolve to influence public policy. Americans continue to hold Congress in low regard. Popular support for Congress fell throughout the 1970s, and Ronald Reagan has continued to point the finger of blame at Congress for economic woes in the 1980s. In addition, Congress has been rocked by a series of episodes or scandals throughout the era. There was Koreagate (so dubbed because it followed close after Watergate), in which Korean businessman Tongsun Park bribed some congressmen in return for their continued support for U.S. economic and military aid to Korea. Then, in 1980, came operation **ABSCAM,** the revelation that FBI agents posing as Arab representatives bribed several congressmen. As a result of ABSCAM, six congressmen and one U.S. senator were convicted of accepting bribes. All are out of Congress now.

The plight of the presidency does not mean that Congress automatically becomes more powerful. Some critics charge that its seniority system and committee process make Congress slow and inefficient, and that the body is incapable of responding to a crisis or to the president. Legislators seem more concerned with reelection than with their constituents. Congress retains an image of a stuffy, unrepresentative body that would rather talk than fight.

The Bureaucracy

The symbol of big government, the bureaucracy, has grown to employ 16 million people: 3 million federal, 3.7 million state, and 9.5 million local government employees. The 3 million federal employees administer a budget of more than $900 billion, and overall public employees spend more than $1 trillion annually! Spending that much money is seen as waste and inefficiency; the bureaucracy has become a hideaway for inefficient and overpaid officials. Citizens have long wondered what bureaucrats do with their time and with the taxpayers' money.

The costs of government have risen dramatically. The Great Society added new and expensive programs to the federal budget, often with little or no attention to their administration. And as society has become

ABSCAM: ABSCAM was an FBI undercover investigation begun in 1978 to lure people involved in organized crime into selling stolen securities and art objects. FBI agents posed as representatives of Arab businessmen and sheiks (hence Arab Scam or ABSCAM). Eight congressmen were approached and asked to use their positions to help Arabs to conclude real estate deals or to obtain such things as U.S. residency and gambling licenses. These deals were tape recorded and videotaped. Ultimately, six members of the House and one senator were convicted of accepting bribes. Many people considered FBI tactics to be a form of entrapment. A 1983 congressional act would allow "sting" operations only when "reasonable suspicion of criminal conduct" exists.

more mobile and technologically sophisticated, government has assumed many of the functions considered private only a few years ago. This increase in government activity has produced a myriad of regulations, agencies, and bureaucrats. To the average citizen—and sometimes to the public official—the bureaucracy seems an impenetrable maze. Ronald Reagan made the bureaucracy a central issue in his campaign for the presidency, claiming that the government needed to go on a diet. He said there was no virtue in extensive use of federal power.

Watergate, too, contributed to the problems of the bureaucracy. White House personnel were placed in agency positions in order to report on progress in implementing presidential objectives. The IRS was asked to harass political enemies by auditing their tax returns; the CIA was directed to participate in the Watergate cover-up. To the bureaucracy's credit, most of these efforts were resisted, but this very resistance caused more concern. Can the bureaucracy be autonomous? To whom is it responsible?

Democracy and the Process of Change

Consent of the Governed: *the belief that political power originates with the popular approval of the people.*

Democracy: *rule by the people.*

Republic: *a form of government in which people do not govern directly but consent to representatives who make and administer laws for the people.*

Representative Democracy: *a government in which the people select representatives to make and enforce laws on their behalf.*

Democracy in the United States has never been a simple process. The framers of the Constitution were careful to distinguish **consent of the governed,** for which there was widespread approval as the original source of political power, from **democracy,** which they took to mean direct government by the people and in which they had little confidence. The framers declared the new government to be a **republic,** a government founded on the consent of the governed but whose power was carefully circumscribed by a written Constitution.

The word *democracy* comes to us from Greece, where the power of rule (*kratia*) by the people or populace (*demos*) literally means people power—rule by the people. As used by the Greeks, particularly the Athenians, democracy was disdained as blind, ignorant rule by the populace—almost mob rule. This the Greeks contrasted to rule by an enlightened few (aristocracy) or rule based on military achievements (timocracy).

Americans have embraced the principle that power originates with the people. Except for the New England town meetings and a few colonial efforts, however, Americans have not seriously tried to involve all citizens directly in lawmaking. We are not a pure or direct democracy. That concept was limited to the Greek city-state of a few thousand citizens, not a nation of four million in 1790 and of 226 million people today. We prefer the term *republic,* in which the people do not govern directly but consent to representatives who make and administer the laws *for* the people. We can call the United States a **representative democracy** (see Figure 1.12).

Public officials are selected by the people to make public policy, and although not all officials are elected, we hold them all accountable for the exercise of their power. The framers of the Constitution combined de-

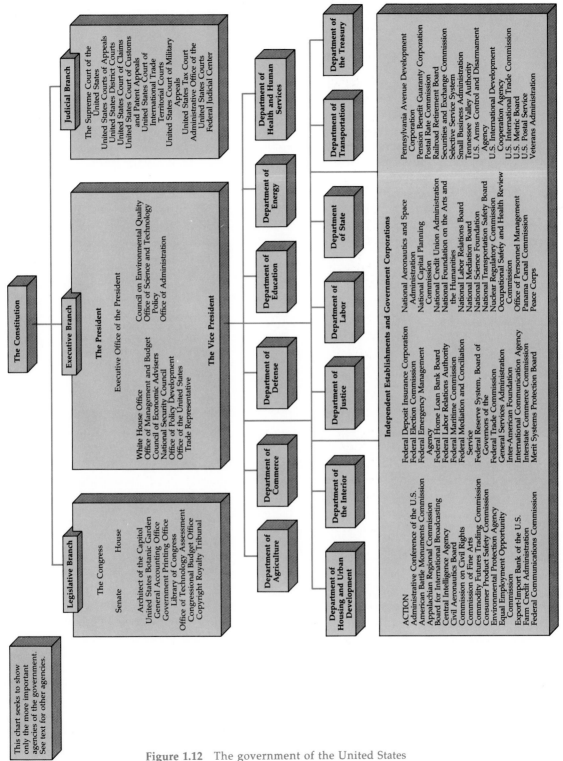

Figure 1.12   The government of the United States

Changing Consensus: Privatization of the Federal Government

A "For Sale" sign hanging on government buildings? As strange as it may sound, that is what the Reagan administration has proposed. In 1986 President Reagan suggested selling off parts of the federal government to private industry, a process that has come to be known as **privatization.** The aim of privatization is to shrink the federal deficit and reduce the size of the federal government, both major concerns of the Reagan administration.

But the idea of selling some familiar and long-term government programs sounds alien to many Americans. Many remember the struggle to create such programs and the difficulty of securing the funds needed to finance the service. For many Americans the expansion of government and government services meant delivery of needed and vital services otherwise unavailable; it also meant a fairer and more equitable way of providing those services. Yet it also has meant larger and more costly government. In the three decades from 1950 to 1980, the size of the federal government budget increased tenfold, to $580 billion. The federal government added one million employees in that same period of time. To the Reagan administration this has meant unnecessary expansion, which they claim the nation cannot afford. Too many programs of questionable value and excessive cost have driven up the deficit. The private sector can do a better job of providing these services at less cost than can the federal government. Hence the decision to seek to sell off parts of the federal government.

According to the Reagan administration, privatization is an idea whose time has come. In 1984 the Private Sector Survey on Cost Control (Grace Commission) said there were a variety of government services that could be more efficiently provided by private enterprise. They

Privatization: *the selling to private enterprise of any number of government functions as a way to reduce the scope and cost of government.*

identified about 11,000 such activities. In Great Britain, for example, Prime Minister Margaret Thatcher has successfully sold off some two dozen state-owned businesses, including the British telephone system and Jaguar cars. The Reagan administration has proposed in 1987 to privatize a number of government programs that compete with private business.

The Reagan plan for privatization has two major directions: the sale of public assets to private enterprise and the use of vouchers. In the first approach public assets would be sold outright. Sales would reduce the size of government and add revenue to the federal budget, thereby reducing the size of the deficit. Programs targeted by President Reagan for sale include:

- *Power marketing administrations* Five power generating and transmission facilities that sell electricity generated by federal dams (the dams would not be sold)
- *Naval petroleum reserves* Oil fields at Elk Hills, California, and Teapot Dome, Wyoming
- *Amtrak* The passenger service railroad
- *LANDSAT* Five remote sensing satellites
- *Crop insurance* To be provided by the private insurance industry
- *Federal Housing Administration* The agency that insures home and apartment house mortgages made by private lenders

The other major method for privatization is to provide vouchers to private citizens and families. These vouchers from the federal government could be used like cash to purchase assistance or services that the government would not directly provide. Reagan has proposed using vouchers in compensatory education for disadvantaged students. Parents could use the vouchers for private schooling instead of relying on public school compensatory programs. He has also proposed housing vouchers to allow low-income families to buy or rent housing privately as an alternative to public housing or public subsidies for low-income housing.

These efforts at privatization remain modest in scope. They hardly balance the budget or dramatically scale back on government. But they do reverse a trend of several generations. For many years government had assumed more and more functions. Many of these had once been performed by private enterprise, but as they became unprofitable for private industry or too costly to be afforded by many citizens, government stepped in to assist. Has the government grown too large and costly to provide many of these services as economically as private enterprise? For many Americans it is difficult to imagine private business providing some of the services and functions government has come to supply in the twentieth century. Yet privatization may become a growing trend in government as our consensus changes on the size and role of the federal government in the lives of Americans.

Constitutionalism: *the principle of granting and limiting political authority under a written or unwritten covenant (constitution).*

mocracy and constitutionalism. Democracy refers to the representational process by which public officials are selected and maintained in office; **constitutionalism** refers to the way in which authority is conferred and limited. We established a system of government in which public officials must receive and re-receive the consent of the people in order to govern. But we have added the safeguard of specific, recognized limits on the power of any officeholder.

Democracy contains two components. There is a procedural process by which the consent of the governed confers legitimacy on public officials, thereby making representation a real and meaningful concept. The heart of **procedural democracy** is the electoral system. Here the majority rules. But there is also a substantive feature of democracy inculcating certain values that are desired for their intrinsic worth. This is our heritage from the Declaration of Independence, the Preamble to the Constitution, and the Emancipation Proclamation. Herein the rights of the individual are protected.

Procedural Democracy: *the process whereby citizens confer legitimacy on public officials. Procedural democracy stresses the importance of the mechanisms for popular government, in particular, the electoral system.*

Procedural democracy stresses the importance of the mechanisms for popular government, the means by which citizens consent to their government. Elections are the key. Four elements are said to be essential for democratic elections:

1. *Regular, periodic elections*   Elections must be conducted at prescribed times and places and at regular and frequent intervals. All elected public officials are required to stand for election and reelection.

2. *Political competition*   Citizens or groups must be free to organize and run candidates for office. The right to vote has little meaning when no alternative exists to serve as a choice or to criticize those in power. Voters have a right to alternative points of view, to all the information.

3. *One person, one vote*   We believe in the principle that one person's vote counts the same as another's, that in the secrecy of the ballot box, bank president and steelworker, millionaire and unemployed each casts but a single vote. The courts have extended this principle to include the drawing of electoral districts so that each district has approximately the same number of people.

4. *Majority rule*   Candidates receiving the most votes win. Whether we endow the majority with special powers or merely find it an expedient excuse for power, majority rules. Losing candidates are obligated to follow the will of the people, and legitimacy is conferred as an expression of the consent of the governed.

Substantive Democracy: *the intrinsic values associated with democracy, such as freedom, equality, and individualism.*

Substantive democracy is part of our political heritage. Out of their English and European past, the colonists shaped and molded the values we associate with American democracy. The line of the Declaration of Independence still rings true: "We hold these truths to be self evident, that all men are created equal; that they are endowed by their Creator with certain inalienable rights."

First, there is a belief in equality, the unique claim of each individual to be treated as an individual whose worth does not have to be proved.

Clearly, Americans have not always practiced this, nor do they fully practice it at present, as the plight of the black American or the native American graphically illustrates. Nor does equality mean all have equal political influence or power. This idea of equality, rather, is a commitment to the basic worth and dignity of the human person.

A second important value is freedom. Americans believe that the individual must be free to select his or her goals. Self-determination is the heart of freedom. Innovation and progress are associated with the spontaneity and variety that are products of freedom. We accept certain rights as basic to our freedom. Such rights as free speech, press, religion, and assembly, guaranteed in the First Amendment, as well as the right to work and live where and how we choose, make freedom a preferred value. Finally, the idea of individualism is basic to democracy. The individual is supreme in democracy. Society exists for no other purpose than to serve the individual. Individual dignity, worth, and value are the premises on which the structure of democracy was erected.

Our democracy is far from perfect, as our recent past shows. The vision of a Great Society remains largely that—a vision. The Vietnam War reminds us that a president can commit thousands of Americans to their death in an undeclared war. Inflation robs millions of lower- and middle-class Americans of their dreams, and of financial security. Watergate and Koreagate have left a citizenry skeptical and distrustful of politics and public officials. Our democracy is a flexible one, however; reports of the death of American democracy are greatly exaggerated. But there is no doubt that our expectations are changing. The processes of democracy will have to adjust; the values of democracy will have to be renewed.

Summary

1. The theme of this textbook is the changing expectations in American politics. The political behavior and government activity of Americans have changed greatly in the last two generations.

2. After two decades of turmoil caused by the Great Society, the Vietnam War, and Watergate, during which there were a loss of trust and confidence in government and a drop in party loyalty, the Reagan administration provides new hope and new direction for the nation.

3. Change has some longer-standing implications as well. Population changes pose political difficulties for America by placing strain on the federal budget and on the social fabric. Employment demands increased education to cope with the developing technology. And while incomes rise, inflation seriously erodes such increases, notably for the retired and minority groups.

4. Reagan has vowed to reverse the trends of the last few decades, in which the number of public employees doubled and federal spending increased to almost one-quarter of the total value of all goods and services in America. The priority for government expenditure has changed

also, with national defense growing in the 1980s after several decades of decline.

5. The result of changing expectations in politics has been a renewed sense of faith and optimism in government but also a slightly more conservative citizenry. Ronald Reagan is a popular president.

6. Democracy is composed of a procedural process and a substantive commitment to the values of equality, freedom, and individuality. The procedural process depends on the mechanisms of regular elections, political competition, equality of the vote, and majority rule.

Research Projects

1. *Attitudes of college-age youth* How do the social and political opinions of your school or your peers compare with the national trends in opinions of college-age youth? This book presents nationwide results from the annual American Council on Education study of college freshmen. These are also published in the Chronicle of Higher Education. Check your student affairs office to find out whether your school participated and compare results. If no local data exist, construct your own questionnaire, using questions from the national survey, and ask students their opinions. Compare the results.

2. *Immigrants and ethnic composition* What is the ethnic mix of your community and state? Using population profiles from the Bureau of the Census, determine how the ethnic composition of your community has changed over the years. Where are recent immigrants to the community and state coming from? The best source is the *Census of Population* reports put out by the Bureau of the Census. There are reports for every state. The General Population Characteristics report is the most helpful, but several other, more specialized, reports are also available from the Census Bureau.

3. *The federal budget* Secure some copies of the federal budget for different years; examine how the budget has increased and what functions receive a smaller percentage of funds over time. You can usually find the federal budget in your college or city library; the *Budget in Brief* is an easy way to review the data. You can also find the data in *Statistical Abstract* or reported in *Congressional Quarterly* or *National Journal*.

Bibliography

Galbraith, John K. *The New Industrial State*. Boston: Houghton Mifflin, 1985.
Galbraith is a readable economist, though not a typical apologist for free enterprise. This work examines American economic life as the product of large organizations—private and public. This characteristic, Galbraith says, obscures and even suppresses capitalism.
Ginzberg, Eli, and Solow, Robert (eds.). *The Great Society*. New York: Basic Books, 1974.

A series of essays that provide a critical evaluation of Great Society programs. The topics of health, education, income, housing, human resources, and civil rights are analyzed by authors in response to a decade of criticism over these basic social programs.
Levitan, Sar, and Taggert, Robert. *The Promise of Greatness*. Cambridge, Mass.: Harvard University Press, 1976.
A fairly comprehensive review of the programs of the Great Society and their impact on the 1970s. The

authors tend to be sympathetic to the policies and programs of the Great Society. Much data and information are included in their analysis.

Lipset, Seymour Martin (ed.). *The Third Century: America as a Post-Industrial Society.* Stanford, Calif.: Hoover Institution Press, 1979.
A group of sixteen scholars look into the future on a wide range of social and political topics. The essays start with the theme of America as a postindustrial society and examine the media, education, ethnic groups, courts, the presidency, and so on.

Lipson, Leslie. *The Democratic Civilization.* New York: Oxford University Press, 1964.
A broad study of democracy, its origins, development, and contemporary dimensions. Lipson centers on the social context, the political and institutional arrangements, and the philosophical ideas of democracy.

Lowi, Theodore. *The End of Liberalism.* New York: W. W. Norton, 1979.
Lowi grasps better than most the profound interconnections among politics, economics, and social well-being. His work questions the value of interest-group liberalism as a theory of politics.

Palmer, John L., and Sawhill, Isabel V. *The Reagan Record.* Cambridge, Mass.: Ballinger, 1984.
A series of essays assessing the Reagan administration's record on domestic public policy. The volume examines the changes brought by Reagan and projects their consequences.

Pynn, Ronald E. *Watergate and the American Political Process.* New York: Praeger, 1974.
A collection of essays on Watergate that examine the impact of Watergate on the political process and the institutions of government. The essays emphasize the larger implications of Watergate.

Reich, Robert B. *The Next American Frontier.* New York: Penguin Books, 1983.
In this discussion of social and economic problems, Reich offers a design for economic recovery to help the U.S. regain world prominence. He stresses high-quality and high-technology production along with the reorganization of various business and governmental practices.

Salamon, Lester M., and Lund, Michael S. *The Reagan Presidency and the Governing of America.* Washington, D.C.: The Urban Institute, 1984.
A series of distinguished scholars examine the effect of the Reagan administration on America's politics and its governing institutions and processes. The volume assesses Reagan's success in changing government policy, focusing especially on relations with other institutions and groups in the political process.

Sundquist, James. *Constitutional Reform and Effective Government.* Washington, D.C.: The Brookings Institution, 1985.
Sundquist discusses proposals to change the fundamental structure of government. The book looks at purported weaknesses in the Constitution such as separation of powers and presidential-Congressional relations. The book raises questions about which changes might work.

White, Theodore H. *America in Search of Itself.* New York: Harper & Row, 1982.
An examination of presidential elections from 1956 to 1980, with special focus on the electoral process, by the author of the famous *Making of the President* series. Theodore White was an astute and long-time commentator on the landscape of American politics.

The Constitution

The tall ships sailed into the harbor, past the Statue of Liberty, and on up the Hudson River. They had come from around the globe to help America celebrate its bicentennial—two hundred years since the signing of the Declaration of Independence. We have now reached the bicentennial of the Constitution. Ours is the oldest constitution in the world. It has survived many vicissitudes of politics: the establishment of the new republic and westward expansion, slavery and the Civil War, social and economic progress, depression and world wars, and, more recently, Watergate. The Constitution, of course, has not solved all our problems, but it has provided a framework for the government of a federal state for two centuries.

The Constitution could not have survived these two hundred years had it not been a flexible set of rules. The particular genius of the American Constitution is its broad, general grants of authority, open to interpretation and change as social, economic, and political conditions change. The Constitution established the basic structure of American government and provided a framework of authority within which government could operate. It contains only a small proportion of the laws, customs, traditions, and political decisions of a nation; however, volumes of statutes and judicial opinions exist to adapt the Constitution to new problems and situations. Ultimately, the strength of this document rests with the people, with their ability and desire to uphold and defend this symbol of their community and form of government.

The Political Foundation

The English Tradition

The Constitution grew out of the political heritage of the English and their government practice in the American colonies. The first arrivals in the New World brought with them the experience and tradition of English politics. But they began almost immediately to shape those practices into a uniquely American set of ideas and patterns of government.

From England the colonists brought with them English law and the traditions of common law and contract. The **common law** was a major part of the English system. It emerged from customary practices and standards of reasonable behavior that judges applied to settle local disputes. Over a period of time the practices and standards evolved into a series of legal rules that became commonly applied. From the common law came the "rights of Englishmen." The **Magna Carta,** signed at Runnymede in 1215, affirmed for Englishmen that the power of their king was not absolute, and with it the tradition of higher law merged with the common law. From the writings of Sir Edward Coke, Americans came to believe in judicial review and that kingly, or executive, authority fell "under the law." Coke argued that the common law was superior to the will of the

Common Law: *a system of judge-made law based on custom and precedent.*

The Magna Carta: *an English document, signed in 1215, affirming that the power of the king was not absolute.*

Baron de Montesquieu was a Frenchman who gave Americans the idea of separation of powers; John Locke was an Englishman who believed in the consent of the governed.

king, and indeed to any political authority, and that judges were bound to review and uphold the law against government abuse. From Sir William Blackstone's *Commentaries on the Laws of England,* widely hailed in the colonies and used as a legal text, came a defense of parliamentary sovereignty, civil liberty, and reason.

A second tradition inherited from England was that of **contract**—the idea that those who govern are responsible to those who are governed. The power of government is limited by the higher law, the constitutional tradition, and customs of the people. Power, to be legitimate, needs the consent of the people.

John Locke's *Second Treatise on Civil Government* presented the analogy of free and equal citizens in a state of nature binding together to form a civil society. In this hypothetical state of nature, Locke argued, individuals possessed certain natural and inalienable rights, among them the rights to life, liberty, and property. But he considered these rights insecure. To secure their rights, Locke wrote, people freely consent to put themselves under the authority of government. This was the social contract—the express consent of the governed binding themselves to a political authority in return for the secure enjoyment of their liberties.

Finally, the colonists brought with them a concept of mixed government, or **republicanism.** Historically this notion evolved as a means for different social classes to share power, a way of balancing interests within society. A republic blended the continuity of the monarchy, the strength of the aristocracy, and the vitality and support of the people necessary to maintain civil authority. Republicanism, then, was a balancing of interests and power. By mixing democracy and aristocracy with monarchy, the danger to political power from any one form of government would be balanced by forces pulling in the opposite direction by the other forms. "Only through this reciprocal sharing of political power by the one, the few, and the many, could the desirable qualities of each be preserved."[1] To James Harrington, a seventeenth-century English republican, a mixed form of government would prevent citizens from having either the interest or the power to subvert government.

The colonists expressed their understanding of mixed government through the concept of a **commonwealth,** whereby separation of interest and function were merged with separation of office. Hence, the colonists emphasized, freedom was best protected when the mixed or republican principle operated and the best men were recruited to government. To this the colonists added a mechanical separation of powers whereby government was divided among separate branches and no branch representing a single class of interests could exercise all the powers or activities of government. Each branch of government would be independent and equal. It was largely through the work of the French theorist Montesquieu that the colonists absorbed the doctrine of the equilibrium of legislative, executive, and judicial powers of government. Even the wise were not to be trusted with too much power. Where powers were separated, liberty was most secure.

Contract: *the idea that government represents a covenant between those who govern and those who are governed. Government power needs the consent of the governed to be legitimate.*

Republicanism: *a system of mixed government intended to preclude men from having either an interest in subverting, or a power to subvert, the government.*

Commonwealth: *a system in which parts of a constitution are independent of each other and each class of interests in society is separate and independent in its political authority and function.*

Colonial Patterns

The colonial experience with government left a mark on American political thinking and institutions. The first settlements were of three types: those founded by merchant capitalists seeking raw materials and trade, those founded by religious leaders seeking freedom of worship, and those founded by royal favorites given grants of land by the Crown.

Commercial expansion in the New World was facilitated when the Crown granted joint-stock charters to English trading companies with a monopoly over area trade. Virginia and Massachusetts Bay, for example, were both founded as **joint-stock colonies,** and their governments were patterned after the joint-stock company. A governor was appointed by the company to administer the affairs of the colony. Gradually, colonial legislatures emerged with some lawmaking authority in order to stimulate local interest in the colonial venture. But the joint-stock enterprise in America did not prove successful; both Virginia, in 1625, and Massachusetts, in 1684, had their charters revoked and were made royal colonies. Governors were appointed by the king and laws passed by the legislative assemblies could be annulled by him; nevertheless, a pattern of government—a framework of legislative and executive authority—had been established.

Compact colonies were established in New England—in Plymouth, Connecticut, and Rhode Island—as a result of ideas borrowed from religious theory. Separatists were accustomed to basing church authority on compact, or mutual consent. Now they had a unique opportunity to extend that theory of organization to society and their political institutions. By compact—the mutual consent of the adult males—they drafted their own basis for government. The Mayflower Compact in 1620 was the most famous of many such covenants. The compact operated as a constitution and provided for the necessary agencies of government. The pattern it provided was a legislature elected by all free men in the colony, which in turn selected the governor. Here were America's first efforts at local self-government. The compact became the colonial symbol for self-government, an instrument created by general agreement and binding to governors and governed alike.

Maryland, New York, New Jersey, Pennsylvania, the Carolinas, and Georgia emerged from royal land grants. These **proprietary colonies,** as they were called, were autonomous principalities. The proprietor was given complete control over the affairs of the colony. Some of the proprietors, such as Lord Baltimore and the Duke of York, at first insisted on exercising complete authority through a locally appointed governor. Others, such as William Penn, moved to establish greater colonial authority with local assemblies. In both cases, the proprietary grants proved awkward. As financial ventures they were largely unsuccessful, and their feudal organizations were unwieldy and out of date. Furthermore, the colonial tendency toward parliamentary authority was more than the proprietors cared to, or were able to, resist. In fact, the proprietary experi-

Joint-stock Colonies: *colonies founded as commercial ventures by English trading companies.*

Compact Colonies: *colonies that based their organization on ideas borrowed from religious theory. Government was created out of consent of the governed.*

Proprietary Colonies: *land grants in America to friends of the Crown, bestowing on the proprietor virtually sole power over the territory.*

ence in America probably promoted the colonists' commitment to parliamentary institutions.

By the close of the seventeenth century, most colonial governments were becoming similar in structure, having like legislative, executive, and judicial systems, and some measure of local authority. Most were to become royal colonies (Virginia in 1625, Massachusetts in 1684, and New York in 1685), and all were increasingly subject to regulation from England. This common experience promoted the development of democracy in the colonies, several distinct elements of which were clearly visible in their governments. The colonies had bicameral legislatures, in which local interests were represented; separate executive authority, both in office and function; judicial appeal to a Privy Council from local courts of law; regular and frequent elections; and an abiding faith in constitutionalism in the conviction that free government required written limits and prohibitions to political power.

Toward Independence

Peyton Randolph of Virginia, first president. Randolph served as president of the First Continental Congress of the United States in 1774. The presiding officers of the Continental Congress and Congress under the Articles of Confederation were called president. There were fourteen presidents before George Washington became the "first" president of the United States under the Constitution of 1789.

By the middle of the eighteenth century, the interests of England and the colonies were diverging. England still viewed the colonies as subordinate political units governed by Parliament and the Crown, but the colonies had begun to see themselves differently. The Sugar and Stamp Acts of 1764 and 1765 illustrated the colonies' growing separation from England. The colonial cry of "Liberty, Property and No Stamps" grew out of England's effort to levy a duty of threepence per gallon on molasses imported into the colonies and to place levies on such imported goods as sugar, coffee, calico, and indigo. The purpose of the acts was to raise revenue—to "defray the expenses of defending, protecting, and securing the colonies." England had long imposed tariffs on the colonies to regulate trade, but a tax affecting commerce and industry was seen by the colonists as a threat to colonial prosperity. James Otis declared the acts void for being "against the fundamental principles of the British Constitution" in his pamphlet *The Rights of the Colonists Asserted and Proved.* Otis argued that natural rights and the British constitution had been violated by a tax levied by a parliament in which the Americans had no representation. To the colonists, England had begun the Revolution.

The removal of the French from Canada had relieved the colonists' military dependence on England. The colonial population was growing, and pressure for westward expansion was increasing. Cultural and economic interests had established themselves and in many respects were considerably unlike English customs and practices. This growing awareness contributed, however subtly, to the "breakdown in sympathy, respect and understanding between the colonists and the mother country."[2]

The Townshend Acts, named for Charles Townshend, British chancellor of the exchequer, proved that America and England were irreconcilably drifting apart. Townshend fashioned a series of taxes on glass, lead, tea, and paper imported into the colonies, disguising the measures to take advantage of the supposed colonial distinction between external and internal taxation. Internal taxation designed to collect revenue and regulate internal matters had been rejected by the colonists, as the Stamp Act crisis demonstrated, but external taxation to regulate trade throughout the empire the colonists viewed as legitimate.

But it was soon obvious that the Townshend Acts had been designed to raise revenue in much the same way as the Stamp Tax had. Colonial reaction was swift and intense. John Dickinson's *Letters of a Pennsylvania Farmer,* which ran in several colonial newspapers, had immediate appeal. Dickinson articulated the view that parliamentary sovereignty over the colonies was limited: Parliament could regulate commerce but it could not tax the colonies. To England, which had always viewed the empire as a single community under parliamentary authority, the distinction Dickinson and the colonists now drew was absurd. If Parliament's authority over the colonies could be denied for "one instance," then it must be denied for "all instances."[3]

The controversy died down with the repeal of the Townshend Acts in 1770 (except for the tax on tea), but Americans were coming more and more to question Parliament's authority over the colonies. James Wilson in 1774 found it difficult to draw the line between colonial and parliamentary authority: "Such a line does not exist; and there can be no medium between acknowledging and denying that power in all cases."[4] The result was a shift in American thinking. By 1774, the colonists were rejecting parliamentary sovereignty. They saw the colonial tie with England resting with the king, claiming that colonial legislatures were independent of parliamentary regulation. As the debate moved forward, the colonists began to set the machinery of revolution in motion. The

The Boston Tea Party revealed the extent of American hostility toward the British.

First Continental Congress met in 1774 to deal with the imperial problem. For a time it considered a plan of union that would give the colonies dominion status, but this was tabled in favor of the Declaration and Resolves of the First Continental Congress, declaring the states "entitled to a free and exclusive power of legislation."

War broke out in 1775, and a Second Continental Congress was called for May 1775. This congress took up the task of raising an army, and it abandoned any hope of reconciliation with Great Britain. Tom Paine's *Common Sense,* which appeared in January 1776, greatly inflamed the public, and urged revolution by attacking loyalty to the king. By the spring of 1776, Congress had declared American ports open to foreign trade, and on May 10, 1776, Congress called for the states to create regular governments. On June 7, 1776, Richard Henry Lee, acting on instructions from Virginia, offered the following resolution to Congress:

> Resolved, that these United Colonies are, and of right ought to be, free and independent states, and that they are absolved from all allegiance to the British Crown, and that all connection between them and the state of Great Britain is, and ought to be, totally dissolved.

A committee of five was appointed to prepare a "declaration to the effect of the said resolution."

On July 1 the committee reported back with a declaration written by Thomas Jefferson. On July 2 a resolution of independence was adopted by a vote of twelve states (New York was undecided and did not vote). Finally, on July 4, 1776, a unanimous Continental Congress adopted the document we now know as the Declaration of Independence.

The Declaration of Independence was an eloquent statement of the eighteenth-century watchwords of constitutional democracy—natural rights, compact, popular sovereignty, and the right of resistance. Separation was achieved, but not independence.

The Articles of Confederation

The Revolutionary War had just begun and would last until 1783. In the meantime, the states had to govern themselves. Virtually all adopted new state constitutions. The Second Continental Congress, in accepting Richard Henry Lee's resolution for independence, also accepted his resolution to draft a constitution for the "United Colonies." The principle of a national government was not entirely new. Benjamin Franklin, at the Albany Conference in 1754, had proposed a scheme to increase colonial cooperation on common problems that amounted to a plan for a federal government. The First Continental Congress in 1774 saw a need for planning and collective action. In 1775, Franklin again proposed a plan for a "league of friendship" that would unite the states under a national Congress. Thus, the federal pyramid of local, state, and national governments was becoming visible. But the system set up by the Articles of Confederation, which were submitted to the states in 1777, maintained the revolutionary arrangement under the Continental Congress and did not solve the problem of sovereignty.

The articles placed full authority for the new national government in Congress while retaining the revolutionary principle of state sovereignty. The provisions of the government under the Articles of Confederation are presented in Table 2.1. Article Two, added by Thomas Burke of North Carolina, stated: "Each state retains its sovereignty, freedom and independence, and every power, jurisdiction, and right, which is not by this confederation expressly delegated to the United States, in Congress Assembled." Burke's addition made the Articles of Confederation a "league of friendship" rather than the basis for a strong national government.

Congress was given the power to make war and peace, to enter into treaties and alliances, to equip an army, to request money from the states,

TABLE 2.1   Major provisions of the Articles of Confederation and Perpetual Union

The States
1. Bound themselves together in a league of friendship, mutual support, and honor
2. Were prohibited from: maintaining standing armies; making war (except in case of invasion) or entering into treaties with another state or a foreign power; levying any impost or duty interfering with the treaties of the United States
3. Were enjoined to: accord free passage, the privileges of trade and commerce, and the privileges and immunities of free citizens in the several states to inhabitants of each state; render up fugitives from justice; to accord full faith and credit to the "records, acts, and judicial proceedings" of other states

The Congress
1. Was appointed annually "in such manner as the legislatures of each state shall direct," and its delegates were subject to recall
2. Could provide for the exercise of an executive power (in fact exercised through committees of the Congress)
3. Had power: to make peace and war and enter into treaties and alliances; to equip an army and navy, requisitioning the states for money, supplies, and men; to borrow money, emit bills of credit, and pledge the credit of the United States; to appoint the superior officers of the United States Army; to provide for the arbitration of boundary and land disputes between states; to provide for a postal system; and to regulate trade with the Indians

In essence, the articles ratified the form of government that had grown up during the war for independence. It was weak government, partly because union is a slow process, whatever the form of government. The central government was also given few powers and could exercise only those that were expressly delegated. Most notable among the disabilities were:

1. Congress lacked the power to tax or to regulate commerce.
2. No provisions were made for enforcing the decisions of the Congress either by sanctions applied to the states or their officers or through laws operating directly upon individual citizens.
3. There was no system of federal courts (except for a Court of Appeals for Admiralty, established in 1780).
4. Congress, when acting with respect to war, commerce, foreign relations, money or requisitions, could act only with the assent of nine states.
5. Amendment required unanimous consent of all the states.

SOURCE: David G. Smith, *The Convention and the Constitution* (New York: St. Martin's Press, 1965), p. 15.

to regulate trade with the Indians, and to establish a postal system. The important matters before Congress—war, foreign relations, and money—required the assent of nine states. Amendments to the articles required unanimous consent. No national executive or court system was created, but two vital powers, taxation and regulation of commerce, were denied Congress. These powers had been central to the dispute with England, and the colonists were not about to encourage centralized authority again. The Confederation, forced to rely on the colonial levy system, came to the verge of bankruptcy. Another weakness was the absence of any enforcement mechanism; the government was obliged to fall back on the states to enforce and carry out the functions of the central government. Since there was no judiciary, no agency existed to resolve questions of authority or enforce policy. Finally, the necessity for nine states to assent frequently proved an obstacle to legislation. Unanimous consent for amendments was impossible, and none were ever ratified.

Under the articles a degree of union was achieved, but problems mounted in the 1780s. The financial difficulties were especially severe. States failed to meet their financial assessments to finance the war, and Congress was unable to pay back even the interest on the large loans it had been granted by the French and Dutch governments. There were problems in foreign affairs as well. Most commercial treaties could not be

Separate states issued their own money during the Confederacy of the 1780s. Having many kinds of currency in circulation proved to be a problem.

negotiated because Congress lacked the power of enforcement, and those treaties that were negotiated were ignored. Britain closed the West Indies to American trade, and states quarreled with one another. New York levied duties on commerce from New Jersey, for example, which in turn taxed commerce from New York.

States ignored Congress and issued their own paper money, making trade and commerce increasingly difficult. Credit and money were either impossible to get or worthless. In Massachusetts in 1786, the paper-money advocates—debtors and small farmers—rebelled in what is known as Shays' Rebellion. The mob, led by Revolutionary War Captain Daniel Shays, closed courts in Massachusetts, thus preventing them from foreclosing mortgages on farms. They threatened to attack Boston proper if money was not made more readily available. The fear of violence in Massachusetts and the worsening economic and political situation heightened the movement for constitutional revision.

Calls for revision of the Articles of Confederation had been heard as early as 1780, before the articles even had been ratified. Alexander Hamilton proposed that Congress call a convention to prepare plans for a "general confederation." In 1781, Congress itself formed a committee to examine the deficiencies of the articles, but it was left for the Annapolis Conference in 1785, formed to consider interstate commerce problems, to move the colonies toward constitutional revision. The Annapolis meeting was a failure; only five states sent delegates, and no trade policy emerged. But Alexander Hamilton of New York and James Madison of Virginia sensed the opportunity and issued a call for a new convention, to meet in Philadelphia the next year, to revise the Articles of Confederation.

The experience of Americans under their first constitution had immense significance for that generation of constitutional thinkers. It was a time of significant social and political problems; it also was a time when people shared a belief that they could shape—and were shaping—the future of a new nation. There were widespread disagreements over what the future should look like, which led to lively and rich debates over political and constitutional issues. There was, however, no debate over the need for and desirability of a new nation. The debate in the 1780s was over the extent and power of the government—in particular, whether the new nation should have a national or a federal government. In the debate over ratification, Madison noted that the Constitution of 1787 was both national and federal. From this the noted historian Merrill Jensen concluded that "while this fact has led to innumerable conflicts of interpretation, it has also been a source of strength; for as one political group after another has gotten control of the central government it has been able to shape the Constitution to its needs and desires. Thus with the single exception of the Civil War, peaceful change has always been possible."[5]

But peaceful change appeared unlikely to the political leaders of the confederacy. The Revolutionary War had yet to be brought to a successful conclusion. In the face of the contending issues of debt, finance, and credit, the problem of establishing a stable economy loomed large indeed. At the same time, political factions pulled the national government in opposing directions. The "federalists" (supporters of state authority) pressed for weak central government, state sovereignty, and local control of finances to provide citizens with credit and land to stave off unemployment, bankruptcy, and the loss of faith in revolutionary ideals. The "nationalists" (supporters of national authority) believed in a national government with ample powers uninhibited by state controls. They wished to erect a national economic system of banking and commerce to facilitate national expansion and growth. Strict interpretation of the powers of Congress and the national government only hindered the task. This was the core of the political controversy that ultimately led to the Philadelphia convention of 1787.

The Constitutional Convention

The delegates assembled in the "large room" of the State House in Philadelphia on the second Monday in May 1787. There were not enough delegates present to represent a majority of states, so the meeting adjourned. On May 25 delegates from nine states opened the Constitutional Convention, and by the end of June, delegates from eleven states were in attendance. Table 2.2 gives a calendar of the events of the convention.

The Delegates

Of the seventy-four delegates appointed, only fifty-five appeared. The real work of the convention was done by fewer than twenty delegates, all eminent men. The gathering included many of America's leading political figures, bankers, merchants, and landowners. They were men well versed in the literature of politics.

But the mood was different from that before the Revolution. As Oliver Ellsworth of Connecticut observed, "A new set of ideas seemed to have crept in since the Articles of Confederation were established." Only eight delegates had signed the Declaration of Independence, though approximately half had fought in the war for independence. Moreover, many of the noteworthy figures of the Revolution were not delegates to the Philadelphia convention. Thomas Jefferson was serving as minister to France, John Adams as minister to Great Britain. Patrick Henry had been selected as a delegate, but "smelt a rat" and declined to participate. Not selected as delegates were such famous figures as Thomas Paine, Samuel Adams, and Richard Henry Lee.

Virginia sent a distinguished delegate, George Washington, a war hero who commanded respect and had the confidence of the other delegates. This undoubtedly was a factor in his being elected president of the convention. James Madison, aged thirty-six, was a strong advocate for the establishment of a national government and largely drafted what was called the Virginia Plan. For this he has been called the Father of the Constitution. Madison was a driving force at the convention. It is from

TABLE 2.2   The Federal Convention of 1787 and Ratification

The Federal Convention of 1787

May 14–24	Preliminary meetings
May 25–28	Organization
May 29	Proposal of Randolph (Virginia) Plan and Pinckney Plan
May 30–June 11	Debate on the Randolph Plan, ending in adoption of its main provisions
June 15	The Paterson (New Jersey) Plan; revolt of the "small state" delegations
June 15–30	Two weeks of debate over the two plans
June 30	The Compromise Committee is appointed
July 5	Report of the Compromise Committee proposing popular representation in the lower house, equal representation in the upper, and origin of all money bills in the lower house
July 5–16	Debate on the Connecticut Compromise
July 16	The Compromise is adopted
July 17	Agree to a judicial negative of unconstitutional state acts
July 23	Adopt the provision for per capita voting in the Senate
July 26	Agree upon a single executive: a president to be chosen for a term of seven years and ineligible for reelection
August 8–10	Agreement upon qualifications of voters and representatives and upon the regulation of elections
August 15–23	Debate on the powers of Congress (Article I, Sections 8 and 9)
August 24–25	Debate on the powers of the president
August 28	Adopt restrictions upon the states
August 29	The "three-fifths" clause; the slave trade; and the commerce clause
August 30	Agree upon the provisions for admission of new states
September 6	Agree to election of the president by electors in the states and with no restrictions upon reelection
September 7–8	Agree upon the annexation of the Senate in the appointive power and in the treaty-making power
September 10	Provision for amendments to the Constitution
September 12	Report of the Committee of Style
September 17	Signing of the Constitution and adjournment

Ratification

Delaware	Thirty members ratified unanimously December 7, 1787
Pennsylvania	Ratified by a vote of 46 to 23, December 12, 1787
New Jersey	Thirty-nine delegates ratified unanimously December 18, 1787
Georgia	Twenty-six delegates ratified unanimously January 2, 1788
Connecticut	Ratified by a vote of 128 to 40, January 9, 1788
Massachusetts	Ratified by a vote of 186 to 168, February 16, 1788
Maryland	Ratified by a vote of 63 to 11, April 26, 1788
South Carolina	Ratified by a vote of 149 to 73, May 23, 1788
New Hampshire	Ratified by a vote of 57 to 47, June 21, 1788
Virginia	Ratified by a vote of 89 to 79, June 25, 1788
New York	Ratified by a vote of 30 to 27, July 26, 1788
Rhode Island	Ratified by a vote of 34 to 22, May 29, 1790
North Carolina	Rejected 193 to 75, August 4, 1788; finally ratified November 21, 1789

SOURCE: David G. Smith, *The Convention and the Constitution* (New York: St. Martin's Press, 1965), pp. 33–34.

his notes of the proceedings that much of the convention's activities have been reconstructed. Also present from Virginia was the governor, Edmund Randolph, who introduced the Virginia Plan to the convention.

Pennsylvania's delegation was equally distinguished. Benjamin Franklin, second only to Washington in reputation and respect, was the oldest delegate, at age eighty-one. A renowned statesman and philosopher, Franklin took little active part in the convention. His presence and spiri-

Fact File
Delegates to the Constitutional Convention

		Occupation	Age at signing	Action regarding the Constitution
New Hampshire	John Langdon	Shipowner	46	Signed
	(John Pickering)*			
	Nicholas Gilman	Politician	32	Signed
	(Benjamin West)			
Massachusetts	(Francis Dana)			
	Elbridge Gerry	Businessman	43	Signed
	Nathaniel Gorham	Businessman	49	Signed
	Rufus King	Lawyer	32	(Approved of)
	Caleb Strong	Lawyer	42	(Approved of)
Rhode Island	No appointment			
Connecticut	William Samuel Johnson	Lawyer/educator	59	Signed
	Roger Sherman	Lawyer/merchant	66	Signed
	Oliver Ellsworth	Lawyer	42	(Approved of)
	[Erastus Wolcott was elected but declined to serve.]			
New York	Robert Yates	Politician	49	
	Alexander Hamilton	Lawyer	32	Signed
	John Lansing, Junior	Lawyer	43	
New Jersey	David Brearley	Lawyer	42	Signed
	William Churchill Houston	Educator	41	
	William Paterson	Lawyer	42	Signed
	(John Neilson)			
	William Livingston	Lawyer	63	Signed
	(Abraham Clark)			
	Jonathan Dayton	Lawyer	26	Signed
Pennsylvania	Thomas Mifflin	Politician	43	Signed
	Robert Morris	Financier	53	Signed
	George Clymer	Banker	48	Signed
	Jared Ingersoll	Lawyer	38	Signed
	Thomas Fitzsimons	Businessman	46	Signed
	James Wilson	Lawyer	44	Signed
	Gouverneur Morris	Lawyer	35	Signed
	Benjamin Franklin	Publisher	81	Signed
Delaware	George Read	Lawyer	53	Signed
	Gunning Bedford, Junior	Lawyer	40	Signed
	John Dickinson	Lawyer	54	Signed
	Richard Bassett	Lawyer	42	Signed
	Jacob Broom	Businessman	35	Signed

	Occupation	Age at signing	Action regarding the Constitution
Maryland			
James McHenry	Doctor	33	Signed
Daniel of St. Thomas Jenifer	Landowner	64	Signed
Daniel Carroll	Landowner	56	Signed
John Francis Mercer	Soldier/politician	28	
Luther Martin	Lawyer	39	
[Charles Carroll of Carrollton, Gabriel Duvall, Robert Hanson Harrison, Thomas Sim Lee, and Thomas Stone were elected but declined to serve.]			
Virginia			
George Washington	Soldier	55	Signed
Edmund Randolph	Lawyer/politician	34	
John Blair	Lawyer	55	Signed
James Madison, Junior	Politician	36	Signed
George Mason	Landowner	62	
George Wythe	Lawyer/politician	61	(Approved of)
James McClurg	Doctor	41	(Approved of)
[Patrick Henry, Richard Henry Lee, and Thomas Nelson were elected but declined to serve.]			
North Carolina			
Alexander Martin	Politician	47	(Approved of)
William Richardson Davie	Lawyer	31	
Richard Dobbs Spaight	Politician	29	Signed
William Blount	Politician	38	Signed
Hugh Williamson	Doctor	51	Signed
[Richard Caswell and Willie Jones were elected but declined to serve.]			
South Carolina			
John Rutledge	Lawyer	48	Signed
Charles Pinckney	Lawyer	29	Signed
Charles Cotesworth Pinckney	Lawyer	41	Signed
Pierce Butler	Soldier	42	Signed
(Henry Laurens)			
Georgia			
William Few	Politician	39	Signed
Abraham Baldwin	Lawyer	32	Signed
William Pierce	Soldier	47	(Approved of)
(George Walton)			
William Houstoun	Politician	32	
(Nathaniel Pendleton)			

*Those whose names are in parentheses did not attend.

SOURCE: Adapted from Max Farrand, *The Records of the Federal Convention of 1787*, vol. 3 (New Haven, Conn.: Yale University Press, 1966).

tual support added credibility to the deliberations, however, and made compromise easier. James Wilson was the scholar of the convention. A legal theorist, Wilson had argued the colonies' case during the Revolution. At the convention, he supported strong central government and direct popular election of the president. (Washington was later to appoint him associate justice of the Supreme Court.) Another supporter of national government from Pennsylvania was Gouverneur Morris, an eloquent debater whose ideas found their way into the final draft of the Constitution.

From New York came Alexander Hamilton, John Lansing, and Robert Yates. Hamilton, at age thirty-two, had achieved national prominence by the time of the convention. Yet his support for a strong national government was continually frustrated, in part by his insistence on a constitutional monarchy and in part by Lansing and Yates, who outvoted him to support weak government. All three left the convention before it had finished its work.

The small states also had their advocates. William Paterson, author of the New Jersey Plan, argued for weak central government and equal representation of states. Also supporting the small states was John Dickinson of Delaware, who had achieved fame during the Revolution and by drafting the Articles of Confederation. The most vocal champion of states' rights, however, was Luther Martin of Maryland. A brilliant lawyer and attorney general of Maryland, Martin was an outspoken critic of centralized authority and nationalistic tendencies. Martin left the convention in disgust before the Constitution was signed by the delegates.

Other delegates deserve mention. Oliver Ellsworth of Connecticut, who had served in Congress, was now Chief Justice of his home state's Supreme Court and was to become chief justice of the United States. Rufus King of Massachusetts became a strong force for national government and won respect as a speaker. Also from Massachusetts was Elbridge Gerry, who refused to sign the finished product, calling it a "monarchial" document. Another who refused to sign was George Mason of Virginia. Mason, a friend of Thomas Jefferson, saw the Constitution as too aristocratic. John Rutledge of South Carolina, an important southerner, argued for stronger national authority.

By the end of May the convention had organized and settled its preliminary business. Washington was unanimously elected to preside, each state was to have an equal voice in voting, and all meetings were to be secret. Many of this assembled body had already distinguished themselves in public service, and more would distinguish themselves under the new government. Their average age was slightly over forty-three years.

The Virginia Plan

On May 27, 1787, Edmund Randolph opened the session with the Virginia Plan. Thus, on its very first day of business the convention was faced not with a plan to revise the articles, but with an entirely new plan of union. As John Roche has suggested,

> [The Virginia Plan's] consequence was that once business got underway, the framework of discussion was established on Madison's terms. There was no interminable argument over agenda; instead the delegates took the Virginia Resolutions—"just for purposes of discussion"—as their point of departure. And along with Madison's proposals, many of which were buried in the course of the summer, went his major premise; a new start on a Constitution rather than piecemeal amendment.[6]

The Virginia Plan occupied the delegates for more than two weeks. It was a nationalistic plan for strong central authority that more than remedied the weaknesses of the articles. Congress could legislate where "the separate states are incompetent, or where the harmony of the United States may be interrupted." A national executive was provided for. A Council of Revision had veto power over both national and state legislation, and Congress could negate any law passed by the states (see Table 2.3).

It appeared that the Virginia Plan would be adopted. The articles had been discarded and debate centered on the method of electing representatives to Congress and apportioning them among the several states. Apparently the delegates accepted the concepts of a two-house legislature, popular elections, strong executive authority, a national judiciary, and a national veto power. The small states preferred state representation and

---

TABLE 2.3 Major provisions of the Virginia Plan

1. A national legislature consisting of two houses, with representation in both houses based on population
2. One branch of the legislature elected by the people; the second branch elected by the first branch from persons nominated by state legislatures
3. The powers of the legislature include:
   a. to legislate on all cases in which the separate states are incompetent
   b. to legislate on all cases in which the harmony of the United States may be interrupted by the exercise of individual state legislation
   c. to negate all laws passed by the several states contrary to the constitution
   d. to call forth the forces of the union against any member of the union failing to fulfill its duty
4. A national executive chosen by the legislature for a fixed (unspecified) term and ineligible for reelection
5. A Council of Revision, composed of the executive and members from the national judiciary, to review acts of the legislature and of state legislatures, with the power to veto such acts
6. A national judiciary consisting of a supreme court and inferior courts established by the legislature; judges hold offices for life
7. Provision to be made for the admission of new states; every state to be guaranteed a republican form of government
8. Provision to be made for amendments to the constitution such that the approval of the legislature is not required

---

SOURCE: Max Farrand, *The Records of the Federal Convention of 1787*, vol. 1 (New Haven, Conn.: Yale University Press, 1966), pp. 20–22.

state control of the legislature; they would also have liked equal representation of states. The large states favored the Randolph proposals but were prepared to compromise, allowing one chamber of Congress to be selected by state legislatures. Having secured a compromise on state control of elections for the Senate, the small states acceded.

A plan for ratification of the Virginia Plan was outlined on June 10, 1787. The convention adjourned so that "leisure might be given" to thoughts on securing ratification, but now the small-state delegates—Paterson, Martin, Elbridge Gerry, and others—realized their situation. They used the recess to declare the Virginia Plan unacceptable, because it pushed too far beyond the articles. William Paterson of New Jersey was then asked to draft a "purely Federal" plan that might serve as an alternative.

The New Jersey Plan

The New Jersey Plan differed little from the Articles of Confederation, although it did remedy some of its defects (see Table 2.4). It would establish a "supreme tribunal," but with little enforcement power. A plural executive would be given only limited authority. The rights to tax and regulate commerce were added to the powers of Congress. But the New Jersey Plan was truly a federal plan: the states selected the representatives to Congress, Congress would be a single chamber, and states would be equally represented. The New Jersey Plan was voted down, but for two weeks the merits of the two plans were debated while tempers shortened. At the center was the growing schism over state sovereignty and

TABLE 2.4   Major provisions of the New Jersey Plan

---

1. Congress to consist of one house, with representation based on states, each state to have one vote
2. The powers of Congress, in addition to those presently existing under the Articles of Confederation, include:
   a. to raise revenue by levying duties on imported goods, by a stamp tax, and by postage
   b. to regulate interstate and foreign commerce
   c. to requisition funds from states in proportion to population (white citizens and three-fifths of all others)
3. A plural (number unspecified) executive elected by Congress for a fixed term and ineligible for reelection. Executive may be removed by Congress upon the application of a majority of state executives. The powers of the executives include:
   a. to execute the federal acts
   b. to appoint federal officers
   c. to direct all military operations
4. One supreme court with judges appointed by the executive for life (no inferior national courts)
5. All laws and treaties of the United States to be the supreme law of the respective states, and the judiciary of the several states to be bound thereby in their decisions
6. Provision to be made for the admission of new states
7. Rules for naturalization to be the same in every state
8. Full faith of law and punishment to be extended to citizens of other states

---

SOURCE: Max Farrand, *The Records of the Federal Convention of 1787*, vol. 1 (New Haven, Conn.: Yale University Press, 1966), pp. 242–243.

nationalism. And the nationalists knew the convention would not succeed without support from the small states.

The Great Compromise

A majority of the states remained committed to proportional representation; small-state delegates were equally determined to fight for equal representation. A compromise was necessary. When the delegates voted to accept proportional representation in the lower house at the end of June, moderates on both sides saw their opportunities: proportional representation for the lower house, equality for the upper chamber. A committee of eleven was quickly appointed, and on July 5 it recommended that

- in the lower house each state be allowed one member for every forty thousand inhabitants;
- all bills for raising or appropriating money originate in the lower house, and not be amended by the upper;
- each state have an equal vote in the upper house.

This was the Great Compromise, or the Connecticut Compromise, named after Roger Sherman of Connecticut, who had been the first to suggest the solution. From then on, the convention made steady progress. There was no more talk of adjournment, and the outline of the Constitution began to take shape. The issue of federalism occupied and divided the convention for better than a month, with sectional rivalries clearly in evidence. The admission of new states and the disposition of western lands was one problem. The East had few such lands and was suspicious of cheap land for farmers. Easterners were more interested in federal power to regulate trade and commerce. The South, joined by a few northern states, opposed Congress's monopoly on trade and its power of direct taxation. These conflicts brought to the surface the issues of slavery and the slave trade, which with the arguments over trade, were unavoidable. Still, solutions evolved. The delegates sifted the issues, and ultimately fashioned a series of compromises:

1. There would be a unified national power to regulate commerce, with the promise that there be no state taxation of imports or federal taxation of exports.
2. Direct taxation would be apportioned according to population and all excises would be uniform.
3. The slave population would be counted at three-fifths, for both taxation and representation.
4. Congress was empowered to impose conditions for the admission of new states.
5. The slave trade could continue until 1808 (for twenty years).[7]

The problem of federalism was also visible in the debate over the executive and the judiciary. Both sides recognized the lack of an executive under the articles. One side wanted a weak executive, responsive to the legislative will. The other side, the convention's nationalists, argued for a national executive possessing independent authority. The conflict focused on the mode of the election. The Randolph Plan called for election by Congress; the nationalist position was ambiguous. James Wilson called for direct election, but most delegates rejected this proposal as too democratic and foreign to American experience. The solution, of course, was the **electoral college**—people in the various states would choose electors, who in turn would elect the president. Each state would choose electors "in such a manner as its legislature may direct." Thus the electors might be popularly elected; but they would be independent. If no candidate received a majority of the electoral votes, the House of Representatives would elect the president.

Electoral College: *the group of electors, appointed by the states, who select the president. To be elected president, a candidate must receive a majority of electoral votes.*

The debate over the judiciary went to the heart of the federal question. Here the problems of the Articles of Confederation were obvious: how would states enforce national policy, and how would jurisdictions of the states and the national government be interpreted? The Virginia Plan empowered a national government to legislate directly. A Council of Revision would have authority to suspend acts of the states. Congress, in turn, would presumably interpret the limits of its authority, since it had, under the Virginia Plan, the authority to negate any law contravening the articles of the union. The net result was that Congress would have to review every act passed in every state in order to determine whether it contravened federal legislation or the Constitution. This criticism, along with the objection that laws contrary to the union would not be recognized by the courts, led the convention to abandon the proposal.

But what should replace it? Luther Martin suggested a phrase from the New Jersey Plan. After a short debate, the convention unanimously accepted Martin's suggestion. It read as follows:

> This Constitution, and the Laws of the United States which shall be made in pursuance thereof; and all treaties made, or which shall be made, under the authority of the United States, shall be the supreme Law of the Land and the Judges in every state shall be bound thereby, anything in the Constitution or Laws of any state to the contrary notwithstanding.

From this proposal came the second paragraph of Article VI of the Constitution.

The delegates also removed Congress's right to contravene laws contrary to the Constitution. Some delegates felt that that power rightly belonged with the court; others disagreed. James Wilson, Elbridge Gerry, and Gouverneur Morris spoke in favor of the power of the federal judiciary to declare federal law unconstitutional. John Dickinson, on the other hand, stated that "no such power ought to exist." The Committee on Detail's resolution setting forth the jurisdiction of the Supreme Court was amended to extend the Court's jurisdiction to "all cases arising under the Constitution and laws of the United States." Madison records that the delegates generally agreed that the jurisdiction "was constructively limited to cases of a judiciary nature." But in outlining the jurisdiction of the federal judiciary, the delegates inserted no provision for judicial review. If the delegates intended the courts to pass on the constitutionality of laws, they did not say so in Article III of the Constitution.

By early September, only forty-two delegates remained at the convention. A Committee on Style was appointed to draft and edit the final document, with Gouverneur Morris doing most of the writing. The draft was accepted almost without alteration. On September 17, 1787, 127 days after convening, 39 delegates stepped to the table at the head of the long

The Constitution was signed at the State House in Philadelphia in 1787 by the remaining delegates to the Constitutional Convention.

room in the State House in Philadelphia and affixed their signatures to the Constitution.

Ratification

If one drew a line fifty miles west of the sea from Maine to Georgia, it would quite accurately separate the tidewater Federalist supporters of the Constitution from the inland anti-Federalist opposition (Figure 2.1). Merchants, shippers, bankers, and landowners, primarily residing on the seacoast, were in favor of a government that would protect commerce and establish a sound national economy and financial system. But the interior was inhabited by small farmers, trappers and traders, and frontiersmen who cared little for commerce or land speculation. To them, the Constitution meant the end of paper money and easy access to land for settlement.

Ratification was not only an economic dispute. People of all economic classes in Delaware, Virginia, and Pennsylvania supported the Constitution. The cities of New York and Philadelphia favored the new Constitution, as did predominately rural New Jersey. At the center was a serious political issue: the Constitution took sovereignty away from the states; the Articles of Confederation had been discarded. The framers even ignored state legislatures for the purpose of ratification.

The convention had declared the Constitution ratified when approved by "popularly elected conventions in nine of the thirteen states." In a sense, the method was illegal. The Articles of Confederation required

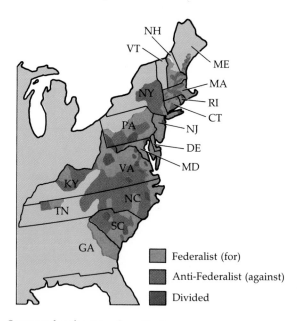

Figure 2.1 Support for the new Constitution

that amendments be submitted to state legislatures and approved by all thirteen states. This, the delegates knew, would be almost impossible to secure. Many delegates also felt that popular approval in the states would enhance the Constitution's national appeal.

The Debate

The debate over ratification was public. Newspaper articles, pamphlets, and speeches were plentiful on both sides. The most widely circulated piece of anti-Federalist literature was Richard Henry Lee's *Letters From a Federal Farmer*. The Federalist position was set out in a series of articles by Alexander Hamilton, James Madison, and John Jay published in New York under the pseudonym Publius. In all, eighty-five essays appeared; they were known as *The Federalist* and they remain the clearest and most articulate statement of the principles behind our system of government.

Anti-Federalists: *opponents of the Constitution drafted in 1787. They favored local government and a weak central government.*

Some of the issues in the debate were trivial; others went to the heart of the Constitution. The **anti-Federalists** questioned whether a national government with centralized power could govern a large and culturally diverse nation. They feared that local and state interests would be ignored and that the increased power of the national government would be an invitation to despotism. And, of course, they noted that no Bill of Rights existed to protect individuals from a powerful national government.

Federalists: *eighteenth-century Americans who supported a strong central government and favored ratification of the Constitution.*

The **Federalists** countered by stressing that a Bill of Rights was unnecessary because the new government was one of enumerated powers. The addition of a Bill of Rights was a bargaining point, however, and in the ratification conventions the Federalists pledged to adopt a Bill of Rights should the convention support ratification.

After ten months, the ratification process was coming to an end. Five states ratified quickly and with little opposition, but in four others the vote was close, and two states (New Hampshire and Rhode Island) at first rejected the Constitution. New Hampshire was the ninth state to ratify on June 21, 1788, on a second vote, and the Constitution became the supreme law of the land. At this point New York and Virginia had not yet ratified, and without the largest and strategically most important states, the new Constitution had little chance of success. Virginia soon ratified, however, and New York followed a month later.

Ratification was achieved in large measure because of the political skills of the Federalists. They were astute politicians who used the addition of a Bill of Rights to their advantage and left their opponents with only one choice: ratify the Constitution or keep the articles, and continue to endure political chaos and economic ruin. The Federalists had stressed the federal nature of the union and the republican basis of authority. The Constitution was not perfect, but it was the best available remedy and the work of the best minds the nation had to offer.

The Constitutional Framework

Benjamin Franklin was approached one day as the convention was drawing to a close and asked, "Well, doctor, what have we got—a republic or a monarchy?" "A republic," replied the doctor, "if you can keep it." The "patchwork of compromises" sent to the states for ratification had become the basis for a new and "more perfect" union based on republican principles.

Representation

The delegates at Philadelphia were committed to wise and virtuous representation. They believed not in majority rule, but in representatives for the people as the most efficient solution for problems and the best defense of liberty. Madison noted that a republic differs from a democracy only in that a republic is "a government in which the scheme of representation takes place." We commonly use the phrase democratic republic, meaning that our representatives are chosen by the democratic principle of **majority rule.** The framers were distrustful of direct democracy. John Adams distrusted its instability, and Elbridge Gerry remarked to the convention during the debate over election procedures for Congress "that the decline in virtue is caused from the excess of democracy."

Majority Rule: *the principle of democracy that holds that the greatest number of citizens should have their way, as in elections or in choosing policy.*

The cure for the excesses of democracy was the republican principle. Madison particularly argued for republicanism. His *Federalist No. 10* was a classic statement on the nature of republicanism. A republic could ensure representation of the people through the franchise, he wrote. Yet in a country as large and diverse as America, representation would discourage the formation of a majority. Madison fervently believed that in the "extended republic," among the great variety of interests, parties, and sects within America, no majority could develop. Coalitions would have to form in order to govern, a process that would temper majorities and allow the democratic system to function freely.

Titles of Nobility

It was fairly clear from the outset of the debate over representation that the delegates wished to abolish hereditary titles of nobility and hereditary offices. The trend had begun in the states and was carried to the convention. The delegates clearly believed that every citizen ought to be judged on merit. The people have a right to pass judgment on their public officials at the polls: "No qualification of wealth, of birth, of religious faith, or of civil profession is permitted to better the judgment or disappoint the inclination of the people," declared the *Federalist No. 57.*[8] Only through an open electoral process could public officials earn the esteem and confidence of the citizens.

Periodic Elections

It was assumed from the outset that regular and periodic elections were the way to ensure the consent of the governed. The *Federalist No. 52* explained it this way:

> As it is essential to liberty that the government in general should have a common interest with the people, so it is particularly essential that the branch of it under consideration should have an immediate dependence on, and an immediate sympathy with, the people. Frequent elections are unquestionably the only policy by which this dependence and sympathy can be effectually secured.[9]

Tenure in Office

A prime means of preventing majorities or demagogues from abusing their powers was to establish, for different offices, differing terms and differing modes of election. The term for the House of Representatives was fixed at two years, that for the Senate at six years, and that for the presidency at four years, while judges would serve for life. In addition, the House was to be directly elected by the people. The Senate was indirectly elected; state legislatures would fix the mode of selection. The president would be indirectly elected through the electoral college. The framers' purpose was not to prevent popular control; indirect election is admittedly less democratic than direct election, but it is still a representative system.

James Madison
Best known as the chief architect of the Constitution, James Madison served as a Virginia legislator and later as vice-president and the fourth president of the United States. It is Madison's notes of the Constitutional Convention that provide us today with the most complete record of the proceedings. Madison penned several of the *Federalist* essays with John Jay and Alexander Hamilton. He was an early supporter of Hamilton, who abandoned the Federalists to become a close friend of Thomas Jefferson.

Separated Powers

Madison put the issue of power directly in the *Federalist No. 37:* "[We must combine] the requisite stability and energy in the government with the inviolable attention due to liberty and to the republic form."[10] The delegates labored long and hard to set up a government that could rule effectively and yet not oppressively. The nationalists wanted a strong central authority; the small states demanded protection for states' rights.

The Constitution tried to balance the power of the central government against that of the states—to unite a national government and thirteen separate states within a federal system. The Constitution also balanced the powers of the national government into three separate but related branches of government—legislative, executive, and judicial.

Federalism   The Constitution did not solve the problem of sovereignty: states' rights would always be a problem. What the Constitution did was to expand the powers of the national government, giving it authority to operate directly on the people. At the same time, the states' authority to legislate their affairs was reserved to them. This was a masterpiece of political engineering: from two contradictory positions of authority the framers fashioned a workable compromise.

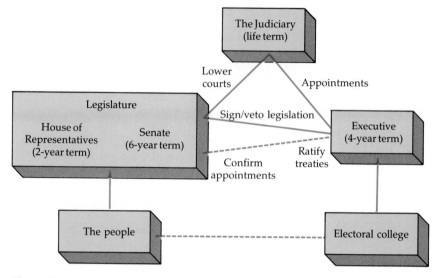

Figure 2.2a   American separation of powers

The Separation of Powers   Federalism had been a compromise thrust on the delegates because of the debate over sovereignty. **Separation of powers,** on the other hand, was a seventeenth- and eighteenth-century political concept designed to protect liberty and prevent tyranny. From the writings of John Locke, and from the French writer Montesquieu's *The Spirit of the Laws* (1748), the colonists took the idea of dividing the power of the national government into three distinct branches: the legislative, executive, and judicial. The delegates wanted power to be separated so that no one branch could take over the powers and responsibilities of the other branches.

Separation of powers gives constitutional authority to each of the three branches of the national government (see Figure 2.2a). None is dependent on the others for the source of its authority, but none of the three can operate without sharing authority. The framers made sure there would be **checks and balances** to authority by making the domains of the branches overlap. For example, the legislature passes laws, but the laws become valid only after the president signs them. It is the chief executive who conducts foreign affairs and makes treaties with foreign countries, but he does so with the advice and consent of the Senate. The courts act as a "watchdog" over the Constitution, exercising the power of judicial review to declare acts of Congress or of state legislatures unconstitutional. Supreme Court judges are appointed by the president and confirmed by two-thirds vote of the Senate.

Limited Authority

It is often said that we have a government of laws, not of people. Article VI declares that the Constitution and the laws and treaties of the United

Separation of Powers: *a seventeenth- and eighteenth-century political theory that was incorporated into the Constitution. To ensure that no single branch of government became too powerful, authority was distributed among the three main branches.*

Checks and Balances: *a system by which each branch of government exercises a check on the actions of the other branches of government.*

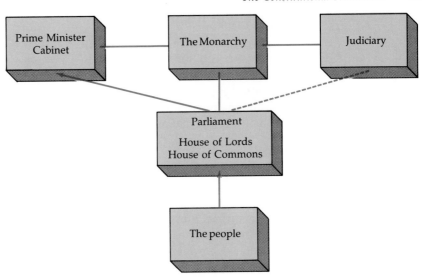

Figure 2.2b   British division of powers

States are the supreme law of the land. The Constitution both grants and limits political authority. The framers of the Constitution enumerated and limited power wherever they felt it was necessary. In Article I, the delegates enumerated the powers of the new Congress. They also placed some specific prohibitions on the powers of Congress in Section 9 of Article I, while in Section 10 they placed limitations on the states. Years of change and interpretations by courts and Congresses have significantly altered this framework. But the principle remains: power should be limited.

The power of the judiciary was likewise restricted in Article III. The judiciary was to hear only "cases and controversies," and then only where federal law or parties of different states were concerned. The Supreme Court was not to make policy. In a most real sense, then, constitutionalism meant limited government.

Legislative Prohibitions   Article I, Section 9, of the Constitution placed some specific restrictions on the powers of Congress. Among these were some basic English rights that the framers felt government must not violate. Foremost was the right to a **writ of habeas corpus,** which Congress was prohibited from suspending unless compelled by rebellion or invasion. The writ of habeas corpus is a basic right of citizens to a judicial order directing an official holding a person in custody to show cause why that person can be legally detained. Congress was also prevented from passing a **bill of attainder.** A bill of attainder was a legislative declaration of guilt naming the individual, crime, and punishment without benefit of trial. Finally, Congress was denied the right to make **ex post facto laws.** Such laws are retroactive criminal statutes that declare actions a crime after they have been committed and permit punishment.

Writ of Habeas Corpus: *a court order requiring that a person held in custody be brought before the court to show cause for his or her detention.*

Bill of Attainder: *a law declaring a particular individual guilty of a crime and naming the punishment without benefit of trial.*

Ex Post Facto Laws: *laws that impose punishment for an act that was not a crime when it was committed.*

The Bill of Rights

Added to the Constitution shortly after ratification, the Bill of Rights protected individuals' rights against the power of the national government. The first ten amendments to the Constitution form the Bill of Rights. They were a distillation of rights under English law and state constitutions growing out of the American Revolution. In effect, the original Constitution is commonly viewed as the Constitution *plus* the Bill of Rights. A strong part of our tradition, having been the focus of debate during the ratification debate, the Bill of Rights is accepted as part and parcel of the Constitution.

The First Amendment freedoms of religion, speech, press, assembly, and petition are designed to protect the individual and ensure a democratic political process. The Second and Third Amendments (ensuring the right to keep and bear arms and prohibiting the quartering of troops in homes) are largely eighteenth-century protections little applied to twentieth-century problems. The Fourth Amendment (prohibiting unreasonable search and seizures), Fifth Amendment (ensuring grand jury indictment of evidence, no double jeopardy for the same crime, and no self-incrimination), and the Sixth Amendment (allowing the right to a jury trial and the right to confront witnesses) are procedural guarantees of fairness and due process when citizens confront the law. The Seventh Amendment extends jury trials to civil matters, and the Eighth Amendment prohibits excessive bails and cruel and unusual punishment. These latter two are known as substantive guarantees. The Ninth Amendment was designed to protect emerging rights not enumerated in the Constitution, since no one assumed that all rights could be listed or anticipated. The Tenth Amendment is a protection for the states and the people of the states meant to reserve powers to them not delegated to the national government. Taken together, the amendments forming the Bill of Rights stand as an impressive guarantee of individual liberty against a possibly oppressive government.

The Bill of Rights was added to the Constitution at the insistence of the anti-Federalists due to fears of abuses by the national government. Yet the fact remains that most of the charges of abuse to the freedoms contained in the Bill of Rights have been leveled at the states, not the national government. It is a strange irony that the great concern over federal abuse to individual liberty should have resulted in protection of individuals from state abuse. Much of our effort to enforce freedom of speech, separation of church and state, and proper criminal investigations, and to define obscenity and corporal punishment, are the result of state intrusions, not federal action.

The Question of Motives

Perhaps because Americans have so venerated the Constitution, it becomes somewhat difficult to interpret the motives behind its formulation.

Early on, critics of national power such as Thomas Jefferson and John C. Calhoun would construct a constitutional theory defending states' rights and restricting national power. After the Civil War, the age of "Constitution worship" began. John Fiske's *The Critical Period in American History, 1783–1789*,[11] argued that under the Articles of Confederation the nation was on the verge of economic chaos and political disunion. The Constitution warded off anarchy and tyranny, yet preserved liberty and popular government through a republican process of government. The Constitution had saved the union. In the twentieth century, the framers' motives were challenged. J. Allen Smith and especially Charles Beard, in *An Economic Interpretation of the Constitution*, questioned the portrayal of the framers as patriots. Beard's charge was the strongest and most influential: the Constitution was "an economic document drawn with superb skill by men whose property interests were immediately at stake."[12] Beard cast the convention in an altogether different light. The Articles of Confederation adversely affected the economic interests of certain classes, and it was the men who met in Philadelphia to draft the Constitution who were thus affected. Beard argued that they drafted the Constitution to protect their own personal economic interests.

Generations of scholars have argued over Beard's thesis. Robert E. Brown[13] attacked it: he held that economically the framers lost as much as they gained by ratification of the Constitution. Forrest McDonald[14] argued that ratification of the Constitution in the states did not come as Beard would have predicted. He suggested that the states whose economic interests were promoted did not overwhelmingly favor adoption.

The Constitution's democratic character was also challenged. J. Allen Smith drew this conclusion: "We are trying to make an undemocratic Constitution the vehicle of democratic rule."[15] Smith, and later Vernon Parrington,[16] stressed the aristocratic character of the delegates and their disdain for democracy.

More recently Garry Wills has written that the Founding Fathers were influenced by eighteenth-century Scottish concepts of the moral sense. In *Explaining America* he offers a view of Madison and Hamilton as moved by public virtue owing to Hume's political essays. The vision of the *Federalist*, says Wills, is of the virtuous ruler "serving not for private gain but out of pride in his own virtue; impartial, not consulting any interest but the 'permanent and aggregate interests of the community.' That is the vision of the *Federalist*."[17]

None of these criticisms and interpretations is totally accurate, yet they all serve a useful purpose. They help us to see the delegates not as gods or saints, but as eighteenth-century politicians with all the shortcomings of human beings, fashioning a government with the tools at hand.

The Evolving Constitution

John Marshall, the great chief justice of the Supreme Court from 1801 until 1835, said of the Constitution in *McCulloch* v. *Maryland*,

This is a Constitution intended to endure for ages to come, and consequently, to be adapted to the various crises of human affairs. To have prescribed the means by which government should in all future time, execute its powers, would have been to change entirely the character of the instrument, and give it the properties of a legal code. It would have been an unwise attempt to provide, by immutable rules, for exigencies which . . . can be best provided for as they occur.[18]

The framers were generally agreed that the Constitution would have to be changed from time to time and that changing conditions would necessitate alteration. They provided, in Article V of the Constitution, a formal method for changing it. But one of the reasons the Constitution has been formally amended so little is that ways exist to change it informally. The Constitution has been changed by congressional and presidential actions that have defined and given substance to its vague language. Finally, and most significantly, the Constitution has been kept up-to-date by the courts, which continually interpret events in accordance with constitutional principles.

Formal Amendment

Formal amendments may be proposed by two methods: a two-thirds vote of both houses of Congress or a national convention called by Congress at the request of the legislatures of two-thirds of the states.

The national government would initiate the process: Congress would call for a national convention at the request of the legislatures of two-thirds of the states. Is Congress obligated to call such a convention upon receipt of a petition from two-thirds of the states? The language of Article V of the Constitution would imply that this was so: "The Congress . . . *shall* call a convention. . . ." But the language of Article IV for returning fugitives charged with a crime is equally imperative: A person fleeing from justice and found in another state "*shall* on demand of the executive authority of the state from which he fled, be delivered up. . . ." Yet the courts have ruled that they lack any enforcement powers to compel a governor to comply. Could the courts compel Congress to call a constitutional convention? How would they enforce such a decree? Furthermore, would the subject matter necessarily be limited to the topic proposed by the states in the petition? One must remember that the only constitutional convention ever convened did not limit its work to "amending the Articles of Confederation."

Nearly four hundred petitions for constitutional conventions have been filed with Congress over the years; few, however, have come close to obtaining the consent of the required number of state legislatures. Between 1963 and 1971, thirty-three states (one short of the required two-thirds) petitioned Congress to call a convention to reverse a Supreme Court decision requiring state legislatures to be reapportioned on the basis of population. But no such convention was ever called.

At present, the National Taxpayers Union is leading a campaign in which thirty-one state legislatures have petitioned Congress for a convention to initiate an amendment to balance the federal budget. The drive picked up momentum in the early 1980s with the conservative mood of the nation and President Reagan's support. Leading the drive have been conservative members of the Senate, notably Orrin Hatch of Utah, Strom Thurmond of South Carolina, and Dennis DeConcini of Arizona. They succeeded in securing Senate approval for a balanced-budget amendment proposal. However, the House has forestalled any further action, and approval appears unlikely. Congress shows little sign of using the convention method to propose amendments to the Constitution.

Amendments that are proposed are ratified by the states in one of two ways: by the legislatures of three-fourths of the states or by special ratifying conventions in three-fourths of the states. Congress determines which of the two methods is to be used (see Figure 2.3).

Equal Rights Amendment: *a proposed constitutional amendment, recently before the states for ratification, that would prohibit sex-based classifications. It was not ratified.*

The fact remains that securing amendments to the Constitution is quite difficult. The most recent effort to ratify the **Equal Rights Amendment** (ERA) is a case in point. It was submitted to the states for ratification in 1972. In June 1982, after ten years before the states, it fell three states short of the needed number to become part of the Constitution. In fact, the Constitution has rarely been amended. With the Bill of Rights correctly considered part of the original Constitution, and ignoring Prohibition and its repeal (one amendment effectively canceling out another), there have been only fourteen amendments added to the Constitution—fewer than one per decade since 1789. It is simply difficult to pass anything in three-fourths of the states.

Proposed

by two-thirds vote of both houses of Congress

or

by a national convention called by Congress on request of the legislatures of two-thirds of the states

Ratification

by legislatures in three-fourths of the states

or

by ratifying conventions in three-fourths of the states

========= traditional

————— once used

- - - - - - - never used

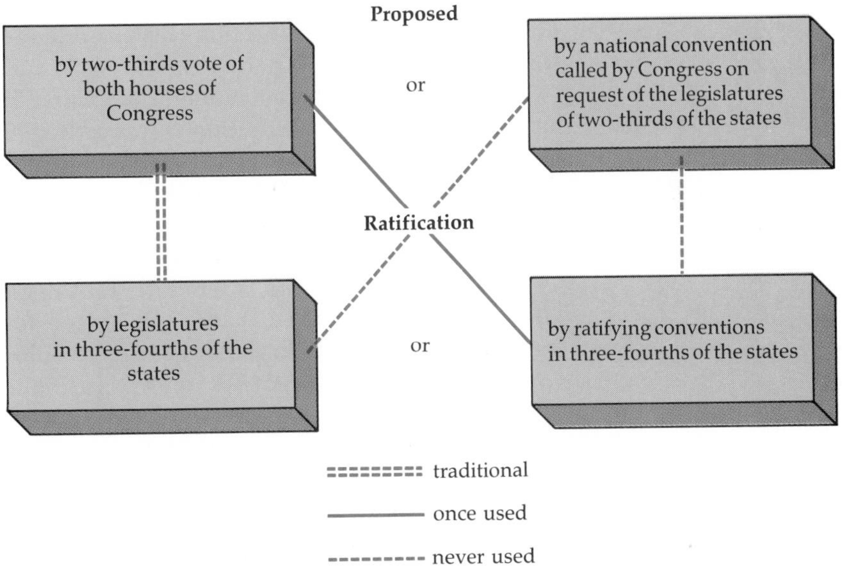

Figure 2.3 Amending the Constitution

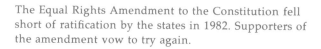

The Equal Rights Amendment to the Constitution fell short of ratification by the states in 1982. Supporters of the amendment vow to try again.

Of the twenty-six amendments that have been passed, only the Twenty-first, repealing prohibition, was submitted to ratifying conventions. States normally have seven years in which to ratify, although Congress determines the amount of time to be provided. Where the time is unspecified, the courts have concluded that seven years is reasonable. Congress has generally followed this practice, although with the Equal Rights Amendment, ratification was extended for thirty-nine months beyond the seven-year period.

A state can ratify an amendment after first having rejected it. But the question of undoing ratification is less settled. Some states have voted to rescind their ratification of the Equal Rights Amendment; but is such recision valid? State ratification is now monitored by the General Services Administration (GSA), which certifies the ratification and keeps the count of states. Previously, the secretary of state performed this duty.

The Supreme Court has entered the ERA dispute. In late 1981 an Idaho district court judge ruled that the extension for ratification of ERA was unconstitutional. He also ruled that states could rescind their ratification. Women's groups and the GSA quickly petitioned the Supreme Court to rule on the question. Before the Court did so, the ERA deadline had expired and the Reagan administration had petitioned the Court to dismiss the suit as moot. In 1982 the Supreme Court did just that. It vacated the district court's order and remanded the case back to the district court with instructions to dismiss the suit. In the meantime, the ERA was reintroduced into the 98th Congress.

Policy and the Separation of Powers

The Founding Fathers contemplated the formulation of public policy as a structural process wherein each of the three branches of the national government would have delegated powers and functions. The primary responsibility for formulating policy was vested with Congress in Article I, Section 8, which sought to articulate the range of policy areas. The president could veto legislation; otherwise, he was to administer the formulated policy. The Court would interpret policy and rule on its constitutionality.

The distribution of power and necessary cooperation, however, have changed greatly over two hundred years. Today the policy-making process is the result of the shifting balance of power within separation of powers. A contemporary review of the process must note the following relevant factors:

1. *Bureaucracy*   There is now almost universal recognition that bureaucracy is significantly involved in public policy. The administration of policy includes discretionary authority. The implementation of policy requires rule making.

2. *Subgovernment phenomena*   A broad range of policy making and implementation is conducted by subgovernments. The most relevant subgovernments are influential congressmen and subcommittees, administrative agencies with policy jurisdiction, and affected interest groups. The subgovernment is normally involved with routine administration; hence prerogatives become established that are difficult to alter.

3. *Courts*   Judicial review has given the courts great influence over policy in the United States. Courts are frequently called upon to interpret statutes and to legitimate courses of action. More and more groups and individuals are turning to the courts to enjoin government or private actions or, conversely, to prompt government action in a policy area.

4. *Interest groups*   As the source of much demand for policy adoption, interest groups represent interests before government and provide criticism for policy implementation. Interest groups concerned with public policy proliferated in the 1970s and early 1980s, many of them focusing on narrow, single-issue policy concerns.

The change in the policy process necessitates close interaction between official and unofficial participants. Subgovernment dominance in policy areas creates a need for this close interaction, and the influence of government and nongovernment participants changes with the interaction and policy areas.

A useful basis for classifying policy formulation is that which identifies the nature of decision making. Three types of policy formulation are

1. *Incrementalism*   This is a congruent process whereby decisions are patterned after previous decisions. There is no reformulation of policy, and decisions differ only incrementally from existing policies. A well-established base exists, therefore, from which to predict policy consequences. Subgovernment participation is strongest in this type of formulation.

2. *Imitative*   Problems of government are treated by analogy. What has worked in the private sector, particularly business, can be imitated for the public sector. Cost-benefit analysis and management by objectives are examples. The executive, courts, and interest groups are likely participants.

3. *Innovation*   New policies are proposed that have no tradition or equivalence in the private sector. They suggest new directions for solutions of problems of public policy. True innovative policies are uncommon and typically face opposition. Hence their adoption is uncertain. The chief executive normally dominates this area.

Changes in the Constitution have occurred through formal amendments. We might categorize these changes as follows:

1. *Authority of government*   The Eleventh Amendment removed from federal court jurisdiction suits against a state by citizens of another state or a foreign citizen. The Thirteenth Amendment abolished slavery and empowered Congress to legislate its enforcement. The Sixteenth Amendment empowered Congress to levy a graduated income tax. The Eighteenth Amendment prohibited the manufacture, sale, and transportation of alcoholic beverages. The Twenty-first Amendment repealed the Eighteenth and empowered states to regulate alcohol. The proposed balanced-budget amendment, were it to be passed and ratified, would require Congress to submit a balanced budget before each fiscal year and allow deficit spending in a fiscal year only by a three-fifths vote of all members of Congress.

2. *Power to the citizen*   The Fourteenth Amendment made the former slaves citizens of the state wherein they resided and extended to them the "privileges and immunities" of citizenship as well as "due process of law" and "the equal protection of the law." The Fifteenth Amendment barred prohibitions to voting on the basis of race, color, or previous condition of servitude. The Seventeenth Amendment gave citizens the direct vote to elect U.S. senators. The Nineteenth Amendment assured women the right to vote. The Twenty-fourth Amendment abolished the poll tax as a prerequisite for voting. The Twenty-sixth Amendment extended the franchise to all persons eighteen years of age and older. If ratified, the proposed Twenty-seventh Amendment will extend equality of rights on the basis of sex.

3. *Structural changes*   The Twelfth Amendment provided for the separate election in the electoral college of the president and vice-president. The Twentieth, or lame-duck, Amendment changed the dates on which terms of office for Congress and the president began. The Twenty-second Amendment limited a president to two terms. The Twenty-third Amendment expanded the electoral college by adding three votes for the District of Columbia. The Twenty-fifth Amendment, on presidential succession and disability, clarified the procedure for succession when a vacancy or disability occurs in the presidency. A proposed amendment before Congress would extend representation in Congress to the District of Columbia.

Informal Changes

The Constitution, as a frame of government, cannot provide for every situation. It has to be adapted to the crises of the moment as they occur. In fact, the body of constitutional law is primarily the result of informal changes, of applying the Constitution to the various legal, economic, social, and political problems the nation has encountered. These informal changes are basic to the American constitutional system.

Congress, in acting on the authority specified in the Constitution, frequently fills in the details of the Constitution. In 1789 Congress passed the Judiciary Act, which established the basic lower court structure we have today. The federal bureaucracy is the result of the authorization by Congress of the organizations and functions of the executive branch established but left undescribed in Article II.

In 1974 Congress moved to fill in the meaning of "high crimes and misdemeanors" when the Judiciary Committee of the House of Representatives undertook Articles of Impeachment against President Nixon as a result of Watergate. The committee did not believe impeachable offenses had to be criminally indictable offenses. It voted three articles of impeachment: obstruction of justice in the Watergate cover-up, abuse of power in the misuse of governmental agencies and violating the oath of office, and contempt of Congress in willfully disobeying congressional subpoenas. We do not know whether Congress would have voted to accept this interpretation, since Richard Nixon resigned his office prior to a full congressional vote.

Presidential practice has defined the power of the chief executive. There have been no changes in the formal powers of the president since 1789, yet the office and its powers have changed markedly over the years. World war, the growth of a world economy, and a host of other events have modified the Constitution as the presidency has grown with the changing national and international environment.

The Watergate tapes gave rise to the constitutional issue of executive privilege: are presidential conversations by right confidential?

Executive Privilege:
the power of a president to withhold information from Congress and the judiciary.

In the Watergate debate over the confidentiality of presidential conversations, President Nixon claimed **executive privilege** for presidential conversations, tapes, and documents. *U.S.* v. *Nixon*[19] required the president to turn over the material but also formally, for the first time, recognized the principle of executive privilege as rooted in the Constitution. Here is a presidential practice that has been accepted under the Constitution (subject to review by the courts, however, as *U.S.* v. *Nixon* made plain) since Thomas Jefferson's day.

Custom and practice over the years have also established a number of other procedures. The clearest example is the presidential nominating convention. The Constitution made no mention of how candidates were to be nominated. Over the years, political parties developed and gradually devised the convention method for nominating candidates. In 1972, George McGovern was soundly defeated for the presidency, but no one disputed his right to challenge Richard Nixon. He had secured the Democratic endorsement and therefore had won the right to challenge Mr. Nixon.

Watergate also affords an example here. In the years following Watergate, several civil damage suits were filed, some against the former president himself. The Supreme Court held that the Constitution affords a president absolute immunity from civil damages for all official actions taken while in office, even where those actions were in violation of the law. Said Mr. Justice Powell, "We consider this immunity a functionally mandated incident of the President's unique office, rooted in the Constitutional tradition of the separation of powers and supported by our history."[20]

Toward the Third Century

Is our Constitution obsolete? Can a Constitution drafted more than 200 years ago govern the nation into the twenty-first century? When the Constitution was framed, the United States was a small, rural, and relatively unimportant country. Most Americans lived within 100 miles of the Atlantic Ocean: Philadelphia had 42,000 residents, New York 33,000, and Boston 18,000. Ninety-five percent of the population lived in towns containing fewer than 2,500 people. The industrial revolution had not yet occurred, the Civil War was 70 years in the future, and the Depression and federal grants-in-aid were undreamt of.

Today we are a mass society, highly mobile and urban. Travel from one coast to another takes only a few hours. Some corporations' assets rival the wealth of most nations. Interest groups and multiple elites dominate the decision-making process. New technology sweeps over us, bewildering and changing the labor market. Nuclear weapons have forever changed our presence and responsibility in world affairs.

We say that political institutions evolved and that they have been entrusted with responsibility to meet the changes, but have they changed so as to become unrecognizable to their creators? Can the separation of powers, a Bill of Rights, as well as congressional, judicial, and presidential offices established and empowered on the basis of ideas drawn from the eighteenth century remain relevant to a people moving into their third century of governance?

The future of our constitutional structure poses some interesting and important questions. What are some of the major problems government will have to confront?

1. *Limited growth* The allocation of scarce resources will be a major concern. The depletion of nonrenewable resources such as coal, oil, and gas and the damage caused to the environment by securing and using these resources will have to be weighed against the need for jobs and industrial growth. Can the nation continue to use the growth of the GNP as the measure of progress? The problem of redistribution of resources is equally troubling. Food, population, and human services all demand attention. How do we bring the problems under control and still protect individual liberty? Problems of regulation and distribution involve the issues of separation of powers and big government.

2. *The postindustrial society* The postindustrial society is an advanced industrial society dominated by sophisticated technology, a service economy, and rapid change—and it is the projection for America in the future. Government will be increasingly important as a provider of social benefits. The society will be educated, mobile, and service oriented. The tendencies for meritocracy and social stratification confront theories of democracy. In a service economy, new property and new income depend on governmental policy and spending. Individuals need protection from themselves. Government regulation becomes social policy. Public planning becomes a necessity. New groups and clienteles are emerging, and the old politics will have to give way and accommodate new realities.

3. *International relations* Multinational corporations and global economic policies already temper our political process. The demand for new policies, and for Congress and the president to work together to coordinate foreign and domestic policies, is an emerging imperative. OPEC already alters our domestic economy. National security and secrecy, human rights, and international cooperation are all values to be judged within the context of the international environment. The need for governmental accountability in foreign affairs is perhaps the most important change needed.

4. *Political values and ideas* Whether the postindustrial society is a reality or not, American political values are already changing. Americans are distrustful and cynical of government. They are fearful of increased taxes. Political alignments are polarizing within both parties. (There are already strains on the political process because of the open-convention system and disarray of the parties.) Single-issue voting is increasing. The traditional values of an open, pluralistic political system stand in contrast to the growing resistance of interest groups to governmental regulation,

Changing Consensus: Terrorism

Constitutions are the documents of civilized nations. The rule of law inherent to constitutionalism is taken as a serious means by which the powers of the governors are circumscribed and the rights of the governed are protected. Throughout our history we have endeavored to act on the adage "a government of law, not men." This has meant that government officials approach problems with solutions that conform to the authority vested with their office. It has further meant that individual citizens treat one another, publicly and privately, by standards accepted by civilized people—those standards fixed in law. But the contemporary wave of terrorism directed at Americans challenges that essential standard of constitutionalism.

Terrorism has grown dramatically in the 1980s, and from kidnapping to bomb attacks to airplane hijacking, Americans increasingly have become targets. Even an incomplete listing of terrorist acts against Americans since the Iranian hostage crisis of 1980 reveals the frightening reality of the phenomenon.

April 1983 Car bombing of U.S. embassy in Beirut; 63 deaths, including 17 Americans

October 1983 Car bombing of U.S. military headquarters in Beirut; 241 U.S. Marines killed

January 1984 Murder of Malcolm Ken, president of American University in Beirut

September 1984 Car bombing of U.S. embassy in Beirut; 23 killed, 2 Americans

December 1984 Kuwait airplane hijacked in Teheran; 2 Americans killed

June 1985 TWA airplane hijacked in Athens; 1 American killed

October 1985 Hijack of cruise ship *Achille Lauro* in Egypt; 1 American killed

March 1986 Bomb exploded aboard TWA airplane; 3 Americans killed

March 1986 West Berlin disco bombed; 2 Americans killed

Although all these terrorist attacks occurred overseas, the FBI claimed in 1985 that it had foiled twenty-three terrorist plots within the United States, six of which were directed from abroad.

Innocent citizens are most vulnerable to terrorism. Terrorists strike at targets of opportunity, which often include places and people innocent of any hostile action against the terrorists or their cause. Vacation travelers, airplanes, market squares, public buildings, and other public places are all favorite targets for terrorists. Terrorism can strike when and where we least expect it.

The Reagan administration has pledged "swift and effective retribution" against terrorists. But combatting terrorism and terrorist organizations calls for measures that frequently strain our civilized tradition of constitutional government. The urge to retaliate is strong, yet it raises unsettling questions of power and justice within our constitutional framework. So do many of the other suggested responses to combat terrorism. Here is a list of the most common proposals:

- Preemptive attack on terrorist groups or camps located in the U.S. or in foreign lands
- Increased CIA and FBI discretion in intelligence gathering on known or suspected terrorists
- Baggage and personal searches of passengers using air or sea transportation
- Barricades around public buildings, including restricted or prohibited public access to such buildings
- Boycott of travel or shipments to or from areas with high risk of terrorism

Each of these suggestions raises potential problems. How much security and personal search is compatible with privacy? The American people value their freedom and mobility, which

terrorism potentially restricts. For example, can Americans be denied access to the U.S. Capitol or other public buildings and landmarks? We are confronted with the problem of balancing personal freedom against the need for protection from wanton violence. But the context of this problem is a new one, for terrorism is not directed at classes of persons or specific objects. Its very randomness is what makes it so difficult to combat within a constitutional framework. It requires broad or inclusive measures that may affect innocent people as much as do the acts of terrorism themselves.

Citizens protesting the neutron bomb are expressing their rights within a democratic political system.

voluntary wage controls, and affirmative action practices. The growth in the size and complexity of government may produce veto groups that will destroy separation of powers.

5. *Mass communication*   From a political standpoint, we are already seeing the effects of mass communication. Presidential candidates no longer need political parties; elections are conducted through the communications media, and candidates' advertising budgets have soared. Issues have been shaped and dramatized by the media; much of what Americans learn and know about political issues is what the media present. There is growing concern about an opinion-shaping ideological bias in mass communications.

6. *Violence*   In recent years, violence has become a national political problem. The assassinations of President Kennedy, Robert Kennedy, and Martin Luther King; the killings at Kent State; the attempted assassination of Ronald Reagan; and terrorist violence abroad, such as the assassination of Anwar Sadat and the attempt on Pope John Paul II, all seem to indicate a trend toward settling problems by violence. There is a tendency for small groups to pressure public authority with hijackings and kidnappings. Street crime is increasing. The obligations of society to victims of violence have become a major new area of law and civil liberties. How to keep the political process open and peaceful yet accommodating is a major issue that will test the flexibility of our constitutional system.

Summary

1. America's political heritage is the result of English political traditions—the common law and republicanism—and colonial political experience, notably legislative authority, free elections, and constitutionalism.

2. The Articles of Confederation were the United States's first attempt at national self-government. They established a weak central government and left real power to the separate states. The Constitution was a new plan for national government in which national power operated directly upon the people.

3. The Constitution represents some basic American political principles. Representation requires decision makers to stand for election by the people. Powers are separated so that no institution or officeholder is entrusted with too much power. Limited authority prevents abuse of political office. Over the years, however, our thinking on limited authority has changed. Finally, individual liberty is protected by a Bill of Rights added to the Constitution.

4. There has been a continuing debate over the Constitution, over the motives of the Founders in drafting the Constitution, and over the distribution of power between the national government and the states. The Constitution has been made adaptable to meet the changing expectations of the American people.

5. The Constitution is shaped and will continue to be shaped by the important political problems America faces. While these problems will test the ability of constitutional government to respond, the Constitution is likely to endure—as it has for nearly two hundred years.

Research Projects

1. *A new constitution*   The present Constitution is nearly two hundred years old. If a new constitutional convention were to be held, what changes would you propose for the convention? Write out some new articles or amendments for the Constitution. If you have no changes to propose, why is the present document adequate? Some interesting efforts discussing redrafting the Constitution you may wish to consult are Rexford Tugwell, *The Emerging Constitution* (Harper's Magazine Press, 1974) and Leland Baldwin, *Reframing the Constitution* (ABC–Clio, 1972).

2. *Ratification of the Constitution*   Debate over ratification of the Constitution was between Federalists and anti-Federalists. Write an essay describing the struggle for ratification. Include such issues as (a) what kind of people the Federalists and anti-Federalists were; (b) how the delegates to state conventions were selected; (c) what the geographical distribution of Federalists and anti-Federalists was; (d) what issues emerged over the

Constitution; and (e) how the states voted on ratification. Would you conclude that the struggle was profound or minor? Fast or slow? Was ratification easy or difficult to achieve?

3. *The frameworks for government*   Line off four columns on a sheet of paper and compare item by item the Articles of Confederation, the Virginia Plan, the New Jersey Plan, and the Constitution. Compare such features as structure and representation in Congress, delegation of power to Congress, presidential power, mode of electing the president, structure of the courts, court jurisdiction, admission of new states, and enforcement.

Notes

1. Gordon S. Wood, *The Creation of the American Republic, 1776–1787* (New York: W. W. Norton, 1969), p. 198.
2. Alfred Kelly and Winfred Harbison, *The American Constitution,* 4th ed. (New York: W. W. Norton, 1970), p. 64.
3. William Knox, *The Controversy Between Great Britain and Her Colonies Reviewed* (London, 1769), pp. 50–51. Reprinted in *Old South Leaflets,* no. 210 (S. E. Morison, ed.) Boston: Directors of the Old South, 1907.
4. James Wilson, *Considerations on the Nature and Extent of the Legislative Authority of the British Parliament. The Works of James Wilson,* James Andrews, ed. (Chicago: Callaghan, 1896), vol. II, p. 506.
5. Merrill Jensen, *The New Nation* (New York: Alfred A. Knopf, 1958), p. xiv.
6. John P. Roche, "The Founding Fathers: A Reform Caucus in Action," *American Political Science Review* 55 (December 1961): 803.
7. David G. Smith, *The Convention and the Constitution* (New York: St. Martin's Press, 1965), pp. 50–51.
8. Alexander Hamilton, James Madison, John Jay, *The Federalist Papers,* Clinton Rossiter, ed. (New York: The New American Library, 1961), p. 351.
9. Hamilton, Madison, Jay, *The Federalist Papers,* p. 327.
10. Ibid., p. 226.
11. John Fiske, *The Critical Period in American History, 1783–1789* (New York: Houghton Mifflin, 1888).
12. Charles A. Beard, *An Economic Interpretation of the Constitution of the United States* (New York: Macmillan, 1960), p. 188.
13. Robert E. Brown, *Charles Beard and the American Constitution* (Princeton, N.J.: Princeton University Press, 1956).
14. Forrest McDonald, *We The People: The Economic Origin of the Constitution* (Chicago: University of Chicago Press, 1958).
15. J. Allen Smith, *The Spirit of American Government* (New York: Macmillan, 1907), p. 31.
16. Vernon L. Parrington, *Main Currents in American Thought* (New York: Harcourt, Brace, 1930).
17. Garry Wills, *Explaining America* (Garden City, N.Y.: Doubleday, 1981), p. 269.
18. *McCulloch* v. *Maryland,* 4 Wheat. U.S. 316 (1819).
19. *United States* v. *Nixon,* 418 U.S. 683 (1974).
20. *Nixon* v. *Fitzgerald,* 457 U.S. 731 (1982).

Bibliography

Bailyn, Bernard. *The Ideological Origins of the American Revolution.* Cambridge, Mass.: Harvard University Press, 1967.
An excellent discussion of the sources and ideas from the eighteenth century with which the American colonists fashioned the Revolution. Bailyn looks at the Revolution through its ideas and intellectual development.

Becker, Carl. *The Declaration of Independence.* New York: Vintage Press, 1942.
A now classic study on the ideas and events surrounding the Declaration of Independence. Following the trend of ideas, Becker sees the declaration as a culmination of dominant eighteenth-century thought.

Burns, James McGregor. *The Vineyard of Liberty.* New York: Alfred A. Knopf, 1982.
A fresh blending of history and biography concerning the shaping of our republic from the Constitutional Convention to the Civil War. Burns discusses how the spirit of liberty has been central to our formative years. Considered are the contributions of several little-known people who helped to shape events in these formative years.

Corwin, E. S. *The Constitution and What It Means Today.* Harold Chase and Craig Ducat (eds.). Princeton, N.J.: Princeton University Press, 1981.
A section-by-section discussion of the Constitution in the light of contemporary Supreme Court decisions and political practices. A useful book for understanding the present interpretation or meaning of the Constitution.

Farrand, Max. *Records of the Federal Convention of 1787.* New Haven, Conn.: Yale University Press, 1937.
The most extensive and comprehensively indexed

record of the debates of the federal convention. Farrand has reconstructed, largely from Madison's notes, the debates and results of the constitutional convention. The best source on the subject.

Hamilton, Alexander, Madison, James, and Jay, John. *Federalist Papers.* New York: New American Library, 1961. As close as America comes to original political theory, the *Federalist Papers* seek to explain and justify the new Constitution. Many of the original essays give valuable insight into the philosophy of the Constitution and the delegates who penned it.

Jensen, Merrill. *The New Nation: A History of the United States During the Confederation.* Boston: Northeastern University Press, 1981. The foremost scholar on the period of the confederation, Merrill Jensen focuses on the events and conflicts between the Revolution and the Constitution. Jensen examines America's first efforts to govern the new nation and the problems the nation faced.

Kelly, Alfred, Belz, Herman, and Harbison, Winfred. *The American Constitution.* New York: W. W. Norton, 1983. A well-written treatment of constitutionalism in America from its earliest origins up to the present. Kelly and Harbison present excellent discussions of early issues and conflicts and the legal precedents surrounding them. These then are carried forward as constitutional history.

Peltason, Jack. *Understanding the Constitution.* New York: Holt, Rinehart & Winston, 1982. An excellent discussion of the Constitution, its origins and present meaning. Peltason's is a readable source book for understanding any article or section of the Constitution and for understanding present construction of the Constitution.

Rakove, Jack N. *The Beginnings of National Politics.* Baltimore: Johns Hopkins University Press, 1979. A very fine study of the history of the Continental Congress. This book fills in an important period of American history prior to the Constitution, focusing on America's first national legislature.

Rossiter, Clinton. *The Seedtime of the Republic.* New York: Harcourt, Brace & World, 1953. A masterful history of colonial and revolutionary America. Rossiter provides a very readable account of colonial life—social life, economics, government, and revolutionary thought—and the men and ideas that influenced the Revolution. Rossiter seeks to describe the environment in colonial and revolutionary America.

Rossiter, Clinton. *1787, The Grand Convention.* New York: Macmillan, 1976. A well-written, lively account of the Constitutional Convention and struggle for ratification. The book contains much useful and interesting information on the convention deliberations as well as on its delegates.

Wills, Garry. *Inventing America.* Garden City, N.Y.: Doubleday, 1978. A fresh look at the events surrounding the Declaration of Independence. Much of the book is devoted to Jefferson's draft of the declaration, seeking to explain Jefferson's meaning and how it differs from other interpretations of the declaration.

Wills, Garry. *Explaining America: The Federalist.* Garden City, N.Y.: Doubleday, 1981. The second work in a planned four-volume series on the American Enlightenment, Wills offers a new interpretation of the *Federalist* that differs from the more common view focusing on separated powers and balanced government. Wills's view is that particular Scottish values from the Enlightenment shaped the Founding Fathers' political theory.

Wood, Gordon S. *The Creation of the American Public.* Chapel Hill, N.C.: University of North Carolina Press, 1969. A scholarly examination of the ideology of the American Revolution, state governments, and politics until the Constitutional Convention. Wood methodically discusses the creation of an American science of politics prior to 1787.

Federalism

The history of federalism is a history of intergovernmental cooperation and tension. The framers had no grand design; their novel experiment in shared sovereignty would necessarily adapt to the changing environment of the nation and the states. Federalism is as much an attitude—a pragmatic, decentralized approach to problem solving—as it is a legal–constitutional arrangement for separating the powers of a national government and its component states. An Englishman, M. J. C. Vile, described federalism this way:

> Americans have a "federal attitude" towards government which colours their whole approach to governmental problems, which insures that the solutions found to these problems will be within a particular pattern. This attitude is . . . vague and meandering, and contains contradictory elements. It is a way of thinking which enables considerable changes necessary in order to adapt to new conditions, changes which can be brought by compromises, the elements of which are easy to find in the rich and varied ideas of American history.[1]

Federalism has its origins in shared decision making and a decentralized party system as much as in the Philadelphia Convention. Morton Grodzins and Daniel Elazar spoke of federalism not as a layer cake with each level a neat, separate sphere of decision-making authority, but rather as a marble cake, in which the functions of government penetrate all levels of government, each of which shares in making public policy.[2] No federal, state, or local functions are separate and distinct. From the Northwest Ordinances, in which states set aside federal land to finance education as a condition for settlement, to the new Department of Education, the school lunch program, and New York's request for federal aid, "the history of the American governments is a history of shared functions."[3]

As a system of authority, federalism is a method of dividing powers between the central, or national, government and the constituent units, or states. It gives substantial and independent authority to each. No level of government is dependent on another for its authority or is in a position to change the distribution of power. The attributes of federalism can be summarized as follows:

1. There is a constitutional division of governmental functions such that each level is autonomous in at least one sphere of action.
2. Each government is final and supreme in its constitutionally assigned area.
3. Both levels act directly on citizens (unlike a confederation, where only the regional units act directly on the citizens, while the central government acts only on the regional governments).
4. Both levels derive their powers from the "sovereign" (that is, the people or the Constitution), rather than from one another.
5. Therefore, neither can change the relationship unilaterally.
6. The regional divisions (that is, states) exist on the basis of their own right.[4]

Unitary Government: *a system of government in which all authority is derived from the central government.*

Confederation: *a system of government in which legal authority is held by constituent governments that, in turn, may choose to create and delegate authority to a central government. This was the type of government system created by the Articles Confederation.*

Formally, then, federalism can be distinguished from a **unitary system of government.** A unitary system derives all authority from the central government, and all local governments exist at the pleasure of the central government. The central government delegates authority and functions to local governments as it chooses. This describes the situation in Great Britain and the relationship between American states and their cities and counties. A **confederation,** on the other hand, places legal authority in the hands of constituent governments that, in turn, may choose to create and delegate authority to a central government. The central government does not have authority to regulate individuals directly; rather, it operates at the direction of the states and acts upon them. This system existed under the Articles of Confederation in 1783. Figure 3.1 shows the system of government under a confederation, a federation, and a unitary government.

As a legal theory, federalism stresses the independence of each level of authority; the Constitution grants exclusive authority to each level of

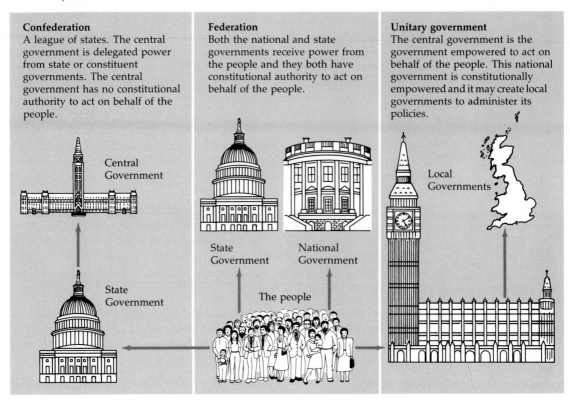

Confederation
A league of states. The central government is delegated power from state or constituent governments. The central government has no constitutional authority to act on behalf of the people.

Central Government

State Government

Federation
Both the national and state governments receive power from the people and they both have constitutional authority to act on behalf of the people.

State Government

National Government

The people

Unitary government
The central government is the government empowered to act on behalf of the people. This national government is constitutionally empowered and it may create local governments to administer its policies.

Local Governments

Figure 3.1   A confederation, a federation, and a unitary government

government. But in fact the real brilliance of federalism rests with its shared responsibilities. Federalism is a dynamic relationship allowing for decentralized authority and joint activity. It provides a relatively efficient method of problem solving.

Whether the framers intended federalism to be a cooperative problem-solving device or a contractual, constitutional division of powers is a question of some dispute. States' rights lawyers are likely to argue for the latter; but much discussion of federalism revolves around problem solving. Part and parcel of our changing expectations regarding federalism is increased intergovernmental cooperation in managing our problems. From cleaning the air to providing recreational facilities to saving New York City, people want efficient and effective solutions to problems.

The History of Federalism

The American experience with federalism began with the colonies and the Articles of Confederation. Working out an acceptable relationship between central and state authorities was a familiar problem for the delegates at Philadelphia.

Early Cooperation and Conflict

By 1765, when the British abandoned their so-called policy of salutary neglect, a beneficial policy of ignoring the colonies, colonial self-government was well entrenched. Foreign affairs and trade were commonly recognized to be under the Crown, but in domestic matters local legislatures had developed the habit of governing for themselves. Stephen Hopkins, the brilliant governor of Rhode Island, compared the British Empire to a federal state in 1765. Parliament could legislate on such matters as commerce, money, and credit, but "each of the colonies hath a legislature within itself, to take care of its interests." In the Albany Plan, Benjamin Franklin had proposed a "grand council" to which the colonies would delegate the power to raise military forces, legislate, make war and peace with the Indians, and levy taxes and collect customs duties. Earlier still, in 1643, Massachusetts Bay, Plymouth, Connecticut, and New Haven formed the Confederation of New England. Motivated by fear of the Indians, the Dutch, and the French, and confronted by common problems and religious interests, they signed the Articles of Union, which provided for two representatives from each colony and gave them power to declare war, make peace, and settle boundary disputes.

The Articles of Confederation were a "league of friendship," with the states retaining final authority. They failed in important ways to give Congress sufficient authority to legislate, and they were cumbersome and impossible to amend. Yet the articles displayed the growing federal character of the new nation and were an attempt to provide a national government with powers to meet common problems.

The Constitutional Convention took up where the articles left off. The Virginia Plan created a national government, and while it recognized the states, it left little authority to them. The New Jersey Plan was more in accord with the articles, closer to what the small states felt the convention ought to draft. Out of the debate over these two plans emerged the final federal form. Actually, this result represented a series of compromises between the large- and small-state delegates, between the nationalists and the states'-righters. Over the question of representation in Congress, and in matters of federal supremacy, court jurisdiction, congressional authority, and the electoral college, the delegates found a middle ground between a unitary government and a confederation, a way of building on their experience in dividing power between two levels of government. This middle ground was federalism.

Changing Expectations

The framers had fashioned a series of compromises based on their experience. Federalism had been a means to solve the problem of union, but, as we have seen, this cooperative venture had built-in tensions. The small states wanted state equality and state sovereignty. They remained concerned that the new federal venture would be unable to maintain the diversity of interests and localism necessary to good and free govern-

Alexander Hamilton
Hamilton was born in the British West Indies in 1757. By the time he was 34, he had been appointed by George Washington as secretary of the treasury. He was an ardent nationalist, served in Washington's revolutionary army, and was noted for his hot temper and intense pride. Hamilton called the Constitutional Convention a "mere waste of time" and his major goal was a national system of commerce financed by national banks. He looked upon public debts as a "national blessing." He was killed in a duel with Aaron Burr in 1804.

ment. Madison and Hamilton argued in the *Federalist* that the states, rather than the national government, would have the upper hand. Over the years, the interpretation of the Constitution and our attitude toward federalism have changed considerably. We still have a federal system, but it is far different from what the framers imagined it would be.

The early years of the country were a period of adjustment between the national and state governments. Instead of operating on the states, the national government operated directly on the people; its power derived from the Constitution, not the states. This view was most obviously put forth by a Supreme Court heavily weighted with Federalists, who successfully sought to extend the powers of the national government at the expense of the states. The competitive federalism of the early years was the result of an effort to identify "proper spheres of governmental jurisdiction" and to define boundaries of authority as clearly as possible. It was also a period of national growth. The Supreme Court expanded national authority in interstate commerce in *Gibbons* v. *Ogden* (1824), giving Congress exclusive and broad powers to regulate interstate commerce. In *McCulloch* v. *Maryland* (1819) implied powers broadened the enumerated powers in Article I. The sequence of constitutional amendments after the Civil War worked against the states: the Reconstruction amendments required states to protect the rights of blacks (the Thirteenth Amendment freed the slaves, the Fourteenth Amendment made freed slaves citizens of the state in which they resided, and the Fifteenth Amendment extended the right to vote to former slaves); the income tax (Sixteenth Amendment) dramatically increased the taxing power of the national government; and the Seventeenth Amendment removed the election of senators from state legislatures.

Evolving Federalism

Dual Federalism:
a nineteenth-century concept of government recognizing a duality of power between national and state governments, each having a distinct sphere of authority and jurisdiction.

Dual Federalism   The effort to define jurisdictions led, in the late nineteenth century, to the concept of **dual federalism.** The Civil War had settled many questions. The doctrine of union as a compact among sovereign states was discredited. The nationalist view of a perpetual union emanating from the people was clearly in ascendancy. A national government of broad, implied powers had superseded the view of enumerated powers. Yet dual federalism sought to preserve the powers of the states— that is, to separate the spheres of governmental authority and protect political autonomy. Dual federalism was designed as a constitutional duality of powers between the national government and states, both levels having their own spheres of authority and distinct jurisdictions. Each level of government would handle a separate domain, having derived its authority from the Constitution, and neither level would need to infringe on the other. Dual federalism also operated "to perfect the free economy." It existed during the period of industrial growth, and the laissez-faire economic policies it produced worked to keep federal regulation to a minimum.

Dual federalism was perpetuated largely by the judiciary. The Supreme Court would sanction state action in some areas and federal action in others. The Court upheld state police powers in a wide range of social and economic areas while it left relatively undisturbed the power of Congress to regulate commerce and to levy taxes. States exercised nearly exclusive authority in the areas of family and criminal law, elections, local government, and commercial law. Civil rights, in the wake of *Plessy* v. *Ferguson*'s[5] separate-but-equal doctrine allowing states to maintain separate facilities for blacks, remained under state jurisdiction.[6] At the same time, Congress had wide latitude in financing agriculture, building rail transportation, and promoting commerce.

But as the courts sought to delineate separate domains of authority, several developments worked to undermine the concept of dual federalism. The marble-cake intermingling of authority could not be denied, and by the first decade of the twentieth century dual federalism was giving way to **cooperative federalism.** By this time, America was much changed. Industrial growth had created economic interdependence, and urbanization and the elimination of the frontier had made great changes in American life. Government was growing. Technological developments strained the social and economic systems. The Sixteenth Amendment enabled the national government to raise tremendous amounts of revenue and funnel it back to the states. The Agricultural Extension Service established a state aid program, the federal highway program was begun, and by 1930 the government was moving toward a permanent grant-in-aid system. In 1935 came the Social Security Act, the landmark legislation that first made the federal government responsible for the welfare of Americans.

Cooperative Federalism: *an interpretation of federalism that emerged in the 1930s. This interpretation is characterized by a sharing of governmental powers for the purpose of joint problem solving.*

The New Deal permanently changed federal–state relations by developing the Works Progress Administration (WPA) and other public employment programs.

Cooperative Federalism   In cooperative federalism no effort was made to maintain a clear distinction between powers and jurisdictions. Rather, the goal was a sharing of powers for the purposes of joint problem solving. Cooperative federalism rejects the neat labeling of discrete federal, state, and local functions. According to Grodzins and Elazar, cooperative federalism is based on the following premises: that responsibilities for virtually all functions should be shared by federal, state, and local governments; that strengthening state governments will not materially reduce the functions of the federal government; that federal, state, and local officials are colleagues, not adversaries; and that the American system is best conceived of as one government serving one people.[7]

The development of cooperative federalism came without any formal change in the Constitution. Much of it occurred when the national government entered areas that were previously in the domain of the states, such as education, public welfare, and health care. The Depression of the 1930s hastened the process. The economic crash in 1929 forced the na-

Grant-in-Aid: *a form of money payment from the national (or state) government to state (or local) governments for specified programs, under whatever conditions the granting authority wishes to impose.*

tional government and the states to cooperate to solve the mounting economic crisis. **Grants-in-aid** were a favored technique. Federal money was made available to states and localities for specific projects, and during the Depression these included welfare, employment, health care, housing, and school lunches. By 1933, aid totaled a half-billion dollars, or 13 percent of federal expenditures. In 1935, at the height of the Depression, federal support totaled $2 billion, or almost 50 percent of all state revenues. From World War II through the 1960s, federal programs continued to proliferate, and grant programs grew extensively in the 1960s. Federal grant programs during that decade included those to hospitals, urban renewal, clean air, crime control, rat control, and depressed areas. By 1971, some $30 billion was being spent for federal grants-in-aid, four times the amount of a decade earlier.

Creative Federalism: *a form of cooperative federalism extending federal grants-in-aid beyond general governments to special districts and private organizations.*

Creative Federalism   Cooperative federalism entered a new phase during Lyndon Johnson's administration. **Creative federalism** succeeded in realizing the tenets of cooperative federalism on a grand scale. The federal government and grants-in-aid entered into a new era, but, as David Walker noted, "The forces that were unleashed by this sweeping victory in turn produced the 'overload' system of the seventies—and the concomitant collapse of cooperative federalism."[8]

Creative federalism redefined the cooperative partnership to include cities, financial districts, and private nonprofit organizations. In several cases it bypassed states altogether in the disbursement of federal funds. This trend increased by a great deal the complexity of federal–state relations and created an intricate structure for the administration of programs, with bureaucratic and local interest-group relationships becoming tightly interwoven. The result was an emphasis on moving money to urban jurisdictions, in which three-quarters of the American people resided.

Creative federalism was intended as the basic tool for creating the Great Society. More than two hundred new grant programs were established between 1963 and 1968, and grant outlays doubled, from $10 billion to $20 billion, for the period, taking about 12 percent of the federal budget. But beyond generating numbers, creative federalism encouraged experimentation regarding federal–state relations. Government came to rely heavily on project grants, which specifically defined project purposes, identified targeted applicants by outlining eligibility, and allowed federal administrators discretion so they could bypass obstructionist units of government. This system emerged without any real national debate within or outside the hall of government over the role of the national government in administering new programs.

Creative federalism, in common with its predecessor, cooperative federalism, is premised on the shared responsibility for governmental functions and on the assumption that the clear delineation of separate federal, state, and local responsibilities is impossible. But creative federalism differs from cooperative federalism in magnitude and kind. By including local governmental units and nonprofit organizations, it expanded the partnership, and by emphasizing city and urban areas over rural regions it redefined the purpose of government. Finally, by expanding grant programs, the implementers of creative federalism established new entitlements to federal money and programs—Medicare and urban renewal—in order to ease urban problems, and the federal government became inextricably committed to underwriting the financial security of millions of Americans.

New Federalism   Richard Nixon first used the phrase new federalism to describe a reaction against the weight of creative federalism. David Walker has described the new federalism as "anti-centralization, anti-categorical, and anti-administrative confusion."[9] New federalism was designed to move power away from Washington by giving states and local governments more discretion in managing programs. The federal administration of grants was streamlined and local units were afforded more flexibility and authority in administering grants. Several project-grant programs were consolidated into block grants so that states would have program discretion. Proponents of new federalism preferred working through general governments and their elected officials to going through special government units or private organizations. New federalism sought to strengthen the position of state and local governments, and to do so without denying them access to the federal revenues that were so much a part of Johnson's creative federalism. The solution: revenue sharing.

Revenue Sharing:
returning a portion of the federal tax revenues to state and local governments to spend as they see fit with no conditions or requirements imposed by the national government.

Revenue sharing was the cornerstone of new federalism. Passed in 1972, general revenue sharing made available to states and localities fed-

The Food Stamp program supplements the incomes of twenty-two million Americans who are entitled to buy food with these coupons.

Changing Consensus: Reagan's New Federalism

onald Reagan unveiled his version of new federalism in his 1982 State of the Union address. Calling the growth in federal programs pervasive and the programs themselves intrusive, unmanageable, ineffective, costly, and above all unaccountable, Reagan proposed as a solution the swapping of some $47 billion in federal programs with the states. The latter would take over the programs, and the federal government would assume total responsibility for Medicaid. "In a single stroke," Reagan said, "we will be accomplishing a realignment that will end cumbersome administration and spiraling costs at the federal level . . . ." As the culprit in making government unaccountable he named the overpowering growth in federal grants-in-aid programs. Reagan's new federalism called for a reduced federal presence in federal grants-in-aid, with the swap being the most novel approach to overhauling federal–state relations.

President Reagan's new federalism is based on a clear delineation of the roles of the federal government and the states and localities. Besides calling for a reduced role for the federal government, he wants to implement a common-sense approach to making government more efficient and responsive by taking the following steps: leaving to private initiative those functions that individuals can perform privately; using the level of government closest to the community for all the public functions it can handle; and reserving federal government action for "those needed functions that only the national government can undertake." One objective of reducing the federal presence is to decrease the federal rate of spending; Reagan called for reductions of $41 billion in entitlement programs and proposed to limit increases in federal spending to 4.5 percent in 1983, down from 17.5 percent in 1980.

The heart of new federalism was the program swap. In his 1982 State of the Union message

sage Reagan proposed trading AFDC and food stamps ($16.5 billion) to the states for federal responsibility for Medicaid ($19.1 billion). In addition, the federal government would turn back sixty-one social and community development programs to the states ($30.2 billion). To compensate the states for the turnback programs, the national government would create a trust fund ($28 billion) from excise taxes until 1991 to pay for the program costs. Reaction to the proposal was cool; several governors feared that welfare was an escalating cost, and others saw inequitable funding in the proposal that would hurt the less wealthy states. Congress refused to take up the proposal. Then, in July 1982, President Reagan presented a revised swap. Food stamps would no longer be returned to the states, and the sixty-one programs were pared to thirty. The states would assume AFDC and thirty programs at a cost of $39 billion. The federal government would assume Medicaid at a cost of $18.3 billion, and a $20.5 billion trust fund would pay the remainder of costs for eight years until it was phased out and the cost of the thirty programs became state responsibility.

The lack of enthusiasm for new federalism has forced President Reagan to retreat from his bold initiatives of 1982. But he has not abandoned the philosophy or direction of that aborted start. Since the swap proposal, Reagan has come to rely upon block grants to achieve his purpose of reducing federal involvement in the affairs of state and local governments. Noting that 18 percent of federal revenues pass through to state and local governments, Reagan said that federal grants-in-aid have "distorted state and local decisions and usurped state and local functions." Traditional categorical grants attach rules, mandates, and requirements that make them unmanageable, while block grants, he noted, give states discretion on program administration. In 1981 some thirty categorical programs were consolidated into seven new block grant programs. In 1983 and again for the 1987 budget Reagan called for the consolidation of categorical grants into block grants. In 1985 he directed the Domestic Policy Council to form a working group on federalism in order to continue to search for block grant possibilities. In this manner, Reagan intends to restore authority to state and local governments.

The final component of the new federalism scheme was deregulation of industry. This aspect made good Reagan's pledge to leave to private initiative those functions best performed by private individuals. The Reagan administration placed the cost to the economy for government regulation at more than $100 billion, a cost that it considered "unnecessary or counterproductive." Reagan's argument was that the marketplace is the best arena in which to ensure cost and quality control. Industry competition and consumer cost consciousness are more effective in raising productivity and reducing costs, he has claimed, than government rules and federal bureaucrats. Reagan moved to deregulate several industries, removing restrictions, rules, or restraints on doing business. Included were such businesses as airlines; banks; broadcasting companies; bus, trucking, and shipping companies; railroads; health care services; and energy companies. In addition, he created the President's Task Force on Regulatory Relief to get a comprehensive picture of existing regulations and to coordinate the review and revision of regulations. With an executive order, Reagan mandated a cost–benefit analysis before any new regulations could be promulgated. And he imposed a sixty-day regulatory freeze to incorporate these concepts into pending rules. Deregulation of industry thus formed another basis of new federalism. According to Murray Weidenbaum, Reagan's former chairman of the Council of Economic Advisors, deregulation was done with the "full knowledge that the forces of competition in the marketplace, more often than not, are the most effective mechanisms for achieving the high level of economic well-being that is the true end product of the business system."[*]

*Murray Weidenbaum, "The Changing Relationship between Government and Business," *Vital Speeches* 42, May 1, 1981, p. 420.

eral revenues that could be applied to a wide range of objectives. The concept incorporated the best of both worlds. The federal government's superior revenue-generating sources would make money available to states and local governments ($6 billion annually) with no strings attached. General governments (states, cities, townships, and counties) would be allowed to use the money as they saw fit—to reduce taxes, augment existing services, or initiate new programs. Thus, state and local governmental discretion was enhanced.

Nixon's new federalism was in no way a return to dual federalism, for it very much retained the cooperative partnership, as revenue sharing well illustrates. Yet Nixon's approach sought to reverse the trends of creative federalism, attempting to move power away from the federal bureaucracy and give states and localities more discretion. Block grants greatly increased the states' latitude in decision making, and revenue sharing provided them total freedom in dispersing money. Nixon's preference for general government made special districts and private organizations ineligible for federal funds or grants-in-aid. In these ways Nixon's new federalism was a transition in the evolution of federal–state relations.

Ronald Reagan sounded round two of new federalism in his State of the Union message for 1982. In that speech he proposed a $46.7 billion swap of programs with the states. The federal government would turn over to the states some sixty federal programs along with Food Stamps and Aid to Families with Dependent Children (AFDC). In turn, the federal government would assume complete responsibility for Medicaid and would set up a trust fund to assist states in assuming the costs of the new programs. The trust fund was to start in 1984 and gradually phase out by 1991. Reagan subsequently modified the proposal.

There was considerable opposition to the swap proposal. States, already in deep financial crisis, worried about their ability to assume the program costs over time. Many governors felt welfare costs would continue to escalate, thereby placing more strain on already tight budgets. Congress was not quick to give up programs over which it had power and from which political benefits were reaped. Interest groups charged that new federalism was a device to cut welfare funding, that states would stop or lower their assistance for the poor, minorities, and handicapped. Big-city mayors grumbled that money to cities would be reduced. They demanded that their role in grants-in-aid continue and that levels of funding for cities be maintained. The net result was that Congress did not take up any of the new federalism initiatives in 1982. No bill was ever sent up to the Hill by the Reagan administration in 1982.

In 1983 President Reagan offered a scaled-back version of new federalism. His 1984 budget proposal called for a more modest program involving thirty-four programs at a cost of $21 billion. Gone were the program swap idea and the trust fund. The revised package of new federalism altered little the existing levels of funding or local authority. It was based on four block grants—three to states and one to local governments.

Behind these proposals is a broader outline of new federalism. President Reagan wants to sort out federal responsibilities from state and local responsibilities and to engender a greater reliance on state and local government as well as the private sector. Reagan feels that federal grants-in-aid programs have usurped state and local functions and violated traditional understandings about the roles of each level of government. Reagan's new federalism actually approaches dual federalism, for the president sees the Constitution as providing clear distinctions between the roles of the federal government and those of the states and localities. Federal grants-in-aid have distorted the distinctions, he claims, and in his new federalism Reagan expects a "major sorting out of federal, state, and local responsibilities, and [that] the federal presence and intervention in state and local affairs will gradually diminish."[10] However, the National Governors' Conference is not so sure. At their Winter 1983 meeting the governors approved a resolution calling for the exploration of federalism alternatives but insisted that "we are not prepared to accept, and will strongly oppose, attempts to shift current federal costs back to states and localities under the guise of federalism."[11]

Reagan's new federalism also places particular emphasis on private initiative. His economic recovery program is based on supply-side economics, letting business invest and expand so as to increase productivity. He sees the competition of the marketplace as the most efficient means of raising productivity and increasing the wealth of Americans. Thus, he has moved to deregulate several key industries to free them from control and regulations that inhibit their risk-taking entrepreneurial activities. Reagan sees private economic enterprise and volunteerism as more efficient and productive than government in providing social and economic well-being for American citizens.

With new federalism, and particularly Ronald Reagan's interpretation, federal–state relations have entered a new era. Our changing expectations regarding national power and responsibility call for a reduced federal presence. Will Reagan's new federalism be lasting? That remains to be seen. What is clear is that the Constitution can be interpreted and applied differently at different times to achieve the nation's goals. With shifts in power and the availability of resources, the government can accommodate the changing needs of the nation and its states.

The Distribution of Powers and Responsibilities

The Constitution has been correctly described as a living document, one whose provisions change with interpretations to keep it abreast with the times. And since we accept change more readily when the names remain the same, we are likely to continue to think of federalism as a distribution of power between the national government and the states. As we shall see, however, that distribution is much changed from the early days of the republic.

Enumerated Powers: *the powers of the national government specifically provided for and listed in the Constitution.*

Implied Powers: *the powers of the national government that can be inferred from enumerated powers.*

Elastic Clause: *the clause in the Constitution that gives Congress the power to make all laws "necessary and proper" to execute enumerated powers. This clause allows for the existence of implied powers.*

Inherent Powers: *powers of the national government that flow not from the Constitution but from the fact that it exists as a government, such as the power to conduct foreign relations.*

The Powers of the National Government

The powers of the national government are largely outlined in the first three articles of the Constitution, which establish the three branches of the national government—legislative, executive, and judicial. First, there are the **enumerated powers,** the powers of the national government specifically provided for and listed. The powers of Congress in Article I include the power to coin money, to establish post offices, to promote the progress of science, and to regulate commerce. In addition, the Constitution and the courts allow for **implied powers,** which can be inferred from the enumerated powers. The Constitution gives Congress the power to make all laws "necessary and proper" to execute the enumerated powers. This is the so-called **elastic clause** of the Constitution that has allowed government to meet all kinds of new demands.

The third kind of national government power is **inherent power.** This power flows not from the Constitution itself, but from the fact of the government's existence. Every nation must deal with other countries. In matters of war and peace, exploration, and occupation of territory, the national government has power "as necessary concomitants of nationality." The Supreme Court made this position clear in *United States* v. *Curtis–Wright Export Corporation* (1936). The national government would have powers to make war and peace, enter into treaties, and maintain diplomatic relations with foreign countries even if the Constitution did not enumerate or confer them.

The Powers of the States

Reserved Powers: *the term used in reference to state powers. The Tenth Amendment reserved for the states all powers not granted by the Constitution to the national government or prohibited to the states.*

The powers of the states are generally referred to as **reserved powers,** meaning that states retain all powers not granted by the Constitution to the national government or prohibited to them. The Tenth Amendment to the Constitution is the source of reserved powers: the powers not delegated to the United States by the Constitution, nor prohibited by it to the states, are reserved to the states, respectively, or to the people. Today, it is also the source of misunderstanding. The common assumption is that enumerated powers of a national government and reserved powers for states constitute a clear, common line of separation between national and state powers. Nothing is further from the truth.

After Roosevelt's "court-packing fight" (an attempt by the president to expand the size of the Supreme Court in order to have more justices sympathetic to his New Deal programs) and its resulting victory for the expansion of federal power, the Tenth Amendment fell into disuse. This development has been called the "switch in time that saved nine." The Tenth Amendment does not seriously restrict national power; rather, the courts viewed it as a truism "that all is retained which has not yet been surrendered."[12] Then in 1976 the Supreme Court began to breathe life back into the Tenth Amendment. In the case of *National League of Cities* v. *Usery,* the Court decided that the Tenth Amendment did provide states protection from federal interference in the conduct of their "traditional" or "integral" functions. However, the Court refused to extend that definition too broadly, holding that the Tenth Amendment did not prohibit federal laws to regulate strip mining, energy conservation, or age discrimination.

Then in a dramatic reversal of itself the Supreme Court once again ruled, in *Garcia* v. *San Antonio Metropolitan Transit Authority* (1985), that Congress is free of specific constitutional limits in the regulation of commerce. The Court ruled not only that Congress could apply the Fair Labor Standards Act to city employees of a city-owned transit system but also that states and cities had no further access to federal courts to challenge acts of Congress that infringed on state prerogatives.

The majority on the Court said it had proved so difficult to separate state and city functions protected from federal control that the effort must now be abandoned. The Constitution created a structural rather than a substantive limitation on the power of Congress to interfere in state affairs.

Already Congress has moved to act on the implications of *Garcia.* It has adopted the national 55-mile-per-hour speed limit and a 21-year minimum drinking age by directing the states to make such changes in state laws or lose federal highway funds. In this fashion Congress can simply compel states to pass legislation.

Concurrent Powers: *powers exercised by both national and state governments, such as the power to levy taxes or regulate commerce.*

Powers not denied the states or exclusively given to the national government may be exercised as **concurrent powers** by both national and state governments. Article VI of the Constitution states that there can be no conflict between national and state law; national law is supreme. Yet the structure of federalism is largely erected on the ability of states and the national government to exercise power concurrently. For example, both the national government and the states levy taxes, regulate commerce, and protect the welfare of citizens.

Much of the history and growth of federalism has been the expansion of the national government into intergovernmental affairs without preempting state activity. The great sharing of responsibility has continued even while the national government has grown. This enduring result defies the idea of a neat separation of functions and yet illustrates the strength of federalism: the ability to meet changing expectations without destroying the Constitution or precipitating a crisis over jurisdictions.

This is not to say there are no conflicts over or restrictions on the power of the states. The Constitution itself places certain restrictions on the states: they may not make treaties, grant letters of marque and reprisal, coin money, emit bills of credit, pass a bill of attainder or ex post facto law, impair the obligation of contracts, grant any title of nobility, lay duties on imports or exports, keep troops in peacetime, or enter into an agreement with another state without the consent of Congress. State regulation cannot become an "undue burden" on the powers of the national government. What constitutes an undue burden and who decides the issue? Ultimately, it is the courts that decide.

The Supreme Court as Umpire

Federalism is a mutually accommodating system, but it still engenders conflicts that need resolution. The Supreme Court plays the role of umpire in the federal system, partly by design and partly due to the twists of history. Under a system of rule by law, it is principally by lawsuit that our system of power is challenged. This fact necessarily involves the Court in the political thicket of federal–state relations. Yet these legal issues disguise a political struggle for power and problem solving. The Supreme Court recognizes its role in modernizing the Constitution and keeping the nation "armed" constitutionally to keep abreast of social problems. As a branch of the national government, the Court has often been charged with favoring national power over state and local control, and the Court's history would appear to bear this out. For example, the Court decided in the nineteenth century that Maryland could not tax the national bank in order to interfere with its operation, and in the twentieth century that New York could not ban the SST from landing or taking off at its airports. The federal system needs a way to maintain peaceful accommodation, however, and the Supreme Court is the "least dangerous" branch because it does not initiate policy or carry it out.

Obligations to the States

The Constitution imposes some national obligations on the states. Article IV contains a set of guarantees to the states that require the national government to

1. guarantee to every state in the union a republican form of government;
2. protect each state against invasion and domestic violence;
3. provide for the admission of new states and protect the jurisdiction of present states.

The guarantee of a republican form of government has never been clearly outlined except to say that enforcement is a congressional responsibility. When the initiative and referendum were challenged in the states as violating the republican principle, the courts refused to hear the cases, stating that the question was one for Congress to decide. The national government is also obligated to protect states against invasion or domestic violence. Congress, or the president, to whom Congress has delegated authority, can send troops to quiet disturbances at the request of a state. For example, at the height of the 1967 Detroit riot, President Johnson, at the request of Michigan's Governor George Romney, sent in federal troops to help state and local officials stop the violence.

Congress must also provide for the admission of new states. No territory has a right to statehood; granting it is a discretionary power of Congress. Congress normally provides for an "enabling act" preparing the way, and when the people draft a constitution for the state, Congress must approve it. Congress can place restrictions on a territory as a condition for admission as a state—provided, of course, it does not impair the jurisdiction of existing states without their consent. Utah, for example, as a condition for statehood in 1894, was obliged to provide for religious toleration in the state and to prohibit polygamous marriages. In 1910, Arizona was denied the power to recall judges as a condition of admission. After admission, however, the Arizona constitution was promptly amended, and Congress could do nothing about it; Arizona was now a state with all the powers of a state.

Horizontal Federalism

Horizontal Federalism: *the federal relationship between states, including the obligations imposed by Article IV of the Constitution.*

Article IV of the Constitution imposes on the states certain obligations in their relationships with one another. The **full faith and credit clause** requires states to accept the laws, records, and court decisions (in non-criminal cases) of another state. Several technicalities complicate this clause, but in practice it means that the civil court judgments of one state are honored in another state. Should a court in New York render a verdict for a landlord for back rent and the tenant move to Illinois, the landlord would not have to bring suit again in Illinois. Illinois courts would have to give full faith and credit to the New York verdict without retrying the case. Divorce is a common example: couples who are divorced in one state and then move to a different state or states are recognized as single under full faith and credit. The technicalities emerge if we change the example a bit. If the couple go to another state for a divorce—say, Nevada, with its short residency requirement—and return to the home state, are they legally divorced? Not necessarily. The courts have held that under specific circumstances the state of residence may rule that the divorce-granting state lacked jurisdiction.

Full Faith and Credit Clause: *a clause in Article IV of the Constitution requiring states to accept the laws, records, and court decisions (in non-criminal cases) of other states.*

Privileges and Immunities: *a clause in Article IV of the Constitution extending to citizens of other states the full protection of state law, access to state courts, and nondiscriminatory treatment.*

States must extend to citizens of other states the **privileges and immunities** granted to their own citizens. Thus, citizens of other states are entitled to the full protection of the laws of the state, to the use of the courts, and to nondiscriminatory treatment. The speed limit is the same for all motorists, not 55 mph for residents and 45 mph for nonresidents. State tax rates are the same for residents and nonresidents alike. Unfortunately, this clause is fraught with ambiguity and technicalities. For example, tuition to attend college or a university can be set at a higher rate for out-of-state students without violating the privileges and immunities clause. Out-of-state fishing and hunting licenses are also acceptable. And privileges and immunities do not extend to political rights, such as voting or serving on juries.

Extradition: *a constitutional provision whereby a state shall surrender a fugitive to the state within whose jurisdiction the crime was committed.*

Third, the Constitution holds that a state shall deliver up a fugitive from justice to the state wherein the crime was committed when requested to do so by the latter. **Extradition** means the governor of the state shall return such fugitives to the state in which they are accused of the crime. Normally governors comply with such requests. Despite the word *shall*, however, in some noteworthy examples governors have refused to comply with extradition requests, and courts have decided that no enforcement mechanisms exist for the extradition clause.

Interstate Compacts:
legal and binding agree-
ments between states
made with the consent of
Congress.

Finally, the Constitution permits states, with the consent of Congress, to enter into **interstate compacts.** Of little importance prior to the twentieth century, these compacts are being used with increasing frequency to solve metropolitan and multistate problems. They are legal and binding agreements on all states signing the compact. The Port of New York Authority, for instance, is the result of an interstate compact between New York and New Jersey. And thirty-three states are signatories to an interstate oil compact designed to prevent federal control over oil.

The Growth of National Government

On all levels, over the decades government has expanded into new fields and taken on additional functions. The result has been more intergovernmental cooperation and frequent interaction between states and the national government. Some commentators claim the growth of the national government as a victory for nationalism over states' rights. From a constitutional perspective this view is correct, but it ignores the purpose and cooperative nature of federalism. The growth of the national government should be viewed, rather, as a changed expectation to solve problems that once were local in nature but now are national.

McCulloch v. *Maryland*

McCulloch v.
Maryland: the 1819
Supreme Court decision
affirming that Congress
had certain implied
powers in addition to
those specifically
enumerated in the
Constitution. This set the
stage for expansion of
national authority.

The growth of national powers was early advanced by the Supreme Court in the famous case of *McCulloch* v. *Maryland* (1819). The ruling of Chief Justice John Marshall laid the cornerstone for the implied-powers doctrine of enumerated powers and strongly curtailed state authority to interfere with the national government.

The case involved the Bank of the United States, Alexander Hamilton's idea of some years earlier. The bank had been created to handle the government's monetary and financial problems, in the hope of stabilizing credit and fostering commerce. Yet by 1819, a Second National Bank had neither checked speculation nor improved financial conditions. Some branches of the bank were badly managed and a few even engaged in fraud. The branches were becoming increasingly unpopular in several states. Among these was Maryland, whose legislature in 1818 placed a heavy tax on the Baltimore branch. Maryland demanded that James W. McCulloch, cashier of the bank, pay the $15,000 annual tax. McCulloch refused, and Maryland brought suit. The Maryland court upheld the Maryland law, and the bank appealed the case to the Supreme Court. Daniel Webster and William Pinckney argued the case for the bank, while Luther Martin defended Maryland. On March 6, 1819, after three days of argument, a unanimous Supreme Court handed down its verdict. Congress had the constitutional power to charter a national bank; the Court denied Maryland's right to interfere with its operation, thereby declaring unconstitutional Maryland's law taxing the bank.

The first issue disposed of by Chief Justice Marshall in rendering the verdict was that of the power to incorporate a bank. Using the doctrine of national sovereignty, Marshall held that the federal government derived its power directly from the people. He admitted that authority was divided between the states and the national government but said that, though limited, the national government's power "is supreme within its sphere of action." Marshall then set forth the broad construction of implied powers. Creating the bank was admittedly not one of the enumerated powers of Congress, but the Constitution also gave Congress powers to carry out and execute its enumerated powers. The creation of a national bank was implied by the enumerated power to coin and regulate money. As Marshall argued, "it can never be to their [the people's] interest and cannot be presumed to have been their intention, to clog and embarrass its execution, by withholding the most appropriate means." Marshall was following the principle laid down by Hamilton in 1791: "Let the end be legitimate, let it be within the scope of the Constitution and all means which are appropriate, which are plainly adopted to that end, which are not prohibited, but consistent with the letter and spirit of the Constitution, are Constitutional."[13]

The second question in the case was Maryland's constitutional right to tax the bank, an issue of dual federalism. Using the principle of federal supremacy, Marshall ruled that the "power to tax involves the power to destroy." Since the bank was a legal instrument of federal authority, an act of Congress must supersede any state effort to control or limit the bank's functions. The supremacy clause in Article VI made the laws and treaties of the United States the supreme law of the land; therefore, the Maryland law was unconstitutional.

Thus at a very early point in the nation's history, the stage was set for the broad interpretation of national powers. Two additional constitutional provisions have supported national growth and adaptability: the power to regulate interstate commerce, and the authority to tax and spend for the general welfare.

The Commerce Clause

Commerce Clause: *the power granted Congress in Article I, Section 8 of the Constitution to "regulate commerce with foreign nations and among the several states." The clause has been interpreted so as to give Congress broad authority over a variety of activities affecting the several states.*

The interstate **commerce clause** (to regulate commerce among the several states) was interpreted broadly to include all "intercourse" between the states, not merely the buying and selling of goods.[14] John Marshall, using the same approach he had five years earlier, ruled in *Gibbons* v. *Ogden* (1824) that the operation of boats on New York waters constituted interstate commerce because passenger vessels were engaged in "intercourse" between states.

The commerce clause has also been used to support legislation that has nothing to do with commercial affairs. The 1964 Civil Rights Act prohibiting discrimination in public accommodations was upheld by the Supreme Court because of the disruptive effect racial discrimination has on interstate travel.[15] In 1985 the Supreme Court declared Congress free of

The interstate highway is a classic symbol of our federal–state partnership and of the grant-in-aid approach to problem solving.

specific constitutional limits in its regulation of commerce.[16] In what amounted to the overturn of a 1976 decision holding that the Tenth Amendment did afford states some protection from Congress's commerce power, the 1985 decision of *Garcia* v. *San Antonio Metropolitan Transit Authority* freed Congress of constitutional limits on regulation of commerce, even when such regulation curtailed the power of the states. With broad reach, the decision said the states' protection within the federal system rested on "special restraints on federal power over the states [inherent] principally in the workings of the national government itself, rather than in discrete limitations on the objects of federal authority." In other words, if there were to be limits on the federal commerce power, those restraints would have to come from "state participation in federal government action. The political process ensures that laws that unduly burden the states will not be promulgated."

Critics, including some Supreme Court Justices, charge that the Court strains the commerce clause. In dissenting in *Garcia*, Mr. Justice Lewis Powell said, "This decision substantially alters the federal system embodied in the Constitution." By looking to the political process for congressional restraint in using its commerce power, Justice Powell argued, the Court "radically departs from long settled constitutional values and ignores the role of judicial review in our system of government." But the fact is that the commerce clause has been adapted to our changing economic and social life: the lives of city dwellers, for example, are affected by the feed a Colorado rancher uses for his cattle. It is this growing interdependence that determines the growing scope of the regulation.

The Power to Tax and Spend

The taxing and spending powers of the national government have also helped national authority to grow. This power raises the question whether Congress can tax and spend for the general welfare or whether that power has to be related to its enumerated powers. The Supreme Court has concluded that Congress may tax and spend to promote the general welfare, thus providing for functions it would otherwise be unable to legislate. The Supreme Court does not inquire into the motive behind an appropriation. Congress may use taxation as a means of regulation. In fact, Congress frequently attaches regulations to appropriations measures, thus legislating while it is spending. Nor does the Court make judgments or place conditions on the general-welfare clause of the taxing and spending power. The conditions for taxing and spending are to be set by Congress.

In fact, until recently Congress could tax and spend for the general welfare as it saw fit, attaching whatever conditions or regulations it deemed appropriate. Taxpayers or states could not challenge that power in the courts.[17] But in 1968[18] the Supreme Court modified this stand slightly to allow taxpayers to bring suits based on a specific constitutional challenge. The courts have cautioned as recently as 1974, however, that they are not a haven for taxpayers to press "generalized grievances" against government.[19]

The Politics of Federalism

The growth of the national government points to one overriding development: a nationally dominated system of shared powers and shared functions.[20] This growth has been facilitated by constitutional interpretation; the national government has come to have the major responsibility for providing services and regulating activities. Much of the growth in federal activity came as a result of the Depression and Franklin D. Roosevelt's New Deal. The states then had neither the financial resources nor the jurisdiction to respond; the federal government did. Since that time, in areas ranging from social security and unemployment assistance to law enforcement, resource management, civil rights, and consumer protection, the federal government has maintained its increased level of activity. The continued growth of the bureaucracy illustrates this increase: Health and Human Services, Housing and Urban Development, Transportation, Energy, and Education are all new or reorganized cabinet-level departments.

But the rise of the national government points to another unmistakable trend: the increased activity of government at all levels. State and local governments are providing more services and spending more money than at any time in the past. Table 3.1 shows the relative growth in spending for all three levels of government in the twentieth century.

The increases and changes are closely related to key events of the twentieth century. The Depression, coupled with military spending during World War II, accounted for the great increase in federal spending in the 1930s and 1940s. That increased level of spending was maintained throughout the 1950s and into the Great Society of the 1960s. The greatest decline has come in local expenditures as a percentage of the total. At one time local spending accounted for more than half the total expenditures; now local spending is only one-quarter of the total public money spent.

Ronald Reagan is intent on reversing the trend of dwindling local spending. His budgets call for increased state and local obligations in several programs. The 1982 proposal included a $47 billion package of increased obligations for states. The revised new federalism proposal called for a more modest $21 billion set of block grants. Total grants-in-

TABLE 3.1   Government spending (in billions of dollars)

	1902 $	1902 %	1922 $	1922 %	1932 $	1932 %	1940 $	1940 %	1950 $	1950 %	1960 $	1960 %	1970 $	1970 %	1980 $	1980 %	1985 $	1985 %
Federal	0.6	35	3.6	39	4	32	9.2	44	42.4	60	90.3	60	196.5	55	579.5	61	946	65.5
State	0.1	6	1.1	12	2	16	3.6	18	11.9	16	22.2	15	56.2	17	156	16.5	195	13.5
Local	1	59	4.6	49	6.4	52	7.7	38	17	24	38.8	25	92	28	213	22.5	304	21

SOURCE: Data for 1902–1974 are from Bureau of the Census, *Pocket Data Book*, Washington, D.C., 1976; 1980 data are from *Statistical Abstract*, 1981; 1985 data are from *Federal-State-Local Fiscal Relations*, Department of the Treasury, 1985.

aid to states decreased by $6.5 billion in 1982. The major reason federal spending does not decline is the increased outlays for national defense in the Reagan budgets.

Fiscal Federalism

Fiscal Federalism: *shared responsibility between the national and state (and local) governments for taxing and spending policies.*

Walter Heller, former chairman of the Council of Economic Advisors under President Kennedy, said, "Prosperity gives the national government the affluence and the local governments the effluence."[21] It is precisely this connection between federal resources and local problems that creates the need for increased federal assistance. The coupling is a fiscal mismatch. The national government can readily increase tax revenues yearly, while state and local governments cannot. Yet the demand for services and problem solving is heard primarily at state and local levels. The result, Michael Reagan argues, is that "state–local ability to meet public demands goes down, while their dependence on federal funds and their indebtedness both increase."[22] For the state and local governments to raise sufficient revenues in the coming decades to meet their needs not only would bankrupt them but, as Congressman Henry Reuss (D.-Wisc.) explains, would be socially undesirable and politically improbable, since state taxes are "inequitable and inflexible."[23] State and local taxes are inequitable because they are based primarily on regressive taxes that hit lower-income groups proportionately harder than higher-income groups, and because resources are not equal from state to state. State and local taxes are inflexible because they are commonly based on authorized limits fixed by law or state constitutions. Taxpayers are now moving to establish authorization limits where none exist as a means of venting their anger over rising taxes. So only federal taxes have the progressiveness to equalize resources and the flexibility to adapt to shifting, multistate problems.

Each of the three major categories of taxes—income tax, sales tax, and property tax—serves as the primary source of tax revenue for a different level of government. Income taxes are the primary source of tax revenue for the federal government, accounting for 60 percent of revenues in 1980; the general sales tax is the primary tax of states, constituting 50 percent of tax income for 1980; for local governments the property tax is the backbone of revenues, making up 76 percent of the total in 1980. Collectively, for 1980, income taxes provided 64 percent of all tax revenues. Since the income tax serves as the national government's primary taxing source, it is no surprise that the national government dominates the revenue picture. This is the primary cause of our current system of fiscal federalism—grants-in-aid, categorical grants, block grants, and, until 1986, revenue sharing.

Grants-in-aid, as suggested earlier, are a form of money payments from the national (or state) government to state (or local) governments for specified programs under whatever conditions the granting authority

The loss of federal dollars has forced many organizations to find other sources of funds.

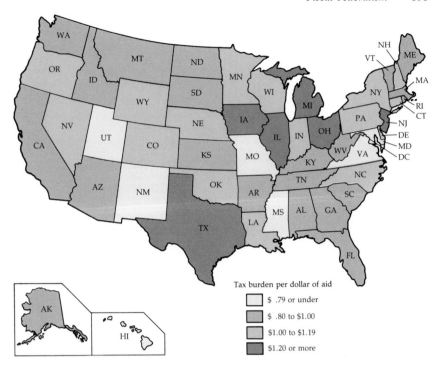

Figure 3.2 Federal taxes allocated to each state per dollar of federal aid received. (SOURCE: *Statistical Abstract*, 1981).

wishes to impose. (See Figure 3.2.) The actual administration of the programs for which money is received is the responsibility of the state or local government. The conditions depend in large measure on the kind of grant at issue. The traditional categorical grants were designed for specific and narrowly defined purposes, leaving states and localities little flexibility in administering them. Block grants, on the other hand, are broad grants in some area (health or education) that leave unspecified the purposes for which the money can be spent. These give local officials more discretion in setting goals and spending money. Closely related, but different again, is revenue sharing. The money returned to state and local governments in general revenue sharing has no prior specifications of purpose or conditions attached to its spending. Such money may be spent by state and local governments as they think wisest, no strings attached.

Grants-in-Aid   The best proof that there is shared responsibility in federalism is the grant-in-aid system, which uses a fiscal–federal relationship as its basis for cooperation. This system embodies the marble-cake principle of federalism suggested by Morton Grodzins.

    The Advisory Commission on Intergovernmental Relations estimated that in 1974 a total of 530 grant-in-aid programs existed. Office of Management and Budget figures show that another 279 programs were added

TABLE 3.2   Historical trend of federal grant-in-aid outlays (fiscal years; dollar amounts in millions)

| | Total grants-in-aid | Federal grants as a percent of | | | |
| | | Federal outlays | | State and local expenditures | Gross National Product |
		Total	Domestic		
Five-year intervals					
1950	$ 2,253	5.3	9.3%	10.4%	0.8
1955	3,207	4.7	13.7	10.1	0.8
1960	7,019	7.6	17.1	14.7	1.4
1965	10,910	9.2	17.5	15.3	1.6
1970	24,065	12.3	22.0	19.3	2.4
1975	49,791	15.0	20.9	23.0	3.3
Annually					
1980	91,451	15.5	20.6	26.3	3.4
1981	94,762	14.0	18.7	25.2	3.2
1982	88,195	11.8	16.1	21.9	2.8
1983	92,496	11.4	15.8	21.6	2.8
1984	97,577	11.5	16.0	21.2	2.6
1985	105,897	11.2	15.6	21.0	2.7
1986 estimate	108,802	11.1	15.6	NA	2.6
1987 estimate	99,094	10.0	14.3	NA	2.2
1988 estimate	99,208	9.7	14.0	NA	2.0
1989 estimate	99,593	9.4	13.8	NA	1.9
1990 estimate	101,572	9.3	13.9	NA	1.8
1991 estimate	102,400	9.1	13.9	NA	1.7

between 1974 and 1980. The increase in the number of grants is matched by the growth of funds appropriated by the grant programs. Appropriations for grants-in-aid have risen almost tenfold since 1960. The figures in Table 3.2 show this remarkable growth as well as Reagan's effect on grants-in-aid.

Categorical Grants   Until the Depression, federal grants totaled less than $100 million annually. The major areas of spending were agricultural extension, highways, and vocational education. But the Depression added fourteen new programs and the New Deal brought federal supervision and conditions to the grant process. Faced with a mounting urban crisis in the 1960s, Congress expanded grants almost fourfold and set up the **categorical grant** system. Congress determined the programs and provided funds. States seeking to participate in a program must commit a certain percentage of state money to match the federal funds, create a state agency to administer the program, submit written plans for administering and spending the money, and be willing to be reviewed periodically by federal officials.

Categorical Grant:
a system of national aid to state and local governments for a specific purpose, allowing the recipient little discretion in use of the money.

State and local governments have some role in shaping the administration of the programs, although it is Congress that determines the programs and their conditions. The latter condition allows Congress to set priorities and determine needs. In 1965–1966 alone, sixty-seven new programs emerged: twenty-one in health, seventeen in education, and the

Individual rights and liberties lose much of their vitality for the homeless and hungry, especially since funding for programs that would help them has been cut during recent years.

Block Grant: *a form of federal aid to state and local governments for broadly defined purposes within which local officials have discretion on the specific programs to be operated.*

rest in resource development, employment, urban affairs, and economic programs. The expansion in the Great Society years saw federal aid go directly to local governments and to nongovernmental agencies such as community action groups, professional associations, and private businesses. Under Medicare, Congress has contracted with insurance companies to process the claims and, with professional associations, to determine the eligibility of participating institutions. Reagan's new federalism is changing the picture, however. After two decades of steady growth, the number of grant programs is being reduced, as is the money allocated to states. The number of categorical grant programs has been reduced from 428 in 1980 to 280 in 1982.

Until 1972, almost all grants-in-aid were categorical grants—there were five hundred such programs. A major issue in creating them was the setting of priorities. To receive money, states had to apply to Washington, get approval, follow the conditions laid down by Congress, and match the grants with some of their own money. This system, critics argued, gave Washington too much control; not only did it affect the budget priorities of states and local governments, but the federal "strings" controlled the states' goals and added regulatory purposes tangential to the grants' intent.

The proliferation of grants also gave rise to the criticism that the number of programs made efficient administration impossible. The federal government often threatened to withhold funds if agencies did not comply with federal regulations. Often programs would be competing and jurisdictions would overlap. Water and waste treatment grants, for example, were available from four departments: Interior, Commerce, Housing and Urban Development, and Agriculture. Coordination was weak, and delays in granting approval were common.

Block Grants The mounting pressure for reform of the grant system led President Nixon in the 1970s to propose consolidating many categorical grant programs into **block grants,** grants to state and local governments for broadly defined purposes within which local officials have discretion on the specific programs to be operated. They permit greater state control than categorical grants, impose fewer conditions, and allow increased flexibility in spending. States typically submit only a master plan for approval. The Crime Control and Safe Streets Acts of 1968 provided the first block-grant money to states and cities to fight crime. In the 1970s most of the consolidation to block grants occurred in the areas of health care, law enforcement, employment training, and education.

Block grants, too, have been controversial. Members of Congress and federal officials are reluctant to give up control. They fear a "waste" of money if state and local governments control priorities. Congress also worries that it will be unable to satisfy constituents and interest groups if it lacks control over spending. Many beneficiaries of categorical grants have also raised objections. Civil rights and welfare groups have been particularly outspoken critics of the consolidation, and law enforcement

Fact File

Geographic Distribution of Federal Funds, 1980

Federal Information Exchange System
Comparison of Federal Funds Made by Major Federal Organizations and Ranked by States

Total department funds, in millions	Agriculture $27,960		Commerce $3,284		Defense $127,136		Education $11,299		Energy $10,697		Health & Human Services $194,955		Housing & Urban Development $8,003		Interior $5,737		Justice $1,703	
State	Rank	%	Rank	%	Rank	%	Rank	%	Rank	%	Rank	%	Rank	%	Rank	%	Rank	%
Alabama	23	1.8	20	1.4	19	1.6	14	2.4	33	.2	21	1.6	21	1.7	40	.4	27	1.0
Alaska	45	.3	19	1.4	34	.6	40	.6	44	.0	51	.1	50	.1	5	6.0	43	.3
Arizona	34	1.2	34	.5	23	1.3	28	1.4	46	.0	31	1.0	31	.9	1	8.9	11	1.9
Arkansas	22	1.8	32	.5	37	.5	30	1.1	47	.0	30	1.0	28	1.0	42	.4	36	.4
California	1	7.2	4	6.3	1	17.5	2	8.5	2	10.5	1	10.2	2	8.4	2	8.2	2	11.1
Colorado	20	1.9	6	3.5	25	1.3	31	1.1	8	4.3	35	.9	30	.9	3	8.0	21	1.2
Connecticut	42	.5	31	.5	8	3.3	34	1.0	27	.4	24	1.4	22	1.5	46	.2	26	1.0
Delaware	51	.1	43	.3	43	.3	48	.3	48	.0	48	.2	46	.2	48	.2	48	.2
District of Columbia	6	3.5	2	13.5	16	1.8	12	2.5	14	2.9	25	1.4	9	3.4	4	7.5	1	20.0
Florida	9	2.8	10	2.8	5	4.0	8	3.1	23	.7	4	5.2	11	3.0	24	1.2	6	3.9
Georgia	10	2.8	21	1.3	13	2.3	15	2.1	31	.2	16	2.0	15	2.0	18	1.5	8	2.5
Hawaii	44	.4	33	.5	24	1.3	44	.5	39	.1	43	.3	42	.3	44	.2	38	.4
Idaho	37	1.0	40	.3	47	.2	47	.3	15	2.8	42	.3	48	.2	16	1.8	47	.2
Illinois	5	3.7	17	1.6	18	1.8	5	4.3	6	4.8	5	4.9	3	6.4	30	.8	5	4.0
Indiana	26	1.6	12	2.2	21	1.5	26	1.5	32	.2	14	2.1	18	1.8	38	.5	19	1.3
Iowa	7	3.1	42	.3	42	.3	29	1.3	30	.2	26	1.3	32	.8	43	.2	37	.4
Kansas	15	2.3	35	.5	28	1.1	33	1.0	42	.0	33	1.0	33	.8	41	.4	24	1.1
Kentucky	27	1.5	25	.8	30	.9	21	1.8	10	3.7	23	1.5	26	1.1	31	.8	18	1.5
Louisiana	17	2.2	5	6.1	27	1.2	17	1.9	12	3.2	22	1.5	14	2.1	32	.7	29	1.0
Maine	43	.4	36	.5	35	.5	37	.8	49	.0	37	.5	38	.5	47	.2	35	.4
Maryland	32	1.3	1	14.5	11	3.1	24	1.7	7	4.6	15	2.1	20	1.7	28	.9	16	1.5
Massachusetts	35	1.1	13	2.2	6	3.5	10	2.8	21	1.1	10	3.0	10	3.3	21	1.3	14	1.7
Michigan	16	2.2	16	1.6	17	1.8	7	3.4	26	.4	8	4.2	7	4.0	33	.7	9	2.3
Minnesota	4	4.0	30	.6	29	1.0	23	1.7	34	.2	19	1.7	12	2.6	22	1.2	23	1.2
Mississippi	25	1.6	23	.8	26	1.2	25	1.6	40	.1	32	1.0	27	1.0	29	.8	39	.3

	Agriculture $27,960		Commerce $3,284		Defense $127,136		Education $11,299		Energy $10,697		Health & Human Services $194,955		Housing & Urban Development $8,003		Interior $5,737		Justice $1,703	
State	Rank	%	Rank	%	Rank	%	Rank	%	Rank	%	Rank	%	Rank	%	Rank	%	Rank	%
Missouri	8	3.0	22	1.2	9	3.3	18	1.9	16	2.7	11	2.3	13	2.4	26	.9	10	2.2
Montana	38	1.0	47	.3	49	.1	43	.5	28	.4	44	.3	44	.3	12	2.4	41	.3
Nebraska	11	2.7	48	.3	39	.4	38	.7	43	.0	36	.6	37	.5	39	.5	45	.2
Nevada	47	.2	46	.3	44	.3	50	.2	13	2.9	47	.4	45	.2	13	2.2	42	.3
New Hampshire	49	.2	38	.4	36	.5	46	.4	45	.0	41	.4	43	.3	49	.1	49	.2
New Jersey	30	1.4	18	1.5	14	2.1	11	2.6	19	2.1	9	3.4	8	4.0	37	.5	12	1.9
New Mexico	39	.9	37	.4	33	.7	35	.8	3	9.0	39	.4	40	.5	6	6.0	32	.6
New York	3	6.1	3	8.6	4	5.3	1	8.6	11	3.4	2	9.6	1	10.4	23	1.2	4	7.2
North Carolina	14	2.4	15	1.8	15	1.9	9	3.0	38	.1	13	2.2	17	1.8	34	.7	20	1.2
North Dakota	33	1.3	49	.3	45	.2	45	.4	35	.1	46	.3	47	.2	19	1.5	46	.2
Ohio	13	2.5	14	1.9	12	2.6	6	3.9	5	6.1	7	4.5	6	4.5	27	.9	17	1.5
Oklahoma	31	1.4	29	.7	22	1.3	27	1.4	24	.7	27	1.2	25	1.3	20	1.4	28	1.0
Oregon	19	2.1	27	.7	41	.4	32	1.1	18	2.1	28	1.1	34	.6	7	4.1	31	.6
Pennsylvania	12	2.5	9	2.8	7	3.5	4	4.6	17	2.6	3	6.1	4	6.2	15	1.8	7	3.5
Rhode Island	50	.2	44	.3	40	.4	41	.5	41	.0	38	.5	36	.6	50	.1	44	.2
South Carolina	29	1.5	28	.7	20	1.5	19	1.8	9	3.7	29	1.1	29	.9	45	.2	34	.5
South Dakota	36	1.0	45	.3	48	.1	42	.5	50	.0	45	.3	41	.3	14	1.8	50	.1
Tennessee	18	2.1	24	.8	31	.9	16	2.0	1	12.3	18	1.8	16	1.9	36	.5	25	1.1
Texas	2	6.5	11	2.7	2	7.9	3	5.6	20	1.4	6	4.6	5	5.0	17	1.6	3	8.6
Utah	40	.7	41	.2	32	.7	39	.7	37	.1	40	.4	39	.5	11	2.8	40	.3
Vermont	48	.2	50	.1	50	.1	49	.3	51	.0	49	.2	49	.2	51	.1	33	.6
Virginia	28	1.5	7	3.4	3	6.8	13	2.5	22	1.0	17	1.8	19	1.8	10	2.9	13	1.8
Washington	24	1.6	8	3.3	10	3.2	22	1.7	4	7.9	20	1.6	24	1.4	9	3.0	15	1.7
West Virginia	41	.6	39	.3	46	.2	36	.8	25	.5	34	1.0	35	.6	25	1.0	30	.9
Wisconsin	21	1.8	26	.8	38	.5	20	1.8	36	.1	12	2.2	23	1.4	35	.6	22	1.2
Wyoming	46	.2	51	1.1	* 51	.1	51	.2	29	.3	50	.1	51	.1	8	3.1	51	.1

(continued)

Geographic Distribution of Federal Funds, 1980 (continued)

Total department funds, in millions	Labor $15,211		State $547		Transportation $19,622		Treasury $11,580		Environmental Protection Agency $5,812		General Services Administration $3,753		National Aeronautics & Space Administration $5,366		Veterans Administration $22,107		All Other $53,915		Total State Funds
State	Rank	%	Rank	%	Rank	%	Rank	%	Rank	%	Rank	%	Rank	%	Rank	%	Rank	%	Millions
Alabama	14	2.0	21	.1	23	1.4	25	1.2	22	1.4	17	1.2	6	4.2	17	2.0	15	2.1	8,829
Alaska	37	.5		.0	17	1.7	44	.3	48	.3	32	.4	36	.0	51	.2	49	.2	2,124
Arizona	25	1.2	23	.0	31	.9	28	1.0	39	.5	27	.5	19	.6	26	1.5	26	1.0	6,217
Arkansas	33	.8	36	.0	36	.7	35	.7	31	.8	41	.2	45	.0	25	1.6	36	.7	4,506
California	1	9.6	11	.8	3	6.8	1	10.7	1	9.5	2	8.1	1	41.3	1	9.4	3	8.2	61,464
Colorado	29	.9	29	.0	27	1.3	27	1.0	27	1.2	12	2.6	11	1.7	30	1.3	23	1.3	6,950
Connecticut	30	.9	19	.2	32	.9	26	1.1	21	1.5	31	.4	9	2.1	35	1.0	29	.9	8,906
Delaware	43	.3	32	.0	51	.2	45	.3	45	.4	22	.7	40	.0	47	.3	51	.2	1,319
District of Columbia	6	5.5	1	74.1	1	8.8	3	5.9	3	6.8	1	23.7	13	1.3	13	2.4	7	4.4	16,073
Florida	11	3.1	12	.8	5	5.0	10	2.8	14	2.3	18	1.0	2	9.1	4	5.5	9	4.1	22,822
Georgia	15	1.9	18	.2	13	2.4	12	2.5	13	2.4	8	3.7	25	.1	10	2.6	17	2.0	11,089
Hawaii	39	.5	31	.0	34	.8	40	.4	36	.6	47	.1	30	.1	46	.3	39	.5	3,151
Idaho	42	.4	44	.0	49	.3	43	.3	40	.5	43	.2	49	.0	45	.3	44	.3	1,995
Illinois	7	3.8	13	.6	6	4.8	6	4.4	11	3.1	5	6.6	22	.2	7	3.5	1	9.6	23,033
Indiana	10	3.3	8	1.0	22	1.4	23	1.5	10	3.1	23	.7	20	.5	22	1.7	20	1.4	9,260
Iowa	35	.6	41	.0	33	.9	32	.9	23	1.4	40	.2	28	.1	33	1.1	31	.9	5,214
Kansas	36	.6	37	.0	30	1.0	36	.7	26	1.2	33	.4	32	.1	34	1.1	28	1.0	5,419
Kentucky	20	1.6	43	.0	25	1.3	19	1.6	17	1.8	19	.8	38	.0	24	1.6	22	1.4	7,210
Louisiana	24	1.3	24	.0	21	1.4	21	1.6	28	1.2	35	.3	8	3.2	21	1.7	27	1.0	7,799
Maine	41	.4	46	.0	45	.4	38	.5	34	.6	38	.2	47	.0	38	.7	40	.4	2,577
Maryland	17	1.7	4	2.1	9	3.7	17	1.7	16	1.9	11	2.9	4	7.9	27	1.4	11	2.8	13,419
Massachusetts	12	2.5	15	.5	10	3.3	9	3.1	15	2.0	14	2.3	15	1.0	8	3.1	13	2.3	15,119
Michigan	3	7.6	7	1.2	15	2.0	7	3.7	5	5.1	15	2.2	23	.2	9	2.8	16	2.0	16,108
Minnesota	28	1.0	10	.9	26	1.3	22	1.5	24	1.3	26	.5	24	.1	20	1.7	21	1.4	8,089
Mississippi	27	1.0	26	.0	39	.6	31	1.0	35	.6	37	.3	18	.6	29	1.3	32	.8	5,456

| | Labor $15,211 | | State $547 | | Transportation $19,622 | | Treasury $11,580 | | Environmental Protection Agency $5,812 | | General Services Administration $3,753 | | National Aeronautics & Space Administration $5,366 | | Veterans Administration $22,107 | | All Other $53,915 | | Total State Funds |
Total department funds, in millions	Rank	%	Rank	%	Rank	%	Rank	%	Rank	%	Rank	%	Rank	%	Rank	%	Rank	%	Millions
Missouri	13	2.1	20	.1	16	2.0	13	2.1	12	2.8	3	7.0	26	.1	16	2.2	14	2.1	13,271
Montana	44	.3	48	.0	38	.6	42	.3	43	.4	39	.2	48	.0	44	.4	42	.3	1,802
Nebraska	46	.3	45	.0	40	.6	37	.5	37	.6	42	.2	46	.0	37	.7	33	.8	3,568
Nevada	45	.3	42	.0	37	.6	47	.3	41	.4	45	.1	39	.0	43	.4	46	.3	1,857
New Hampshire	48	.2	33	.0	43	.4	46	.3	32	.7	46	.1	35	.0	42	.4	43	.3	1,973
New Jersey	8	3.6	9	.9	11	2.7	11	2.7	8	3.7	9	3.6	16	.7	15	2.2	12	2.7	14,253
New Mexico	34	.6	22	.1	41	.5	39	.4	47	.3	29	.4	21	.3	36	.7	38	.6	4,231
New York	2	8.4	2	9.2	2	7.8	2	10.1	2	9.3	4	7.0	14	1.0	2	7.0	2	8.2	40,742
North Carolina	22	1.4	6	1.3	24	1.4	15	1.8	7	4.2	20	.8	31	.1	11	2.6	19	1.4	10,173
North Dakota	49	.2	50	.0	44	.4	50	.2	49	.3	48	.1	31	.1	49	.3	48	.2	1,667
Ohio	5	5.6	17	.2	12	2.4	8	3.4	4	5.9	13	2.4	7	3.7	6	3.8	8	4.3	19,756
Oklahoma	31	.9	38	.0	18	1.6	33	.9	29	1.0	36	.3	34	.0	23	1.7	24	1.2	6,560
Oregon	26	1.1	27	.0	28	1.2	20	1.6	33	.7	25	.6	33	.0	31	1.2	30	.9	5,218
Pennsylvania	4	6.1	14	.5	4	6.5	5	4.8	9	3.7	10	3.0	10	1.9	5	4.7	6	4.5	25,174
Rhode Island	40	.5	35	.0	48	.3	41	.3	42	.4	44	.2	37	.0	41	.5	41	.4	2,164
South Carolina	32	.8	28	.0	42	.5	30	1.0	38	.5	28	.4	41	.0	28	1.4	34	.8	6,226
South Dakota	47	.2	49	.0	46	.4	48	.2	50	.3	51	.1	43	.0	40	.5	47	.2	1,627
Tennessee	19	1.7	34	.0	20	1.5	14	1.9	30	.8	21	.7	29	.1	14	2.3	4	6.0	11,571
Texas	9	3.5	3	2.9	7	4.4	4	5.2	6	4.5	7	4.3	3	9.0	3	6.6	5	4.8	29,331
Utah	38	.5	39	.0	35	.7	29	1.0	44	.4	34	.3	12	1.3	39	.5	37	.6	3,096
Vermont	50	.2	40	.0	50	.2	49	.2	51	.2	49	.1	42	.0	48	.3	50	.2	1,021
Virginia	18	1.7	5	2.0	14	2.3	16	1.8	19	1.6	6	4.4	5	4.6	12	2.5	10	3.2	17,128
Washington	16	1.8	16	.3	8	4.1	24	1.2	18	1.6	16	2.1	17	.7	18	1.9	18	1.7	12,013
West Virginia	23	1.3	30	.0	19	1.6	34	.9	25	1.3	30	.4			32	1.2	35	.7	3,896
Wisconsin	21	1.5	25	.0	29	1.1	18	1.7	20	1.6	24	.7	27	.1	19	1.8	25	1.2	7,557
Wyoming	51	.1	47	.0	47	.3	51	.3	46	.4	50	.1	44	.0	50	.3	45	.3	1,026

The organizational units were chosen as traditionally tabulated items of general use, which are the agency categories similar to those shown in the federal budget.

GET a real JOB.

HELP A TEACHER THROUGH SCHOOL. GIVE!

MEMORIAL TO THE UNKNOWN TEACHER

© Tom Whittemore/ROTHCO

officials have objected that the 1968 Crime Control Act gave too much money to suburban police departments and too little to urban forces, which dealt with far more crime. Mayors were unhappy as money was channeled to states rather than localities; they felt urban problems were not receiving enough attention or support.

Block grants have become the centerpiece of President Reagan's federalism. With both his unsuccessful 1982 swap proposal and his subsequent budgets Reagan has continually pressed for consolidation of grant programs into block grants. His 1987 budget asserts that more than 85 percent of the estimated federal obligation is now concentrated in 25 programs. And with the termination of revenue sharing in 1986, block grants may take on additional importance for fiscal federalism in the future.

Revenue Sharing

Soon after his inauguration in 1969, Mr. Nixon proposed the new federalism that was designed to rebalance the federal–state relationship. Central to the new federalism was revenue sharing. As noted earlier, the president proposed that the federal government turn back tax revenues to the states to spend, with only the stipulation that states "pass through" a portion of the money to the cities and local governments. When Nixon proposed revenue sharing, he said it was time to stop the expansion of

Melvin Laird
Melvin Laird first
introduced revenue
sharing to the Congress
in 1958. Laird, a Re-
publican congressman
from Wisconsin from
1953 until 1969, went
on to become secretary
of defense in Nixon's
first administration.
Laird's original
revenue-sharing bill
contained the essentials
of the bill enacted into
law in 1972; however,
the 1958 bill received
little consideration as
long as the federal
deficit produced by the
Vietnam War was seen
as a problem.

the national government. Revenue sharing, Mr. Nixon argued, "marks a turning point in federal–state relations, the beginning of decentralization of governmental power, the restoration of a rightful balance between the state capitals and the national capital."

Revenue sharing is not new. Andrew Jackson once distributed a federal budget surplus among the states. In 1958, Melvin Laird, then a Republican congressman from Wisconsin and later secretary of defense for President Nixon, proposed returning tax money to the states. In 1960, Walter Heller, who was to become chairman of the Council of Economic Advisors under Presidents Kennedy and Johnson, presented a plan to the same effect. But neither proposal received much attention or support. By 1967–1968, however, more than one hundred bills with some thirty variations of revenue sharing had been introduced into the Congress.[24] Congressmen and senators were beginning to endorse the idea; both presidential candidates in the 1968 election supported the proposal.

In 1972, Congress passed the State and Local Fiscal Assistance Act, authorizing a sum of $30.2 billion to be returned to state and local governments over a five-year period, with one-third of the funds for states and two-thirds of the funds to be distributed to local governments. Considerable opposition had been raised prior to passage of the act. Democrats were suspicious; Wilbur Mills, then chairman of the powerful House Ways and Means Committee, was flatly opposed. Organized labor was opposed. Mayors were fearful because they worried that states would eat up the funds and cities would receive little aid. Thus, Congress delayed action on the proposal. Then the Vietnam War ended and revenue sharing no longer threatened existing programs; the categorical grants-in-aid were to remain. A substantial percentage of money would go to local and urban governments, thus pacifying the mayors. As the president had requested, relatively few strings were attached regarding use of the funds: money could be spent for needed services, whatever they were. More than $6 billion annually was to be distributed, calculated from a formula that included population, tax effort, and per capita income.

Revenue sharing was extended for four years in 1976 and then renewed again in 1980 and 1983. The 1976 extension retained all the original features of revenue sharing (two-thirds of funds going to local governments and one-third to the states) and added provisions against discrimination and for greater public participation in deciding how the funds were to be used. Public meetings had to be held and publicized in the newspapers before any decision on budgeting the money could take place. The 1980 extension of revenue sharing dropped state governments as fund recipients because many states were enjoying budget surpluses. President Reagan further recommended the continuation of revenue sharing from 1983 to 1986, but at a constant level of $4.6 billion annually. He threatened to veto any bill authorizing a higher level of spending. In Reagan's new federalism proposals, revenue sharing would have been shifted over into a local block grant.

Public Policy: Offshore Oil Leases

In response to the OPEC boycott of oil in the 1970s, the hunt for alternative sources of energy began. Part of that effort was a search for new domestic sources of oil. There was widespread consensus that large-scale oil imports were a danger to our security and adversely affected the domestic economy. Oil companies widened efforts to find oil on land, hoping for another find like the one at Alaska's Prudhoe Bay, but they focused on exploring for oil in the ocean. Petroleum geologists estimate that as much as 60 percent of United States oil reserves are under the ocean floor, most of it in California and the Gulf of Mexico. That is the problem. Whose oil is it, and under what conditions should oil leases be granted?

The potential bonanza of oil from offshore leases has produced a conflict between states and the national government. The Department of Interior has encouraged industry to drill offshore for oil. It uses as justification the 1978 Outer Continental Shelf Lands Act, which calls for offshore oil exploration to "assure national security, reduce dependence on foreign sources and maintain a favorable balance of payments in the world trade." Although the law was passed during the energy crisis, which is at least temporarily over, Secretary of the Interior James Watt and his successors used it in the 1980s to attract oil exploration by offering large offshore areas for lease.

State opposition to federal offshore leasing is strong. States control drilling and receive revenues from leasing within three miles of their coastlines (ten miles for Texas and part of Florida due to a previous agreement with the national government). Beyond the three miles, ownership and jurisdiction rest solely with the federal government. The states also contend that they are entitled to split revenues with the federal government from leases on another three-mile zone, which straddles the state–federal boundary. The federal government does share revenue from this area with states but it has no obligation to do so.

Environmental concerns provide another area of contention. States worry that increased oil exploration, particularly in deep water, increases environmental danger. Oil spills threaten many coastlines with scenic or wilderness value. Increased drilling also causes air pollution and may damage the fishing industry. Broadening the area for leasing increases the environmental risks.

The federal–state conflict is most obvious in the matter of offshore oil revenues. The national government argues that expanded leasing brings revenue into the treasury and helps reduce the deficit. States contend that they must deal with the problems associated with oil drilling and so are entitled to part of the money. The states accuse the Reagan administration of holding a giant "fire sale" and of insensitivity to state problems. As the two levels of government continue to squabble, an escrow fund of $6 billion in oil royalties has piled up. The federal government proposes giving coastal states 27 percent of the revenues and using the remaining $4 billion to reduce the federal deficit. States say they are entitled to between 33 and 50 percent of the escrow fund. The Interior Department argues that states should receive only those monies actually obtained from oil and gas drained from state lands by federal wells—1 to 4 percent of the total.

Here is an example of the federal–state partnership and how the drive for revenue can alter federal relations. At one time Americans were quite content to let states control offshore oil leasing. But as the quest for energy independence grew and as the federal deficit widened, the national government moved in to preempt a good deal of state action—and revenue. Now we have a protracted conflict between the national government and the coastal states over offshore drilling leases. At stake are billions of dollars in potential revenue and the future of the federal partnership between the national government and the states.

In 1986, however, the debate over revenue sharing ended. President Reagan called for its elimination, stating that the nation could no longer afford revenue sharing, and Congress allowed the program to expire. With the federal deficit continuing near $200 billion in the mid-1980s and with the improvement in revenue-generating ability of local tax systems, the time had come to end this fourteen-year practice of sharing federal revenues with local governments. Declared President Reagan in his 1987 budget,

> In an austere federal budget, national priorities must be met first. Local priority needs that are appropriate for federal financing can be achieved through block grants and other broad based support that provides flexible federal funding in areas such as health, community development, and job training.

The Future of Federalism

The federalism debate is by no means over. For two hundred years we have experimented with a federal arrangement. The Constitutional Convention did not settle the issue. If anything, the convention heightened the potential of the issue to generate conflict. Historical events have often focused attention on the federal basis of the union. The Civil War and the question of slavery are prime examples of such conflicts. Still other issues have dramatized the failure of the federal system simply or clearly to distribute power and solve problems: the Depression, civil rights, urban living, poverty, environmental regulation, and urban bankruptcy have all altered our thinking on federalism. Some settled issues of federal–state relations are court decisions on commerce, federal supremacy, and taxing authority.

Revenue sharing had its measure of success, but proved to be no panacea. In fact, money distributed in this way amounted to only 11 percent of the federal revenue shared with state and local governments. Newer reforms are likely to alter the balance of power between Washington and the states. The problems facing America in the 1980s transcend the simplistic idea of federalism as a neat tripartite division of power among three layers of government. For a nation spending a trillion dollars annually, political life is much too complex for such an approach.

In the future, American federalism will continue to be intimately related to national politics. The continual shifts in population, both growth and migration, will affect the resources of states as well as the nature of their problems. Economic development and social conditions in the nation generally are reflected in the individual states. Employment, urban blight, and technology are all problems that must be faced. The plight of the cities means more federal assistance. Demands for services and support for disadvantaged citizens conflict with those of overburdened taxpayers unhappy with the spiraling cost of government services. States and localities will become more and more dependent on the federal dollar, particularly so since revenue sharing has been eliminated. Categorical grants will remain a part of fiscal federalism. But if national financing is to play a central role, the sharing of services will have to continue. It seems unlikely that the federal government will take over or control more services. New federalism points in the opposite direction. Decentralization of federal financial assistance will continue.

The trend of the future is probably toward multistate regionalism—that is, several states joining together to work on a common problem. This seems a midpoint between federal control and the untenable position of state and local programs extending beyond local legal boundaries. It is a recognition that crime, pollution, energy development, and transportation transcend localities. Regional organizations promote interstate cooperation and aid in solving interstate conflicts. They enable a group of states to pursue solutions within an area without concern for established jurisdictions. They are also a means to decentralize administrative decision making and improve coordination. Such regional organizations have been successful in the past. The Tennessee Valley Authority, for example, provides power, irrigation, and water management to the Tennessee valley; the Delaware River Basin Commission manages water resources and prevents pollution in the Delaware basin (which affects New York, New Jersey, Pennsylvania, and Delaware); and the Appalachian Regional Commission administers special financial assistance programs for the depressed regions of thirteen states. More pressing is the need for metropolitan organizations to address the problems affecting urban America. The ability of cities and states, backed by federal resources, to launch coordinated programs will be a major priority in the future.

Finally, pragmatic federalism as a variation of cooperative federalism is likely to remain. The constitutional issues are likely to win some supporters and to continue to shape federalism by enabling the system to undertake and cooperate in problem solving. It has become clear, however, that the demands of citizens for government to meet new needs and solve problems form an institutional imperative. The people want problems solved, not jurisdictional stalemates; what works, whatever the authority or level, is the essence of pragmatic federalism. The faith of a people in their government is at stake. People are pessimistic and cynical. Taxpayers revolt, demanding efficiency and economy in government. Yet the essence of federalism is the system's ability to adjust and to adapt to new situations. The movement throughout the 1970s has been for more state and local autonomy in spending federal funds.

The 1980s suggest even greater emphasis in the direction of unencumbered state and local spending. It is likely that the period will become one in which national priorities are established and federal and state responsibilities sorted out. Yet it is clear that the federal system is flexible enough to accommodate changes and our attitude toward federalism pragmatic enough to permit them.

Summary

1. Federalism, as a system that divides authority between the national government and the states, has its origins in shared decision making to solve common problems.

2. The history of the nation–state relationship changed with the development and growth of the nation. From early efforts to define separate boundaries to more recent cooperative ventures, federalism has proven a flexible set of standards. There has been very little concern over constitutionally separated power.

3. In the distribution of power, the national government has enumerated powers while the states retain reserved powers. Interpretation of the powers of the national government, however, has greatly broadened those powers. Yet states remain strong and viable entities in the federal scheme.

4. Fiscal federalism illustrates the dependence of state and local governments on federal-government spending as federal aid has been pumped into communities as a means of maintaining the federal partnership. State and local governments are likely to remain heavily dependent on the federal dollar in support of public programs.

5. Revenue sharing provided federal money to states and localities for fourteen years. It ended in 1986; block grants remain the principal means under the Reagan administration to provide federal dollars to states and local governments.

Research Projects

1. *Multiple governments*   How many government jurisdictions are there in your city or area? First make a list of government units you are aware of without consulting any reference source. Next use the phone book to see if you can locate any more. Finally, consult the *Blue Book* for your state and the *Census of Governments–Governmental Organization* published by the Bureau of the Census to find a complete listing of government units. (Hint: Don't forget school districts, park districts, airport authorities, and water-management districts.)

2. *The federal dollar*   How much federal money does your state and city or town receive? The most complete source for this information is the *Geographical Distribution of Federal Funds,* published each year by the Community Services Division of the Executive Office of the President. Other good sources are the *Census of Government–Compendium of Government Finances,* published by the Bureau of the Census, and the *Book of the States,* printed each year by the Council of State Legislatures.

3. *Block grants*   In examining federal funds in your state and city, can you find out how many grants, and how much money, your city receives?

In what areas are these grants? The *Catalog of Federal Domestic Assistance*, published by OMB, is the best source for these data. Another source is city hall; the city auditor can provide the information. The Census Bureau also publishes federal expenditures by state for each fiscal year.

4. *National priorities*   Do national issues take precedence over state or local matters? Is the national government the center of our attention? Watch a local television newscast (not national news) and compare numbers of stories on national, state, and local affairs. Do the same for a local or state newspaper (*The New York Times* would *not* be a good example) to examine coverage of events on the national, state, and local levels. You might have to do this for more than one day, since unique news events may prejudice the results.

Notes

1. M. J. C. Vile, *The Structure of American Federalism* (New York: Oxford University Press, 1961), p. 39.
2. Morton Grodzins and Daniel Elazar, "Centralization and Decentralization in the American Federal System," in Robert A. Goldwin, ed., *A Nation of States* (Chicago: Rand McNally, 1963).
3. Ibid., p. 7.
4. From *The New Federalism* by Michael Reagan. Copyright © 1972 by Oxford University Press, Inc. Reprinted by permission.
5. *Plessy* v. *Ferguson*, 163 U.S. 537 (1896).
6. David B. Walker, *Toward a Functioning Federalism* (Cambridge, Mass.: Winthrop Publishers, 1981), p. 56.
7. Morton Grodzins and Daniel Elazar, "The American Federal System," in Goldwin, *A Nation of States*, 1963, pp. 21–22.
8. Walker, *Toward a Functioning Federalism*, p. 100.
9. Ibid., pp. 104–105.
10. 1982 Budget Message of the President, February 8, 1982.
11. *National Journal*, March 5, 1983, p. 519.
12. *United States* v. *Darby*, 312 U.S. 100 (1941).
13. *McCulloch* v. *Maryland*, 4 Wheaton 316 (1819).
14. *Gibbons* v. *Ogden*, 9 Wheaton 1 (1824).
15. *Heart of Atlanta Motel* v. *United States*, 379 U.S. 241 (1964).
16. *Garcia* v. *San Antonio Metropolitan Transit Authority*, 469 U.S. 528 (1985).
17. *Frothingham* v. *Mellon*, 262 U.S. 447 (1923); *Massachusetts* v. *Mellon*, 262 U.S. 447 (1923).
18. *Flast* v. *Cohen*, 392 U.S. 83 (1968).
19. *United States* v. *Richardson*, 418 U.S. 166 (1974).
20. Reagan, *The New Federalism*, p. 145.
21. Walter H. Heller, *New Dimensions of Political Economy* (Cambridge, Mass.: Harvard University Press, 1967), p. 129.
22. Reagan, *The New Federalism*, p. 34.
23. Henry S. Reuss, *Revenue Sharing: Crutch or Catalyst for State and Local Governments?* (New York: Praeger, 1970), p. 39.
24. Reagan, *The New Federalism*, p. 90.

Bibliography

Elazar, Daniel. *American Federalism: A View from the States.* New York: Harper & Row, 1984.
  A basic work on federalism. Elazar approaches federalism as a partnership, and he discusses federalism as it has changed over the years. Much of the book looks at federalism from the states' viewpoint. Elazar has much good information on the states, including their political culture.

Glendening, Parris, and Reeves, Mavis Mann. *Pragmatic Federalism.* Pacific Palisades, Calif.: Palisades Publishers, 1984.
  A very good treatment of federal–state relations with particular attention to the political environment within which they operate. The view here is that federalism is an evolving, pragmatic effort to work out solutions to issues as they arise.

Goldwin, Robert A. (ed.). *A Nation of States.* Chicago: Rand McNally, 1963.
  A collection of essays on federalism. Some essays examine the history and intent of federalism, while others defend or criticize the national government's role in federalism.

Grodzins, Morton. *The American System.* New Brunswick, N.J.: Transaction Books, 1983.
  An extensive history of federalism from the perspective that federalism has always meant shared responsibility.

This is a valuable source book that provides an indispensable understanding of federalism and the various areas of shared authority.

Hawkins, Robert B. *American Federalism: A New Partnership for the Republic.* San Francisco: Institute for Contemporary Studies, 1982.

A collection of papers from a conference on federalism, the book treats federalism in the 1980s. Considerable attention is given to the Reagan administration as well as to the views of state and local public officials. This is the best work to date on Reagan's federalism.

Howitt, Arnold. *Managing Federalism: Studies in Intergovernmental Relations.* Washington, D.C.: Congressional Quarterly Press, 1984.

Written from an unusual perspective, this book gives readers an understanding of how intergovernmental relations operate. It uses several case studies to show the system at work and the problems people encounter along the way.

Reagan, Michael D., and Sanzone, John G. *The New Federalism,* 2nd edition. New York: Oxford University Press, 1981.

A sharp and insightful discussion of federalism. Reagan and Sanzone are critical and politically astute. New federalism is intergovernmental relations in which policy expands government largely through federal grants-in-aid. This, the authors write, alters our understanding and approach toward federalism.

Riker, William. *Federalism: Origins, Operation, Significance.* Boston: Little, Brown, 1964.

Riker provides the most critical assessment of federalism. The book, however, seeks to develop a theory of federalism by examining federal governments in Europe and elsewhere as well as in America.

Sharkansky, Ira. *The Maligned States.* New York: McGraw-Hill, 1978.

A defense of states. Sharkansky feels state autonomy and flexibility in dealing with problems has considerable merit. While noting differences among states, he observes that on balance state accomplishments in providing services and dealing with social problems have been good.

Walker, David B. *Toward a Functioning Federalism.* Cambridge, Mass.: Winthrop Publishers, 1981.

This volume traces the evolution of American federalism from its beginnings to 1980. It focuses on the judicial, financial, service, and political developments that make up the changing character of federalism. Contemporary federalism is seen as dramatically different and increasingly dysfunctional.

Wright, Deil. *Understanding Intergovernmental Relations.* Monterey, Calif.: Brooks/Cole, 1982.

A very good study of intergovernmental relations. Wright provides a strong measure of analysis to accompany his description and discussion of intergovernmental relations. Much of the volume focuses on finances and attitudes toward intergovernmental activities.

The First Amendment Liberties

"The preservation of the sacred fire of liberty, and the destiny of the republican model of government, are justly considered as deeply, perhaps as finally, staked on the experiment entrusted to the hands of the American people." So said George Washington at his first inaugural. Washington was voicing the eternal problem of balancing individual liberty and the authority vested in a community. This balance is difficult to achieve, particularly in a democratic society. A constitutional republic was a government of limited and enumerated powers emanating from a written constitution and was devised to protect individual liberty. Civil liberties are those individual freedoms spelled out in the Constitution and the Bill of Rights that guarantee protection to persons, ideas, and property from arbitrary interference by government. At the convention, Charles Pinckney said of the Constitution, "Our true situation appears to me to be this—a new, extensive country containing within itself the materials of forming a government capable of extending to its citizens all the blessings of civil and religious liberty, capable of making them happy at home."

James Madison stated the problem clearly in *Federalist No. 51:* "In framing a government which is to be administered by men over men, the great difficulty lies in this: you must first enable the government to control the governed; and in the next place, to control itself." The Supreme Court has understood the issue in exactly this way; it has been a staunch defender of civil liberties. The rule of law that the justices are sworn to uphold is the substance and sustenance of civil liberty. As Mr. Justice Black wrote, "The worst citizen no less than the best is entitled to equal protection of the laws of his state and his nation."[1]

Fundamental Freedoms

Fundamental Liberties: *individual rights so basic to liberty and justice that they need not be enumerated in order to be protected.*

Democratic government is created for the well-being of its citizens. Constitutional government must protect civil liberties and rights. But how? And which liberties and rights were to be considered basic and inviolable, an individual's **fundamental liberties**? Mr. Justice Cardozo wrote in *Palko* v. *Connecticut* (1937) that there were two categories of rights: those that were implicit in the concept of ordered liberty and those that were not. Those liberties not implicit must be enumerated, as in a Bill of Rights, to be protected, but those inherent to ordered liberty need not be listed to be protected. Rather, they flow from a "principle of justice so rooted in the traditions and conscience of our people as to be ranked as fundamental."[2] The distinctive characteristic of fundamental freedoms was that they were indispensable for liberty and justice, and courts were to give more judicial protection for them than for other parts of the Constitution. Unfortunately, neither Mr. Justice Cardozo nor the Supreme Court has ever articulated a list of fundamental freedoms. The Court has refused to call all liberties within the Bill of Rights fundamental freedoms. In recent years, however, the Court has spoken of such rights as abortion, racial equality, free speech, and criminal justice as preferred rights.

Yet it was of the first ten amendments, the Bill of Rights, that Mr. Justice Cardozo was speaking. These amendments were added to the Constitution in 1791, thus fulfilling the promise of the Founders to add protection for civil liberties in order to secure ratification. Various states already had bills of rights in their state constitutions, and the absence of such basic protections in the national Constitution caused distrust and fear of centralized power. The Bill of Rights was directed at the national government, and in an early nineteenth-century case the Supreme Court held that the Bill of Rights applied only to the national government and not to the state governments.[3]

Can the liberties of the Bill of Rights be labeled as fundamental, thereby obligating the states as well as the national government? Justice Cardozo thought so, but the Supreme Court has refused to bind states by declaring freedoms fundamental. The Court has, however, used the Fourteenth Amendment, which does apply to states, to impose on the states

Fact File
The Process of Selective Incorporation

Provision	Amendment	Year	Case
"Public use" and "just compensation" conditions in the taking of private property by government	V	1896 and 1897	Missouri Pacific Railway Co. v. Nebraska, 164 U.S. 403, 17 S.Ct. 130; Chicago, Burlington & Quincy Railway Co. v. Chicago, 166 U.S. 226, 17 S.Ct. 581
Freedom of speech	I	1927	Fiske v. Kansas, 274 U.S. 380, 47 S.Ct. 655; Gitlow v. New York, 268 U.S. 652, 45 S.Ct. 625 (1925) (dictum only); Gilbert v. Minnesota, 254 U.S. 325, 41 S.Ct. 125 (1920) (dictum only)
Freedom of the press	I	1931	Near v. Minnesota, 283 U.S. 697, 51 S.Ct. 625
Fair trial and right to counsel in capital cases	VI	1932	Powell v. Alabama, 287 U.S. 45, 53 S.Ct. 55
Freedom of religion	I	1934	Hamilton v. Regents of Univ. of California, 293 U.S. 245, 55 S.Ct. 197 (dictum only)
Freedom of assembly, and, by implication, freedom of association	I	1937	DeJonge v. Oregon, 299 U.S. 353, 57 S.Ct. 255
Free exercise of religious belief	I	1940	Cantwell v. Connecticut, 310 U.S. 296, 60 S.Ct. 900
Separation of church and state; right against the establishment of religion	I	1947	Everson v. Board of Educ., 330 U.S. 1, 67 S.Ct. 504
Right to public trial	VI	1948	In re Oliver, 333 U.S. 257, 68 S.Ct. 499
Right against unreasonable searches and seizures	IV	1949	Wolf v. Colorado, 338 U.S. 25, 69 S.Ct. 1359
Exclusionary rule as concomitant of right against unreasonable searches and seizures	IV	1961	Mapp v. Ohio, 367 U.S. 643, 81 S.Ct. 1684
Right against cruel and unusual punishments	VIII	1962	Robinson v. California, 370 U.S. 660, 82 S.Ct. 1417
Right to counsel in all felony cases	VI	1963	Gideon v. Wainwright, 372 U.S. 335, 83 S.Ct. 792
Right against self-incrimination	V	1964	Malloy v. Hogan, 378 U.S. 1, 84 S.Ct. 1489; Murphy v. Waterfront Com'n, 378 U.S. 52, 84 S.Ct. 1594
Right to confront witnesses	VI	1965	Pointer v. Texas, 380 U.S. 400, 85 S.Ct. 1065
Right to privacy	Various	1965	Griswold v. Connecticut, 381 U.S. 479, 85 S.Ct. 1678

Other incorporated provisions	Amendment	Year	Case
Right to impartial jury	VI	1966	Parker v. Gladden, 385 U.S. 363, 87 S.Ct. 468
Right to speedy trial	VI	1967	Klopfer v. North Carolina, 386 U.S. 213, 87 S.Ct. 988
Right to compulsory process for obtaining witnesses	VI	1967	Washington v. Texas, 388 U.S. 14, 87 S.Ct. 1920
Right to jury trial in cases of serious crime	VI	1968	Duncan v. Louisiana, 391 U.S. 145, 88 S.Ct. 1444
Right against double jeopardy	V	1969	Benton v. Maryland, 395 U.S. 784, 89 S.Ct. 2056
Right to counsel in all criminal cases entailing a jail term	VI	1972	Argersinger v. Hamlin, 407 U.S. 25, 92 S.Ct. 2006
Right of petition	I		Included by implication of other First Amendment incorporations
Right to be informed of the nature and cause of the accusation	VI		Included by implication of other Sixth Amendment incorporations

	Amendment	Provision(s) not incorporated
Provisions of the first eight amendments not incorporated	II	All
	III	All
	V	Right to indictment by grand jury
	VII	All
	VIII	Right against excessive bail; right against excessive fines

SOURCE: Harold Chase and Craig Ducat, Constitutional Interpretation, 2nd ed. (St. Paul, Minn.: West, 1979).

Practicing Politics: How to Get a Passport

*I*f you are unmarried and over the age of thirteen, you must have a passport in your own name to travel abroad. Here is how to go about obtaining one:

1. Have your picture taken by a passport photographer, who will give you prints of the required size and quality. Two 2 × 2 inch photographs, front view and full face in ordinary street dress, are needed. They may be black and white or color. Sign your name on the back of each.

2. You need your birth certificate (an original certified copy) or other evidence to prove you hold U.S. citizenship.

3. You will need proof of your identity such as a previous passport or a driver's license (a credit card or a social security card is not acceptable).

4. You must appear personally at a U.S. passport agency, before a clerk of any federal court or state court of record, before a judge or clerk of any probate court accepting applications, or at a post office designated to accept passport applications. U.S. passport agency offices are located in Boston, Chicago, Detroit, Honolulu, Houston, Los Angeles, Miami, New Orleans, New York, Philadelphia, San Francisco, Seattle, Stanford, and Washington, D.C.

5. Obtain and fill out the application, submit your documents, and pay the necessary fees. If all is in order, you will receive your passport in the mail, usually within two weeks.

6. U.S. passports are valid for ten years from the date of issue. The passport will contain a list of countries for which it is not valid; this list changes depending on the international situation.

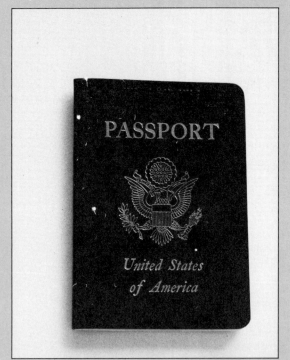

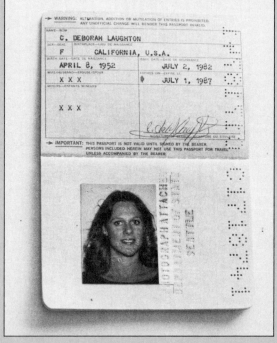

Selective Incorporation: *the gradual process whereby Supreme Court decisions have included provisions of the Bill of Rights as applying to limit state governments.*

many of the freedoms named in the Bill of Rights. In fact, today much of the Bill of Rights has been interpreted as limiting state governments. The due process clause says that no state shall "deprive any person of life, liberty, or property, without due process of law." Using the due process clause of the Fourteenth Amendment, the Supreme Court began a gradual process of **selective incorporation.** *Gitlow* v. *New York*, in 1925, was the landmark case: for the first time the Court held that a provision of the Bill of Rights—the First Amendment rights of free speech and a free press—could not be impaired by states any more than it could by the national government. The decision said, "[These] are among the fundamental personal rights and liberties protected by the due process clause of the Fourteenth Amendment from impairment by the states." Since 1925, the Supreme Court has moved to include more provisions of the Bill of Rights as fundamental personal rights protected from impairment by states under the due process clause of the Fourteenth Amendment. The Court has been unwilling to say that the Fourteenth Amendment referred to the entire Bill of Rights, but today virtually all of the latter's provisions (including the right to privacy) have been applied to the states. Many of the fundamental personal rights and liberties are contained within the First Amendment, to which we now turn our attention. The First Amendment protects the freedoms of religion, speech, press, assembly, and other forms of expression.

First Amendment Freedoms

Freedom of Religion

It is not surprising that the first right mentioned in the First Amendment is freedom of religion. Puritan colonists came to America to escape religious persecution, and for them freedom of religion was a necessity. Thus, the first words of the First Amendment are clear and emphatic: "Congress shall make no law respecting an establishment of religion, or prohibiting the free exercise thereof."

Establishment Clause: *the part of the First Amendment that prohibits the federal government or any state from setting up a church, passing laws to aid any religion, or preferring one religion over another.*

No-Preference Position: *the doctrine that holds that government may support religion, but that government cannot show any preference to one religion over another.*

The Establishment Clause   The **establishment clause** prevents the federal government or any state from setting up a church. Nor can any government pass laws to aid any religion, or prefer one religion over another.[4] Some critics argue that the establishment clause was not intended to prevent government support for religion, only favoritism for a particular religion or religions. But this **no-preference position** has not been accepted by the Supreme Court. The Court has adhered to the idea of a "wall of separation between church and state," a doctrine set forth by Mr. Justice Black in the 1947 decision *Everson* v. *Board of Education.* It was on this basis in 1962 that the Court struck down prayer in schools as "wholly inconsistent with the establishment clause,"[5] and outlawed Bible reading as a daily requirement in public schools.[6]

The wall-of-separation doctrine has drawn considerable opposition, particularly regarding the prayer and Bible-reading decisions. It is true that the distinction between church and state is not easy to draw; the Court has walked a very fine line at times. Not every law that confers an "indirect" or "incidental" benefit to religion, the Court has said, is necessarily invalid.[7] For example, after having apparently laid down its narrow interpretation of permissible support in *Everson*, the Court went on to hold that reimbursement to parents for transportation to and from parochial schools was not a violation of the **wall-of-separation principle.** Such reimbursement was not aid to religion, but rather was a contribution to the child's welfare and safety.

Wall-of-Separation Principle: *the phrase used by the Supreme Court in interpreting the First Amendment prohibition against establishment of a church, thereby preventing public aid or support for religious activity.*

In 1970 the Court declared that property tax exemptions for churches have a secular purpose and provide only incidental aid to religion, and therefore do not violate the establishment clause.[8] But what exactly would constitute a violation was left unarticulated. A year later the Court, in the case of *Lemon* v. *Kurtzman* (1971), did clarify the establishment clause by creating a three-part test for any program to meet in order not to violate the establishment clause: (1) it must have a clear secular purpose; (2) it must neither advance nor inhibit religion; and (3) it must avoid causing "excessive government entanglement with religion."[9]

The 1971 case involved state attempts to subsidize the cost of parochial school education, which the Court found to be unconstitutional. Here the effort to supplement teachers' salaries in private schools was held to cause excessive administrative entanglement, even though the Court found acceptable the program's secular purpose of promoting the education of young children.

However, the three-part test in *Lemon* has been applied differently in various circumstances. In 1981 the Court determined that where open meetings of religious groups are held on state-supported college campuses, the colleges are not thereby sponsors of the groups. A state university or a public high school cannot prevent a student religious group from using its facilities for worship or discussions when such facilities are available to other student groups. This equal access policy for student religious groups is not incompatible with the establishment clause. In 1983 Congress passed the Equal Access Act, which prohibits any public high school receiving federal aid from denying access to its facilities by student religious groups. And the Court has said colleges may not prohibit the use of university buildings and grounds for religious worship or religious teaching. "An open forum in a public university does not confer any imprimatur of state approval on religious sects or practices."[10]

Child-Benefit Theory: *a Court position that state aid for parochial education does not violate the establishment clause when the principal benefit is to the child.*

Over the years, the relationship between financial aid to parochial schools and the establishment clause has been a knotty problem. In *Everson* v. *Board of Education*, while laying down its wall-of-separation doctrine, the Court held that aid to parochial education did not in itself violate that doctrine. Where the primary benefit was to the child, state aid would not necessarily be invalid. The **child-benefit theory** has survived as the Court has struggled to determine when aid was primarily secular in purpose and benefited the child, and when it violated the three-part test of *Lemon* and was public support to religion. The Court has rejected direct subsidies for salaries as unconstitutional; it has accepted the use of tax funds to purchase textbooks, provide diagnostic health services, reimburse parents for bus transportation, administer state-prepared tests, and support recordkeeping and reporting activities. In 1983, in *Mueller* v. *Allen,* the Court declared tax deductions for private school tuition to be permissible, calling it a secular matter of public policy and not aid to religion.[11] "An educated populace is essential to the political and economic health of any community and a state's effort to assist parents in meeting the rising costs of educational expenses plainly serves this secular purpose of ensuring that the states' citizenry is well educated." But in 1985 the Court refused to allow cities or school districts to send publicly paid school teachers into parochial schools to conduct remedial or enrichment classes. Such classes have the effect of advancing religion.[12]

State support for religious schools is another issue. Very little state aid may go to parochial elementary and secondary schools without violating the establishment clause. The Supreme Court has ruled that these schools are permeated with religious teaching. At the college and university level, however, the Supreme Court has been more generous in allowing state support for nonpublic education. There still cannot be support for religion, and a two-part test has been devised to judge such aid. The test says (1) the institution's secular function must not be permeated with a religious atmosphere, and (2) there must be assurances by the college or university that the aid will not be used for religious teaching or activities. On this basis in 1976 the Court approved, for the first time, annual grants to support the operation of religious colleges in Maryland.[13]

Because of the wall of separation in the establishment clause, prayers and Bible reading have been outlawed in the public schools. No official sponsorship or approval of religious beliefs is permitted.[14] Even nondenominational prayers are prohibited.[15] Released time for religious instruction may be permissible, provided the instruction is not given on school premises during the school day. Bible study is permissible if it is presented as an academic subject.

Conservatives in Congress, buoyed by the 1980 elections and President Reagan's endorsement, have pushed for a constitutional amendment for voluntary prayer in public schools, though without much success. Conservatives in America have made school prayer one of their issues for the political agenda of the nation. The amendment before Congress would bar the federal courts, including the Supreme Court, from hearing any cases on voluntary school prayer. To date, Congress has shown little inclination to pass the proposal and submit it to the states. Many critics think such a limitation of federal court jurisdiction would be not only an unwise precedent but probably unconstitutional as well.

Several states have sought ways around the school prayer ban. Some states have passed laws permitting a daily period of silence for personal

meditation or prayer or personal beliefs. It was hoped that by not specifically referring to prayer or religion the establishment clause would not be violated. But the Supreme Court, in *Wallace* v. *Jaffree* (1985), struck down state laws permitting one-minute periods of school time for "meditation or voluntary prayer."[16] While the Court did not say all moments of silence without mention of prayer were unconstitutional, it left little reason to believe states could permit prayer under the label of meditation. Such state statutes typically have a purpose, and that purpose is, in reality, voluntary prayer. This, the Court said, is an endorsement "not consistent with the established principle that the government must pursue a course of complete neutrality toward religion."

The establishment clause has also been used to prevent schools and churches from vetoing liquor license applications. Statutes that give churches and schools power to veto liquor licenses within a 500-foot radius of a church or school affront the First Amendment's establishment clause; they delegate to private, nongovernmental entities a power reserved for government. This, then, advances religion in violation of the establishment clause.[17]

A long-smoldering issue over the establishment clause has been the use of Christian symbols during the Christmas season in public buildings. From the singing of traditional Christmas carols by school children to the display of nativity scenes in parks and city halls, the question of traditional celebration and religious faith has been raised. For several years lower courts have ruled both ways on the issue—some courts calling creche sets or nativity scenes legitimate traditional celebration, others saying such activities foster a Christian set of values and so violate the establishment clause. Finally in 1984 the Supreme Court received the question and ruled, in *Lynch* v. *Donnelly,* that city nativity scenes depicting traditional Christmas elements do not violate the establishment clause.[18]

In a five to four decision, Chief Justice Burger wrote for the majority, saying that the Constitution "affirmatively mandates accommodation, not merely tolerance, of all religions, and forbids hostility toward any." The Court was saying the wall-of-separation doctrine was not complete or totally accurate. "No significant segment of our society and no institution within it can exist in a vacuum or in total or absolute isolation from all other parts, much less from government."

Chief Justice Burger went on to acknowledge a long-standing tradition of religion in American political life. "There is an unbroken history of official acknowledgment by all three branches of government of the role of religion in American life from at least 1787." He cited the motto "In God We Trust," the pledge "One nation under God," and religious paintings hanging in publicly supported art galleries. In deciding the case, Burger concluded that Christmas creche scenes have a secular purpose, depicting the historical origins of Christmas. The benefit to one's faith is "indirect, remote and incidental."

The Free-Exercise Clause   If the First Amendment prohibits the establishment of religion, it also protects the individual's right to worship freely. This means that people are free to worship or believe what they will or to hold no religious beliefs whatsoever. In the **free-exercise clause** government is absolutely prohibited from proscribing any religious belief and is also required to make some accommodations for the practice of religion. Further, government may not burden an individual or confer any benefits upon an individual because of religious beliefs.

The results can often appear confusing. In 1985 the Supreme Court ruled that a state law requiring the photograph of a person on his or her driver's license violated the First Amendment.[19] But in 1986 the Court refused to stop the federal government from using the Social Security number of a child simply because the family believed such numbers were evil. Said the Court, a citizen "may no more prevail on his religious objection to the government's use of a Social Security number for his daughter than he could on a sincere religious objection to the size or color of the government's filing cabinets."[20]

The Constitution itself prohibits any religious tests as a condition for office in the federal government. In 1961, the Supreme Court invalidated

Free-Exercise Clause: *the part of the First Amendment that protects the right of individuals to worship as they choose.*

Church and State: A Judicial Thicket in Lower Federal and State Courts

The freedom of religion guaranteed in the First Amendment continues to perplex courts in spite of Supreme Court rulings. The Supreme Court sought to provide a policy for lower courts and public officials to follow in implementing permissible forms of activity. In *Lemon* the Court established its three-part test for church–state relations. Yet in the past several years, courts have been pressed with church–state issues, often resulting in conflicting applications. Here are some of the issues lower federal and state courts have been faced with regarding church–state relations.

1. *Invocations and benedictions at high school graduation ceremonies*   A Michigan district court did not think such brief prayers violated the establishment clause (*Stein* v. *Plainwell*, U.S. District Court for Western Michigan, 5-85); but an Iowa district court did not see it that way, holding that invocations and benedictions at public ceremonies *did* violate the establishment clause. (*Graham* v. *Central Community School District of Decatur*, U.S. District Court for Southern Iowa, 5-85.)

2. *Ten Commandments in the classroom*   Posting the Ten Commandments of the Christian faith is unconstitutional in North Dakota (*Ring* v. *Grand Forks Public School District No. 1*, N.D. U.S. District Court, 1-80), but constitutional in Kentucky. Apparently in Kentucky the placards showing the Commandments were financed by voluntary contributions and were no more religious than the Preamble to the Kentucky Constitution. (*Stone* v. *Graham*, Kentucky Supreme Court, 4-80.)

3. *Smoking marijuana*   Members of the Coptic church may be prevented from smoking marijuana as part of their religious worship. The Florida Supreme Court said that the state's interest in public health and safety outweighed the free exercise of their religion (*Town* v. *Florida*, 11-79), but in North Dakota the U.S. District Court said members of the Native American church were permitted to smoke peyote as part of their worship.

4. *Employment discrimination for religion*   The First Amendment accords persons wide latitude to practice their religion, but what happens when that practice conflicts with their employment? Worldwide Church of God members must be given sufficient days off to observe their holy days, says a Court of Appeals for the Second Circuit (*Philbrook* v. *Ansonia Board of Education*, 3-84), while a Sikh employee refusing to shave in order to wear a gas mask safely could be transferred to a lower-paying job. (*Bhatra* v. *Chevron USA, Inc.*, Court of Appeals for the Ninth Circuit, 6-84.) Then in Ohio a Court of Appeals refused to prevent an Ohio Christian School from not renewing a teacher's contract after she became pregnant. The church school said a "mother's place is in the home." (*Dayton Christian Schools* v. *Ohio Civil Rights Commission*, Court of Appeals for the Sixth District, 6-85.)

5. *City maintenance of religious displays*   In *Lynch* v. *Donnelly* the Supreme Court ruled that traditional Christmas displays on public property do not violate the establishment clause, but the issue is not fully settled. What if the display is limited solely to a nativity scene? The District Court for Eastern Michigan thinks city placement and maintenance of such a scene violates the establishment clause. (*ACLU, Oakland County* v. *City of Birmingham*, 7-84.) On the other hand a District Court in Rhode Island thinks an "unknown child" memorial bearing biblical inscriptions and donated by anti-abortion citizens can be maintained by a city without violating the establishment clause. (*Fausto* v. *Diamond*, U.S. District Court for Rhode Island, 6-84.)

6. *Interracial romance* A private fundamentalist Christian school's expulsion of a white female student believed to be having a romantic relationship with a black male classmate violated the female student's rights. The Court of Appeals for the Fourth Circuit could find no official church doctrine opposing interracial romance; therefore, as no valid religious belief had been called into question, it was not necessary for the court to decide whether the student's rights were more important than the church's doctrine. (*Fiedler* v. *Marumsco Christian School*, 10-80.)

7. *Creationism and evolution* The Court of Appeals for the Fifth Circuit overturned a Louisiana statute requiring public schools to teach "creation science" whenever "evolution science" is taught. The court rejected the statute as violating the establishment clause, saying it served no legitimate state purpose because creationism was a religious belief. (*Aguillard* v. *Edwards*, 7-85.)

The Supreme Court ruled in 1984 that it is constitutional to display Christmas nativity scenes like this one in a public park.

state laws that required a religious oath as a condition for state employment.[21] Yet governmental accommodation to religious beliefs does not mean that the practice of one's religion is not subject to limitation. The profession of faith is absolute; the practice of one's faith is not. In 1879, Mormons were prohibited from practicing polygamy. The Supreme Court held that Congress was free to prohibit any action, regardless of its religious implication, provided it did not prohibit a belief.[22]

A balance has had to be struck between the free-exercise clause and government regulation through its police powers. Sunday closing laws have been upheld, when challenged by Orthodox Jews, as having a secular purpose—that of setting aside a day for rest, recreation, and tranquility.[23] School vaccinations and medical treatment may be administered over the religious objections of parents or other individuals.[24] In 1972, however, the Supreme Court held that a state could not compel Amish children to attend public school beyond the eighth grade.[25] Nor could Jehovah's Witness children be required to salute the flag or participate in any public ceremony that offended their religion.[26] In fact, New Hampshire was prevented from levying a fine on a Jehovah's Witness citizen who covered over the license plate motto "Live Free or Die." In 1981 the Court ruled that a state could not deny unemployment compensation to a Jehovah's Witness who quit his job for religious reasons rather than allow himself to be transferred to a department engaged in the production of military weapons.[27] Government cannot even pass legislation granting employees an absolute right not to work on their Sabbath. "Government must guard against activity that infringes on religious freedom, and must take pains not to compel people to act in the name of any religion."[28]

Persons claiming an exemption from government regulation on religious grounds must demonstrate that such regulation burdens the practice of their religion. In this area, there are several recurring problems. One is exemption from military service on religious grounds. The Selective Service Law originally permitted exemption from combat for persons belonging to "well recognized" religions whose creeds prevented them from participating in war, a condition interpreted as requiring belief in a Supreme Being. In 1965 the Supreme Court broadened the exemption to apply to all whose nontheistic beliefs occupied the place of a religion in their lives;[29] in 1970 the exemption was extended to those whose sincere beliefs required them to refuse to participate in war.[30] The Vietnam War brought a greater challenge, however, as critics of the war sought to argue that their religion required them to refrain from participation in "unjust" wars. The Supreme Court rejected the argument, holding that the exemption applied only to persons opposed to participation in any war.[31] The other recurring problem is in health and medicine. Court decisions have permitted vaccinations, medical treatment of children, and blood transfusions over religious objections. Modern medical techniques, life-support devices, and the "right to die" present serious issues involving the free-exercise clause that have not yet been resolved by the Court, at least not on the grounds of the free exercise of religion.

Freedom of Speech

Freedom of speech is basic to democracy. As Mr. Justice Holmes once observed, "It is not free thought for those who agree with us, but freedom for the thought that we hate" that makes this freedom so important. Democratic government depends on free expression: public elections, the power of the press, interest groups, congressional investigations, and public entertainment all depend on the substantive guarantees in the First Amendment for a free and open society. Yet free speech also provokes controversy. President Nixon claimed that the Vietnam War protesters aided and comforted the enemy and impaired the American war effort. Today, many people feel that obscenity and pornography have been protected to the detriment of American life. Public officials complain that freedom of information and sensational journalism prevent them from receiving frank opinions and making strong decisions because of the "fish-bowl environment" they must operate in.

These challenges to free speech grew louder in the 1960s as courts expanded the umbrella of protection for free expression, notably in the area of obscenity and protest against the Vietnam War. There is a surprisingly low level of support for free expression among the American public; as one moves from abstract concepts to specific situations, the American people exhibit little tolerance for Mr. Justice Holmes's "marketplace of ideas."[32] Government and the courts frequently do place limits on free

Demonstrators protesting cuts in funding for the needy stage a "sleep-in" in Lafayette Park, opposite the White House.

Oliver Wendell Holmes
Serving on the United
States Supreme Court
from 1902–1932, Oliver
Wendell Holmes was a
staunch supporter of
individual freedom.
Known for his liberal
dissents from the
bench, Holmes turned
many a powerful
phrase with his skillful
command of the lan-
guage. Holmes, accord-
ing to one biographer,
was not merely "a
commanding American
legal figure but a
significant figure in the
history of civilization."

expression. This in itself is the source of some controversy, since the courts apply different tests and take different attitudes in different cases.

A recent example of the need to balance interests comes from political demonstrations and protests. The Court has ruled that cities may ban political posters and signs on public property,[33] such signs constituting a visual clutter that is within a city's power to prohibit. Likewise the national government can prohibit "sleep-ins" in national parks that are intended to dramatize the plight of the nation's poor and homeless.[34] The Court said the government has an interest in keeping parks attractive and intact, "readily available to the millions of people who wish to see and enjoy them by their presence." Finally public utility companies cannot be compelled to disseminate other groups' views in the "extra space" available on their billing envelopes.[35] To distribute consumer group statements or other points of view with which the firm may disagree impermissibly burdens the utility companies' rights of free speech.

Balancing Interests   The strongest position for freedom of expression was taken by Mr. Justice Black, who argued that free speech was an absolute right as expressed by the framers in the words "Congress shall make *no law* . . . abridging the freedom of speech." Justice Black would allow no law abridging freedom of speech or press, including laws for slander and libel. For him, First Amendment rights enjoyed a *preferred position*, not to be "balanced away whenever a majority of [the] Court thinks that a State might have an interest sufficient to justify abridgment of those free-

The public presence of American Nazis tests the meaning and strength of the First Amendment.

doms." Yet Justice Black was never able to persuade a majority of the Court to adopt the preferred position or absolutist view. The Court has consistently looked for some means, or test, to *balance* the constitutional protection of individual expression with the requirements of public order and safety.

Balancing Doctrine: *the Court view that an individual's right to liberty must be balanced against the needs of public order and safety.*

This **balancing doctrine** resulted from a series of opinions and dissents written by Justices Holmes and Brandeis early in the twentieth century. With what was called the **clear-and-present-danger test,** the Court sought to restrict freedom of expression for the benefit of society only when such expression constituted a clear and present danger to society. The two cases arose out of the Espionage and Sedition Acts of 1917 and 1918, when some Socialists were arrested and convicted for mailing out leaflets protesting the draft.[36] The convictions were upheld; the Supreme Court saw the leaflets as an immediate threat to national security. Writing in *Schenck* v. *United States,* Justice Holmes expounded the clear-and-present-danger doctrine:

Clear-and-Present-Danger Test: *the test proposed by Supreme Court Justice Holmes for determining when government had the right to restrict free speech. Only when speech provoked a "clear and present danger" were restrictions permissible.*

> [The] character of every act depends upon the circumstance in which it is done. . . . The most stringent protection of free speech would not protect a man on falsely shouting fire in a theater and causing a panic. It does not even protect a man from an injunction against uttering words that may have all the effect of force. . . . The question in every case is whether the words used in such circumstances are of such a nature as to create a clear and present danger that they will bring about the substantive evils that Congress has a right to prevent. It is a question of proximity and degree.[37]

In the *Abrams* case, the majority of the Court found that criticism of the war effort produced a "bad tendency" and that speech could be prohibited when it tended to bring harmful results. In *Gitlow* v. *New York,*[38] the Court went further and adopted the **bad-tendency test** to balance state regulation of seditious activity. In this case, the Court upheld a New York law prohibiting the advocacy of violent overthrow of the government.

Bad-Tendency Test: *a test established by the Supreme Court in 1925 to deal with the prohibition of speech threatening the overthrow of the government.*

By the 1940s, the Court had begun to use the clear-and-present-danger test to examine free expression. The justices began to look at Justice Black's reasoning that the "substantive evil" that follows as a result of the speech "must be extremely serious and the degree of imminence extremely high before utterances can be punished."[39] This trend has continued into the present; the Court has focused on protecting the advocacy of unpopular ideas and the printing of allegedly prejudicial pretrial material or classified documents in the press. In *Watts* v. *United States,* the Supreme Court reversed the conviction of a man protesting the draft. Watts had said that, if drafted and forced to carry a rifle, the first man he would aim the rifle at would be the president. The Court viewed this as "symbolic speech" and not a threat to incite violence.[40] It also refused to allow the conviction of a Ku Klux Klan member for advocating and teaching political violence.[41] The Court now appears to be saying that clear and present danger must provoke incitement to violence, imminent lawless

Citizens protesting the banning of books are taking a stand against censorship.

action, or a court determination of the objective meaning of the speaker's words before free speech can be limited. This interpretation provides fresh and strong protection for the First Amendment freedom.

The Burger court has demonstrated that it is equally serious with regard to protection for free speech. It has refused convictions for disorderly conduct for a speech that did not result in imminent lawless behavior.[42] It struck down, as unconstitutionally overbroad, a Massachusetts law allowing the conviction of a person wearing the American flag on the seat of a pair of blue jeans.[43] It has also added **commercial speech**—advertising of professional services—to the constitutional protection of the First Amendment.

In 1982 the Court refused to allow a school board to ban books from high school and junior high school libraries because the school board viewed the books as "anti-American, anti-Christian, anti-Semitic, and just plain filthy." Nine books had been removed, including Kurt Vonnegut's *Slaughterhouse Five*, Desmond Morris's *The Naked Ape*, Richard Wright's *Black Boy*, and Eldridge Cleaver's *Soul on Ice*. The Court recognized the school board's role in judging curricula and determining the school environment, including the content of the school library, but felt that the First Amendment placed limitations on the discretion of such boards to remove books from school libraries. "In sum, just as access to ideas makes it possible for citizens generally to exercise their rights of free speech and press in a meaningful manner, such access prepares students for active and effective participation in the pluralistic, often contentious society in which they will soon be adult members."[44]

The balancing approach is very much in evidence when it comes to the draft and registering for Selective Service. The Supreme Court has upheld the right of the government to enforce the Selective Service registration requirement passively—that is, to prosecute only those persons who report themselves as having violated the law.[45] The restriction of freedom of speech is no greater than is essential to the furtherance of the government's substantial interest in raising a military to ensure its security. Added to an earlier decision permitting the denial of federal financial assistance to students failing to register for the draft,[46] this case gives the government ample resources to compel compliance with Selective Service registration.

The balance was also applied when the Court upheld a school's authority to discipline students for vulgar and offensive language in public places.[47] The school was allowed to suspend the student for "lewd and indecent" speech in a high school assembly. The Court said "schools must teach by example the shared values of a civilized social order," and they must be given discretion to punish "inappropriate" speech in classrooms and assemblies.

Prior Restraint: *the power of government to require approval before information can be communicated. In most instances, prior restraint is prohibited under the First Amendment.*

Prior Restraint   Action that would restrain freedom of expression before the activity occurs is called **prior restraint.** Prior restraint of free expression is considered by the courts to be equally or more serious than the actual impairment of freedom of expression. Although not all forms of prior restraint are unconstitutional, notably where obscenity is involved, "the government carries a heavy burden of showing justification for the imposition of such a restraint."[48] Areas of concern include the public forum for speeches, motion pictures, use of the mail, press reporting at trials, and, of course, the press.

The most famous case of prior restraint in recent years was the Pentagon Papers case, in which the United States government sought to prevent the *New York Times* and *Washington Post* from publishing a classified report on the history of policy making in Vietnam. The Supreme Court, in a six to three decision producing nine separate opinions, ruled that the prohibition sought by the government was an unconstitutional example of prior restraint. Justices Black and Douglas were of the opinion that any and all forms of prior restraint were unconstitutional and that limiting the publication of news would make a shambles of the First Amendment. The majority opinion, however, declared that there were situations in which the government might legitimately seek restraint for the publication or expression of material. The government bore a "very heavy burden," however, to demonstrate that such publication would cause "immediate and irreparable damage" to the nation. In this case the majority held that the publication of the Pentagon Papers posed no such threat to the security of the nation.[49]

In *Nebraska Press Association* v. *Stuart* (1976), the Supreme Court extended the argument over prior restraint to the publication of materials relating to criminal proceedings in a trial court. The Nebraska Press Association had sought to publish confessions made by a defendant in a murder trial. It was restrained from doing so by the trial court because the statements were "strongly implicative" of the accused. A unanimous Supreme Court held the order invalid. Again, prior restraint was a formidable barrier. As Chief Justice Burger said, due process and a fair trial may be reasons for such restraint, but the deprivation of a fair trial does not necessarily come about from publicity surrounding sensationalized crimes.[50]

Freedom of the Press

It is difficult to separate freedom of speech and freedom of the press. Both are forms of expression; both are protected under the First Amendment. In fact, in this era of electronic journalism and instant communications, it is primarily through newsprint and television that information is broadcast. The tradition of a free press is basic to the democratic tradition. As early as 1735, in the John Peter Zenger trial, freedom of the press was upheld as a freedom from oppression and persecution. Zenger was acquitted of charges of libeling the royal government in a New York newspaper.

Freedom of Information   Freedom of the press, however, does not guarantee the right to broadcast or televise what may be spoken or published elsewhere. In the regulation of the airways it is the right of the listening or viewing public that is paramount, not the right of broadcasters. There is no First Amendment right to a radio or television license; the Federal Communications Commission (FCC) may deny licenses in the public interest without violating freedom of speech.[51]

The privilege of an operating license also involves responsibility. What standards of fairness must a broadcaster follow in exercising the right of free speech? The Court has ruled that the FCC may require stations operating under an FCC license to follow the **fairness doctrine** by providing time for replies in cases of personal attack and political editorials.[52] The Court has also ruled, however, that this doctrine does not require stations to provide air time to groups seeking to make known their views on controversial issues. Unlimited access to the public airways does not best serve the public interest, and there exists no such right to access under the First Amendment.[53]

Fairness Doctrine: *a requirement by the Federal Communications Commission that radio and television broadcasters provide time for replies in cases of personal attack and political editorial.*

The Court has declared that no general right of access to the media exists; however, in 1981 the Court did create a limited right to *reasonable access* for federal candidates to public office in an election.[54] The government can require broadcasters to sell air time to presidential and congressional candidates once a campaign is under way.

The Supreme Court has rejected legislative efforts to apply the fairness doctrine or the right of access to newspapers. In *Miami Herald Publishing Co.* v. *Tornillo* (1974), the Court struck down as violating the First Amendment a Florida law requiring newspapers to provide free space to political candidates whom the newspaper had criticized. The First Amendment erects a "virtually insurmountable barrier" between the critical process of editorial judgment and government regulation of the print media.[55]

In 1974, the Freedom of Information Act (FOIA) was passed to increase the public's access to government information. The act, passed over President Ford's veto, makes available to citizens upon request all documents and records of the federal government and its agencies—except those falling into such exempt categories as national security, personnel information, trade secrets, interagency and intra-agency memos, law enforcement investigations, and the like. The FOIA has greatly expanded public information on the federal government's operations and has worked to restore open government. Yet the act has proved controversial, and many agencies have attempted to shield sought-after information by declaring it exempt from disclosure under the law.

The Freedom of Information Act was designed to provide for the disclosure of information, not for its withholding. It does not *require* the government to withhold material just because it falls within one of the exempted categories.[56] Yet determining what can be exempted has proven difficult. When Henry Kissinger was national security advisor to President Nixon, his office-telephone conversations were beyond the reach of the Freedom of Information Act.[57] Transcripts of these calls were not agency records obtainable under the act because persons working for

---

Freedom of Information-Privacy Acts Request

Date: _____

Your Complete Name: _____ Your Telephone No.: _____

Your Address: _____

_____

_____

Name of Subject of Your Request (if yourself, indicate "same"): _____

_____

Date and Place of Birth of Subject of Your Request (if individual(s)): _____

_____

Additional information which would assist in identifying and locating the records you seek:

Previous Residence(s) of Subject: _____

Place of Employment of Subject: _____

_____

Other: _____

Your Signature: _____

If mailed please have signature notarized: _____

If subject of your request is another living individual, you must provide the individual's notarized authorization to furnish records to you.

If this form is mailed, address to:

Director
Federal Bureau of Investigation
9th and Pennsylvania Avenue, N.W.
Washington, D.C. 20535

Attention: Freedom of Information-Privacy Acts Section

FOIPA requests are handled in chronological order based on the date of receipt. Your request will be handled as soon as possible and all documents which can be released will be made available at the earliest possible date.

- -

(Do Not Write in the Spaces Below - For Bureau Use Only)

Identification Required:

One Photo ID _____
           or
Two Nonphoto IDs with name and address: _____

Initials _____   Date: _____

FBI/DOJ

The Freedom of Information Act, passed in 1974, has greatly enhanced the public's access to federal government records.

the president in the White House are not defined as agencies. Likewise, the names and addresses of persons counted by the Census Bureau are exempted from disclosure.[58] Cities challenging the 1980 census are not allowed access under the law to names and addresses to examine for error. Also protected are the names of, say, Iranian nationals holding valid U.S. passports. The State Department denial of the request was sustained as "an unwarranted invasion of personal privacy."[59] The FBI also could prevent disclosure of "namecheck" summaries of information prepared for the White House on individuals who had criticized the presidential administration. The Court found that such summaries were compiled for political rather than law-enforcement purposes but that the summaries contained information originally compiled for law-enforcement purposes. Hence, the summaries retained their exemption as law-enforcement investigatory information.[60]

In 1985 the Supreme Court created an exemption for the CIA from the Freedom of Information Act, saying the director has broad authority to protect from disclosure all sources of intelligence information, not just those sources to which the CIA had to guarantee confidentiality in order to obtain information.[61]

The Reagan administration has tried to limit the use of the Freedom of Information Act by making it more difficult for private citizens and the media to get information. A series of changes before Congress in 1983 would authorize the attorney general to close government files to citizen requests in a number of areas. The types of information that would be protected from disclosure are investigations of organized crime and terrorism. In addition, government agencies would have a longer time span to respond to requests for releasing records, and it would become more difficult to obtain information submitted by businesses to the government. Higher fees would be charged for copying requested documents.

Free Press and Fair Trial   Freedom of the press meets its most serious challenge when it comes into conflict with another basic right, the right to a fair trial. When the details of a crime and the subsequent arrest and trial of a suspect are reported by the media, the right to a fair and unbiased trial is jeopardized. Juries may find it impossible to separate fact and trial evidence from rumor and sensational reporting. In the celebrated Sam Sheppard murder trial, the conviction of Dr. Sheppard for the murder of his wife was overturned because the court failed to protect the defendant, the jurors, and the witnesses from the overwhelming and often prejudicial publicity.[62]

In 1980, however, the Supreme Court forthrightly declared that press coverage of trials per se does not jeopardize the right to a fair trial. In the case of *Richmond Newspapers* v. *Virginia* the Court said the public and the press have a First Amendment right to attend criminal trials. Chief Justice Burger wrote the opinion, saying, "We hold that the right to attend criminal trials is implicit in the guarantees of the First Amendment; without the freedom to attend such trials, which people have exercised for centuries, important aspects of freedom of speech and of the press could be eviscerated."[63] Then in 1984 the Court extended the right of the press to cover pretrial hearings.[64] This right was further extended in 1986 when the Court ruled that pretrial hearings could be held in secret only as a last

The Supreme Court has ruled that media coverage does not prevent a fair trial.

resort to assure a fair trial and only after saying why it is necessary to exclude the public.[65] The case applies only to criminal cases; the Court has never said the public has a constitutional right to attend civil trials. Chief Justice Burger wrote that pretrial proceedings "cannot be closed unless specific, on the record findings are made demonstrating that closure is essential to preserve higher values and is narrowly tailored to serve that interest."

Presumably this decision will restrict efforts to bar the public from trials and hearings. It will markedly cut back on protective orders, called **gag rules,** to prevent the printing of information that might violate the right of a defendant or prejudice a prospective juror. But it still does not give the public absolute access to criminal court proceedings. Nor does it allow information to be withheld from such proceedings.

The media thus have access to trials. In fact, it may even be permissible to televise or otherwise broadcast coverage of a criminal trial. The Constitution, on its face, does not prohibit public media coverage of trials, nor does such coverage necessarily compromise a jury's ability to judge fairly, and states are free to experiment with such programs of coverage.[66]

Journalists and reporters have no constitutional right to withhold confidential information or protect confidential sources. Reporters have long argued for this right, but in 1972 the Supreme Court ruled otherwise. It said that requiring newspaper reporters to appear and testify before state or federal grand juries does not abridge the freedom of speech and press guaranteed under the First Amendment.[67]

Gag Rule: *a court order restricting the printing of information about criminal proceedings in cases where publication might violate the rights of a defendant or prejudice a prospective jury.*

Libel: *written or spoken statements, known to be false, that defame a person's character or reputation.*

Libel   Libel is another form of speech not protected under freedom of speech and press. Traditionally, courts have made it exceedingly difficult to prove libel with respect to public officials. The Supreme Court has held that to libel a public official, one must prove that the statements were made with "malice." That is, that the statements were made with the knowledge that they were false or with reckless disregard of their truth or falsehood.[68] The category of "public official" has been broadened to include "public figures," those who are candidates for public office and even other persons involved in public affairs or events of general public interest.[69]

Recently, however, the Court has redefined the standard for libel. First, not all controversies of interest to the public are necessarily public controversies.[70] In the case *Time* v. *Firestone*, the Supreme Court awarded libel damages to Mrs. Firestone for *Time's* reporting that her husband was divorcing her on grounds "of extreme cruelty and adultery." Second, nonpublic figures suing for libel need not prove actual malice in establishing the basis for libel.[71] In 1985 the Court said the First Amendment does not preclude awards of both actual and punitive damages, even without proof of malice on the part of libeling parties in private matters.[72] However, private parties cannot recover damages from the media unless they can show statements made in the media were false. The Court said

William Proxmire
A Democratic senator from Wisconsin since 1957, William Proxmire is an eccentric and maverick in Congress. Known for his tireless energy, he has answered over 7,000 roll calls in the Senate since 1966 without a miss. Proxmire is a persistent critic of waste and extravagant spending in the government. Since 1975 he has presented his monthly "Golden Fleece" award for the "biggest or most ridiculous or most ironic example of government waste." The military is a favorite target for his Golden Fleece award.

in 1986, "The common law presumption that defamatory speech is false cannot stand."[73] Henceforth the plaintiff must bear the burden of proof of falsity.

Third, the "public official" protection does not extend to activities of public officials outside the performance of their official responsibilities.[74] Senator William Proxmire could be sued for libel in awarding his "Golden Fleece" award—an award for the most waste or unnecessary project by a U.S. government agency. Fourth, a reporter's "state of mind" can be probed in a libel trial to discover his or her thoughts, opinions, and conclusions during the editorial process in order to establish evidence of reckless or knowing disregard for the truth.[75] The Court explained there is no First Amendment protection that keeps a person from inquiring of those who write, edit, or produce information whether they knew or suspected the publication was in error.

Finally there is no absolute immunity for persons libeling or expressing damaging falsehoods to public officials under the banner of "redress of grievances."[76] The right to petition government for redress of grievances is no shield against libel suits and enjoys no greater constitutional protection than other First Amendment expressions.

In recent actions, however, the Court has broadened the basis for persons to bring suit against so-called exploitative or sensationalist magazines and newspapers. In *Keeton* v. *Hustler Magazine* the Court said libel suits need not be initiated in the state of a magazine's corporate headquarters, but may take place in the state of the magazine's circulation.[77] "There is no unfairness in calling it [the magazine] to answer for the contents of that publication wherever a substantial number of copies are regularly sold and distributed." In *Calder* v. *Jones* the Court said a libel suit could be filed in state court even if the defendant is a resident of one state and the corporation (*National Enquirer*) is headquartered in another state, the point being that the state is the focal point of the story, and the effects from the story are suffered in that state.[78]

Freedom of Assembly and Association

The First Amendment protects the right of people "peaceably to assemble and to petition the government for a redress of grievances." This right, the Supreme Court has said, is as "equally fundamental" as the other First Amendment freedoms. Speech, association, assembly, and petition are all considered to be part of the constitutionally protected right of free expression under the First Amendment. The courts have long recognized citizens' right to use public places to assemble peaceably and petition.[79] This includes the right of labor organizations to hold meetings and to picket,[80] civil rights groups to march and demonstrate,[81] and organizations such as the Communist party to hold political rallies.[82]

The right of assembly is not an unlimited right, however. The assembly must be conducted in a law-abiding, peaceful manner. Cities and states may require licenses for parades and demonstrations. A group is not free to block traffic, incite riot, or otherwise disrupt the public or public buildings. The government may make regulations concerning the manner in which such an assembly may occur, although it may not use its regulatory power to interfere with the lawful right of a people to assemble. The line is a thin one. The Court has upheld laws prohibiting picketing near a courthouse as an undue influence on a judge, juror, or witness that would interfere with the trial.[83] The American Nazi party was allowed to parade through Skokie, Illinois, the home of many Jews who had survived Nazi concentration camps. Freedom of association is closely allied with freedom of assembly. The Court ruled in *Bates* v. *Little Rock* that a list of names of individuals participating in an assembly does not have to be furnished to governmental authorities, and that such a requirement would be an unnecessary infringement of personal liberty.[84] Under freedom of association, the right of student organizations to exist has been upheld regardless of their parent organizations' previous record;[85] the NAACP may assist individuals with civil rights grievances,[86] and union officials may aid members in labor disputes with an employer.[87] But the major issues of association have centered on loyalty and security questions.

The clash results from the inclusion of advocating the overthrow of the government in free expression and the need to protect the nation's peace and security. The major tests have come from the perceived threat of Communism in the 1950s and at time of war or dangerous international situations. During and after World War II, the Soviet Union was viewed as pressing for world domination; groups expounding socialist or revolutionary ideas were frequently viewed as "fronts" for the Soviet Union. Senator Joseph McCarthy (R–Wis.) is infamous for his efforts in the 1950s to root out alleged Communists and communist sympathizers in the federal government. It was Senator McCarthy's campaign that caused Americans to recognize that First Amendment rights were being trampled in the name of national security. Nevertheless, the courts have long recognized that the government does have a legitimate right to protect national security and regulate subversive activity.

Seditious Speech: *advocation of the violent overthrow of the government of the United States. It is considered a crime only when people are specifically urged to commit acts of violence.*

The Smith Act of 1940 made it a crime for anyone to advocate the violent overthrow of the United States government (referred to as **seditious speech**). In 1951, the Supreme Court upheld the constitutionality of the Smith Act, thus allowing the conviction of eleven Communist party leaders for advocating "overthrow of the government."[88] Subsequently, however, the Court restricted the interpretation of the Smith Act to persons actively intending to overthrow the government. No longer would mere advocacy of an abstract doctrine of revolution (i.e., Marxism) be adequate for prosecution under the Smith Act.[89] It was, however, still a crime to be a member of the Communist party, as the Smith Act provided.

The anti-communist campaign was stepped up during the Korean conflict with the passage of the McCarran Act, which required Communists and communist organizations to register with the Subversive Activities Control Board as communist agents or communist front groups. At first

Changing Consensus: Mandatory Drug Testing

Americans have discovered a drug epidemic. Newspapers, magazines, and television have labeled it the nation's Number One menace. The president and first lady have embarked on a crusade to mobilize citizens against drugs. "Drug abuse is a repudiation of everything America is," declared President Reagan in a televised address in 1986, "the destructiveness and human wreckage mock our heritage." Added Nancy Reagan, "There's no moral middle ground. Indifference is not an option."

Drug use and drug trafficking have long been a source of concern, but in 1986 our attention was riveted by their extent. This was in large part due to revelations of widespread drug use in the entertainment and sports fields. The public was shocked to learn of the cocaine-associated deaths of promising basketball star Len Bias and pro football player Don Rogers, and of extensive drug use on movie sets. In 1985, the President's Commission on Organized Crime reported the following statistics.

- There were 5 million regular users of cocaine.
- 20–24 million had tried cocaine.
- There were 563 cocaine-related deaths.
- 30 percent of all college students will have tried cocaine by their fourth year.
- 42 percent of all college students have tried marijuana.
- There were 500,000 estimated hard-core users of heroin.*

As a result, the government has declared war on drugs: putting more money into enforcing anti-drug laws, passing new legislation, and requiring testing for drug use.

Mandatory drug testing has become a popular panacea, used by more and more organizations to combat drugs on the job. Many corporations have instituted either random screening or testing of all employees, in the name of safety and corporate productivity. Some use drug testing to create favorable public opinion or to bolster morale. A fifth of all Fortune 500 companies reportedly use drug testing; that number is expected to double by 1987.** The National Football League wants unannounced tests for all its athletes during the season. Major league baseball has written drug testing into its contract with players. And President Reagan has proposed an executive order requiring that most civilian federal employees be tested for drug use (military personnel are already subject to examination).

But is drug testing really such a good idea? Apparently the American public thinks so. Three-fourths of the people questioned in a 1986 Gallup Poll said that testing of airline pilots, police, athletes, and government workers was a good idea, and 60 percent thought that high school students should be tested. There was a fairly even split only on the question of whether to test all employees on the job: 50 percent favored testing and 44 percent did not.[†]

Popular opinion aside, there are some very real practical problems with instituting mandatory drug testing. Those who have had a statistics course may recall Type II errors that have to do with accepting a false hypothesis. Remember, we are dealing with probabilities and testing, and no matter how stringently we set the parameter, we cannot be certain that every single test will be accurate or correct. The most commonly-used test for drug use has a one-in-twenty rate of false positives.[‡] Just imagine the consequences for someone who doesn't use drugs and who tests positive: loss of employment, possible criminal prosecution, personal embarrassment, and rejection by co-workers and friends. The inaccuracy of testing makes many researchers and testers wary of making it mandatory on a broad scale.

Required drug testing also involves serious legal issues. Critics raise contractual, procedural, and constitutional objections. The most serious of these charges invoke Fourth Amendment guarantees against unreasonable searches and seizures and the invasion of privacy. Mandatory drug testing or random screening does not presume probable cause; it is conducted in school or at the workplace without any reasonable suspicion that the person uses drugs.

Many see this as a gross invasion of privacy and the kind of unreasonable search and seizure prohibited by the Constitution. Other challengers note the absence of due process and of procedures to protect individuals who are subjected to drug testing. Typically, no hearings are held, and individuals who test positive often have no opportunity to dispute or explain the results. Unions, such as the NFL Players Association, contest that drug testing violates collective bargaining agreements and union contracts. Courts in Iowa, New Jersey, and New York have struck down drug test requirements for public employees and students.[§] A congressional critic of drug testing, Gary Ackerman (D-N.Y.), concludes, "Testing is not only inappropriate for our society, but it is also impractical."

Changing consensus is asking for toughening laws against drugs and drug use. Apparently, mandatory testing is seen as an acceptable tactic in this new war. Yet there are some very real and very serious problems asociated with such a practice. The true solution to our society's problem with drugs lies not so much in the urine-filled specimen bottle as in convincing individuals to say no to drugs.

*Newsweek, August 11, 1986, p. 15.
**National Journal, April 12, 1986, p. 916.
†Newsweek, August 11, 1986, p. 16.
‡U.S. News and World Report, July 28, 1986, p. 51.
§National Journal, April 12, 1986, p. 916.

Rallies and demonstrations are a form of symbolic speech; here, hundreds of thousands of civil rights advocates gather around the Washington Monument during the 1963 March on Washington.

Symbolic Speech: *nonverbal behavior generally covered as a form of free expression by the First Amendment.*

the power of the board was upheld by the Supreme Court, and the Communist party could thus be compelled to register as a communist action organization. But then, in 1965, the Supreme Court ruled that to require individual Communists to register violated their Fifth Amendment right against self-incrimination.[90] Subsequent decisions have further restricted the use of the McCarran Act.

In the 1950s, loyalty oaths had become a common practice in public employment. The Court at first upheld the oaths on the basis that employment was a privilege and not a right. But by the 1960s the oaths were more and more frequently being invalidated, though more often than not on the grounds that they were too vague. Finally, in 1967 the Court struck down loyalty oaths for both state and federal employment as a form of guilt by association that violated the First Amendment. Political affiliation could no longer be a condition for public employment.[91] In 1980 the Supreme Court added, in *Branti* v. *Finkel*, that political party affiliation alone was insufficient cause to remove an appointee from public office. Here the Court argued that the right to belong to a different political party than the employer—even in patronage public positions— was protected under the First Amendment.[92]

Other Forms of Speech

Symbolic Speech   So far, we have been treating nonverbal behavior as a form of free expression. Generally the Court has been willing to look upon nonverbal behavior as free expression covered by the First Amendment, but whenever there is a question of action, or **symbolic speech,** rather than just verbal speech, the problem of reconciling individual liberty with social needs for peace, order, and security becomes more complex. The Supreme Court has wrestled with this issue, trying to distinguish between speech and action and to balance the interests of each. Draft-card burning was held to be a form of action, not symbolic speech, and hence the individual could be prosecuted. Yet public school children could not be compelled to salute the flag. Civil rights protesters and antiwar demonstrators have argued that their rights to assemble and demonstrate are rights under the First Amendment.

Symbolic speech as a constitutionally protected form of free expression under the First Amendment was recognized as early as 1931. It was not, however, until the civil rights campaigns and the Vietnam War that symbolic speech was put to the test. In 1963 civil rights demonstrators had their conviction for breach of peace overturned when they demonstrated on the grounds of a state capitol. The demonstrators had been peaceful and, the Court reasoned, they had not impeded pedestrian or vehicular traffic.[93] Three years later, the Court upheld a sit-in by blacks in a library protesting segregated facilities, even though the sit-in extended beyond the normal activities of a library.[94] In *Tinker* v. *Des Moines School District*, the Court said school officials could not expel or punish students for wearing black armbands to protest the war in Vietnam. The Court

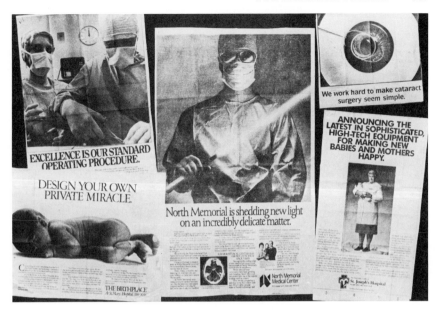

Since the 1975 Supreme Court ruling that commercial speech is a First Amendment right, such legal activities as the practice of medicine can be advertised.

reasoned this was a symbolic "silent, passive expression of opinion" that in no way disrupted the operations of the school.[95] The Court has also permitted desecration or alteration of the flag under certain circumstances as a constitutionally protected form of free expression.[96] Finally, the Court has ruled for a motorist's right to obscure the license plate motto "Live Free or Die" as symbolic speech.[97]

Commercial Speech:
protection of legal advertising from government regulation as a First Amendment form of free speech.

Commercial Speech   Until 1975, advertising was not protected from governmental regulation as free speech. In *Bigelow* v. *Virginia*, however, the Supreme Court ruled that if an activity is legal, the state cannot prohibit the advertising of it.[98] The *Bigelow* case involved newspaper advertising of abortions. The Court ruled that the advertisement was of interest to the public and extended the First Amendment freedom to cover such advertisements. The Court was careful to point out that it was sanctioning the advertising of a legal activity—the constitutional right to an abortion—and not illegal abortions. Subsequently, the Supreme Court added the advertising of prescription drug prices,[99] "for sale" signs on homes in racially integrated communities,[100] contraceptives,[101] advertising by physicians or contracting by physicians with Health Maintenance Organizations (HMOs),[102] and legal fees for attorneys.[103] In fact, in 1985, the Court said a state could not discipline an attorney for soliciting legal business by advertising truthful and nondeceptive information, including illustrations, about potential clients' legal rights if they had used a contraceptive known as the Dalkon Shield Intrauterine Device.[104]

Billboards are a more complex problem. Long recognized as a well-established medium of communication covered by the First Amendment, outdoor advertising may be regulated to control traffic hazards or for city beautification under commercial speech. But it cannot be banned per se, since to do so would violate the protection of noncommercial speech under the First Amendment.[105]

But just because advertising is legal does not mean it falls under the protection of commercial speech. The Court has said states may ban or restrict advertising "of products or activities deemed harmful, such as cigarettes, alcoholic beverages, and prostitution."[106] In other words, government can sometimes ban truthful advertising of products and services that are legal to sell. The 1986 case involved Puerto Rico's restrictions on advertising for casino gambling, which is legal in the territory. The Supreme Court said such restrictions by states were permissible: If it would be constitutional for a state to prohibit the sale of a product "deemed harmful," then a state could also take the lesser step of banning or restricting advertising of the product without banning its sale. In this way the Court drew a distinction from previous cases on commercial speech in which "the underlying conduct that was the subject of the advertising restriction was constitutionally protected and could not have been prohibited by the state."

Political Speech:
political advertising and campaigning are forms of free speech covered under the First Amendment. Political speech is basic to the democratic process.

Political Speech   Political campaigning is, of course, basic to our democratic process, and candidates have the "untrammeled right of free speech." The competition for votes requires an environment in which candidates can freely express an opinion and voters can learn about the candidates and their platforms. Political campaigning and advertising, however, are subject to increased regulation by the states. The Court has ruled that military bases may prohibit political rallies and the distribution of campaign literature, since the principal function of a military base is the training of soldiers.[107] The Court has also ruled that a municipal transit system can refuse to sell political advertising space even though it sells commercial advertising on its buses. The bus is not a public forum and the riders are a captive audience.[108] We have already noted the Court ruling by which newspaper editors are not required to provide space for replies to critical editorials. But in 1981 the Court did say broadcasters must sell broadcast time to candidates for presidential and congressional elections—that candidates have the right to access to media time.[109]

Informing the public on controversial issues of the day does not depend upon the identity of the source—even when the source is a corporation. The Court, in 1980, permitted public utility firms to advertise and to place bill inserts in their mailings to promote their position on controversial issues of public policy.[110] And as we observed earlier, such utility firms are not required to provide equal space to groups with opposing views in their bill inserts or envelopes.[111] In 1984 the Supreme Court also struck down bans on editorials on public radio or public television stations. Such bans were aimed at precisely the form of speech the framers of the Bill of Rights were most anxious to protect—speech that was defined by its contents.[112]

The Court continues to be cautious in limiting the right to contribute to or spend money for political purposes. In 1976, in *Buckley* v. *Valeo*, the Court refused to accept spending limitations for federal elections.[113] In 1982 it refused to prohibit expenditures of more than $1,000 by political action committees (PACs) to further a presidential candidate's chances.[114] The Court had found local ordinances limiting individual contributions for or against local ballot measures a violation of the First Amendment rights of association and expression.[115]

Obscenity: *a lewd or indecent publication expressing or presenting something offensive that appeals to the prurient interest.*

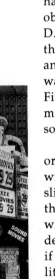

The issue of obscenity is complex, and no satisfactory definition of the term has been established. Scenes like this remain common in many cities.

Obscenity   **Obscenity** is not a constitutionally protected form of free speech. In *Roth* v. *United States* (1957), the Supreme Court held that such protection is not extended by the First Amendment, saying, in part, "implicit in the history of the First Amendment is the rejection of obscenity as utterly without redeeming social importance."[116] The principle of *Roth* still governs obscenity cases today: the question is not constitutional protection for obscenity, but what constitutes obscenity. No issue has caused the Court more difficulty in recent years. Changing standards of morality and changing expectations for state regulation of individual sexual behavior have produced an array of court cases dealing with the issue of obscenity and sexually explicit material. From Erskine Caldwell and D. H. Lawrence a generation ago, to the more recent questions raised by the movie *Deep Throat* and by *Hustler* publisher Larry Flynt, the standards and bounds of permissible expression have continually been tested. It was Justice Brennan, writing in 1973, who said, "No other aspect of the First Amendment has, in recent years, commanded so substantial a commitment of our time, generated such disharmony of views, and remained so resistant to the formulation of stable and manageable standards."

The *Roth* case declared obscenity to be outside the area of free speech or press, but went on to say that material, to be obscene, must be "utterly without redeeming social importance." Therefore, any ideas having the slightest redeeming social importance must have the full protection of the First Amendment. It was Justice Brennan, writing for the majority, who outlined the test for judging material as obscene. Material could be declared obscene and without constitutional protection, Brennan stated, if such material appealed to the prurient interest in sex; had no serious literary, artistic, or political merit; and on the whole was offensive to the average person under contemporary community standards.

In the abstract, the Court had set guidelines for judging obscenity. In practice, though, these criteria did not help much, and the Court would be faced with determining specific questions and circumstances. The language in *Roth* was ambiguous. How was one to establish an appeal to prurient interest using some contemporary community standard as understood by the average person? Subsequent cases sought to clarify the various elements of the test. The Court held, in a case involving the book *Fanny Hill*, that all elements of the test must be applied independently and the work must fail all three parts to be obscene. *Fanny Hill* might, under community standards, appeal to the prurient interest in sex, but it was not "utterly without redeeming social value."[117] The meaning of "contemporary community standards" was never agreed upon by the justices. For some, it meant local standards; for others, it meant a national standard.

As a result of the ambiguous language of *Roth* and the difficulty of applying it to specific circumstances, subsequent cases had the effect of removing the more prohibitive restrictions on sexually explicit material. Adult bookstores sprang up in almost all metropolitan centers. More sexually explicit movies began playing in neighborhood theaters. Nudity in movies, magazines, and night clubs became more common. As a result of *Memoirs* v. *Massachusetts,* which limited obscenity to material without redeeming social value, many argued that not even hard-core pornography could be outlawed by the state.

In 1973 the Supreme Court addressed the issue again. It abandoned the direction of *Memoirs,* which had required the state to prove the negative—that material was utterly without redeeming social value. Consequently, when a California restaurant manager took offense at Marvin Miller's sexually explicit solicitation to purchase four books and sued Mr. Miller, the Court was ready to abandon the "utterly without redeeming social value" test and allow states greater latitude in regulating obscenity. In *Miller* v. *California* (1973), Marvin Miller's conviction was upheld in a narrow five to four vote, and the Court set a new test for obscenity: (a) whether the average person, applying contemporary community standards, would find that the work, taken as a whole, appeals to the prurient; (b) whether the work depicts or describes, in a patently offensive way, sexual conduct specifically defined by the applicable state law; and (c) whether the work, taken as a whole, lacks serious literary, artistic, political or scientific value.[118]

Community Standards: *the Court test to determine obscenity. Each community must determine for itself its standard for judging obscenity.*

The Court had said that local communities should apply their own **community standards** in judging obscenity. Although a national standard never commanded a majority of the Court, adherence to a national standard seemed to inhibit the applicability of any local standard. Now the Court specifically faced that issue and rejected a national standard in favor of local community standards. Note too that the negative proof and language of *Memoirs* were absent in *Miller:* "utterly without" is replaced with "serious," and "redeeming social value" changed to read "literary, artistic, political or scientific value." The decision was intended to pave the way for greater efforts by state and local authorities to exercise their judgment in controlling the stream of sexual publications and films.

Only one year later, however, the Supreme Court warned local communities that, although they were to apply community standards to judge obscenity, local juries did not have *unbridled discretion* in determining what was patently offensive.[119] The Court here overturned a state conviction that had found the movie *Carnal Knowledge* obscene. Their own viewing convinced the justices that the film was not obscene. Subsequent decisions reinforced the unbridled-discretion limitation on local efforts to ban movies and activities as obscene. Drive-in movies could not ban movies with nudity per se.[120] The musical *Hair* could not be banned without a proper judicial hearing.[121]

The Court has further made it clear that normal criminal procedures must be followed in prosecuting for obscenity. In 1980 the high court overturned convictions for obscenity because such procedures were not followed. A Texas statute, which enjoined movie theaters from showing films suspected of being obscene on the basis that the theaters had been found to show obscene films in the past, was invalidated. This was an unconstitutional form of prior restraint.[122] But a bookstore selling sexually explicit material could be closed down as a public nuisance because of evidence of homosexual and heterosexual conduct, incuding solicitation for prostitution.[123] The latter activity created the public nuisance; the store was not accused of illegally selling obscene books or movies. Also, the Court would not permit the conviction for obscenity where twelve cartons of obscene material were mistakenly delivered to the wrong person and subsequently turned over to the FBI. The use of the evidence by the FBI amounted to a warrantless illegal search and seizure. The proper addressees on the packaging label had every right to expect their privacy to be protected.[124] However, the nature of the material being seized makes a difference. The Court allowed a warrant for confiscating obscene material described only as "patently offensive." The Court reasoned that the seizure of material presumptively protected by the First Amendment raises concerns other kinds of seizures do not.[125]

The intent of *Miller* was the elimination of hard-core pornography, although some people question whether that happened, since special cases have come to be considered along with the *Miller* decision. The private possession of obscene materials is not a crime,[126] but the state can prohibit their transportation, even for private use.[127] Also, the state may prohibit the use of the mail as a means of receiving obscene material.[128] In *Young* v. *American Mini Theaters, Inc.*, the Court accepted the use of zoning ordinances to regulate the location of adult movie theaters.[129] But in 1981 the Court warned that the use of zoning cannot be overly broad. Zoning ordinances that exclude all forms of live entertainment, including nonobscene nude dancing, violate the First Amendment. "The zoning power is not infinite and unchallengeable."[130] Zoning can, however, be an effective tool to restrict the spread of adult theaters. Local governments may use zoning either to concentrate adult theaters in one area or to disperse them. They are prevented only from prohibiting them altogether. "The First Amendment requires only [that a community] refrain from effectively denying respondents a reasonable opportunity to open and operate an adult theater within a city."[131]

With regard to children and child pornography, the Court sees the state as having a special interest in protecting children and gives it

© *Hy Rosen*, Albany Times-Union, N.Y./ROTHCO

"greater leeway in the regulations of pornographic depiction of children." In the 1982 case of *New York* v. *Ferber*, the Court gave the state such
leeway, upholding a New York statute prohibiting people from knowingly producing, directing, or promoting material that visually depicts
sexual conduct by children under 16.[132] The Court gave five reasons for
this greater leeway: (1) a need existed for safeguarding the physiological,
emotional, and mental health of children; (2) the *Miller* standard was not
a satisfactory standard for the child pornography problem; (3) the advertising and selling of child pornography provided an economic motive
and were thus integral parts of the production of such materials, an activity illegal throughout the nation; (4) the value of permitting live per-
formances and photographic reproductions of children engaged in lewd
sexual conduct was exceedingly modest, if not *de minimis;* and (5) recognizing and classifying child pornography as a category of material outside the protection of the First Amendment was not incompatible with
earlier decisions.

Schools have the authority to discipline students for "lewd and indecent" speech. In a 1986 decision, the Court gave school officials broad
authority to prohibit the use of vulgar and offensive language in public
places.[133] When a student used "sexual innuendo" in a speech before a

school assembly, the Court said such speech was obscene and inappropriate and that school officials could suspend the student from school. "Surely it is a highly appropriate function of public school education to prohibit the use of vulgar and offensive terms in public discourse," wrote Chief Justice Burger. "The schools, as instruments of the state, may determine that the essential lessons of civil, mature conduct cannot be conveyed in a school that tolerates lewd, indecent, or offensive speech and conduct such as that indulged in by this confused boy."

The Right to Privacy

The right to privacy may well be "the most comprehensive of rights and the right most valued by civilized people."[134] This right has been associated with personal freedom and limited government in democratic theory. Constitutionally, it has been associated with protection from unreasonable searches and seizures and the protection of private property. Justice Brandeis defined the right to privacy as the right to be left alone—a protection for the individual, in private matters, from governmental intrusion.

The right to privacy is not specifically mentioned in the Bill of Rights. It was first raised as a constitutional protection in 1890 by Louis Brandeis and Samuel Warren in a law review article in which they suggested that individuals ought to have their private affairs protected from publication in newspapers.[135] As a Supreme Court justice, Mr. Brandeis held the view that government may not violate the "privacy of the individual" under the Fourth Amendment to the Constitution. A majority on the Supreme Court, however, did not come to hold this view until 1965. In *Griswold* v. *Connecticut*, the Court recognized, or created, the right to privacy as a constitutionally protected freedom.

Penumbras

The *Griswold* case arose over a Connecticut law that forbade the use of contraceptive devices or the dispensing of medical advice on the use of such devices. Griswold, a physician and the executive director of the Planned Parenthood League, was convicted of providing medical advice and information to married couples regarding means of birth control. The Supreme Court reversed the conviction. Justice Douglas, writing for the Court, found that the law impermissibly limited the right to privacy of married couples. To ground the right to privacy in the Constitution, Justice Douglas turned not to the Fourth Amendment, which prohibited unreasonable searches and seizures, nor to the Ninth Amendment, which provided for the enumeration of additional rights not specifically pro-

Penumbras: *zones of privacy emanating from several provisions in the Bill of Rights, particularly the First Amendment. Penumbras were used by the Supreme Court as the basis for its 1965 recognition of the right to privacy as a constitutionally protected freedom.*

vided for in the Bill of Rights, but to **penumbras,** zones of privacy emanating from several provisions in the Bill of Rights, particularly the First Amendment.

> Specific guarantees in the Bill of Rights have penumbras, formed by emanations from those guarantees that help give them life and substance . . . various guarantees create zones of privacy.[136]

The First Amendment freedom of association created such a zone of privacy: the right to educate a child in a parochial school and the right of an organization to protect its membership list. The Third, Fourth, and Fifth Amendments created penumbras protecting the individual from intrusions by government. Justice Douglas noted the historical basis for recognizing the right to privacy as supporting the Court's decision in ruling invalid the Connecticut statute: "We deal with a right of privacy older than the Bill of Rights—older than our political parties, older than our school system," he said.

Justice Goldberg concurred, but he reasoned that the due process clause of the Fourteenth Amendment also embraced fundamental personal rights. Thus, states would be barred from infringing on the concept of liberty, including the right of marital privacy, even though the right is not mentioned in the Constitution. This rationale was supported by the intent of the framers as evidenced in the Ninth Amendment, in which, Justice Goldberg argued, the Court can find support for its activity in broadening personal rights not enumerated in the Constitution.

Seven years later, the Court held that there was no legitimate way to distinguish between married and unmarried couples as to the use of contraceptives. In *Eisenstadt* v. *Baird*, the Supreme Court ruled invalid a state law prohibiting the distribution of contraceptive devices to unmarried persons as a violation of equal protection. Justice Brennan wrote for the majority, stating, "If the right to privacy means anything, it is the right of the individual, married or single, to be free from unwanted governmental intrusion into matters so fundamentally affecting a person as the decision whether to bear or beget a child."[137] In 1977, the Court held invalid a law restricting the sale of contraceptive devices by licensed pharmacists to persons over the age of 16.[138] The Court, without a majority opinion, apparently reasoned that the denial of contraceptives to children did not deter them from sexual activity.

But the Court has been reluctant to extend the right of privacy too far; it has refused to create the same privacy rights for prisoners as it does for ordinary citizens. In two cases in 1984, the Supreme Court said prisoners have far less protection of privacy than other citizens. Prisoners are subject to random searches of their cells at any time, and their right of property is not violated by prison guards' intentional destruction of inmates' personal property such as letters, photographs, and books legally in inmates' possession.[139] Nor do inmates have any constitutional right to "contact visits" at which they are permitted to embrace or touch spouses, family, or friends.[140]

Abortion

Undoubtedly the greatest, and by far the most controversial, extension of the right of privacy came in the 1973 ruling that extended the right of privacy to include the right to an abortion. In two cases, *Roe* v. *Wade* and *Doe* v. *Bolton*, the Supreme Court declared, "This right to privacy, whether it be founded in the Fourteenth Amendment's concept of personal liberty and restrictions upon state action, as we feel it is, or . . . in the Ninth Amendment's reservation of rights to the people, is broad enough to encompass a woman's decision whether or not to terminate her pregnancy."[141]

The Court skirted the issue of whether the fetus was a person from conception. It found no *legal* basis for such a conclusion, but did not rule it out on religious or philosophical grounds. Rather, the Court focused on the interests of the mother as the compelling issue controlling legislation on abortions.

The Burger Court has shown no reluctance to extend the right to abortion as part of the right of privacy. In *Planned Parenthood* v. *Danforth*, the Supreme Court ruled that a state could not require parental or spousal consent for a legal abortion.[142] However, the Court would accept parental notification of abortions for minors as a means of protecting both family integrity and the well-being of the adolescent. The Court did distinguish between parental notification and parental consent, saying notification does not unconstitutionally burden the abortion decision.[143] The Court also ruled that a state could not make maturity or competence a judicial criterion for women under eighteen obtaining abortions.[144]

© 1986, *New York News, Inc. Reprinted with permission.*

The Burger Court reaffirmed these rights in June 1983 when, in a series of six to three decisions, it declared unconstitutional state laws that sought to restrict the abortion decision in the following ways: requiring women more than three months pregnant to have abortions performed in hospitals, not doctors' clinics; making doctors tell women seeking abortions about possible birth-giving alternatives, abortion risks, and that the fetus is a "human life"; insisting on a twenty-four hour waiting period between signing an abortion-consent form and the performance of the medical abortion; and requiring all pregnant, unwed girls under fifteen, no matter how "mature," to obtain a parent's consent or a judge's approval before having an abortion.[145] Mr. Justice Powell, speaking for the majority, said hospitalization for an abortion in the second trimester of pregnancy imposed a "heavy, and unnecessary, burden on women's access to a relatively inexpensive, otherwise accessible, and safe abortion procedure." As for information on abortion alternatives, Justice Powell said such information was "designed not to inform the woman's consent, but rather, to persuade her to withhold it altogether." Finally the Court did acknowledge maturity as a factor, but said state law cannot assume all minor girls too immature to make the abortion decision for themselves.

Again in 1986 the Supreme Court resolutely rejected state efforts to complicate or burden the woman's abortion decision. Writing for a five to four Court, Justice Blackmun, author of the *Roe* v. *Wade* decision, declared, "Few decisions are more personal and intimate, more properly private, or more basic to individual dignity and autonomy, than a woman's decision—with the guidance of her physician and within the limits specified in *Roe*—whether to end her pregnancy. A woman's right to make that choice freely is fundamental. Any other result, in our view, would protect inadequately a central sphere of liberty that our law guarantees equally to all."[146] The case centered on a Pennsylvania statute admittedly designed to discourage women from choosing abortions. The law required women seeking abortions to give their "informed consent" to the procedure, meaning they had to be informed of the risks of abortion and carrying a child to term, told of medical assistance available if they chose to bear the child, and given material describing characteristics of the fetus at two-week intervals. The law further required physicians to report to the state certain information concerning the woman, the abortion, and fetal viability. The law required a physician performing an abortion after fetal viability to take care to save the fetus's life. The Court found each provision of the Pennsylvania law unconstitutional; the statute had a "chilling" effect on a woman's exercise of her right to choose an abortion.

In declaring the informed consent provision unconstitutional, Justice Blackmun called the Pennsylvania law "nothing less than an outright attempt to wedge the Commonwealth's message discouraging abortion into the privacy of the informed consent dialogue between a woman and her physician." In rejecting the reporting requirement, Blackmun noted that such requirements "raise the spectre and harassment of women who choose to have an abortion." Justice Blackmun linked the decision to the Court's previous cases and affirmed those precedents. "Our cases have long recognized that the Constitution embodies a promise that a certain sphere of individual liberty will be kept largely beyond the reach of government." In strong words he concluded, "That promise extends to women as well as men."

The Court did note in *Maher* v. *Roe* that the right to an abortion meant only freedom from governmental interference in exercising the right; it did not include the right to have government pay for a nontherapeutic abortion.[147] The most controversial extension of this principle was the Hyde Amendment, by which in 1976 Congress prohibited federal funds for abortions except in situations necessary to save the woman's life or for cases of rape or incest. The amendment had been challenged in federal court as violating the due process clause of the Fifth Amendment and the religious clause of the First Amendment. In 1980 the Supreme Court upheld the constitutionality of the Hyde Amendment. The Court reasoned that the amendment placed no government obstacles in the path of women choosing to terminate their pregnancies, but that there was no constitutional entitlement to the financial resources of the federal government in order "to realize all the advantages of that freedom."[148]

January 1983 marked the tenth anniversary of the Supreme Court's decision legalizing abortions. That decision remains a matter of national public controversy. Opponents of the decision are fighting hard to overturn the *Roe* decision—either by a constitutional amendment banning abortions or by legislation defining the origin of life as being at conception. Advocates are equally resolved to fight for the right of a woman to make a private decision on terminating a pregnancy. The efforts of both groups have led to a national struggle that involves a high level of emotion and is politically divisive.

Figures from the Center for Disease Control show the number of legal abortions to have risen from 23,000 in 1969 to over 1.5 million in 1980. The 1.5 million abortions constitute about one-fourth of all annual pregnancies in the country. Abortion has become one of the most common surgical procedures.

There have been fifteen Supreme Court decisions concerning abortion since 1973. Almost all substantially support and enlarge the original 1973 decision. The Burger Court, in its 1983 decisions, shows equal resolve in affirming these earlier decisions; it is not willing to back away from its 1973 decision. Yet, several states and communities have enacted restrictive abortion laws, many ending up in the federal courts only to be struck down as incompatible with the Supreme Court's decision.

At the heart of the dispute is a nonjudicial issue concerning when life begins. Abortion opponents like the Right to Life Association insist life begins at conception and that fetal destruction is murder. Supporters of abortion argue that there is no true person until a fetus can survive outside the womb—usually after twenty-four weeks. Until that time, a woman's control over her own body is the only "right" at stake.

Opponents of abortion, including President Reagan and Senator Jesse Helms (R–N.C.), have supported an amendment to the Constitution overturning the *Roe* decision. More recently Senator Helms has introduced a "human life" bill into the Congress. The bill declares that human life begins at conception and states that there is no right to an abortion. The advantage of the human life bill from the abortion opponents' point of view is that it requires only a congressional majority and would not need to be submitted to the states.

The public's feelings about abortion are apparently mixed. Polls by NBC News and Lou Harris in 1984 found widespread support for abortion. Seventy-three percent of the NBC News poll sample agreed with the statement, "The decision to have an abortion should be left to the woman and her physician," and 60% from the Lou Harris poll opposed a constitutional amendment to ban abortion. Yet only 40% of a CBS/*New York Times* poll agreed that "abortion should be legal as it is now," and 62% said, in a January 1985 Gallup survey, that they "favor a ban on all abortions except in the case of rape, incest, or when the mother's life is endangered." It appears that many persons are personally uncertain concerning abortion but are unwilling to impose any view on others.

Homosexuality

There is no constitutional right to engage in homosexual conduct. In a bitterly divided five to four decision the Supreme Court ruled in 1986 in the case of *Bowers* v. *Hardwick* that homosexual activity falls outside the zones affording privacy to individuals.[149] The case concerned an act of sodomy between two consenting male adults in the bedroom of one of the participants.

Justice White, writing for the Court, drew a sharp distinction from heterosexual choices and made it clear that homosexual activity is not a constitutional right of privacy. "None of the rights announced in those cases [heterosexual cases] bear any resemblance to the claimed constitutional right of homosexuals to engage in acts of sodomy that is asserted in this case. No connection between family, marriage, or procreation on the one hand and homosexual activity on the other has been demonstrated. . . . Moreover, any claim that these cases nevertheless stand for the proposition that any kind of private sexual conduct between consenting adults is constitutionally insulated from state prescription is unsupportable."

Efforts to base protection for homosexual conduct between adults on the Constitution the Court found "unsupportable" and "facetious." Justice White found that neither the concept of fundamental freedoms nor the right to privacy includes homosexual rights. Nothing in the history of fundamental freedoms could be so construed; nor was the Court willing to create a new fundamental freedom for homosexual activity. As for privacy in the home for consenting adults, homosexual conduct, even if victimless, can be made illegal by states. The Court said, "The right pressed upon us here has no similar support in the text of the Constitution, and it does not qualify for recognition under the prevailing principles for construing the Fourteenth Amendment."

While the decision did not address discrimination against homosexuals in other contexts, the case clearly was a blow to gay rights activists. It most likely will encourage states to pass new legislation prohibiting various forms of homosexual behavior. Justice Blackmun, dissenting, wrote, "The right of an individual to conduct intimate relationships in the intimacy of his or her own home seems to me to be at the heart of the Constitution's protection of privacy." But a majority on the Supreme Court differed with Justice Blackmun, ruling that homosexual conduct falls outside the constitutional protection and is not a personal right of privacy.

The Right to Die

Does a person have a personal right to choose to die? Is such a right to die covered by the right of privacy? In the case of a brain-dead girl, Karen Quinlan, argued before the New Jersey Supreme Court in 1976, the contention that self-determination and the right of privacy are synonymous was put forth. The court avoided the issue by holding the question to be whether a guardian could make a decision for an incompetent adult. It held that Karen Quinlan's father could act in her best interests, including removing life-support devices, based on his religious beliefs. It is likely that it will be only a matter of time before this question will have to be confronted by the Supreme Court.

Summary

1. Civil liberties are basic to a democratic government. Some individual rights are fundamental freedoms that must be protected. Originally interpreted to apply to the national government only, the Bill of Rights, which contains our basic civil liberties, has been gradually extended to cover the states as well.

2. Freedom of religion prohibits government intrusion into religious worship. This does not mean there is no government support or regulation of religious activity, only that the Supreme Court has been very careful to keep government intervention to a minimum.

3. Freedom of speech is not an absolute right but one that must be balanced against the imminent threat to public order. There is a long history of protection, however, for this basic right. Democracy is dependent on the freedom of speech as well as the other First Amendment freedoms.

4. Newer forms of expression today also receive protection under the First Amendment. These include symbolic speech, commercial speech, and political speech.

5. Obscenity has never been protected as a form of expression within the First Amendment. The Supreme Court, however, has never satisfactorily arrived at a definition of obscenity. Presently, the Court allows communities to define obscenity for themselves, although within circumscribed boundaries.

6. The right of privacy has emerged as the most recent fundamental freedom to receive protection under the First Amendment and the entire Bill of Rights. It may well be the most important right, for it protects individuals from unnecessary government invasion into their lives. This includes the right of women to choose an abortion.

Research Projects

1. *Summarize a Supreme Court case (called a* brief*)*   Try to digest an important Supreme Court decision. In the library there will be several books on constitutional law that contain Supreme Court cases. Pick an interesting case. In one or two pages, summarize the case. You should follow a common format: (a) state the facts of the case—who did or said what, and what the first court verdict was, based on what grounds; (b) constitutional issue—what constitutional principles are in question; (c) decision—what did the Supreme Court rule; (d) reasoning—outline the logic of the Court's basis for making its ruling; and (e) precedent—what broader implication does the ruling hold?

2. *Support for the First Amendment freedoms*   Construct a brief questionnaire on First Amendment rights to ascertain the level of support for these basic freedoms. You can give this questionnaire to some of your college friends and acquaintances. Then you might also give it to neighbors or friends of your parents, noting any differences in the responses of the groups. Here are some questions you could ask:

- Should people be allowed to vote even if they can't do so intelligently?
- Do you agree that we do not have to allow known Communists to speak because they do not believe in the American system?
- Is it true that no one has a right to treat the flag or other symbols of our country with disrespect?
- Should we respect people's freedom of worship even if we do not like their religion?

3. *Obscenity*   In your community, how readily available is "adult literature"—material with a sexual appeal? For example, are R- or X-rated movies shown, are there adult bookstores, and how and where are adult magazines such as *Hustler, Playboy, Oui,* and *Playgirl* displayed? Is there any effort to control this by the use of zoning laws? You might wish to interview city officials on their views of the problem and their efforts to zone areas in order to control obscenity.

4. *Press coverage and fair trial*   Try to find a pending trial case and examine the press coverage surrounding the case. Now put yourself in the place of a juror. Do you think you could render an impartial verdict? What parts of the press coverage might be labeled sensational? If you were the newspaper editor, what parts of the story might not have been printed and yet protect the people's right to know?

Notes

1. *Bell* v. *Maryland,* 378 U.S. 226 (1964).
2. *Palko* v. *Connecticut,* 302 U.S. 319 (1937).
3. *Barron* v. *Baltimore,* 7 Peters 243 (1833).
4. *Everson* v. *Board of Education,* 330 U.S. 1 (1947).
5. *Engel* v. *Vitale,* 370 U.S. 421 (1962).
6. *Abington School District* v. *Schempp,* 374 U.S. 203 (1963).
7. *Committee for Public Education and Religious Liberty* v. *Nyquist,* 413 U.S. 756 (1973).
8. *Walz* v. *Tax Commission,* 397 U.S. 664 (1970).
9. *Lemon* v. *Kurtzman,* 403 U.S. 602 (1971).
10. *Widmar* v. *Vincent,* 454 U.S. 263 (1981).
11. *Mueller* v. *Allen,* 463 U.S. 388 (1983).
12. *School District of City of Grand Rapids* v. *Bell; and Aguilar* v. *Felton,* ____ U.S. ____ (1985).
13. *Roemer* v. *Maryland Public Works Board,* 426 U.S. 736 (1976).
14. *Abington School District* v. *Schempp,* 374 U.S. 203 (1963).
15. *Engel* v. *Vitale,* 370 U.S. 421 (1962).
16. *Wallace* v. *Jaffree,* ____ U.S. ____ (1985).
17. *Larkin* v. *Grendel's Den,* 459 U.S. 116 (1982).
18. *Lynch* v. *Donnelly,* 465 U.S. 668 (1984).
19. *Jensen* v. *Quaring,* ____ U.S. ____ (1985).
20. *Bowen* v. *Roy,* ____ U.S. ____ (1986).
21. *Torcaso* v. *Watkins,* 367 U.S. 488 (1961).
22. *Reynolds* v. *United States,* 98 U.S. 145 (1879).
23. *Braunfeld* v. *Brown,* 366 U.S. 599 (1961).
24. *Jacobson* v. *Massachusetts,* 197 U.S. 11 (1905).
25. *Wisconsin* v. *Yoder,* 406 U.S. 205 (1972).
26. *Board of Education* v. *Barnette,* 319 U.S. 624 (1943).
27. *Thomas* v. *Indiana Employment Security Division Review Board,* 450 U.S. 707 (1981).
28. *Estate of Thornton* v. *Calder Inc.,* ____ U.S. ____ (1985).
29. *United States* v. *Seeger,* 380 U.S. 163 (1965).
30. *Welsh* v. *United States,* 398 U.S. 333 (1970).
31. *Gillette* v. *United States,* 401 U.S. 437 (1971).
32. See for example James W. Prothro and Charles Grigg, "Fundamental Principles of Democracy: Bases of Agreement and Disagreement," *Journal of Politics* 22 (Spring 1960); Herbert McClosky, "Consensus and Ideology in American Politics," *American Political Science Review* 58 (June 1964); Robert Erickson, Norman Luttbeg, and Kent Tedin, *American Public Opinion,* 2nd ed. (New York: Wiley, 1980), pp. 84–88.
33. *Los Angeles City Council* v. *Taxpayers for Vincent,* 466 U.S. 789 (1984).
34. *Clark* v. *Community for Creative Non-Violence,* 468 U.S. 288 (1984).
35. *Pacific Gas & Electric* v. *Public Utilities Commission of California,* ____ U.S. ____ (1986).
36. *Schenck* v. *United States,* 249 U.S. 47 (1919); *Abrams* v. *United States,* 250 U.S. 616 (1919).
37. *Schenck* v. *United States,* 249 U.S. 47 (1919).
38. *Gitlow* v. *New York,* 268 U.S. 652 (1925).
39. *Bridges* v. *California,* 314 U.S. 252 (1941).
40. *Watts* v. *United States,* 394 U.S. 705 (1969).
41. *Brandenburg* v. *Ohio,* 395 U.S. 444 (1969).
42. *Hess* v. *Indiana,* 414 U.S. 105 (1973).
43. *Smith* v. *Goguen,* 415 U.S. 566 (1974).
44. *Board of Education, Island Trees Union Free School District* v. *Pico,* 457 U.S. 853 (1982).
45. *Wayte* v. *United States,* ____ U.S. ____ (1985).
46. *Selective Service System* v. *Minnesota Public Interest Research Group,* 468 U.S. 841 (1984).
47. *Bethel School District* v. *Fraser,* ____ U.S. ____ (1986).
48. *Organization for a Better Austin* v. *Keefe,* 402 U.S. 415 (1971).
49. *New York Times Company* v. *United States,* 403 U.S. 713 (1971).
50. *Nebraska Press Association* v. *Stuart,* 427 U.S. 539 (1976).
51. *National Broadcasting Co., Inc.* v. *United States,* 319 U.S. 190 (1943).
52. *Red Lion Broadcasting Co.* v. *Federal Communications Commission,* 395 U.S. 367 (1969).
53. *Columbia Broadcasting System* v. *Democratic National Committee,* 412 U.S. 94 (1973).
54. *Columbia Broadcasting System, Inc.* v. *Federal Communications Commission,* 453 U.S. 367 (1981).
55. *Miami Herald Publishing Co., Inc.* v. *Tornillo,* 418 U.S. 241 (1974).
56. *Chrysler Corporation* v. *Brown,* 441 U.S. 281 (1979).
57. *Kissinger* v. *Reporters' Committee for Freedom of the Press,* 445 U.S. 136 (1980).
58. *Baldridge* v. *Shapiro,* 455 U.S. 345 (1982).
59. *U.S. Department of State* v. *Washington Post,* 456 U.S. 595 (1982).
60. *Federal Bureau of Investigation* v. *Abramson,* 456 U.S. 615 (1982).
61. *CIA* v. *Sims,* ____ U.S. ____ (1985).
62. *Sheppard* v. *Maxwell,* 384 U.S. 333 (1965).
63. *Richmond Newspapers* v. *Virginia,* 448 U.S. 555 (1980).
64. *Waller* v. *Georgia,* 467 U.S. 39 (1984).

65. *Press Enterprise Co.* v. *Superior Court,* _____ U.S. _____ (1986).
66. *Chandler* v. *Florida,* 449 U.S. 560 (1981).
67. *Branzburg* v. *Hayes,* 408 U.S. 665 (1972).
68. *New York Times* v. *Sullivan,* 376 U.S. 254 (1964).
69. *Curtis Publishing Company* v. *Butts,* 388 U.S. 130 (1976); *Rosenbloom* v. *Metromedia,* 403 U.S. 29 (1971).
70. *Time, Inc.* v. *Firestone,* 424 U.S. 448 (1976).
71. *Wolston* v. *Reader's Digest Association,* 443 U.S. 157 (1979).
72. *Dun and Bradstreet* v. *Greenmoss Builders,* _____ U.S. _____ (1985).
73. *Philadelphia Newspapers, Inc.* v. *Hepps,* _____ U.S. _____ (1986).
74. *Hutchinson* v. *Proxmire,* 442 U.S. 111 (1979).
75. *Herbert* v. *Lando,* 441 U.S. 153 (1979).
76. *McDonald* v. *Smith,* _____ U.S. _____ (1985).
77. *Keeton* v. *Hustler Magazine,* 465 U.S. 770 (1984).
78. *Calder* v. *Jones,* 465 U.S. 783 (1984).
79. *David* v. *Massachusetts,* 167 U.S. 43 (1897).
80. *Thomas* v. *Collins,* 323 U.S. 516 (1945).
81. *NAACP* v. *Alabama,* 356 U.S. 449 (1958).
82. *DeJonge* v. *Oregon,* 299 U.S. 353 (1937).
83. *Cox* v. *Louisiana,* 379 U.S. 559 (1965).
84. *Bates* v. *Little Rock,* 361 U.S. 516 (1960).
85. *Healy* v. *James,* 408 U.S. 169 (1972).
86. *NAACP* v. *Button,* 371 U.S. 415 (1963).
87. *Brotherhood of Railroad Trainmen* v. *Virginia,* 377 U.S. 1 (1964).
88. *Dennis* v. *United States,* 341 U.S. 494 (1951).
89. *Yates* v. *United States,* 354 U.S. 298 (1957).
90. *Albertson* v. *Subversive Activities Control Board,* 382 U.S. 70 (1965).
91. *Keyishian* v. *Board of Regents,* 385 U.S. 589 (1967); *United States* v. *Robel,* 389 U.S. 258 (1967).
92. *Branti* v. *Finkel,* 445 U.S. 507 (1980).
93. *Edwards* v. *South Carolina,* 372 U.S. 229 (1963).
94. *Brown* v. *Louisiana,* 383 U.S. 131 (1966).
95. *Tinker* v. *Des Moines School District,* 393 U.S. 503 (1969).
96. *Street* v. *New York,* 394 U.S. 576 (1969); *Spence* v. *Washington,* 418 U.S. 405 (1974).
97. *Wooley* v. *Maynard,* 430 U.S. 705 (1977).
98. *Bigelow* v. *Virginia,* 421 U.S. 809 (1975).
99. *Virginia State Board of Pharmacy* v. *Virginia Citizens Consumer Council, Inc.,* 425 U.S. 748 (1976).
100. *Linmark Associates, Inc.* v. *Township of Willingboro,* 431 U.S. 85 (1977).
101. *Carey* v. *Population Services International,* 431 U.S. 678 (1977).
102. *American Medical Association* v. *Federal Trade Commission,* 455 U.S. 676 (1982).
103. *Bates* v. *State Bar,* 433 U.S. 350 (1977).
104. *Zauderer* v. *Disciplinary Counsel of Supreme Court of Ohio,* _____ U.S. _____ (1985).
105. *Metromedia, Inc.* v. *San Diego,* 453 U.S. 490 (1981).
106. *Posados de Puerto Rico* v. *Tourism,* _____ U.S. _____ (1986).
107. *Greer* v. *Spock,* 424 U.S. 828 (1976).
108. *Lehman* v. *City of Shaker Heights,* 418 U.S. 298 (1974).
109. *Columbia Broadcasting System* v. *Federal Communications Commission,* 453 U.S. 367 (1981).
110. *Consolidated Edison Co. of New York, Inc.* v. *Public Service Commission of New York,* 447 U.S. 530 (1980); and *Central Hudson Gas and Electric Corp.* v. *Public Service Commission of New York,* 447 U.S. 557 (1980).
111. *Pacific Gas & Electric* v. *Public Utilities Commission of California,* _____ U.S. _____ (1986).
112. *FCC* v. *League of Women Voters of California,* 468 U.S. 364 (1984).
113. *Buckley* v. *Valeo,* 424 U.S. 1 (1976).
114. *Common Cause* v. *Schmitt,* 80-847 and 80-1067.
115. *Citizens Against Rent Control* v. *Berkeley,* 454 U.S. 290 (1981).
116. *Roth* v. *United States,* 354 U.S. 476 (1957).
117. *A Book Named "John Cleland's Memoirs of a Woman of Pleasure"* v. *Attorney General of Massachusetts,* 383 U.S. 413 (1966).
118. *Miller* v. *California,* 413 U.S. 15 (1973).
119. *Jenkins* v. *Georgia,* 418 U.S. 153 (1974).
120. *Erznoznik* v. *City of Jacksonville,* 422 U.S. 206 (1975).
121. *Southeastern Promotions, Ltd.* v. *Conrad,* 420 U.S. 546 (1975).
122. *Vance* v. *Universal Amusement Co., Inc.,* 445 U.S. 308 (1980).
123. *Arcara* v. *Cloud Books,* _____ U.S. _____ (1986).
124. *Walter* v. *United States,* 447 U.S. 649 (1980).
125. *New York* v. *P. J. Video, Inc.,* _____ U.S. _____ (1986).
126. *Stanley* v. *Georgia,* 394 U.S. 557 (1969).
127. *United States* v. *Orita,* 413 U.S. 139 (1973).
128. *United States* v. *Reidel,* 402 U.S. 351 (1971).
129. *Young* v. *American Mini Theaters, Inc.,* 427 U.S. 50 (1976).
130. *Schad* v. *Mount Ephraim,* 452 U.S. 61 (1981).
131. *City of Renton* v. *Playtime Theatres,* _____ U.S. _____ (1986).
132. *New York* v. *Ferber,* 458 U.S. 747 (1982).
133. *Bethel School District* v. *Fraser,* _____ U.S. _____ (1986).
134. Justice Brandeis, dissenting in *Olmstead* v. *United States,* 277 U.S. 438 (1928).
135. See Louis Brandeis and Samuel Warren, "The Right to Privacy," *Harvard Law Review,* 193 (1890).
136. *Griswold* v. *Connecticut,* 381 U.S. 479 (1965).
137. *Eisenstadt* v. *Baird,* 405 U.S. 438 (1972).
138. *Carey* v. *Population Services International,* 413 U.S. 678 (1977).
139. *Hudson* v. *Palmer,* 468 U.S. 517 (1984).
140. *Block* v. *Rutherford,* 468 U.S. 576 (1984).
141. *Roe* v. *Wade,* 410 U.S. 113 (1973).
142. *Planned Parenthood* v. *Danforth,* 428 U.S. 52 (1976).
143. *H. L.* v. *Matheson,* 450 U.S. 398 (1981).
144. *Bellotti* v. *Baird,* 440 U.S. 904 (1979).
145. *City of Akron* v. *Akron Center for Reproductive Health, Inc.,* 462 U.S. 416 (1983); *Planned Parenthood Association of Kansas City, Mo., Inc.* v. *Ashcroft,* 462 U.S. 476 (1983); *Simopoulos* v. *Virginia,* 462 U.S. 506 (1983).
146. *Thornburgh* v. *American College of Obstetricians & Gynecologists,* _____ U.S. _____ (1986).
147. *Maher* v. *Roe,* 432 U.S. 464 (1977).
148. *Harris* v. *McRae,* 448 U.S. 297 (1980).
149. *Bowers* v. *Hardwick,* _____ U.S. _____ (1986).

Bibliography

Abraham, Henry. *Freedom and the Court.* New York: Oxford University Press, 1982.

A standard work that discusses civil rights and liberties, including freedom of speech, religion, race, and due process. The book is current and sufficiently detailed to provide an excellent survey of rights and liberties as interpreted by the Court.

Emerson, Thomas. *Toward a General Theory of the First Amendment.* New York: Random House, 1966.

Emerson takes the approach that the First Amendment confers an absolute right to free speech on citizens. Nevertheless, Emerson raises several issue areas and relates Supreme Court decisions to them, making for lively reading.

Krislov, Samuel. *The Supreme Court and Political Freedom.* New York: Free Press, 1968.

A reasoned discussion of the Supreme Court's attempts to unravel some thorny issues regarding political freedoms. Rather than concentrating on case law, Krislov looks for standards or reasoning by the Court to establish principles for political freedoms.

Mason, Alpheus T. *The Supreme Court: Palladium of Freedom.* Ann Arbor, Mich.: University of Michigan Press, 1962.

Mason views an important role of the Supreme Court to be the protection of minority rights. He provides a good historical discussion of the Court's treatment of political freedoms.

Morgan, Richard. *The Supreme Court and Religion.* New York: Free Press, 1975.

In this overview of church–state relations, Morgan looks at the sources of conflict and the groups involved. He gives only minor attention to law and court decisions on church–state matters.

Sigler, Jay. *American Political Policies.* Homewood, Ill.: Dorsey Press, 1975.

A discussion of the First Amendment policies as developed by the Supreme Court, containing an especially good analysis of implementing rights. The work affords a good overview of political rights, including the rights of such minority groups as women, Indians, and the handicapped.

Sorauf, Frank. *Wall of Separation.* Princeton, N.J.: Princeton University Press, 1976.

The best and most extensive treatment of the First Amendment right to freedom of religion. Sorauf analyzes not only the issues and parties to church–state suits but also the political and legal context for such suits, making use of empirical data.

Sunderland, Lane. *Obscenity.* Washington, D.C.: American Enterprise Institute, 1974.

A review of major court decisions and legislative proposals relating to obscenity. The first chapter presents a good historical overview of obscenity decisions.

Young, J. B. (ed). *Privacy.* New York: Wiley, 1978.

A sophisticated collection of articles on privacy. The first sections seek to examine the role and value of privacy, while the remainder of the articles look at privacy and social policy. Included are topics on government, law enforcement, media, and several professions.

Equality and Due Process

The Fourteenth Amendment to the Constitution produced a civil revolution. It changed the way America acts and thinks. The amendment says that no state shall deny to any of its citizens the equal protection of the laws. No other phrase in the Constitution has meant more for the protection of the civil rights and personal liberty of individuals. The Fourteenth Amendment has been the vehicle for securing justice for racial and other minorities and the source of support for aid to the poor; it is also the basis for the challenge by women of sex discrimination.

The Fourteenth Amendment introduced into our concept of equality the specific requirement that states treat individuals equally with respect to the law. This constitutional guarantee of equality has been extended to apply to both the states and the national government. It is a principle that is important to Americans; but in practice, equality remains elusive.

Racial Justice

The most dramatic use of the equal protection clause of the Fourteenth Amendment has been to secure justice for racial minorities. The Court's application of the Fourteenth Amendment has produced a revolution in public education, and the amendment has been further used to secure voting rights, jobs, and housing for racial minority groups. The impact of the Fourteenth Amendment has produced changes, but no one can say that racial discrimination has ended. Severe problems continue: racial tension often runs high; unemployment for black Americans is substantially greater than the average for white workers; the educational level for blacks is below that of their white counterparts, as is blacks' median income; and infant mortality is higher among blacks than whites. Housing conditions for blacks remain substandard. Yet, were it not for the Fourteenth Amendment, there would be little constitutional basis for attacking any of these situations.

Separate but Equal

The Reconstruction amendments, also referred to as the Civil War amendments, were ratified shortly after the end of the Civil War. The Thirteenth Amendment, ratified in 1865, abolished the institution of slavery. The Fourteenth Amendment, proposed in 1866 and ratified in 1868, extended citizenship to the freed slaves and included the rights and privileges pertaining thereto. The last of the three amendments, the Fifteenth, was ratified in 1870 and gave black American citizens the right to vote in federal and state elections.

Jim Crow: *a term used to refer to racial discrimination or segregation.*

Yet **Jim Crow** and segregation lived on. The constitutional amendments abolished slavery and declared equal protection of the laws, but they said nothing about personal association and treatment. For example, in 1882, the Supreme Court ruled valid a state law that provided for more stringent penalties for adultery and fornication if the couple was composed of people of different races than if the two were of the same race.[1] In 1883, the Supreme Court ruled that the Fourteenth Amendment prohibited not discrimination by private individuals, but only state actions that were discriminatory.[2] And in 1896 the Court adopted the constitutional position that public accommodations could legally be separate if they were equal, known as the **separate-but-equal doctrine.**

Separate-but-Equal Doctrine: *the doctrine adopted by the Supreme Court in 1896, which affirmed that public accommodations could legally be separate if they were equal.*

Louisiana railways were required by law to maintain separate but equal accommodations. Homer Plessy, one-eighth African, boarded one such train, sat in a coach reserved for whites, would not move when asked, and was arrested. The Supreme Court in *Plessy* v. *Ferguson* refused to deny the arrest as a violation of the Fourteenth Amendment. In short, the Louisiana statute requiring separate but equal accommodations was deemed compatible with the Constitution. "It [the Fourteenth Amendment] could not have been intended to abolish distinctions based upon

The long struggle for racial justice has been both painful and inspiring.

color, or to enforce social, as distinguished from political equality, or a commingling of the two races upon terms unsatisfactory to either."[3]

Justice Harlan was the lone dissenter in *Plessy* v. *Ferguson*. His view was that the Civil War amendments had made the Constitution "color-blind." To impose a categorical distinction of separate but equal was to perpetuate and protect "classes among citizens." In time, Justice Harlan prophesied, the decision would "prove to be quite as pernicious as the decision made by this tribunal in the *Dred Scott* Case" (the decision to force a runaway slave in a free state to be returned to his owner).

It was not until 1954, however, that the Court rectified its decision. The Court really never took equal accommodations seriously. It allowed the closure of black schools for "purely economic reasons" and the merger of black children into overcrowded schools,[4] and it extended the concept of separate but equal educational facilities to races other than blacks, thereby prohibiting blacks' admission to white schools.[5] It was in public education particularly that the separate-but-equal doctrine was most consistently applied. And it was in public education that the revolution in racial justice began.

Linda Brown
It was because Linda Carol Brown, when seven years old, had to travel an extra fourteen blocks to attend an all-black elementary school that Linda's father, Oliver Brown, sued the school board in 1950. The case resulted in the landmark Supreme Court case that overturned legal segregation in this country. Linda Brown had to walk between railroad tracks for six blocks to catch her bus for the mile ride to school; an all-white elementary school was only seven blocks from her home. In 1976 Linda Brown was a divorced mother with two children working and living in Topeka, Kansas. Her children attended public schools in Topeka that are 35 percent black.

The Revolution in Public Education   In 1954 the Supreme Court, in *Brown* v. *Board of Education of Topeka, Kansas*, overturned the separate-but-equal doctrine, declaring simply, "In the field of public education the doctrine of separate but equal has no place."[6] The Court argued that segregated facilities were not and could not be equal. It was not the tangible signs—buildings, teachers' salaries, books, and so forth—that were inequitable, but rather the effects of segregation on the children directly and presently. "We cannot turn the clock back to 1868 when the Amendment was adopted, or even to 1896 when *Plessy* v. *Ferguson* was written. We must consider public education in the light of its full development and its present place in American life throughout the nation."

The Court asked itself this question: "Does segregation of children in public schools solely on the basis of race, even though the physical facilities and other tangible factors may be equal, deprive the children of the minority group of equal educational opportunities?" The Court unanimously agreed that it did. Separate educational facilities were inherently unequal; segregated facilities deprived citizens of the equal protection of the laws guaranteed by the Fourteenth Amendment.

Technically, the *Brown* decision applied only to public educational facilities. The Supreme Court moved swiftly and resolutely, however, to extend the desegregation principle to buses, public parks, golf courses, restaurants, municipal auditoriums, and the like. Such cases merely cited *Brown* to strike down ordinances that segregated facilities on a separate-but-equal basis.

It was one thing, though, to desegregate public facilities and quite another to order their integration. In *Brown* v. *Board of Education*, 1955 (*Brown II*), the Court had to consider the scope and timing for its previous decision. The Court ruled that public schools should proceed with "all deliberate speed" to desegregate their facilities.[7] But events in the South and elsewhere indicated just how slow and difficult a process that was going to be. In 1957, President Eisenhower had to send in federal troops to quell a disturbance and help escort black students seeking to attend high school in Little Rock, Arkansas. In 1962, the University of Mississippi was integrated only after rioting on campus had claimed the lives of two men. A year later, the governor of Alabama, George Wallace, physically blocked black students from entering the University of Alabama.

The Court was growing impatient. It recognized the need for time in desegregating school facilities, but it would not tolerate unnecessary delay or direct and open violation of its rulings. In 1964, the Court ruled "the time for mere deliberate speed has run out."[8] In *Green* v. *County School Board,* the Court not only repeated its statement about prompt action, but required the school board to put forward a plan that would work, "and promises realistically to work now."[9] More and more school systems would have to take action to eliminate racial discrimination.

Over the years, one thorny issue has been racial segregation practiced by private schools. Since they were most often private church-affiliated schools or academies, they were beyond the pale of public orders for desegregation. Yet as church schools, they enjoyed protection under the First Amendment and were tax exempt. The Internal Revenue Service long has sought authority to deny tax-exempt status to private schools that practice racial discrimination. In 1983, the Supreme Court gave the IRS that power.[10] The Court ruled the IRS was correct in denying tax-exempt status to Bob Jones University and the Goldsboro Christian Schools.

In writing for an eight-person majority, Mr. Chief Justice Burger said that to be eligible for tax-exempt status, an institution "must serve a public purpose and not be contrary to established public policy." And racial discrimination in education was contrary to public policy! The Court acknowledged the schools' claim that racial integration was contrary to the schools' religious belief but said the nation's interest in eradicating racial discrimination in education "substantially outweighs whatever burden denial of tax benefits places on . . . (these schools') exercise of their religious beliefs." One year later, however, the Court ruled that private citizens could not bring suit to force the IRS to move on denying tax-exempt status to such schools—that parents of black school students lacked legal standing to sue the IRS for being too lenient in granting tax-exempt status.[11]

Busing

No affirmative action proposals have caused more controversy than the court-ordered remedy of forced busing to overcome intentional discrimination against racial minorities. In 1971, *Swann* v. *Charlotte–Mecklenburg Board of Education* established the readiness of the Court to impose judicial remedy for school systems perpetuating a dual, or segregated, system.

Where a federal court found intentional discrimination, where de jure (legal) segregation was present and no adequate plan for desegregation existed, the court was authorized to provide specific remedy.[12] What the Supreme Court did in this case was to order an extensive program of two-way **busing** of students between Charlotte and Mecklenburg County to break up segregated schools. Students would be bused out of their neighborhood schools, to schools some distance from home if necessary, to break the pattern of segregation.

Busing: *a court-ordered remedy to overcome intentional discrimination against racial minorities. Students are transported out of their neighborhoods to schools some distance from home, if necessary, to break the pattern of segregation.*

District courts around the country were quick to follow suit. A federal district court judge in Detroit, Michigan, ordered area-wide busing in the fall of 1971. Richmond, Virginia, was ordered to bus students across city and county lines in 1972. Judge Garrity of Boston ordered blacks bused into South Boston and Charlestown in 1974. By 1975, Louisville, Kentucky, had been added to the list. And in 1978, after several delays, the city of Los Angeles undertook the most massive busing of students to date.

Court-ordered busing of schoolchildren has produced strong criticism and even violence. But the Court has not backed down. In 1979 Columbus and Dayton, Ohio, were required to bus students. A resolute Court said that the affirmative duty to disestablish dual school systems "is beyond question."[13]

The Court has allowed voters to limit the use of busing for school desegregation by ballot initiative but only if such action does not narrow rights guaranteed by the U.S. Constitution or place special burdens on blacks.[14] Thus, Los Angeles was permitted to limit busing, but a voter initiative in Seattle, Washington, was invalidated because it went too far by prohibiting the school board from using busing to correct social imbalance.[15]

Busing is a well-established tool for judicial relief to provide Fourteenth Amendment rights of equal protection of the law where intentional legal segregation exists in public education. But it is precisely this tool that angers many conservatives. They feel that court-ordered busing is a violation of the Constitution because it uses the law for social activism not mandated by Congress. Busing critics, notably Senator Jesse Helms (R–N.C.), would offer legislation preventing the Justice Department from bringing any legal action that could lead to court-ordered busing. To date Congress has shown little inclination to pass antibusing legislation, but the New Right and other conservatives vow to continue to make busing a social issue for the 1980s.

The Reagan administration has been a strong opponent of busing. It has sought to restrict the scope of *Swann* by allowing judges to choose remedies other than busing. The Reagan administration's solicitor general has gone to the Supreme Court to ask that a 1981 district court decision involving Nashville, Tennessee public schools be reinstated. In that case the district court judge said that elementary school children benefit more from attending their neighborhood schools than from being bused to more racially balanced schools. The Reagan administration wants the

Supreme Court to permit a more permissive reading of *Swann,* allowing judges to consider "competing educational, social, and economic costs" or considering transportation effects that "risk the health of the children or significantly impinge on the educational process."

Desegregation in Public Facilities

The revolution produced by the *Brown* decision spread quickly. Throughout the last half of the 1950s, racial barriers began to fall. The Court invalidated segregation in parks, buses, athletic contests, restaurants, auditoriums, and the like. But the change was not easy. Demonstrations, boycotts, sit-ins, and protests occurred throughout the South. In 1956, to end segregation on bus lines, Martin Luther King, Jr., organized a boycott in Montgomery, Alabama. Sit-ins occurred at several segregated restaurants and lunch counters in the early 1960s. And in 1963 Dr. King organized a massive demonstration against segregation in Birmingham, Alabama. The demonstrators were met in that city by fire hoses, well-protected police officers, and police dogs. The resulting scenes of violence and brutality touched the conscience of the nation. Two hundred thousand people jammed the Mall in Washington, D.C., in August 1963 to participate with Dr. King in the March on Washington. Civil rights for black Americans was a national concern; America would have to respond.

Congress had not passed a meaningful civil rights act for nearly a century when President Kennedy sent in a comprehensive civil rights bill in 1963. President Johnson, upon the death of President Kennedy, urged Congress to act swiftly. The bill was passed and signed into law by President Johnson on July 2, 1964. The new law, the Civil Rights Act of 1964, made it a federal crime to discriminate on the basis of race, color, religion, national origin, or sex in places of public accommodation, including hotels, motels, restaurants, gas stations, theaters, sports arenas, movie houses, or other places of entertainment involved in interstate commerce. It also forbade discrimination in employment. Further, the act prevented the application of differing standards to voting; empowered the attorney general to bring suit to enforce the desegregation of public accommodations; and permitted the executive branch to cut off federal funds to those agencies or organizations continuing to practice discrimination.

Voting Rights

By 1964, the civil rights movement was turning its attention to the political process. The Fifteenth Amendment was meant to sweep away racial barriers to voting, yet the percentage of eligible black voters remained low well into the twentieth century. No more than 15 percent of black voters were registered to vote as of 1948. Southern states had devised means to prevent blacks from voting. The so-called white primary excluded blacks from voting, not in a general election but in the primary. This practice was declared unconstitutional in 1944. The poll tax as a condition for voting was eliminated in federal elections by law and passage of the Twenty-fourth Amendment to the Constitution in 1964. Two years later the Supreme Court removed the last vestiges of the poll tax by declaring remaining state poll taxes unconstitutional. But *literacy tests* were still used to disqualify voters unable to read or write and *grandfather clauses* sought to restrict voting to descendants of eligible voters a generation earlier. And if these measures failed, there was always outright intimidation.

The battle for the ballot was long, involving slow changes in the law. Under the leadership of the Supreme Court, racial prohibitions to voting were being swept away, but gradually, on a case-by-case basis. However, in 1965 Congress passed the Voting Rights Act. Instead of outlawing discriminatory practices as the 1964 act had done, the act empowered federal officials to register voters and to supervise the conduct of elections. Literacy tests were suspended and heavy fines were set for intimidation of voters or interfering with voting rights. In 1980 the Court affirmed the 1965 act, preventing Rome, Georgia, from altering its electoral system from a plurality electoral system to a majority vote for members of the city commission because the change, though not intended to be discriminatory, would have effectively been so.[16] And in 1982, the Court used the act to invalidate a Mississippi election procedure for school board elections, holding that the procedures had not been cleared as nondiscriminatory by the Justice Department.[17]

The results were immediate and direct: the registration of eligible black voters increased dramatically. By 1971, more than half the eligible voters in the South were registered. And for the first time since Reconstruction, blacks were candidates for public office. By 1970, close to five hundred blacks had been elected to public office.

The Voting Rights Act has thrice been extended, and each time the scope and power of the law have been broadened. In 1970 all literacy tests were suspended and residence requirements to participate in federal elections were reduced to thirty days from the traditional six months to two years. In 1975 Congress acted to incorporate other minorities under the provisions of the law, including the printing of election materials in bilingual form for non–English speakers.

The Voting Rights Act came up for renewal in 1982. The extension was seen as a test of the commitment of Congress and the president to black civil rights. The bill found widespread popular and congressional support, not only nationwide but in the South, where most of the bill's enforcement was directed. The president, although at first somewhat reluctant, signed the bill into law. The act now requires nine states and parts of thirteen others to secure Justice Department approval before changing their election laws and procedures. This "preclearance" test was the heart of the bill; these states had to preclear their election law changes before putting them into effect. Congress extended this preclearance enforcement section of the law for 25 years. This issue was central because Congress said voting rights violations could be proved by showing that an election law or procedure resulted in discrimination. This reversed a 1980 Supreme Court decision that limited voting rights violations to cases involving an intent to discriminate. President Reagan had supported limiting the act to intent to discriminate. Congress chose, however, to exclude intent in favor of the result or effect of voting rights procedures and laws. The law directed courts to look at the "totality of circumstances" in determining whether a voting rights violation had resulted. Finally, the act declared that in lawsuits there is no right to proportional representation for any minority group and that the lack of proportional representation was only one circumstance for a court to consider.

Public Accommodations, Employment, and Housing

The migration of blacks from the South to the cities of the North in the 1940s and 1950s produced black ghettos in those cities. Unemployment, poverty, and substandard housing left millions of Americans hopeless and desperate.

Public Accommodations   The 1964 Civil Rights Act had attacked private discrimination in places of public accommodation. Title II of the 1964 act made it a federal offense for a person to discriminate on the basis of race, color, religion, or national origin in places of public business or occupancy. The law specifically included inns, hotels, motels, and public boardinghouses. It also listed businesses serving the public: restaurants, gasoline stations, and any place serving food or selling products that have moved through interstate commerce. Also included were such places of public occupancy as motion picture houses, theaters, concert halls, sports arenas, and other settings for entertainment. The attorney general was empowered to bring suit to effect **desegregation** as well as intervene in cases brought by individuals.

Desegregation: *abolishing the practice of racial segregation.*

The major provisions of the act were quickly challenged; notably under fire was the authority of Congress to use the interstate commerce clause to desegregate public accommodations. In 1964, a unanimous Supreme Court upheld the constitutionality of the act in *Heart of Atlanta Motel v. United States.*[18] The result has been the effective desegregation of public facilities.

Employment   Title VII of the 1964 Civil Rights Act made it an unfair labor practice for any employer engaged in interstate commerce to discriminate on the basis of race, color, sex, religion, or national origin. Congress created the Equal Employment Opportunity Commission (EEOC) to enforce the fair employment portions of the act, and the commission was strengthened with the passage of the Equal Employment Opportunity Act of 1972. The EEOC works primarily to aid disadvantaged groups seeking employment opportunities.

Efforts to eliminate discrimination in employment, particularly the work of the EEOC, were supplemented by Executive Order 11246 in

The promise of racial equality remains unfulfilled for many black Americans.

1965, which prohibits discrimination in employment by employers doing business with the federal government (the order was amended in 1967 to prohibit sexual as well as racial discrimination). Under the threat of withholding federal funds—or disbarment from eligibility for federal grants—employers, contractors, and public universities have been required to adopt affirmative action plans to redress the past effects of discriminatory practices. Recruitment plans, salary schedules, retirement programs, and fringe benefits are all screened to ensure compliance with federal rules and law.

A major civil rights issue that arose in the 1980s centers around seniority systems and union bargaining agreements. The Supreme Court generally has held that employers cannot be held responsible—or liable—for the effects of discrimination without any intent to discriminate. The Court has refused to invalidate seniority systems on the basis of their being discriminatory. Showing a disparate impact alone is insufficient; there must be a discriminatory purpose as well.[19] "Differentials among employees that result from a seniority system are not unlawful employment practices unless the product of an intent to discriminate." It is the responsibility of the employees to prove that a seniority system had been adopted with the intent to discriminate. The Court's reading of the 1964 Civil Rights Act requires that challengers of a labor practice prove not only "effect" but also "intent" to discriminate.[20]

More generally, the Court has decided that employers do not bear the burden of proving that their reasons for hiring were legitimate and nondiscriminatory. Employers need only prove that the reasons for their actions were nondiscriminatory, not that a person hired or promoted was better qualified than another.[21] On the other hand, employers cannot wipe away charges of employment discrimination by producing "bottom line" figures on the total number of minorities employed or promoted as a complete defense. The principal focus is the protection of the individual employee; "bottom line" defense is seen to confuse unlawful discrimination with discriminatory intent.[22]

Of particular concern to civil rights groups has been the conflict between two legitimate plans: union contracts with seniority rules and affirmative action plans. Minorities have typically been the "last hired, first fired" under rules of seniority systems in many industries, which has had the effect of softening the impact of affirmative action. Particularly in an era of fiscal austerity and budget cutbacks, layoff orders fall inordinately heavily on minorities. The question is, does the blunting of affirmative action hiring by valid seniority systems of layoff constitute discrimination? In the 1984 case of *Firefighters Local Union* v. *Stotts,* the Supreme Court ruled that affirmative action plans and minority employee protection plans do not override valid seniority systems.[23] For affirmative action to take precedence over a seniority system, the Court said a person must demonstrate that the seniority system worked to the detriment of specifically identified victims of an employer's proven practice of discrimination. Membership in a group that was the target of discrimination is insufficient; each individual must prove that the discriminatory practice had an impact on him or her.

On a related issue, the Court ruled in the 1986 case of *Wygant* v. *Jackson Board of Education* that a collective bargaining agreement containing layoff provisions cannot override seniority in order to achieve its racial goal of affirmative action. The Jackson school board had negotiated an agreement with its teachers that in case of layoffs it would retain minority teachers with less seniority in order to preserve affirmative action goals.

The Court said the layoff provisions violated the equal protection clause of the Fourteenth Amendment. The school board's use of race to lay off nonminority teachers with more seniority was an intrusive burden, even if done under terms of a collective bargaining agreement. "In cases involving valid hiring goals, the burden to be borne by innocent individuals is diffused to a considerable extent among society generally. Though hiring goals may burden some innocent individuals, they simply do not impose the same kind of injury that layoffs impose. Denial of a future employment opportunity is not as intrusive as loss of an existing job."[24]

Housing   In 1962, President Kennedy ordered the federal government to stop allowing the use of federal money for housing projects operated on a segregated basis. In 1968, Congress passed the Civil Rights Act of 1968, which prohibited discrimination in the sale or rental of private property listed through a real estate agent. The legislation covered the bulk of housing in the nation. Private individuals selling their own homes were exempted, but real estate brokers and public housing projects were all included. The act forbade discrimination not only in the sale of private property, but also in the advertising of homes for sale.

The Supreme Court also moved to outlaw discrimination in the sale of private homes. In *Jones* v. *Mayer Co.*, the Court upheld an 1866 civil rights act that prevented discrimination in the sale of private property. The case did not involve state action and therefore the decision could not be held unconstitutional under the Fourteenth Amendment. Rather, the 1866 act was upheld as banning private acts of discrimination under the Thirteenth Amendment. Private discrimination was seen to create a **badge of slavery**—burdens and disabilities placing restraints on fundamental rights, equivalent to slavery—and was thus impermissible under the Thirteenth Amendment.[25] That amendment, the Court reasoned, allowed Congress to outlaw not only indentured servitude but also badges of slavery. Private acts constituted badges of slavery, and Congress could pass legislation to eliminate them.

Under the Fourteenth Amendment, state action was necessary for the Court to strike down state law as violating equal protection of the laws. Congress could act only in its areas of competence, such as interstate commerce, but here the Court was allowing Congress to attack purely private discrimination under the Thirteenth Amendment. In *Runyan* v. *McCrary*, the Supreme Court extended the reasoning of *Jones* to prohibit private nonsectarian schools from denying admission to students because of their race.[26] The private school had violated the contractual rights of blacks by failing to offer services equally to white and nonwhite students. Although the Court has not extended this reasoning to every situation—a private social club can limit membership on the basis of race and yet not lose its liquor license[27]—the authority of Congress is established to legislate under the Thirteenth Amendment to attack private as well as public acts of discrimination.

Badge of Slavery: *private acts of racial discrimination that violate the Thirteenth Amendment.*

Equal Protection: *the phrase in the Fourteenth Amendment that has been the basis for overturning laws that seek to unreasonably classify people on the basis of race.*

Equal Protection of the Laws

The thrust of the Supreme Court's reading of the Fourteenth Amendment and its reviews of congressional acts has been to examine laws that distinguish or classify people by race. The Court has never held that laws cannot classify by race (or for that matter by sex or age). Rather, the Court has said that such laws cannot *unreasonably* classify people. An unreasonable classification is one in which there is no relationship between the classes of people created and the legitimate goals of government to be advanced. There must be some *compelling state interest* to permit classification of people by race. The Court treats such laws with great suspicion and subjects them to rigid scrutiny before sustaining them. Race has become the most suspect classification, but the category of laws is being extended for classifications based on sex, age, and physical disability.

A recent example of the application of equal protection is a 1986 Supreme Court decision rejecting the peremptory challenge of jurors by prosecutors. The Court said peremptory challenges to exclude jurors solely on racial grounds violated the equal protection rights of both defendants and prospective jurors.[28] In fact, exclusion of jurors of the defendant's race or ethnic group constituted a prima facie case of purposeful discrimination in violation of the equal protection of the laws.

Affirmative Action: *the policy of providing special assistance to minorities in an effort to equalize results in areas such as education and employment.*

Reverse Discrimination   A more interesting problem arises for laws that promote benign racial classification—laws that use classifications to benefit or promote a racial or ethnic minority. The recent **affirmative action** plans, racial-balance programs in education, and quotas for employers and contractors have all raised questions regarding equal protection of the laws. Should these laws be viewed as suspect as well, or is there a compelling state interest in overcoming the social, political, and economic effects of past discrimination?

The issue first arose in the *De Funis* case in 1974. Marco De Funis was denied admission to law school in favor of some minority applicants screened by separate standards. A trial court in the state of Washington ordered him admitted. The state supreme court reversed the decision, holding that the setting aside of seats for minority students was a compelling state interest in promoting racial equality and integration. De Funis appealed to the Supreme Court. Justice Douglas stayed the Washington supreme court order until the full Court could consider the merits of the case. But this never happened; De Funis was in his last year of law school by then, and the Supreme Court dismissed the case without discussing the merits of benign classification.[29]

But the issue could not long be avoided. In 1973 and 1974 Allan Bakke had been denied admission to the University of California at Davis medical school in favor of some minority applicants, under Davis's special admissions program to increase the proportion of "disadvantaged" medical students. In both years, disadvantaged applicants were admitted with lower scores on admission tests than those achieved by Bakke. Bakke sued, charging the special admissions program excluded him from medical school because of his race, thereby denying him the equal protection of the laws guaranteed by the Fourteenth Amendment. He charged the school with **reverse discrimination.** The Supreme Court agreed, but on narrow grounds and in a divided opinion.

Reverse Discrimination: *the practice of aiding minority groups to the exclusion of white Americans. The use of quotas is a telling feature of reverse discrimination.*

Allan Bakke was to be admitted to medical school. The explicit use of quotas (setting aside a specific number of seats for disadvantaged students) was deemed a violation of the Fourteenth Amendment. "It tells applicants who are not Negro, Asian, or Chicano that they are totally excluded from a specific percentage of the seats in an entering class." Indeed, this was the fatal flaw in the Davis admission program. Justice Powell wrote for the Court that race can be taken into consideration as a factor for admission. It may be deemed a "plus" in an applicant's file, yet it must not isolate the individual from all other candidates. Furthermore, the Court ruled that a program based solely on race does not promote the state's interest in ethnic diversity, although ethnic diversity is a worthwhile educational objective.[30] Schools may use race as a factor, but they cannot make it the sole factor. The Court was walking a fine line. Affirmative action was to continue: "The state has a legitimate and substantial interest in ameliorating, or eliminating where feasible, the disabling effects of identified discrimination." Yet the use of quotas was not permissible. In *Steelworkers and Kaiser Aluminum* v. *Weber* (1979), the Court specifically confronted positive programs to recruit minority personnel for union and private-industry trainee openings. The Court found no objection. This was a private, voluntary plan; no state action was involved. Here affirmative action did not violate equal protection of the laws.[31]

In 1986 the Supreme Court stated more clearly that minority job preference at the expense of white employees is permissible where there has been persistent discrimination or the lingering effects of pervasive discrimination.[32] The decision, involving two cases, amounted to an endorsement of affirmative action in the workplace to cure past discrimination against minority groups. The companion cases involved the Cleveland firefighters, where minority members were given preferential treatment in hiring and promotion, and the New York sheet metal workers union, where a lower federal court judge had imposed a goal of twenty-nine percent minority membership upon the union. The Court accepted both these plans, even recognizing that the beneficiaries would not necessarily be limited to identified victims of discrimination.

Allan Bakke
It was Bakke's lawsuit against minority quotas that produced the Court ruling against reverse discrimination. Bakke was subsequently admitted to medical school, and is presently a practicing physician.

The Court said affirmative action plans may use race-conscious remedies such as goals and relevant population numbers. The Court stopped short of an outright acceptance of racial quotas, which it had declared unconstitutional in *Bakke,* but the Court did admit that federal judges have broad discretion to approve decrees in which employers, over the objection of white employees, settle discrimination suits by use of affirmative action plans to hire or promote minority employees through specified racial goals or quotas. Wrote Justice Brennan for the Court, "In appropriate circumstances affirmative action, race-conscious relief as a remedy for past discrimination ... may be appropriate where an employer or a labor union has engaged in persistent or egregious discrimination, or where necessary to dissipate the lingering effects of pervasive discrimination."

The Court did enter a note of caution. Racial preference should not be necessary to cure discrimination in most cases, and such plans should not be used routinely or merely to create a racially balanced work force. It also shied away from the word "quota." The percentage used in the New York plan was the available labor pool of minority workers; the Court called this a goal to be reached for, not a rigid quota.

Yet the decision has the effect of endorsing numerical hiring and promotion goals. Indeed, it permits broader affirmative action remedies through a consent decree than might otherwise result from litigation. While not an acceptance of racial quotas, it does permit companies and unions to use race-conscious plans to remedy past patterns of racial discrimination.

The Court also upheld the minority-business-enterprise provision of the Public Works Employment Act of 1977, which required that at least 10 percent of federal funds used for local public works projects be set aside for minority businesses. Congress, the Court noted, seeks to overcome the effects of prior discrimination by ensuring that minority business enterprises are not denied equal opportunity to participate in federal grants to state and local governments and that racial and ethnic criteria are valid means of accomplishing Congress's objective. In pressing for equal economic opportunity, "Congress has necessary latitude to try new techniques such as the limited use of racial and ethnic criteria to accomplish remedial objectives."[33]

Sex and Age Discrimination

Sex Discrimination

Until recently the courts never looked seriously at sex discrimination as a violation of the Fourteenth Amendment. Men and women were treated differently under the law, and married women in particular were subject to several limitations. Women were discriminated against in employment, inheritance, ownership of property, and even jury duty.

By 1971, the situation had begun to change. For the first time, in *Reed v. Reed*, the Supreme Court offered equal-protection guarantees against sex discrimination under the Fourteenth Amendment.[34] At issue was an Oregon statute that gave mandatory preference to a male in the selection of an administrator for an estate. The Supreme Court ruled unanimously that the arbitrary preference for males could not be justified under the Fourteenth Amendment.

The decision stopped short of declaring sex a suspect category; it did not question a legislature's power to use gender as a basis for classification. It simply stated, "To give a mandatory preference to members of either sex over members of the other, merely to accomplish the elimination of hearings on the merits, is to make the very kind of arbitrary legislative choice forbidden by the Equal Protection Clause of the Fourteenth Amendment." But in 1973 Justice Brennan found sex to be a suspect class, though not in the same way in which race is viewed as suspect.[35]

In 1981, the Court reiterated this view when it refused to invalidate a California statute prohibiting males, but not females, from having sexual relations with persons of the opposite sex under age eighteen. The Supreme Court said that gender-based classifications are not "inherently suspect" and thus do not need "strict scrutiny" by the Court. Gender-based classifications would be upheld if they bore a "fair and substantial relationship" to legitimate state ends. The upholding of such statutes reflects the fact, the Court said, "that the sexes are not similarly situated in certain circumstances."[36] Thus, it appears that a declaration of sex as a suspect category like race will depend on the fate of the Equal Rights Amendment, which failed to be ratified in 1982 but was reintroduced in that same year.

In subsequent decisions, the Supreme Court has struck down laws that exempted women from jury duty,[37] provided for social security benefits based on the earnings of the deceased husband differently from the earnings of a deceased wife,[38] created differing ages of majority for males and females in cases of support,[39] favored alimony for women,[40] set gender-based Aid to Families with Dependent Children unemployment benefits,[41] discriminated between the sexes in the sale of beer,[42] and allowed unilateral disposal of property held in joint ownership.[43] The Court has also rejected a women-only admission policy for a state-supported school of nursing.[44] And in 1984 it ruled that the male-only Junior Chamber of Commerce (Jaycees) could not continue to forbid the membership of women.[45]

The Court has been willing to sustain sex distinctions in law with regard to property-tax exemptions for widows, however, since women are more likely than men to face an unsympathetic job market.[46] The Court allowed a male naval officer passed over for promotion to be discharged while retaining in service a female passed over for promotion,[47] and it permitted greater social security benefits to women "to compensate women for past economic discrimination."[48] It would, however, not allow workmen's compensation to deny benefits to men unless they were actually dependent on a deceased wife's earnings, while widows need not prove dependence on their husband's earnings.[49]

The greatest recent controversy was over the all-male draft. President Carter, in 1980, reactivated the draft, and three days before registration was to commence, a district court found that the act violated the due process clause of the Fifth Amendment. The district court made clear that it was deciding not whether women should serve in combat, but only whether women should be required to register for the draft. Because of the immediacy of the issue, the government appealed the decision to the

Fighting Discrimination:
Equal Employment Opportunity Commission

The Equal Employment Opportunity Commission (EEOC) has been around since 1965. It is responsible for initiating and investigating charges of job discrimination against private and public employers, and under its direction the federal government has endeavored to fight society's historically biased treatment of blacks, Hispanics, and women. The EEOC has taken to court employers with discriminatory job practices in hiring, training, retention, and promotion. It has set rules and regulations for contractors doing business with the federal government, requiring them to demonstrate their commitment to affirmative action. Traditionally this has meant the establishment of numerical goals for recruitment, training, and promotion of minorities and women. It also has meant setting timetables for reaching those goals.

The Reagan administration, however, wants to change the approach taken by the EEOC. Having already had the opportunity to appoint all members on the commission, the administration now asks the EEOC to back away from numerical goals, timetables, and the more stringent elements of affirmative action. The EEOC has been instructed by its chairman, Clarence Thomas, to relax its numerical standards for judging compliance with affirmative action requirements and to ease its rules for bias-free tests in judging worker abilities. The underlying philosophy of the Reagan administration toward equal employment opportunity laws requires only color-blind personnel policies, not preferential treatment. This philosophy, they assert, is bolstered by a changed consensus in American society and the workplace toward equal employment opportunity.

Several federal agencies have already fallen into line. The Department of Labor, responsible for monitoring contractor compliance in hiring, is revamping rules that place less weight on raw numbers. The Office of Personnel Management is moving toward automatically approving most professionally designed hiring tests, even if they seem to favor white males. The U.S. Commission on Civil Rights has resolved to reject as precedent all previous commission policies. And the EEOC is concentrating on individual cases of discrimination rather than identifying company-wide or industry-wide patterns of bias.

What has emerged with the EEOC is a changed approach to job discrimination in three areas. First there is an attitude of suspicion toward discrimination charges based on statistics rather than evidence of bias against specific workers. Second, remedies for past biased practices should be tailored more narrowly, aiding particular persons injured by bias rather than requiring company-wide or industry-wide changes in employment practices. Third, the definition of affirmative action should be changed to emphasize recruiting techniques and training programs more than hiring of specific minorities.*

This new approach to addressing job bias is not without critics. Many companies over the last twenty years have implemented EEO programs and are well accustomed to demonstrating compliance. In 1985 the National Association of Manufacturers (NAM) voted at its convention not to support proposals that weaken equal employment rules, strongly endorsing affirmative action as a social policy that has worked and should be kept.* "We're accustomed to setting goals," said William S. McEwen, Monsanto Co. equal employment director and head of NAM's panel; "business has always set objectives." The last twenty years has produced wide agreement on equal employment standards. Disputes are quickly settled today.

Critics also point to a decline in suits filed

in court against employers. In 1981, the EEOC brought 358 suits; in 1983 the number declined to 195. Of particular concern to women is the lack of action to enforce the 1963 Equal Pay Act. Known as "comparable worth," the 1963 act directs "equal pay for substantially equal work," yet women point out that the EEOC has yet to bring suit for comparable worth; in fact it has no official policy on comparable worth.

Like many other agencies under the Reagan administration, the Equal Employment Opportunity Commission is part of a changing consensus toward government activism and social policy. Will America's historic commitment to equal opportunity be better served by Reagan's changed philosophy of focusing on individual cases of job bias? Only in a workplace free of discrimination can minorities and women find the opportunity to realize their true worth. Nothing less can be the goal of a nation professing the values and ideals the United States has nurtured over two hundred years.

*Business Week, March 11, 1985, p. 42.

The consideration of race as a factor in hiring was sanctioned by the Court's decision that under the Fourteenth Amendment it is permissible to advance the interests of minorities.

The battle against discrimination on the basis of sex has resulted in women serving in the U.S. military; in this case, the Marine Corps.

Supreme Court for a quick review. In June 1981 the Supreme Court handed down its decision: the all-male draft was constitutional; it did not violate the Fifth Amendment.[50] The Court said that in terms of both military policy and fitness for combat women were not "similarly situated" with men. The six to three decision stated, "The Constitution requires that Congress treat similarly situated persons similarly, not that it engage in gestures of superficial equality." Mr. Justice Marshall was vocal in dissent: "The Court today places its imprimatur on one of the most potent remaining public expressions of 'ancient canards about the proper role of women.'"

A novel effort to attack sex discrimination was put forth in the case of *American Booksellers* v. *Hudnut*. The case had sought to argue that pornography was sex bias because it depicted women as sex objects, typically presenting them in scenes of exploitation, degradation, or abuse. The Supreme Court, however, summarily dismissed the case, affirming a lower court order rejecting the contention.[51] That Court of Appeals had said, "Under the First Amendment the government must leave to the people the evaluation of ideas."

Another recent concern is the status of maternity leaves. In 1974 the Supreme Court ruled that mandatory leaves for teachers violated due process,[52] placing heavy burdens on women in personal matters of mar-

"The opportunity is equal, but the pay isn't."

GRIN AND BEAR IT by Lichty & Wagner © Field Enterprises, Inc., 1983. By permission of News America Syndicate.

riage and family. Using the same logic, the Court struck down a statute that exempted pregnant women from employment-leave benefits owing to pregnancy.[53] But the Court has allowed the exclusion of pregnancy from the conditions that legally yield disability benefits to employees.[54]

In 1979 the Court began providing some additional avenues for women to redress sex discrimination, most specifically in education. The Supreme Court ruled in *Cannon* v. *University of Chicago* that the Title IX regulations for the educational amendments of 1972 created a right for a private individual to bring suit for sex discrimination.[55] But then in 1984 the Court said that Title IX restrictions against sex discrimination were limited to departments receiving federal aid and not to the entire institution.[56] The ruling has the effect of limiting the impact of Title IX amendments by not bringing all of an institution's program under their jurisdiction. Federal assistance may be terminated only to the specific areas not in compliance.

In 1982 the Court said that Title IX covered discrimination against institutional employees as well as students and other beneficiaries. Thus, Title IX prohibits educational institutions from discriminating in employment on the basis of sex.[57] In another important decision, *Washington County* v. *Gunther*, the Supreme Court said the 1964 Civil Rights Act allows women to file suit for sex discrimination as well as for racial discrimination. Hence women need not prove that they were denied "equal pay for equal work," but only that sex was used against them in determining a pay scale—that is, that they were paid less than men or paid less than wage surveys of similar jobs say the job is worth.[58]

Comparable Worth: *an attempt to provide equal pay for equal work for women by comparing the skills and tasks required for every job. Dissimilar jobs requiring equivalent skills or efforts would have the same pay.*

Comparable Worth   The most significant recent movement to attack sex discrimination is the "comparable worth" campaign. On the basis of the 1963 Equal Pay Act and the 1964 Civil Rights Act, women are now pressing to receive pay equal to that of men for what they perceive to be equal work. Women say they have long been the subject of job discrimination that has artificially held down their wages. Whether or not as the result of a conscious policy, pay for women is considerably lower than for men. In 1970 the state of Washington, which has been a leader in seeking to implement comparable worth, initiated a job evaluation that assigned point values to particular jobs. The result showed that for comparable jobs, female employees had a lower wage rate.

Many persons challenge the concept of comparable worth. They argue that it is virtually impossible to compare worth fairly across occupations, and that in a market economy supply and demand should determine wages. Furthermore any attempt to provide equal pay for the sexes would add a significant burden to the economy, placing additional costs on business.

Yet comparable worth is making inroads. First in Washington in 1973 and more recently in Minnesota and Iowa, comparable worth plans are being implemented. A federal district court in Washington has upheld Washington's efforts at comparable worth, holding the state guilty of discriminating against women. The judge's order requires the state to spend an estimated $500 million in the next six years. The Reagan administration has shown little sympathy toward comparable worth, and the Supreme Court has yet to rule on the issue. Hence the future of Washington's plan and comparable worth in general remains in doubt.

The Equal Rights Amendment   The Equal Rights Amendment (ERA), which would write a prohibition of sex discrimination into the Constitution, fell three states short of the thirty-eight needed for ratification by the time of the deadline for ratification on June 30, 1982. The amendment was originally passed by Congress in 1972 and given a ratification deadline of 1979, but in 1978 that deadline was extended to 1982. Even before the deadline expired, a resolution was introduced in Congress to resubmit the ERA as a constitutional amendment. The reintroduced ERA is identical to the original proposal.

The ERA would prohibit sex-based classification. Section I of the amendment reads, "Equality of Rights under the law shall not be denied or abridged by the United States or by any state on account of sex." The intent of the amendment is to eliminate sex-based classifications. It would appear that, should the amendment succeed, sex classifications would be treated like race classifications, if the logic of treating suspect classifications through constitutional language is a proper analogy.

The Rights of the Disabled and Aliens

The Developmentally Disabled

The major piece of legislation protecting the rights of the developmentally disabled is the 1975 Developmentally Disabled Assistance and Bill of Rights Act. This law established a federal grant program to aid states in creating programs to care for and treat people with developmental disabilities. It included a bill of rights stating that mentally retarded people have a right to (1) appropriate treatment, services, and habilitation for their disabilities, and (2) treatment and services provided in the least restrictive setting possible. The act further stated that the federal government and states have an obligation to provide such services and follow

Great attention has been focused on the rights and abilities of handicapped people in recent years. This man owns and operates a furniture manufacturing plant.

minimum standards. However the Court has interpreted the act to express a congressional preference, and not mandate new substantive rights to be funded by states.[59] Nonetheless, even though no new rights are conferred by the act, mentally disabled persons are entitled to safe conditions and freedom of movement within institutional care facilities. Here, for the first time, were articulated some substantive rights of involuntarily committed mentally retarded persons. Specifically, the Supreme Court ruled that such patients have a constitutional right to "safe conditions" and "minimally adequate training" and may not be subjected to "unreasonable bodily restraints."[60] Yet the Court, in 1985, refused to declare mental retardation a suspect or quasi-suspect category. Laws that differentiate the mentally retarded from other persons are not required to meet a higher standard of scrutiny than are laws that make distinctions based on sex or race. Laws may treat the mentally retarded differently from other citizens so long as the laws are a rational means to a legitimate end.[61]

With regard to physically handicapped persons, the pattern of support is similar. In 1975 Congress passed the Education for All Handicapped Children Act, designed to provide federal money to assist state and local agencies in educating handicapped children. Congress had discovered that a majority of handicapped children in the United States "were either totally excluded from schools or sitting idly in regular classrooms awaiting the time when they were old enough to drop out." Congress required that states, to qualify for federal assistance, had to demonstrate that they had programs that assured handicapped children the right to a "free appropriate public education."

The Court entered the debate in 1982 when the issue arose as to whether schools were obligated to provide specialized services to allow students to achieve their "full potential." For example, must a school district provide a signer for a partially deaf student? The Court said no. School districts must provide enough specialized services to allow handicapped students to benefit educationally, the Court ruled, but they need not require schools to provide an opportunity "to maximize each child's potential commensurate with the opportunity provided other children."[62] The Court in 1984 said schools must provide those support services necessary for a child to remain in school.[63]

The rights of handicapped persons were given a boost in 1984 when the Supreme Court ruled in *Consolidated Rail Corporation* v. *Darrone* that the Rehabilitation Act of 1973 prohibits private employers from discriminating against the handicapped.[64] The decision was sufficiently broad to cover an employer receiving federal funds, even if providing jobs was not the purpose of the funds. The case extended to the entire organization, not just to the program receiving federal funds or contracts.

However, protecting the rights of the handicapped does not extend to forcing hospitals to provide aggressive treatment for severely handicapped infants over the objections of parents. In its 1986 "Baby Doe" decision, the Supreme Court ruled that Congress had not authorized the Health and Human Services secretary to intervene or issue rules requiring that parents, hospitals, or state officials provide aggressive treatment for severely handicapped infants to preserve their lives.[65] The Court found no evidence that parental or hospital decisions to allow such infants to expire constituted discrimination. In fact, the Court said that HHS regulations clearly were designed not to bar discrimination but rather to enforce treatment: the regulations were based on a "manifestly incorrect perception that withholding of treatment in accordance with parental instructions necessitates federal regulations." The Court found that, on the contrary, state agencies were doing a satisfactory job of protecting the interests of handicapped infants.

Aliens

During the first years of the 1980s, aliens entered the United States in increasing numbers. Asian children fathered by American servicemen in Southeast Asia were brought to the U.S., and thousands of Cuban and Haitian "refugees" streamed into the country in 1980. Mexicans continually cross the southern U.S. border in search of employment and a better life. Several immigration reform bills before Congress would curb the flow of illegal aliens into the United States and offer amnesty for millions already in the country.

Mexican immigrants apprehended by the Border Patrol represent thousands of illegal aliens from many countries. Their presence causes serious social problems in the United States.

While some of these aliens have immigrated to the country legally and others have been granted "refugee" status, many aliens reside here illegally. Illegal aliens often take employment in this country, and employers are often all too willing to employ them at illegally low wages, since such workers are not free to protest. Other aliens add to the welfare rolls, thereby placing greater financial burdens on states already faced with budget problems. The status of aliens in America is a major issue for the 1980s.

What actions can be taken to solve problems involving immigrants? Clearly, those who came to the United States illegally can be detained and deported, but are they entitled to the equal protection of the laws? In 1982 the Supreme Court ruled that they were so entitled. In *Plyler* v. *Doe* the Court wrote that the provision in the Fourteenth Amendment that prevents a state from denying to *"any person* within its jurisdiction the equal protection of the laws" applies to illegal aliens. The state of Texas had argued that undocumental aliens were not persons within their jurisdiction. But the Court rejected that claim, saying, "Whatever his status under the immigration laws, an alien is surely a person in any ordinary sense of that term." Thus, even aliens residing in the country illegally are recognized as persons guaranteed due process of law and the equal protection of the laws under the Fourteenth Amendment.[66] Law enforcement officials, however, have some latitude, as they do not need a warrant to stop and question aliens at a place of work. Aliens may be questioned and detained for some hours without violating their Fourth Amendment protections.[67] Illegal aliens are protected by federal labor laws. In *Sure-Tan* v. *NLRB* the Court said illegal aliens deported because companies report them to immigration could get their jobs back if they could find a legal way back into the country.[68]

A specific issue in *Plyler* v. *Doe* was a Texas statute requiring illegal aliens to pay public school tuition. The Court struck down this statute, ruling that a free public education could not be denied to the children of illegal aliens. Such children, if so denied, would suffer an "enduring disability." Mr. Justice Brennan, writing for the five to four majority, said, "The school has a fundamental role in maintaining the fabric of our society. We cannot ignore the significant social costs borne by our nation when select groups are denied the means to absorb the values and skills upon which our social order rests."

Later the same year, the Court expanded the rights of alien children when it said that a state could not exclude nonimmigrant aliens from in-state status and the lower state college and university tuition rates that apply to state residents.[69]

However, states and localities do have a lawful right to exclude a broad category of aliens from public service jobs. The Supreme Court found that a general requirement of citizenship for certain public jobs was not a deficiency but "a necessary consequence of the community's process of political self-definition."[70] Aliens are outside the community.

A growing issue has to do with political aliens. Many aliens, particularly from El Salvador, citing human rights violations in their home country, have sought refuge in the United States. They claim they are persecuted for their political views and that to return home would cause them great harm—even death. Some church groups and communities have taken up the cause, offering these illegal immigrants **sanctuary** in their churches or communities. They have declared themselves safe havens for fleeing Central Americans.

Sanctuary: *providing political refugees illegally in the United States protection from deportation or prosecution by allowing them to reside in churches or communities where federal officials are reluctant to apprehend them.*

The Reagan administration is not sympathetic to the sanctuary movement. It has pressed for prosecution of persons or groups harboring these illegal aliens, claiming that such aliens either are here for economic reasons or cannot prove valid concerns for their well-being. In 1984 the Court added support for the Reagan position by refusing to make it more difficult for the INS to deport such aliens. In order to resist deportation, the Court said, aliens must prove they personally face a "clear probability" of persecution.[71]

Age Discrimination

Like laws on race and sex, those that discriminate on the basis of age are increasingly coming under attack. Although age discrimination is not itself an unreasonable or arbitrary distinction, an increasing number of laws and administrative rules prohibit discrimination on the basis of age. The 1967 Age Discrimination in Employment Amendment to the 1964 Civil Rights Act added age to the list of prohibited bases for discrimination that constituted an unfair labor practice. The Older Americans Act of 1975 extended the protections against unreasonable discrimination based on age by permitting the federal government to withhold federal funds from any program that unreasonably discriminates or withholds benefits because of age. The act empowered the United States Commission on Civil Rights to identify such programs and report them to the secretary of health, education, and welfare.

More recently, Congress extended the mandatory retirement age from sixty-five to seventy years of age for most nonfederal workers. The law passed in 1978 extends protections of the 1967 Age Discrimination Amendment to those between sixty-five and seventy years of age. In effect, this legislation prohibits forced retirement before age seventy. The act was affirmed in a 1985 Supreme Court decision, which declared that employers may not force retirement of workers under seventy years of age without substantial justification. At question was whether an airline could force retirement at age sixty. In rejecting the airline's retirement age the court created a two-part test to justify early age qualifications for retirement: (1) employers had reasonable cause to believe all or substantially all persons over the age specified would be unable to perform safely the duties of the job, or (2) that it is highly impractical to deal with older employees on an individual basis, as with individualized testing.[72]

Changing Consensus: Double Discrimination: The Older Woman

In the America of a generation ago, most women, whether or not they worked before marriage, retired from the salaried work force on their wedding day. This generally posed no problem, for marriages were stable. According to the social consensus, a woman who spent her life as a homemaker could expect to be supported throughout her life. Whether to consider homemaking a career and whether one had prospects in the labor force outside the home simply were not issues.

Today, the circumstances are quite different. A woman left without support because of death of a spouse or divorce when she is in her late forties or fifties is a person completely outside the system. She is not yet eligible for social security benefits (which in any case are tied to her husband's years of work and earnings); social agencies can offer her little. She is not eligible for unemployment insurance, and the job market is a nightmare for women her age. When a recently widowed fifty-year-old woman walks into an employment agency looking for a job, she finds herself quickly shuffled out with the suggestion that she do volunteer work. Even if she held a job for a few years before her marriage, that experience is no longer considered relevant. And it is almost impossible for her to get training: training programs are for those who will be working for years and so will repay an employer's investment in them. She is a nonperson by virtue of her age, sex, and life history.

What makes this discrepancy between the American dream and reality so poignant is that, as of the 1980 census, 38 percent of American women over forty have no husbands, and more than a million widowed or divorced women under sixty are out of the labor force. In addition, more than six million are married homemakers—but the fact is that one out of every three marriages ends in divorce.

These changes—and the obviously changed consensus on the pattern of giving up work for marriage—are part of the ferment that has revitalized the women's movement and organizations of older people such as the Gray Panthers. And these shifts have motivated an attempt to pass federal legislation to provide job training and develop special community-service positions for older women. Perhaps because discrimination issues are so closely tied to the reality of economic survival and to the American ideal of justice and opportunity for all, a new consensus may be emerging. If it is not, we may soon be forced to forge one, for our population is aging and, statistically, American women outlive men.

Older women, like this one working in an aircraft manufacturing plant, face discrimination on several levels when they attempt to enter the work force.

Due Process

Political power involves a trust that can easily be abused. The Founding Fathers were well aware of the danger of concentrating too much power in the hands of the government. In addition to the Bill of Rights, they wrote due process protections into the Constitution. Article I, Section 9, outlined specific guarantees, while the Fifth Amendment provided broader guarantees—that no one could be deprived of life, liberty, or property without due process of law. **Due process** is of two kinds: **procedural due process,** which refers to the fairness with which laws are enforced, and **substantive due process,** which relates to the reasonableness of the law itself.

Due Process: *legal, constitutional protections of personal rights and liberties.*

Procedural Due Process: *the aspect of due process that refers to the fairness with which laws are enforced.*

Substantive Due Process: *the aspect of due process that deals with the fairness of the law itself.*

Substantive Due Process

Substantive due process is an ancient concept: there have always been some rights that government could not violate, rights considered basic natural rights of free people.

In the early part of the twentieth century, substantive due process was needed to protect freedom of contract—that is, the Supreme Court would strike down almost any law that impaired economic liberty. The right of property was almost inviolable. The Court would not accept minimum wage laws, price controls, regulations for working hours, or working conditions as legitimate state interests. It argued that the right of contract could be impaired only where legislation had some reasonable relation to a legitimate end of government. And only when the health and safety of the public were at stake could the Court be convinced to sustain legislation.

With the Great Depression and the New Deal in the 1930s, the Court began to abandon this view. Today the Supreme Court will no longer apply the liberty-of-contract view of substantive due process to economic legislation. It prefers to think that the reasonableness of the use of property and economic regulations is a legislative responsibility. As long as it can find some relationship between legislation and public welfare, the Court will not interfere.

The Court has now turned its attention to the protection of fundamental constitutional rights. The Court will use the equal protection clause and the due process clause to limit *any* government from interfering with the fundamental constitutional rights of citizens. Once a right has been given the status of a fundamental right, only a compelling state interest will induce the Court to sustain legislation limiting that right. The Court has proceeded cautiously in lengthening the list, but there is no reason to believe its attitude toward the protection of fundamental rights, such as the right to vote, will change.

Class Action Suit: *a lawsuit brought by a group of persons with a common legal concern who are willing to share the costs of bringing suit.*

One technique citizens may use to protect fundamental constitutional rights is to bring a **class action suit.** This is a lawsuit brought by a group of persons with a common legal concern who are willing to share the costs of bringing suit. The Supreme Court has held that parties to the suit must have some personal interest in the suit, not just a general interest in the outcome for a third party. Class action suits are most commonly used by taxpayers and public interest groups, but women have also sued to prevent sex discrimination in employment and retirement benefits, while doctors have successfully prevented restrictions to the doctor–client relationship. But the Court is not eager to encourage general challenge to laws. Taxpayers are not allowed to challenge the secrecy of the Central Intelligence Agency, since they suffered no injury, nor can citizens bring suit to unseat members of Congress. Furthermore, parties to a class action must demonstrate some substantial personal interest, at least $10,000 individually (the group cannot total all losses to arrive at $10,000).[73]

Procedural Due Process

The language of the Fifth and Fourteenth Amendments—which prohibit the national and state governments from depriving citizens of life, liberty, or property without due process of law—is the basis for procedural due process. This requires that the government be fair in providing a process to consider a person's interests when it acts to deprive someone of life, liberty, or property. In other words, the government must give the individual his or her "due."

It is in the area of criminal justice that procedural due process is most evident and most frequently criticized. An accused citizen must be afforded all rights guaranteed by the Bill of Rights plus a fair hearing. There are rules by which evidence may be used against a defendant. The government must prove beyond any *reasonable doubt* that a crime was committed. The primary sources of procedural due process rights in the Constitution are the Fourth, Fifth, and Sixth Amendments to the Constitution.

Due Process and the Criminal Justice System

Searches and Seizures

The Fourth Amendment protects persons against unreasonable searches and seizures. Not all searches and seizures are unconstitutional, but persons are to be "secure in their persons, houses, papers, and effects against unreasonable searches and seizures." It is the definition of unreasonable, however, that has produced what Justice Lewis Powell called a "twilight zone."

Probable Cause: *the basis upon which a search warrant is issued and, thus, a necessary condition for police searches.*

In general the Fourth Amendment requires a search warrant, issued by a judicial officer on the basis of **probable cause,** for a search to be constitutional. There are two main procedural requirements: first, the warrant is to be issued by a nonpolice officer who has a neutral and detached outside view of the issue; second, the place to be searched and the person or things to be seized are to be specifically described.

Self-Incrimination: *the Fifth Amendment protection of the people's right to refuse to bear witness against themselves.*

The Court has held that the Fourth and Fifth Amendments' protection against **self-incrimination** prevents authorization of the seizure of mere evidence to establish a criminal charge against someone, since such seizure would compel self-incrimination. In other words, a court cannot authorize a "fishing expedition" by issuing a warrant to search a house in order to see if something can be found that would allow bringing charges against the individual. In *Dunaway* v. *New York*, the Court forbade taking a suspect into custody without probable cause for purposes of interrogation in the hope that "something might turn up."[74] Nor can police detain a criminal suspect in order to take fingerprints without consent or without probable cause.[75] The mere-evidence rule seems to preclude any self-incriminating evidence, but this is not the case. The Supreme Court, in *Schmerber* v. *California*, ruled that taking blood samples to introduce as evidence to prove drunk driving did not violate the right to be protected against self-incrimination.[76] The Court interpreted the Fifth Amendment as not requiring individuals to bear witness against themselves, but it did not prohibit the introduction of physical evidence as the object of a reasonable search and seizure. But reasonable it must be. In *Winston* v. *Lee* the Court rejected mandatory surgery, under general anesthetic, to remove a bullet as physical evidence.[77] The Court said surgical intrusion into an individual's body in a search for evidence involves violations of privacy and security of such magnitude that the intrusion may be "unreasonable" even if likely to produce evidence of a crime.

The mere-evidence rule has been sufficiently modified to allow evidence aiding in the apprehension and conviction of those accused. In *Warden* v. *Hayden*, the Court said, "There must, of course, be a nexus—automatically provided in the case of fruits, instrumentalities or contraband—between the item to be seized and criminal behavior. Thus in the case of 'mere evidence,' probable cause must be examined in terms of cause to believe that the evidence sought will aid in a particular apprehension or conviction."[78]

In 1983, the Supreme Court significantly modified and eased the basis for evaluating the sufficiency of probable cause for issuing a search warrant, specifically, where a search warrant was issued on the basis of an informant's tip. Until 1983 police had to establish probable cause using a two-pronged test that demonstrated the informant's veracity and reliability as well as the informant's basis of knowledge in giving such information. But with *Illinois* v. *Gates* the Court discarded that test in favor of a more lenient rule that allows a court to consider the "totality of circumstances" surrounding police requests for a search warrant.[79] "The task of the issuing magistrate is simply to make a practical, common sense decision whether, given all the circumstances set forth in the affidavit before him, including the 'veracity' and 'basis of knowledge' of persons supplying hearsay information, there is a fair probability that contraband or evidence of a crime will be found in a particular place."

What, then, is subject to seizure? Generally speaking, it must be evidence relating to proof that a crime was committed or is about to be committed, and it must be described plainly and adequately in the search warrant. Police officers can seize other property if that property is related

Plain View Evidence:
*evidence of a crime un-
covered as a result of a
legitimate search for
evidence for an unrelated
crime. Courts allow such
evidence to be admitted in
a trial even though it was
not the product of a
search warrant.*

to the property described in the warrant or if it is contraband. They cannot, however, use as evidence property unrelated to the property described in the warrant, such as shotgun shells found in a locked trunk when the warrant was for alcohol. The courts do allow **plain view evidence** as an exception: if in the process of a legitimate search the police inadvertently come across a piece of incriminating evidence, they may seize the evidence under the prior justification for which the warrant was issued.[80] But, the Court has cautioned, "the plain view doctrine may not be used to extend a general exploratory search from one object to another until something incriminating at last emerges."

As a general rule, searches and seizures conducted without a warrant are unreasonable, but there are important exceptions. For example, school officials do not need a warrant or probable cause to search public school students.[81] Officials need only "reasonable grounds" to search a student or a student's belongings for contraband or evidence relating to a crime. Warrantless, naked-eye observation from aircraft of a fenced-in backyard of a home also is permissible.[82] Individuals who leave an area open to view from above retain no constitutional expectation of privacy from aerial surveillance. Most arrests are made without a warrant, and an arrest is a seizure under the Fourth Amendment. A police officer may make an arrest without a warrant if a crime was committed in the presence of the officer or if the police officer has probable cause to believe a felony has been committed and that the accused committed the felony. The Supreme Court recently reaffirmed this position in not requiring warrants for felony crimes in pressing situations. A postal inspector was allowed to arrest a suspect without a warrant upon the probable cause that he possessed stolen credit cards.[83] The Court would not, however, accept the right of the Occupational Safety and Health Administration (OSHA) to make warrantless inspections of businesses and industries, because it "devolves almost unbridled discretion upon executive and administrative officers, particularly those in the field, as to when to search and whom to search."[84] But if Congress can fashion a regulatory scheme for the warrantless search of commercial property, the Court will sustain such a search.[85] In *Donovan* v. *Dewey*, the Court allowed warrantless inspections of federal mines, since mine owners do not have the same privacy interests as do individuals in their homes. Also, the Court said that administrative searches of commercial property differed significantly from the sanctity accorded an individual's home.

Third-Party Warrant:
*a search warrant issued
for a person or place not
suspected of criminal ac-
tivity. The only require-
ment is that police have
probable cause to believe
the person has, or the
place contains, evidence
relating to a crime.*

There must be some assurance that a search is reasonable and has a purpose. The Court accepts third-party warrants as valid under these criteria. A **third-party warrant** allows the search of a place where no arrest is intended. The Fourth Amendment does not prevent the state from issuing a warrant simply because the owner or occupant of the place searched is not suspected of criminal activity. Thus, law enforcement officials in California could secure a warrant to search student newspaper offices at Stanford University for pictures of demonstrators who had assaulted police at a demonstration. The significant element in a reasonable search is that there exists reasonable cause to believe that evidence is located on the premises to be searched.[86] But third-party searches do require search warrants. Police armed with a valid search warrant still need to obtain another search warrant before entering a third-party residence. They cannot use any valid search warrant as a justification to search any home without the owner's consent or without some exigent circumstances.[87]

The Court has moved to restrict police officers without a warrant from entering private homes to make routine felony arrests. In the past, police, acting with probable cause, often entered private homes in order to effect an arrest. The Court held that it was a basic principle of the Fourth Amendment that searches and seizures inside a home without a warrant are presumptively unreasonable. This was the intent of the framers, the Court argued, and such an entry constitutes an invasion of the sanctity of the home. "In terms that apply equally to seizures of property and to seizures of persons, the Fourth Amendment has drawn a firm line at the entrance to the home. Absent exigent circumstances, that threshold may not reasonably be crossed without a warrant." Thus, police officers are forbidden to enter homes to make warrantless arrests and are allowed only limited authority to enter homes to make arrests when they have an arrest warrant and probable cause.[88]

No issue seems to have presented more problems than lawful searches. Courts permit the search of automobiles without a warrant if police have probable cause to believe the automobile contains evidence relating to a crime, and the Court considers a motor home to be included within this warrantless search coverage.[89] But until 1981, when an automobile was routinely stopped in traffic, a police search was restricted to visual evidence in plain view, and police were prohibited from examining the passenger compartment or the trunk. The Burger Court changed these standards and now permits the search of the closed passenger's compartment as incident to a lawful custodial arrest.[90] In 1982, the Court extended this permission even more broadly to cover the entire vehicle. Police officers who have legitimately stopped an automobile and who have probable cause to believe that contraband is concealed somewhere within it may conduct a warrantless search as thorough as any judge could authorize in a warrant. Thus, police who have legitimately stopped any vehicle may search every part of the vehicle and its contents, including containers and packages.[91] "If probable cause justifies the search of a lawfully stopped vehicle, it justifies the search of every part of the vehicle and its contents that may conceal the object of the search." The principle was extended further in 1985 when the Court permitted objects or packages removed from a searched vehicle to be inspected several days later. The warrantless search of an automobile and all containers need not be immediate, nor does later inspection of those removed contents require issuance of a search warrant.[92]

Police also may monitor a car's progress on public roads by use of a radio transmitter or "beeper" without invading the occupant's privacy.

Such a warrantless monitoring of a car is neither a search nor a seizure under the Fourth Amendment.[93] The Court said that privacy does not extend to visual observation from public places; motorists on public roads have no such reasonable expectation to privacy. The Fourth Amendment does not prohibit police from augmenting their sensory facilities.

Stop and frisk is another area of considerable controversy. In 1979 the Court said police cannot randomly stop automobiles under the guise of checking the operator's license or vehicle registration in order to "aggressively patrol" high-crime districts.[94] Police officers may stop and frisk a suspect on the street if they have reason to believe the individual is armed and dangerous. But the stopping of pedestrians without reasonable suspicion of criminal activity violates the Fourth Amendment.[95] Even patrons in a bar being investigated with a search warrant cannot be searched without probable cause.[96] In 1983 the Court made this provision even stronger when it invalidated California's loitering law.[97] California law had allowed police to arrest anyone stopped on suspicion of a crime if they failed to provide "credible and reliable" identification. The Court held the law contained no standard for determining what a suspect had to do to satisfy the requirement of proving "credible and reliable" information. In effect, the law amounted to arbitrary enforcement in violation of the Fourteenth Amendment's due process clause. "As such, the statute vests virtually complete discretion in the hands of police to determine whether the suspect has satisfied that statute and must be permitted to go on his way in the absence of probable cause to arrest."

However, if a person is the object of an investigation relating to a crime, he or she may be briefly stopped, asked questions, or have identification checked without police having probable cause concerning that person. In *U.S.* v. *Hensley*, police, acting on a Wanted flyer circulated from another police department, stopped and detained the person named in the flyer, though the detaining police had no direct evidence or warrant for the suspect. The Court said police officers from one department may rely on a flyer or bulletin from another department. Such a brief, nonprobable cause stop promotes strong government interests in combatting crime that outweigh the individual's interest.[98]

Once police have probable cause to perform a legal search, however, they are accorded considerable discretion. Police may detain persons as long as reasonably necessary to effect their purpose, not by an arbitrary time limit.[99] The police may detain all occupants of a building while executing a valid search warrant—that is, a person need not be the object of the warrant to be detained.[100] Detention is held to be less intrusive than the search itself. Police have strong justification for detention—preventing flight, violence, or the destruction of evidence. Thus, the Court established a new Fourth Amendment exemption to detention as seizure—detention pursuant to the execution of a valid search warrant. And once a person has been placed in custody, police may monitor the detainee's

Stop and Frisk: *the police practice of stopping suspects on the street to determine whether they are concealing evidence or illegal weapons.*

movements, even by entering his or her domicile and executing a plain view search for contraband.[101] In the relevant case, a college student in his dorm was arrested for possession of alcohol because he appeared to be underage. The security officer accompanied him into his dorm room and discovered drugs. The Court held that the plain view rule applied and the search was legal; once he had made the arrest, the officer had the right to "remain literally at the defendant's elbow at all times."

Deadly Force: *the use of all necessary force, including shooting to kill, to effect an arrest.*

Deadly force may not be used in executing a search and seizure to prevent apparently unarmed, nondangerous suspects from escaping. "A police officer may not seize an unarmed, nondangerous suspect by shooting him dead."[102] In the rather controversial decision of *Tennessee* v. *Garner*, the Supreme Court, in its six to three decision, invalidated the Tennessee law permitting a police officer, after notice of intent to arrest and where the suspect flees or forcibly resists, to "use all the necessary means to effect the arrest." The Court said police cannot use such deadly force unless the police officer finds it necessary to prevent the escape and has probable cause to believe the suspect poses a significant threat of death or serious physical injury to the officer or others.

Under the Fourth Amendment, the courts have only one device to ensure protection against unreasonable searches and seizures, and that is to exclude from evidence material unconstitutionally obtained as the result of an illegal search and seizure. This is known as the **exclusionary rule.** In *Mapp* v. *Ohio*, the Supreme Court extended the exclusionary rule to state criminal proceedings.[103] For example, fingerprints and a confession to a robbery cannot be used as evidence if the arrest was illegal—that is, if it was based on uncorroborated evidence and executed without warrant or probable cause.[104] The intent was to deter police from violating the constitutional rights of citizens. But critics have charged that the ruling permits criminals to go free. The Burger Court was sensitive to this charge and cut back on the scope of the exclusionary rule. In 1974 the Court ruled that the exclusionary rule does not extend to grand jury proceedings, at which witnesses may be required to answer questions based on illegally obtained evidence.[105] And in 1976, the Court restricted the right of federal courts generally to review state court convictions where questions of improper evidence had been raised.[106] If the state court considered the question and rejected the contention of illegal evidence, federal courts were not free to order a new trial on the basis of the exclusionary rule. In 1980 the Court permitted the use of illegally obtained evidence to impeach a defendant's false statements as long as the testimony was in response to proper cross-examination reasonably suggested by the defendant's direct examination.[107]

Exclusionary Rule: *the court device of excluding from a trial evidence that was obtained as a result of an illegal search and seizure.*

More importantly, the Supreme Court has significantly restricted the scope of the exclusionary rule. It overturned the automatic-standing rule, which gave defendants standing to challenge searches and seizures in crimes of possession, thereby restricting the federal courts' ability to apply the exclusionary rule.[108] And in 1984 the Supreme Court created two large exceptions to the exclusionary rule: (1) an inevitable discovery exception, and (2) a good faith exception.

The inevitable discovery exception permits the use of evidence collected through police misconduct when such evidence would inevitably have been discovered anyway.[109] The 1984 case, *Nix* v. *Williams*, involved the 1968 Christmas killing of a 10-year-old girl. The defendant told police of the body's whereabouts as he was being transported in a car. His original conviction was overturned because the evidence of the body's location was obtained as a result of an illegally obtained statement. Williams was later retried, not on the basis of his statements, but using evidence as to the location and condition of the body. This the Court said was permissible, because such evidence would inevitably be found: "If the prosecution can establish by a preponderance of the evidence that the information ultimately or inevitably would have been discovered by lawful means," the evidence is admissible in court.

The good faith exception, established in the case of *U.S.* v. *Leon*, allows the admission of evidence obtained from an illegal search and seizure if that evidence was obtained in the reasonable belief that the search or seizure was legal at the time police conducted it.[110] As long as police acted in "good faith" in the belief that the warrant was valid and the evidence seized was legally obtained, it does not matter that the warrant was invalidly issued or the evidence illegally seized; the evidence is admissible in court: "The exclusionary rule is designed to deter police misconduct rather than to punish the errors of judges and magistrates."

Complicated questions arise now because of new technology and the wide availability of sophisticated listening devices and recording equipment. The Founding Fathers thought in terms of physical objects— homes, papers, and documents—when drafting the Fourth Amendment. Indeed, early in the twentieth century, the Supreme Court held that the Fourth Amendment applied only to physical objects or physical entry into a home.[111] But by 1967 the issues of electronic eavesdropping and wiretapping, the right to privacy, and security under the Fourth Amendment could no longer be avoided. In *Katz* v. *United States*, the Supreme Court said that conversations captured electronically were subject to search and seizure rules under the Fourth Amendment.[112] The seizure of a telephone conversation without a warrant, the Court ruled, violated Fourth Amendment rights: "Wherever a man may be, he is entitled to know that he will remain free from unreasonable searches and seizures."

The *Katz* decision meant that warrants would be required for wiretapping, and that courts would now have to contend with the issue as a search and seizure question. The Omnibus Crime Control and Safe Streets Act of 1968 clarified the matter somewhat by requiring federal agents to secure a warrant from a federal judge before doing any wiretapping and outlining a broad range of potential crimes for which wiretapping warrants might be issued. The act similarly allowed state officials, namely the attorney general, to apply for warrants to wiretap in state situations where a crime had been or was about to be committed. The act set up a procedure by which the attorney general of the United States would grant permission for wiretapping after securing the necessary warrant. Richard Nixon's attorney general, John Mitchell, interpreted the law as allowing him, *without* court approval, to sanction electronic surveillance in cases involving a threat to the internal security of the United States. In the only case to emerge on the question, the Supreme Court rejected Mr. Mitchell's contention and ruled that the law did not include the right to authorize surveillance for domestic conspiracy.[113] The Court left open the possibility of electronic surveillance of foreign agents for purposes of national security, but stated directly, "The danger to political dissent is acute when the government attempts to act under so vague a concept as the power to protect domestic security." In the wake of Watergate and the subsequent revelations regarding past presidents and warrantless wiretapping, Congress has been considering legislation that would prohibit all government wiretapping, for any reason, unless undertaken with a judicial warrant.

Rights of the Accused The Fifth and Sixth Amendments are the foundation of the procedural guarantees affording due process of the law to persons standing accused of a crime. The Supreme Court has played a prominent role in extending these rights, particularly from federal courts to state courts. Its liberalization of the rights of the accused in the 1960s produced public criticism that the courts were "coddling criminals" and ignoring the rights of law-abiding citizens. Nonetheless, the Court's aim has been to extend the ancient and sacred principles of innocence and burden of proof to all persons standing before the bar of justice.

The Fifth Amendment protects citizens by requiring that the government present evidence to a grand jury to determine whether it is sufficient to justify a criminal trial. It also protects citizens from having to incriminate themselves: the burden of proof rests with the state. The Sixth Amendment provides for a jury trial for all criminal prosecutions; the right to be informed of charges, to be confronted with witnesses, and to have the assistance of counsel are also Sixth Amendment rights in federal prosecutions.

In 1983 the Supreme Court said that refusal to take a blood-alcohol test may be used against a person in a trial without violating the Fifth Amendment privilege against self-incrimination. The Court was specifically upholding the **implied consent** law used to attack the problem of drunk drivers. Securing a driver's license carries with it the implied consent to a blood-alcohol test if stopped on suspicion of driving while intoxicated. Refusal to take the blood-alcohol test may then be admitted in court as evidence against the motorist. Adding this penalty to the exercise of a right—refusing the blood-alcohol test—does not constitute impermissible coercion.[114] Implied consent thus withstands the challenge of self-incrimination.

Implied Consent: *a law in several states that says that by holding a driver's license a person also has given consent to a blood-alcohol test if stopped on suspicion of driving while intoxicated.*

However, the Fifth Amendment protection against self-incrimination does not apply to proceedings to commit persons to a psychiatric hospital when these persons are said to be "sexually dangerous."[115] The Court labeled such activity as treatment, not punishment. The state may serve its purpose of treating rather than punishing sexually dangerous persons by committing them to an institution for a lengthy, even indefinite, period.

In federal prosecutions, it has always been a principle that people accused of crimes are protected against self-incrimination. Coerced confessions are not permitted as evidence; an individual has the right to remain silent. It was not until 1936 that the principle was extended to include state prosecutions, although these cases dealt with the trial stage and said little about pretrial interrogation and custodial treatment. Rule 5 of the Federal Rules of Criminal Procedure requires the accused to be presented "without unnecessary delay" before a committing officer. Confessions obtained during an unlawful detention are inadmissible. Rule 5(b) states,

> [The Commissioner] shall inform the defendant of the complaint against him, of his right to retain counsel and of his right to have a preliminary examination. He shall also inform the defendant that he is not required to make a statement and that any statement made by him may be used against him.

The Supreme Court has used this rule to give it supervisory powers over lower federal courts on the admissibility of evidence. The rule was applied in *Mallory* v. *United States,* when the Court overturned a rape conviction on the basis that the confession was exacted with an undue delay in arraigning the defendant.[116]

This still left open the question of when exactly during a police interrogation counsel must be provided and a suspect informed of the right against self-incrimination. In *Escobedo* v. *Illinois,* the Court voided a murder conviction because the defendant was denied counsel and not told of the right to remain silent during police interrogation.[117] The full range of those rights was then made clear in **Miranda *v.* Arizona,** in which the Court detailed the principles governing interrogation:

*Miranda v. Arizona:
the Supreme Court
decision that detailed the
principles governing police
interrogation.*

> Prior to any questioning, the person must be warned that he has a right to remain silent, that any statement he does make may be used as evidence against him, and that he has a right to the presence of an attorney, either retained or appointed. . . . If he indicates in any manner and at any stage of the process that he wishes to consult with an attorney before speaking, there can be no questioning.[118]

Chief Justice Warren made it clear there would be no federal or state convictions if defendants were denied the due process of law from the moment they were taken into custody or otherwise deprived of their freedom. These have come to be known as the *Miranda* rights; they are

Ernesto Miranda
It was the overturned conviction of Ernesto Miranda by the Supreme Court that led to the articulation of the rights of the accused, known as the *Miranda* rights. Miranda had been convicted of the rape-kidnapping of an eighteen-year-old woman. He signed a written confession after two hours of police interrogation. The Supreme Court overturned the conviction on the basis that he had not been told his rights. After the Supreme Court decision, the state of Arizona retried and convicted Miranda, largely on evidence from his girlfriend, who testified that Miranda admitted to her that he committed the crime. Miranda was paroled from prison in 1972 and four years later he was stabbed to death in a barroom quarrel—on the tenth anniversary of the *Miranda* decision.

the due process rights that must be explained to all persons held in custody by federal or state law enforcement officials.

The *Miranda* decision extended the scope of protection from the trial to the point of origination of custody, for both federal and state criminal proceedings. In 1986 the Court extended the *Miranda* protection to arraignment proceedings. The right to counsel is no less significant, and the need for safeguards no less clear, at arraignment than for post-arraignment, custodial interrogations.[119] But *Miranda* rights do not extend to questioning about traffic offenses.[120] Drivers stopped by police for questioning about traffic offenses need not be advised of their constitutional rights. However, if arrested, even for the traffic offense, they must then be advised of their *Miranda* rights.

The appointment of Warren Burger to the Supreme Court in 1969, and the subsequent appointments of five new members, produced a Supreme Court decidedly more cautious than the Warren Court in protecting the rights of the accused. Early in 1971 this Court began to restrict the extent of the *Miranda* ruling. In *Harris* v. *New York*, the Court ruled that statements given to police who had not followed *Miranda* guidelines could be used to impeach testimony. (The statements, however, would not be admissible as evidence for the prosecution.)[121] In *Michigan* v. *Tucker* (1974), the Court further restricted *Miranda* by applying it only to the defendant's own testimony, not to incriminating statements made by a friend whom the defendant voluntarily named to police.[122] In *Michigan* v. *Mosley* (1975), it allowed a conviction based on a confession to a crime when the defendant had been interrogated and informed of his rights for a separate crime.[123] The right to remain silent and to be informed of that right does not prejudice prosecution for another crime. In 1979 the Court further restricted *Miranda* when it held that explicit waiver of the right to counsel was not necessary once the *Miranda* rights had been made known to a defendant.[124] In 1980 the Court said that interrogation within the meaning of *Miranda* applies to express questioning and not to a suspect's susceptibility. *Miranda* comes into play whenever police question or say or do things they should know are incriminating. It does not extend to routine conversation or off-hand remarks between police not intended to invite a response from a suspect. In such a context, suspect susceptibility to make self-incriminating responses is not limited by the *Miranda* principles.[125] In 1985 the Court refused to suppress a confession, made after proper *Miranda* warnings and a valid waiver of rights, because police had obtained an earlier voluntary but unwarned admission. Despite "letting the cat out of the bag," the initial, voluntary statement itself is inadmissible as evidence since unwarned, but it does not taint or make inadmissible a subsequent confession made by a defendant knowing he or she has already confessed.[126]

The Court has further moved to create a "public safety" exception for *Miranda* rights.[127] The concern for public safety must be paramount and takes priority over the literal language of *Miranda*. In the case of *New York* v. *Quarles*, an armed rape suspect apprehended in a supermarket after a

Practicing Politics: Your Due Process Rights

If you are legally placed under arrest for a misdemeanor or a felony, the arresting officer will read you the **Miranda warning,** which is a statement of your due process rights. This is a copy of the actual form used by the Grand Forks Police Department:

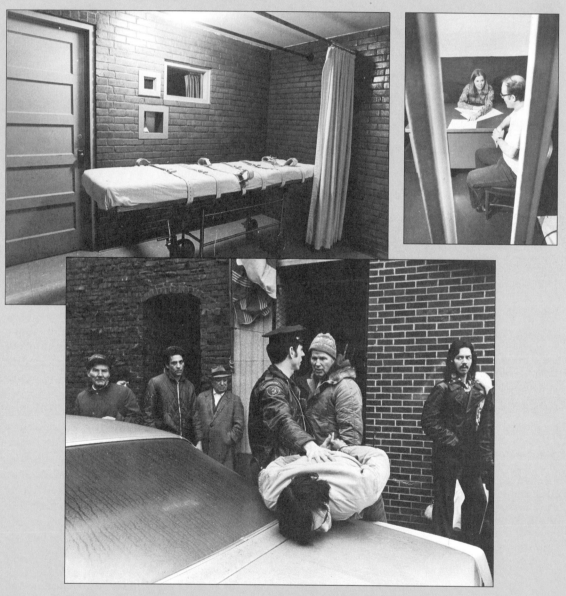

The criminal justice system can ensure that those who break the law face severe, sometimes even tragic, consequences.

MIRANDA WARNING

1. You have the right to remain silent.
2. Anything you say can and will be used against you in a court of law.
3. You have the right to talk to a lawyer and have him present with you while you are being questioned.
4. If you cannot afford to hire a lawyer one will be appointed to represent you before any questioning, if you wish one.

If you are detained by the police, you have the following due process rights:

1. *Detention for investigation* The degree and length of detention for investigation, for which there must be probable cause and not mere suspicion, are unclear. However, this is considered custodial interrogation, and your *Miranda* rights apply.
2. *Arrest* If you are placed under arrest, you have the right to know the charges. Police must bring you for arraignment on specific charges or release you. (These charges are not binding; it is the prosecutor who decides the charge.) If you are acquitted or the charges are dismissed, it may be possible to have the arrest expunged from the record. The case law varies, but it can and has been done.
3. *Arraignment* Within a period of time (it varies from state to state), police must bring you before a judicial officer to determine whether the arrest was lawful and whether sufficient evidence exists to charge you with a crime. At this point you are either formally charged with a crime or set free. If you are charged, usually a preliminary hearing is held to test the evidence. You (your lawyer) can challenge the probable cause for the charges, and charges can be dropped or reduced.
4. *Bail* For all but the most serious charges—murder or treason—you are eligible for bail once you are booked and arraigned. Bail is based on the presumption of innocence since you have not yet been proved guilty. The amount of bail required depends on the seriousness of the charges, the evidence, your employment, financial resources, character, and past criminal record.

chase was asked for the location of the gun used in the crime. The Court said both the gun and the statement locating the gun could be admitted into evidence. Locating the gun to protect public safety in this situation took priority over reading the defendant his rights.

In a 1986 decision, *Moran* v. *Burbine,* the Supreme Court refused to extend *Miranda's* reach to police who are less than forthright in their dealings with an attorney or if they fail to tell a suspect of a lawyer's unilateral efforts to contact him or her.[128] The Court said *Miranda* rights were not violated because police failed to inform a suspect that a lawyer hired to defend him was trying to reach him, nor were *Miranda* rights jeopardized when police gave the hired lawyer misleading information about when the suspect was going to be questioned. When a suspect voluntarily waives his *Miranda* rights, Ms. Justice O'Connor wrote for a six to three majority, police are not required to provide him with "a flow of information to help him calibrate his self-interest in deciding whether to speak or stand by his rights." Justice O'Connor refused to extend *Miranda* rights to cover this form of police deception.

Nevertheless, if the Court has seen fit to restrict *Miranda,* it has not indicated any readiness to discard the ruling. The case of *Rhode Island* v. *Innis* expanded the meaning of *interrogation* beyond express questioning. The Court refused to restrict *Miranda* to direct questioning but did include "any words or actions on the part of police . . . that the police should know are reasonably likely to elicit an incriminating response from the suspect."[129] Nor can police use a government informer to record conversations in order to elicit postindictment statements from a defendant for use in a trial.[130] Police had wired a codefendant, who was a government informer, to record the defendant's conversations at a meeting with the codefendant in which both defendants, without counsel, planned to discuss their defense strategy and which police knew or should have known would produce incriminating statements. The codefendant, feigning poor memory, talked and reminisced with the defendant about their criminal activity. "By concealing the fact that (the codefendant) was an agent of the state, the police denied (the defendant) the opportunity to consult with counsel and thus denied him the assistance of counsel guaranteed by the Sixth Amendment."

Furthermore, the right to counsel, once invoked, can only be waived voluntarily, and then only when done so knowingly and intelligently. Responding to police-initiated interrogation in itself is not a waiver of that right.[131]

Included under *Miranda,* then, are those factors that are the "functional equivalent" of express interrogation. In 1975, in *Doyle* v. *Ohio* and *Wood* v. *Ohio* the Court ruled that the exercise of *Miranda* rights could not be used against a defendant as evidence in a trial; the state cannot use silence as an indication of guilt.[132] This principle was further reinforced in 1986 when the Court said a state may not use postarrest silence against a defendant who pleads not guilty by reason of insanity.[133] The silence cannot be introduced as evidence to prove the defendant's sanity.

The Right to Counsel   Closely related to the right against self-incrimination and, indeed, part of the *Miranda* ruling, is the right to counsel. As originally stated in the Sixth Amendment, the right to have "the assistance of counsel" extended only to the right of the accused to employ counsel; the state had no obligation to provide that counsel. Furthermore, the Court made it clear in *Betts* v. *Brady* (1942) that the Fourteenth Amendment requirement of due process did not guarantee the Sixth Amendment right to counsel in state criminal proceedings.

All that changed in 1963. The landmark decision of *Gideon* v. *Wainwright* required that everyone accused of a serious crime be given the opportunity to be assisted by counsel. If the defendant could not afford to employ counsel, the state was obligated to provide such assistance.[134] The Court said, "Any person haled into court, who is too poor to hire a lawyer, cannot be assured a fair trial unless counsel is provided for him." The ruling applied to all felony proceedings, both federal and state. The Court expanded on the *Gideon* decision in 1972 when it extended the right to counsel not only to felony cases, but also to misdemeanors or so-called lesser offenses.[135] The Court felt that deprivation of liberty—even for short periods of time—was a serious matter and that lack of legal assistance impinged on due process. In 1979 the Court ruled that the right to counsel did not extend to persons charged with state crimes who were not sentenced to jail, even though they stood charged with crimes punishable by jail sentences.[136] And in 1981 the Court said that the right to counsel did not apply to all parental-status-termination suits. Only if a person was deprived of physical liberty would due process require appointment of counsel.[137]

Nor does the Sixth Amendment guarantee a "meaningful attorney-client relationship."[138] A defendant whose attorney became ill and was hospitalized could not receive a continuance but had to accept another attorney, even though the defendant claimed the new attorney was unprepared (contrary to the attorney's claim). The subsequent trial did not violate the defendant's rights. Criminal defendants cannot claim that they have been denied effective counsel unless they can show that counsel's performance fell below "objective standards of reasonableness," which so prejudiced the defense that the results of the proceeding would have been different.[139] And a disagreement between a lawyer and a client in which the attorney attempts to dissuade the client from committing perjury does not deprive a person of the Sixth Amendment right to counsel.[140] Finally, as we have already observed, failure of police officers to inform a suspect that an attorney is attempting to reach the suspect or police officers' giving the attorney misleading information regarding their intention to interrogate a suspect does not interfere with the attorney–client relationship.[141]

In 1978 the Court overturned a state conviction for three defendants because they were not each afforded counsel after repeated requests to be separately represented. The Supreme Court ruled that each defendant was entitled to separate counsel to ensure adequate assistance and to prevent a potential conflict of interest.[142] The Court reiterated its position in *Bounds* v. *Smith* when it held that prison inmates not only have a fundamental constitutional right of access to the courts, but that prison authorities have an obligation to assist inmates in their right of access.[143] This includes allowing inmates to file writs and other legal motions, making available adequate legal library resources, and providing competent legal counsel.

Trial by Jury   The Sixth Amendment also protects the oldest and most treasured right in the Constitution: trial by jury. Jury trial is guaranteed in Article III of the Constitution as well as in the Sixth Amendment. Article III, Section 2, reads:

> The trial of all crimes, except in cases of impeachment, shall be by jury; and such trial shall be held in the state where the said crimes shall have been committed.

The Sixth Amendment reads:

> In all criminal prosecutions the accused shall enjoy the right to a speedy and public trial, by an impartial jury of the state and district wherein the crime shall have been committed.

Trial by jury has been falling into disuse, however; courts have traditionally held that petty offenses do not require trial by jury. And, of course, an individual may waive the right to trial by jury, subject to approval of the court.[144] Several states have reduced the number of jurors from the traditional twelve or altered the unanimity requirement for conviction. In 1970, the Supreme Court ruled that a state need not provide a twelve-person jury to fulfill the Sixth Amendment trial by jury provision. A jury conviction for robbery and a subsequent sentence of life imprisonment were upheld even though Florida provided only a six-person jury.[145] Ruled the Court, in *Williams* v. *Florida*, "The fact that the jury at common law was composed of precisely 12 is an historical accident, unnecessary to effect the purpose of the jury system and wholly without significance 'except to mystics.'" There must be at least six, however; the Court ruled that a five-person jury was too small.[146] The number six will also satisfy the Seventh Amendment requirement of a jury trial in civil suits.[147]

States have also reduced the requirement of unanimity for juries to reach a verdict for conviction. Oregon's constitution permitted guilty verdicts in criminal cases, except first-degree murder, where ten of the twelve jurors so voted. The Supreme Court upheld the provision.[148] As in *Williams*, the Court said, "After considering the history of the 12-man requirement and the function it performs in contemporary society, we concluded that it was not of constitutional stature. We reach the same conclusion today with regard to the requirement of unanimity." But unanimity is necessary for six-person juries. Six is the minimum number necessary for juries and for convictions without violating the Sixth and Fourteenth Amendments.[149]

In a major decision in 1986, *Batson* v. *Kentucky,* the Court ruled that a prosecutor's use of peremptory challenges to exclude jurors solely on racial grounds violated the equal protection rights of both defendants and prospective jurors.[150] In fact, a prima facie case of purposeful discrimination can be made, the Court said, when members of a defendant's racial group are excluded from the jury. Such exclusion raises the inference that the exclusion was based on race.

Cruel and Unusual Punishment   Derived from the English Bill of Rights, the Eighth Amendment protection from **cruel and unusual punishments** sought to regulate both the manner of punishment and its severity. Supposedly the framers had in mind such practices as drawing and quartering, burning at the stake, crucifixion, and tarring and feathering, but more recently the Eighth Amendment has been invoked to overturn a California statute making it a misdemeanor for a person to "be addicted to the use of narcotics." And in 1980 the Court said mandatory life imprisonment for convictions on three nonviolent property crimes (total value: $229) was not cruel and unusual punishment.[151] In recent years, the major issue under scrutiny in this context, however, has been that of **capital punishment.**

Cruel and Unusual Punishment: *a phrase used in the Eighth Amendment provision intended to regulate the manner and severity of criminal punishment.*

Capital Punishment: *the use of the death penalty as a form of criminal punishment.*

As early as 1879 the Supreme Court ruled that capital punishment did not violate the Eighth Amendment as long as the death penalty was carried out without unnecessary cruelty, but in this century citizen groups have waged campaigns to abolish capital punishment. In the 1950s and 1960s several states did abolish the death sentence, but the goal of these groups has been to get the Supreme Court to make an authoritative ruling. The question of capital punishment has sparked lively debate over the years. Opponents argue that the death penalty is a cruel and unusual punishment that has no effect in deterring crime. The function of sentencing ought to be rehabilitation, not punishment. Proponents respond by noting the rising crime rate and the need to provide the criminal justice system with the tools adequate to meet the challenge. They argue that swift and sure justice is the best cure for rising crime.

In 1972, in *Furman* v. *Georgia,* the Court ruled that the death penalty, as presently administered by the states, did constitute cruel and unusual punishment.[152] By a five to four vote, the Court ruled that the death sentence had been applied in a wanton and capricious manner, discriminated against the poor and minorities, and left too much discretion to juries. Only two justices argued that the death sentence was cruel and unusual punishment in itself, however; the rest of the majority were speaking specifically about the handling of the death sentence.

States were left in a quandary. Did *Furman* ban the death sentence as unconstitutional, or would states have only to tighten the discretionary elements in the law? Most states felt it prudent to suspend the death sentence until the Court had an opportunity to review the issue. That opportunity came in 1976, when the Supreme Court reviewed the laws of five states: Georgia, Texas, Florida, North Carolina, and Louisiana. Two of the state laws that provided for a mandatory death sentence were ruled unconstitutional. The remaining three laws were upheld, however, because they provided for proper discretionary power of imprisonment or death as a separate decision once guilt had been established.[153]

Gregg v. *Georgia* clearly stated that capital punishment itself was not unconstitutional as a form of cruel and unusual punishment: "We hold that the death penalty is not a form of punishment that may never be imposed, regardless of the circumstances of the offense, regardless of the character of the offender, and regardless of the procedure followed in reaching the decision to impose it." The Court did, however, indicate that there must be careful review and use of the death sentence only for certain specified crimes. In *Coker* v. *Georgia,* the Court ruled that capital punishment for rape was cruel and unusual punishment because the sentence was excessively disproportionate; there was no loss of life to the victim.[154] In *Godfrey* v. *Georgia* the Court overturned a Georgia statute as being unconstitutionally vague because it permitted the death penalty for murder when the murder was "outrageously or wantonly vile, horrible or inhumane in that it involved torture, depravity of mind, or an aggravated battery to the victim."[155] And in *Beck* v. *Alabama* the death penalty was overturned because the jury was not given the opportunity to consider a verdict of guilty to a lesser included, noncapital offense.[156] Any jury considering a sentence of death must recognize "the gravity of its task and proceed with the appropriate awareness of its truly awesome responsibility. Furthermore, for a state to minimize a jury's sense of responsibility by suggesting that the jury does not have the final say in imposing the death penalty is inconsistent with the Eighth Amendment.[157]

Indeed, in recent years concern about jury attitude has been growing. Both defendants and prosecutors have brought claims based on it. The Supreme Court has said defendants may insist that prospective jurors in trials involving interracial crimes be informed of the victim's race and questioned on the issue of racial bias.[158] Prosecutors have a right, the Court also agreed, to remove prospective jurors who are so opposed to capital punishment that they would be unable to perform their duties at the sentencing phase.[159] Affording the prosecutor such a right does not affect a jury's ability to be impartial.

The 1980s have seen the Court delineate more carefully the conditions and circumstances for imposing the death penalty. A defendant convicted of murder under a statute later invalidated as unconstitutional (as precluding consideration of a lesser verdict) was not given a new verdict or permitted a new trial; the constitutional flaw was deemed irrelevant to the case.[160] On the other hand, the death penalty cannot be imposed on a retrial once the sentencing proceeding of the first trial has declined to impose that punishment.[161] But a judge can disregard the jury's recommendation for a life sentence and impose the death penalty.[162] Nothing in the Constitution requires that only a jury make the decision to sentence someone to die.

The Court has also declared it unconstitutional to impose the death penalty on persons who aid and abet felonies ending in murder but who themselves do not kill, attempt to kill, or intend to kill.[163] "The death penalty is disproportionate as applied to him."

The issue of proportionality has been a ticklish one. Must courts be consistent in ensuring that penalties of death are imposed only in similar cases? In 1984 the Supreme Court said no, refusing to overturn a sentence of death because the state court failed to conduct a "comparative proportionality review" before affirming the death sentence.[164] Courts need not compare sentences with penalties imposed in similar cases, even if so requested by prisoners.

If the death penalty cannot be given to those who don't pull the trigger, can it be applied to juveniles? The Supreme Court has yet to confront the issue directly, although in 1982 a related case came before the Court. Oklahoma convicted a sixteen-year-old of killing a police officer. The boy was tried as an adult and sentenced to death. The Court overturned the conviction, not because the youth was a minor, but because the trial court had failed to consider all relevant mitigating factors surrounding his childhood and family life. The Court said, "We are not unaware of the extent to which minors engage increasingly in violent crime. Nor do we suggest an absence of legal responsibility where crime is committed by a minor. We are concerned here only with the manner of the imposition of the ultimate penalty: the death sentence imposed for the crime of murder upon an emotionally disturbed youth with a disturbed child's immaturity."[165]

Protection for Victims and Witnesses

The Burger Court showed more inclination to protect society's rights than the Warren Court did. In numerous areas of the criminal justice system, the Court accorded protection for society against the individual. The actions of the Court appear to be consistent with the thrust of public demands for a response to the rising crime rate and for protection. President Ford, in a message to Congress in 1975, stated: "For too long, the law has centered its attention more on the rights of the criminal than on the victim of the crime. It is high time we reversed this trend and put the highest priority on the victims and potential victims." Victims are often persons in the criminal justice system. Rape victims, for example, have been subjected to enormous pressure on the witness stand to recount the details of the crimes, and were often faced with the accusation that they had somehow encouraged the defendant. Witnesses for the prosecution were often bullied into testifying by police, and then given no protection from threats by a defendant. The system offered little sympathy and even less compensation for the disruption caused victims and bystander witnesses.

With the 1970s came a wave of programs to assist witnesses and the victims of crime. Funded largely from the Law Enforcement Assistance Administration (LEAA), the new services have included the following:

> Referring victims to social services; assisting victims in obtaining benefits; supplying information, such as advice about residential security measures, the status or disposition of the criminal case in which the victim is involved, and the rights of victims to insurance, restitution, compensation, or other benefits; comforting or counseling the victim after the crime; advising the victim as to what he or she can expect as a witness; assisting in obtaining witness fees; providing transportation or sitting services for witnesses; providing a special witness notification system designed to prevent unnecessary trips to the courthouse; ensuring that witnesses have their property returned once it has been used as evidence; providing lounges in courthouses; and arranging for victim-offender confrontations designed to allay victim fears and improve the offender's chances for rehabilitation.[166]

The area attracting the greatest interest now is compensation and restitution for victims of crime. More than a dozen states have initiated such programs. **Restitution** programs require the offender to make reparation to the victim; in **compensation** programs, the state compensates the victim just as an insurance company pays a damage claim.

The movement gained momentum and notoriety in 1982 with California's Proposition 8—The Victim's Bill of Rights. Passed by California voters with a 56 percent vote, the proposition marked sweeping changes in California's criminal laws by cutting back the rights of defendants. It made easier the admission of evidence as well as the detention of suspects. Congress, too, passed a crime victim's protection act in 1982. This act allowed prosecutors to seek court orders to protect victims or witnesses from intimidation. It also required judicial sentencing reports to include a "victim's impact statement" on the financial, social, psychological, and physical impact of the crime on the victim. Finally, it authorized the judge to order restitution to victims in cases involving loss of property or personal injury to cover uninsured medical expenses, property losses, or funeral and burial expenses.

Restitution: *the principle of requiring an offender to make reparation to the victim of a crime.*

Compensation: *government programs to aid victims who have suffered loss or injury as a result of a crime.*

Summary

1. The Fourteenth Amendment to the Constitution has been the basic constitutional device by which equal rights and due process of law are extended to citizens in states. Most effectively used to secure rights for black Americans, the amendment is also used by the poor, American Indians, and women.

2. The struggle for racial justice has been long and incomplete. Attacked in the courts, segregation was declared unconstitutional in 1954. Yet it would be another decade before advances took place in voting,

housing, and employment. Even today blacks lag behind whites in almost all these areas.

3. Today the issue of racial justice turns from eliminating laws that bar equality to more active governmental support for racial integration, such as affirmative action in redressing past discriminatory practices.

4. Sex and age discrimination are increasingly coming under attack. Yet, to date, the Supreme Court has not put these discriminatory practices in the same suspect category as racial discrimination.

5. We recognize two forms of due process protection for citizens: procedural due process, requiring fairness in enforcing laws, and substantive due process, requiring law itself to be reasonable.

6. In the criminal justice system citizens are not to be subject to unreasonable searches and seizures. Persons may not be arrested or detained without cause or knowledge of their rights. In short, government may not interfere with citizens' lives without justifiable reason.

7. The principal issue in the Eighth Amendment ban on cruel and unusual punishment has been the death penalty. The Court has said that the death penalty per se is not a form of cruel and unusual punishment.

Research Projects

1. *Equal employment opportunity*   Your college or university undoubtedly has a set of rules and procedures for Equal Employment Opportunity, and these are likely to be mandated by the federal government. Find out what these rules and procedures are and where they came from—that is, if they were locally developed or adopted from federal rules and regulations. Who monitors their implementation? You might wish to compare your findings with those of the Bureau of National Affairs, *The Equal Employment Act of 1972*, or the *Supervisors EEO Handbook* published by Executive Enterprise Publications.

2. *Capital punishment*   Write an essay on capital punishment, setting forth the arguments for and against capital punishment. Does your state use capital punishment? If it does, what procedures are followed in its implementation? How do local lawyers and prosecutors feel about the subject?

3. *Black civil rights*   Analyze the progress made by black Americans in the United States since 1960. Compare them with their white counterparts in the areas of income, education, employment, and housing. Much of these data can be found in the *Statistical Abstract* or *Social Indicators* published by the Bureau of the Census. A useful reference work is Levitan, Johnson, and Taggart, *Still a Dream* (Harvard University Press).

4. *Miranda rights*   After reviewing and listing the *Miranda* rights and noting how the courts have recently interpreted these rights, go to your local police department and interview some police officers on the effect of *Miranda* rights on the performance of their responsibilities. Be sure to explain to the police department what you are doing and why. Do you

sense any confusion or hostility on their part toward these rights or toward the courts?

5. *Sex discrimination*   Make a list of jobs in your school: librarian, custodian, secretary, computer programmer, and so on. Look up the sex and salary of persons in those positions to see whether people with comparable jobs receive equal pay. Note that length of service and merit evaluations can influence comparisons; but in a large enough organization with several employees, these should be fairly equal. Is there a pattern of men occupying higher paying positions? What is the sex of the supervisory personnel?

Notes

1. *Pace* v. *Alabama*, 106 U.S. 583 (1882).
2. Civil Rights Cases, 109 U.S. 3 (1883).
3. *Plessy* v. *Ferguson*, 163 U.S. 537 (1896).
4. *Cummings* v. *Board of Education*, 175 U.S. 528 (1899).
5. *Gong Lum* v. *Rice*, 275 U.S. 78 (1927).
6. *Brown* v. *Board of Education of Topeka, Kansas*, 347 U.S. 483 (1954).
7. *Brown* v. *Board of Education (Brown II)*, 349 U.S. 294 (1955).
8. *Griffin* v. *Prince Edward County Board of Education*, 377 U.S. 218 (1964).
9. *Green* v. *County School Board*, 391 U.S. 430 (1968).
10. *Bob Jones University* v. *U.S.; Goldsboro Christian Schools* v. *U.S.*, 461 U.S. 574 (1983).
11. *Allen* v. *Wright*, 468 U.S. 737 (1984).
12. *Swann* v. *Charlotte-Mecklenburg Board of Education*, 402 U.S. 1 (1971).
13. *Columbus Board of Education* v. *Penick*, 441 U.S. 903 (1979) and *Dayton Board of Education* v. *Brinkman*, 441 U.S. 903 (1979).
14. *Crawford* v. *Los Angeles Board of Education*, 458 U.S. 527 (1982).
15. *Washington* v. *Seattle School District #1*, 458 U.S. 457 (1982).
16. *City of Rome, Ga.* v. *United States*, 446 U.S. 156 (1980).
17. *Hathorn* v. *Lavorn*, 457 U.S. 255 (1982).
18. *Heart of Atlanta Motel* v. *United States*, 379 U.S. 421 (1964).
19. *Pullman–Standard* v. *Swint*, 456 U.S. 273 (1982).
20. *American Tobacco Company* v. *Patterson*, 456 U.S. 63 (1982).
21. *Texas Department of Community Affairs* v. *Burdine*, 450 U.S. 248 (1981).
22. *Connecticut* v. *Teal*, 457 U.S. 440 (1982).
23. *Firefighters Local Union No. 1784* v. *Stolts*, 467 U.S. 561 (1984).
24. *Wygant* v. *Jackson Board of Education*, ____ U.S. ____ (1986).
25. *Jones* v. *Alfred H. Mayer Co.*, 392 U.S. 409 (1968).
26. *Runyan* v. *McCrary*, 427 U.S. 160 (1976).
27. *Moose Lodge No. 107* v. *Irvis*, 407 U.S. 163 (1971).
28. *Batson* v. *Kentucky*, ____ U.S. ____ (1986).
29. *De Funis* v. *Odegaard*, 416 U.S. 312 (1974).
30. *University of California Regents* v. *Bakke*, 438 U.S. 265 (1978).
31. *Steelworkers and Kaiser Aluminum* v. *Weber*, 440 U.S. 954 (1979).
32. *Firefighters* v. *Cleveland*, ____ U.S. ____ (1986) and *Local 28* v. *Equal Employment Opportunity Commission*, ____ U.S. ____ (1986).
33. *Fullilove* v. *Klutznick*, 448 U.S. 448 (1980).
34. *Reed* v. *Reed*, 404 U.S. 71 (1971).
35. *Frontiero* v. *Richardson*, 411 U.S. 677 (1973).
36. *Michael M.* v. *Superior Court of Sonoma County*, 450 U.S. 464 (1981).
37. *Taylor* v. *Louisiana*, 419 U.S. 522 (1975); *Duren* v. *Missouri*, 439 U.S. 890 (1978).
38. *Weinberger* v. *Wiesenfeld*, 420 U.S. 636 (1975).
39. *Stanton* v. *Stanton*, 421 U.S. 7 (1975).
40. *Orr* v. *Orr*, 440 U.S. 268 (1979).
41. *Califano* v. *Westcott*, 440 U.S. 944 (1979).
42. *Craig* v. *Boren*, 429 U.S. 190 (1976).
43. *Kirchberg* v. *Feenstra*, 450 U.S. 455 (1981).
44. *Mississippi University for Women* v. *Hogan*, 458 U.S. 718 (1982).
45. *Roberts* v. *U.S. Jaycees*, 468 U.S. 609 (1984).
46. *Kahn* v. *Shevin*, 416 U.S. 190 (1976).
47. *Schlesinger* v. *Ballard*, 419 U.S. 498 (1975).
48. *Califano* v. *Webster*, 430 U.S. 313 (1977).
49. *Wengler* v. *Druggists Mutual Insurance Co.*, 446 U.S. 142 (1980).
50. *Rosteker* v. *Goldberg*, 453 U.S. 57 (1981).
51. *American Booksellers Association, Inc.* v. *Hudnut*, ____ U.S. ____ (1986).
52. *Cleveland Board of Education* v. *LaFleur*, 414 U.S. 639 (1974).
53. *Turner* v. *Department of Employment*, 423 U.S. 44 (1975).
54. *General Electric Co.* v. *Gilbert*, 429 U.S. 125 (1976).
55. *Cannon* v. *University of Chicago*, 441 U.S. 677 (1979).
56. *Grove City College* v. *Bell*, 465 U.S. 555 (1984).
57. *North Haven* v. *Bell*, 456 U.S. 512 (1982).
58. *Washington County, Oregon* v. *Gunther*, 452 U.S. 161 (1981).
59. *Pennhurst State School* v. *Halderman*, 451 U.S. 1 (1981).

60. *Youngberg* v. *Romeo*, 457 U.S. 307 (1982).
61. *City of Cleburne* v. *Cleburne Living Center*, ____ U.S. ____ (1985).
62. *Hendrick Hudson Board of Education* v. *Rowley*, 458 U.S. 176 (1982).
63. *Irving Independent School District* v. *Tatro*, 468 U.S. 883 (1984).
64. *Consolidated Rail Corporation* v. *Darrone*, 465 U.S. 624 (1984).
65. *Bowen* v. *American Hospital Association*, ____ U.S. ____ (1986).
66. *Plyler* v. *Doe*, 457 U.S. 202 (1982).
67. *INS* v. *Delgado*, 466 U.S. 210 (1984).
68. *Sure-Tan* v. *NLRB*, 467 U.S. 883 (1984).
69. *Toll* v. *Moreno*, 458 U.S. 1 (1982).
70. *Cabell* v. *Chavez-Salido*, 454 U.S. 432 (1982).
71. *Immigration and Naturalization Service* v. *Stevic*, 467 U.S. 407 (1984).
72. *Western Air Lines* v. *Criswell*, ____ U.S. ____ (1985).
73. *Zahn* v. *International Paper Co.*, 414 U.S. 291 (1973).
74. *Dunaway* v. *New York*, 442 U.S. 200 (1979).
75. *Hayes* v. *Florida*, ____ U.S. ____ (1985).
76. *Schmerber* v. *California*, 384 U.S. 757 (1966).
77. *Winston* v. *Lee*, ____ U.S. ____ (1985).
78. *Warden* v. *Hayden*, 387 U.S. 294 (1967).
79. *Illinois* v. *Gates*, 462 U.S. 213 (1983).
80. *Collidge* v. *New Hampshire*, 403 U.S. 443 (1971).
81. *New Jersey* v. *T.L.O.*, 469 U.S. 325 (1985).
82. *California* v. *Ciraolo*, ____ U.S. ____ (1986).
83. *United States* v. *Watson*, 423 U.S. 411 (1976).
84. *Marshall* v. *Barlow, Inc.*, 436 U.S. 307 (1978).
85. *Donovan* v. *Dewey*, 452 U.S. 594 (1981).
86. *Zurcher* v. *The Stanford Daily*, 436 U.S. 547 (1978).
87. *Steagald* v. *United States*, 451 U.S. 204 (1981).
88. *Payton* v. *New York*, 445 U.S. 573 (1980).
89. *California* v. *Carney*, ____ U.S. ____ (1985).
90. *New York* v. *Belton*, 453 U.S. 454 (1981).
91. *United States* v. *Ross*, 456 U.S. 798 (1982).
92. *U.S.* v. *Johns*, ____ U.S. ____ (1985).
93. *U.S.* v. *Knotts*, 460 U.S. 276 (1983).
94. *Delaware* v. *Prouse*, 440 U.S. 648 (1979).
95. *Brown* v. *Texas*, 440 U.S. 903 (1979).
96. *Ybarra* v. *Illinois*, 444 U.S. 85 (1979).
97. *Kolender* v. *Lawson*, 461 U.S. 352 (1983).
98. *U.S.* v. *Hensley*, 469 U.S. 221 (1985).
99. *U.S.* v. *Sharpe*, ____ U.S. ____ (1985).
100. *Michigan* v. *Summers*, 452 U.S. 692 (1981).
101. *Washington* v. *Chrisman*, 455 U.S. 1 (1982).
102. *Tennessee* v. *Garner*, ____ U.S. ____ (1985).
103. *Mapp* v. *Ohio*, 367 U.S. 643 (1961).
104. *Taylor* v. *Alabama*, 457 U.S. 687 (1982).
105. *United States* v. *Calandra*, 414 U.S. 338 (1974).
106. *Stone* v. *Powell*, 429 U.S. 874 (1976); and *Wolff* v. *Rice*, 429 U.S. 874 (1976).
107. *United States* v. *Havens*, 446 U.S. 620 (1980).
108. *United States* v. *Salvucci*, 448 U.S. 83 (1980).
109. *Nix* v. *Williams*, 467 U.S. 431 (1984).
110. *U.S.* v. *Leon*, 468 U.S. 897 (1984).
111. *Olmstead* v. *United States*, 277 U.S. 438 (1928).
112. *Katz* v. *United States*, 389 U.S. 347 (1967).
113. *United States* v. *United States District Court for the Eastern District of Michigan*, 407 U.S. 297 (1972).
114. *South Dakota* v. *Neville*, 459 U.S. 553 (1983).
115. *Allen* v. *Illinois*, ____ U.S. ____ (1986).
116. *Mallory* v. *United States*, 354 U.S. 449 (1957).
117. *Escobedo* v. *Illinois*, 378 U.S. 478 (1964).
118. *Miranda* v. *Arizona*, 384 U.S. 436 (1966).
119. *Michigan* v. *Jackson*, ____ U.S. ____ (1986).
120. *Berkemer* v. *McCarthy*, 468 U.S. 420 (1984).
121. *Harris* v. *New York*, 401 U.S. 222 (1971).
122. *Michigan* v. *Tucker*, 417 U.S. 433 (1974).
123. *Michigan* v. *Mosley*, 423 U.S. 96 (1975).
124. *North Carolina* v. *Butler*, 441 U.S. 369 (1979).
125. *Rhode Island* v. *Innis*, 446 U.S. 291 (1980).
126. *Oregon* v. *Elstad*, ____ U.S. ____ (1985).
127. *New York* v. *Quarles*, 467 U.S. 649 (1984).
128. *Moran* v. *Burbine*, ____ U.S. ____ (1986).
129. *Rhode Island* v. *Innis*, 446 U.S. 291 (1980).
130. *Maine* v. *Moulton*, ____ U.S. ____ (1985).
131. *Edwards* v. *Arizona*, 451 U.S. 477 (1981).
132. *Doyle* v. *Ohio* and *Wood* v. *Ohio*, 423 U.S. 823 (1975).
133. *Wainwright* v. *Greenfield*, ____ U.S. ____ (1986).
134. *Gideon* v. *Wainwright*, 372 U.S. 335 (1963).
135. *Argersinger* v. *Hamlin*, 407 U.S. 25 (1972).
136. *Scott* v. *Illinois*, 440 U.S. 367 (1979).
137. *Lassiter* v. *Social Services Department of Durham, North Carolina*, 452 U.S. 18 (1981).
138. *Morris* v. *Slappy*, 461 U.S. 1 (1983).
139. *Strickland* v. *Washington*, 466 U.S. 668 (1984).
140. *Nix* v. *Whiteside*, ____ U.S. ____ (1986).
141. *Moran* v. *Burbine*, ____ U.S. ____ (1986).
142. *Holloway* v. *Arkansas*, 435 U.S. 475 (1978).
143. *Bounds* v. *Smith*, 430 U.S. 817 (1977).
144. Rule 23(a), Federal Rules of Criminal Procedure; *Singer* v. *United States*, 380 U.S. 24 (1965).
145. *Williams* v. *Florida*, 399 U.S. 78 (1970).
146. *Ballew* v. *Georgia*, 435 U.S. 223 (1978).
147. *Colgrove* v. *Battin*, 413 U.S. 149 (1973).
148. *Apodaca* v. *Oregon*, 406 U.S. 404 (1972).
149. *Burch* v. *Louisiana*, 441 U.S. 130 (1979).
150. *Batson* v. *Kentucky*, ____ U.S. ____ (1986).
151. *Rummel* v. *Estelle*, 445 U.S. 263 (1980).
152. *Furman* v. *Georgia*, 408 U.S. 238 (1972).
153. *Gregg* v. *Georgia*, 428 U.S. 153 (1976), and four other cases.
154. *Coker* v. *Georgia*, 433 U.S. 584 (1977).
155. *Godfrey* v. *Georgia*, 446 U.S. 420 (1980).
156. *Beck* v. *Alabama*, 447 U.S. 625 (1980).
157. *Caldwell* v. *Mississippi*, ____ U.S. ____ (1985).
158. *Turner* v. *Murray*, ____ U.S. ____ (1986).
159. *Lockhart* v. *McCree*, ____ U.S. ____ (1986).
160. *Hopper* v. *Evans*, 456 U.S. 605 (1982).
161. *Bullington* v. *Missouri*, 451 U.S. 430 (1981).
162. *Spaziano* v. *Florida*, 468 U.S. 447 (1984).
163. *Enmund* v. *Florida*, 458 U.S. 782 (1982).
164. *Pulley* v. *Harris*, 465 U.S. 37 (1984).
165. *Eddings* v. *Oklahoma*, 455 U.S. 104 (1982).
166. This excerpt is adapted from "Criminal Justice and the Victim: An Introduction" by William McDonald and is reproduced from *Criminal Justice and the Victim* (*Sage Criminal Justice System Annuals* Volume 6), William McDonald, editor, copyright 1976, pp. 17–55, by permission of the publisher, Sage Publications, Inc. (Beverly Hills/London).

Bibliography

Berger, Raoul. *Death Penalties: The Supreme Court's Obstacle Course.* Cambridge, Mass.: Harvard University Press, 1982.

No friend of judicial activism, Berger examines the history and meaning of the Eighth Amendment's cruel and unusual punishment clause. He believes the judiciary should keep out of state efforts to legislate capital crimes.

Fellman, David. *The Defendants' Rights Today.* Madison, Wis.: University of Wisconsin Press, 1977.

A basic and extensive work that treats defendants' rights from beginning to end. Arrest, preliminary hearing, and basic trial rights are discussed in a fairly nontechnical manner. The procedures are clearly presented.

Franklin, John H. *From Slavery to Freedom.* New York: Alfred A. Knopf, 1974.

The standard work on the history of the black struggle in America. The volume provides excellent coverage of slavery and colonial life as well as Reconstruction and emergence into the twentieth century.

Freeman, Jo. *The Politics of Women's Liberation.* New York: David McKay, 1975.

A complete analysis of the women's liberation movement in terms of its political impact. Freeman provides history, contemporary activities, and policy impact of the women's movement.

Kluger, Richard. *Simple Justice.* New York: Vintage Books, 1976.

A fascinating and detailed study of the history of school desegregation and the *Brown* decision. For its length, the book is not overly technical or complicated; rather, it reviews the history and drama surrounding that historic case.

Lewis, Anthony. *Gideon's Trumpet.* New York: Random House, 1964.

The gripping story of Clarence Gideon and his efforts to be represented by counsel. Anthony Lewis is the Supreme Court reporter for the *New York Times* and wrote the absorbing account of the Supreme Court case that culminated in a landmark decision.

Sindler, Allan. *Bakke, De Funis, and Minority Admissions.* New York: Longman, 1978.

A discussion of recent court decisions on reverse discrimination and affirmative action. The volume offers considerable supplementary information surrounding the two cases.

Spurrier, Robert L. *To Preserve These Rights: Remedies for the Victims of Constitutional Deprivations.* Port Washington, N.Y.: Kennikat Press, 1977.

A fairly technical work, the book examines constitutional remedies for persons accused of crimes. Covered are such topics as the exclusionary rule, suits against arresting officers, and victim compensation.

Wilson, James Q. *Thinking About Crime.* New York: Basic Books, 1983.

A series of essays seeking to understand crime and the way society deals with crimes. Not content with the way criminologists and politicians have dealt with crime, Wilson offers some suggestions for improvement.

Wise, David. *The American Police State.* New York: Vintage Books, 1978.

A journalistic, well-documented account of how government agencies with police powers abuse their powers. Focuses on the activities of the FBI, CIA, and IRS.

ublic Opinion

Increasingly widespread dissatisfaction with politics has surfaced throughout the United States. Old patterns of opinions and consensus have deteriorated; new patterns of cynicism and distrust have created a disquieting environment. Political parties are weak and voter participation in elections is declining. The reputations of public institutions have dropped and then surged back upward again. Public concern centers on nothing less than the traditional assumptions of democratic politics. One contemporary student of public opinion has concluded, "Much that has been said in the recent past about stability, orderliness, legitimacy, efficaciousness, and widespread consensus in American political life has come to appear quite vulnerable."[1] The 1950s and 1960s produced some fundamental alterations in public opinion, and, according to Nie, Verba, and Petrocik, the last decades of the twentieth century will see politics quite unlike that of the previous generation:

In case of nuclear accident kiss your children good bye. no nukes

One way citizens can influence their government is by influencing public opinion.

In the 1950's the public was only mildly involved in politics, was relatively content with the political process, and had long-term commitments to one or the other of the major parties. Today it is more politically aroused, more detached from political parties than at any time in the past forty years, and deeply dissatisfied with the political process.[2]

The basic fabric of public opinion has changed. Professor Dawson cites three conditions in contemporary American political life that helped shape the current sense of political malaise.[3] First, the past few decades have witnessed a growing disquiet and sense of frustration. The coalitions of the New Deal and the Democratic and Republican parties have disintegrated; the Great Society represented a significant political and social departure from the goals of the New Deal, and the social and political coalitions it created now seek recognition and power. Second, the disquiet and disarray have altered the forms of political concerns: "There have been changes in the types of issues that are most salient to the public and in the socioeconomic conditions and groupings that structure political outlooks and consequently political conflict and consensus."[4] Third, these changes in issues and political outlook have made it difficult for political institutions and leaders to respond clearly and effectively to the people's strongest concerns.

The patterns of contemporary disarray are easily discernible. First, the period of the Great Society, democratic reform, and taxpayer revolution has seen the emergence and politicization of groups such as blacks, minorities, women, welfare recipients, blue-collar workers, and middle-income taxpayers. These groups have come to dominate the new issues, expressing frustration and disaffection with the political process. Second is the decline in Americans' attachment to their political process. Turnout in presidential elections has been declining steadily since 1960. The public opinion polls have also reported the decline in political party identification. Fewer and fewer people adhere to a partisan label, and among young voters independents outnumber partisan identifiers altogether. Congress and the presidency have labored to raise their reputations. The bureaucracy has borne the brunt of protest by taxpayers and become a symbol of waste and inefficiency. Courts and law enforcement officials have also suffered from the erosion of confidence. A third pattern of contemporary public opinion has been the shift in issue salience. The newer issues are not dividing the population into traditional patterns, nor are the newer patterns exhibiting the stability characteristic of the traditional issues. Owing to their salience, the issues of fiscal accountability, governmental responsibility, and abortion have produced new, increasingly politicized groups. For such groups, traditional issues of economic welfare, governmental intervention, and civil rights appear less important than in prior decades, and overall single-issue politics are coming to dominate the political scene.

What Is Public Opinion?

Public opinion is a rich mix of opinions from the diverse segments and political groups composing American society. There is the general, mass distribution of opinion, often broken down into special publics to identify patterns of conflict or consensus within the opinion expressed by the American people. Students of public opinion have also found it useful to separate out the opinions of political leaders and media representatives—that is, **elite opinion** (see Figure 6.1). The characteristics of elites, or opinion leaders, have particular relevance in shaping and protecting the opinions of the public. Finally, the impact of institutions on opinions must be examined. Opinions are formed and shaped under the influence of the family, the school, elections, interest groups, and governmental institutions. These institutions mediate between public opinion and elite opinion.

Elite Opinion: *the opinions of political leaders and media representatives.*

The Components

Public opinion is important in a democracy, for it forms the basis of political life. Yet we cannot assume that government can or even ought to discern public opinion, let alone act on the basis of it. Public opinion varies in stability and intensity, and not all opinions are relevant to politics. V. O. Key once defined public opinion as "those opinions held by private persons which governments find it prudent to heed." We are concerned here specifically with those opinions that relate to and affect the policies and practices of politics.

Public opinion is the assembling of individual attitudes, whether these attitudes are individually generated or formed as a result of interest-group or party affiliation. Individual attitudes on political matters differ in several important ways.

Salience: *the degree of importance an issue holds for a specific individual.*

Salience   People differ over which issues are important for politics—that is, which have **salience.** Salient issues are those issues that people feel are important to their lives. For the homeowner, the most press-

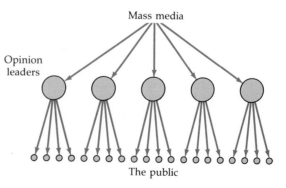

Figure 6.1 The two-step flow of communication and public opinion

ing political problem may be property-tax relief; the assembly-line auto worker might worry about unemployment and inflation. The more closely the issue is viewed as affecting the life of a citizen, the more salient the issue will be to that citizen.

Salience differs with individuals; it also changes with time. For a majority of Americans in the 1930s, employment, income, and economic security dominated politics. In the 1940s and 1950s, war and communist aggression were salient concerns. Social issues such as racial justice, poverty, and the Vietnam War moved to the fore in the 1960s. By 1980, Americans were again personally aroused over jobs, inflation, and income security as various forces worked to threaten their standard of living. In 1985 foreign policy reemerged with Reagan's bombing of Libya in response to a wave of terrorism. The fear of terrorism caused people to reassess administration policy as well as change personal plans for travel.

Stability: *the resistance to change in a political opinion.*

Stability   While some opinions change rapidly, others resist change and endure for long periods. Americans with consistent political values and a continuous interest in an issue maintain a stable pattern of opinions that does not change with time. People who remain in the same job, reside in the same locality, and associate with the same circle of friends have the most stable opinions. For a generation, partisan preference and group identification were stable opinions, and these were easily identifiable with job, income, and ethnic factors. We could reliably predict that groups of people would behave in consistent ways. Now these factors are changing. Democrats, for example, do not necessarily vote Democratic, nor do they always believe that more government is helpful.

Intensity: *the strength of the political opinions held by a given individual.*

Intensity   The most elusive aspect of public opinion is its **intensity.** People vary greatly in the strength of the opinions they hold. Some may mildly agree with a position—say, more stringent penalties for crimes— while others are violently opposed. Then, of course, there are those who have no opinion. It is not always easy to equate intensity with the general character of public opinion. Intensity can be short-lived or of long duration; people may hold intense feelings on particular concerns, or an individual may be just "letting off steam" through vehemence. Officials must be cautious in assessing the intensity of public opinion.

Consistency and Knowledge   Public opinion is often based on a minimum of knowledge. Students of public opinion prefer to distinguish mass public opinion from attentive or elite public opinion. Even with the increase in issue concern, many Americans regularly pay little or no attention to politics. Opinion formation is often personal and emotional, and unknowledgeable opinion holders can produce unstable and inconsistent public opinion: "The point here is that if a person lacks opinions on many issues, for whatever reason, then it will be impossible for him to demonstrate any consistent ideological pattern of thinking."[5] Free and Cantril, for example, distinguish between operational and ideological liberalism–conservatism.[6] **Operational liberals** are people who approve

Operational Liberals: *persons indicating approval for specific programs involving government policy and power, such as compulsory medical insurance and low-rent housing.*

George Gallup
The dean of American pollsters, George Gallup is the originator of the Gallup Poll. Since 1935 the American Institute of Public Opinion in Princeton, New Jersey, has been surveying public attitudes on political, social, and economic matters. The Gallup Poll is world famous, having caught public attention in 1936 with its accurate prediction of the presidential election using a survey of only 3,000 people. Since then the Gallup Poll has become an American institution with its accurate predictions of elections and popular attitudes.

Random Sample: *a method used in opinion polling in which people surveyed are selected completely by chance.*

Quota Sample: *a method used in opinion polling in which members of various groups are surveyed in proportion to their percentage in the population as a whole.*

of specific programs involving government policy and power (such as compulsory medical insurance or low-rent housing). Free and Cantril counted two-thirds of the public as operational liberals. On measures that separated people on an ideological scale from liberal to conservative, such as general attitude toward governmental power, local control, and individual initiative, 50 percent were opposed to government and national control—that is, they *thought* conservatively. According to the authors, "For a large proportion of the American people, there is clearly not only a separation of but a conflict between their attitudes toward practical governmental operations and programs, on the one hand, and their ideological ideas and abstract concepts about government and society, on the other."[7]

Measuring Public Opinion

There are several reasons why we measure public opinion. First, people are curious about how other Americans feel on issues of public concern. In newspapers and magazines and on television, journalists report public attitudes on everything from presidential popularity to the length of skirts and the price of hamburger. Second, market polls are used by industry and politicians to test attitudes toward products, including political candidates. Business will test market a product to assess public acceptance; political candidates test public response to campaign activity, including how and where to campaign. Third, scientific opinion polling provides information for political scientists and other scholars seeking to improve their understanding of public opinion. Results of scientific polling have yielded, for example, knowledge of the relationship between beliefs and partisanship.

Public opinion is measured by means of the survey method. We ask people to register their opinion or their preference. Can we get an accurate representation of American public opinion this way?

Accurate polling depends on two distinct factors: (1) the sample's ability to represent a more general population, and (2) the wording of questions. First, it is necessary to know that we have a representative sample. Pollsters cannot—nor do they need to—sample everyone. A representative sample can give a relatively accurate picture of the whole body (with usually 3 percent error either way). It is necessary, however, that the sample truly represent the population to be surveyed. A **random sample,** in which the people surveyed are selected completely at random, is best. In some cases, a **quota sample** is adequate. As long as the people surveyed fall within the percentage for age, sex, income, occupation, and so on, of the larger population, we can assume the sample is reasonable. Professional pollsters have developed their skill to the point where a few thousand, or even as few as 1,500 people, can give an accurate picture of public opinion.

Next, we know that the way we ask questions will, in large measure, determine the answers we get in return. It is difficult to write a question that does not affect the respondent's answer. The words must convey a clear meaning but without prejudicing the response. For example, in asking a question on abortion, use of the phrase *unborn child* implies that the fetus is a person and that abortion is murder. Also, if we ask people to agree or disagree with a statement, we are not necessarily giving the respondents a fair range in which to express an opinion. We can avoid limiting respondents' answers by using a multiple-choice form. If we ask open-ended questions (where the respondent supplies all information for the answer), we get an even better reflection of opinion but we will have difficulty summarizing and tabulating answers. Such questions also assume that the respondent has enough information or interest to be able to answer. Forced answers, however, give a false sense of knowledge and salience. In short, measurement of public opinion is a tricky business. The way in which people come to have political opinions, however, is now a fairly clear process.

Political Socialization

Political opinions are formed early in life, and much of what children learn about politics shapes their later attitudes. Political socialization is the process through which persons acquire political orientations and patterns of behavior.[8] Awareness begins in the preschool years, and a fairly concrete set of opinions and partisan preferences emerges in the primary school years. In other words, most of our political attitudes and behaviors are learned. The "agents" most responsible for transmitting political values and opinions are, by and large, the same agents responsible for nonpolitical socialization: family, school, peer groups, and the mass media.

The Learning of Political Orientations

The early awareness of politics is limited to vague symbols; apparently children view government as a person. Easton and Dennis report that in the early grades, students view the president as the government. Only gradually do the more differentiated symbols, such as Congress or voting, expand the meaning of government.[9] Yet even by the eighth grade the president remains a dominant, benevolent symbol, "the person who helps you and your family most."

The first attitude of a child toward politics is a positive sense of trust and support for the government. Reported Easton and Hess, "The sentiments of most children with respect to their political community are uniformly warm and positive throughout all grades, with scarcely a hint of criticism or rate of dissatisfaction."[10] This sense of trust and support remains with children throughout grade school, though it diminishes slightly with age. Easton and Dennis report finding 72 percent of fourth graders feeling that the president rarely or almost never errs; this response dipped to 51 percent for eighth graders.[11]

Party identification is an acquired belief, coming primarily from the parents. By age seven or eight, a majority of children identified with one or the other of the two major political parties. Reported Easton and Hess, "a strong majority in each grade from two (age 7–8) through eight (age 13–14) state that if they could vote they would align themselves with [one] of the two major parties in the United States."[12]

Partisan awareness begins in the early school years and closely follows the identifiable partisanship of the parents. By grade six, all but 4.5 percent of students in one study had some appreciation of the party labels Democrat or Republican, although the authors pointed out that these labels were vague and were really only words that students "rooted for." There is growing evidence now that the generation coming of age in the late 1960s and 1970s rejected parental partisanship in favor of political independence—a rise in independence unmatched in the parental generation.[13] The difference in party loyalty may be a generational effect. "It seems likely that this trend is still continuing, with the end of the 'independent generation' not yet in sight."[14]

Jennings and Niemi found evidence, in their study of generations, of the emergence of a generational shift when they compared high school senior classes of 1965 and 1973. The 1973 seniors were distinctly less strongly imbued with the traditional virtues associated with civic training. Politics was less important to their lives, and they exhibited greater skepticism and cynicism about people and societal institutions. "Not surprising, dirty politics was more salient in 1973—Watergate was taking its toll."[15] Yet in many ways the 1965 group of seniors was less typical than the 1973 group. They showed no continual movement away from parental views. To the extent that the 1965 seniors differed from their parents, that pattern was not as evident in the seniors a decade later. On many issues, the 1973 seniors were more like their parents than were the 1965 seniors. Jennings and Niemi concluded, "For the concerns that we have studied here, the tendency has been for parent and offspring generations to be drawn together, and on most political attributes for the 1973 seniors to shift in such a way as to reduce whatever parent-offspring differences had existed in the mid-1960s."[16]

Agents of Political Socialization

The Family   The family is the most pervasive socializing agent, and it shapes the child's political orientation in fundamental ways. We have already noted that party labels are largely inherited. Jennings and Niemi reported in 1974 the overwhelming adoption of partisanship from the family among high school seniors; only 20 percent differed in party identification from their parents (see Table 6.1). Even more striking was the finding that, as adults, two-thirds of those surveyed continued to identify with the political party they inherited from their parents. Only 10 percent had changed parties; the remainder called themselves independents.

TABLE 6.1 Parent and child agreement in party identification

Students	Parents			
	Democratic	*Independent*	*Republican*	
Democrat	66%	29%	13%	(43%)
Independent	27	54	36	(36)
Republican	7	17	51	(21)
Marginals[a]	(49)	(24)	(27)	100

[a]The marginal totals present the proportion of parents and students that hold a particular party prefer-ence. For example, looking at the column marginals we can see that 49 percent of the parents are Demo-crats. Looking at the row marginals we can see that 43 percent of the students in the sample are Democrats. SOURCE: Adapted from M. Kent Jennings and Richard G. Niemi, *The Political Character of Adolescence: The Influence of Families and Schools* (Copyright © 1974 by Princeton University Press): Table 2.2, p. 41. Re-printed by permission of Princeton University Press.

The transmission of party identification from parent to child has thus been quite strong. But what happens in an age of changing political ori-entation? Do younger generations continue to mirror parental opinions and partisanship? In a remarkable study of two generations of individ-uals over a seventeen-year period, M. Kent Jennings and Gregory B. Markus chronicle the declining commitment to political parties among the younger generation.[17]

Using the data in Table 6.2, Jennings and Markus note that the genera-tion that started their political careers in 1965 "began their adult political lives strikingly less committed to political parties than were their par-ents, and they have remained less committed for nearly two decades.[18] The parents' generation remained quite stable in their political orienta-tions with a fairly high level of partisanship. The children's generation also exhibited some stability, though less than their parents', and at a consistently lower level of partisanship. In addition, the children's parti-sanship did not crystallize until they were in their late twenties.

> Based on our preliminary analysis, it appears that the period between the mid-twenties and mid-thirties witnesses a surge in the crystalliza-tion of a variety of sociopolitical attitudes, not simply partisan ones.[19]

With a generation of growing independents, one must wonder about the future socialization of partisanship and the fate of political parties in the years to come.

The transmission of political values other than party identification from parent to child was far weaker. Only meager parental influence was found in the comparison of political attitudes of parents and children on policy issues, political activity, and political cynicism.[20] Children were quite likely to be in disagreement with their parents on issues of govern-mental activity, voting, political efficacy, and feelings about groups in society. The reasons for this differ considerably from generation to generation. Jennings and Niemi found that the frequency of political communications within a family affects parent–child agreement. This fac-tor in turn is affected by the degree of consistency on issue orientation

TABLE 6.2   Party identification at three points in time

	Parents			Offspring		
	1965	*1973*	*1982*	*1965*	*1973*	*1982*
Strong Dem.	26%	18%	20%	19%	9%	8%
Weak Dem.	24	27	24	24	25	24
Independent	24	26	28	36	48	43
Weak GOP	13	17	15	13	12	17
Strong GOP	12	12	14	8	6	7

SOURCE: M. Kent Jennings and Gregory B. Markus, "Partisan Orientations over the 'Long Haul'," *American Political Science Review* 78 (December 1984): 1003.

among the parents. Apparently adolescent rebellion is not a cause of political disagreement. Lane and Sears concluded,

> Rebellion against parental beliefs does not play a large role in determining the political opinions of American voters. . . . The rebelling adolescent is much more likely to rebel in terms which are more important to his parents, such as in his dress, his driving, his drinking, his obedience to the law, his sexual behavior and so forth. Only in rather rare instances does it have political effects as well.[21]

The School   Education plays a significant role in the political socialization of children. In school, children learn the values of the political system: they memorize the pledge of allegiance, sing patriotic songs, and learn about great leaders, notably such presidents as George Washington, Abraham Lincoln, and John Kennedy. In later grades, they receive formal instruction in civic education and democracy. The classroom teacher creates a political environment that students learn from or accept. Teachers report giving considerable attention to citizenship duties in the classroom. In fact, the teacher is a most salient agent in the socialization of the school child. Hess and Torney, for example, reported finding an increasing compatibility of beliefs between students and teachers[22] as students progressed from second to eighth grade.

School, then, is an important socializing agent. It transmits information on substantive issues to the child and teaches the duties and responsibilities of citizenship. School is not responsible for the affective domain of trust and loyalty, nor for partisanship. In fact, there is no reliable trend toward any party with increased education.[23] But teachers do have an appreciable effect on the political beliefs of their students. Students expect to be taught in school, so there is fairly high receptivity to messages; however, civics courses—the courses specifically designed to instruct students in politics and democracy—have only a marginal impact on political attitudes. Langton and Jennings found the number of civics courses taken to be almost unrelated to attitudes, political knowledge, sense of efficacy, or levels of toleration. The only major exception was among black students,[24] for whom there was a significant increase in political knowledge, efficacy, and tolerance after taking civics courses. For blacks, civic

Children reciting the pledge of allegiance demonstrate how well schools instill political values.

education presents new material, but for white students, civic education is redundant.[25]

The Peer Group   We have long known that groups with which we identify influence our thinking. Therefore, it is not surprising that children are influenced by their peers, although the extent of the influence is difficult to sort out. Children are politicized when friends of the same age talk about politics. In the school years it is difficult to disentangle the effects of family, school, and peer-group influences because these are mutually reinforcing sources. What peer groups seem to do is reinforce already formulated political attitudes.

Friendship has been found to be a major component in peer-group political socialization. Substantial political agreement occurred between people designated as best friends, particularly among girls, indicating that girls are more sensitive than boys to the views of those around them.[26] With age and a career, some stability and homogeneity in the social environment result. Social class, work associates, and ethnicity affect political attitudes. Some time ago, Berelson, Lazarsfeld, and McPhee found that relationships with those who held similar political beliefs increased with age.[27]

Jennings and Niemi found that older adults do change their attitudes in response to their political and social environments. While young adults change more frequently than older persons and the likelihood of change grows smaller as one gets older, older adults do change their views. "But just as major political events occurring prior to the advent of maturity can deflect a new generation from the paths set down by the previous one, events can shake up existing generations including the older members of those generations."[28]

The Mass Media We have come to accept the ability of the media to sell commercial products and shape the taste, preferences, and life-styles of Americans, so it is not surprising that the mass media shape political opinions as well. The impact of the media on children is uncertain. The child is clearly exposed to politics through the media, and television is the primary source of this exposure. For younger children, television dominates; as the child grows older, newspapers come to be an increasingly important source of information. Among the poor, television remains the dominant medium. Table 6.3 shows the sources of most of our news.

TABLE 6.3 The public's view of television and newspapers, 1959-1980

Question: First, I'd like to ask you where you usually get most of your news about what's going on in the world today—from the newspapers or radio or television or magazines or talking to people or where?

Source of most news:	1959	1961	1963	1964	1967	1968	1971	1972	1974	1976	1978	1980
Television	51%	52%	55%	58%	64%	59%	60%	64%	65%	64%	67%	64%
Newspapers	57	57	53	56	55	49	48	50	47	49	49	44
Radio	34	34	29	26	28	25	23	21	21	19	20	18
Magazines	8	9	6	8	7	7	5	6	4	7	5	5
People	4	5	4	5	4	5	4	4	4	5	5	4
Don't know/ no answer	1	3	3	3	2	3	1	1	—	—	—	—

Question: If you got conflicting or different reports of the same news story from radio, television, the magazines, and the newspapers, which of the four versions would you be most inclined to believe—the one on radio or television or magazines or newspapers?

Most believable:	1959	1961	1963	1964	1967	1968	1971	1972	1974	1976	1978	1980
Television	29%	37%	36%	41%	41%	44%	49%	48%	51%	51%	47%	51%
Newspapers	32	24	24	23	24	21	20	21	20	22	23	22
Radio	12	12	12	8	7	8	10	8	8	7	9	8
Magazines	10	10	10	10	8	11	9	10	8	9	9	9
Don't know/ no answer	17	17	18	18	20	16	12	13	13	11	12	10

SOURCE: Adapted from *Public Opinion Magazine* (August/September 1979): 31–32. 1980 data from Gallup Poll.

It is difficult to document direct media influence on political attitudes, although recent studies are finding the mass media to be a principal source of political information for young children. N. Hollander labeled the media "the new parent" in recognition of the role they play in transmitting political learning to the child. Children report the media as being influential: S. H. Chaffee and associates reported that students rate the media as the most important source of opinion influence, over parents, teachers, and friends.[29]

The Patterns of Public Opinion

Conflict and Consensus

Most political commentators have viewed the past two decades as a period of change. Whether one uses the label *revolution* or *crisis,* the changes in economic life, race relations, foreign affairs, and family life have been pronounced. Government has had difficulty adjusting and responding to new attitudes and changing demands.

Patterns of conflict and consensus are important if a government is to represent a people. The distribution of opinion helps government decide whether it should or should not act and if so, in what way (see Figure 6.2). The long-term stability of opinions in an area lends legitimacy to governmental policy. It also affords policymakers a fair measure of predictability in contemplating policy changes. By 1968, however, those traditional patterns were breaking down. And as yet, a new stability has not formed.

Domestic Welfare and Economic Issues Domestic welfare and economic issues have long been central in politics. Since the Depression and the New Deal, government has been deeply involved in domestic welfare and economic policies, and this involvement has been the source of an enduring and stable conflict. Democrats, labor, minorities, and low-

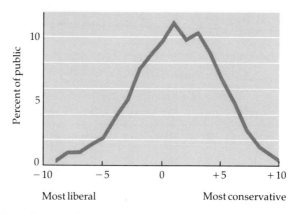

Figure 6.2   Distribution of public opinion over 10 issues, 1976

income groups have supported government involvement in general, and welfare and economic regulation specifically. Republicans, business, and the higher income groups have generally been opposed.

The New Deal coalition is crumbling, however; there is an increasing fragmentation of the American public over domestic welfare and economic issues. Note Harry Holloway and John George: "The original coalition was thought to draw potentially from six somewhat overlapping groups: the poor, blacks, the unions, Catholics and Jews, the white South, and the central cities. . . . But by the late 1960s neither the poor nor the South were firm elements of the coalition. . . . By 1976 other changes were evident. Blacks and labor supported Carter, but the Carter coalition differed in its appeal to Protestants, to the suburbs, to rural areas, and to a biracial South."[30]

The fragmentation of domestic issues results from the intrusion of new people and new issues into politics. We have already noted the changing population patterns and the shifting coalition base for the political parties. The result may be nothing short of a generational realignment of the American public.[31] The new social issues divide America and do it in ways that cross the older, established economic and class divisions.

The election of Ronald Reagan and his early success in Congress signaled a growing conservative trend in domestic welfare and economic assistance issues. Reagan has been successful in cutting social welfare and entitlement programs, and indicators on social welfare questions of public opinion have suggested approval for this position. On three issues—government guarantees of employment, government provision of national health care insurance, and the power of the federal government generally—the proportion of the population giving liberal responses has declined. In 1964 nearly 40 percent gave liberal responses to these issues; in 1976 the figure was 20 percent,[32] and by 1984 liberal support had slipped to near 15 percent. But it is important to note that this conservative trend does not support repeal of social welfare programs or the undoing of New Deal or Great Society legislation. "Rather, it suggests opposition to further government growth, experimentation, and intervention in the social welfare policy area."[33]

New social issues have emerged that divide the American public. These social issues have to do with abortions, marijuana, aliens, and divorce. We see from the sampling of opinion in Table 6.4 that public intolerance regarding these issues has grown. While there has been some conservative movement on the issues over the past two decades, these topics continue to be the source of bitter disagreement among large numbers of Americans.

Foreign Affairs   Traditionally foreign policy, war, and the threat of communism have been major focuses of concern for Americans. All during the Cold War years of the Eisenhower administration and into the early 1960s, foreign affairs was *the* dominant concern. With the end of the post-World War II world, however, the domestic emphasis of

TABLE 6.4   Opinion distribution on social issues

		Liberal	*Conservative*
Divorce:	Do you think divorce should be more difficult or easier to obtain than it is now? (National Opinion Research Center, 1982)	Easier, 46%	More difficult, 54%
Marijuana:	I favor legalizing the possession of small amounts of marijuana for personal use. (Gallup, 1985)	Favor, 30%	Do not favor, 70%
Homosexuality:	Do you think homosexual relations between consenting adults should or should not be legal? (Gallup, 1985)	Should, 44%	Should not, 47%
Abortion:	A woman should be able to get an abortion if she decides she wants one. (ABC/*Wash. Post,* 1984)	Agree, 62%	Disagree, 38%
Illegal aliens:	I favor a law making it illegal to hire an immigrant who has come to the U.S. without proper papers. (Gallup, 1982)	Do not favor, 35%	Favor, 65%
Drug testing:	Would you tell me whether periodic drug testing should or should not be done for all current employees by their companies? (Roper, 1985)	Should, 46%	Should not, 49%
Handguns:	Do you favor or oppose the registration of all handguns? (Gallup, 1985)	Favor, 70%	Oppose, 25%

Lyndon Johnson, and subsequent economic and inflationary problems in the 1970s, the public's concern for foreign affairs as a pressing problem dropped from a high of 63 percent in 1962 to 10 percent in 1973.

Left: President Reagan explains the American raid on Libya; *right:* Tripoli after the attack.

From World War II through the 1960s, Americans readily accepted active involvement with other parts of the world. Three-fourths of the American people viewed favorably our direct concern with foreign affairs. From 1956 through the late 1960s, support for foreign affairs consistently increased. Vietnam changed that consensus. Between the beginning of our active involvement in Vietnam and the negotiated withdrawal of American troops in 1973, public opinion made a complete change.

The 1980s again bring foreign affairs into focus for the American people. The Panama Canal Treaty was attacked as an "American giveaway." SALT II has increased worry over military strength and preparedness vis-à-vis the Soviet Union. The Soviet invasion of Afghanistan in 1979 raised questions about our ability to contain the Russians and protect our interests around the globe. The extended crisis in Iran, where fifty Americans were held hostage in the U.S. Embassy, further prompted Americans to reemphasize foreign policy and military affairs.

President Reagan has made foreign policy a central issue of public opinion. His call for a 50 percent increase in defense spending, his push for new weapons systems—the B-1 bomber and the MX missile—and his invasion of Grenada and bombing of Libyan terrorist camps have renewed concern for defense and foreign policy. There was early support for President Reagan's call for increased defense spending. Two-thirds of the people said the United States needed to increase expenditures for defense or else fall behind the Soviets, and 52 percent said they trusted

President Reagan inspired public controversy in 1985 when he visited Bitburg, West Germany, where 49 Nazi soldiers are buried.

TABLE 6.5   Responding to the threat of terrorism

	Approve	Disapprove
Meet the demands of terrorists for money or the release of other terrorists from jail in order to save lives.	15%	77%
Put more money and effort into gathering intelligence information.	69	21
Put more money and effort into strengthening security measures at our embassies and overseas military headquarters.	74	17
Strike back with American military forces against terrorists who have attacked U.S. facilities, even though some innocent people might be killed.	38	47
Attack known forces first if we think they are planning to attack us, even though innocent people might be killed.	24	63

SOURCE: Roper Organization, January 1986.

Ronald Reagan to make the right kind of decisions about controlling nuclear weapons. In Reagan's second term, the people believe that his objective for defense spending has been achieved and express their support and confidence in his handling of relations with the Soviets. A majority of Americans say defense spending should be kept at its present level; only 17 percent want it increased and 26 percent want it reduced. On Reagan's ability to handle relations with the Soviets, his standing with the public in his second term rose steadily from 50 percent on the eve of reelection to 64 percent support in 1986.

But on issues involving the Middle East and Central America, President Reagan is on shakier ground with the American public. Feelings about his actions in the Middle East have been fairly evenly split, while his Central American policy of aiding the anti-Sandinista rebels in Nicaragua found favor with only a quarter of the people. Many Americans expressed their concern that the U.S. would be drawn into war in Nicaragua. The American people want no more Vietnams.

Reagan's standing with the public was seriously eroded in late 1986 by revelations of a secret arms deal with Iran, and of the funneling of profits from that deal to Contra rebels in Nicaragua. With the news of the arms sale itself and of the president's failure to inform Congress and high-level public officials about it, Reagan's public approval rating was cut in half.

Terrorism provides another perplexing problem for both the Reagan administration and the American people. Many Americans think the U.S. must take some action, but they are divided on what that action should be. Forty percent of Americans, in a 1986 CBS poll, said U.S. military action against suspected terrorists would help reduce terrorism, while forty-nine percent thought military action would only make things worse. As Table 6.5 indicates, the American people do want action taken on terrorism but they do not share President Reagan's commitment to strike back militarily.

Reverend Jesse Jackson's Rainbow Coalition united diverse groups in support of his 1984 presidential bid.

Civil Rights Concern for race relations has been an enduring issue since the late 1950s. After two decades of protests, demonstrations, and legal battles, the issue of black America remains unsettled in the minds of many Americans. There are conflicts over the rights of blacks and other minorities, including the role of government in supporting those rights, and there are deep cleavages within racial groups.

Over the years, public support for government intervention in the racial integration of jobs, schools, and public accommodations has been divided. The percentage supporting government activity is more than a majority, and the proportions have varied very little over the years. Yet many Americans refuse to embrace desegregation openly as a position. The most common response is something in between. Many Americans also apparently feel that civil rights leaders are pushing too fast for change, while only a handful, principally blacks, think the process of change has been too slow. Two newer areas of conflict to emerge over civil rights are busing and affirmative action plans. There is widespread disagreement over the desirability of both. A 1979 poll showed that 80 percent of the American people opposed busing children across town for interracial education, and 75 percent of whites thought that blacks were "entitled to no special consideration and must make it strictly on merit."

Democratic Values

It may be recalled that democracy is based on some fundamental principles. In particular we spoke of individual freedom, equality of opportunity, majority rule, and open political participation. Can we assume that Americans believe in and support these values?

Studies conducted over the years reveal a strikingly consistent pattern: on the level of abstract generality, the American people are united and supportive of basic American values; on the level of application of those principles to specific situations, they are far less supportive and are di-

Fact File
What the American Public Is Worried About

	The economy	Foreign affairs	(Vietnam)[a]	Social problems	Government malperformance	Energy	Others	Don't know
Oct.–Nov. 1967	16	50	(50)	21	—	—	—	13[b]
May 1968	12	42	(42)	43	—	—	9	3
June–July 1968	12	52	(52)	44	—	—	6	1
Aug. 1968	10	51	(51)	41	—	—	12	2
Jan. 1969	12	40	(40)	40	—	—	16	2
May 1970	10	36	(22)	56	—	—	16	2
Feb. 1971	29	40	(28)	28	—	—	15	2
June 1971	27	40	(33)	37	—	—	14	1
Nov. 1971	41	23	(15)	28	—	—	19	4
April 1972	30	41	(29)	29	2	—	12	2
June 1972	30	40	(32)	17	1	—	13	3
July 1972	28	30	(25)	28	2	—	16	2
Sept. 1972	30	37	(27)	23	3	—	13	3
Feb. 1973	39	10	(3)	32	3	—	20	9
May 1973	48	9	(3)	26	14	2	8	3
Sept. 1973	69	7	(1)	16	14	3	11	3
Jan. 1974	30	6	—	7	22	46	7	3
May–June 1974	48	6	—	11	26	6	19	4
Oct. 1974	82	—	—	3	11	3	15	2
Feb.–Mar. 1975	80	5	—	15	7	7	18	3
July 1975	72	—	—	10	12	5	20	2
Jan. 1976	70	5	—	12	4	3	25	3
April 1976	62	5	—	18	17	2	25	3
Oct. 1976	78	6	—	9	10	1	23	4
July 1977	51	10	—	14	6	15	17	8
Oct. 1977	61	7	—	13	5	18	14	3
Feb. 1978	57	9	—	9	5	23	11	4
Feb. 1979	66	18	—	6	3	14	8	3
May 1979	62	5	—	6	3	33	8	2
Oct. 1981	75[c]	4	—	8	4	2	15	2
Jan. 1982	84	5	—	9	3	2	5	2
Aug. 1982	64	10	—	7	2	—	16	2
July 1983	69	17	—	6	2	—	6	3
Oct. 1983	57	23	—	10	2	—	7	4
Feb. 1984	44	23	—	11	2	—	11	4
Sept. 1984	38	60	—	11	3	—	22	—

[a]Vietnam percentages are included in the foreign affairs total.
[b]Others and don't know are combined in 1967.
[c]Combines inflation and unemployment.
SOURCE: Adapted from Gallup Polls.

vided in their support. James Protho and Charles Grigg found in 1960 that Americans could agree on and support such statements as "Every citizen should have an equal chance to influence government policy," and "People in the minority should be free to try to win majority support for their opinions." When these same citizens were asked how they felt regarding statements applying the principles to concrete situations, however, the agreement quickly melted away. There was very little support for the statements on application. On ten statements concerning items such as barring blacks from office, allowing only taxpayers to vote, permitting antireligious speeches, or allowing communist speeches only three of the statements generated agreement among 75 percent or more of those polled. The percentage was somewhat higher for people with more education, but even here half the questions left the educated in disagreement.[34]

TABLE 6.6   Democracy's "rules of the game"[a]

Items	Political influentials (N = 3,020)	General electorate (N = 1,484)
	% Agree	
There are times when it almost seems better for the people to take the law into their own hands rather than wait for the machinery of government to act.	13.3	26.9
The majority has the right to abolish minorities if it wants to.	6.8	28.4
We might as well make up our minds that in order to make the world better a lot of innocent people will have to suffer.	27.2	41.6
If congressional committees stuck strictly to the rules and gave every witness his rights, they would never succeed in exposing the many dangerous subversives they have turned up.	24.7	47.4
I don't mind a politician's methods if he manages to get the right things done.	25.6	42.4
Almost any unfairness or brutality may have to be justified when some great purpose is being carried out.	13.3	32.8
Politicians have to cut a few corners if they are going to get anywhere.	29.4	43.2
People ought to be allowed to vote even if they can't do so intelligently.	65.6	47.6
To bring about great changes for the benefit of mankind often requires cruelty and even ruthlessness.	19.4	31.3
Very few politicians have clean records, so why get excited about the mudslinging that sometimes goes on?	14.8	38.1
It is all right to get around the law if you don't actually break it.	21.2	30.2
The true American way of life is disappearing so fast that we may have to use force to save it.	12.8	34.6

[a]Since respondents were forced to make a choice on each item, the number of omitted "don't know" responses was, on the average, fewer than one percent, and thus has little influence on the direction or magnitude of the results reported.

SOURCE: Herbert McClosky, "Consensus and Ideology in American Politics," *The American Political Science Review* 58 (June 1964).

Herbert McClosky found much the same results in his 1964 study. McClosky sampled the general electorate as well as a group of delegates to the national party nominating conventions; the latter he labeled *influentials*. He asked both groups—electorate and influentials—a series of questions on the democratic "rules of the game" and social and political equality (see Table 6.6). On the rules of the game, McClosky found that the general public could not reach consensus (75 percent or more in agreement) on any of the questions asked. When the same questions were put to the influentials, consensus was achieved on eight of the twelve

TABLE 6.7   Application of democracy to social, political, and economic equality

Items	Political influentials (N = 3,020)	General electorate (N = 1,484)
	% Agree	
Political equality		
The main trouble with democracy is that most people don't really know what's best for them.	40.8	58.0
Few people really know what is in their own best interest in the long run.	42.6	61.1
"Issues" and "arguments" are beyond the understanding of most voters.	37.5	62.3
Most people don't have enough sense to pick their own leaders wisely.	28.0	47.8
It will always be necessary to have a few strong, able people actually running everything.	42.5	56.2
Social and ethnic equality		
We have to teach children that all men are created equal but almost everyone knows that some are better than others.	54.7	58.3
Just as is true of fine race horses, some breeds of people are just naturally better than others.	46.0	46.3
Regardless of what some people say, there are certain races in the world that just won't mix with Americans.	37.2	50.4
When it comes to the things that count most, all races are certainly not equal.	45.3	49.0
The trouble with letting certain minority groups into a nice neighborhood is that they gradually give it their own atmosphere.	49.8	57.7
Economic equality		
Labor does not get its fair share of what it produces.	20.8	44.8
Every person should have a good house, even if the government has to build it for him.	14.9	28.2
I think the government should give a person work if he can't find another job.	23.5	47.3
The government ought to make sure that everyone has a good standard of living.	34.4	55.9
There will always be poverty, so people might as well get used to the idea.	40.4	59.4

SOURCE: Herbert McClosky, "Consensus and Ideology in American Politics," *The American Political Science Review* 58 (June 1964).

questions. For the values of democracy, McClosky asked a series of questions in which matters of social, political, and economic equality were raised in specific situations. The pattern of responses was similar (see Table 6.7). The general public could achieve consensus (75 percent agreement) in none of the areas; the rate for the influentials was not much better. The latter achieved consensus on only a few questions, though they did score closer to the needed 75 percent on many more questions than the electorate. McClosky concluded,

> American politics is widely thought to be innocent of ideology, but this opinion more appropriately described the electorate than the politically active minority. . . . The evidence suggests that it is the articulate classes rather than the public who serve as the major repositories of the public conscience and as the carriers of the Creed. Responsibility for keeping the system going, hence, falls most heavily upon them.[35]

Group Differences and Public Opinion

The consequences and impact of public opinion can be readily and meaningfully assessed when we understand the groupings that differentiate it. At the outset we said that public opinion was a rich mix created by the diversified groups composing society. In fact, one may argue that there is no public opinion, only the opinions of many subpublics. In other words, we break down public opinions into categories, or groupings, that we think are politically relevant. The usual divisions are formed from social class, income, age, race, religion, and sex. Using these, social scientists can look for clusters within mass public opinions that command a consensus in a specific group or segment. The focus on group differences is helpful in understanding conflict and consensus within American society, and particularly in understanding changing opinions as new issues and new people come to the fore.

The traditional stability of opinion groupings is changing. New polarities by race, age, and education are emerging. This is true for party support and for a number of other issues as well. We will briefly examine four groupings that have relevance for the 1980s: (1) the persistence of ethnic or racial divisions; (2) the decline of class and economic differences; (3) the growth of a generation gap caused by differences of age and education; and (4) the reemergence of religious differences.

Racial Differences

As noted earlier, America came out of the 1970s more polarized along racial lines than at the start of the decade. Racial divisions persist. Concludes Alan Monroe, "For whatever reason, the difference between black and white opinions on issues is the greatest of any social cleavage. This cleavage in opinion is reinforced by several factors. Individuals are aware of being black or white and, what may be important, they know that others are aware."[36]

The depth of racial divisions is evidenced in opinions on political issues. The differences are even more pronounced when the issues are pointed toward race. Erickson, Luttbeg, and Tedin report finding different attitudes on desegregation. Data gathered by the Survey Research Center at the University of Michigan in 1976 showed black and white responses to be markedly different when respondents were asked whether they favored desegregation, strict segregation, or something in between. Three out of four blacks favored desegregation as compared with two out of five white respondents; 50 percent of the whites favored something in between compared with only one-quarter of the blacks. Furthermore, blacks were far less convinced that desegregation has moved along fast enough (45 percent said not fast enough), while whites thought desegregation was proceeding at about the right pace or too fast (44 percent said too fast).[37] On the more volatile issue of busing, blacks are likely to approve (67 percent in a 1980 Gallup Poll), while whites equally strongly disapprove (82 percent).

Ethnic differences persist on all issues. Blacks are more likely to take liberal positions on issues of public policy, such as spending, guaranteed annual income, and government medical care.[38] Electorally, blacks remain firm in their support for the Democratic party. Their support for Lyndon Johnson and then Hubert Humphrey in 1968 was overwhelming. By 1972 whites were fleeing the Democratic party; blacks remained solid. The 1976 election saw blacks less enthusiastic but nonetheless voting Democratic, while whites were evenly divided. And in the 1980s the racial split again approached 1972 proportions. Blacks overwhelmingly supported the Democratic candidates—nearly nine of ten blacks so voted—while only one-third of white voters cast a ballot for Jimmy Carter in 1980 and Walter Mondale in 1984.

Class and Economic Differences

With the acceptance of the policies of the New Deal, economic and class differences have declined. In economic terms, most Americans see themselves as middle class. As incomes have increased, the traditional disputes over wages and tax policies have diminished. The welfare-state notion no longer evokes strong protest. This is not to say that economic issues and unemployment are not concerns for Americans. In 1979, 75 percent of Americans rated inflation and economic health as the most serious problems facing America. The point is that differences of opinion are not following economic or class lines.

On noneconomic social issues, class or social status is affected by other factors, such as education and race. We find, for example, less tolerance for civil rights and rights of the accused among lower-income groups. But whether this is a function of class status or low education is unclear, since most lower-income people have lower education levels. Lower socioeco-

Isolationism: *a theory of foreign policy that opposes international alliances, foreign aid, or trade with communist nations.*

Working-Class Authoritarianism: *a willingness to accept authority and follow it, even if it violates individual rights.*

nomic groups also take a more **isolationist** view of foreign policy, opposing foreign aid or trade with communist nations. These opinions are commonly cited to prove the existence of a **working-class authoritarianism.** The problem is that a similar attitude is not in evidence on social welfare issues or even in a careful analysis of foreign policy issues. State Erickson, Luttbeg, and Tedin, "The accumulation of survey evidence indicates that economic status has virtually no impact on the aggressiveness of one's foreign policy stance."[39]

In short, class divisions seem to be declining. Postwar affluence has eroded the meaningful distinctions based on class status, and there is a consensus on governmental and social goals. What conflicts do occur are largely the result of ethnicity, age, or other factors. The distinctions of class remain, but the impact is limited.

Education and Age Differences

Education is a relevant variable for public opinion, but as educational levels increase throughout the nation, the differences diminish. Recent events have also blurred educational distinctions. Traditionally, college-

TABLE 6.8   Age and opinions on selected political issues

Opinion[a]	Percent holding such opinions		Difference
	Under 30 years old	Over 50 years old	
I oppose stricter community standards regarding sale of sexually explicit materials. (Gallup, 1977)	67	32	−35
I favor legalizing the possession of small amounts of marijuana for personal use. (Gallup, 1982)	48	15	−33
The TV/media reflect permissive, immoral values which are bad for the country. (Yankelovich, 1981)	50	74	−24
Homosexual relations should be legal between consenting adults. (Gallup, 1982)	56	33	−23
I am in favor of prayer in public schools. (Gallup, 1984)	60	76	−16
I favor busing children to achieve racial balance in the public schools. (Gallup, 1982)	37	23	−14
The AIDS epidemic has changed my opinion of homosexuals for the worse. (Gallup, 1985)	34	47	−13
I favor a ban on federal financing of abortions. (Gallup, 1982)	39	47	−8
I favor a freeze on the production of nuclear weapons whether or not the Soviet Union agrees to do the same. (Gallup, 1982)	52	45	−7
I support maintaining cost-of-living increases for social security benefits. (Gallup, 1984)	88	90	−2

[a]For Gallup data, percentages may be in error by about one percent, since they were recalculated from original tables in which nonopinion holders were included in the percentage base.

educated persons have been more tolerant and supportive of dissent. Yet support for Nixon and criticism of the Watergate investigation were highest among the better educated. Education makes some difference in opinions, but we are cautioned by students of public opinion to "put aside stereotypes of the less educated as authoritarians ranked against the enlightened college-educated elites."[40]

Age appears to be a salient variable for opinion differences. It is readily apparent from Table 6.8 that a generation gap does in fact exist. On all ten items, young people take the more liberal position; on seven of the ten the differences are dramatic. Particularly on marijuana and obscenity, young adults take a strikingly more permissive position. Politically, the differences by age are most evident in the refusal of young voters to accept partisan labels. In 1976, half the voters under age twenty-five called themselves independents. If this trend continues or accelerates in the 1980s, the generational impact could cause a partisan realignment or a serious undermining of political parties altogether.

Religious Differences

Religion has been an historic factor in differences of opinion. Yet in the 1960s religious differences did not widen or become significant political divisions for the American people. Religious differences in political party support were evident then and remain today, but on a whole range of social issues—capital punishment, Vietnam amnesty, defense spending, and busing—religious differences were not significant.

By 1976, however, a "religious renewal" had surfaced. Jimmy Carter, a so-called born-again Christian, was elected president, religious groups and cults spread across college campuses and the nation, and new social issues divided opinions along religious lines.

Fundamentalist religious movements have become intensely political. In 1980 the Moral Majority was formed to back conservative Christian candidates for public office—including presidential winner Ronald Reagan. In 1986 the Moral Majority combined with several other fundamentalist religious groups and renamed itself the Liberty Federation. The group is predominately Protestant, white, and middle class, an outgrowth of video evangelist Jerry Falwell's following.

In 1981 video preacher Pat Robertson created the Freedom Council in order to get "moral citizens deeply involved in the political process." The Freedom Council has sought to elect GOP convention delegates to aid Robertson in his presidential drive in 1988.

Several additional Christian groups formed Christian Political Action Committees (PACs) to influence elections. Such groups no longer shun preaching politics from the pulpit, establishing voter registration desks in backs of churches, or creating "Christian hit lists." These largely evangelical Christian groups actively campaigned and contributed money for or against candidates they targeted on moral and religious grounds.

The efforts of the Moral Majority and the Christian right met with considerable success in 1980. Together they raised more than $1 million

Ah, there you are, my lovely!

© *Dennis Renault*, Sacramento Bee, *Cal./ROTHCO*

in campaign funds, and many of the candidates on their "hit lists" were defeated at the polls. With this success, and its support of Ronald Reagan, the religious right sensed that America was ready for its political agenda. Conservatives in Congress, led by Senator Jesse Helms (R–N.C.), introduced a series of bills that embodied the bulk of their social program. They called for a balanced-budget amendment to the Constitution, the restoration of prayer in schools, the prohibition of forced busing to achieve racial integration, a pro-life amendment denying women access to abortions, and the elimination of sex education from school curricula. But their immediate success was short-lived. In 1982 only one candidate targeted for defeat lost his bid for reelection, and few Americans—only 6 percent of the public—reported strong support for the Christian right's political agenda. In 1984 the results were no more heartening. While the Christian groups continue to raise substantial dollars, engage in mailing and publicity, and boost large memberships, they have been unable to repeat their successes of 1980.

The Media and Public Opinion

The impact of the mass media on public opinion appears immense. More than 60 million newspapers are sold daily; nearly 10,000 weekly, semi-monthly, and monthly periodicals are published; and 95 percent of American homes contain at least one television set. The mass media reach a wide audience, as shown in Figure 6.3, and yet social scientists remain uncertain of the role the media actually play in shaping public opinion.

By persuading their vast audience that certain issues are of primary importance, the media set the agenda for significant political activity.

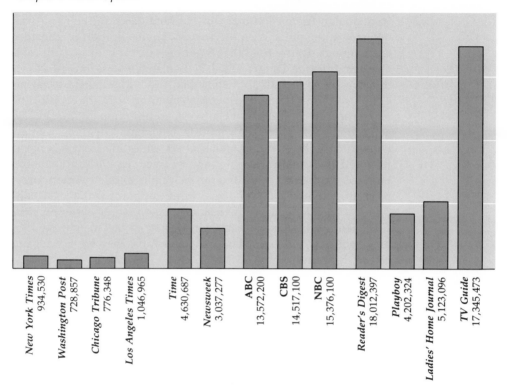

Figure 6.3   Audience reached by selected media.

Nearly two-thirds of Americans report television as the prime source of most of their information, followed by newspapers (44 percent) and radio (18 percent). Television remains the most believable of the news media, with 51 percent of respondents citing television as most believable in 1980 to 22 percent for newspapers. Less educated and lower-social-status individuals tend to rely on television exclusively; with more education, there is a tendency to use multiple sources of information. Those who read newspapers with strong reputations were found to be more politically informed than readers of less notable newspapers.[41]

Agenda Setting: *the identification of important issues. The media perform what is called the agenda-setting function.*

Agenda Setting   There is little question that the media influence the public on the question of which issues are important. In fact, the media perform what is called the **agenda-setting function,** telling people which issues and activities are important and deserve to be considered by the public. Further, evidence shows that the more exposure people have to issues in the media, the more they regard those issues as important. Television is particularly adept in performing this function. It has two unique advantages. First, it can reach millions of people instantaneously and simultaneously with the same message. Second, visual images are more powerful than the printed word. Such was surely the case with the

Public Opinion and Agenda Setting for Policy

We are constantly reminded that public opinion forms the boundaries for a democratic government. Individuals and groups make demands, and these demands help shape the policy agenda for democratic government. We recognize that much public opinion is uninformed and disorganized. Many of the policy decisions made, as V. O. Key said, are where "extremely small proportions of the general public have any awareness of the particular issue, much less any understanding of the consequences of the decision."* Policymakers must be keenly aware of the volatility of public opinion. In measuring the impact of public opinion on public policy, two features must be considered: the type of policy agenda involved and the character of public opinion.

1. Roger Cobb and Charles Elder have identified two types of policy agenda:
   a. *Systematic agenda*—all issues commonly perceived by members of the political community as meriting public attention.
   b. *Governmental agenda*—those problems to which public officials give serious and active attention.**
2. In characterizing the public, the main question is how issues are raised from the systematic agenda to the governmental agenda. A characterization follows:
   a. *Mass public*—80% of the people possess only rudimentary political information and interest. While they may vote, they remain passive observers of politics.
   b. *Attentive public*—15% of the people regularly concern themselves with political issues and communicate those ideas among persons with whom they are associated.
   c. *Mobilized public*—5% of the people concern themselves with political issues and seek to mobilize support on behalf of those issues by first-hand contact with public officials.†

It is to the attentive, and more specifically to the mobilized, public that the agenda-setting function of public opinion falls. "For all practical purposes the attentive public is the public between elections."‡ While we cannot suggest that governmental agendas are determined by attentive publics (a great deal of public policy proceeds independently of public opinion or what the public may be mobilized to do), the attentive and mobilized publics do make important contributions to the policy process. James Rosenau suggests three policy roles that the attentive public could perform as a form of citizenship between elections:

1. *As an unorganized audience* As a sounding board for policy debate, leaders carry on discussion and argumentation leading to policy choice. The attentive public provides the boundaries for choices.
2. *As organized groups* The attentive public may build support or criticism for public policy by pressing their attitudes and demands upon governmental officials. This reinforces or diminishes the preference for policy positions by policymakers.
3. *As surrogate electorate* Because they are an audience for policy issues and because they press their demands before government, the attentive public provides evidence of what may happen at the next election. This links public opinion and the attentive public to the mass public. They expose public officials to currents of thought and provide them a measure of their political vulnerability.§

*V. O. Key, *Public Opinion and American Democracy* (New York: Alfred A. Knopf, 1961), p. 14.

**Roger W. Cobb and Charles D. Elder, *Participation in American Politics: The Dynamics of Agenda-Building* (Boston: Allyn and Bacon, 1972), p. 85.

†James N. Rosenau, *Citizenship Between Elections* (New York: Free Press, 1974), p. 106.

‡Rosenau, p. 4.

§Rosenau, pp. 6–16.

Walter Cronkite
Longtime anchor of the CBS Evening News, Walter Cronkite became the most watched newsperson in America. Cronkite worked as a war correspondent for UPI during WW II. Soon thereafter he went to work for CBS, becoming anchorman for the 1952 political conventions. Subsequently, he became anchor for the CBS Evening News and then managing editor. During the Watergate affair, the Nixon administration blamed CBS News for turning a small burglary into a scandalous TV story. The results of a poll in 1973, the year the Watergate affair became public, found Cronkite the "most trusted man in America." He retired from CBS in 1981.

Gatekeepers: *media personnel who make the decisions on what information is used as news in the media.*

Iranian hostage crisis. Printed descriptions of blindfolded and bound Americans and the burning of the American flag couldn't approximate the impact of moving images transmitted almost simultaneously with the events themselves.

Most Americans readily accept the media's agenda of importance. Most citizens scan the front page of the newspaper, expecting to find the most important stories headlined, and they watch daily newscasts on television, waiting to hear and see the major developments of the day. Doris Graber reports evidence of the agenda-setting influence of the media. In one study, several thousand persons reported quite similar judgments about the importance of current events. The list of issues mentioned corresponded to cues in their news sources.[42] The evidence is that the presentation and focus on events in the media control the political agenda and establish the issues people perceive as important.

Deciding the News   The motto of the *New York Times* is "All the news that's fit to print." Cynics like to turn the motto around to read "All the news that fits, they print." What is unmistakably clear is that far more news is generated in the world daily than any media source can use. Thus, those controlling the media must make choices as to which stories to use and how to use them. People who make decisions about what the media use as news are called **gatekeepers.** They decide whether camera pictures of violent demonstrations should be used in place of pictures of the bargaining going on across a table. For instance, during the Iranian hostage crisis, scenes of wild demonstrations by Iranian students shouting anti-American slogans were featured on television and in newspapers. The emphasis was on the students and the chaotic situation. Only later was time given to the Iranian government's grievances against the shah and against American interests in Iran.

How is the decision made to choose a news story? We must not forget that the media are private corporations concerned with profit and advertising and competing with each other for viewers and subscribers. Yet the news people take seriously their role in protecting the public interests and its right to know. The two concerns must be balanced. Doris Graber finds that there are five criteria used in choosing news stories, all relating to audience appeal. To be newsworthy, stories must (1) have a *high impact* on readers or listeners; (2) have an element of natural or manmade *violence, conflict, disaster,* or *scandal;* (3) have an element of *familiarity* of situations or well-known people; (4) be events that occur *close to home;* and, finally, (5) the news should be *timely* and *novel.*[43] Herbert Gans, in his book *Deciding What's News,* found that 70–85 percent of the stories about people in the news featured well-known persons, most specifically presidents, presidential candidates, federal officials, and well-known violators of the law. As to activities in the news, Gans found that stories most frequently concerned government conflicts, government decisions and ceremonies, government personnel changes, protests, crimes and scandals, and disasters.[44]

The worry is that publishers focus on the sensational, to the detriment of more sober, informational stories. They become more concerned with attracting readers and viewers than with news content, and they sacrifice real news gathering for cheap stories that pander to their audience. Rupert Murdoch is the most notorious example. The Australian-born publisher, owner of some 80 newspapers and magazines, took the staid British *Times* of London and turned it into a sensationalist paper with screaming headlines and rank gossip. Murdoch also has built a media empire in the United States. He bought several floundering newspapers and magazines, including the *New York Post, Chicago Sun-Times, Boston Globe,* and the *Village Voice.* Concern heightened when Murdoch followed his London example in New York by making the *Post* a steamy tabloid replete with banner headlines crying out "Youth Gulps Gas, Explodes," "The Sheiks Hit the Fan," and "Headless Body in Topless Bar."

Murdoch is a no-nonsense, aggressive businessman known for turning declining papers around to show a profit. What concerns some journalists is his use of cheap sensationalism to increase profits. To Murdoch's credit, however, his purchase of the Boston and Chicago papers has not produced more *National Enquirer*-type newspapers. In 1985 Murdoch concluded a deal to purchase seven Metromedia television stations in major markets around the country. To conclude the deal, however, Murdoch had to sell some of his newspapers; the FCC prohibits majority ownership of newspapers and broadcast stations in the same city. There is little doubt that Rupert Murdoch is a media force to be reckoned with, leaving a good deal of traditional journalism foundering in his wake.

But if the media can set the agenda for a nation, can they direct public opinion? Here the evidence is far less clear. There has been a high correlation between newspaper endorsement and electoral success, particularly where there was a long ballot and voter information was low.[45] Yet Thomas Patterson and Robert McClure's *The Unseeing Eye* found little evidence of the public being taken in by television ads. Viewers were not "duped" by political ads; if anything, they became more knowledgeable: "To put it bluntly, spot political commercials educate rather than hoodwink the voters."[46] Michael Robinson's study of military news reporting put the impact negatively: broadcast reports give rise to cynical and negative attitudes toward the issue. There was growth in negative feelings toward the political system, an attitude Robinson labeled **video-malaise.**[47]

Video-Malaise: *a term used by Michael Robinson to describe the growth in negative feelings toward the political system that is attributed to media reporting.*

Over the years, many charges of biased reporting have surfaced. In the 1950s, Senator Joseph McCarthy (R-Wis.) labeled Edward R. Murrow and CBS News as part of the "jackal pack" of communist sympathizers. In 1984 Senator Jesse Helms and his Fairness in Media organization attempted to buy up shares of CBS in order to correct what he perceived to be the network's liberal bias. Do the media, in fact, have a liberal bias, and does such a bias influence the audience?

A 1984 survey by the *Los Angeles Times* of 2,700 news and editorial staff members from some 600 newspapers around the country did find a liberal bent among journalists. "A majority of the journalists, compared with less than a quarter of the public, call themselves liberals. While the public in our sample includes slightly more conservatives than liberals, among newspaper journalists, liberals outnumber conservatives by over three to one."[48] But if the journalists were liberal, the public surveyed did not strongly detect such a bias in the daily newspapers. Barely half said they could identify their paper as liberal or conservative, and they were evenly divided: 25 percent called their paper liberal and 24 percent called it conservative. Almost all readers, 96 percent, said their own newspapers were doing a very good or fairly good job. There was no popular perception of a leftist bias in the press.

> In terms of either general political orientation or specific issues, there is no evidence that people perceive the newspapers they read as biased strongly to the left. On issues like support for President Reagan, school prayer, and the death penalty, those with an opinion see their newspapers as sharing the public's (more conservative) views, not the prevailing liberalism of the reporters and editors.[49]

Michael Robinson's study of television network coverage of the 1984 election found no evidence of liberal bias. Democrats did receive slightly more air time (26,000 seconds for Mondale/Ferraro to 25,000 seconds for Reagan/Bush), but a search of news stories found practically no issue bias whatsoever.[50] Of the 826 news pieces Robinson studied, only 21 suggested a point of view. Eleven of the stories implied a liberal point of view; ten carried a conservative slant. This hardly constituted a liberal bias. "More important, the majority of those twenty-one pieces that showed bias were *commentaries*, the appropriate place for policy opinion. In the end, none of the networks displayed much ideology, and CBS News was as innocent as the rest."[51]

In fact, what takes place is a good deal of selective perception. People focus on issues that are salient to them, and issues that appear to affect them personally are most likely to be salient issues. They also apply **selective perception** in registering the content of the news. People focus on issues and facts that support their own concerns and biases. The "facts" are screened and combined by the individual according to his or her attitudes and opinions. We select the points that support our positions. The difference between what is presented and what is heard can be startling.

Selective Perception: *the tendency of individuals to screen the contents of the news by focusing on only those issues and facts that support their own concerns and biases.*

Yet the impact of the various media cannot be ignored; they have the power to change opinion and change it dramatically. Television particularly has an immediacy and directness the print media cannot match. This same advantage, however, provides ample opportunity for misuse. The dramatization of events may make them appear more critical than they are. Events or comments can be selected out of context and convey inaccurate impressions. Such was the case at the 1980 Republican national convention when, pressed for news, the networks centered on Reagan's discussions with Gerald Ford about the vice-presidency. It was the respected CBS anchor Walter Cronkite who coined the phrase "co-presidency" to characterize the discussions, a term used by neither Ford nor Reagan.

Bandwagon Effect: *the tendency of people to vote for the apparent winning candidate. The reporting of election results from the East before polls close in the West is believed by some to influence voters to vote for the candidate reported to be winning in the East. This is a controversial practice.*

Studies indicate that television does not appear to create a **bandwagon effect**—that is, reporting an election result from the East before the polls have closed in the West does not change results in the West. William Glaser's study of television's impact on voter turnout concluded that people who rely on television for campaign information are no more likely to vote than any other citizens.[52] The major influence of television has been a change in the way we conduct campaigns. It has removed campaigning from the party professionals and party activists. Candidates now rely on the media rather than on the party to reach more people, and to reach them more quickly and more dramatically. Media managers create an image, market a candidate, and use media campaigns based on market research to maximize votes in much the same manner that Ford spurs sales of its automobiles.

Public Trust

Ultimately, the test of public opinion can be measured by the confidence people express in their political system. In a democracy, where consent of the people is vital, the erosion of confidence is of serious concern. Some suggest that the loss of confidence impairs effectiveness, gives rise to instability, and even threatens the survival of democratic government. Whether we go this far or not, public confidence does indicate public satisfaction with government.

During the 1970s and the early 1980s, manifestations of distrust and cynicism reached epidemic proportions (Table 6.9). Trust and responsiveness indicators declined sharply; more than half of all Americans expressed distrust and cynicism toward national institutions. The erosion of confidence affected the president, Congress, and the courts, but was not limited to politics: all major institutions suffered. With the Reagan years, trust and confidence have begun to reappear, most dramatically with the

TABLE 6.9   Levels of public trust and confidence in institutions

	1973	1974	1976	1978	1980	1982	1984
Television news	41%	31%	28%	35%	31%	25%	29%
Medicine	57	50	42	42	34	32	43
Military	40	33	23	29	28	31	45
Press	30	25	20	23	19	14	18
Organized religion	36	32	24	34	22	20	24
Major companies	29	21	16	22	16	18	19
Congress	29	18	9	10	18	13	28
Executive branch	19	28	11	14	17	20	42
Organized labor	20	18	10	15	—	8	12
Average	33	28	20	25	—	21	31

SOURCE: *Public Opinion* (October–November 1979). Published bimonthly by the American Enterprise Institute for Public Policy Research. 1980s data from Gallup Polls.

Practicing Politics: Joining a Local Community or Block Association

$\mathscr{M}$any people prefer to participate in politics at the local level and devote their time and energy to solving community problems. There are thousands of local organizations all over the country. Here are some ways to go about locating and joining those in your area:

1. Check bulletin boards at local shops and supermarkets; specialty bookstores in particular often serve as information clearinghouses for a local area.
2. Talk to friends, neighbors, and local community leaders.
3. Check your local library: it may have a community bulletin board, and librarians often know about local groups. The *Encyclopedia of Associations*, a standard reference work in most libraries, contains profile listings of organizations and projects, including when the group was founded, size of membership, staff, activities, and publications. Regional and local directories may also be available; ask the reference librarian.

Once you have located the organization(s) that seems to suit your needs and talents, find out all you can about it. Go to the office or to a meeting and volunteer to help. If you have an idea for a project that is not on the group's agenda, offer to carry it out if the group approves.

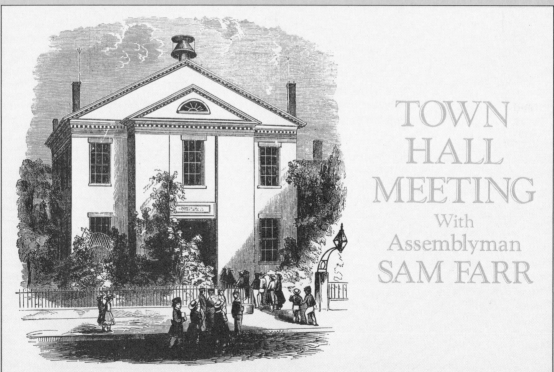

America's first form of democratic government was located in the town hall, which continues to draw citizens. Most people make contact with their government on a local level.

executive branch. And just as all institutions suffered during the decline, so now all institutions appear to be part of the recovery. We see growing faith in the military, medicine, organized labor, and the press.

It would appear that trust and confidence change cyclically. As a period of malaise sets in, as with Watergate and the presidency, its cynicism sweeps over all major institutions. But as the presidency bounces back, so too a mood of forgiveness arises for all sectors of society. Let us hope that Jack Citrin's analysis is correct: "Political systems, like baseball teams, have slumps and winning streaks. Having recently endured a succession of losing seasons, Americans boo the home team when it takes the field. But fans are often fickle; victories quickly elicit cheers. And to most fans what matters is whether the home team wins or loses, not how it plays the game."[53]

Summary

1. Much of what we know about public opinion is changing. Old patterns of opinion and consensus are deteriorating. New people and new issues are producing new patterns of political conflict.

2. Political socialization explains much of what people believe about politics by examining how they acquire their political attitudes. By adolescence a child has a well-developed set of political attitudes. The commingled influences of family, peers, education, and media produce a political picture that remains fairly stable throughout adult life.

3. Traditional social and economic conflicts, which divided Americans for two generations, are being resolved today. The expanded role for government policy has won approval from most Americans. Newer social issues such as abortion, gay rights, and pornography have surfaced to divide the people.

4. We can have little confidence that the American people are united in their support of democratic values. On abstract generalities the people are supportive, but on the application of values to particular settings and people, there is little commitment to democracy. This is one reason we differentiate between elite and mass opinion.

5. Public opinion groupings dramatize the social cleavages in America. Race continues to be a persistent and deep division, while social class has diminished in importance. Newer cleavages by education and age are growing in importance. These trends are likely to continue in the coming years.

6. The media exert a persuasive influence on Americans. The source of most political information, the media—particularly television—set the agenda for important political issues. Instantaneous technology has the capacity to inform and educate; when abused, it also has the ability to cause irreparable harm.

Research Projects

1. *Political socialization*   Has the process of socialization into politics for you and your friends been similar to that described in the text? Ask yourself and five to ten of your friends some questions and compare the answers with the results from the studies on political socialization.

- What is your party affiliation?
- What are your father's and mother's party affiliations?
- What is your degree of interest in politics?
- How often did your parents talk about politics with you?
- What political events stand out in your mind? How do you feel about those events?
- How do your parents feel about those events?
- Can you describe the party identification and attitude toward politics of three close friends? Are they similar to yours?

2. *Public opinion poll*   Conduct your own public opinion poll. You could poll a class you are taking, the neighborhood where you or your parents live, or, if the school has a little money, you could mail a questionnaire to city residents by randomly selecting them from the telephone book. Ask those you question to agree or disagree with statements on relevant contemporary issues—for example:

- We should use force, if necessary, to achieve the release of political hostages.
- All women should be permitted to have abortions if they so desire.
- The government has become too large and wasteful to be effective.
- Blacks and minorities should be given preference for employment and admission to colleges and universities.
- No one has the right to advocate the violent overthrow of the American government.

You will need to examine the results by social–economic characteristics, so include a couple of questions on age, sex, and race of respondent. Carefully examine the results. Do they differ from those of other studies? How? Was your sample scientifically drawn? How could your sampling technique account for the differences?

3. *Trends in public opinion*   The Gallup Poll puts out the monthly *Gallup Opinion Index;* there are also volumes of Gallup Polls, *The Gallup Poll, 1935–1971, The Gallup Poll, 1972–1977,* and yearly volumes thereafter. Trace the changes in opinion on major issues over time. Many of the polls break down answers by social–economic characteristics. Note how the responses differ by age, income, race, and sex. Select one or two issues to trace over the years; select a more recent issue and analyze the results. What are the demographic patterns? What is the conclusion on stability and change toward issues by the American public?

4. *The media*   Do the media set the agenda of issues for the American public? Compare and analyze national circulation newspapers—the *New*

York Times and *Washington Post*—a national network TV newscast, and a state or local newspaper. What stories are covered? Are the stories the same? Are lead TV stories matched by front-page stories in the papers? What priorities can you discern in each source? How much overlap between media sources is there?

Notes

1. Richard E. Dawson, *Public Opinion and Contemporary Disarray* (New York: Harper & Row, 1973), p. 1.
2. Norman Nie, Sidney Verba, and John Petrocik, *The Changing American Voter* (Cambridge, Mass.: Harvard University Press, 1976), p. 1.
3. Dawson, *Public Opinion and Contemporary Disarray*, p. 3.
4. Ibid.
5. Alan D. Monroe, *Public Opinion in America* (New York: Dodd, Mead & Co., 1975), p. 162.
6. Lloyd Free and Hadley Cantril, *The Political Beliefs of Americans* (New York: Simon and Schuster, 1968).
7. Ibid., p. 46.
8. David Easton and Jack Dennis, *Children in the Political System* (New York: McGraw-Hill, 1969), p. 7.
9. Easton and Dennis, *Children in the Political System*, p. 116.
10. David Easton and Robert D. Hess, "The Child's Political World," *Midwest Journal of Political Science* 6 (1962): 236–237.
11. Easton and Dennis, *Children in the Political System*, pp. 179–181.
12. Easton and Hess, "The Child's Political World," p. 245.
13. M. Kent Jennings and Richard G. Niemi, *Generations and Politics* (Princeton, N.J.: Princeton University Press, 1981), p. 205.
14. Ibid., p. 207.
15. Ibid., p. 226.
16. Ibid., p. 229.
17. M. Kent Jennings and Gregory B. Markus, "Partisan Orientations over the Long Haul: Results from the Three-wave Political Socialization Panel Study," *American Political Science Review* 78 (December 1984): 1000.
18. Ibid., p. 1015.
19. Ibid., p. 1016.
20. M. Kent Jennings and Richard G. Niemi, "Transmission of Political Values From Parent to Child," *American Political Science Review* 62 (March 1968): 177–179.
21. Robert Lane and David Sears, *Public Opinion* (Englewood Cliffs, N.J.: Prentice-Hall, 1964), p. 25.
22. Hess and Torney, *The Development of Political Attitudes in Children*, pp. 200–202.
23. Eleanor E. Maccoby, Richard E. Mathews, and Anton S. Morton, "Youth and Political Change," *Public Opinion Quarterly* 18 (1954): 37.
24. Kenneth P. Langton and M. Kent Jennings, "Political Socialization and the High School Civics Curriculum in the United States," *American Political Science Review* 62 (September 1968): 852–877.
25. Ibid.
26. S. K. Sebert, M. K. Jennings, and R. Niemi, "The Political Texture of Peer Groups," in M. K. Jennings and R. Niemi, *The Political Character of Adolescence* (Princeton, N.J.: Princeton University Press, 1974).
27. Bernard R. Berelson, Paul F. Lazarsfeld, and William N. McPhee, *Voting* (Chicago: University of Chicago Press, 1954), p. 97.
28. Jennings and Niemi, *Generations and Politics*, p. 389.
29. S. H. Chaffee, L. S. Ward, and L. P. Tipton, "Mass Communication and Political Socialization," *Journalism Quarterly* 47 (1970): 647–659.
30. Harry Holloway and John George, *Public Opinion* (New York: St. Martin's Press, 1979), pp. 25–26.
31. Nie, Verba, and Petrocik, *The Changing American Voter*, especially Chapter 5.
32. David H. Everson, *Public Opinion and Interest Groups in American Politics* (New York: Franklin Watts, 1982), p. 125.
33. Ibid.
34. James Protho and Charles Grigg, "Fundamental Principles of Democracy: Basis of Agreement and Disagreement," *Journal of Politics* 22 (1960): 282.
35. Herbert McClosky, "Consensus and Ideology in American Politics," *The American Political Science Review* 58 (June 1964): 369.
36. Monroe, *Public Opinion in America*, p. 93.
37. R. Erickson, N. Luttbeg, and K. Tedin, *American Public Opinion*, 2nd ed. (New York: Wiley, 1980), pp. 168–169.
38. Ibid., p. 169.
39. Ibid., p. 162.
40. Holloway and George, *Public Opinion*, p. 106.
41. Erickson, Luttbeg, and Tedin, *American Public Opinion*, p. 134.
42. Doris A. Graber, *Mass Media and American Politics*, 2nd ed. (Washington, D.C.: Congressional Quarterly Press, 1984), pp. 133–134.
43. Ibid., pp. 63–65.
44. Herbert J. Gans, *Deciding What's News* (New York: Pantheon Books, 1979), pp. 8–18.
45. John E. Mueller, "Choosing Among 133 Candidates," *Public Opinion Quarterly* 34 (Fall 1970): 395–402; Michael Hooper, "Party and Newspaper Endorsement as Predictors of Voter Choice," *Journalism Quarterly* 43 (Summer 1969): 302–305.
46. Thomas Patterson and Robert McClure, *The Unseeing Eye* (New York: Putnam's, 1976), p. 23.
47. Michael J. Robinson, "Public Affairs Broadcasting and the Growth of Political Malaise: The Case of the Sell-

ing of the Pentagon," *The American Political Science Review* 70 (June 1976).

48. William Schneider and I. A. Lewis, "Views on the News," *Public Opinion* (August/September 1985): 6.
49. Ibid., p. 8.
50. Michael J. Robinson, "The Media in Campaign '84: Wingless, Toothless, and Hopeless," *Public Opinion* (February/March 1985): 44–45.
51. Ibid., p. 45.
52. William A. Glaser, "Television and Voting Turnout," *Public Opinion Quarterly* 29 (Spring 1965): 71–86.
53. Jack Citrin, "The Political Relevance of Trust in Government," *The American Political Science Review* 68 (September 1974): 987.

Bibliography

Dawson, Richard, Prewitt, Kenneth, and Dawson, Karen. *Political Socialization.* Boston: Little, Brown, 1977.
An excellent summary of the findings on political socialization. Contains a discussion of the process of political socialization, integrating the results of studies of that process.

Erickson, Robert, Luttbeg, Norman, and Tedin, Kent. *American Public Opinion.* New York: Wiley, 1980.
The most complete and up to date study of public opinion. There are several good chapters covering public opinion and ideology, democracy, differences, elections, parties, and pressure groups.

Free, Lloyd, and Cantril, Hadley. *The Political Beliefs of Americans.* New York: Simon and Schuster, 1968.
A basic work that looks at the beliefs of Americans along liberal–conservative dimensions. Free and Cantril provide a good insight into the value process of forming and expressing opinion.

Gans, Herbert J. *Deciding What's News.* New York: Pantheon Books, 1979.
A study of news gathering and news gatherers. Gans examines two nightly television news programs and two weekly news magazines, analyzes the coverage of news, and discusses how news is put together by journalists.

Graber, Doris A. *Mass Media and American Politics.* Washington, D.C.: Congressional Quarterly Press, 1984.
The best available general discussion of the role of the media in American politics. Graber covers all the basic topics and summarizes findings on the media.

Holloway, Harry, and George, John. *Public Opinion.* New York: St. Martin's Press, 1985.
An excellent text on public opinion that examines coalitions of opinions and their impact on elites in society. There is extensive coverage of the opinion grouping of mass opinion.

Jennings, M. Kent, and Niemi, Richard. *The Political Character of Adolescence: The Influence of Families and Schools.* Princeton, N.J.: Princeton University Press, 1974.
A basic work on political socialization that underscores the importance of family and schools as agents of socialization. Explains the process of socialization, what family values students bring with them to school, and how school alters those beliefs.

Jennings, M. Kent, and Niemi, Richard. *Generations and Politics.* Princeton, N.J.: Princeton University Press, 1981.
A recent study on political socialization. This study focuses on young adults and their parents; what makes it appealing is that the authors were able to restudy the groups eight years later.

Patterson, Thomas, and McClure, Robert. *The Unseeing Eye.* New York: Putnam's, 1976.
Suggests that television may not be an all-powerful generator of public opinion. Patterson and McClure seek to assess the impact of television on public opinion, notably regarding candidates and election issues. They find the impact less than overwhelming.

Shaw, Donald, and McCombs, Maxwell. *The Emergence of American Political Issues: The Agenda Setting Function of the Press.* St. Paul, Minn.: West, 1977.
A collection of essays on the role of the press in establishing the priority of issues for Americans. The book discusses how issues are prioritized from news and how susceptible people are to the influence of the press.

$\mathcal{I}$nterest Groups

The 236 million people who live in the United States are spread among metropolitan centers, urban ghettos, suburban tracts, rural towns, and farms and ranches. Our population reflects a vast mix of backgrounds and cultures. No matter how we look at the United States, the picture is always a diverse one. This same diversity is reflected in the groups and organizations that represent the special interests of our citizens.

Americans have always been inclined to divide into special interest groups. James Madison called these groups *factions* and felt that their existence was explained by the unequal distribution of property. In the 1830s, Alexis de Tocqueville, traveling in the United States, was impressed with the number and assortment of special interest groups: "Americans of all ages, all conditions, and all dispositions constantly form associations." Tocqueville called America a society of joiners, and his assessment still holds true. In 1976, 57 percent of all Americans reported being active in a voluntary association.[1] At present some nineteen thousand groups and associations exist nationwide. Some are ethnic and cultural, others were formed on the basis of members' economic and oc-

247

cupational status, still others were generated by particular issues of concern to citizens.

Individuals seek the support and resources of others to achieve common goals. When the purpose of any group includes pressuring government to enhance the group's objectives, the organization is known as a political pressure group, clearly an entity of interest to the study of American politics.

Political pressure groups, once felt to be a "normal" and healthy part of the American political process, have recently come under attack along with other institutions. A 1973 study by the Senate Committee on Government Operations revealed that three out of four Americans felt "special interests get more from the government than the people do." A 1975 Harris Poll showed that 72 percent of Americans believed Congress to be too heavily influenced by special interest lobbies. Americans see the political processes as dominated by special interest groups, and government as serving the purposes of a few big interests, not those of the general public.

The decline of trust and confidence in the political system has deeply affected interest groups. It is common to hear charges that politicians are captives of special interests and that big business runs the country. Many feel that the present malaise in government can be laid at the feet of interest groups. Former lobbyist Robert Winter-Berger writes, "Without the lobbyists, corruption in government would be minimal, simply because the efforts to corrupt would be so disorganized, so diffuse."[2]

Interest Groups and Public Policy

The public sees interest groups as powerful brokers dominating and controlling the political process. Yet students of interest groups are far from agreed on their influence. According to Lewis Dexter, "Washington representatives would no more bribe or threaten government officials than a professional author would bribe or threaten editors. . . ."[3] And Lester Milbrath, summarizing his interviews with lobbyists, concluded, "The weight of the evidence . . . suggests that there is relatively little influence or power in lobbying per se."[4] Others who have traced the lobbying efforts of an organization or followed a particular issue find considerably more evidence of power and influence.[5]

Interest Group: *a group of individuals who band together seeking the support and resources of others to achieve common goals. When the goal becomes to pressure government to enhance the group's objectives, it becomes a political pressure group.*

The problem stems in part from the nature and functions of **interest groups.** Some people see interest groups as the key variable in political activity. David Truman, for example, viewed politics as the interaction of groups in American society. He defined an interest group as "a shared-attitude group that makes certain claims upon other groups in the society through any of the institutions of government."[6] Whether one goes so far as to call public policy the result of competing group interaction, it is clear that interest groups are important, active, and influential in the policy process.

TABLE 7.1   Types of voluntary organizations in the United States

Category	Number	Percent
Trade, business, and commercial	3719	19.4
Public affairs	1934	10.1
Health and medical	1885	9.9
Cultural organizations	1633	8.5
Social welfare	1449	7.6
Hobby and avocational	1298	6.8
Education	1187	6.2
Religious	952	5.0
Scientific, engineering, and technical	909	4.8
Agricultural	881	4.6
Athletic and sport	736	3.8
Legal, government, public administration, and military	657	3.4
Fraternal, foreign interest, nationality, and ethnic	491	2.6
Greek letter, and related	330	1.7
Veterans, hereditary, and patriotic	292	1.5
Labor unions, associations, and federations	251	1.3
Chambers of Commerce	141	0.7

SOURCE: Katherine Gruber, editor, *Encyclopedia of Associations*, 20th ed. (Detroit: Gale Research Co., 1986).

What Is an Interest Group?

Carol Greenwald's definition of an interest group differs from Truman's, cited above. Writes Greenwald, "An interest group is a combination of individuals who seek to pursue shared interests through a set of agreed upon activities."[7] Any group becomes a political pressure group when a number of individuals seek to pursue shared interests by attempting to influence decisions within the policymaking system.

Table 7.1, which lists voluntary organizations in the United States, shows that economic, social welfare, health, and education groups dominate. Many of these organizations make use of the political process when it suits their needs and goals. They differ as to where they apply pressure on the political process, and their goals lead them to different forms of action. Agricultural groups, for instance, may find the executive branch, which sets commodity-exchange policies, and a sympathetic Department of Agriculture logical places to lobby if they seek to influence policy. Social welfare groups may find new legislation necessary to further their goals. They might therefore lobby Congress and the appropriate committees, asking them to write legislation that would further the mission of their groups. Fraternal organizations may be concerned about other matters, such as tax-exempt status. Very few organizations, however, are totally committed to political activity.

Interest Groups in Action

Political pressure groups seek to influence government. Lobbying is a form of communication whereby an interest group interacts with public officials for the purpose of influencing decision making. The federal gov-

Lobbying: *a form of communication whereby an interest group interacts with public officials for the purpose of influencing decision making.*

Access: *the contact with public officials that forms the basis for lobbying activity. Access depends on reaching key decision makers at key points in the political process.*

ernment defines lobbying as the solicitation of money for the purpose of influencing congressional legislation. Yet lobbying need not be limited to soliciting money nor to influencing Congress.

Lobbying is the politics of **access.** Groups seek access to public officials who make policy to present the group's goals and objectives. Any group may seek to contact a public official, but the effective interest group seeks systematically to communicate its position and maximize its access. Carol Greenwald argues that lobbyist communication is an attempt to affect the behavior of individuals by supplying information. The most effective way, Greenwald suggests, is to influence the official's job security or public image.[8]

Interest-Group Functions

Interest groups perform several functions, three of which are worth looking at in detail: material, social, and political. The most common function associated with interest groups is to promote members' material rewards and benefits. Labor organizations, for example, strive to push up wages to keep earning power ahead of inflation. General Motors opposes tougher emission standards for automobiles because they drive up the cost of automobiles and can thus reduce sales and profits. In a less political context, groups provide material benefits to their members directly. Members of the American Association of Retired Persons, for instance, qualify for low-cost generic drug and vitamin purchases. Consumers Union tests and rates brand-name merchandise for its members so that they can get the best value for their dollar.

Groups may also perform social functions. These can have both intrinsic worth for individual members and extrinsic worth for the group. In personal terms, membership in a group can reinforce one's identity. For example, the National Organization for Women (NOW) and Association of Retired Persons provide such personal reinforcement. By stressing women's concerns, members of NOW can feel that they are working to solve women's common problems and are thus expressing and asserting their own identity. And membership in the Association of Retired Persons, which argues that life does not end at sixty and that retired persons can lead active and full lives, enables people to express and contribute to these beliefs. The social function also works to promote social solidarity and rapport within the group. Like-minded people join together to advance their interests collectively. The Right to Life Association was formed as a direct result of the Supreme Court's decision on abortion. The Sierra Club and the Audubon Society are made up of individuals dedicated to protecting the environment and maintaining wilderness areas. These people join in the hope of achieving collective success in situations in which individuals would be less powerful.

The political function interest groups perform is essentially a linkage function. Groups become the primary means by which social issues and demands can be formulated and articulated to government in a more or

Practicing Politics: How to Join a Women's Group

*I*f you want to focus your political activity on achieving opportunities and rights for women, here are some national organizations you can contact for information about the groups and activities in your area.

Groups active on all issues related to women:

Center for the American Woman and Politics A nonpartisan research and educational center. Eagleton Institute of Politics, Rutgers University, New Brunswick, New Jersey 08901.

League of Women Voters A long-established group dedicated to nonpartisan political action and education; state and local branches exist throughout the country. 1730 M Street NW, Washington, D.C. 20036.

National Organization for Women (NOW) A group dedicated to using politics, education, and legal resources to improve the status of women. 1401 New York Avenue NW, Suite 800, Washington, D.C. 20015.

Clearinghouse on Women's Issues A nonparti-

san group for national, state, and local women's groups and civil rights organizations; its purpose is "to exchange and disseminate education information and materials on issues related to discrimination on the basis of sex or marital status." P.O. Box 70603, Friendship Heights, Maryland 20813.

Groups focused on electing women to office:

National Women's Education Fund Provides information and technical training for women who want to seek political office. 1410 Q Street NW, Washington, D.C. 20009.

National Women's Political Caucus Provides information and training for women candidates. 1275 K Street NW, Suite 750, Washington, D.C. 20005.

Women's Campaign Fund A nonprofit group that raises money to support women candidates for national and state office. 1725 I Street NW, Washington, D.C. 20006.

In every city are organizations whose members serve as advocates for women and seek to advance their interests.

less systematic manner. What individuals alone cannot achieve, groups stand a realistic chance of securing. Groups fill a void by representing interests to government, thereby providing legislators and other public officials with a sense of what segments of the American public think about the major issues before them. There is widespread agreement, however, that interest groups have been usurping power from political parties. There are a growing number of single-interest groups as well as groups that take uncompromising stands. There is less willingness on the part of interest groups to work with political parties, to compromise, or to form broad alliances of shared power.

Influence

Political observers disagree about the extent to which groups influence politics, and there is no easy way to measure such influence. Rising medical costs do not necessarily mean that doctors or hospital groups are influential in preventing government agencies from regulating costs. A visit with a member of Congress does not equal influence peddling. And not all groups are equally powerful. An association of independent dry cleaners, for example, does not possess the resources or opportunities of General Motors or AT&T. In fact, General Motors may not need to lobby in the traditional sense of the term; a news release, a phone call to an old friend, or a plant closing can produce the desired effect. Many means of influence are simply not visible.

Objective Influence: *the ability of an interest group to make good its demands upon government through direct personal contact with political officials.*

Robert Presthus has sought to understand interest-group influence, which he perceives as the ability of an interest group to make good its demands upon government. He distinguishes between **objective behavioral influence,** deriving from direct personal contact with political officials, and **subjective influence, or reputational, judgments** of the behavior and legitimacy of groups.[9] In general, he found that groups with the most experience and resources committed to lobbying government were the most successful, and groups actively engaged in lobbying were more successful than groups that were not. The more interaction there was between lobbyists and public officials, the greater was the level of influence.[10]

Subjective Influence, or Reputational Judgments: *the influence of an interest group based on perceptions and its standing in the community; that is, its reputation with public officials.*

Categories of Interest Groups

Groups can be categorized in countless ways. Here we will classify them under the headings of occupational, issue-oriented, and ethnic and religious groups.

Occupational Groups: *a classification of interest groups by occupation. This typical categorization of interest groups is dominated by business and labor groups.*

Occupational Groups

Since a principal function of interest groups is attaining material benefits for its members, it is logical that **occupational groups** should be the largest category. Occupational groups are dominated by business and labor, but agriculture and professional associations exist as well.

Business   Business groups form the oldest, largest, and most heterogeneous category of groups.[11] For example, the National Association of Manufacturers, founded in 1895, represents some 12,000 firms throughout the nation. It is a leading spokesman for "big business," actively opposes labor, and promotes free enterprise. In addition, many large corporations maintain their own lobbyists. Most corporations prefer to retain a Washington law firm specializing in lobbying to look after the company's interests. And many small businesses belong to trade associations or join together to employ a law firm in Washington. Business groups focus on regulatory activities and the federal bureaucracy as much as or more than they do on Congress.

Since World War II the National Association of Manufacturers has suffered a decline in membership and come more and more to represent big business. But, report Norman Ornstein and Shirley Elder, "a diminishing membership has been accompanied by a growing aggressiveness in political affairs."[12] The U.S. Chamber of Commerce, with a broader membership, represents some 4,000 local chambers of commerce with individual, trade association, and business memberships of more than 70,000. The total membership of the U.S. Chamber of Commerce stands at 4.5 million. Its budget of $16 million is chiefly raised from membership dues. The Chamber uses standing committees to initiate policy positions and its professional staff, working with the committees, then seeks to lobby government to implement those policies. Recent issues have included common-site picketing (allowing a union with a grievance against one contractor to picket an entire construction site and stop work for all contractors), tax laws, and government regulation.

In recent years, the Business Roundtable, founded in 1972, has become a vocal organization in defending business interests. Composed of corporate chief executives from nearly 200 of America's largest and most prestigious corporations, the Roundtable was established because of dissatisfaction with the efforts of the other business lobbies. Since the Business Roundtable is composed of corporate chiefs, it prefers to work through members and not lobbyists or law firms; a major corporate executive is far more likely to have direct personal contact with a senator or departmental secretary than is a hired representative. The Roundtable addresses major areas of concern to business such as the Arab boycott, Consumer Protection Agency proposals, and antitrust legislation.

The energy crisis increased the number of energy lobbying groups. After 1974, for example, more than fifty petroleum interest groups registered as Washington lobbyists.[13] The oil industry is represented by its trade association, the American Petroleum Institute, but many separate industry associations also exist. Almost all the major oil companies maintain Washington lobbyists. The American Gas Association represents pipeline and distributing companies, and the International Natural Gas Association represents interstate pipeline companies and the gas-transportation industry.[14] Several individual gas-producing firms also register as lobbyists, as do electric utility companies. In fact, almost every gas and electric utilities company has some sort of lobby representation in Washington. The number of citizen groups lobbying on energy matters has also grown. A recent count showed more than twenty such groups lobbying in Washington, including the Consumer Energy Council of America, Critical Mass Energy Project, the Energy Committee of America, Solar Lobby, and Friends of the River.

Labor   Dominated by the AFL–CIO, organized labor is often seen as a single-interest group. In fact, the AFL–CIO (American Federation of Labor/Congress of Industrial Organizations) is an umbrella for 95 separate affiliated unions whose 14 million members are a diverse assortment of laborers, teachers, and white-collar workers. In addition, organized labor includes other individual unions such as the United Auto Workers, the United Mine Workers, and the Teamsters.

It is the AFL–CIO that sets the tone for organized labor, however, and the organization is a powerful force in American politics. The president, Lane Kirkland, presides over the Executive Council, composed of affiliate union presidents. The union maintains a separate legislative department with eight professional lobbyists. In addition, lobbyists are employed by the affiliate unions. The most potent political arm of the AFL–CIO, however, is its political department, COPE (the Committee on Political Education). COPE employs seven professionals, fifteen assistants, and eighteen field representatives. The primary responsibilities of this committee are fund raising, voter-registration drives, political-party support, and electioneering. COPE spends more than a million dollars in a federal election supporting House and Senate candidates endorsed by the AFL–CIO.

In recent years, the AFL–CIO has adapted to the political realities of postpartisan politics. It concentrates less on parties and more on issues and candidates sympathetic to labor and continues to mobilize resources and voters to support its lobbying efforts. To use George Meany's term (the former AFL–CIO president for 25 years until his death in 1980), the AFL–CIO is a political machine.[15] In part this change is due to the recognition that labor is no longer a single bloc of voting power: 43 percent of labor families voted for Reagan in 1980 and 48 percent in 1984. This split occurred despite endorsement of the Democratic candidates by a majority of union leadership.

Organized labor, even the AFL–CIO, cannot speak for all workers. The American labor movement has never been united. Walter Reuther and his United Auto Workers split with the AFL–CIO in 1968 and became an independent union, with a membership of 1.1 million. The Teamsters, with 2.3 million members, are another large and separate group. Farm workers have begun to organize under the militant Cesar Chavez. Public

Numerous foreclosures have brought the plight of farmers to the attention of the nation, and resulted in fundraising ventures such as the Farm Aid concert organized by Willie Nelson.

employee unionization has been growing and labor has been divided over their striking and disrupting essential services.

Agriculture   American farmers represent a large interest group. Nearly 4 million people are members of farm organizations. They are a clientele group (that is, a particular interest receiving benefits from the government), long recognized as vital to the nation. The Department of Agriculture was established in 1862 to support and work with farm and agribusiness interests. Yet the farmer remains an independent political actor: farm groups have never united and spoken with one voice.

The largest of the three national farm organizations is the American Farm Bureau, with approximately 3 million members. The Farm Bureau has a close association with the Department of Agriculture. Bureau and Agricultural Extension agents work closely on farming techniques and crop and livestock productivity. With its strength primarily in the Midwest, the Farm Bureau has come to oppose government regulation in agriculture and to support the free-market economy. It opposes the price-support program for crops.

The Farm Bureau generally speaks for the larger, more successful producers; the National Farmers' Union, however, with a membership of 300,000, draws from the smaller, less profitable farmers, primarily in the upper midwestern and western states. Calling itself the champion of the dirt farmer, the Farmers' Union supports high levels of price supports for crops and livestock. In more recent years, the Farmer's Union has supported efforts to protect migrant farm workers.

The oldest of the national farm groups, founded in 1867, is the National Grange. It has a membership today of some 400,000, with primary support in the New England and the Mid-Atlantic states. Historically, the Grange has been a social organization concerned with the welfare of the farm family, but in recent years this group has adopted the more political approach of backing price supports for farmers.

Recently, we have witnessed a growing militancy among farm interests. The National Farmer's Organization (NFO) calls for withholding produce from the market to increase the price paid to producers. The 1978 "tractorcade" to Washington sought to dramatize the plight of the farmer caught between low prices for products and the high costs of farming. The United Farm Workers won a five-year boycott against grape growers in California in 1970. To organize lettuce field workers, Chavez's National Farm Workers again called for a nationwide boycott, this time of iceberg lettuce.

The 1980s have witnessed an increasingly heavy debt for many farmers and an unprecedented number of farm foreclosures, notably in the Midwest. Large numbers of farmers have been forced to leave farming. Some farmers have gone on welfare, and popular country singer Willie Nelson has organized several farm-aid concerts to assist financially strapped farmers. The farm crisis has generated a number of new support groups and militant organizations dedicated to dramatizing the plight of the farmer.

Professional Associations   There are currently hundreds of professional groups operating in the United States. Many maintain registered lobbyists in Washington; others are involved in politics in other ways.[16] Two of the best established and most powerful groups are the American Bar Association and the American Medical Association. These groups exercise control over lawyers and doctors through licensing and training standards, and both are active on political issues. The American Bar Association rates the fitness of all judicial candidates to serve on the federal bench. The American Medical Association has recently opposed national health care insurance and efforts to further regulate the health care industry. Professional associations also exist for bankers, teachers, bureaucrats, historians, political scientists, and any number of other groups. These groups are not regularly or constantly active, but they do lobby when an issue affects them.

Issue-Oriented Groups

Issue Groups: *interest groups that are formed in direct response to a specific public controversy. For example, the Right to Life Association was founded in response to the controversy over the 1973 Supreme Court decision permitting abortions.*

Issue groups are those formed in direct response to a public controversy. The Right to Life Association was founded after the 1973 Court decision permitting abortion; Environmental Action, Inc., was founded to protest, by means of Earth Day, threats to the environment. Issue groups may, of course, take a broader focus on political issues or be directed toward narrower or single-issue politics. More recently, public interest groups have emerged. A public interest group is one that seeks a goal that "will not selectively and materially benefit the membership or activists of the organization."[17]

California Senator Alan Cranston (center) waves some of the million-plus signatures, collected by the Sierra Club, that called for the resignation of Secretary of the Interior James Watt. Also on the steps of the Capitol are House Speaker Tip O'Neill (*right*), and Sierra Club President James Fontaine (*left*).

Environmental Groups   With concern rising for the environment, there has been a proliferation of environmental interest groups. The number of ecology-oriented groups grew following the oil embargo in 1973, and recent air pollution incidents and oil spills have generated more. But some environmental groups are long-standing, well-established organizations. The Sierra Club, founded in 1892, has a membership of more than 350,000. It lobbies for clean air and clean water and opposes construction activity that spoils scenic areas. The National Wildlife Federation has 4.2 million members and a budget of more than $24 million. These groups tripled their membership in the decades of the 1960s and 1970s. Newer groups include Friends of the Earth, Inc., Environmental Action, Inc., and the Wilderness Society. These groups have memberships ranging from fifteen thousand to one hundred thousand, their budgets run up to $1 million, and they are political pressure groups with a direct-action orientation. Currently some five hundred issue groups concerned with the environment, ecology, and energy hold meetings, disseminate information, and lobby.[18]

Environmental groups have become far more visible in the 1980s under the Reagan administration. The environmentalists were particularly angered with the policies of Reagan's first secretary of the interior, James Watt. Secretary Watt's brash style and laissez-faire policies rallied environmental groups to action, increasing their memberships in the process. Watt was the first cabinet secretary ever to receive a petition with one million signatures calling for his resignation. Secretary Watt not only opened federal lands to coal mining, but also encouraged offshore oil drilling and proposed granting oil and gas leases within wilderness areas for the exploration of energy. He also proposed removing 805,000 acres of Bureau of Land Management land from possible designation as wilderness area. This infuriated environmental groups such as the Wilderness Society and the Sierra Club. In fact, in January 1983, six groups—the Wilderness Society, Sierra Club, Environmental Defense Fund, National Audubon Society, National Wildlife Federation, and Natural Resource Defense Council—went to court to stop the action.

In 1985 Reagan appointed Donald Hodel as secretary of the interior. A former undersecretary of Interior and secretary of the Department of Energy from 1982 to 1984, Hodel is known as a more moderate, less flamboyant manager, who is able to get along with Congress. He won praise for his efforts on the 1982 nuclear-waste disposal bill, although environmentalists continue to doubt his commitment to conservation, pointing to his support for nuclear power and the coal-leasing programs.

The environmental movement is going through something of a midlife crisis.[19] By the end of 1985 half a dozen major environmental groups, among them the Sierra Club and the National Audubon Society, will have new chief executives. There is more effort at coalition building, including efforts to build alliances with farmers, labor, and, yes, even industry. Many organizations are redirecting their focus to state capitals, rather than trying to mobilize grass roots support in response to Washington activity.[20] Environmental groups made their point with the public during the Watt years. Their actions were able to delay dams, power plants, and offshore drilling, and they heightened public awareness of toxic waste disposal. Now environmental groups, with mature policies, must work with consumers and industries to sustain those victories by changing the planning and operation of these environment-threatening systems.

Public Interest Groups: *interest groups that claim to seek goals that will benefit society in general rather than narrow, special interests.*

Public Interest Groups   Jeffrey Berry, in a 1972–1973 study of public interest groups, identified eighty-three such groups in areas ranging from the environment, general politics, consumerism, church, poverty, and civil rights, to peace.[21] Much public interest activity can be traced to Ralph Nader and his efforts to protect the American consumer. Nader, with the aid of some law students and lawyers, began a series of investigations into business and consumer affairs. Eventually he established an organization called Public Citizen, Inc., which solicited funds for a mass-based membership and now supports most of the Nader investigations. In all, Nader heads some fifteen public interest groups in the areas of consumer affairs, energy, health care, and governmental regulation. Some of the more well known are Congress Watch, which researches and lobbies Congress and disseminates information on its activities; Critical Mass, devoted to nuclear power concerns, notably safety standards for nuclear power plants; and the Public Interest Research Group, which seeks to establish chapters on college campuses and supports research on public interest issues.

Common Cause is another leading public interest group, founded in 1970 by former Secretary of Health, Education, and Welfare John Gardner. Its original efforts to solicit money and members met with success; more than 100,000 citizens joined and paid $15 a year in dues. Today Common Cause has a membership of more than 250,000, and a professional staff of lawyers, lobbyists, field organizers, public relations experts, and citizen volunteers to work for reform of the American political system. Major efforts have been directed at the seniority system in Congress, public financing of campaigns, and public disclosure of receipts and expenditures by candidates and lobbyists.

Public interest groups claim to broaden political participation and speak for the national will, but Berry suggests we view them with caution:

> If it is common sense to assume that interest groups are a necessary ingredient of our present political system, it is also common sense to realize that public interest groups are not the savior of that system. Giving the views of public interest groups greater credence, or tailoring public policy more closely to what they advocate, will not necessarily make the governmental decisions more reflective of the national will. Nor is representation through interest groups *per se* an adequate supplement to elected representatives in government. The fact that 30 percent of the public interest groups in the sample have

Ralph Nader
Ralph Nader is a champion of consumer rights. While an attorney in Hartford, Connecticut, Nader became alarmed over the large number of auto fatalities. To alert the public to the danger of automobiles, he wrote *Unsafe at Any Speed* in 1965. The book propelled Nader into the public eye and made him unpopular with automobile industries. Since that time, Nader has been a leader in the consumer movement. He has formed the Center for the Study of Responsive Law, Public Citizen, Inc., and Center for Auto Safety. His organizations attract young people, called "Nader's Raiders," to work on projects during their summer vacations.

no real membership attests to the problems of organizing individuals around certain interests that they ostensibly share.[22]

There are problems in labeling any group a public interest group. Some groups may use the designation as a means for increased access to government or to add greater legitimacy to their activities. There is no standard definition or membership requirement to qualify as a public interest group. In any event, public interest groups have proliferated and added more voices to be taken into account by government, thereby making it increasingly difficult for Congress to accommodate all points of view. The reformist attitude of many of these groups, while laudable in spirit, can result in unintended or unwanted consequences. The reforms of campaign contributions and spending are an example. Rather than limiting contributions and spending, the reforms gave rise to political action committees (PACs) and more interest-group spending.

Single-Interest Groups   With a factioned electorate developing as party cohesion breaks down, more and more single-minded special interest groups appear and become militant voices. For example, pro-life forces became active in the late 1970s in opposing abortion and political candidates supporting abortion. Farmers have tractored to Washington to demand higher prices for grain and other farm products. Truckers have blocked gas pumps to dramatize rising fuel costs. And native Americans have camped out at the White House to symbolize the poor treatment they have received. Gay rights has become a major issue in several places, including San Francisco, California, and Dade County, Florida.

Single-issue groups have given American politics an increasingly emotional and militant tone. An alarming example is the emergence of fringe groups such as the Covenant, Sword, and Arm of the Lord and the Posse Comitatus. The Covenant, Sword, and Arm of the Lord is a militarist, survivalist organization located in the Midwest and West. The Posse Comitatus (Latin meaning "power of the country") is a loosely organized, ultraconservative group that believes in no government authority above the county level. Citing roots in English common law, the Posse claims that the law vests sheriffs with authority to seek civilian assistance; hence members carry guns and often act as vigilantes. They also reject paper currency and the income tax system. Such groups appeal to bankrupt farmers and small town folk who feel victimized by urban and corporate power.

Ethnic and Religious Groups

Ethnic and religious groups have had a long and rich tradition in American politics. A major demand of minority groups has been for economic equality, but ethnic and religious interests transcend economic issues. In America's early development, ethnic groups—Irish, Italian, Polish, German, and others—sought to integrate themselves into American society while preserving their cultural heritage. By the twentieth century, black

Changing Consensus: Abortion and Single-Issue Politics

One of the ways in which American politics—and the American consensus—has changed in recent years is in the rise of single-issue politics. Americans all over the country have banded together not on the basis of class, party, ethnic group, or region, but in support of or in opposition to some particular issue—for example, the environment, nuclear power, control of the schools, urban renewal, or the Vietnam War. The kind of consensus that once left individual decisions to government and confined battles over policies to the drafting of party platforms and national political conventions has vanished. The abortion, or right-to-life, issue is a good case in point.

On this one issue—whether abortion should be a matter of choice—strong forces on both sides have set up national organizations whose supporters may not agree on anything else. Since abortion laws were liberalized in Colorado in 1967, the controversy has gained momentum: nine versions of a Human Life amendment to the Constitution are in congressional committees, and seventeen states have requested that constitutional conventions be called. Right-to-life forces have polled legislators and worked to defeat those who do not hold their view on this one issue. In 1977, the passage of the Hyde Amendment, a rider to the Department of Labor and HEW appropriations bills, prohibited the use of federal funds for abortion unless the life of the mother was in danger. Pro-choice forces challenged the amendment in court. In June 1980, however, the Supreme Court in *Harris* v. *McRae* upheld the constitutionality of the Hyde Amendment. This decision meant the end of Medicaid coverage for abortion for about 300,000 poor women each year. Pro-life forces were heartened—the Supreme Court appeared ready to limit the right to an abortion. But not so. In 1983 the Supreme Court struck down restrictive state laws interfering with a woman's right to an abortion. Only three justices dissented—Justices O'Connor, Rehnquist, and White—but their dissents indicated a readiness to alter *Roe* v. *Wade*. The Court, however, straightforwardly told state legislatures to stop trying to influence a woman's private decision on whether to terminate her pregnancy. Anti-abortion groups were surprised by the decision but vowed to renew their efforts to amend the Constitution to ban abortions.

For some that effort has taken a violent turn. According to federal authorities there have been thirty instances of bombing or arson directed against family planning clinics since May 1982, twenty-four in 1984 alone. The most notable of these was the Christmas Day 1984 bombing of three abortion clinics in Pensacola, Florida. In 1985, the home of Supreme Court Justice Blackmun, the author of the *Roe* v. *Wade* decision, was fired upon by an unknown assailant. Such violence illustrates the strength of the political passions that may arise from a single issue.

The result of all this activity and pressure is that politicians, once free to campaign as liberal, conservative, or middle-of-the-road candidates, find themselves forced to pick their way delicately along heavily mined campaign trails. One misstep and a whole bloc of voters can be turned away. Parties face the same problem and lose more and more control over candidates and platforms. And the electorate must sometimes make choices on the basis of issues that have nothing to do with the fundamental problems facing American society as a whole. Single-issue politics can be important in solving local problems and in bringing injustices to public attention, but on the national level it can so fragment our society's consensus that we are left without a common purpose and common goals. After all, if I will not speak to you because you disagree with me over abortion, how are we going to work together to solve the problems of energy, unemployment, and inflation?

groups had begun forming to advance the cause of racial equality. The move for the Court's reinterpretation of the Fourteenth Amendment was dramatized in no small measure by the efforts of black civil rights groups. Religious groups, too, have a history of organization and of voicing political concerns.[23]

The black movement grew out of white repression after the Civil War. The oldest organization, the National Association for the Advancement of Colored People (NAACP), was formed in 1909. In its earliest years the NAACP avoided direct confrontation or mass action, preferring instead to use the courts. Its Legal Defense and Educational Fund developed legal expertise and won many important victories through the years. Even today, the NAACP prefers the marble corridors of the court to the asphalt of the streets. Growing militancy in the 1960s gave rise to newer, mass-based, direct-action organizations. In 1957 Dr. Martin Luther King, Jr., formed the Southern Christian Leadership Conference and successfully used tactics of nonviolent protest. In 1968, the Black Panthers were formed by activists impatient with the results of the other organizations.

Church groups are usually less directly involved in the policy process of government, yet they too have organizations that are occasionally involved in politics. The United States Catholic Conference is the most established Catholic organization. In the 1960s it opposed aid to education that excluded support for parochial schools.

In 1982, the National Conference of Catholic Bishops took an almost unprecedented action by drafting a pastoral letter to Catholics condemning the nuclear arms race. This gesture was strongly opposed by the Reagan administration. The letter represented a break with the tradition of bipartisan foreign policy and the silence of the church on matters of foreign policy. The Catholic bishops felt they had "a special obligation" to make available the moral and religious resources of the Catholic tradition on the issue of nuclear armament.

The Christian Right   There are five principal Christian Right organizations: the Moral Majority (renamed Liberty Federation in 1985), the Religious Roundtable, the Christian Voice, the National Christian Action Coalition, and the Freedom Council. All these organizations have Washington lobbyists and engage in traditional lobbying activities. By far the best known of the group is the Moral Majority, founded by "Old Time Gospel Hour" evangelist Jerry Falwell. The Moral Majority claims chapters in all fifty states and a membership of 72,000 ministers and four million people. Falwell renamed the Moral Majority the Liberty Federation in 1985 to move away from pastor organization activity, saying it was time to create "moral activity committees" of parishioners in interested churches to do the work. This restructuring may have been in response to some criticism that ministers were becoming too politically involved. The Freedom Council, created in 1981 by video evangelist Pat Robertson, is a "Christian, non-profit organization formed to help maintain the great gift of religious freedom which we have enjoyed in this

Jerry L. Falwell
Independent Baptist minister and founder and president of the Moral Majority, Rev. Jerry Falwell became a national figure during the 1980 election. A native of Lynchburg, Virginia, Falwell was ordained in 1956. That year he founded the independent, fundamentalist Thomas Road Baptist Church in Lynchburg. Today the church has over 17,000 members. Falwell is an exponent of the "electronic church." He claims to reach 18 million people each week on the "Old Time Gospel Hour," broadcast over more than 400 radio and 390 TV stations. His Moral Majority, established in 1979, reportedly has 4 million members committed to the group's ideals of conservative politics and Christian values in politicians.

land." Robertson aims to get citizens who embrace Christian moral principles deeply involved in the political process. He is a candidate for the 1988 GOP presidential nomination.

The Christian Right has made effective use of technology in pressing their moral message to the nation. They have televised ministries and the Christian Broadcast Network, as well as refined and extensive computerized mailing lists, which they use most effectively to raise money, distribute literature, and advance political candidates. Richard Viguerie, labeled the postmaster general of the Right, has been the genius behind the computerized mail solicitations.

On the surface the success of new Right conservatives and Christian political groups such as the Moral Majority and their affinity with Ronald Reagan would seem obvious. These groups succeeded in including their issues in the 1984 GOP party platform: voluntary school prayer, a constitutional amendment banning abortions, opposition to ERA, and no new taxes. President Reagan has endorsed their views and moved the governmental agenda to the right. Yet the Christian Right complains that President Reagan, and to an even larger extent the GOP, have ignored the conservative agenda. They argue that Reagan has not pushed strongly enough for their program, and has even surrounded himself with moderates and Washington establishment politicians.

The Reagan administration has unquestionably been a boon to conservative groups as a political and social force. Conservative organizations are appearing nationwide, on college campuses and in churches, and evangelical ministers are organizing and coordinating activities. For 1984 Christian Right groups concentrated on voter registration drives, the recruitment and training of Christian political candidates, and pushing "family issues." They continue to raise and spend money in support of Christian candidates and Christian political issues.

However, the Christian Right's success is also the source of its problems. With the proliferation of groups and activities, the new Right is becoming decentralized. There no longer exists a unity within the movement or a national spokesman for its agenda. While the Rev. Jerry Falwell continues to enjoy national prominence, the Liberty Federation can no longer lay claim to the consciousness of the new Right. Says Peter Weyrich of the emerging decentralization, "It's now divided into spheres of influence and spheres of operation, and these operate . . . independently of each other. Five years ago, the leadership was clear, and people were in a definite hierarchy. But that's changed. . . . Now they have their own leadership and are independent."[24]

The other problem is the grass roots mobilization to dominate local and state GOP parties. As evangelical churches mobilize and even form coalitions with other groups such as the Right to Life organization, they are meeting resistance from traditional GOP party activists and business interests. Long-time conservative activist Richard Viguerie no longer believes that the new Right can operate within the traditional GOP party.

"I've come to realize in the last few years that the big business community . . . has their hooks so solidly into the Republican Party that I'm not sure you can really make the Republican Party a vehicle that will be responsive to the populist people at the grass-roots level."[25] Hence Viguerie and others are calling for a "populist conservative" party to become the vehicle for the new Right and Christian political groups.

Government

It may seem unreasonable to include branches of the government as pressure groups, yet congressional committees, caucuses, administrative bureaus, executives, and foreign governments can and do lobby. Government employees are also organized and lobby for benefits and issues of concern to their organizations.

Much lobbying involves the pressuring of one branch or level of government by another. For example, the Department of Education may lobby for increased educational monies from a House committee on education. During the Watergate years an executive agency, the Office of Economic Opportunity, sued its boss, Richard Nixon, to release impounded funds for the continuation of the agency and its activities. The Executive Office has a legislative relations staff to keep in constant contact with members of Congress and to monitor the progress of legislation; every department has a congressional liaison or assistant secretary to keep in touch with Congress, key legislators, and committees on items that pertain to that department.

Within Congress it is widely conceded that the members themselves are the absolute best lobbyists for all types of bills. They are renowned for their ability to secure projects and benefits for their districts and constituents. Bills costing millions of dollars pass Congress on the lobbying skills of veteran legislators. Congressional committee meetings often are where interests are protected, guaranteeing that no bill gets written without particular interests being accommodated. Congress is made up of lobbyists, each representing home districts and constituents as well as particular issues of concern.

Government pressure groups may take the form of associations such as the National Municipal League, the National Conference of State Legislatures, and the Governors' Conference. Government policymakers at the state and local levels have formed associations to examine common problems and find efficient ways to deal with them. Here governmental organizations are taking policy positions and asking themselves or other branches or levels of government to respond.

Koreagate: *a Congressional scandal of the late 1960s and early 1970s involving the testimony of Korean businessman Tongsun Park that he bribed congressmen for their continued support of U.S. economic and military aid to Korea.*

The **Koreagate** scandal illustrated how foreign governments lobby Congress. Most major foreign powers keep lobbyists in Washington to look out for their interests on a number of fronts. Public employees are another potent force. Unionization is growing at the state and local levels, and today some 4 million public employees are union members.

Groups: Leaders and Members

Why do individuals join interest groups? Studies of political participation reveal that, however widespread, participation in interest groups remains selective. Many Americans do not participate in any interest group. And for those who do, politics may not be the reason. Table 7.2 shows participation in interest groups and the civic concern of the membership. Most groups report a high level of civic involvement and a moderately high concern for political affairs.

Individuals may be motivated to join interest groups for a variety of reasons. Mancur Olson stresses the collective action of a group to provide "benefits" or "rewards" to the individual.[26] Olson argues that membership in an interest group is calculated in terms of "costs" and "benefits." Robert Salisbury offers a different explanation. He suggests that a mutual exchange of incentives between members and leaders would support group membership and participation.[27] According to Salisbury's exchange theory, members and leaders trade mutually reinforcing incentives for group participation. He cites three kinds of incentives: material (tangible

TABLE 7.2   Civic participation by members of voluntary organizations

Type of organization	Population who report membership (in percent)	Members who report the organization is involved in community affairs (in percent)	Members who report that political discussions take place in the organization (in percent)
Political groups such as Democratic or Republican clubs, and political action groups such as voters' leagues	8	85	97
School service groups such as PTA or school alumni groups	17	82	54
Service clubs, such as Lions, Rotary, Zonta, Jr. Chamber of Commerce	6	81	64
Youth groups such as Boy Scouts, Girl Scouts	7	77	36
Veterans' groups such as American Legion	7	77	56
Farm organizations such as Farmer's Union, Farm Bureau, Grange	4	74	61
Nationality groups such as Sons of Norway, Hibernian Society	2	73	57
Church-related groups such as Bible Study Group or Holy Name Society	6	73	40
Fraternal groups such as Elks, Eagles, Masons, and their women's auxiliaries	15	69	33
Professional or academic societies such as American Dental Association, Phi Beta Kappa	7	60	57
Trade unions	17	59	44
School fraternities and sororities such as Sigma Chi, Delta Gamma	3	53	37
Literary, art, discussion, or study clubs such as book-review clubs, theater groups	4	40	56
Hobby or garden clubs such as stamp or coin clubs, flower clubs, pet clubs	5	40	35
Sports clubs, bowling leagues, etc.	12	28	30

SOURCE: Sidney Verba and Norman H. Nie, *Participation in America: Political Democracy and Social Equality* (New York: Harper & Row, 1972), pp. 178–79. Copyright © 1972 by Sidney Verba and Norman H. Nie. Reprinted by permission.

rewards such as money), solidary (friendship or community building), and purposive (issue positions or ideology).

Size and Cohesion

We normally base our estimate of a group's potential political impact on its size. For example, the AFL–CIO has 14 million members (and if we count families, almost 50 million), which is more than 6 percent of the entire population. By contrast, professional organizations such as the American Medical Association and American Bar Association have much smaller memberships but contain a higher percentage of eligible members. The AMA counts 50 percent of all doctors as members; the Bar Association claims 65 percent of all lawyers. Although size is a factor in the political power of a group, unity is equally important for success. The AFL–CIO may be large, but it does not speak with a united voice on many issues. In fact, the larger the group, the more difficult unity becomes.

Overlapping Membership: *the tendency for individuals to belong to more than one interest group. These memberships may be "crosscutting" and lead to a conflict in views and activities.*

People often have **overlapping memberships;** they belong to more than one interest group. These memberships may be "crosscutting," leading to a conflict in views or activities. An individual may be a member of a union that supports abortion, a member of the Catholic Church, which opposes abortion, and a member of the Veterans of Foreign Wars, which is more concerned with the Panama Canal than with abortion. Faced with the "threat" of conflict, individuals may lose interest in politics and the organizations or alter their level of participation. Again, the larger the group, the greater the opportunity for overlapping memberships that can endanger unity.

Leadership

The task of the interest-group leader is "to maximize the sources of internal group cohesion and act as group spokesman vis-à-vis the outside world."[28] Sinclair holds that effective leadership depends on three factors: (1) communication between leaders and followers, (2) the makeup of the membership, and (3) the distribution of power in the organization.[29]

As Carol Greenwald notes, the internal leadership's ability to develop cohesion is directly affected by the size and heterogeneity of the group. Groups with diversified memberships, such as national labor unions and such federations as the American Federation of Teachers, are difficult to unify. Time and resources must be expended to mobilize the membership for some political goal. Because of the communication problem, Common Cause, for example, regularly polls its members on items of concern. Leaders of smaller, more homogeneous organizations are more likely to concentrate on strategy and tactics in lobbying public officials for the organization.

Internal governance of interest groups is not typically democratic. The president, an executive council, and paid professional staff frequently dominate. They spend full time on organization and goals; members cannot do so. Leaders are the most visible and control the communications

Practicing Politics: Lobbying

*I*f you want to influence government directly, one of the best ways is to become a lobbyist. Persuade policymakers that a certain policy is the right one or that a certain problem needs legislation in order to be solved. Just writing a letter or sending a telegram to a legislator is lobbying. But if you want to work on a broader and more systematic level, you can join an issue group such as Common Cause, which engages in public interest lobbying, or any one of the thousands of organizations listed in the *Washington Information Directory*. This directory is published annually by Congressional Quarterly, Inc., in Washington, D.C., and is available in most libraries.

If you work for a group, it is important to plan an effective strategy. Here are two basic steps:

1. Find out what kinds of decisions are needed to reach your goals, and who in government can make them. Don't overlook administrators, who often have much local discretion.
2. Be prepared; understand the political context in which decision makers work, and draft a policy or a bill so that concrete action can result.

Here are some of the tasks you can perform for your group:

- Research and gather evidence to support the group's position.
- Organize letter-writing campaigns.
- Attend hearings to present information or monitor what is being discussed.
- Assist in drafting position papers and material to generate publicity.
- Organize fundraising activities and events.

Getting Through To Washington

A letter to Washington is not a waste of time. Congressmen want to hear from their constituents and will listen to what voters have to say.

Here are a few pointers for writing to your elected officials. (The same holds true for any elected official, whether in Washington, D.C., in your state capitol, or on the local city council.)

- **K.I.S.S.** Keep it short and simple. No one wants (or has the time) to read a five page, single-spaced letter which rambles and never gets to the point. Make it clear and concise. It will stand a better chance of being read and have greater effect.
- **No postcards or form letters, please.** Write your own letter in your own words just as you would write to anyone else. Mass-produced form letters or postcards which flood congressional offices don't convey the sincerity and concern of an individual letter and risk winding up in file 13.
- **Courtesy pays.** Angry, insulting or threatening letters serve only to antagonize and alienate. Be polite. Be constructive. Explain how you feel pending legislation will affect you. *Urge* their support (or opposition) for such legislation, but don't *demand* it. When discussing a particular bill, try to refer to it by name and number.
- **Flattery is fine, too.** If you agree with your legislator's position or vote on an issue, let him/her know. Everyone appreciates praise for a job well done. However, if they displease you, let them know that, too. But remember the preceding point, try to be constructive in your criticism and above all . . . be courteous.
- **Write again.** If your legislator's reply is just a brief acknowledgement of your own letter and doesn't answer your initial concerns, write again to ask for specific information. Be conscientious, however. Don't constantly write and expect replies on every issue under the sun.
- **Focus.** Don't waste time writing to every representative and senator in Congress. Write only those who represent your congressional district or state.
- **Address it to:**

The Honorable (Name)   The Honorable (Name)
House of Representatives   United States Senate
Washington, D.C. 20515   Washington, D.C. 20510
Dear Mr./Mrs. (Name):   Dear Senator (Name):

process. Although they may be removed or their recommendations challenged, the process is normally not an easy or a likely alternative. National conventions are cumbersome, and procedural requirements thwart unskilled members. Elections have not historically been contested for most organizations.

How representative of its members is the leadership? There is no universal or simple answer; simply because most organizations are not internally democratic, we cannot conclude that they are unrepresentative. Groups do change and challenge leadership. The United Mine Workers has, in recent years, faced several challenges to its leadership. John Gardner recently stepped aside as president of Common Cause to allow new people to lead the organization. One must measure the responsiveness of leadership by the achievement of goals, the relative satisfaction of the membership, and the opportunity for member participation in the political process.

The Process

Access depends on reaching top decision makers at key points in the political process. Generally speaking, interest-group activity takes three forms: monitoring political activity, opposing governmental action, and initiating governmental action.[30]

All political interest groups monitor political activity. Significant amounts of any organization's time and resources are put into keeping abreast of legislative proposals, administrative rules and regulations, court cases, and foreign governmental activity. The task is massive. Just reading the *Congressional Record* and the *Federal Register* can be full-time occupations. Yet keeping current is not enough. The earlier one knows what is happening, the quicker one can develop a strategy and gain access. Often, an "early warning system" will allow a group to get access to a key policymaker or mobilize its members before the issue is finalized.

Fighting for the status quo is easier than trying to initiate political change. Many groups spend a good deal of their time opposing governmental action. The oil lobby has worked to prevent the end of the oil depletion allowance. Energy and conservation groups fought against the deregulation of natural gas and construction of the Alaskan pipeline. Indeed, in a political process such as ours, with its checks and balances, it is easier to block policy at any one point than to initiate and guide new policy through all the steps. People and policymakers are cautious concerning change. And the growing opposition to big government, more regulation, and impersonal or inefficient government all work to facilitate opposing governmental action.

We know, however, that groups can be successful in seeking change. Dam construction along the Tennessee River has been halted and new nuclear power plants have been suspended or postponed as consumer groups have lobbied the White House or gone to court for an injunction.

To seek a change in policy is difficult because a group must know exactly what it wishes to achieve and how to achieve it. Goals must be effectively translated into definite public policy.

Influence Techniques

Direct Contact   Lobbyists consider direct contact most effective. Presenting information or data to an administrator or legislative committee is viewed as the best way to persuade and impress officials: "In direct relationships lobbyists try to become auxiliaries to decision makers, providing information to activate, reinforce, strengthen, and remind the official of his commitment to the issue."[31] This access is difficult to achieve. For the executive branch, a visit with a secretary or bureau chief might be the goal; in Congress, direct contact means seeing members or testifying before a legislative committee.

It is possible to overrate direct contact. Committee hearings generally produce no changes of votes. Speakers are scheduled to testify to dramatize a point more than to present information. Attendance at hearings is spotty at best. Executive contact is also uncertain. Departmental secretaries are not always on top of their organizations; clientele groups may exercise as much influence as the secretary. Presidential politics usually intervenes, and the bureaucracy can always plead anonymity or lack of jurisdiction.

Letter Writing   Almost every group uses letter writing or constituent-initiated contact at some time or other (see Figure 7.1). The intent is to convince public officials that broad support for or opposition to some issue exists. These campaigns also serve to inform the public on an issue of concern for a group and to create a favorable atmosphere of public opinion. Finally, letter writing serves to politicize and satisfy the membership that the organization and its leadership are working to implement the group's goals.

Letter-writing campaigns seek to involve a group's membership to impress upon officials the level of support for a group's position. The National Rifle Association frequently exhorts members to write Congress on pending legislation, even going so far as to include sample letters in its publication, *The American Rifleman.* One drawback of such a technique is

	Active	Symbolic
Conventional	Voting Writing letters to congressmen	Fourth of July parades
Nonconventional	Sit-ins	Riots

Figure 7.1   Forms of political participation

© 1981, *Interlandi*/Los Angeles Times

that policymakers can usually spot such campaigns and discount much of the activity as inspired by the group's leadership and not representative of the total membership. Only 15 percent of the population engage in letter writing on public issues, and only 3 percent do so on a regular basis.[32] Yet citizens feel that letter writing is an effective means of influence. Berry found that 47 percent of the public interest groups surveyed considered letter writing "an effective tool.[33]

Media Campaigns   Pressure groups also use the media. Television in particular has become a favorite: groups pay for ads to publicize their positions, to inform the public, and to recruit support. The American Petroleum Institute and the major oil companies, for example, have used ads on television since 1973 to explain the high cost of energy and to describe what the oil industry is doing to combat the problem. Environmentalists have done the same to dramatize pollution and the hazards it poses to life and health. Such campaigns are expensive and require the skills of professionals to be successful.

The media can be effective, if expensive, ways to reach the public, but they do not necessarily influence policymakers. The major impact of media campaigns is on agenda setting. "Here may lie the most important effect of mass communication, its ability to mentally order and organize our world for us. In short, the mass media may not be successful in telling us what to think, but they are stunningly successful in telling us what to think about."[34]

Businesses are pressured to divest their interests in South Africa as a means of opposing apartheid.

Direct Action   A form of influence increasingly in use by at least some interest groups is direct action. We are seeing a tendency on the part of some groups to protest, picket, and even threaten violence as a form of lobbying activity. Direct action has become a useful device for small groups seeking to increase their bargaining power.[35] Consumer and environmental interest groups have been most prone to boycotts, pickets, and demonstrations. These can be effective techniques to dramatize and crystallize public opinion and force public-policy activity, but they involve obvious risks. If the public does not see the actions as legitimate, they invite strong response and may result in a loss of power or prestige for the organization. Such activities are most strongly identified with minorities, the disadvantaged, and the poor. When white middle-class protesters engage in direct action, however, such as in the antibusing campaigns, such techniques inspire less opposition.

The evidence collected by Michael Lipsky seems to suggest that protest action does gain media coverage, and that protest can affect policymakers in the political system. The chances for successful direct action, however, remain slim. Public officials are likely to respond to their traditional publics, not to protest groups.[36]

Social and Technical Services   Lobbyists seek to provide services in order to enhance their standing with policymakers. Much of this activity is legitimate, but some lobbyists feel a need to make their presence known by providing entertainment. In some cases, the services are in the form of gratuities, free theater tickets, or meals. In recent years concerns about conflict of interest have quelled many of the more flagrant forms of gift giving. More common services are those based on friendship and mutual concerns. Lobbyists will trade information, often providing detailed reports based on painstaking research for a public official. Often they will write speeches for a representative or a public official. Information a lobbyist is party to may help an overworked and underinformed bureaucrat or enhance a legislator's own career or position vis-a-vis the departmental secretary or committee.

The greater the extent to which any group can be viewed as a source of technical information and expertise on a subject, the greater will be the reliance on it by legislators and bureaucrats. Professional groups such as the American Medical Association and the American Bar Association traditionally enjoy an advantage. When the American Medical Association comments on health care or the American Bar Association on judicial qualifications, their areas of expertise offer little base for challenge.

Lobbyists may also use social events as opportunities to bring decision makers and lobbyists together. The country club and the cocktail circuit are familiar approaches used by the lobbyist. These are partially deductible expenses for an organization. President Carter sought to tighten controls over such spending. In fact, reformers urge broader registration laws for lobbyists and more detailed accounting of expenses and activity to assure the public that influence buying does not take place.

Electoral Activities   Nominally, interest groups maintain a position of political neutrality. Their concern is to influence the policy of government, whether Democrats or Republicans are in control. Group effectiveness, however, is frequently thought to be advanced by electoral activities. The association of the AFL–CIO with the Democratic party is of long standing; the Chamber of Commerce more closely resembles the Republican party in philosophy and outlook.

The extent of electoral activity depends on the resources of interest groups—that is, their money and votes. As political parties and political candidates need both, interest groups become a major electoral resource: "Interest groups that are capable of coordinating their members' activities can function alongside the operation of the regular party organization, providing a welcome supplement to the party's activities."[37]

There are several reasons why interest groups seek an alliance with political parties. Carol Greenwald has noted three. First, party cooperation is another way to ensure a group's access to public officials. Second, groups with sufficient resources (membership or money) can make use of the electoral process to display and maximize these resources. Third, participation in party politics provides an opportunity to shape campaign issues and party platforms in ways acceptable to the group. This forces candidates to take stock of interest-group positions and either support them or be aware of the consequences of nonsupport.[38]

More recently, some writers on political parties have suggested that party organization and traditional support have collapsed. Political parties are only umbrella organizations for interest groups. Interest groups are not uniting and compromising in an alliance, but demanding that the party and candidate move to the group's position. The increasing number of amateurs in politics, including groups seeking convention delegates, forces the political parties into a difficult position. They must appeal to interest groups and yet struggle to maintain a majoritarian interest in order to elect candidates to public office.

Political Action Committees (PACs): *a legal method for labor unions, professional associations, corporations, or other organizations to solicit funds to be spent for political purposes.*

Campaign Contributions   Elections cost a great deal of money. One of the prime resources an interest group can provide is money. In 1976, congressional campaigns cost $100 million; in 1982 the figure was $300 million. Much of the money comes from interest groups, notably their political action committees (PACs). A **political action committee** is a legal method for labor unions, professional associations, corporations, or any other organization to solicit funds to be spent for political purposes. In the wake of Watergate and illegal corporate contributions, the formation of PACs has given business firms a legal opportunity to solicit employees and stockholders for political contributions. PACs are now a potent force in congressional elections. "PAC receipts grew from $19.2 million in 1972 to $137 million in 1980; their expenditures rose from $19 million in 1972 to $133 million in 1980; and their contributions to congressional candidates increased from $8.5 million in 1972 to $55.3 million in 1980. The proportion of PAC receipts going to congressional candidates in general election campaigns increased from 13.7 percent in 1972 to 25.3 percent in 1980."[39]

Political action committee growth has been phenomenal. In 1970 there were only 90 PACs, in 1974 there were 600, and by 1978 the number had risen to 1,653. This staggering growth continued into the 1980s, as is evident from Table 7.3; by 1984 there were 4,300 PACs. Their influence has grown as dramatically as their number. In 1974 PACs spent $12 mil-

TABLE 7.3   The growth of political action committees

Type of PAC	1974	1976	1978	1980	1982	1984
Corporate	89	433	808	1,226	1,500	1,809
Labor	201	224	217	318	350	438
Ideological	—	—	73	241	644	1,146
Trade, member, and health	318	489	451	490	613	757
Other	—	—	104	276	43	197
Total	608	1,146	1,653	2,551	3,150	4,347
Contributions to congressional candidates (in millions)	$11.6	$21.5	$32	$57.25	$85.7	$113.0

SOURCE: Federal Election Commission, 1984.

lion. That figure tripled to $32 million in 1978. For 1980 the 1978 figure nearly doubled, to $57 million. In 1984 the money donated to congressional candidates reached $113 million—representing a tenfold increase in only one decade. The PAC contributions to congressional candidates now account for one-third to one-half of all money received by the candidates.

PACs play a dominant role in many congressional races, and their proliferation, particularly in corporate and ideological groups, has flooded campaigns with money. Their recent growth has aided conservative candidates and has rebalanced the liberal and labor bias that existed in the earliest PACs. In 1982 the coffers of conservative and corporate PACs gave GOP and conservative candidates a large financial boost. The lion's share of PAC contributions goes to incumbents, where chances for re-election are the greatest. (See Table 7.4.)

One of the oldest and best-known political action committees is the AFL–CIO's Committee on Political Education (COPE). Indeed, in the early years of PACs, labor groups dominated the scene. Today that picture is reversed, and presently some 1,800 corporate PACs are in existence. Almost every major corporation has a PAC. In addition, almost all trade associations—such as the National Association of Realtors and the

TABLE 7.4   Political action committees' political financing, 1984 (in millions of dollars)

	Funds			Race			Congress					
	Raised	Spent	Contributed to federal candidates	President	Senate	House	Incumbent	Challenger	Open	Dem.	GOP	Other
Corporate	66.3	59.2	39.0	.7	14.3	24.0	30.2	3.9	4.1	14.9	24.1	—
Labor	51.1	47.5	26.2	.3	5.6	20.3	16.7	5.9	3.2	24.7	1.5	—
Ideological	102.8	97.4	15.3	.2	5.8	9.3	7.8	5.0	2.3	8.0	7.3	—
Trade, member, health	59.3	54.0	28.3	.2	7.3	20.8	22.3	3.1	2.7	13.9	14.4	—
Other	9.1	8.7	4.1	.1	1.1	3.0	3.5	.3	.3	2.5	1.6	—
Total	288.6	266.8	112.9	1.5	34.1	77.4	80.5	18.2	12.6	64.0	48.9	—

SOURCE: Federal Election Commission, 1984.

American Medical Association—have established PACs. The most recent proliferation of PACs has occurred among ideological groups. The conservative movement in the 1980s has been led by the National Conservative Political Action Committee (NCPAC), dubbed "Nick-Pac." This committee took the lead in defeating several liberal congressmen in 1980. It is well financed and uses modern campaign mail and advertising techniques to influence voters.

Do political contributions produce success? There is no question that more money goes to incumbents and that incumbents very often win reelection. Furthermore, there is recent evidence that money is crucial to the success of any challenger. It is nonincumbents who need the attention and recognition of voters, and spending money is the way to achieve recognition. "The more the challenger spends, the smaller the incumbent's victory margins."[40] There is also evidence that contributors, particularly PAC contributors, concentrate on legislators on committees dealing with group areas of interest. Fred Wirtheimer of Common Cause has reported that Representative Blouin of the House Education and Labor Committee, in a tough reelection battle, received campaign gifts from two dozen unions. Members on the House Agriculture Committee received large contributions from dairy industry PACs, and maritime unions gave extensively to Democrats on the House Committee on Merchant Marine and Fisheries.

Regulation

In recent years, interest groups increasingly have come under attack. The charges of special-interest peddling, captive public policy, and influence buying are all frequently heard. The word lobbyist connotes sinister motives. In a reform-minded environment, where political scandal and campaign money have worked to erode public trust and confidence, it is not surprising that interest-group regulation and reform should surface. In 1975, a Harris Poll found three-fourths of the American people agreeing that "Congress is still too much under the influence of special interest lobbies." It is the abuses to the constitutional right of speech under the First Amendment that have led to demands for reform. The Ninety-fourth and Ninety-fifth Congresses struggled with lobby reform, but without much success. Watergate, Koreagate, and the phenomenal rise of political action committees have speeded the pace of reform. Yet Congress is cautious about impinging on the First Amendment or damaging its own basis of support and contributions.

The basic regulations are still those of the 1946 Federal Regulation of Lobbying Act. Passed by Congress as part of the Legislative Reorganization Act of 1946, this act was directed toward congressional activity and merely required individuals receiving money from an individual or group for the purposes of lobbying Congress to register with the House and Senate. Lobbyists were required to register, identify their employer, list their general legislative objectives, and file quarterly expense reports, as were the parent groups.

The act contained as many loopholes as it did regulations. It defined lobbying narrowly as the solicitation and collection of money for influencing legislation. Groups or individuals that spent money on their own behalf were exempt from registering. Lobbyists could define for themselves what expenditures were required to be reported as lobbying expenses. Large sums and considerable activity could be excluded at a group's discretion. More critically, the law was specifically directed at individuals and groups making direct contact with legislators for the "principal purpose" of influencing legislation. Groups not making direct personal contact or those able to argue that their principal purpose was other than lobbying did not have to register. For thirty years the National Association of Manufacturers did not register, claiming it served numerous purposes other than lobbying.[41] The act specifically exempted testimony before congressional committees and did not cover regulatory agencies or the federal bureaucracy.

In the wake of Watergate, Congress worked on several new versions of lobby legislation. A Senate bill required registration based on a new definition of lobbying: a group was considered to be lobbying Congress when it had one paid officer or employee and retained a law firm or raised $5,000 in solicitations. This bill applied only to Congress. The Senate bill included far more extensive and detailed reporting requirements. The House passed reform legislation in 1976, but the House bill differed from that of the Senate by defining a lobbyist as an individual or group spending $1,250 a quarter to lobby and spending 20 percent of an employee's time for lobbying activities. The two chambers could not agree on a compromise, so although each chamber had drafted legislation, no new law emerged from the Ninety-fourth Congress.

The Ninety-fifth Congress did not prove any more successful, though once again it sought lobby-reform legislation. The House Judiciary bill was similar to its predecessor but set the lobbying expense figure at $2,500 a quarter and the number of days a person was employed to lobby at thirteen or more in a quarter. This bill also included a significant disclosure provision for grass roots efforts. The Senate proposed its own version, which was significantly stronger than the House bill. However, Congress adjourned before any joint action could take place.

In 1979 a group of lobbyists banded together, calling themselves the American League of Lobbyists. The group is committed to improving the image, if not the conduct, of lobbyists. They have proposed a "Lobbyists' Code of Ethics," which asks lobbyists to "place the public's interest above all others, giving loyalty to the highest ethical principles and to the nation, above loyalty to employer, client, or personal interest." Their ten standards of conduct require lobbyists to be honest, to avoid conflicts of interest, and to report all violations of the principles. The group remains small but, in the absence of greater federal regulation, offers some prospect for self-regulation.

The Changing Nature of Group Influence

Back during ratification of the Constitution, James Madison warned Americans in his *Federalist No. 10* about the mischiefs of faction (groups), about a factious spirit that tainted our public administration, caused distrust of public engagements, and led to preoccupation with private rights. Madison said, "The regulation of these various and interfering interests forms the principal task of modern legislation and involves the spirit of party and faction in the necessary and ordinary operations of government." Are interest groups too powerful? The American public thinks so, but influence is too elusive a quality to measure. Public opinion and governmental activity are much changed since David Truman wrote *The Governmental Process,* which describes public policy as the result of group interaction. Recent scandals and campaign abuses have contributed to a cynical and distrustful atmosphere: the reforms proposed in the 1970s would have been labeled un-American during the 1950s.

Government has changed since the 1950s. The federal budget has more than quadrupled and governmental activity has expanded into new areas. The federal bureaucracy and government regulation are new issues; the characteristic liberal–conservative debate of the 1950s has been transformed into one of economy and efficiency in the 1980s. We now accept as legitimate a range of governmental activity that a few years ago would have been the source of great ideological concern.

In this context, interest groups seek to organize, operate, and compete for access to the decision-making process. The belief that they dominate public policy through influence peddling is a naive view of the contemporary political system. As government expanded and increased its efforts, new programs created new clientele groups. This does not make policymaking more difficult; rather, it makes change less likely. "The competition of interest groups does not, in the long run, make it more difficult for the government to start doing things, it only makes it difficult for the government to stop."[42]

James Wilson's point in the above quote was that the expanded scope of government settled the primary issue dividing interest groups. The issue became in the 1970s not the right of government to act but the way in which it would and how much money it would spend. Advocacy of an issue became a matter of public interest. As Wilson put it, "It is difficult to take negative positions on these matters without appearing to defend, out of one's stake and without a philosophical fig leaf, private advantage."[43] This is the atmosphere in which we must confront single-issue politics today.

Single-issue groups are on the rise. The changes in governmental activity and the changes in attitudes among the American people have spawned numerous separate and single-minded groups. Such groups are ideologically and politically inflexible; they reject much of the shared consensus and political-party activity of the past generation. Single-issue groups take on private and narrow interests, push them onto the public agenda, and demand satisfaction as a moral responsibility.

This development has some important consequences for interest groups. One such change has been to identify clientele groups more closely with governmental agencies. For example, the Office of Economic Opportunity "lobbied" for welfare rights and benefits. It makes more difficult the politicization of any group in terms of group benefits. A private good is transformed into a public good.

The increased scope of government confers a new legitimacy on interest groups and denies to other groups their traditional legitimacy. Public interest groups have arisen in recent years with the goal of making government accountable. This has provided them with a status and mission that a decade ago would have attracted little interest. Tax reform groups also attract interest in the wake of Proposition 13, the measure initiated in California to reduce taxes and limit future taxes. By contrast, labor and business groups that have traditionally opposed one another on basic economic terms have suffered. Both labor and business are seen as protected; the public turns to regulation and controlling wages and prices. The traditional issues of free enterprise, collective bargaining, and a minimum wage are seen as "givens." Increased protection for the public via regulation is now more relevant.

The rise of new interest groups in the 1960s and 1970s and the mobilizing of small constituencies has changed expectations. The newer groups carry an ideological commitment in the name of the public. They may act as "veto groups," thereby preventing change. Their support for political parties appears to be waning; alliances have become more difficult to form. The result is that issues get on the public agenda, traditional political practices are criticized, but little change is produced. Whether this is democracy in action is open to debate.

Summary

1. There is no clear-cut evidence on the influence of interest groups on the political process. We know interest groups can exercise considerable power, but not all groups are equal in their ability to influence. We still do not know how to measure influence accurately.

2. Interest groups are important to the political process because they provide a means of representing individual interest to government. Yet Americans are skeptical about groups as "influence peddlers." Newer issue groups have narrowed their focus, concentrating on single issues.

3. Traditional interests such as business and labor continue to function but are being challenged for influence by new environmental and public interest groups. Many group members find membership valuable for the individual satisfaction of participation and tangible rewards.

4. The success of an interest group depends on the size and cohesion of the group, the skills of the organization's leadership, and the nature of

the action required to advance its goals. Generally, groups opposing governmental action are more successful than groups needing to initiate new policies.

5. A key factor in interest-group influence has been the growth in political action committees. PACs have provided a legal means for organizations to contribute money to political campaigns. In recent years PACs have come to dominate the financing of election campaigns. Calls for reform and spending limits are increasingly heard.

Research Projects

1. *Group lobbying* Select a group in your city or area—for instance, a labor union, a corporation, or an environmental group. The telephone book can be of help. Make an appointment and send letters of inquiry regarding the group's political interest and activity on some issue. You might wish to inquire as to the group's

   a. goals—does it want new legislation, will it prevent new legislation, and is it involved with regulatory agencies?
   b. staff—are there full-time, paid personnel employed to lobby?
   c. budget—how much money is devoted to lobbying?
   d. techniques—what kinds of activities does the group engage in (testimony, letters, litigation, public relations)?

2. *Group testimony* Select a bill that is before Congress. Read the *Congressional Record* and review the testimony on the bill in committee. What percentage of the people testifying on the bill represent interest groups? What groups support and oppose the bill? Can you assess the nature of support and opposition? Finally, determine the quality of the testimony based on facts, thoroughness, and skill of presentation as best you can from the record.

3. *Interest profile* Select an issue you are concerned about. How many interest groups exist that are concerned with that issue, both nationally and locally? The *Encyclopedia of Associations* will list the number of national groups and their addresses; the telephone book can help you locally. You may wish to join one of them.

Notes

1. Samuel H. Barnes, "Some Political Consequences of Involvement in Organizations," paper delivered at the American Political Science Association Annual Meeting, 1977.
2. Robert Winter-Berger, as cited by Carol S. Greenwald in *Group Power* (New York: Praeger, 1977), p. 324.
3. Lewis Anthony Dexter, *How Organizations Are Represented in Washington* (Indianapolis, Ind.: Bobbs-Merrill, 1969), p. 7.

4. Lester Milbrath, *The Washington Lobbyist* (Chicago: Rand McNally, 1963), p. 353.
5. See Robert Engler, *The Politics of Oil* (Chicago: University of Chicago Press, 1967); Mark Nadel, *Corporations and Political Accountability* (Lexington, Mass.: D. C. Heath, 1976); and Russell Warren Howe and Sarah Hays Trott, *The Power Peddlers: How Lobbyists Mold America's Foreign Policy* (New York: Doubleday, 1977).

6. David B. Truman, *The Governmental Process* (New York: Alfred A. Knopf, 1951), p. 37.
7. Greenwald, *Group Power*, p. 15.
8. Ibid., p. 63.
9. Robert Presthus, *Elite Accommodation in Canadian Politics* (New York: Cambridge University Press, 1975), p. 173. Compare with his "Interest Group Lobbying: Canada and the United States," *Annals of the American Academy of Political and Social Science* (May 1974): 44–57.
10. Presthus, "Interest Group Lobbying," especially pp. 49–50.
11. V. O. Key, Jr., *Politics, Parties and Pressure Groups* (New York: Thomas Y. Crowell, 1958), p. 82.
12. Norman J. Ornstein and Shirley Elder, *Interest Groups, Lobbying and Policymaking* (Washington, D.C.: Congressional Quarterly Press, 1978), p. 38.
13. Greenwald, *Group Power*, p. 29.
14. Ornstein and Elder, *Interest Groups, Lobbying and Policymaking*, pp. 40–41.
15. Harry Holloway, "The Political Machine of the AFL–CIO," *Political Science Quarterly* 94 (Spring 1979): 132.
16. There are several interesting and revealing case studies of these associations and their political activities. Robert Alford, *Health Care Politics: Ideological and Interest Group Barriers to Reform* (Chicago: University of Chicago Press, 1975); Stephen Bailey, *Education Interest Groups in the Nation's Capital* (Washington, D.C.: American Council of Education, 1975); Joel B. Grossman, *Lawyers and Judges: The ABA and the Politics of Judicial Selection* (New York: Wiley, 1965); and Richard Harris, *A Sacred Trust* (Baltimore: Penguin Books, 1969).
17. Jeffrey M. Berry, *Lobbying for the People: The Political Behavior of Public Interest Groups* (Copyright © 1977 by Princeton University Press), p. 7. Reprinted by permission of Princeton University Press.
18. Greenwald, *Group Power*, p. 181.
19. Neal R. Peirce, *National Journal* (August 3, 1985): 1808.
20. Ibid.
21. Berry, *Lobbying for the People*, p. 14.
22. Ibid., p. 291.
23. There are some interesting studies of ethnic, race and religious groups in politics. See Ronald H. Baylor, *Neighbors in Conflict: The Irish, Germans, Jews and Italians of New York City, 1929–1941* (Baltimore: Johns Hopkins University Press, 1978); Stephen Isaacs, *Jews and American Politics* (Garden City, N.Y.: Doubleday, 1974);

Richard Kluger, *Simple Justice: The History of Brown v. Board of Education* (New York: Alfred A. Knopf, 1975); and Richard Morgan, *The Politics of Religious Conflict* (New York: Pegasus, 1968).
24. *Congressional Quarterly, Weekly Report* (August 25, 1984): 2085.
25. Ibid., 2086.
26. Mancur Olson, *The Logic of Collective Action: Public Good and the Theory of Groups* (Cambridge, Mass.: Harvard University Press, 1965).
27. Robert H. Salisbury, "An Exchange Theory of Interest Groups," *Midwest Journal of Political Science* (February 1969): 1–32.
28. Greenwald, *Group Power*, p. 48.
29. John E. Sinclair, *Interest Groups in America* (Morristown, N.J.: General Learning Press, 1976), p. 21.
30. Ornstein and Elder, *Interest Groups, Lobbying and Policymaking*, pp. 54–58.
31. Greenwald, *Group Power*, p. 69.
32. James N. Rosenau, *Citizenship Between Elections* (New York: The Free Press, 1974), p. 209.
33. Berry, *Lobbying for the People*, p. 233.
34. Donald Shaw and Maxwell McCombs, *The Emergence of American Political Issues: The Agenda-Setting Function of the Press* (St. Paul, Minn.: West, 1977), p. 5.
35. See Michael Lipsky, "Protest as a Political Resource," *American Political Science Review* 62 (December 1968): 1144–1158.
36. Ibid., pp. 1157–1158.
37. Sinclair, *Interest Groups in America*, p. 29.
38. Greenwald, *Group Power*, p. 119.
39. M. Margaret Conway, "PACs, the New Politics, and Congressional Campaigns," in Allen Cigler and Burdett Loomis, eds., *Interest Group Politics* (Washington, D.C.: Congressional Quarterly Press, 1983).
40. Stanton Glantz, Alan Abramowitz and Michael Barkart, "Election Outcomes: Whose Money Matters?" *Journal of Politics* 28 (November 1976): 1038. See also Gary Jacobson, "The Effects of Campaign Spending in Congressional Elections," *American Political Science Review* 72 (June 1978).
41. Ornstein and Elder, *Interest Groups, Lobbying and Policymaking*, p. 104.
42. James Q. Wilson, *Political Organizations* (New York: Basic Books, 1973), p. 341.
43. Ibid., p. 343.

Bibliography

Berry, Jeffrey M. *Lobbying for the People: The Political Behavior of Public Interest Groups.* Princeton, N.J.: Princeton University Press, 1977.
   The best survey of the growth of public interest groups in the political process. The book provides both an overview of characteristics and a detailed discussion of the activity of a few such groups.
Cigler, Allen, and Loomis, Burdett. *Interest Group Politics.* Washington, D.C.: Congressional Quarterly Press, 1986.
   A collection of essays, the volume covers the internal workings, electoral activity, and policymaking role of interest groups.
Dexter, Lewis A. *How Organizations Are Represented in Washington.* Indianapolis, Ind.: Bobbs-Merrill, 1969.
   A basic work that surveys representational efforts of groups in Washington, D.C. Discusses the means and activities of lobbyists seeking to represent interests before government. Dexter understands representation to be more inclusive than lobbying.

Greenwald, Carol S. *Group Power*. New York: Praeger, 1977.

  The best work to date on interest groups. Provides an excellent overview of interest group activity, resources, and strategies. Spiced with examples.

Ornstein, Norman, and Elder, Shirley. *Interest Groups, Lobbying and Policymaking*. Washington, D.C.: Congressional Quarterly Press, 1978.

  An excellent, readable discussion of interest groups lobbying the national government. The book provides a good introduction with theories of group activity and three case studies illustrate lobbying activity.

Rosenau, James. *Citizenship Between Elections*. New York: The Free Press, 1974.

  A complex and sophisticated treatment of political participation taking nonelectoral forms. By surveying citizens, Rosenau seeks to explain kinds and amounts of participation and whether activities were self-initiated.

Sabato, Larry. *PAC Power: Inside the World of Political Action Committees*. New York: Norton, 1985.

  A detailed discussion of political action committees and their various forms of political activity, especially campaign financing. Sabato's look at how PACs operate is based on interviews with several PAC leaders; it provides an in-depth account of the role of PACs in American politics.

Schlozman, Kay, and Tierney, John. *Organized Interests and American Democracy*. New York: Harper & Row, 1986.

  In this survey, the authors place interest group activity in Washington within the larger framework of American politics. They examine the influence of interest groups within the confines of a democratic political system. They claim that interest groups, while expanding in number and activities, are not about to overrun American politics.

Verba, Sidney, and Nie, Norman. *Participation in America*. New York: Harper & Row, 1972.

  An extensive survey of the forms and extent of political participation in America. Makes heavy use of data and becomes technical in places, yet the treatment is thorough and informative on varieties of participation.

Ziegler, L. Harmon, and Peak, Wayne. *Interest Groups in American Politics*. Englewood Cliffs, N.J.: Prentice-Hall, 1972.

  A basic textbook on interest groups that covers the full array of topics. There are good chapters on the role of interest groups in American politics as well as separate chapters on business and labor groups.

olitical Parties

Nowhere have the changing expectations of American politics been more dramatic than in the case of political parties. American political parties are in a state of decline. For two decades, partisan attachment to the two major parties has been weakening. "Strong" Republicans (GOP) and "strong" Democrats have decreased by a third in each party, and national nominating conventions now largely ratify presidential candidate decisions made by voters in primaries and caucuses months prior to the convention. Ticket splitting has become increasingly common. Writes Everett Ladd, a perceptive student of political parties, "American political parties manifest a diminished institutional presence. As labels, as names on the ballot, they are alive and well, but as organizations they have withered."[1]

Several commentators have written on the impact of contemporary society on political parties, the pressures that have been eroding political party support, and the parties' organizational structures. Figure 8.1 shows the changes in the American electorate. Several important consequences have emerged as a result of changing economic and social relationships

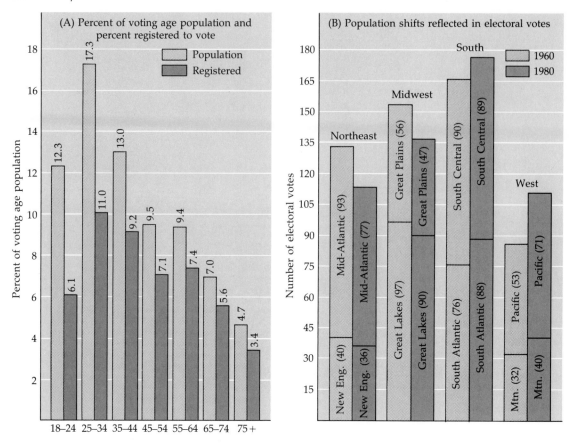

Figure 8.1 (A) Percent of population that has reached voting age and percent registered to vote (B) Population shifts reflected in electoral votes

in "postindustrial" America. The change to sophisticated technologies, notably computer data processing, public polling, and media campaigning, has weakened party control over the electoral process. Candidates and the public are now in direct contact. The increasing educational level of the American electorate means that issues have become more important. Citizens today are more likely to enter the political process out of a sense of commitment to a candidate or to an issue than at any time in our history. Public interest concerns are replacing the more narrowly defined concerns of interest groups, which once dominated the parties. Labor, for example, no longer dominates the Democratic party. Republicans have become increasingly alarmed over the charge that big business interests dictate their policy. In a political environment where politics is becoming more technologically complicated and the electorate more independent, political parties find a diminished role. "Anti-partyism" has become a popular stance.

The Decline of the Parties

Three factors play a role in the decline of political parties: the weakening of party loyalty, changes in campaigning and campaign organizations, and reforms in the nominating process.

Party Loyalty

No factor has received more public attention in the media than the shifting of party loyalty among the American electorate since 1960. From 1960 through 1984, partisans lost numbers to the ranks of independents (see Table 8.1). The loss, particularly among strong party identifiers, was most evident through the 1970s, during which the number of independents increased 50 percent. The Reagan years have seen some evidence of growth in Republican party identifiers. Overall the growth remains small, but as a recovery from the 1970s the GOP turnaround takes on greater significance. The GOP particularly made strong gains among voters under age 30. Apparently the mood of confidence and popular support for Ronald Reagan in the 1980s is having its greatest impact among those voters who have most recently entered the political process. This reverses a trend: in 1977, 41 percent of voters under 30 years of age called themselves independent; today less than 30 percent under 30 call themselves independent (see Table 8.2).

Ticket Splitting: *when party identifiers vote for some candidates of the opposing party on the election ballot.*

The declining loyalty to political parties can also be seen in the dramatic rise in **ticket splitting,** as shown by the increased percentage of congressional districts carried by a presidential candidate and congressional candidates of opposing parties. The rise of ticket splitting parallels the decline in partisan identification. Fifty percent of the voters are not voting for all candidates of one party, but are exercising independent judgment and casting ballots for individual candidates.

Finally, as partisan voting has declined, issue voting has increased. Voters today are much more likely to evaluate candidates and parties in terms of their issue positions and to be influenced by those stances. With the decline in party identification, issues have become a far more reliable indicator of a person's vote.[2] According to Nie, Verba, and Petrocik,

TABLE 8.1 Party identification of the electorate 1960-1984

	1960	1964	1968	1972	1976	1978	1980	1982	1984
Strong Democrats	20%	27%	20%	15%	15%	15%	18%	20%	17%
Weak Democrats	25	25	25	26	25	24	23	24	20
Independents	23	23	30	35	37	38	34	30	34
Weak Republicans	14	14	15	13	14	13	14	14	15
Strong Republicans	16	11	10	10	9	8	9	10	12
Apolitical, other	3	1	1	1	1	3	2	2	2

SOURCE: Center for Political Studies, University of Michigan. (Figures do not add up to 100% due to rounding.)

TABLE 8.2   Party preference by age

	18–30	31–44	45–60	61 and over
1980				
Republican	35%	33%	34%	41%
Democrat	54	60	57	55
Independent	5	5	7	2
1985				
Republican	47	43	39	43
Democrat	47	48	51	51
Independent	4	6	9	5
Change				
Republican	+12	+10	+5	+2
Democrat	−7	−12	−6	−4

SOURCE: ABC/*Washington Post* Poll, reported in *National Journal* (October 5, 1985): 2275.

"Over the two-decade period (1952–1972), party evaluations have come to have less effect on the vote. . . . When it comes to issue evaluations, the increase in their impact on the vote comes from the increased numbers who evaluate candidates in issue terms."[3]

Changing Campaigns

The year 1972 was a landmark one for political parties. In that year both parties faced insurgent, or nonparty, campaign organizations by candidates for the presidency. George McGovern's supporters used the reform rules of the Democratic party to "capture" a majority of the convention delegates and nominate their candidate. They did so at the expense of the party regulars and partisan support. On the Republican side an incumbent president, Richard Nixon, set up a totally autonomous campaign organization—the Committee to Re-Elect the President—to finance and operate his reelection drive. The Republican party became superfluous to the campaign; the money raised was spent to reelect the president, not to support GOP candidates, and organization staff was drawn from the White House, not the party. In some cases, the committee supported Democratic candidates considered closer to the president than their Republican challengers.

This trend in campaigning has been gaining momentum for some time. Technology has heightened the ability of candidates to forsake political parties and has accentuated the *four Ms of politics*—mobility, media, money, and machines (computers). With their new mobility, Americans no longer have the deep-seated loyalties or roots that characterized earlier generations. Attachments to parties cannot develop and grow, so voting is tied more to issues and personalities.

Campaigns are now conducted largely through the media, particularly television, which is an instantaneous vehicle for reaching large masses of people. Television is also extremely personal: the candidates can speak directly to the people in settings they control. This way of campaigning accentuates the importance of personality and image. Rather than party loyalty, characteristics such as reliability, honesty, and competence are dramatized. Previously, candidates needed to rely on campaign organizations, door-to-door volunteers, whistle-stop tours, and billboards. Today a candidate needs an advertising specialist, prime time, and money.

Technological sophistication costs money—a great deal of money. The cost of elections has soared. A presidential election (primary contest and general election) costs nearly $200 million, and congressional races can run into the millions. Most of the money is used first to poll and analyze issue trends and voting patterns. Such data processing has heightened the need for machines—notably computers—to provide detailed, sophisticated information on contemporary electoral behavior. Once the concerns have been targeted, a media campaign is set in motion. Radio, television, and newspaper ads are designed and placed, using the most specialized and effective communication techniques available. There is little need for a political party in the process.

Coattail Effect: *the power of a presidential candidate to attract voters so that congressional candidates of the same party are elected to office.*

Incumbency: *public officials in office running for reelection. Incumbents often attract voters because of their office and greater name recognition.*

Two important effects of this more personal campaign style are the decline of **presidential coattails** in elections and the advantage of **incumbency** in running for election. Throughout the century, one pattern has been consistent: in election years presidential candidates have succeeded in carrying with them congressional candidates of their party, while in off-year elections success for congressional candidates of the president's party has declined. The regularity of this pattern had been impressive, but now the coattail effect is disappearing and congressional races are becoming insulated from the presidential contest. During the 1930s the average gain or loss for the Democrats was forty-eight seats,[4] but in the 1970s the net change severely diminished. In the 1980s, President Reagan's coattails early on served the Republican party well. But by 1984 the average gain in seats dropped appreciably. In 1986 Reagan campaigned for GOP congressmen and senators, calling the election a referendum on his administration. The result was almost no change in House seats, but the loss of GOP control in the Senate, where Republicans lost eight seats.

Incumbency is increasingly an asset for political candidates. Whether due to ticket splitting, the ability to raise campaign revenue, or the media, it is a political fact that incumbents win reelection and win handily. In the post–World War II years, incumbent candidates to the House of Representatives won 90 percent of their elections; incumbent senators were only slightly less successful, winning approximately 80 percent of their elections. In better than two-thirds of these cases, the results were not even close; the incumbent won with more than 55 percent of the popular vote.

Reforms of the Nominating Process

The theme of party reform has been a strong one in the past decade. Since 1968, the Democrats have struggled with internal reforms. The GOP has made less sweeping changes, but has become increasingly con-

Jesse Jackson, Walter Mondale, and Gary Hart: the three principals at the
Democratic National Convention in 1984.

cerned about party reform. A longer-standing reform has been the use of
the primary election as the means of nominating candidates and convention delegates; the primary takes candidate selection out of the hands of
party regulars and places it with the citizen-voter.

Democratic party reforms have encouraged more participation in the
party through the open caucus. This development has facilitated participation by political activists—the amateurs who come to politics out of an
ideological commitment to issues and/or a candidate. The **political amateur** is rewarded by party reform and ideological commitment, not party
stability. State Soule and McGrath, "The political world of the amateur is
defined by internal party democracy, by intense commitment to policies
and programs, and by a reluctance to compromise even though the consequences may spell electoral defeat."[5]

Reform of the presidential nominating conventions has meant that 50
percent of convention delegates are selected by primary elections. The
parties have lost control of the delegate selection process: "Serious candidates have to create elaborate personal organizations to wage the costly
and far-flung campaigns that are a precondition of winning."[6] Educated,
issue-oriented activists dominate the convention and candidate selection.
Party harmony is no longer a concern, as the McGovernites showed in
1972 when they refused to compromise on seating delegates and rejected
Mayor Richard Daley and the Chicago delegation. In 1984 the Democrats
were again plagued by disunity as Gary Hart and Rev. Jesse Jackson challenged Walter Mondale for the Democratic nomination.

The electoral primary has greatly enhanced this personalized style
of campaigning. In 1976, the "outsider" to national Democratic politics,

Political Amateurs:
*individuals who are
politically motivated by
issues or attachment to
a candidate, not party
loyalty.*

Jimmy Carter, benefited directly from the primaries by building upon his success in them to win the Democratic nomination. In 1984 both presidential candidates—Reagan and Mondale—came to the convention with primary-selected delegates. This made the balloting a foregone conclusion and left the conventions with no meaningful choices, although both Hart and Jackson sought to persuade pledged delegates to either switch their votes or boycott the first ballot in an unsuccessful effort to derail Mondale's bid for the nomination.

Primaries take nominations out of the hands of the party, or at least weaken partisan control in the name of democracy, and place potential candidates directly before the voters. Reliance on the media and appeal to volatile issues enhance candidate success but weaken party responsibility. In 1984 the Democrats started out with eight candidates for the presidential nomination. Everett Ladd likens the presidential-nominee selection process to a flea market:

> Thus the U.S. has been reduced in presidential-nominee selection to a system of chaotic individualism. Each individual entrepreneur (the candidate) sets up shop and hawks his wares, that is, himself. The buyers—the voters—do not find the same choice of merchandise in all the states, and one seller, who may attract only a small segment of all the buyers, is finally granted a monopoly. Candidates are able to win, then, because of crowded fields, low turnouts, and strategic miscalculations by their opponents, but above all because there is no one in charge. Increasingly there is no formal party mechanism in place with substantial authority to plan for the outcome.[7]

Shaping the Party System

The parties are durable institutions, however; they have survived challenge and change before. In fact, they survive because there is no coherent party organization or clearly identifiable membership. Both parties compete for the same citizen support; both are decentralized coalitions of candidates, interest groups, party activists, and citizen identifiers. They function sporadically—at election time. At the national level, the parties function once every four years when coalitions must mass to nominate a party candidate for the presidency.

Historical Development

The framers of the Constitution did not foresee the development of parties as we understand them; the Constitution does not even mention political parties. Yet the framers were well aware of the tendency to associate in groups. James Madison's *Federalist No. 10* warned of this tendency to disregard the public good "in the conflicts of rival parties." The convention itself split into two factions over ratification, with the Federalists supporting the new Constitution and the anti-Federalists opposing it.

Left: In 1868, the Democratic convention included a torchlight parade in Union Square, New York City. *Right:* The Republican convention more than a hundred years later.

President Washington, in his farewell address upon leaving office, warned the nation against what he viewed as "the baneful effects of the spirit of Party."

Political parties began to take root during Washington's administration (see Figure 8.2). Alexander Hamilton, as Washington's secretary of the treasury, promoted a national banking system and strong, centralized government authority. This position earned him the support of bankers, manufacturers, large landholders, and commercial interests (we often call this group the Whig party). Alarmed over this aristocratic concentration of power, Thomas Jefferson and James Madison became the spokesmen for a coalition of republican democrats, farmers, trappers, frontiersmen, debtors, and laborers. This was the first Republican party.

These groups, however, remained largely coalitions. The election of 1800 saw the ascendancy of Jefferson and republican democracy. The Republican coalition remained more or less intact until 1824, when competition between factions within the party broke out. One group supported John Quincy Adams; the other supported Andrew Jackson. With the election of 1832, groups of supporters came together to nominate and campaign for a "party" candidate. This was the origin of genuine political parties as we understand them today.

After 1832, the Adams supporters called themselves National Republicans, and the Jacksonian backers called themselves Democratic Republicans. From then on these two parties (the Democratic Republicans dropped the label Republican and called themselves Democrats; the Republicans were replaced by the Whigs in the 1830s, only to be replaced by Republicans in the mid-1850s) nominated, supported, and tried to control candidates running for public office.

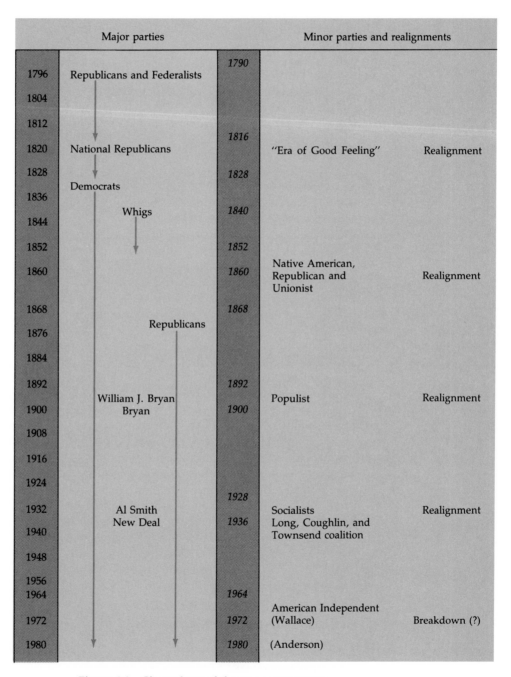

	Major parties			Minor parties and realignments	
1796	Republicans and Federalists	1790			
1804					
1812					
1820	National Republicans	1816	"Era of Good Feeling"	Realignment	
1828		1828			
1836	Democrats				
1844	Whigs	1840			
1852		1852			
1860		1860	Native American, Republican and Unionist	Realignment	
1868	Republicans	1868			
1876					
1884					
1892	William J. Bryan Bryan	1892	Populist	Realignment	
1900		1900			
1908					
1916					
1924		1928			
1932	Al Smith New Deal	1936	Socialists Long, Coughlin, and Townsend coalition	Realignment	
1940					
1948					
1956					
1964		1964			
1972		1972	American Independent (Wallace)	Breakdown (?)	
1980		1980	(Anderson)		

Figure 8.2 Chronology of the two-party system

From the third decade of the nineteenth century until the present, political campaigning has been dominated by two large coalitions nominating and supporting candidates for public office. In the 1850s and 1860s, slavery and the nature of the union dominated the parties. A North–South split began to replace the East–West, urban–rural divisions. At the turn of the century, populism and reform were gathering momentum. The Democrats nominated William Jennings Bryan in 1896. Theodore Roosevelt led the Republicans in the first decade of the twentieth century. World War I shattered America's isolation and the hold of the Democratic party. The Republicans dominated the 1920s while the economy prospered and big business grew as a result of new mass-production techniques for a growing number of consumer products.

Critical Realignment:
a long-term change in party identification with a relocation of groups across party lines.

The Depression of 1929 and the election of Franklin D. Roosevelt in 1932 brought a **critical realignment** of the American electorate. Since 1932, there has been a Democratic majority in America. Between 1932 and 1968, there were only eight years of Republican administration (Eisenhower's), and Congress has been in the hands of the Democratic majority for every session except two (1947–1948 and 1953–1954). Since 1968, the Democrats have continued to control one or both houses of Congress, but they held the presidency only with the victory of Jimmy Carter in 1976. In 1980 Republicans gained control of the Senate and they retained control in the 1982 and 1984 elections. Does this mean that a Republican majority is emerging, as some have suggested, or are political parties diminishing as vehicles? Are presidential races autonomously directed?

This brief historical sketch serves to illustrate the nature of the grand coalitions we have had under the two-party system. Now the Democratic New Deal coalition of Franklin Roosevelt is breaking apart. When George McGovern challenged the party in 1972, his support differed markedly from the FDR coalition of previous years. Jimmy Carter apparently pieced together enough of the "old coalition," plus the support of blacks and minorities, to gain a narrow victory in 1976. But neither Carter nor his successor in 1984, Walter Mondale, could hold the coalition together. Much of the Republican success at the presidential level since 1976 has been with traditional Democratic components of the old coalition: labor, blue-collar workers, Catholics, and the South. Add to this GOP success among whites, the middle class, and conservatives in the electorate, and the Republicans stand poised to replace the Democrats as the majority party. Some commentators today suggest that the American electorate is ready for a critical realignment, a refashioning of electoral loyalties owing to the change in political party support.

Institutional Factors

The American electoral process has been very compatible with the two-party system. Our institutional arrangements have given it support and worked to the disadvantage of minor political parties.

Single-Member District: *the method used in Congressional elections. Each of the designated number of representatives for a state is elected from a separate, single district.*

Plurality: *the largest number of voters.*

Congressional elections are conducted by districts. We use **single-member districts:** each of the designated number of representatives for a state is elected from a separate, single district and the highest vote-getter is elected. Thus, rather than using proportional representation, which apportions seats on a proportional basis, with each party entitled to a percentage of representatives based on its proportion of the popular vote, we require each party candidate to receive a **plurality** in each congressional district (if there are ten districts and the Democratic candidates each receive 40 percent of the vote and the Republican candidates each receive 60 percent of the vote, the Republicans elect ten representatives to Congress, not six; this is the winner-take-all system). Under such a system, minor parties cannot hope to capture a plurality.

The electoral college for the selection of the president operates in much the same way; a candidate needs a majority of electoral votes to be elected. A state's electoral votes *all* go to the candidate receiving the largest popular vote (a plurality gives unanimous support to a party candidate). To receive that majority, a candidate has to gain pluralities in enough states to receive the necessary number of electoral votes. The more parties there are, the less likely the majority. The dominance of the presidency in American politics keeps the electoral college coalition alive.

Ideological Factors

A final factor helping to shape the party system is political ideology. A great tradition exists in America of identifying political parties on a liberal–conservative basis. Whenever the conservative party wins seats in Congress or captures the presidency by a substantial margin, we are commonly told that the nation has shifted to the right. When Ronald Reagan was elected in 1980 and several liberal congressmen were unseated, political commentators talked about "thunder on the right."

There has always been a sense in which Americans have used ideology to relate to political parties. Traditionally ideology served as a reference point, with voters retaining little attachment to issues, but rather supporting parties more out of loyalty. Citizens separated parties more on the basis of group benefits or the nature of the times; thus, Republicans became the party of prosperity and Democrats the party of labor. People saw Democrats vaguely as liberal and more willing to use government to support economic and social programs, and they deemed Republicans conservative and opposed to government intervention in social or economic areas. Still, voters exhibited no consistent concern for issue stands in making their choices. Recently, though, growing evidence suggests that an ideological separation of the parties has occurred and that voters are attracted to parties because of their issue stance.

Issue Voting: *a growing tendency on the part of voters to take clear positions on issues and to cast their ballots on the basis of issues, instead of party identification or group affiliation.*

With the decline in party loyalty noted above, **issue voting** has increased. More and more voters have been taking clear, consistent positions on issues, and more citizens say issues are important in determining how they cast their ballots. Issue voting and party voting are coming together; they need not be incompatible.

That parties do differ in their approach to issues can be seen in a comparison of party **platforms.** The drafting of elaborate stands on contemporary issues is seen by some as a meaningless gesture, but Gerald Pomper reports considerable evidence that platform promises are fulfilled and, moreover, that they center on important programs.[8] Changes in the nation are reflected in party platforms. Reports Pomper, "Changes in the platform correspond in time with critical party realignments. A new issue brings with it a new party coalition to deal with that issue. Important changes in the content of public policy then result."[9]

The 1980s may suggest just such a realignment, although there is no common agreement on this subject. Several years ago Kevin Phillips's book, *The Emerging Republican Majority,*[10] spoke of Richard Nixon's success in attracting white urban voters, voters from the South and West, Catholics, and working-class voters to the GOP party in a trend toward conservatism. It now appears that Ronald Reagan is more likely to make Phillips's prophecy come true. In fact, since 1968 the Democrats have had limited success with voters in these groups, the only exception being Jimmy Carter's one-time success in 1976 (see Figure 8.3). The South, for example, has not voted solidly Democratic since 1960, with Democrats winning the electoral votes of Louisiana, North Carolina, South Carolina, Alabama, Mississippi, and Florida only once or twice since that year. More GOP-type voters have been migrating to the Sun Belt, which has become the home of the new conservatism, causing many to point to the South as the base for the GOP's hoped-for new majority.

The 1980 Republican victories in the presidential election and the Senate were considered evidence of a conservative shift, and Reagan's reelection sweep in 1984 was further evidence of the slide to the right. Certainly the GOP has become decidedly conservative. Both the 1980 and

Platform: *the document, written at the national convention, that specifies a party's position on issues.*

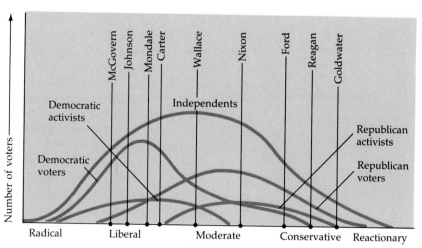

Figure 8.3 Types and examples of political positions in the United States

1984 GOP platforms took strong conservative stands on the issues, opposing ERA, abortion, forced busing, and gay rights and supporting school prayer, deregulation, tax cuts, and reduced federal spending. Yet the signals are mixed. There has been no marked change in numbers of congressional seats, with the House firmly in the Democrats' control and the Democrats regaining control of the Senate in 1986. Public support for conservative stances, while it has grown somewhat, does not command a majority. Many commentators attribute GOP success in the 1980s more to the personal popularity and skill of the "great communicator," Ronald Reagan. How intense and real realignment and conservatism in America really are will be revealed in the years to come—and will be hotly debated in the interim.

Toward Responsible Parties

The need for effective party structures is generally conceded. Political parties are the basic intermediary structures between citizens and their government, yet they have remained fragmented and loosely organized organizations with little national cohesion. Neither political party can mobilize its members in Congress or the executive branch behind a coherent party program. Moreover, the lack of party responsibility in government spills over to the electorate, who are thus unable to make clear voting decisions based on partisan distinctions. This lack of party responsibility has often been lamented.

In 1950 a committee of the American Political Science Association issued a series of reforms aimed at making political parties more programmatic, more cohesive, and more accountable. Their report became known as the "responsible party model" for political parties. It followed a long tradition of urging party loyalty and discipline. To prevent the disintegration of the two major political parties, the committee called for the following:

1. parties to bring forth programs to which they commit themselves
2. parties with sufficient internal cohesion to carry out their programs
3. a sense of responsibility by both parties to the general public as enforced through elections and by party leaders to the party membership[11]

Among the specific proposals advanced by the 1950 committee were that a national party council be formed to recommend candidates for Congress and to discipline state and local parties; that smaller but more frequent conventions be held (every two years), with the platform binding on all party officeholders; that there be closed primary elections; and that there be a national presidential primary. Only a few of the recommendations have ever been adopted and little has been accomplished in making parties more responsible. Concludes Samuel Eldersveld,

> The idea of cohesive, program-oriented, disciplined, centralized parties with 1) candidates selected because of their commitment to

programs; 2) party workers recruited on the basis of programs; 3) voters identifying with parties and supporting them primarily on the basis of programs is a conception of the American party system which clearly, in its major outlines, has not been embraced and is probably not attainable.[12]

Political Party Functions

Political parties have served and continue to serve several important functions, though in a diminished capacity. These functions center around one mission—to elect candidates to public office. Everett Ladd has identified three characteristics essential to the success of the party process: competition, representation, and organization.[13]

Competition

Political parties compete for political power. Successful candidates who assume public office organize and direct the affairs of that office; they formulate, enact, and administer public policy. The party in power knows that if it is unsuccessful, it will be replaced by the other party. A competitive two-party system keeps the party in power attentive to the public interest, responsible in formulating policy, and honest in administration. The challenging party formulates alternative positions and offers criticism so that, at election time, the voter has a choice and a basis on which to evaluate past performance.

Party competition is considered compatible with democracy because it results in alternative positions being organized and offered to the citizens. It allows the voters to express their views and to replace the party in power by peaceful, acceptable means. Party competition seeks to transcend factionalism, sectionalism, and generation as it combines individuals running for office and citizen influence in the political process. Political parties remain the major means of linking separate electoral contests so that individual citizens can exercise some measure of popular control.

Representation

Political parties present alternatives in terms of both candidates and public policy. Parties simplify the issues for the citizen so that the costs of political activity and support are not greater than the average citizen can afford. Moreover, parties afford the opportunity for candidates, interest groups, and citizens to come together to fashion a mutually acceptable set of issues and candidates in return for political support. That American parties are really coalitions has been one of their real strengths. Different people and groups have found support and representation through polit-

Practicing Politics: How to Use a Voting Machine

Some places in this country still use paper ballots and ballot boxes, but most heavily populated areas have switched to voting machines. Here is how to vote by using a voting machine:

1. Make a list of your choices or study the sample ballot at the polling place. You may carry a sample ballot into the voting booth with you.
2. Walk into the booth after you have been checked in the roll book and given a number. Move the red handle to the voting position to close the curtains.
3. Move the small black levers next to the names of the candidates you want. As you move each lever, an X will appear beside the name for which you vote. Leave the levers in position.
4. If you have made a mistake or changed your mind, move the small lever back up and press the correct one(s).
5. If you do not like any of the candidates, follow the directions for a write-in vote. Use a ballpoint pen.
6. If you have a problem, do not touch anything; put your head through the curtains and ask for help.
7. Check what you have done; then pull the red handle back to the original position. The levers go up and your vote is recorded before the curtains open.

The ballot is both symbol and substance of the political process enacted in the voting booth.

ical parties. Groups often find that their views are adopted by parties and eventually enacted into public policy.

This representational function has offered parties a constant, steady stream of potential leaders and candidates. It has kept issues and policy responsibility before the party. By uniting diverse segments of the population, the party system has played down social conflicts; aspiring leaders have had to prove ready to compromise in order to preserve the coalition.

Organization

Political parties remain the basis for organizing the government. Parties, having competed for public office and promised to represent interests, have the responsibility for running the government.

It is true that the United States does not have a system of party responsibility. Parties have little control over their members once they are in power, but they still form the basis for the organization of the government. In Congress party committees allocate committee assignments for representatives, and the president forms an administration largely from party loyalists and advisers.

Political parties are the conduit for public opinion. It is principally through political parties that the mass of citizens can exert influence over the political process and hold public officials accountable. If the control is not direct or always effective, the fundamental premise remains intact: popular control of policymakers requires organization, and political parties provide a meaningful measure of public control without unreasonably raising the costs of political participation.

Changing Functions

The American system places a heavy burden on political parties: they must organize the affairs of government while representing the public interest. This has never been easily or perfectly achieved. The process of uniting millions of people into a coalition and translating their will into public policy is bound to result in distortions. Parties have few mechanisms for ensuring partisan loyalty, and they respond sluggishly. In recent years the functions of political parties have proved even more difficult to carry out. Parties are going through a period of transition. The Republican party is making a comeback after a period of being relegated to the status of a minor party. The GOP has had control of the presidency for sixteen of the twenty years since 1968, yet has controlled the House not at all and the Senate for only eight years in that time span. The strength of the party's conservative wing is propelling its representational character in a direction different from that of its recent history.

On the other hand, internal competition among the Democrats has created an organizational morass. The New Deal coalition has faced the challenge of young and minority political activists, and the Democrats have experienced increasing difficulty in holding the coalition together. Women, Hispanics, young voters, and environmentalists have all been demanding a pivotal place within the party, at the expense of the traditional labor and black partisans.

Party nominations for the presidency have, in recent years, been more ideological and unrepresentative of the people, if election results are any measure. Goldwater in 1964 was able to gather only 38.5 percent of the popular vote for the Republicans. In 1972 McGovern won only 37.5 percent of the vote as the Democratic candidate. Twelve years later, Democrat Walter Mondale could garner barely 40 percent of the popular vote. Challengers for the nomination are also increasingly ideological: for example, McCarthy in 1968, Reagan and Harris in 1976, Crane and Kennedy in 1980, and Jackson in 1984.

Nowhere has the parties' loss of representation and control been more in evidence than in the presidential nominating process. The open caucus and the primary have opened the nomination to a wide spectrum of candidates and groups using the presidential nominating process as a platform or vehicle to dramatize issues. Their concern is less with winning than with airing their ideological commitment. This has often been the mark of minor or third parties.

Third Parties

Doctrinal Party: *a minor political party that professes a particular doctrine and nominates candidates to the presidency over several elections.*

Transient Party: *a short-lived political party that emerges out of economic protest and secessionist movements.*

Third parties are about as old as America. Almost as soon as the Republican Democrats and Whigs emerged, Americans were given third alternatives: the Anti-Masons (1832), the Know-Nothings (1856), and the Greenbackers (1880). Although none has seriously challenged the two major parties, third parties have been a vehicle for minority viewpoints. Only five times in our political history has a minor party polled more than 10 percent of the popular vote: the Know-Nothing party in 1856 got 21.1 percent of the popular vote on an anti-Catholic, anti-Irish platform; in 1860, with the division of the union, Southern Democrats and Constitutional Unionists combined to take 31 percent of the total vote; in 1912 the Progressive (Bull Moose) party of Theodore Roosevelt won 27.4 percent of the vote; in 1924 Wisconsin's Robert LaFollette won 16.6 percent of the vote as the Progressive candidate for president; and in 1968 George C. Wallace, running as the American Independent party nominee, secured 13.5 percent of the popular vote.

V. O. Key has classified minor parties into two broad categories: **doctrinal parties,** which profess a particular doctrine and nominate candidates to the presidency over several elections, and short-lived **transient parties,** which emerge out of economic protest and secessionist movements.[14]

The minor parties that endure are largely unsuccessful in influencing the election results. The Socialist and Communist parties are examples. They continuously nominate candidates for public office, including the presidency, yet they can secure no better than a small fraction of the vote.

John Anderson
An independent candidate for president in 1980, Anderson collected 7 percent of the popular vote. He began his political career as a member of the House of Representatives in 1960. In 1969 he became GOP conference chairman in the House. Known as a staunch conservative during his early years, Anderson moderated his views to become a critic of the Vietnam War and was the first GOP congressional leader to complain about the escalating nuclear arms race. As an independent candidate for the presidency in 1980, Anderson impressed people with his articulate, informed stands on issues. Critics claimed that his bid for the high office spoiled Carter's chances. This criticism proved to have been mistaken.

They survive because of a small band of dedicated supporters. Doctrinal parties exercise little influence on the electoral process and in this sense can be said to be outside the system.[15] The Populists, the Greenback party, and the Progressives of 1924 all arose as a form of economic protest. Secessionist parties develop by splitting away from one of the major parties. The Progressives of 1912 and the Dixiecrats of 1948 are examples of such movements. Minor political parties are not to be judged only by their lack of electoral success. Doctrinal minor parties seek to promote a program that runs counter to those of the major parties. Parties seeking economic reform call attention to new issues and advocate unpopular policies whose time has not yet come. The Progressive party warned of concentration of economic power and the growth of monopolies. The Prohibitionist party continues to struggle for the prohibition of the sale of alcoholic beverages. The impact of minor parties must be judged, in part, by their impact on the major parties. The secessionist parties have alerted the major parties to dissent on public issues. The Dixiecrats of 1948 gave the Democrats warning that the South and civil rights would be controversial and troublesome. The Bull Moose bolt in 1912 was a warning about changing attitudes toward big business.

The impact of third parties can be to deny the two major parties a majority of electoral votes in a presidential contest. There was much suspicion that the Wallace campaign in 1968 was designed to deny a clear majority to either party and throw the election into the House of Representatives, where some compromise could be fashioned. Some said Eugene McCarthy's bid in 1976 was designed to take electoral votes away from Jimmy Carter.

As much as anything, however, minor parties popularize issues and ideas. They serve as a sounding board for the two major political parties. Their representation functions as a pressure that forces the major parties to adjust to, and even to adopt, minor-party positions in subsequent years. For many third-party supporters, this is reason enough for the existence of third-party politics.

Has the ability of the two major parties to absorb minor-party positions diminished? Has the brokerage role of political parties, the ability to accommodate diverse points of view, broken down to a point where political activists, being denied access to the nomination, form their own parties? In short, has the decline of parties opened the way for new third-party movements? To date this has not happened, but clearly it becomes an increasing possibility given the reforms to political parties and the unwillingness of aroused delegates to compromise.

What we have seen is the rise of the independent candidate. John Anderson's independent bid for the presidency followed Eugene McCarthy's 1976 campaign. However, Anderson's 1980 run for the presidency attracted more support and affected partisan voting to a degree that influenced both major political parties.

The Supreme Court, in 1983, gave a boost, of sorts, to third-party and independent political candidates. The Court declared unconstitutional an

Running as an Independent: Elections and Public Policy

In late April 1980, John B. Anderson dropped out of the race for the Republican endorsement for the presidency and became an independent candidate. But as an independent he followed an unusual policy in American presidential politics.

In his bid for the presidency, Anderson stressed that he was not forming a third party—the routes taken by Bull Moose Theodore Roosevelt in 1912 and American Independent George Wallace in 1968. Although there have been third-party candidates on the ballot in several states—for example, in the Socialist Labor party, the Prohibition Party, and most recently, Lester Maddox as the presidential candidate from Wallace's American Independent party—Anderson chose to run alone. This was the second presidential election in a row in which there was an independent candidate; Eugene McCarthy ran as an independent in 1976.

Essentially, there are three problems of running as an independent for the presidency: ballot access, money, and votes.

The major problem is access to the ballot in the separate states. Each state sets its own laws. First, there are filing dates, and many states have filing dates in May and June. The Supreme Court, in *Anderson* v. *Celebrezze* (1983), eased this restriction by declaring unconstitutional state laws that impose an early filing date for independent presidential candidates. A second problem is the signed petitions required for filing as a candidate. For some states, only a minimal number of voter signatures are necessary, but many states require large numbers of signatures obtained according to complex rules. California requires 1 percent of all registered voters; Massachusetts requires petitions from individual towns. Other states demand the naming of a vice-presidential running mate or the selection of presidential electors.

The problem of money is far less complex but no more pleasing to an independent candidate. Independent candidates for the presidency are not entitled to public funds from the Federal Election Commission. Anderson's Democratic and Republican counterparts each received $30 million to run their fall contests. So the independent candidate must rely on voluntary private contributions to finance the campaign. The FEC did rule Anderson eligible for retroactive election funding if he achieved 5 percent of the popular vote, which he did.

Voter response is speculative, and independents have not been very successful. McCarthy garnered only 1 percent of the popular vote and no electoral votes; Anderson took 7 percent but no state's electoral votes. Most commentators suggest that the impact of these candidates was to rob major candidates of votes. Two schools of thought persist: one that Anderson hurt Carter by drawing the votes of disenchanted liberals, the other that he hurt Reagan by siphoning off some of the anti-Carter protest vote. The greatest potential of an independent candidate is to deny either major candidate an electoral majority. While this did not happen in Anderson's case, his campaign did evidence dissatisfaction with the two-party system.

Major Minor Parties

Year	Party	Popular votes (percent)	Electoral votes
1824	Democratic–Republican (Henry Clay)	12.99	37
	Democratic–Republican (William Crawford)	11.17	41
1832	Independent Democrat	0	11
	Anti-Masonic	7.78	7
1836	Independent Democrat	0	11
	Whig (Hugh White)	9.72	26
	Whig (Daniel Webster)	2.74	14
1840	Liberty	0.28	0
1844	Liberty	2.30	0
1848	Free Soil	10.12	0
1852	Free Soil	4.91	6
1856	Whig–American	21.53	8
1860	Southern Democrat	18.09	72
	Constitutional Union	12.61	39
1872	Straight Out Democrat	0.29	0
1876	Greenback	0.9	0
1880	Greenback	3.32	0
1884	Greenback	1.74	0
	Prohibition	1.47	0
1888	Prohibition	2.19	0
	Union Labor	1.29	0
1892	Populist	8.50	22
	Prohibition	2.25	0
1896	National Democrats	0.96	0
	Prohibition	0.90	0
1900	Prohibition	1.50	0
	Socialist	0.62	0
1904	Socialist	2.98	0
	Prohibition	1.91	0
1908	Socialist	2.82	0
	Prohibition	1.70	0
1912	Progressive	27.39	88
	Socialist	5.99	0

Year	Party	Popular votes (percent)	Electoral votes
1916	Socialist	3.18	0
	Prohibition	1.19	0
1920	Socialist	3.42	0
	Farmer–Labor	0.99	0
1924	Progressive	16.56	13
	Prohibition	0.19	0
1928	Socialist	0.72	0
	Communist	0.13	0
1932	Socialist	2.22	0
	Communist	0.26	0
1936	Union	1.96	0
	Socialist	0.41	0
1940	Socialist	0.23	0
	Prohibition	0.12	0
1944	Socialist	0.16	0
	Prohibition	0.16	0
1948	States Rights Democrat	2.40	39
	Progressive	2.38	0
1952	Progressive	0.23	0
	Prohibition	0.12	0
1956	Constitution	0.17	0
	Socialist–Labor	0.07	0
1960	Socialist–Labor	0.07	0
		(Harry F. Byrd)	15
1964	Socialist–Labor	0.06	0
	Socialist Workers	0.05	0
1968	American Independent	13.53	46
	Socialist–Labor	0.07	0
1972	Libertarian	0	1
	American	1.40	0
1976	People's	0.10	0
	Eugene McCarthy, independent candidate	1.00	0
1980	John Anderson, independent candidate	6.58	0
	Libertarian	1.04	0

SOURCE: *Guide to U.S. Elections, Congressional Quarterly*, 1975: 219–260, 300–307.

Ohio law requiring independent candidates for the presidency to file statements of candidacy and nominating petitions very early in an election year. This law placed an undue burden on voting rights and the associational rights of independent voters and candidates.[16] "A burden that falls unequally on new or small political parties or on independent candidates impinges, by its very nature, on associational choices protected by the First Amendment. It discriminates against those candidates and—of particular importance—against those voters whose political preferences lie outside the existing political parties."

Party Machinery

American political parties are decentralized, unlike the Labor and Conservative parties in England and parties in West Germany, which are organized around a parliamentary system of government. Because of the federal nature of our political system, personal candidate organizations, and a once-every-four-years presidential nomination, parties are organized on the state level. As Pendleton Herring noted some time ago, "In the federal sphere, our political parties are temporary alliances of local leaders held together by the hope of winning the Presidency."[17]

State parties vary in organization, structure, and strength. Usually there is a state committee and a state party chair. State committee membership is determined by state party rules; members are usually elected to office by the state convention or in state primary elections. The national party committee and the national chairman try to oversee state party activity, but state committees and chairs are not responsible to the national organization.

Party organizations at the different levels are independent; the national committee has little control. To the extent that the national organization functions at all, it does so largely during presidential election years. Local organizations do not respond well to direction from the state party. Local party chairs and precinct committees become active during elections; they support locally nominated candidates and some state candidates. The most significant achievement of the local party organization, which may benefit the national and state parties as well as the local party, is to "get out the vote." With this loose organizational structure it is not surprising, then, that local party "bosses" (strong party leaders who control politics in their city) have been able to control political parties in metropolitan areas and that national candidates have set up their own election organizations.

The boss system was maintained in America because the local party organization had control over the nomination of candidates to public office as well as the selection of delegates to the national conventions. There were patronage jobs (that is, appointments based on political loyalty and support) in addition, which public officials could pass around to reward loyal support. Typically a **party caucus,** a closed meeting of party

Party Caucus: *the party conference, consisting of all party members in the legislative chamber.*

Richard J. Daley
A lifetime resident of Chicago, Richard J. Daley was mayor of the city from 1958 to 1975. "Boss" Daley was the undisputed authority in Chicago and leader of the Democratic party in Illinois. During his tenure as mayor, he reformed the police and fire departments, ran a tight city hall, and contributed to Democratic victories in Illinois elections. In the late 1960s his position was challenged. Black leaders urged him to end discrimination in Chicago, and the 1968 Democratic National Convention, which was held in Chicago, ended with rioting in the streets. In 1972 his Illinois delegation was unseated from the Democratic convention and his power ended.

Direct Primary: *popular elections used to determine party nominees for public office and to select state and national convention delegates and party officers.*

© *Mike Peters*, Dayton Daily News

leaders, would select the candidates of the party. This small band of local party faithfuls would meet, screen candidates, and produce a slate for the November ballot. Thus the nominating process remained in the hands of a party elite and brought accusations of backroom deals. Candidate slates created in this way often failed to represent the party membership or the general electorate. Throughout the nineteenth century, however, the party caucus was the preferred method of candidate selection.

State law now prescribes the method by which political parties may nominate candidates for public office. In the Populist and Progressive eras, the spirit of reform led to the initiation of the **direct primary** in virtually every state of the union. By the mid-1920s, popular elections were held to determine party nominees for public office. Party caucus or convention nominees, and any insurgent candidate filing enough signatures on a petition, ran in a primary election to secure party endorsement for the general election. Today, primaries are used not only to nominate candidates, but also to select state and national convention delegates and party officers. The primary has become the principal method of nominating candidates to office and in the process has weakened party control and effectiveness.

Candidates can direct personal campaign efforts to secure the nomination and win public office, and they have thus become less dependent on a party for endorsement or support. This trend has weakened party control. The personalized style of campaigning creates ticket splitting, which further weakens party cohesion. The mood of cynicism and hostility toward parties, combined with ticket splitting and the primary, make it exceedingly unlikely that political parties will become stronger in the near future.

The National Party Organization

National Committee:
the national party organization responsible for setting up the process for the national nominating convention.

The national party organization is a relatively simple structure consisting of a **national committee** (see Figure 8.4). Each party constitutes its national committee differently. Until the reforms of 1972–1974, the Democratic committee consisted of one man and one woman from each state. Today it is a committee of 365 persons: the state party chairs and highest ranking officers of the opposite sex (110 members), representatives apportioned to each state on the basis of party vote and population (200 members), and representatives from the Democratic Governors' Conference, the House and Senate, and affiliated groups represented in the party (approximately 50–60). The Republican National Committee con-

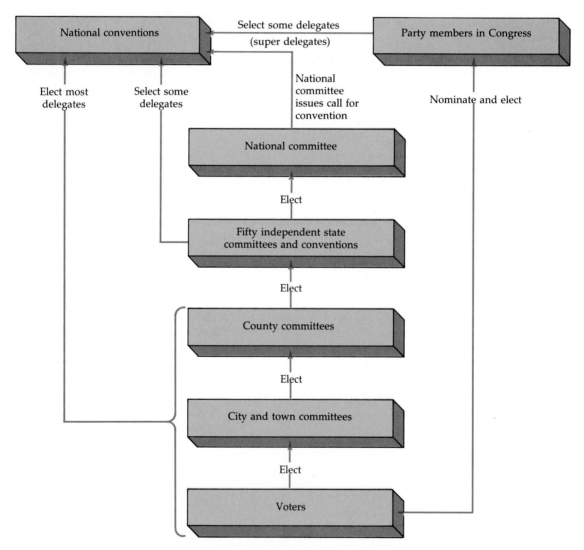

Figure 8.4   Organization of national parties

sists of 162 persons with 3 representatives from each state, including the state party chairs. Also included in both party organizations are representatives from the District of Columbia, Puerto Rico, and other U.S. territories. The national convention elects the national committee members, but this election is little more than a formality. The national committee has responsibility for the well-being of the party, but in fact it seldom meets and exercises no real authority. The committee's main task is to set up the process for the national nominating convention.

The national party chairperson is selected by the national committee of each party. In fact, he or she is selected by the incumbent president or party presidential nominee at the close of the convention. The position is not one of power; the chair helps to facilitate the presidential campaign, moderates state party disagreements with the national convention, and keeps the peace within the party. The selection of a national chair is usually the product of a compromise with state party leaders. The positions of national party chair and national committee members change frequently, and the chair changes with each new presidential nominee. In 1972, Nixon replaced Robert Dole with George Bush. The Democrats replaced Larry O'Brien with Robert Strauss, a party moderate, in the wake of George McGovern's defeat. In 1980, it was Bill Brock for the GOP and John White for the Democrats. For 1984 the Democrats selected Charles T. Monatt and the Republicans divided their responsibility. Frank J. Fahrenkopf, Jr. was chosen chairman of the Republican National Committee in charge of day-to-day operations for the RNC. Senator Paul Laxalt (R-Nev.), a long-time friend of President Reagan, was selected General Chairman. As such, he directed election strategy and coordinated all three GOP political arms—the Republican National Committee, GOP House Campaign Committee, and GOP Senate Campaign Committee. In 1985 the Democrats chose national committee treasurer Paul G. Kirk to replace Monatt as the party's chairman.

The national committee officers are not the directors of the presidential campaign. The machinery of the national party is largely ignored. The president or presidential nominees establish their own organizations, which they organize around key advisers and supporters who helped launch the nomination drive. Congressional candidates also forsake the national party. Incumbency itself is the major asset. Candidates for the House and Senate also have established personal organizations. They have key backers in their districts, independent access to campaign money, and their own information networks. Congressional and senatorial campaign committees are also created by party members in the House and Senate. These committees campaign for party candidates by raising money, bringing in speakers, providing advice to challengers, and generally supporting party members' bids for reelection.

The National Convention

The crowning achievement of the national party is the national convention. The nomination of a presidential candidate and the subsequent cam-

The gala festivities of the presidential nominating convention belie its serious purpose.

paign are the essence of the national party. The very existence of the national party is continued by convening to nominate a candidate for the office of the presidency. Although formally the convention has supreme authority for policymaking—it writes the platform, determines the rules, elects the national committee, and arbitrates disputes—it exercises little real authority. The four days of the convention every four years are a time of celebration, usually as the party endeavors to keep its national image intact. The convention is really designed to achieve one objective: nominating a presidential candidate. But other items of business—adopting rules, settling delegate seating disputes, and approving the platform—are important, and on occasion they can be dramatic. Take, for example, the rules revisions of the Democrats in 1972, the abortion planks in the party platforms in 1976, and the open-convention fight by Kennedy supporters in 1980 to free committed delegates. There was also the complaint by Hart and Jackson in 1984 that primary election rules reduced their delegate counts. Mondale won 39 percent of the votes in primary elections but received the votes of 56 percent of convention delegates, while Hart received 36 percent of the vote in all primaries but got only 30 percent of the delegates. Jackson's election figure was 18 percent while his convention total was 12 percent. Yet the delegates were present in those percentages because of the rules and reforms of the delegate-selection process. Delegates to the Democratic and Republican conventions are selected according to state law and party rules. Reforming the selection process has become a major concern for both political parties.

Reform Results

What have these delegate-selection reforms accomplished? They have increased reliance on the state presidential primary as a means of selecting convention delegates. In fact, the state primary has become the most prevalent way of selecting delegates. By 1980, approximately two-thirds of all delegates were picked or bound to vote according to the results of ballots cast by voters in the primaries (the fraction dropped to 50 percent in 1984). State caucuses or conventions no longer retain the right to nominate or control the balloting of convention delegates. The Democrats have moved to limit the impact of primaries by creating a category of "super delegates"—automatically seated public officials or party officers. This affords party regulars greater influence within the national presidential convention. In 1988, super delegates constituted nearly 20 percent of the total delegate count.

Largely as a result of rules reform, most convention delegates are political amateurs without much prior convention experience. They are frequently motivated to become involved in politics by their commitment to a presidential candidate or issues. Table 8.3 illustrates the number of convention delegates over the years who had never before attended a presidential nominating convention. Reforms have meant that upwards of three-quarters of the delegates were newcomers to the political nomination process.

The socioeconomic composition of delegates also has changed, in that delegates were far more representative of the general public in 1980 and 1984 than they were in 1968 (see Table 8.4). The reform rules have worked in this regard.

TABLE 8.3   Convention delegates who had never before attended conventions

	1944	1968	1976	1984
Democrat	63%	67%	80%	74%
Republican	63	66	78	69

SOURCE: Barbara Farah, "Delegate Polls: 1944–1984," *Public Opinion* (August/September 1984): 44.

TABLE 8.4   Socioeconomic makeup of Democratic convention delegates

	Women	Blacks	Youth[a]	Other[b]
1968	13%	5.5%	4%	NA
1972	38	15	21	5%
1976	36	7	14	NA
1980	49	15	11	8
1984	51	18	8	7

[a]Eighteen to thirty years of age.
[b]Includes delegates of Spanish-speaking or Indian origins; not available for 1968 or 1976.
SOURCE: *The Party Reformed, Final Report of the Commission on Party Structure and Delegate Selection* (Washington, D.C.: Democratic National Committee, July 7, 1972), pp. 7–8; Congressional Quarterly, *Guide to the 1976 Election;* 1980 data, CBS news survey, in the *New York Times,* August 11, 1980 and August 23, 1984.

Finally, the reliance on primaries and an open delegate-selection process have made the national convention anticlimactic. The distribution of delegates becomes fairly well established before the convention. Rules prohibit the "wheeling and dealing" that marked past conventions. Delegates are bound to candidates for one, two, or even three ballots. Since 1960, no party has used more than one ballot to nominate a presidential candidate. The Ford–Reagan nominating contest was bitterly fought, but it was still decided on the first ballot. It might also be noted that since 1960, the conventions have been televised nationally. The parties and the candidates are very well aware of the image they convey to viewers and voters; any hint of corrupt politics could be fatal for the election.

The conventions may be anticlimactic because the results are predictable. The new rules may also have changed our expectations regarding the role of the political party:

> This trend may underline the importance of nonparty resources—early candidacy, strong personal organization, money, successful polls and media, political personality—in the contest for nomination. The continuation of these tendencies may lead to a further decline in the role played by party leaders in the presidential nominating process.[18]

Political Parties: A Critical Realignment

We have been studying the functioning of political parties in a changing environment, a political environment in which presidential landslide victories have become commonplace. Equally impressive has been the declining ability of the victorious presidential candidate to translate that vote margin into congressional seats for the party. The argument is commonplace by now: the electorate has changed its expectations about the political process and the role of political parties within that process. The American electorate may be heading toward a critical realignment. Will the changes result in greater partisan support, or in the dissolution of political parties as we have come to know them? We have seen this realignment cut across traditional partisan affiliation. The consequence has been an acceleration of the process of party decomposition.

Dealignment: *the decline of political party loyalty, leading to the ultimate destruction of the party system. Party preference is replaced with political independence.*

The debate centers on dealignment and realignment. **Dealignment** is the erosion of party loyalty with no new emerging partisanship. The decrease in strong partisan loyalty and the rise in independent voters as well as ticket splitters indicate dissatisfaction with parties. Nie, Verba, and Petrocik note that "the issues which loosened party ties were racial conflict and Vietnam, capped off in recent years by Watergate. These issues caused substantial discontent. They led the public to turn against the political process more generally."[19] Dealignment is particularly potent for young voters, for they are most susceptible to reduced party loyalty. They are entering the political arena at a time of weak party loyalty and widespread party defection.

Realignment: *the alteration of political party loyalty by large numbers of persons for an extended period of time. Party preference changes such that the minority party becomes the preferred and dominant party.*

However, dealignment only suggests the decline of partisanship, not the change of party loyalty. **Realignment** means an alteration in the basic pattern of support for political parties. A minority party becomes the majority and dominant party for an extended period. Such periods of realignment are often associated with a series of changes taking place in society, whether sudden or gradual. Evidence cited as supporting movement toward realignment is the shifting social base of political parties—the decline of the New Deal party system[20] or the success of Ronald Reagan and conservatives in 1980. The ideological composition of the party coalitions has changed.

Many commentators argue that no movement toward realignment is taking place. The evidence is mixed. What follows is a brief survey of the forces working toward dealignment and realignment.

The parties are operating within a changed environment. The traditional view of centrist, "accommodationist" parties seeking to build a coalition to capture a majority of the electorate is no longer operative. In the New Deal context, the politics of coalition building kept parties from moving too far from the center, if issues mattered at all. Parties sought to nominate candidates who could appeal to the broad mass of voters and maintain the politics of accommodation and consensus.

Now issues have emerged as an important variable; since 1964, voters have increasingly come to evaluate the parties in terms of their stand on issues. Gerald Pomper has documented this trend of voters to see the Democrats as "liberal" and the Republicans as "conservative,"[21] of which the rise of Barry Goldwater, Eugene McCarthy, George Wallace, George McGovern, and Ronald Reagan is a clear indicator. We see further evidence of the lack of party power with candidates such as fundamentalist Christian Pat Robertson and the ultraconservative Lyndon LaRouche. In fact, LaRouche supporters won nominations for state offices on the Illinois state ballot as Democrats in 1986, upsetting convention-endorsed candidates.

Also associated with the rise of issue awareness has been the tendency of voters to choose candidates on the basis of issues. The issue awareness of voters and the rise of ideological candidates have made issues a significant force in determining the presidential vote. Ideological consistency as a basis for voting helps to explain the rise of political activists and the increases in ticket splitting. These are all symptoms of the current party decline.

We have documented the decline in party identification. There has been a loss of faith among strong party identifiers for both parties. The rise in the number of independents is well known. At the same time that party identification has diminished there has been a rise in ticket splitting. Voters are increasingly likely to vote for candidates of opposing parties. Party labels do not have the force they once had. Almost 50 percent of elections now have split outcomes, where presidential and congressional candidates carrying the district are of differing political parties.

The weakening of party organization also contributes to party decline. Reforms of the delegate-selection process have produced a wave of political activists at presidential nominating conventions. The democratization of party rules through the use of the presidential primary has left the party no control over the direction in which presidential nominating conventions will go.

The rise of political amateurs underlines a change in the nature of the groups seeking access to the political parties. New groups, heretofore largely excluded from participation in the party process, have demanded reforms to facilitate their participation in the party system. These groups include blacks, women, youth, and Hispanic Americans. Such groups have become a major force within the Democratic party, and they are also increasingly active as voting blocs within American society.

As a result of these changes—the rise of issues and the decline of party organization—we have a base for critical realignment from party loyalty to a nonparty adherence to issues. "Groups are relocating across party lines, to be sure, in response to new conflict structures. But equally impressive is the movement of voters away from firm partisan ties generally. We are becoming a nation of electoral transients."[22]

Problems of Representation

Political parties are not representative of the American public. Changes in voter affiliation and organization procedures have left parties weak and disoriented. The electorate voting for a presidential party candidate today is small and unrepresentative of the electorate at large. The new procedures—presidential primaries, proportional representation, and open caucuses—make it increasingly likely that party politics can be captured and dominated by activists seeking reform and ideological candidates. In the words of Ladd and Hadley, we have confused *participation* and *representation* in party politics. Political parties no longer represent large coalitions of people. Parties no longer have the regulars and the organization to promote compromise and consensus. Those who have spent their lives working for the party are pushed aside to facilitate democratic participation within the party.

What we fail to understand, however, is that open participation is not more representative in terms of the general public. Increased participation has democratized political parties, but it has also facilitated the demands of new groups of political activists. The nominating process is open to groups and candidates that seek to capture the presidential nomination and to use it as a forum to advance their causes or issues. The process in no way ensures that such groups or candidates will represent the American public. If anything, where landslide victories occur, just the opposite is the case: candidates unacceptable to the American people succeed in obtaining party nomination. The ability of the party to appeal to its traditional supporters and identifiers is diminished.

It is not that political parties have ever been perfect instruments for representation. Smoke-filled rooms, political bossism, and closed caucuses have all worked to exclude legitimate interests. There has never been a serious move toward responsible party government in this country. Parties have never exercised control over their elected public officials, and party membership has always been loose. Without political parties, however, what would provide the representative function? Everett Ladd has noted that political parties have, in the past, made errors and been dishonest but they also have managed to keep the political process together. Can we continue to govern ourselves in an era where political parties have a diminished presence?[23]

Summary

1. Political parties are in a state of decline, since politics has become more technologically complicated and the electorate more independent. We see the weakened state of political parties in the decline in party identification, changes in campaigning and campaign organizations, and reforms to the nominating process.

2. While parties have declined, they persist in part because the two parties historically have been grand coalitions, and also because the institutional arrangement of the electoral process works to the disadvantage of third parties.

3. Political parties have served one mission rather well: the election of candidates to public office. From this one mission comes support for the democratic ideas of political competition and representation, which these parties have done less well.

4. Third parties have never been very successful if measured by number of votes. They continue to express minority points of view, however, thereby challenging the two-party structure.

5. Party machinery is unwieldy and largely irrelevant for the governance of political parties. It functions only for the presidential nominating convention. The direct primary has replaced party organization in control of political parties.

6. Reforms to the presidential nomination process have weakened party control over presidential selection. The delegate selection process has been opened, allowing insurgent candidates significant opportunity to secure the party nomination for president. There remains little party control or responsibility in presidential campaigning.

Research Projects

1. *Delegates to party conventions* How are political party delegates to conventions selected? Create a flowchart for the political parties in your state—Democrat and Republican—for selecting delegates to local,

district, state, and national conventions. When are they selected? Are caucuses or primary elections held? Is there a proportional system of representation? Write your state party headquarters and ask for the information. *Congressional Quarterly* and the *National Journal* also carry good overviews on delegate selection.

2. *Party platforms*   Do a side-by-side analysis of the party platforms in the 1984 election. List the platforms under major topic headings. Do parties differ significantly in their approach and stand on issues? You can find the platforms in the proceedings of the parties published after each national convention in the presidential election years. Also see the compilation of historical party platforms in Kirk H. Porter and Donald B. Johnson, *National Party Platforms* (University of Illinois Press, 1966, with supplement), so you can do this for earlier years as well.

3. *A national primary*   Write an essay on the concept of a national primary. What are the arguments for and against a national presidential primary? Which ones are most convincing to you?

Notes

1. Everett Carll Ladd, *Where Have All the Voters Gone? The Fracturing of America's Political Parties* (New York: W. W. Norton, 1982), pp. xxiii–xxiv.
2. Gerald M. Pomper, "From Confusion to Clarity: Issues and American Voters, 1956–1968," *American Political Science Review* 66 (June 1972).
3. Norman Nie, Sidney Verba, and John R. Petrocik, *The Changing American Voter* (Cambridge, Mass.: Harvard University Press, 1976), p. 172.
4. Richard W. Boyd, "Electoral Trends in Postwar Politics," in James David Barber, ed., *Choosing the President* (Englewood Cliffs, N.J.: Prentice-Hall, 1974), p. 187.
5. John W. Soule and Wilma E. McGrath, "A Comparative Study of Presidential Nomination Conventions: The Democrats of 1968 and 1972," *American Journal of Political Science* 19 (August 1975): 509.
6. Ladd, *Where Have All the Voters Gone?*, p. 57.
7. Ibid., p. 69.
8. Gerald M. Pomper with Susan S. Lederman, *Elections in America* (New York: Longmans, 1980), p. 167.
9. Ibid., p. 175.
10. Kevin P. Phillips, *The Emerging Republican Majority* (Garden City, N.Y.: Doubleday, 1970).
11. "Toward a More Responsible Two-Party System," *American Political Science Review* 44 (Supplement 1950).

12. Samuel J. Eldersveld, *Political Parties in American Society* (New York: Basic Books, 1982), p. 429.
13. Ibid., p. xvii.
14. V. O. Key, *Politics, Parties and Pressure Groups* (New York: Thomas Y. Crowell, 1964), p. 255.
15. Ibid., p. 255.
16. *Anderson v. Celebrezze*, 460 U.S. 780 (1983).
17. Pendleton Herring, *The Politics of Democracy: American Parties in Action* (New York: Rinehart, 1940), p. 121.
18. Joyce Gelb and Marian L. Palley, *Tradition and Change in American Politics* (New York: Thomas Y. Crowell, 1975), p. 256.
19. Nie, Verba, and Petrocik, *The Changing American Voter*, p. 350.
20. John R. Petrocik, *Party Coalitions: Realignments and the Decline of the New Deal Party System* (Chicago: University of Chicago Press, 1981).
21. Pomper, "From Confusion to Clarity"; see also his *Voter's Choice: Varieties of American Electoral Behavior* (New York: Dodd, Mead & Co., 1975).
22. Everett Carll Ladd and Charles Hadley, *Transformations of the American Party System*, 2nd ed. (New York: W. W. Norton, 1983), p. 320.
23. Ladd, *Where Have All the Voters Gone?*, p. 77.

Bibliography

Burnham, Walter Dean. *Critical Elections and the Mainsprings of American Politics.* New York: W. W. Norton, 1970.
On the decline of political parties and the realignment of the American electorate. Burnham provides insightful historical analysis of the party system and American voting behavior.

Crotty, William. *American Parties in Decline.* Boston: Little, Brown, 1984.

An introductory book on political parties that explains the declining role and significance of political parties in the U.S. The book relates the decline of parties to Congress and congressional–presidential relations.

Eldersveld, Samuel J. *Political Parties in American Society.* New York: Basic Books, 1982.
As a leading student of political parties, the author provides a broad reassessment of parties based on the latest research in the field. He is far from convinced that party realignment has occurred, and argues that parties continue to play a significant role in American society.

Gelb, Joyce, and Palley, Marian L. *Tradition and Change in American Politics.* New York: Thomas Y. Crowell, 1975.
A textbook on political parties with the standard fare of topics. The authors have managed to capture the sense of change in political parties. The book attempts to look at parties as a response to the environment in which they operate.

Ladd, Everett Carll. *Where Have All the Voters Gone? The Fracturing of America's Political Parties.* New York: W. W. Norton, 1982.
A series of essays by Ladd that first appeared in *Fortune,* the volume is a short but penetrating analysis of the problems of political parties. Writing with wit, Ladd examines the two major parties and the perils of party reform.

Ladd, Everett Carll, and Hadley, Charles. *Transformations of the American Party System,* 2nd ed. New York: W. W. Norton, 1983.
A look at the changes in the Democratic and Republican parties since the New Deal. Makes good use of data to explain the breakdown of the old coalition and changed composition of support for political parties.

Maisel, Louis, and Sacks, Paul M. *The Future of Political Parties.* Beverly Hills, Calif.: Sage Publications, 1975.
A collection of essays looking at party decomposition not only in America but also in several states and foreign nations. Some of the articles are specialized and employ technical methods; others, however, give an overview and can be read more easily.

Petrocik, John R. *Party Coalitions: Realignments and the Decline of the New Deal Party System.* Chicago: University of Chicago Press, 1981.
The theme is that the party system has undergone a major if gradual realignment over the past ten to fifteen years. Petrocik explains the reasons for these changes and presents data on the new configurations.

Ranney, Austin. *Curing the Mischiefs of Faction.* Berkeley, Calif.: University of California Press, 1975.
The most complete work on reforms to the political parties, with special attention to 1972, in which Ranney had a personal hand. Ranney tries to weigh the relative merits and pitfalls for parties when they undertake internal reform.

Sorauf, Frank. *Party Politics in America.* Boston: Little, Brown, 1984.
A basic text on political parties, with good coverage of the standard topics—organization, support, electoral performance, and organizing a government. The author sees parties contributing to our notion of representative government.

Sundquist, James. *Dynamics of the Party System.* Washington, D.C.: Brookings Institution, 1983.
A rather extensive and detailed analysis of the history of the party system. Sundquist examines popular support for political parties over time, concluding that party realignment is not likely but that parties are not healthy either.

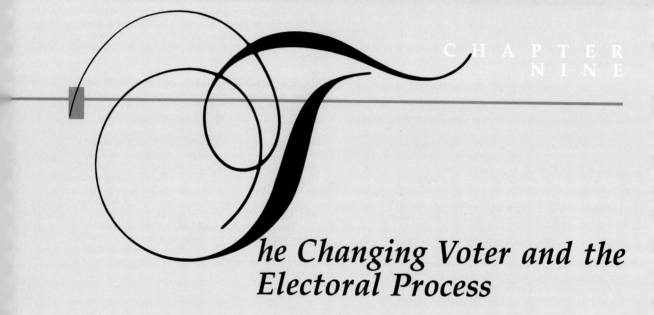

The Changing Voter and the Electoral Process

The last two decades of American electoral politics have been characterized by a variety of forces producing change both in the system and in
the individual voter. Events since our involvement in the Vietnam War
have produced a climate of changing expectations. The 1960s saw the rise
of civil rights activists and a period of social unrest, with civil disturbances and riots. The Great Society sought to engineer America's resources to solve our social ills, but the period of rising entitlements
ended when we became mired in the conflict in Southeast Asia. The
Vietnam War not only drained resources from domestic programs, but
became the most unpopular and divisive war in American history. The
1970s brought revelations of political corruption and scandal, and Watergate left the nation cynical and uncertain regarding the use of presidential power. In the process Watergate tested the limits of constitutional
rule and democratic politics. Economic recession and inflation have
emerged as new issues of concern, along with the high cost of government. Issues have become privatized; citizens are turning away from politics and political parties to more personal concerns.

As politics has changed, so has American political behavior. The American public of 1980 differed considerably from that of 1960. On the eve of John Kennedy's election, the public was relatively unmotivated to participate in politics, was content with the political process and the two major political parties, and demonstrated little concern for issues or issue voting. Today the American electorate is defecting from parties, is intensely aware of issues as new groups enter the political arena, and is searching for an ideology, along with stability and confidence in the whole political system.

The change involving the electoral process has many dimensions. In this chapter we will attempt to focus on several of these dimensions, particularly those that have had the greatest impact on traditional voting patterns and political behavior. The critical realignment of the electorate that has been taking place in the United States has been as much a result of the changing composition of that electorate as of changes in the attitudes and behavior of citizens already participating in the system.[1]

Who Votes

Voter Participation

The basic premise of democracy is citizen participation. A democracy is predicated on the right and ability of a people to choose their own representatives. We frequently evaluate democracy by the extent of the franchise to vote. In the twentieth century, the franchise in America has been extended: the Nineteenth Amendment gave voting rights to women; the 1964 and 1965 civil rights acts, as well as the elimination of the poll tax effected by the Twenty-fourth Amendment, sought to enforce suffrage for black Americans as established in the Fifteenth Amendment; and the Twenty-sixth Amendment lowered the voting age in federal elections to eighteen.

Yet it is one of the ironies of American democracy that as we approached universal suffrage in the 1960s, voter participation in elections began to decline. In 1960, a high of 63.1 percent of the eligible voters went to the polls in the presidential election. Then, for twenty years, there was a steady decline in voter turnout. In 1968, 60.7 percent of the voters went to the polls. In 1972, even with more than 7 million new eighteen- to twenty-one-year-old voters added to the electorate, the turnout rate slipped to 55.6 percent, and in 1980 only 52.6 percent cast a vote in the three-way race between Reagan, Carter, and John Anderson. A slight upturn in voter turnout occurred in the 1984 Reagan–Mondale contest, with 53.3 percent of voters going to the polls (see Figure 9.1).

There are several reasons for nonvoting, not registering to vote appearing to be the principal one. Among those who are registered but do not vote, there are a variety of reasons given for failure to do so: not liking any of the candidates, not being interested in politics, illness, too incon-

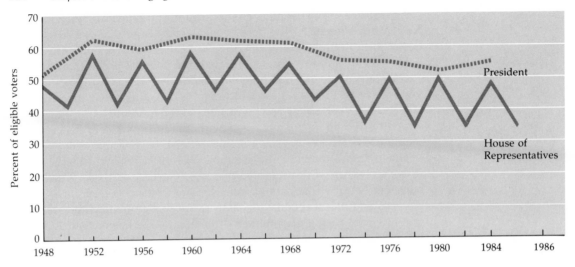

Figure 9.1   Turnout of voters in elections for president and House of Representatives

venient to vote, not able to take time off from work, being out of town, or not being able to get to the polls (see Table 9.1).

The decline in voter participation cannot be blamed on the enfranchisement of eighteen- to twenty-one-year-olds. True, the turnout rate of this group is low, but the 6 percent decline over the eight-year period is greater than the youth vote; "at most, the eighteen-year-old vote accounted for less than two percentage points of the decline from 1968 to 1972."[2] At least part of the explanation for the declining level of participation must be a conscious choice by citizens of all ages to stay away from the polls. Some citizens have always been indifferent; we know that the smaller a person's concern for the outcome of the election, the less likely he or she is to vote. Yet the marked trend in the past two decades sug-

TABLE 9.1   Reasons for nonvoting

	1968	1972	1976	1980	1984
Not registered	34%	28%	38%	42%	31%
Didn't like candidates	12	10	14	17	10
Not interested in politics	7	4	10	5	8
Illness	15	11	7	8	7
Inconvenient	—	—	—	—	7
Working	3	7	2	3	7
Not a citizen	—	—	4	5	6
New resident	10	8	4	4	6
Out of town	6	5	3	3	5
Couldn't get to polls	—	—	2	1	3
Didn't get absentee ballot	2	1	1	—	1
No particular reason	8	13	10	10	8
All others	3	13	5	2	1

SOURCE: *Gallup Report* (November 1984): 11.

Elizabeth Cady Stanton
Elizabeth Stanton was an early leader of the women's suffrage movement. Born in Johnstown, New York in 1815, Stanton, with several other women, called the first women's rights convention in 1848 at Seneca Falls, N.Y. There she insisted a suffrage clause be included in the bill of rights drafted at the convention. In 1852 she formed a lifelong friendship with Susan B. Anthony. Both became national figures in the suffrage movement. That movement gained its first major success in 1869 when Wyoming became the first state to allow women the right to vote. By 1913 twelve states had extended the suffrage right to women, and in 1920 the Nineteenth Amendment to the Constitution was ratified, eighteen years after Stanton's death. Stanton was known as a brilliant orator and journalist who dedicated her life to legal and political rights for women.

gests that people felt there was little to be gained by political participation. Voter disaffection with the political process, distrust, and cynicism created a sense of powerlessness and frustration that manifested itself in nonvoting.[3] And just as trust and confidence are regaining some lost ground in the 1980s, so voter turnout increased with the 1984 presidential election.

We can see in Table 9.2 that the nonvoter is more likely to be young, poorly educated, and of a minority background. Groups with these characteristics are precisely those that have recently been enfranchised. The citizen most likely to turn out to vote is middle-aged, well educated, and white. There may be several reasons for this pattern. One is that such a participant is part of the established middle class, which benefits from the system and appears to have greater confidence in the political process. Years ago a study called *The American Voter* established participation rates based on degree of interest in the campaign, concern over the outcome of the election, and sense of political efficacy. The authors found that the higher the degree of interest, the greater the concern for the outcome, and the greater the sense of political effectiveness on the part of the individual voter, the more likely the citizen was to participate.[4] Those with a stake in the system are more likely to express interest and concern and to have a sense of efficacy. For the disadvantaged or for newly enfranchised groups there seems to be less direct reward for participation. The political climate of cynicism further discourages participation. Such

TABLE 9.2 Voter participation in national election by groups

	1972	1974	1976	1978	1980	1982	1984
White	64.5%	46.3%	60.9%	47.3%	60.9%	49.9%	61.4%
Black	52.1	33.8	48.7	37.2	50.5	43.0	55.8
Spanish	37.4	22.9	31.8	23.5	29.9	25.3	32.6
Male	64.1	46.2	59.6	46.6	59.1	48.7	59.0
Female	62.0	43.4	58.8	45.3	59.4	48.4	60.8
Northeast	—	48.7	59.5	48.1	58.5	49.8	59.7
Midwest	—	49.3	65.1	50.5	65.8	54.7	65.7
South	55.4	36.0	54.9	39.6	55.6	41.8	56.8
West	—	48.1	57.5	47.5	57.2	50.7	58.5
18–20	48.3	20.8	38.0	20.1	35.7	19.8	36.7
21–24	50.7	26.4	45.6	26.2	43.1	28.4	43.5
24–34	59.7	37.0	55.4	38.0	54.6	40.4	54.5
35–44	66.3	49.1	63.3	50.1	64.4	52.2	63.5
45–54	70.8	56.9	68.7	58.5	69.3	62.2	69.8
65 and over	63.5	51.4	62.2	55.9	65.1	59.9	67.7
Employed	66.0	46.8	62.0	46.7	61.8	50.0	61.6
Unemployed	49.9	28.8	43.7	27.4	41.2	34.1	44.0
Eight years or less	47.4	34.4	44.1	34.6	42.6	35.7	42.9
Some high school	52.0	35.9	47.2	35.1	45.6	37.7	44.4
High school grad.	65.4	44.7	59.4	45.3	58.9	47.1	58.7
Some college	74.9	49.6	68.1	51.5	67.2	53.3	67.5
College grad.	83.6	61.3	79.8	63.9	79.9	66.5	79.1

SOURCE: *Statistical Abstract*, 1986.

groups can find no personal meaning or sense of power by participation: "The decline in interest appears to represent more a conscious rejection of politics than a withdrawal into more neutral apathy."[5]

How Voters Decide

Normal Vote: *electoral behavior based on stable patterns of partisan loyalty and group affiliation, which are adjusted for short-term variations. The normal vote examines partisan tendencies within socioeconomic groupings to make predictions.*

Why do citizens vote the way they do? Actually, determining the why of voting is extremely difficult and complex. In the past, we have relied on surveys asking people why they voted as they did, but critics say replies to survey questions do not represent actual behavior. The surveys established the concept of the **normal vote** based on the importance of the long-range effect of party identification and adjusted for short-term deviations due to issues and candidates. As these forces lose their relevance, the notion of a normal vote is less pertinent, although we still find it useful to examine behavior according to various criteria.

One approach is sociological. This method focuses on the socioeconomic background of voters and examines voting behavior of citizens according to income, age, race, education, and group affiliations, as seen in Table 9.3. There continues to be some stability of voting patterns according to sociological variables. The other approach is psychological. Instead of stressing group affiliation or socioeconomic background, we measure motives such as party support, issues, or candidate assessment. The psychological approach attempts to explain voting patterns by identifying relevant concerns in the minds of the voters. Great changes appear to be taking place in the psychological motivations influencing voting behavior.

Sociological Factors

Political scientists have studied sociological factors in voting behavior since the 1940s. *The People's Choice* was an early study examining the relationship between class, income, and voting. Said the authors, "Social characteristics determine political preference."[6] Out of the New Deal alignment of the electorate there emerged some clear, stable connections between voting patterns and socioeconomic position that were predictable and continuous, interrupted only by short-term conditions that were temporary deviations.

The New Deal voting-behavior patterns from the 1930s through the early 1960s showed distinct social and economic differences. The wealthier, professional, better-educated persons voted predominately Republican. The lower socioeconomic classes, blacks, and union members were largely Democrats. And to a certain degree, these patterns continue to hold true.

Social Class   Social class can be measured by income and occupation. We see that the upper classes tend to vote Republican, while manual workers are more likely to support the Democratic party. But a word of caution: the trend in America toward continually higher levels of income and

Changing Consensus: Minorities and Bilingual Education

The consensus that Roosevelt and the Democratic party built in the 1930s included American minorities; the party sought and depended heavily on the support of blacks and the ethnic groups of the large cities. But with the coming of the civil rights movement in the 1960s, this sense of common purpose began to fade as the minorities, eager to participate more fully in the postwar prosperity, turned to exercising their political power for their own benefit. The result has been similar to that of single-issue politics: real problems have been brought to public attention and opportunities have been expanded, but the electorate is again fragmented, and parties and politicians are pressured not for general policies, but on specific issues that may then cost them elections.

The newest of these groups is the Hispanic Americans, whose numbers are growing so fast that they now form the largest single ethnic group after black Americans (more than 19 million). Members of this group want jobs, education, and better immigration policies. Unlike other earlier immigrants, they are less willing to submerge themselves in the wider culture. They want education—but bilingual education. In 1982 the Supreme Court ruled that alien children illegally in the United States are entitled to a free public education. The case of *Plyler* v. *Doe* said that denying alien children public schooling would cause them an "enduring disability." It made no difference whether their parents had arrived in the state legally or not. This decision places great pressure on school systems to provide bilingual materials.

Bilingual education sounds like a good idea: after all, why not be fluent in two languages? But there are also problems: if Spanish–English bilingual programs are set up, should similar programs be established for every language group? And if people who are already handicapped by lack of familiarity with a sophisticated, technological society do not learn good English language skills, will they ever be able to compete for jobs and opportunities? If inefficient bilingual programs result in linguistic subcultures, groups may become permanently cut off from the mainstream culture, the basic unity of our society. The fact that we have all, up to now, considered ourselves Americans first and members of an ethnic group second could be weakened and destroyed.

319

TABLE 9.3 Vote by groups in presidential elections since 1960

	1960 JFK	1960 Nixon	1964 LBJ	1964 Goldwater	1968 HHH	1968 Nixon	1968 Wallace	1972 McGovern	1972 Nixon	1976 Carter	1976 Ford	1976 McCarthy	1980 Carter	1980 Reagan	1980 Anderson	1984 Mondale	1984 Reagan
National	50.1%	49.9%	61.3%	38.7%	43.0%	43.4%	13.6%	38%	62%	50%	48%	1%	41%	51%	7%	41%	59%
Sex																	
Male	52	48	60	40	41	43	16	37	63	53	45	1	38	53	7	36	64
Female	49	51	62	38	45	43	12	38	62	48	51	*	44	49	6	45	55
Race																	
White	49	51	59	41	38	47	15	32	68	46	52	1	36	56	7	34	66
Nonwhite	68	32	94	6	85	12	3	87	13	85	15	*	86	10	2	87	13
Education																	
College	39	61	52	48	37	54	9	37	63	42	55	2	35	53	10	39	61
High school	52	48	62	38	42	43	15	34	66	54	46	*	43	51	5	43	57
Grade school	55	45	66	34	52	33	15	49	51	58	41	1	54	42	3	51	49
Occupation																	
Prof & business	42	58	54	46	34	56	10	31	69	42	56	1	33	55	10	34	66
White collar	48	52	57	43	41	47	12	36	64	50	48	2	40	51	9	47	53
Manual	60	40	71	29	50	35	15	43	57	58	41	1	48	46	5	46	54
Age																	
Under 30 years	54	46	64	36	47	38	15	48	52	53	45	1	47	41	11	40	60
30–49 years	54	46	63	37	44	41	15	33	67	48	49	2	38	52	8	40	60
50 years & older	46	54	59	41	41	47	12	36	64	52	48	*	41	54	4	41	59
Religion																	
Protestant	38	62	55	45	35	49	16	30	70	46	53	*	39	54	6	39	61
Catholic	78	22	76	24	59	33	8	48	52	57	42	1	46	47	6	39	61
Politics																	
Republican	5	95	20	80	9	86	5	5	95	9	91	*	8	86	5	4	96
Democrat	84	16	87	13	74	12	14	67	33	82	18	*	69	26	4	79	21
Independent	43	57	56	44	31	44	25	31	69	38	57	4	29	55	14	33	67
Region																	
East	53	47	68	32	50	43	7	42	58	51	47	1	43	47	9	46	54
Midwest	48	52	61	39	44	47	9	40	60	48	50	1	41	51	7	42	58
South	51	49	52	48	31	36	33	29	71	54	45	*	44	52	3	37	63
West	49	51	60	40	44	49	7	41	59	46	51	1	35	54	9	40	60
Members of labor union families	65	35	73	27	56	29	15	46	54	63	36	1	50	43	5	52	48

*Less than one percent.

NOTE: 1976 and 1980 results do not include vote for minor party candidates.

SOURCE: *The Gallup Opinion Index* (November 1984): 32.

education is weakening these traditional patterns. The New Deal distinctions are less relevant. The under-thirty group in particular contains a large number of independents and new GOP identifiers, and these are the people with rising income and educational levels.

The relationsihp between social class and partisanship is weakening. Many working-class and union families voted Republican in 1980 and 1984, while middle-class and white-collar employees split fairly evenly between the two parties. In fact, since 1952 the difference in partisan preference between working-class and middle-class people has been shrinking. Everett Ladd's study of four elections (1948, 1960, 1968, and 1972) discovered a tendency for well-educated, high-income groups to support Democrats in those years.[7] Further, it appears that while the relationship between class and party has been steadily declining in the North, it has actually increased in the South.

> In the early 1950s in the South, middle- and working-class people were overwhelmingly Democratic; there were virtually no differences between them. Since that time, a modest, class-based partisan alignment has emerged in the South. The middle class has become increasingly Republican, while the working class, particulary the black working class, remains quite solidly Democratic. By 1980, the class alignment in the South was actually stronger than in the North, although in both regions in 1980 the class basis of partisanship was weak.[8]

In short, the social classes continue to show some differences in preference, but the differences have significantly narrowed in the last decade as America has moved toward becoming a middle-class society.

Race Nonwhites have most consistently and dramatically supported the Democratic party. This is the only group to provide a clear majority for the Democratic candidate in *every* presidential election since 1952.

From 1968 to 1972, there was an alarming trend for political parties to be divided on racial lines. In 1972 fewer than one in three white voters who went to the polls voted Democratic, whereas almost all nonwhites voted Democratic. The 1976 election redressed that balance considerably, although the nonwhite support for the Democratic candidate continued. But in the 1980 and 1984 elections the racial division in partisan voting resurfaced, approaching 1972 levels. Blacks and minority groups formed the base of support for the Democratic party; the Republican party remained the party of white voters.

But even within the Democratic party in 1984 race was a divisive factor; it was never far below the surface during the primary campaign and the nominating convention. "Jackson won 77 percent of the black vote but only 5 percent of the white vote. Hart, by contrast, carried the white vote in all but seven states yet won only 3 percent of the black vote. It was Mondale who was consistently able to attract both white and black votes, an ability that saddled his opponents with an insurmountable obstacle."[9]

Religion   There continue to be slight differences in preferences by religion. Catholics align themselves more with Democrats, while Protestants are more likely to prefer the Republican party. This pattern, however, evaporated in the 1984 presidential election. In any case, the distinctions do not rival the potency that religion had in the 1960 election. In that year John Kennedy became the first Catholic to be elected president, winning 78 percent of the Catholic vote and 38 percent of the Protestant vote.

In the 1980s once again religion has become a political force. Ronald Reagan has done equally well with Protestants and Catholics. But this success belies the religious distinction that emerges when one looks at fundamentalist or "born-again" Christians. Here Reagan's appeal to Protestants is strongest. Reagan won 60 percent of the born-again Protestant vote in 1980 against a born-again incumbent president; in 1984 he took fully 80 percent of the born-again Protestant vote. It is this appeal to, and the political involvement of, conservative, fundamentalist Christian groups that has attracted so much attention in the 1980s.

The renewed impact of religion in elections comes from the success of the Moral Majority and other Christian Right groups in the 1980 election. Their support for Reagan and congressional candidates was motivated less by partisanship than by ideological leanings. These groups targeted candidates and made financial contributions to them based on their support for Christian values and a conservative political philosophy.

In 1980 the Christian Right was successful in targeting several Senate candidates for defeat. They contributed several million dollars to "Christian" candidates and worked to defeat candidates opposed to their religious and social values. Although their subsequent electoral success has not matched that of 1980, there is no evidence that the Christian Right plans to reduce its activity or involvement in future elections.

The role of religion was even stronger in the 1984 election. The Christian Right and evangelical Christians actively supported the reelection of Ronald Reagan. For his part, Reagan openly courted fundamentalist Christians with actions like his Dallas prayer breakfast held during the GOP nominating convention and mass mailings to ministers enlisting their support in his reelection. The GOP party platform adopted nearly all the Christian Right's positions on social issues. In turn, fundamentalist Christians overwhelmingly supported Ronald Reagan and the Republican party: 80 percent voted for Reagan in November.

White evangelical Protestants traditionally have been Democrats but have not been very politically active. The Christian Right's involvement in politics has changed that. With their charges of liberal bias in the media and secular humanism in schools, the Christian Right has galvanized evangelical Protestants, who share their concerns over issues like abortion, homosexuality, crime, and pornography. Most have switched their political party affiliation as the GOP has openly appealed to them.

On the Democratic side, the Rev. Jesse Jackson also sought to appeal to religious groups. In seeking the Democratic presidential nomination,

TABLE 9.6   Partisanship and opinion profile of groups, 1950s and 1970s

Group	1950s		1970s	
	Issues	*Party*	*Issues*	*Party*
Middle and upper status native white southerners	Quite a bit to the right	Strongly Democratic	Move further right	Move away from Democratic party, more independent
Lower status native white southerners	Moderately right	Strongly Democratic	Move further right	Move away from Democratic party, more independent
High status northern WASP	Moderately right	Strongly Republican	Move a bit left and split	Less Republican, more independent
Middle and lower status northern WASP	Center	Slightly Republican	Move a bit right	More independent and more Democratic
Blacks	Strongly left	Strongly Democratic	Move even further left	Even more Democratic
Catholics	Moderately left	Strongly Democratic	Move to center	A bit more independent
Jews	Strongly left	Strongly Democratic	Move further left	A bit more independent
Border South	Moderately right	Strongly Democratic	Move a bit further right and split a bit	More independent

SOURCE: Norman Nie, Sidney Verba, and John Petrocik, *The Changing American Voter* (Cambridge, Mass.: Harvard University Press, 1979).

Blacks have increased their liberalism and commitment to the Democratic party. For other groups, attitude changes appear to have produced greater independence rather than partisan attachments.

Redefining Political Behavior

New groups, new issues, and the decline of partisanship have all produced vast changes in electoral behavior. The continuity of the American system of the 1950s has been broken. Civil rights, the Great Society, the Vietnam War, Watergate and political scandal, wage and price controls, economic instability, and taxpayer revolt have left profound marks on American citizens. New groups have entered the political process, cutting across the traditional patterns of party alliances. According to Walter Dean Burnham, "The American electorate is now deep into the most sweeping behavioral transformation since the Civil War. It is in the midst of a critical realignment of a kind radically different from others in American electoral history."[23]

From Party to Issues

The substantial increase in issue concern and voting by the American electorate has not been gradual; it was a marked change that occurred in the late 1960s. Since 1964, presidential campaigns and elections have been characterized by ideological and activist participants. Richard Boyd summarizes the central role of issues today as including (1) issue consistency in attitudes, (2) issue beliefs and partisan loyalties, and (3) issue beliefs and voting.[24]

In the past, surveys revealed an electorate that professed general but confusingly vague attitudes on public affairs. People could be classified liberal or conservative by their stands on issues, but there was no real consistency over a series of beliefs. Being liberal on civil rights did not necessarily produce a liberal opinion on foreign relations with communist nations. People were just as likely to be conservative on one issue and liberal on another. Americans simply were not likely to respond to politics on the basis of issues.

In 1964, however, issues began to play a central role, and since then the public has developed an issue consistency. Democrats have come to be perceived as liberals and Republicans as conservative by voters. An issue polarization has developed between the parties.[25] For the first time, the 1964 election was an ideological contest that challenged the New Deal coalition. The traditional alignments further decayed in 1972 with the infusion of political activists supporting George McGovern.

Gerald Pomper has documented these changes within the American electorate. Since 1968, on four important issues, the relationship between party identification and issues has crystallized: on all four issues—publicly financed medical care, school integration, federal employment guarantees, and federal aid to education—Democrats were decidedly more liberal than Republicans. On some issues, such as medical care and aid to education, the differences were striking. On others, they were less dramatic but still apparent.[26] The result is an electorate that is gravitating to political parties, or to presidential candidates, because of issue stands. We see groups that are liberal over a series of issues—civil rights, welfare, school integration—moving to the Democratic party. Republicans are

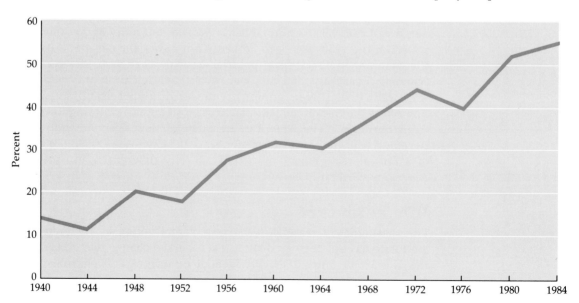

Figure 9.2 Trends in split-ticket voting for president and members of Congress

drawing support from conservative groups—Southerners, business—as a result of the Goldwater and Nixon strategies. Because of these changes, citizens are casting their ballots on the basis of issues and their assessment of a candidate's ability to handle the job.

Ticket Splitting

As a result of the decline in party identification and the increasing importance of issues, a dramatic rise in ticket splitting has occurred. In recent elections, there has been an increase in split outcomes where the presidential candidate of one party and the congressional candidate of another party carried the same congressional district (Figure 9.2). A gradual but consistent trend has emerged since 1952 toward an increased

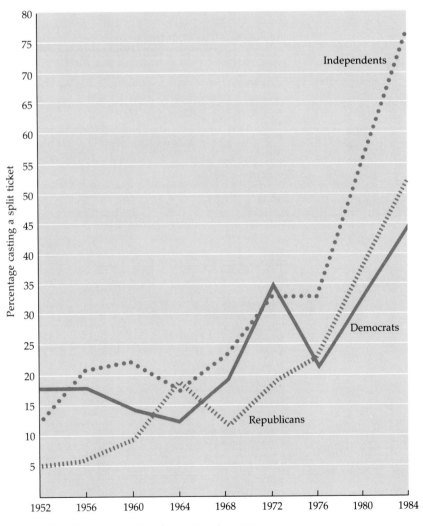

Figure 9.3   Trends in split-ticket voting by party

percentage of split outcomes. In 1972, the increase was dramatic: a 15 percent rise was noted in the level of ticket splitting. We have reached a point now where ticket splitting is greater than straight-party voting.

Walter DeVries and V. Lance Tarrance identify the ticket splitter as the new force in American politics. The traditional self-imposed labels of Democrat, Republican, or independent do not explain how a person actually votes. And when DeVries and Tarrance looked at how people actually had voted, they concluded there was a wide discrepancy between self-perception and actual voting behavior. In 1968, 45 percent of the voters who had identified themselves as Republican split their ticket and voted for at least one Democratic candidate; 47 percent of self-professed Democrats did the same; and 25 percent of independents reported voting a straight party ballot.[27] In 1984 Republicans were slightly more likely to split their ticket: 52 percent reported voting for candidates of opposite

TABLE 9.7 Ticket splitters

	Straight ticket	Different parties	No opinion
National	43%	54%	3%
Sex			
Men	43	55	2
Women	44	54	2
Age			
Under 30	37	60	3
18–24	30	66	4
25–29	49	49	2
30–49	47	52	1
Over 50	41	56	3
50–64	37	60	3
65 and older	43	54	3
Race			
White	40	57	3
Black	69	30	1
Hispanic	41	51	8
Education			
College graduate	40	59	1
Some college	39	59	2
High school graduate	43	54	3
Less than high school	55	42	3
Politics			
Republican	46	52	2
Democrat	54	44	2
Independent	21	76	3
Occupation			
Professional/business	36	62	2
Clerical and sales	45	55	—
Manual	41	56	3
Non-labor force	57	41	2
Religion			
Protestant	46	53	1
Catholic	41	54	5

SOURCE: *Gallup Report* (November 1984): 14.

parties, while 44 percent of Democrats reported doing so (Figure 9.3). Persons most likely to split their ticket were young voters, the well educated, those in professional and business occupations, and those with high incomes (see Table 9.7). In short, the traditional party identifier is exercising independence and voting for the candidates he or she feels are most qualified.

Equally as important is that ticket splitters do not rely on political parties and group affiliations in deciding how to cast their ballots. Say DeVries and Tarrance,

> Many voters—principally the ticket splitters, who make up a sizeable portion of the undecided voters in elections—draw their attitudes about candidates and their positions on issues from the media (principally television) and interpersonal relationships (family and friends).
>
> Ticket splitters do not rely on political parties or their affiliations—they rely on the news media for their information about politics and government.[28]

The ticket splitter is more issue oriented. Much of that orientation comes from the ticket splitter's use of the media, especially television. As a result, the ticket splitter does not identify strongly with either political party. And with the voter under thirty, who professes a strong propensity to reject partisan labels, we can expect further splitting of ballots between candidates of both parties and a further erosion of political parties.

Voting Patterns

Democratic politics is predicated on the right of the individual citizen to participate in the decision-making process by voting. Yet elections represent the collective judgment of a people. We have noted that expectations of voters change as they approach elections and political candidates. The very basis for American political behavior has changed. And while both political parties can depend on a certain measure of public support, traditional patterns have decayed and eroded. A new independence is dominating voting behavior.

So far we have been reviewing the motivations for voting behavior. How does this changing pattern of behavior distribute itself on a national level? Even though many of the changes are related to individual motivation, we can still discern voting patterns that help us to understand a little more clearly how America votes and why citizens vote as they do.

Competitiveness

One of the more remarkable patterns has been the increase in landslide presidential elections. For national politics, the presidency is the focal point of elections, the office most sought by both parties.

TABLE 9.8   Presidential popular vote since 1932

		Democrat	*Republican*	*Other*
1932	FDR	57.4%	39.6%	3.0%
1936	FDR	60.8	36.5	2.7
1940	FDR	54.7	44.8	0.5
1944	FDR	53.4	45.9	0.7
1948	Truman	49.5	45.1	5.4
1952	Eisenhower	44.4	55.1	0.5
1956	Eisenhower	42.0	57.4	0.6
1960	Kennedy	49.7	49.5	0.8
1964	Johnson	61.1	38.5	0.4
1968	Nixon	42.7	43.4	13.9
1972	Nixon	37.5	60.7	1.8
1976	Carter	51.0	48.9	0.1
1980	Reagan	41.2	51.0	7.8
1984	Reagan	40.6	58.8	0.6

SOURCE: *Statistical Abstract*, 1981 and 1986.

In recent elections, we have vacillated from very close elections to one-sided, landslide victories, as shown by Table 9.8. The 1960, 1968, and 1976 electoral contests were all very close; in all three the winning presidential candidates had popular margins of less than 2 percent. By contrast, 1964, 1972, 1980, and 1984 were landslide victories: Lyndon Johnson and Richard Nixon each polled more than 60 percent of the popular vote. Reagan's 10 percent margin in 1980 was equally one-sided in an election most people said was too close to call. Reagan, unlike Carter, had no dif-

TABLE 9.9   Electoral competition for congressional seats

	House (%)								
	1970	*1972*	*1974*	*1976*	*1978*	*1980*	*1982*	*1984*	*1986*
Marginal seats (won with 50% to 55% of the vote)	12.5	14.9	22.3	18.7	17.9	16.8	17.7	13.3	10.8
Safe seats (won with over 55% of the vote)	76.3	75.2	67.4	74.4	71	75	75.9	73.3	73.8
Uncontested	11.2	9.9	10.3	6.9	11	8	6.4	13.3	15.4

	Senate (%)								
	1970	*1972*	*1974*	*1976*	*1978*	*1980*	*1982*	*1984*	*1986*
Marginal seats (won with 50% to 55% of the vote)	42.4	47.1	39.9	33.3	35.3	56	36.4	21.2	47.1
Safe seats (won with over 55% of the vote)	57.5	52.9	57.1	60.6	61.8	41	63.6	75.8	52.9
Uncontested	0	0	3	6	3	3	0	3	0

SOURCE: Data compiled from returns reported in *Congressional Quarterly*, 1970–1986. (Figures may not total 100% because of rounding.)

ficulty with reelection, in 1984 adding an additional eight percentage points to his 1980 margin.

These results testify to the decline of long-term party loyalties and the emergence of the new politics, in which political activists, issues, and personalities dominate elections. Throughout the 1930s, 1940s, and 1950s, the pattern of competitiveness could be predicted, based on traditional patterns of loyalty, but this is the case no longer. The old loyalties are dissolving. Landslides and competitiveness alternate, based on short-term factors such as issues and candidate personalities. The media accentuate these factors. The result is that we have nationalized the presidential election, divorcing it from traditional attachments and loyalties. Voters form their impressions and receive their information from the media. This lays the electorate open to changes and swings on a uniform basis across the nation. Typically, today the presidential ballot is a split ticket, with the voter voting for one party's candidate for president and for another party's candidate for Congress or state offices.

For congressional contests, the pattern is not altogether different. Table 9.9 shows the pattern of electoral competition for congressional seats from 1970 to 1986. The pattern of noncompetitiveness in the House for four out of five seats has remained fairly stable throughout the whole period. There is greater competition in the Senate, but even there fewer than half the seats are contested. Most of the uncontested and noncompetitive elections are won by incumbents.

Incumbency

One of the most remarkable patterns in voting behavior is the success of incumbent politicians in being reelected. The American political tradition has a long history of "throwing out the rascals." But either we have no rascals—which current levels of distrust and cynicism would seem to contradict—or we continue to reelect our politicians for other reasons.

Traditionally, the safest incumbent is the president. Until 1976, when Gerald Ford lost to Jimmy Carter, an incumbent president had not been defeated for reelection since 1932. Since the Civil War, only three incumbent presidents had lost reelection bids until Ford's defeat in 1976. But this trend seems to be slowing down. While not an elected incumbent, Ford lost to Carter in 1976; Carter in turn lost to Reagan. Single-term presidents may well become the norm. Since Eisenhower, no president other than Reagan has completed a second term in office (though not because of electoral defeat in every case). Johnson chose not to run for a second term, Nixon resigned, Ford was defeated in 1976, and Carter was decisively turned back in his 1980 reelection bid.

Table 9.10 depicts the success of congressional incumbents in winning reelection. In the Senate the numbers are smaller and so is the success ratio, yet two-thirds to three-fourths of incumbent senators win reelection bids.

There are several explanations for the success of incumbents. Because congressional races are less visible and less well publicized, the informa-

Jamie L. Whitten
The dean of all members of the House of Representatives, Democratic Representative Jamie Whitten of Mississippi first won election to the House in a special election in 1941. He has won reelection ever since with little more than token opposition. Only since 1978, with the resurgence of the Republican party in Mississippi, has Whitten faced a challenger able to win at least 30 percent of the vote. Whitten's career is the strongest example of the power of incumbency and uncompetitive elections.

TABLE 9.10   Success of incumbents seeking reelection, 1950–1986

	Senate					House			
		Defeated					Defeated		
Year	Seeking reelection	Primary	General	Percent reelected	Year	Seeking reelection	Primary	General	Percent reelected
1950	32	5	5	68.8	1950	400	6	32	90.5
1952	31	2	9	64.5	1952	389	9	26	91.0
1954	32	2	6	75.0	1954	407	6	22	93.1
1956	29	0	4	86.2	1956	411	6	16	94.6
1958	28	0	10	64.3	1958	396	3	37	89.9
1960	29	0	1	96.6	1960	405	5	25	92.6
1962	35	1	5	82.9	1962	402	12	22	91.5
1964	33	1	4	84.8	1964	397	8	45	86.6
1966	32	3	1	87.5	1966	411	8	41	88.1
1968	28	4	4	71.4	1968	409	4	9	96.8
1970	31	1	6	77.4	1970	401	10	12	94.5
1972	27	2	5	74.1	1972	390	12	13	93.6
1974	27	2	2	85.2	1974	391	8	40	87.7
1976	25	0	9	64.0	1976	384	3	13	95.8
1978	25	3	7	60.0	1978	382	5	19	93.7
1980	29	4	9	55.2	1980	398	6	31	90.7
1982	30	0	2	93.3	1982	381	10	29	92.4
1984	29	0	3	89.7	1984	413	3	17	95.1
1986	28	0	7	75.0	1986	393	3	6	98.0

NOTE: Number seeking reelection is the total number of seats up for election less those where the incumbent was retiring or running for office or where a vacancy existed.

SOURCE: Data compiled from returns reported in *Congressional Quarterly,* 1950–1986.

tion and visibility advantage rests with the person in office. Incumbents can generally use their office to attract media attention and use the aura of the office to advance their candidacy. The incumbent generally attracts greater sources of funds, giving the incumbent candidate a greater opportunity for exposure. In the absence of any information, notably any negative information, voters appear to go with the trusted, recognizable name over the uncertainty and anonymity of a challenger. Voters split tickets largely to vote for incumbents. Still others stress that the changes in political behavior affect the national contest for the presidency more than congressional and state elections. Here party loyalties and local alliances are stronger and dominate voting behavior at the local level. Although we have had twenty-four years of Republican administration since 1952, there was a Republican majority in a house of Congress for only four years, starting in 1952. In fact, while Nixon was winning by a landslide in 1972, there was only minimal change in the seats held by the Democrats in Congress. However, the late 1970s and the 1980 election jarred that pattern when several liberal incumbent senators were defeated. But the 1980s have been good news for incumbents: they did better those years than they had for several elections. It seems safe to say that the staying power of members of Congress has insulated congressional elections from the presidential contest. We are likely to continue to see minority presidents or even majority presidents facing unsympathetic Congresses. President Reagan appears to be a case in point.

The Coattail Effect

One of the important consequences of the success of incumbents is the decline of the coattail effect in presidential elections, which historically has connected congressional elections to the presidential contest.

A coattail effect is the power of a presidential candidate to attract voters so that congressional candidates of the same political party are elected to office. The pattern is simple and consistent. In a presidential election year there is a net gain in congressional seats for winning presidential party candidates. In off-year elections, congressional candidates of the president's party lose seats to the opposition party. The historical pattern is impressive. Only four times in this century did a presidential candidate fail to add to the congressional seats for his party in Congress. Only once did an off-year election fail to produce a drop in the number of seats for the president's party.

The regularity of this pattern has been explained by differences in the composition of the electorate at off-year and presidential elections. Angus Campbell suggests that in presidential years the issues, personalities, and attention to the presidential contest produce a larger turnout by adding **peripheral voters** who come out only because of the presidential election.[29] These peripheral voters do not normally vote in off-year elections. The short-term factors that bring them to the polls make them likely to vote for the winning presidential candidate. The **core voters,** by contrast, vote in presidential and off years alike. They are the solid parti-

Peripheral Voters: *individuals who come out only because of presidential elections and normally do not vote in off-year elections.*

Core Voters: *individuals who vote in almost all elections, presidential and off year. Core voters are more likely to hold strong partisan loyalties.*

TABLE 9.11   Coattail effect in elections, net gain or loss of congressional seats for the president's party

	House		Senate	
	Democrats	Republicans	Democrats	Republicans
	(Number of seats)		(Number of seats)	
1950	−29	+28	−5	+5
1952	−23	+22	−2	+1
1954	+21	−18	+1	−1
1956	+1	−3	+1	0
1958	+50	−47	+15	−13
1960	−20	+19	+1	+2
1962	−5	+2	+2	−2
1964	+37	−37	+1	−1
1966	−48	+47	−4	+4
1968	−3	+5	−7	+7
1970	+11	−12	−3	+2
1972	−12	+12	+2	−2
1974	+42	−42	+4	−5
1976	+2	−2	+1	0
1978	−12	−12	−3	+3
1980	−34	+33	−12	+12
1982	+26	−26	0	0
1984	−15	+15	+2	−2
1986	+5	−5	+8	−8

SOURCE: Data compiled from election returns reported in *Congressional Quarterly.*

san loyalists. Peripheral voters are less likely to have a long-standing attachment to a party, but because enough of them vote a straight ticket, the result produces the net gain in congressional seats for the president's party. In off-year contests, the core voters are less swayed by short-term factors, and presidential-party candidates cannot count on the added support of peripheral voters.

Table 9.11 reveals an up-and-down pattern for coattails. As issues intruded into elections in the 1960s and 1970s, congressional elections became increasingly insulated from presidential elections, and the distinctions, based on party identification, of core and peripheral voters became less relevant. Elections in the 1980s saw the up-and-down pattern once again. Ronald Reagan's coattails have proven ragged. Early on, changes in Congressional seats were substantial, near their pre-1970 level. Reagan's popular victory in 1980 produced large gains for the Republicans, followed by a marked drop in seats at the mid-term elections. But the 1984 and 1986 elections were quite different. Coattails dropped off significantly. President Reagan made a strong bid in 1986 to elect Republicans, calling the elections a referendum on his presidency. The plea may have aided GOP in House elections, but cost them control of the Senate, as eight more Democrats were added to the Senate.

Sectionalism

Sectionalism: *a historical pattern of voting in which areas of the nation, such as the South or the West, repeatedly vote for one party as the majority party.*

America has had a historical pattern of sectional voting, or **sectionalism.** The South was long counted in the Democratic column as the Solid South. It produced only Democratic congressmen, governors, and state legislatures from the post-Civil War years through the 1960s. Republican strength was in America's heartland and in New England: the Great Plains, Maine, and Vermont. Since the New Deal, the Plains states (North Dakota, South Dakota, Nebraska, and Kansas) have gone Democratic only once, in 1964 for Lyndon Johnson; Maine and Vermont voted Democratic in 1964, Maine in 1968 (Figure 9.4).

Now these patterns are changing. The South voted for Goldwater in 1964, George Wallace in 1968, Richard Nixon in 1972, and Ronald Reagan in 1980 and 1984. Republican senators and governors are also making an appearance in some southern states. The South today is the base for the emerging American conservatism. Rather than support Democrats, southerners are looking for conservative candidates. Nixon made that part of his southern strategy in 1972, though Carter was able to capture the South in 1976. Reagan with his conservative appeal found support from the South in 1980 and 1984.

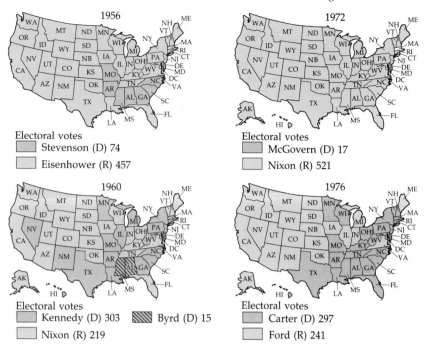

Figure 9.4
Presidential election results by states for 1960 to 1984. Notes: 1968—a North Carolina Republican elector cast his vote for George Wallace, making the official count Nixon, 301; Humphrey, 191; Wallace, 46. 1972—a Virginia Republican elector cast his vote for Libertarian candidate John Hospers, making the official count Nixon, 520; McGovern, 17; Hospers, 1. 1976—a Republican elector from the state of Washington cast his vote for Reagan, making the official count Carter, 297; Ford, 240; Reagan, 1.

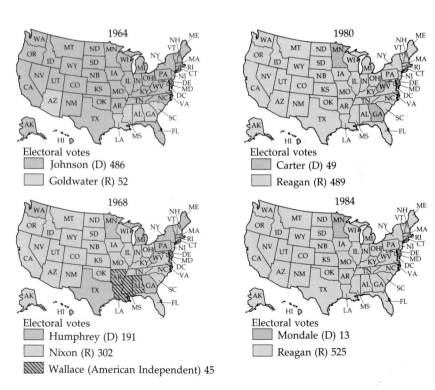

The Sun Belt   There is much discussion of the Sun Belt versus the Frost Belt in American politics. The Sun Belt is that section of the country that includes the South, beginning roughly with Virginia and including Florida, and runs across the Southwest and into California. This section of the country has not voted Democratic since 1960, except in 1976, Carter's victory year, and is considered the base for conservatives. The Sun Belt is attracting people with its climate and economic opportunity; in the 1980 census the Sun Belt states gained twelve House seats and electoral votes.

The migration patterns and politics of the Sun Belt have changed over the years. The Sun Belt is drawing everyone from urban retirees to young job seekers to corporate executives. It also has the highest concentration of Hispanic Americans of any region and is attracting increasing numbers of ethnic-group members. And the old-style southern politics is changing with the changing population. Retirees push politics in a conservative direction while industrial transplants from the northeastern and western states are impatient for change and growth. Rural politics is giving way to urban ways of political life.

While in 1976 the Sun Belt was Carter's stronghold, in 1980 even that native southerner could not hold it. Ronald Reagan won every southern and Sun Belt state in both 1980 and 1984, except Carter's home state of Georgia in 1980.

Midterm Elections as Referenda

There are two kinds of elections: presidential and off-year, or midterm, elections. In presidential election years voter turnout is higher and candidates of the elected president's party do better. In midterm elections voter participation declines and the party opposed to the incumbent president picks up seats in Congress. The trend is consistent, occurring in almost every election since the Civil War.

Though the pattern is clear, the reasons for it are not. As we have seen earlier, some analysts say that a surge of peripheral voters is attracted to the presidential election, and they cast ballots for the party's congressional candidates as well. In the off year the numbers of such voters decrease, resulting in a decline in presidential-party seats. This is the explanation most often used to describe the coattail effect in presidential elections and the subsequent decline of House seats in the off-year election. Others argue that "rational voters" exercise judgment on individual candidates or political-party programs, turning out of office candidates who have not delivered on the promises they or their parties made in the previous campaign. But the most interesting theory is that the midterm election serves as a referendum on the performance of the incumbent president.

The premise that midterm elections are a referendum means that voters take the off-year opportunity to express their sentiments on the president's performance for the past two years. The more popular the president and the more successful his program, the better the president's party does in the off-year elections. But since the president's party invariably loses seats, the midterm election is often seen as a negative referendum of the president's performance. The evidence that the referendum phenomenon exists is impressive. In fact, Ronald Reagan sought to use the 1986 election in this manner, with several specific references to the election as a referendum on his presidency. Throughout the campaign, as he stumped for Republicans, he claimed a vote for a Republican was a vote for Ronald Reagan.

Gerald Kramer has demonstrated that voters are quite responsive to national conditions and that they are particularly sensitive to economic fluctuations, with an "economic upturn helping the congressional candidates of the incumbent party, and economic decline benefitting the opposition."[30] Changes in real personal income seem most crucial in changing votes. Another study, covering the six midterm elections from 1946 to 1966, found that people who disapproved of the president's performance were more likely to vote in off-year elections and to cast their ballot against the presidential-party congressional candidates.[31] Edward Tufte's study of midterm elections since 1938 found that the congressional vote for the president's party changed with the president's popularity and the performance of the economy. Often the number of seats did not change directly owing to vote margins and districting factors, but voters did respond to presidential performance, and that response was reflected in the percentage of the vote for the president's party:

> To be specific: a change of ten percentage points in the President's approval rating in the Gallup Poll is related to a change of 1.3 percentage points in the national midterm congressional vote for the President's political party; and a change of $50 in real disposable personal income per capita in the year of the election is related to a change of 1.8 percentage points in the vote.[32]

The two explanations—the coattails/surge and decline of voters model and the state of the economy/presidential popularity model—both predict seat losses at the midterm election fairly well. James Campbell has worked to integrate the two models into an explanation that effectively measures off-year losses.[33] Campbell discovered that the two models can complement one another and can explain quite effectively most of the off-year loss of seats for the president's party.

The strongest factor associated with seat loss, in Campbell's study, was prior presidential vote. "Losses tend to be greater when the president wins by a large margin in the preceding election. For every additional percentage point of the vote the president wins in the prior election, one can expect his party to lose about three seats at the midterm."[34] The second strongest variable was the public evaluation of the president's job performance at the time of the midterm. "To a significant degree, seat losses tend to be greater when the president is unpopular at the midterm.

For every additional percentage point favorable to the president in the midterm Gallup Poll, one can expect the president's party to save about one seat."[35]

The final variable was the state of the economy. This seemed to have the least direct impact on midterm seat loss. "The effect of economic conditions seemed to be lagged, indirect, and somewhat more modest than previously claimed. A one-percent improvement in economic conditions in the year prior to the midterm enhances the president's popularity enough to save his party about two seats at the midterm."[36]

It is possible to exaggerate the claims of midterm referenda voting. Many factors are at work. For example, incumbents enjoy name recognition and financial advantages, election margins generally are not close, and constituency issues can be significant. Yet the results cannot be denied. Such factors as previous popular vote for president, job assessment, and economic conditions weigh on the minds of voters. If we have nationalized the presidential contest, then the midterm election may be one more opportunity to express approval or disapproval of the state of the nation.

The Electoral System

Political parties and popular elections are the cornerstones of American democracy. The act of choosing between competing candidates vying for public office is the most basic of political freedoms. And when the voter stands alone in the voting booth, exercising the untrammeled right of free choice, the moment represents the culmination of a process that is at the heart of democracy. The Constitution, federal and state laws, and political traditions are all at work to ensure an electoral process that gives the American citizen that right. The electoral system is more than ballots and totals, however; it includes nominations and campaigns as well as electoral institutions. And the electoral process has been changing.

We can view the electoral system as having three stages, though in fact they are not really completely discrete. Nominations provide for the selection of candidates for public office, the narrowing down of would-be contestants to those who actually are candidates for public office. Campaigns provide the most interest and add the most cost to elections. Here candidates seek to convince voters to vote for them and would-be candidates campaign for delegates in order to receive a nomination. The third stage is the process of conducting elections, the laws regarding voter registration, balloting, and tallying results.

Nominations

Basically, political parties nominate candidates for public office, although even in nonpartisan elections there must be a process for narrowing down the number of contestants. The parties as well as the public require

Major contenders for the presidency in 1988 are *top row, left to right:* Howard Baker and Pat Robertson; *middle:* Gary Hart, Bill Bradley, and George Bush; *bottom:* Jack Kemp and Mario Cuomo.

a means of deciding who will run for public office. This is the process of nomination.

The United States Constitution says nothing about nominations; state laws govern this process. The practice of allowing political parties to nominate candidates quickly filled the void left by the Constitution. The technique of letting a party caucus nominate candidates gave way in the twentieth century, however, to the more democratic process of letting the voters decide party nominations through the direct primary.

In this country, where we elect a great many public officials, the control of nominations is a considerable power. In several areas where there is no real party competition, securing the nomination is tantamount to election. Even where real party competition does exist, selecting the right candidate is important because the choice is primarily between two candidates. Third-party candidates may have an easy time being nominated for office, but they are rarely a potent force in the general election.

As a direct result of early twentieth-century political reform, the voters themselves select party nominees by direct primary. Today every state in the country utilizes the direct primary. The state assumes the burden and cost of conducting these primary elections.

The primary has worked to make the candidate-selection process more fair and democratic, but it has also eroded political parties, because they have lost control of nominations. Almost any person who files a petition carrying the minimum number of signatures with the secretary of state can be placed on the primary ballot. Neither would-be candidate nor signers of petitions need be party loyalists. Any qualified voter may vote in the primary. While there may be some restrictions on which party contest the voter can vote on, the election is open to all eligible voters.

There are several kinds of direct primary elections. The most common is the **closed primary,** in which voters must make a prior declaration of party affiliation in order to vote in that party's primary. This limits the primary to party loyalists and gives a truer indication of party sentiment. Yet because party loyalties are not strong anyway, the closed primary does not actually exclude people. In 1986, the Supreme Court ruled state statutes could not require a closed primary against a state party's wishes. Such statutes prohibit political parties from appealing to independent voters by denying independent voters the opportunity to vote in the party's primary election. This violated the First Amendment's associational rights.[36a] In an **open primary,** any qualified voter may participate simply by showing up at the polls. No statement of party support is required; the voter is merely asked to choose one party ballot or the other. This method allows the voter to "cross over" and vote in the other party's race. If one party has no real contest, voters may be attracted to the other party's contest and vote in it. This primary maximizes freedom of choice, but is not necessarily a true expression of partisan or public support. Three states, Washington, Alaska, and Louisiana, now use a **blanket primary,** in which the voter is given both party ballots and can vote back and forth between the parties in choosing nominees for public

Closed Primary: *a form of direct primary in which voters must make a prior declaration of party affiliation in order to vote in the party's primary.*

Open Primary: *a form of political election in which any qualified voter may participate simply by showing up at the polls. No statement of party support is required; the voter is merely asked to choose one party ballot or the other.*

Blanket Primary: *a form of direct primary in which the voter is given both party ballots and can vote back and forth between the parties in choosing nominees for public office.*

office. This type of ballot is the most democratic of all, but it further weakens party support and gives the party little indication of what will happen in the general election.

Nominating the President Presidential candidates are nominated by party conventions, which are the only occasions on which the party meets as a national political organization. Nominally at least, it is the party that controls the nomination for the presidency. Recent reforms in the delegate-selection process, however, have weakened party control of the nomination. Candidates now begin campaigning for state delegates as early as two to three years before the convention, working in state elections, attending fund-raising affairs, and consulting with local party officials. Figure 9.5 shows different paths to the presidential nomination.

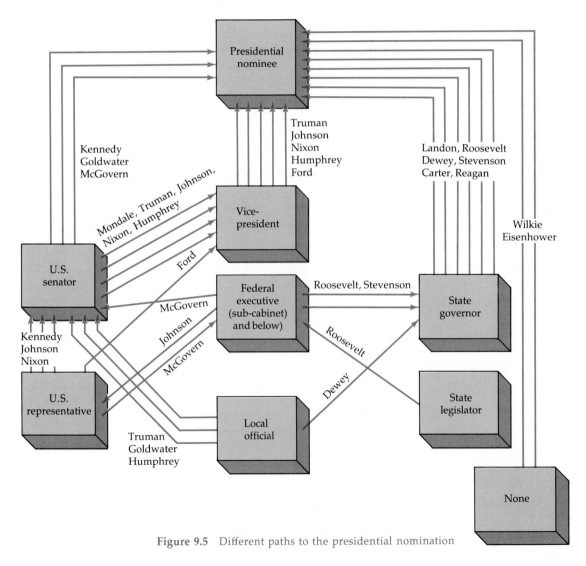

Figure 9.5 Different paths to the presidential nomination

The convention process itself is relatively simple: a candidate must receive a majority of delegate votes at the convention in order to secure the nomination. If no candidate receives a majority on the first ballot, the delegates continue to ballot until a majority is achieved for one candidate. Since 1952, however, no party convention has taken more than one ballot to produce a candidate. The delegates come to the convention pledged or with some level of commitment to a candidate.

Each party apportions its delegates differently. The Democrats had 3,933 delegates in 1984. A state's delegates are determined on the basis of population and popular votes cast for Democratic presidential candidates, so the large, populous states have the advantage. The Republicans used 2,235 delegates in 1984. That number resulted from awarding delegates to states that voted Republican in the previous presidential election and also elected Republican senators, House members, and governors. This system tends to favor the small states, which have been the stronghold of Republican strength in the past several years.

Delegate-selection processes differ with each state and party. But in each state's group of delegates several, such as the congressional delegates, the governor, and state party chairpeople, are automatically seated, or selected by the party leadership.

State conventions may also select delegates. The state convention forms caucuses supporting candidates and chooses delegates for the national convention through majoritarian elections or a proportional distribution. Today the most prevalent method of selecting convention delegates is by presidential primary. Here states may combine the presidential-preference test with the delegate-selection process.

The number of states using the presidential primary has risen. In 1968 sixteen states had such a primary, by 1972 twenty-three states had adopted it, and in 1976 thirty states had primaries. That number has remained relatively constant. Thirty-three states had presidential primaries in 1980 and thirty in 1984. The use of the primary has facilitated the change from control of nominations by party leaders to direct participation by the electorate. The proportion of convention delegates selected in primaries rose to a high of 75 percent in 1980 and then dropped back in 1984 to 50 percent as further Democratic rules reforms produced the first decline in primary-selected delegates since 1968.

Primary election of convention delegates operates differently in the various states. In some states, voters choose convention delegates directly from among contending slates of delegates. These delegates may or may not be committed to a candidate, depending on state law. The other basic variation is for the presidential preference primary to bind convention delegates selected by some other means. These two processes are combined in varying fashions:

1. *Presidential preference only*   Delegates are selected by party caucuses, and the presidential preference vote may or may not be binding on the delegates. If the election is binding, the Democratic party requires

delegates to be appointed according to a proportional representation formula.

2. *Presidential preference and delegate selection*   One vote for a presidential candidate also elects delegates pledged to or supportive of the presidential candidate. Parties may run unpledged slates of delegates.

3. *Presidential preference and separate election of convention delegates*   Here the voter votes once for a presidential candidate and once for convention delegates. The selected delegates may be bound to the winner according to state law. Some states have an advisory preference vote, with delegates listed as pledged or favoring a candidate. Some states use the mandatory preference, in which case the delegates are required to support that presidential primary winner. Again, proportional representation can be used to apportion delegates if mandatory preference is used.

4. *Delegate selection primary*   Under this format, the voter casts a ballot directly for convention delegates from contending slates. No presidential candidates appear on the ballot, although it is no secret which candidates the various contending slates of delegates prefer.

Democratic Rule Changes   The Democrats began to make rule changes in the wake of confrontation in the streets of Chicago in 1968. The McGovern Commission sought to open up the procedures for delegate selection, particularly to "significant groups that have traditionally been identified with the Democratic party." The commission sought to remove control from the party leaders by recommending explicit rules on delegate selection, abolishing the **unit rule** (which required all delegates to cast their ballots as the majority ruled) and establishing affirmative action guidelines to increase representation among youth, women, and minority groups, and requiring all delegates to be selected in the same year as the convention. Although the McGovern Commission did not set quotas on the number of blacks, women, and youth for each state delegation, the 1972 credentials committee for the convention began establishing them when it was faced with challenges from reform advocates regarding the representativeness of state delegations.

The reforms increased the reliance on primaries to select delegates, brought an increase in challenges, and generally radically changed the composition of the convention. George McGovern was a prime beneficiary of the changes, which allowed his liberal activists to capture a majority of the delegate slots and nominate McGovern for the presidency. Owing to the ensuing controversy and McGovern's convincing defeat at the polls in 1972, Democratic officials ended the quota system in 1974 and drafted new rules for the 1976 convention that included affirmative action guidelines but no quotas. The major change was the establishment of proportional representation: all candidates with 15 percent or more support of delegates at any level would receive proportional support in delegates at the state or national convention. There were to be no state winner-take-all primaries, and 75 percent of all delegates were to be se-

Unit Rule: *the rule that requires all convention delegates from a state to cast their ballots as the majority of that state's delegates rule.*

lected at the congressional-district level or lower. The increased emphasis on the primary again provided an easy way to apportion delegates and proved a benefit for Jimmy Carter, who did so well in the primary elections in 1976.

For 1980, the Democrats made further reforms. The proportional representation threshold for eligibility to win delegates was a sliding scale from the current 15 percent to a high of 25 percent for states that began the delegate selection process later in the year. In 1980, Democrats banned election of delegates from single-member districts or loophole, winner-take-all primaries, which had permitted district level, winner-take-all elections in 1976.

Super Delegates: *a special category of convention delegates established by the Democratic party in order to include elected public officials and ranking party officers. This is designed to give party regulars a greater voice at the national presidential nominating convention.*

The major reforms for 1984 included a category of 550 **super delegates**—elected senators and members of the House, governors, state party chairs, and other party or elected officials, who were automatically seated as convention delegates. Constituting 14 percent of the total delegates, they were designed to give party regulars and moderates greater voice in choosing the presidential nominee. The party also reintroduced the loophole, or winner-take-all, primary at the congressional district level. In short, the intention was to give the convention more freedom to make decisions and to increase the power of party regulars. For 1988 the Democratic Fairness Commission hardly altered the 1984 rules. Here is a summary of the Democratic rules for delegate selection to the presidential nominating convention:

1. *Proportional representation*   States will apportion convention delegates in proportion to candidate strength in both caucus and primary states. Caucus states base delegates on the proportion of delegates attending candidate preference caucuses; primary states use the popular vote in the presidential primary to apportion delegates. A threshold level for candidates to qualify for delegates is established at 15 percent in caucus states and most primary states.

2. *Loophole primary*   States may reintroduce the 1980 outlawed winner-take-all primary election at the district level. Voters will ballot for delegates identified with their presidential preference. The entire delegate bloc will be won by the victorious presidential candidate.

3. *Super delegates*   Approximately eight hundred party and elected public officials go to the convention as uncommitted delegates. Almost all members of the House and Senate, selected by the party's congressional caucus, are included, as are all Democratic governors and all members of the Democratic National Committee. For 1988, no super delegates are chosen by the state parties.

4. *Early primaries*   All early primaries and caucuses except the Iowa caucus and New Hampshire's primary have been banned. All caucuses and primaries must be held between the second Tuesday of March and the second Tuesday of June. Any exception requires approval by the party.

TABLE 9.12   Democratic public officials as convention delegates

Year	Senators	Representatives	Governors
1956	90%	33%	100%
1960	68	45	85
1964	72	46	61
1968	68	39	83
1972	36	15	80
1976	18	15	47
1980	14	15	76
1984	62	67	88

SOURCE: *National Journal* (January 2, 1982): 25; 1984 data from *Congressional Quarterly, Weekly Report* (July 21, 1984): 1745.

5. *Candidate loyalty*   Delegates are no longer bound on the first convention ballot to their presidential preference. Delegates are free to respond to changing political conditions. They need only reflect the sentiments of those electing them.

6. *Affirmative action*   Men and women will be equally distributed in state delegations. Goals and timetables for affirmative action will include blacks and Hispanics.

The Democrats proposed abolishing automatic seating. Indeed, from 1968 to 1980 the proportion of senators, House members, and governors as delegates declined. Table 9.12 shows that the percentage of senators as delegates declined from 68 to 14 percent, that of House members from 39 to 15 percent, and that of governors from 83 to 47 percent. The creation of the category of super delegates in 1984 redressed this decline and gave greater power to party regulars to shape the convention decision. In 1984 well over half of Democratic senators and House members were convention delegates. In fact, 22 percent of the delegates to the Democratic convention in 1984 were party and elected officials, most coming from the group of super delegates. For 1984 the expansion of super delegates from 550 to 650 allowed for 80 percent of senators and House members to attend the Democratic convention as delegates.

Republican Rule Changes   Republican rule changes have been much slower and less dramatic. In 1971, the Ginn Commission (headed by Rosemary Ginn, a committeewoman from Missouri) called for reforms to include open participation, no automatic seating of delegates due to office or party position, no proxies, equal representation of men and women, and proportional representation for persons under twenty-five years of age. Although the commission's proposals have generally been supported, they have not been made party rules.

A major source of contention within the Republican party is the victory-bonus system, which rewards states with additional delegates if the state voted Republican in the last presidential, congressional, or gubernatorial election. The Ripon Society of liberal Republicans has challenged the system in court, arguing that it rewards small states and thereby denies the one person–one vote equal protection clause of the Fourteenth Amendment. The Supreme Court has refused to hear the case.

The Republican rules-review committee made no major changes in the 1980s.

Campaigns

With the decline of political parties, the process of conducting campaigns has changed. The nomination of a president has been nationalized, and the new nominating process has changed the approach to and conduct of campaigns. The presidential campaign is now a national campaign.

Political parties as a campaign resource are being replaced by candidate organizations. Since the presidential candidate needed to put together a personal organization to work the states for convention delegates, the same approach is now used for the general election campaign. Candidate organizations are markedly different from the state-oriented groups that dominated the traditional parties. The change began in 1968, when hundreds of out-of-staters converged on New Hampshire and other primary states to work for Eugene McCarthy's challenge to Lyndon Johnson's nomination. They canvassed, knocked on doors, passed out literature, and raised funds apart from, and often in spite of, the state party organization. In 1972, President Nixon placed all responsibility and resources for his reelection in a Committee to Re-Elect the President, thereby bypassing the Republican party altogether. By 1976, the Reagan supporters had become a distinct faction of the GOP party. Jimmy Carter's support

Campaigning requires considerable skill and enormous effort; candidates and their supporters inevitably suffer from stress and fatigue.

came from campaigners moving from state to state to drum up support for him. That this approach is so common today, and draws so little criticism, is quiet testimony to the nationalization of presidential campaigns and the erosion of political parties.

As the campaign for the presidency has become nationalized, it has also become subject to new conditions: (1) the national media have become the principal means of campaigning; (2) the cost of campaigning has skyrocketed and requires organizations to seek out sources of funding; and (3) campaign organizations have become specialized, professionally staffed organs that plan and execute strategy and tactics with the scientific precision of a modern army.

The Media   The standing of candidates today is determined not by party support or leadership commitment, but by a handful of reporters and commentators who follow the presidential campaign. The judgment of the media can make or break a candidate. These commentators are well-recognized persons in the field, work for the largest and most prestigious communication firms, and have the trust and confidence of the American public. Candidates direct their campaigns to winning over the press and to getting widespread and favorable attention in the public media.

The media have greater influence on the nomination process than on the general election. Events move faster: several states hold caucuses or primaries on the same day, and there are several candidates, each with a message or story needing to be told. The rules and procedures for conducting delegate selection and primaries are complex. "Thus the public must rely on the media to keep score—to define the standards of victory and interpret the results—far more than during the general elections."[37] During the primary season, political interest has not yet peaked; the voters' knowledge of the candidates is low and partisan loyalty is not of much help. "The voters are therefore more susceptible than in the fall to both the candidates' paid advertising and the stories that the media choose to emphasize in their news coverage."[38]

This is the age of television and television elections. There are more television sets in American homes than there are bathtubs. We have already seen the extent to which Americans depend on TV for their news and that it is the most important source for political information. Candidates like to use television to campaign since the medium affords them a controlled environment. They can send a message just as intended, packaged and appealing. They can project an attractive image with no undesirable traits, styling themselves as candidates for all people. Moreover, television immediately tells the electorate who is winning, providing instantaneous results of primary elections, delegate counts, and public opinion polls, which are translated by network commentators into gains or losses for candidates.

Media politics has ushered us into a new era. The message projected by the media makes or breaks candidates. Candidates spend thousands and even millions of dollars trying to find, package, and market the right image. Not only is advertising expensive but so too is creating the message to be advertised.

This reliance on the media gives increased importance to media personnel, who in their turn have become kingmakers. Media people have the power to influence the selection of candidates and campaign issues by their choice of featured stories. Calling a primary election a victory and labeling the particular candidate the frontrunner propels that candidate into the spotlight and suggests that he or she is worthy of public attention. This power of the media controller, of course, is not lost upon candidates. Press conferences are always scheduled in major network centers and always before the evening news deadline. Candidates go out of their way to be available to major news commentators. They provide space and time for news personnel on the campaign trail.

Another result of the era of media politics is that candidates are selected for their compatibility with television campaigning. Both political parties seek out potential candidates with an eye to their appeal as projected over the tube. Good-looking candidates with "camera presence," which can cause the voters to identify with them, are much sought after. Many people wonder how candidates in history would have fared before the bright lights of television—Washington with his powdered wig, Lincoln with his dour expression, or Truman with his gruff language. Doris Graber somberly notes that

> Candidates who are short on television performance skills now spend considerable time with professionals to remedy their shortcomings. In recent years, television advisers have become regular members of presidential and gubernatorial staffs. Names of media experts like Gerald Rafshoon, Tony Schwartz, David Garth, Charles Guggenheim, or Joseph Napolitan have become as well-known as the political bosses of yesteryear.[39]

Note, for example, the impact of the media on presidential debates. In 1960 John Kennedy successfully projected an image of youthful vigor and ability, while Richard Nixon appeared tired and sullen. Kennedy's phrase "to get the nation moving again" sounded more attractive to voters when linked to his image projected in the televised debates. In 1976 both Ford and Carter were media conscious and sought to exploit the other's weaknesses. Their three televised debates probably did not have the dramatic impact on voters that the 1960 debate did, but they did succeed in sharpening the differences between the candidates.

The 1980 Carter–Reagan debate was unique. There were, in fact, two debates: an early debate in June involving independent candidate John Anderson and Ronald Reagan without Jimmy Carter, and the Cleveland debate in late October between Reagan and Carter without Anderson. This debate came very late in the campaign and thus had the potential to swing the election.

There were two debates in 1984 between Mondale and Reagan. The media helped to shape the context in both. In the weeks prior to the first

Public Policy and Professional Campaign Managers

Most students of public policy find only an indirect influence on public policy by citizen participation at the polls. Yet democratic public policy requires that citizens select top policymakers. Many feel that the importance of elections is not the selection of policy but the choice of policymakers, who in turn formulate policy in line with broad programmatic promises made in the campaign (platforms). There is evidence that voters have shaped the direction of public policy by selecting one party and its platform over another, that critical partisan realignments have altered national policies, and that voter alignments are organized around substantive policy issues. "Partisan alignments form the constituent basis for governments committed to the translation of the choices made by the electorate during critical periods into public policy over a relatively long period of time."*

Significant policy issues to emerge in recent elections, however, are the breakdown of political parties and a rise in the voter's mood of cynicism, which have led to the hiring of more and more professional election consultants to manage campaigns. In such an atmosphere of mechanical, advertised, and impersonal elections, can the electorate have any real role in policymaking?

Very few voters understand the increasing involvement and growing importance of professional consultants, the paid professionals who plan and manage a candidate's campaign. Such consultants specialize in almost every facet of an election. Here are just some of the activities for which a candidate can get help:

1. *Overall organization* Campaign strategy, campaign management, staff training, counseling, research, fund raising, election-day organization, press relations, precinct organization.

2. *Specific campaign techniques* Polling, electronic media, advertising, mail solicitations, films, voter turnout, graphics, data processing, print media, media-time buying.

3. *Issues* Bonds, women's issues, referenda.

Today there are more than two hundred full-time professional campaign consultants.** Theirs is a highly complex and technical business, utilizing the technologies of the computer and electronic media. More often than not the campaign consultants have backgrounds in industries such as media production, advertising, data processing, and polling. They apply their skills and emergent technology to the field of elections.

What are the most significant implications of professional campaign consultants? Three seem possible, if not evident. The first is for continued antipartyism. The use of consultants is the result of the antiparty feeling in American politics. Personal campaigning and personal campaign organizations feed on this antiparty sentiment and cause it to grow. These features of the new style place the voter directly before the candidate and his or her array of consultants. Both candidates and voters become increasingly vulnerable. Second, campaigning is likely to continue to become more specialized. The various facets of the campaign will produce more specialized technologies, requiring close coordination and making the conduct of elections more complex and costly. Third, elections that are not won or lost, but managed, are subject to manipulation. Usurping control from the voter could thus be the most far-reaching effect of managed campaigns.

*Benjamin Ginzberg, "Elections and Public Policy," *American Political Science Review* 70 (March 1976): 49.

**National Journal* (November 4, 1978): 1772.

debate, the press expected Reagan, the Great Communicator, to dominate. Yet in that debate Reagan faltered in his speaking and was unsure of his facts; Mondale gave a strong, sure presentation. Mondale had won despite predictions to the contrary. Now the media were called upon to make a major reassessment. Would Reagan falter again? Could Mondale deliver a knockout punch in the next debate? Reagan did perform somewhat better in the second debate; that there was no knockout punch by Mondale was a general consensus reached by the media. But what about the issues? It would seem that the press paid little attention to the policy differences between the two candidates. The issues got lost in the drama of personal confrontation staged by the media.

The media have the potential to present issues and candidates directly to the people. They reach a wider audience more directly than any party or campaign organization. They can sharpen issues and personality traits, and provide background and comparative analysis. They can give the voter sufficient information and a context in which to make reasoned and informed judgments. But the media also have the capacity for abuse. The selective decisions regarding which issues or personality features the media concentrate on can distort the image or nature of a campaign. The sensational is too often displayed and emphasized. Since voters are heavily dependent on the media for information, first impressions are critical. Candidates are aware of this and often seek to manipulate the media. Joe McGinniss's *The Selling of the President—1968,* for example, sought to demonstrate how Mr. Nixon used the media in 1968.[40]

Professional Organizations   A second campaign technique is the creation of highly specialized, professional campaign organizations.

Public opinion polling is basic to campaign organizations. Polling helps to identify issues and personality images, and to show the social and political composition of electorates. All presidential candidates employ professional polling firms to target issues and identify groups who are sure to vote for a candidate, those who cannot be won over, and those who are undecided. The polling firm then surveys the groups to determine what issues are relevant, how people feel, and what the candidate must do to "capture" those blocs of voters. Polls keep the candidate abreast of progress or any changes in voter feelings and concerns. With the aid of computers, samples of voters as specific and defined as neighborhoods can be analyzed to give voter profiles. Updated information is added and campaign strategies formulated to capitalize on voter thinking. The campaign strategy is based on the scientific polling of voters. No longer do candidates simply take to the stump, make speeches, shake hands, and eat chicken in union halls. Highly skilled media consultants and advertising firms work with candidates to make use of polling data in presenting the candidate in a most favorable light.

Professional campaign consultants may not have the ability to make a candidate or create issues, but they do have the technical and managerial skills that allow a candidate to present his or her personality and issues in the most efficient and effective manner. They use modern technology—mass media, data processing, direct-mail computer systems, and commercial advertising—to win elections and they are specialists in polling, fund raising, advertising, and public relations. Their job is to assist the candidate and the organization in all areas of the campaign, from fund raising to precinct organizing to creating election-day voter drives. There are now more than two hundred such consulting firms in the United States, and most prefer to work for one party or for candidates with a given ideology.[41]

The result of professional technological campaigning has been to destroy traditional campaign techniques. Party workers and organizations are largely superfluous. Many voters are becoming disillusioned and cynical as they are bombarded with slick, Madison Avenue-type political ads.[42] Candidates, particularly those who have to run every two years, have come to rely heavily on such consultants. This has contributed heavily to the cost of campaigning, since campaign consultants and media campaigning are extremely expensive.

Campaign Finance   Whatever the specific reasons, the American political process has been degraded by rising election costs. Watergate merely illustrated the extent to which money has come to dominate elections. The cost of campaigning has risen continuously since 1952, but most dramatically since 1964. The Citizen's Research Foundation estimated that in 1972 a total of $228 million was spent on elections, with 61 percent of the cost going for the presidential campaign (Figure 9.6). The 1976 figures indicate a total of $212 million. The presidential contest cost approximately $115 million, the Senate costs were $38 million, and campaigning for the House cost $61 million. The presidential contest represented a change, as public financing for the first time limited campaign spending. Public funds for presidential campaign costs amounted to $72.3 million in 1976—$43.6 million for the general election, $24.3 million for the primary elections (money was distributed to fifteen qualifying candidates, thirteen Democrats and two Republicans), and $4.4 million to the political parties to operate the nominating conventions. The escalation of campaign costs slowed down in 1976 as a result of reform efforts: public financing set limits on expenditures; the climate of Watergate made contributors and the public cautious; campaign laws restricted contributions by individual donors; and inflation made political money scarce.

The 1980s have witnessed the renewed rise of election costs with dramatic increases in spending for Senate and House contests. The 1980 total of $394 million was almost equaled in 1982 without the presidential contest: in that year, $200 million was spent on House elections while thirty-three Senate contests cost $138 million. With the presidential election of 1984 costs again escalated—to over half a billion dollars! Presidential spending showed modest increases, while the cost of Senate contests

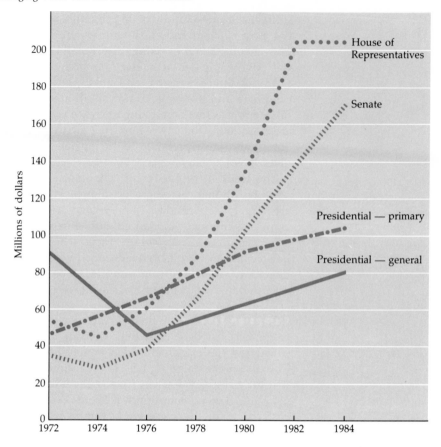

	House	Senate	Presidential		Total
			Primary	General	
1984	203.6	170.5	103.7	80.8	558.6
1982	204.0	138.4			342.4
1980	136.0	102.9	92.3	62.7	393.9
1978	88.0	65.5			153.5
1976	60.9	38.1	66.9	45.9	211.8
1974	45.0	28.9			73.1
1972	54.3	35.5	46.6	91.4	227.8

Figure 9.6 Campaign spending in national elections (in millions of dollars)

jumped 20 percent. There are several explanations for the escalating costs. Foremost among them is the growth of political action committees and the money they contribute to congressional races. The crowded primary field to secure a presidential nomination also increases costs.

Another explanation for the rise in spending has to be inflation. Between 1976 and 1984 the consumer price index rose 35 percent, so spending had to increase by one-third just to remain even. Other costs spiraled, most specifically those associated with electronic technology—computer mailing and public opinion polling. A fourth reason for the skyrocketing cost of elections is an increase in the use of television advertising. More and more candidates are depending on the medium to convey their message. In 1976 almost half of both Ford's and Carter's campaign budgets went for media advertising. Prime-time television ads now cost $300,000 for a minute of network time.

Campaign contributions from large donors have attracted public attention, and up to 1972 the big contributor dominated. More recently, however, reform legislation, bolstered by court decisions, has worked to restrict large contributions and expand the number of small donors. Results of recent polls indicate that 8 to 12 percent of the American public contributes to political campaigns. Herbert Alexander reports that in the 1980 presidential prenomination campaign, individuals contributed $73.6 million directly to the candidates, or about 68 percent of the net campaign receipts. In the same year, individuals accounted for 67 percent of funds contributed to House candidates in the general election and 78 percent of the funds for Senate candidates.[43] Says Alexander, "Although the percentage of funds contributed by PACs has increased steadily since 1972, direct individual contributions also have increased proportionately to help meet growing campaign costs."[44]

Small donors are increasing, in part because of the rise of political activists and computer mass-mail solicitations and in part because of public-financing eligibility requirements. The McGovern campaign in 1972 and George Wallace's drive in 1968 are examples of campaigns financed by small contributions. George McGovern reported receiving from five hundred thousand to a million small donations. One report placed the figure of $100-plus contributors at only 27 percent of total contributors. Wallace backers claimed that 85 percent of the $6.7 million total they raised from February to October 1968 was from contributions of less than $100 each.[45] In 1980 Reagan successfully used mail-order drives, obtaining 45 to 50 percent of his campaign funds from mail solicitation. So did independent John Anderson, who had to rely on contributions that averaged $30 apiece.[46] The Republican National Committee reported that it raised almost $26.5 million in 1980 from small donors—those giving less than $500. But these totals, impressive as they may be, still fall short of a mass-based, grass roots campaign. The totals represent contributions from approximately only 1 percent of the voting-age population.

Campaign-Finance Legislation   The spiraling costs of elections and the scandals surrounding the 1972 election spurred a drive for reform. As a result of illegal corporate contributions in the Watergate affair, twenty-one companies pleaded guilty to illegally contributing more than $980,000—most of it to the Nixon campaign. Lack of contribution limits or public disclosure led to charges of influence peddling and the buying of public favors.

The Corrupt Practices Act of 1925 sought to restrict campaign spending and provide for public disclosure. The Hatch Act of 1940 set a limit of $5,000 for any person's contribution to a federal candidate or political committee, but there was no limit to the number of committees supporting one candidate to which an individual could contribute. President Johnson labeled the 1925 act "more loophole than law," but it remained the basic election law until 1972.

In 1971 Congress passed the Federal Election Campaign Act, which sought to provide for fuller public disclosure of funding and to draw more donors into politics by allowing a tax credit against the federal income tax (50 percent of the contribution up to $25 on a joint return). More specifically, the act set limits on media expenditures, placed ceilings on contributions by candidates to their own campaigns, and required reporting and disclosure of expenditures and contributors. Many of these provisions were modified or replaced by the 1974 amendments to the act. The 1974 amendments came as a direct result of Watergate, and produced significant modifications to the 1971 act. They also gave rise to a Supreme Court decision testing the constitutionality of the law.

The 1974 act set more restrictions not only on contributions but also on campaign spending—$700,000 for congressional candidates and $20 million for each presidential candidate. This legislation also established tighter disclosure and reporting requirements and created a bipartisan Federal Election Commission to oversee enforcement of its provisions. The act further provided for public financing of presidential campaigns, making matching public funds available to eligible candidates—up to $5 million in the primary election, and total public funding in the general election.

The law was promptly challenged in the courts. A group of plaintiffs composed of conservatives and liberals, including Senator James Buckley (conservative–N.Y.) and Eugene McCarthy, brought suit, arguing that the law violated the First Amendment freedoms of speech and association. They also charged that the Federal Election Commission, with its bipartisan composition, violated the separation of powers by giving Congress a right to appoint members. The Supreme Court, in a landmark case, *Buckley* v. *Valeo*,[47] reviewed the constitutionality of the election-law reforms. The Court was mixed in its judgment of the 1974 reforms. The Court found unconstitutional, as an undue restriction of First Amendment freedoms, limits on political expenditures by a person to promote a political cause or candidacy. The Court also ruled unconstitutional limitations on expenditures by a candidate to further his or her own candidacy. The spending of money to communicate with voters is a form of free speech protected under the First Amendment, the Court ruled. But the Court upheld limits on contributions to candidates and political organizations. Here the Court sought to draw a distinction between *spending* and *contributing*. Congress could limit contributions in order to equalize influence and prevent the abuses that large contributions brought to the electoral process. And in the presidential contest, if a candidate took public funds, Congress could legitimately limit spending by those candidates as one of the overall conditions for accepting public money. Finally, the Court found the Federal Election Commission illegally constituted, though it upheld the concept of a regulatory commission.

In the wake of *Buckley* v. *Valeo*, Congress quickly adopted new legislation: the 1976 amendments to the Federal Election Campaign Act. The present regulations governing federal elections are summarized below:

1. *Contribution limits* Individuals are limited to giving no more than $5,000 a year to a political action committee or a political party. Contributions to any candidate in a primary or general election are limited to $1,000 per candidate per election. The total aggregate contribution limit for an individual is $25,000 a year.

2. *Public financing* Matching public funds up to $5 million per candidate are available to eligible presidential candidates for primary elections. To be eligible, a candidate must meet a fund-raising requirement of $100,000 raised in amounts of $5,000 or more in each of twenty states. Only the first $250 of individual private contributions is matched with public funds. Full public funding, on a voluntary basis, is available for major-party presidential candidates in the general election. Minor-party candidates are eligible for partial funding if they win 10 percent or more of the vote in two consecutive presidential primaries. If candidates receive full public funding, no private contributions are allowed. Public funding is also available for presidential nominating conventions. Major parties automatically qualify; minor parties would receive a proportion of federal funds based on votes received in the previous election.

3. *Spending limits* Presidential candidates who accept public funds may spend no more than $50,000 of their own money. For primaries, presidential candidates accepting public money have state-by-state spending limits. Candidates may spend an equivalent of sixteen cents per voting-age resident in each state (adjusted for inflation), with a floor of $264,000 owing to New Hampshire's and Alaska's small populations.

4. *Disclosure* Candidates and committees must file periodic pre- and post-election reports, identifying by name the sources of all contributions totaling more than $200 annually and itemizing all expenditures over $200 by name of person or firm paid and purpose of the expenditure.

5. *Enforcement* The **Federal Election Commission** has overall responsibility to enforce campaign-finance laws and to administer public financing of presidential elections. The six-member bipartisan commission is appointed by the president and confirmed by the Senate.

Federal Election Commission: *a bipartisan commission that has the responsibility to enforce campaign finance laws and to administer public financing of presidential elections. The six-member commission is appointed by the president and confirmed by the Senate.*

Suffrage: *the right to vote.*

Conducting Elections

Suffrage The electoral system centers around the act of voting. The history of the citizen's right to vote—**suffrage**—has been the extension of that right. The extension of the franchise in America has been a long and often controversial process. The nation was founded on the premise that only white, male, property-holding citizens at least twenty-one years of age could participate. A major part of American political history has been the democratic erosion of those restrictions to political participation (see the Fact File on pages 362–363).

Property qualifications were the first to go. Although they did not write it into the Constitution, eighteenth-century thinkers were distrustful of mass citizen participation. The Founding Fathers were inclined to keep from participating those whom they believed had no interest or stake in political matters. Gouverneur Morris stated, "Give the votes to the people who have no property and they will sell them to the rich who will be able to buy them." And Roger Sherman declared, "The people immediately should have as little to do as may be about the government." That the states already had laws restricting suffrage seemed adequate to the framers, and no such prohibitions were added to the Constitution. But by the election of 1832, the mood of the nation had changed. The election of Jackson brought mass campaigning; immigration and the frontier produced a democratization of American life. In short, by the time of the Civil War most states had eliminated property tests for voting.

Extending the franchise to black Americans has been a longer and more bitter struggle. The Fifteenth Amendment guaranteed the right to vote to black Americans, but we have seen that the right was ignored and legally circumvented by southern states after the Civil War. Through the use of the white primary, literacy tests, poll taxes, and registration requirements, blacks were prevented from participating. Throughout the late nineteenth century and into the twentieth, federal law and the U.S. courts worked to eliminate many of the devices used to bar black involvement in the electoral process. The Supreme Court attacked the white primary in 1944, declaring it unconstitutional in *Smith* v. *Allwright*. In 1964 the Court set aside poll taxes in federal elections. The 1965 Voting Rights Act set aside literacy tests and authorized federal authorities to enter states and register voters. Yet even with the legal barriers overcome, black voting remains low.

The all-male electorate began to be challenged by the turn of the century. Wyoming first allowed women to vote in 1864. By 1900, three additional western states followed suit. From then on, the women's suffrage movement spread and gathered momentum. By 1919 Congress had proposed the Nineteenth Amendment, which was quickly ratified, and women were able to vote in the 1920 presidential election.

More recent changes have expanded the electorate further. In 1961, the Twenty-third Amendment to the Constitution was ratified, extending suffrage for the presidential contest to the District of Columbia, giving the seat of the government three electoral votes. However, the District of Columbia still has no representation in Congress; it is managed by Congress, although residents pay the same taxes as everyone else. The greatest recent expansion of suffrage came in 1970, when Congress lowered the voting age to eighteen for all elections. The Supreme Court ruled that Congress had power to do so only in federal elections.[48] Some states followed suit, others did not. The Twenty-sixth Amendment, ratified in 1971, extended suffrage rights in all elections to those eighteen years of age and older. The amendment reportedly added 10.5 million Americans to the voting rolls. Yet their record of participation is the lowest of all groups; only half of eighteen- to twenty-one-year-olds do vote.

Reapportionment   Equally as challenging a concept for democracy as universal suffrage is the notion that every person's vote has equal weight. Yet in the twentieth century, while nation and courts were struggling with universal suffrage, a political imbalance was growing between urban and rural America. State legislatures are required to redraw congressional and state legislative districts every ten years. This is known as **reapportionment.** Yet states often refused to do so or drew the lines along geographical boundaries that favored rural areas. The population explosion and patterns of immigration brought great numbers to urban centers, however. America was becoming an urban nation, but its legislatures failed to reflect the change. By 1960, state legislatures and congressional districts were greatly unbalanced with respect to population. Many states had districts twice as large as others; California had one district four hundred times larger than its smallest.

Legislatures, dominated by representatives benefiting from the system, were reluctant to correct the problem. Representative Emmanuel Celler (D–N.Y.) introduced legislation to require states to reapportion congressional districts to limit population deviance between districts to 15 percent. But Celler's bill failed to muster much congressional support. The courts were also reluctant to address the issue. In 1946, in *Colegrove* v. *Green*,[49] the Supreme Court ruled that the problem of reapportionment was a "political question." The courts lacked jurisdiction, the Court ruled, and the issue could properly be settled only by legislatures. But the case raised an interesting issue. *Colegrove* argued that the population variance among legislative districts within a state constituted a state's denial of the equal protection of the laws as guaranteed by the Fourteenth Amendment. The Court ruled that Congress alone had the authority to determine fair representation in legislative chambers. But by the 1960s, the Court was of another mind. In 1962, in *Baker* v. *Carr*,[50] the Court ruled that the issue of legislative reapportionment could be resolved by the courts. In other words, the Court was inviting suits to challenge malapportioned legislative districts. *Baker* v. *Carr* produced a political revolution. It was a landmark case in constitutional law and it dramatically affected the course of American government and politics.

The Court did not have long to wait for suits. In *Wesberry* v. *Sanders* (1964),[51] the Supreme Court ruled that congressional districts had to be apportioned among the states according to population, citing the language of the Constitution in Article I, Section 2. Said the Court, "As early as is practical, one man's vote in a Congressional election is to be worth

Reapportionment: *the mandatory redrawing by state legislatures of congressional and state legislative boundaries every ten years, after the decennial census.*

Fact File
Voter Registration Information

State or other jurisdiction	Mail registration allowed for all voters	Minimum state residence requirement (days)	Closing date for registration before general election (days)	Persons eligible for absentee registration(a)	Automatic cancellation of registration for failure to vote after ___ years
Alabama		1	10	D,S,T	2
Alaska	*	30	30	(b)	2
Arizona		50	50	S,T	4
Arkansas		—	20	D	4
California	*	29	29	(b)	4
Colorado		32	32	D,S,T	2
Connecticut		—	21(c)	D	
Delaware	*	—	3rd Sat. in Oct.(c)	(b)	4
Florida		—	30	(d)	2
Georgia		—	30	B,D,R,S,T	3
Hawaii		—	30	B,D,E,R,S,T	2
Idaho		30	17/10(e)	B,D,S,T	4
Illinois		30	28	(f)	4
Indiana		30	29(g)	B,D,S,T	2
Iowa	*	—	10	(b)	4
Kansas	*	20	20	(b)	4
Kentucky	*	30	30	(b)	4
Louisiana		—	24(c)	D,T	4
Maine	*	—	Election day	(b)	
Maryland	*	29	29	(b)	5
Massachusetts		—	28	D,T	
Michigan		30	30	D,S,T	10
Minnesota	*	20	Election day	(b)	4
Mississippi		30	10	(f)	4
Missouri	*	—	28	(b)	
Montana	*	30	30	(b)	4
Nebraska		—	10	D,S,T	
Nevada		30	30	S,T	2
New Hampshire		10	10	B,D,R,S	
New Jersey	*	30	29	(b)	4

State or other jurisdiction	Mail registration allowed for all voters	Minimum state residence requirement (days)	Closing date for registration before general election (days)	Persons eligible for absentee registration(a)	Automatic cancellation of registration for failure to vote after ___ years
New Mexico		—	42	T	2
New York	*	30	30	(b)	4
North Carolina		30	21(h)	D	8
North Dakota(i)		30			
Ohio	*	30	30	(b)	4
Oklahoma	*	—	10	D	4
Oregon	*	20	Election day	(b)	2
Pennsylvania	*	30	30	(b)	2
Rhode Island		30	30	D	5
South Carolina		—	30	D,S,T	
South Dakota		—	15	S,T	4
Tennessee	*	50	30	(b)	4
Texas	*	—	30	(b)	
Utah	*	30	5	(b)	4
Vermont		—	17	(d)	4
Virginia		—	31	(f)	4
Washington	*	30	30	(f)	2
West Virginia	*	30	30	(b)	4
Wisconsin	*	10	Election day	(b)	2
Wyoming	21	—	30	B,D,E,S,T	2
District of Columbia	*	30	30	(b)	4
Puerto Rico		—	50	(f)	2
Virgin Islands		45	45	S	4

SOURCE: *The Book of the States, 1984–1985* (Lexington, Ky.: The Council of State Governments, 1984).

Key:

— No residence requirement.

(a) In this column: B—Absent on business; D—Disabled persons; E—Not absent, but prevented by employment from registering; R—Absent for religious reasons; S—Students; T—Temporarily out of jurisdiction.

(b) All voters. See column on mail registration.

(c) Closing date differs for primary election. In Connecticut, 14 days; Delaware, 21 days; Louisiana, 30 days.

(d) Anyone unable to register in person.

(e) With precinct registrar, 17 days before; with county clerk, 10 days.

(f) No one is eligible to register absentee.

(g) Before deputy registrar, 45 days.

(h) Business days.

(i) No voter registration.

as much as another's." In other words, one person, one vote. The same year, in *Reynolds* v. *Sims*,[52] the Supreme Court extended the principle of one person, one vote to cover both houses of state legislatures. The Court relied on the equal protection clause of the Fourteenth Amendment as the basis for making its ruling. As the Court said in *Reynolds*, "Legislators represent people, not trees or acres." Legislative districts are to be apportioned on the basis of population: one person, one vote. And if legislatures cannot or will not reapportion, the federal courts will design an acceptable plan for the state.

The 1964 decisions seemed to imply that some population variance would be permissible. Said the Court in *Reynolds*, "Some deviations from the equal-population principle are constitutionally permissible with respect to the apportionment of seats in either or both of the two houses of a bicameral state legislature." Just how much remained to be seen. The Court rejected a 6 percent variation for congressional districts in 1969[53] and a 4 percent deviance in 1973.[54] A standard of mathematical exactness was being applied for congressional districts. And in 1983 the Court rejected seven-tenths of one percent as not sufficiently equal, saying states must make a "good faith effort to achieve precise mathematical equality."[55] For congressional districts, states must use population census data and must arrive at mathematical exactness. "Adopting any standard other than population equality, using the best census data available, would subtly erode the Constitution's idea of equal representation." For state legislatures, greater deviations were being tolerated. In 1973 the Court let stand a Virginia plan that had a 16.4 percent population variation and otherwise permitted a 10 percent variance in a Texas plan.[56] Summarizing its position in *Chapman* v. *Meier*,[57] the Court said, "As contrasted with congressional districting, where population equality appears now to be the preeminent, if not the sole criterion on which to adjudge constitutionality, . . . when state legislative districts are at issue we have held that minor population deviations do not establish a prima facie Constitutional violation."

Gerrymandering: *the drawing of electoral districts so as to disadvantage a political group at the polls; often results in oddly shaped districts.*

The cases on redistricting did not address **gerrymandering,** the drawing of legislative districts to disadvantage one political group. As long as legislative districts were numerically equal, they could take most any shape or boundary. This was often done by political parties in control. They would manipulate district lines to give themselves an advantage over the opposition political party. In 1986 the Supreme Court said that severe gerrymandering of election districts violated the Constitution.[58] The Court was careful not to throw out all odd-shaped districts, only those that "consistently degrade" a political group's influence. In essence the Court did not reject all gerrymandering, but it drew a narrow line, saying "unconstitutional discrimination occurs only when the electoral system is arranged in a manner that will consistently degrade a voter's or a group of voters' influence on the political process as a whole."

The Court had previously ruled that racial gerrymandering, the manipulating of district lines to dilute the electoral strength of a racial minority, violated the Constitution. This decision marks the first instance of declaring partisan gerrymandering to be unconstitutional as well.

Registration In every state but one (North Dakota), to be eligible to vote a citizen must establish his or her legal qualification to vote. Although the requirements are not great (age and residency), the act of **registering** is a physical imposition that keeps otherwise eligible voters from participating in elections. In 1976 an estimated 45 million voters were kept from the polls because they were not registered to vote. To combat this issue, several states, such as Minnesota, have instituted election-day registration, where registration and voting can be done at the same time and in the same place.

Registration: *the physical act of establishing legal qualification to vote. To be eligible to vote a citizen must meet minimum age and residency requirements.*

Southern states used voter registration to keep blacks off the voter rolls. By moving registration locations or using irregular hours, states kept would-be voters from qualifying and establishing their right to participate. With the 1965 Voting Rights Acts, Congress empowered the Department of Justice to establish registration procedures in areas where blacks had been discriminated against in voting. But President Carter felt this was not good enough; registration provisions still kept too many citizens from participating. Citing the fact that at least twenty other democracies had higher levels of voter turnout, the president proposed a national system of election-day registration. States should be encouraged to adopt such a system, the president noted, for those with election-day registration systems have higher turnout rates of voting.

A major factor in registration was determining what constituted residency. States frequently used a one-year period of residency as a qualification; some states set the time as long as two years. States frequently added county and precinct requirements as well. But the Voting Rights Act of 1970 permitted voting in presidential elections with only a thirty-day residency. Then, in 1972, the Supreme Court ruled that no state, for any election, could require more than a thirty-day residency.[59] The Court modified the ruling somewhat in 1973, however, by allowing a longer residency in state and local elections—a requirement of fifty days was considered reasonable.[60] But the thirty-day limit for voting in presidential elections stood.

Balloting As we walk into the polling place, we usually pay little attention to the nature of the ballot or the placement of candidates' names. Yet research has proved that these factors can affect the outcome. For example, a name placed low on a ballot gathers fewer votes than those higher up because voters have to "dig" to find the candidate. Voting machines make writing in names extremely difficult. And a party-column ballot facilitates straight-ticket voting.

Party Column (Indiana) Ballot: *a form of ballot that lists candidates by parties in straight columns.*

Whether voting is by machine or paper ballot, two principal forms of ballots are used. The **party column (Indiana) ballot** lists candidates by parties in straight columns. This makes party identification considerably easier, and often there is a single party lever or box to enable the voter to vote for all candidates listed for the party. This ballot encourages straight

Office Block (Massachusetts) Ballot: *a form of ballot that lists candidates by the office sought. Party affiliation is noted after the candidate, but straight party voting is difficult.*

Electoral College: *the body that elects the president of the United States. To be elected president, a candidate must receive a majority of electoral votes. The Founding Fathers distrusted direct popular election of the president, choosing instead to create an artificial body called the electoral college. Electors are chosen by states, typically by the political parties within the states.*

party balloting. The **office block (Massachusetts) ballot** lists candidates by the office sought; all candidates running for president, for example, are listed under that office. Party affiliation is noted after the candidate, but straight party voting is made more difficult.

The Electoral College   In every election except that for the president, direct balloting by the people determines the outcome. For the presidency, however, the U.S. Constitution established the **electoral college** to mediate between the people and a legislative election. Electors were to exercise independent judgment.

To be elected president, a candidate must receive a majority of electoral votes. Each state appoints, as the state legislature may direct, a number of electors equal to the total number of senators and representatives the state has in Congress. Normally each party nominates a slate of electors pledged to the party's presidential candidate. Voters in the general election technically vote not for a presidential candidate, but for a slate of electors, even though the electors' names may not appear. The presidential candidate winning a *plurality* of the popular vote receives *all* that state's electoral votes.

Although there is no constitutional requirement that the electors be chosen by the presidential contest, every state does so. The Constitution says a state legislature may select electors in such manner as it may direct. The winning electors meet in the state capital in December, as directed by Congress, and cast their ballots. Officially they may vote for whomever they feel is most qualified to be president. In practice, they cast all ballots for the party candidate to whom they were pledged and who received the most popular votes in the state.

The state transmits the sealed ballots to the president of the Senate. Then, before the House and Senate in early January, the ballots are opened and counted. The candidate receiving a majority of electoral votes for president is declared president-elect. If no candidate receives a majority, the House of Representatives is directed by the Constitution to choose the president from among the top three candidates, each state in the House having one vote. If no candidate receives a majority of electoral votes for vice-president, the Senate must choose from the top two candidates, a majority of senators determining the winner.

The electoral college, with its winner-take-all approach, concentrates electoral votes in the heavily populated states: the urban and suburban centered states such as New York, California, Pennsylvania, Ohio, and Texas. Candidates spend their time campaigning in states with the most electoral votes, states where a shift of a few thousand votes can mean an additional one hundred or so electoral votes. A presidential candidate needs to carry only twelve states to win a majority of electoral votes, and the candidate needs only a plurality of popular votes to capture all the state's electoral votes. Practically, however, campaign strategy dictates the states to campaign in. Some states are viewed as solid, and only minimal attention is given to campaigning there; others show little likelihood of being carried, so they too are given little campaign effort. The remaining states are the battleground. Some of them are small and receive low priority. Hence, the campaign comes down to the large or medium-size states where campaigning can alter the outcome.

Politically the electoral college favors the large states; they have the electoral clout, and it is in those states that presidential candidates campaign (Figure 9.7). The votes in larger states swing elections. On the other hand, small states enjoy a unique status under the electoral college. Proportionally their share of the electoral vote (because each state has two senators) is greater than the percentage of the popular vote nationwide. That may be little consolation, but a shift of relatively few votes here and there makes for electoral margins. If the popular vote were used, shifts in the larger states would also count, but with the electoral college they only increase the margin for winning the same number of electoral votes.

It is precisely because of this electoral distortion, as well as the possibility of defection by electors, that the last decade has seen a rising cry for reform in the electoral college. Such defections occurred in 1960, 1968, and 1976 (one each year). In 1960 Senator Byrd received one electoral vote that had been won by Kennedy. Wallace received a Republican elector's vote in 1968, and Ronald Reagan received a vote in 1976 from the

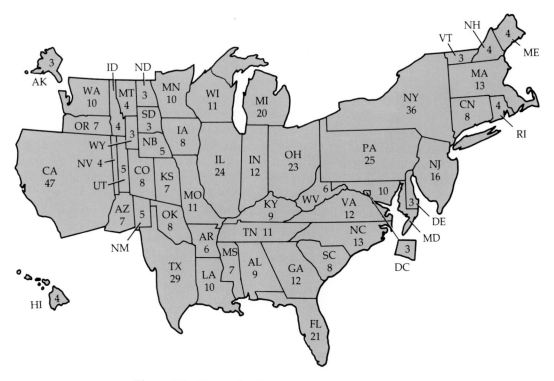

Figure 9.7 Electoral college map of the United States of America. States are drawn in proportion to number of electoral votes, which total 538.

state of Washington, which voted for Gerald Ford. But the most serious questions arose in 1968, when it was feared that George Wallace's candidacy might deny either major-party candidate an electoral majority. (Wallace won forty-six electoral votes.) This would have thrown the election into the House of Representatives, where some speculated that the candidates might have bargained with state delegations in return for their support. There was some fear that Wallace would ask his electors to vote for Richard Nixon in return for concessions. Obviously, the results made all this speculation irrelevant, but dissatisfaction with the whole electoral college was enhanced. Again, in 1980 John Anderson's bid for the presidency raised the possibility that the House would have to select the president. Wild speculation abounded. The House becomes deadlocked; the vice-president serves as president. The Senate refuses to act until the House selects a president; the Speaker of the House serves as acting president. While none of this happened, as in 1968, dissatisfaction with the electoral college increased.

From time to time various reforms for the electoral college have been advanced. The reforms may be summarized as follows:

1. *The automatic plan*   This would make the smallest change. It would retain the electoral college concept and the winner-take-all philosophy and merely abolish the selection of electors and their need to vote. Electoral votes would be automatically assigned to the winning presidential candidate on the basis of the popular vote in the state. This arrangement would eliminate elector defections and the possibility of electoral bargaining as suggested in 1968.

2. *The district plan*   The electoral college would be retained, but votes would be awarded on the basis of a plurality of popular votes in each congressional district. Each of the House districts in the state would have one electoral vote, to be awarded to the presidential candidate with a plurality of popular votes in that district. The remaining two electoral votes (for the two senators) would go to the statewide popular-vote winner. This plan would keep the electoral structure intact, but would more closely reflect popular-vote trends throughout the country. It would also increase the likelihood of a third-party candidate winning some electoral votes, and therefore the possibility that the contest would be thrown into the House. Some district proposals would alter this feature and have a joint session of Congress, voting as individuals, select the president if no electoral majority was achieved.

3. *The proportional plan*   This plan would make the greatest alteration in the electoral college. It would award electoral votes from a state in direct proportion to the percentage of the popular-vote total. So if the two candidates split 52 to 48 percent in the popular vote, one candidate would be awarded 52 percent of the state's electoral votes (with the number of electoral votes determined as now), and the other candidate would get 48 percent. This plan would alter the present arrangement, by which

Practicing Politics: How to Register to Vote

1. In order to vote in any local, state, or national election, you must be registered—that is, you must be entered on the election rolls of your district or area.

2. Registration regulations differ from state to state according to state law, so you will need to write or call your local Board of Elections or your county or town clerk. You can also seek information from the League of Women Voters of the United States, 1730 M Street NW, Washington, D.C. 20036.

3. In some states you must register in person; others allow mail registration. Generally, for first registration, you need proof of age and residence.

4. When you register you may enroll in a party simply by signing and declaring yourself a member. You may also declare yourself independent, but remember that in some states only party enrollment allows you to vote in primary elections.

5. In many states you are permanently registered as long as you vote with a certain frequency (every two years, for example), but check the rules in your state.

6. Usually, residence in a state for thirty to fifty days is sufficient for voting purposes. It is possible to vote in an election in one state and then vote in another election in a different state in the same year, but you will still need to register in both places.

the candidate who wins 52 percent of the popular vote receives all the electoral votes. The plan greatly increases the possibility of a fair split and the opportunity for a third-party candidate to throw the election into the House of Representatives.

4. *Direct election* The final plan would abolish the electoral college altogether and let the people elect the president and vice-president through direct popular election. President Carter advocated such a proposal and suggested that Congress initiate a constitutional amendment to that effect. Such proposals have been heard before. In 1969 the House initiated a constitutional amendment calling for the direct election of the president. The plan required the winning candidate to receive at least 40 percent of the popular vote; if no candidate received the requisite minimum, a runoff election would be held between the top two vote getters. The Senate refused to concur, and the proposal died. Opposition to the direct election centers around two arguments: the federal basis of elections, which keeps states with large numbers of electoral votes more influential, and the opportunity for increased fraud and abuse. Voters may be misled or influenced by media campaigns that create a bandwagon effect across the nation.

Summary

1. Elections are the basic means by which the collective judgment of the people is expressed in a democracy. For several decades such judgments were stable and predictable. This has been interpreted to mean satisfaction with the political system. Changes today in voting behavior raise the possibility of realignment into a Republican majority.

2. We are being forced to redefine political behavior. There is considerable change in the motivation behind voting for candidates. Where party identification once dominated, issues and candidate personality are cited as increasingly important in elections. Issues combine with ticket splitting to reduce partisanship as voters respond more to candidates and personal campaigns than to political parties.

3. Recent voting patterns do not speak strongly for the collective judgment of the people. Landslide elections are increasingly common, incumbents win reelection with striking success, and electoral competition is weak. These trends conflict with the rational voter trends in which voters exercise independent judgments based on issues and personality assessments.

4. Campaigning for the presidency has become nationalized and heavily dependent on the new technologies such as the media, polling, and fund raising. These have placed the presidential candidates directly before the people. The presidential race is divorced from congressional elections and political parties.

5. Campaign costs have risen rapidly in the past two decades. The high cost of campaigning has degraded the electoral process. Reforms in campaign finance have sought to control campaign abuses. The public financing of the 1976 presidential election did succeed in reducing the cost of the presidential campaign.

6. The electoral system has some built-in biases. Many of these preferences have been neutralized by practices such as reapportionment and election-day registration. One major remaining issue of electoral bias still unresolved is the electoral college.

Research Projects

1. *Voter turnout*   What is the voter turnout in your state and city? What are the legal requirements for voting—registration, residency, and balloting? Compare your state and town with others. *The Book of the States* will provide you with legal requirements and restrictions. The *Statistical Abstract* gives turnout by states. Also helpful are the volumes *America Votes* and the *Almanac of Politics,* both of which cover elections by states. You may have to contact your city auditor to determine turnout of eligible voters for your city.

2. *Popular and electoral vote*   As you know, presidential elections are determined by the electoral vote, not the popular vote. How do the popular vote and electoral vote differ? Choose a presidential election, recent or past—possibly compare 1984 with 1960 or 1968—and examine how the electoral-vote percentage differed from the popular-vote totals. How would a regional or congressional district apportionment of electoral votes alter the results? To find the district vote totals, consult *Guide to U.S. Elections, America Votes,* or the *Almanac of Politics* for the appropriate years.

3. *Money and elections*   All federal candidates are required to file periodic and quarterly financial statements as well as a final summary with the Federal Election Commission. These reports are jointly filed with the secretary of state in the state. They are public records, and for a minimal fee you can obtain copies of them. Select a candidate for the House of Representatives or the Senate from your state and examine the financing of the campaign. How much money came in as contributions? What is the source of those contributions? How much money is being spent? in what areas?

4. *Voting and issues*   Numerous commentators on electoral politics have observed the emerging importance of issues in voting behavior. Write an essay describing the change in voting behavior over the past twenty years. How has the importance of party identification, group identification, candidate personality, and issues in campaign and voting changed? Several excellent works cited in the bibliography will be useful in writing this essay.

Notes

1. Norman Nie, Sidney Verba, and John R. Petrocik, *The Changing American Voter* (Cambridge, Mass.: Harvard University Press, 1979), pp. 1–2.
2. Richard Boyd, "Electoral Trends in Postwar Politics," in James David Barber, ed., *Choosing the President* (Englewood Cliffs, N.J.: Prentice-Hall, 1974), p. 183.
3. See Phillip Converse, "Change in the American Electorate," in Angus Campbell and Phillip Converse, eds.,*The Human Meaning of Social Change* (New York: Russell Sage, 1972).
4. Angus Campbell, Phillip Converse, Warren Miller, and Donald Stokes, *The American Voter* (New York: Wiley, 1960), Chap. 4.
5. Nie, Verba, and Petrocik, *The Changing American Voter,* p. 280.
6. Paul F. Lazarsfeld, Bernard Berelson, and Hazel Gaudet, *The People's Choice* (New York: Columbia University Press, 1944), p. 27.
7. Everett Carll Ladd, "Liberalism Upside Down," *Political Science Quarterly* 91, 4 (Winter 1976–1977).
8. William H. Flanigan and Nancy H. Zingale, *Political Behavior of the American Electorate*, 5th ed. (Boston: Allyn and Bacon, 1983), p. 83.
9. Gary R. Orren, "The Nomination Process: Vicissitudes of Candidate Selection," in Michael Nelson, ed., *The Election of 1984* (Washington, D.C.: Congressional Quarterly Press, 1985), p. 68.
10. Scott Keeter, "Public Opinion in 1984," in Gerald Pomper, ed., *The Election of 1984* (Chatham, N.J.: Chatham House, 1985), p. 107.
11. Ibid., p. 101.
12. Ibid., pp. 102–103.
13. Campbell, Converse, Miller, and Stokes, *The American Voter,* p. 273.
14. Norman Nie with Kristi Anderson, "Mass Beliefs Systems Revisited: Political Change and Attitude Structure," *Journal of Politics* 36, 3 (August 1974): 571.
15. Arthur H. Miller, Warren Miller, Alden Raine, and Thad Brown, "A Majority Party in Disarray: Policy Polarization in the 1972 Elections," *American Political Science Review* 70, 3 (September 1976): 778.
16. Gerald Pomper and colleagues, *The Election of 1976* (Chatham, N.J.: Chatham House, 1981), p. 74.
17. Gerald Pomper, *The Election of 1984* (Chatham, N.J.: Chatham House, 1985), p. 81.
18. Ibid.
19. Ibid., p. 82.
20. Walter DeVries and V. Lance Tarrance, *The Ticket Splitter: A New Force in American Politics* (Grand Rapids, Mich.: William B. Eerdmans, 1972), p. 115.
21. Nie, Verba, and Petrocik, *The Changing American Voter,* pp. 267–269.
22. Ibid., p. 267.
23. Walter Dean Burnham, "American Politics in the 1970s: Beyond Party?" in Louis Maisel and Paul M. Sacks, eds., *The Future of Political Parties*, Sage Electoral Studies Yearbook, vol. 1 (Beverly Hills: Sage Publications, 1975), p. 238.
24. Boyd, "Electoral Trends in Postwar Politics," pp. 190–195.
25. Gerald Pomper, "From Confusion to Clarity: Issues and American Voters, 1956–1968," *American Political Science Review* 66 (June 1972): 415–428.
26. Ibid., pp. 418–419.
27. DeVries and Tarrance, *The Ticket Splitter,* p. 51.
28. Ibid., p. 115.
29. Angus Campbell, "Surge and Decline: A Study of Electoral Change," in Angus Campbell, ed., *Elections and the Political Order* (New York: Wiley, 1966).
30. Gerald Kramer, "Short Term Fluctuations in U.S. Voting Behavior, 1956–1964," *American Political Science Review* 65 (March 1971): 140–141.
31. Samuel Kernell, "Presidential Popularity and Negative Voting," *American Political Science Review* 71 (March 1977): 44–66.
32. Edward R. Tufte, "Determinants of the Outcomes of Midterm Congressional Elections," *American Political Science Review* 69 (September 1975): 825.
33. James E. Campbell, "Explaining Presidential Losses in Midterm Congressional Elections," *Journal of Politics* 47 (November 1985).
34. Ibid., p. 1154.
35. Ibid., p. 1155.
36. Ibid.
36a. *Tashjian* v. *Republican Party of Connecticut,* ____ U.S. ____ (1986).
37. Orren, "The Nomination Process," p. 52.
38. Ibid.
39. Doris Graber, *Mass Media and American Politics* (Washington, D.C.: Congressional Quarterly Press, 1980), p. 161.
40. Joe McGinniss, *The Selling of the President—1968* (New York: Trident Press, 1969).
41. *National Journal* (November 4, 1978): 1772.
42. Ibid., p. 1776.
43. Herbert E. Alexander, *Financing Politics: Money, Elections and Political Reform*, 3rd edition (Washington, D.C.: Congressional Quarterly Press, 1984), p. 75.
44. Ibid.
45. David Adamany, "The Source of Money: An Overview," *Annals of the American Academy of Political and Social Science* 425 (May 1976): 22.
46. Ibid., p. 70.
47. *Buckley* v. *Valeo,* 424 U.S. 1 (1976).
48. *Oregon* v. *Mitchell,* 400 U.S. 112 (1970).
49. *Colegrove* v. *Green,* 328 U.S. 549 (1949).
50. *Baker* v. *Carr,* 369 U.S. 186 (1962).
51. *Wesberry* v. *Sanders,* 376 U.S. 1 (1964).
52. *Reynolds* v. *Sims,* 377 U.S. 533 (1964).
53. *Kirkpatrick* v. *Preisler,* 394 U.S. 526 (1969).
54. *White* v. *Weiser,* 412 U.S. 783 (1973).
55. *Karcher* v. *Daggett,* ____ U.S. ____ (1983).
56. *Mahon* v. *Howell,* 410 U.S. 315 (1973); *White* v. *Register,* 412 U.S. 755 (1973).
57. *Chapman* v. *Meier,* 420 U.S. 1 (1975).
58. *Davis* v. *Bandemer,* ____ U.S. ____ (1986).
59. *Dunn* v. *Blumstein,* 405 U.S. 330 (1972).
60. *Murston* v. *Mandt,* 410 U.S. 679 (1973); *Burns* v. *Forston,* 410 U.S. 686 (1973).

Bibliography

Agranoff, Robert. *The New Style Election Campaigns.* Boston: Holbrook Press, 1976.
A collection of essays written on campaigns, many by people active in electoral campaigns. Covered are such topics as campaign management, technology use, media, and ethics and reform.

Alexander, Herbert E. *Financing Politics: Money, Elections and Political Reform.* Washington, D.C.: Congressional Quarterly, 1983.
The best and most complete resource on campaign finance, sources and expenditure of funds, and the impact of campaign reform laws. The book contains up-to-date data on money and its impact on electoral politics.

Asher, Herbert. *Presidential Elections and American Politics.* Homewood, Ill.: Dorsey Press, 1984.
A text on electoral behavior with excellent coverage of party identification, issues, and the role of the campaign. While the analysis is sophisticated, the book contains much useful and understandable information.

Campbell, Angus, Converse, Phillip, Miller, Warren, and Stokes, Donald. *The American Voter.* New York: Wiley, 1960.
The classic work on voting behavior. Attempts to explain the causes of voting behavior based upon an extensive survey of American voters. Party identification is found to be the most powerful cause for voting.

DeVries, Walter, and Tarrance, V. Lance. *The Ticket Splitter: A New Force in American Politics.* Grand Rapids, Mich.: William B. Eerdmans, 1972.
The basic work on an increasingly common phenomenon. The authors dwell less on self-identification than on electoral activity to explain electoral behavior. There is good discussion of changing campaign strategies and ticket splitting.

Flanigan, William H., and Zingale, Nancy H. *Political Behavior of the American Electorate.* Boston: Allyn and Bacon, 1983.
A nice, readable survey of political behavior. The authors examine electoral patterns over several national elections. They include chapters on political socialization, public opinion, campaigns, and voting behavior.

Hill, David, and Luttbeg, Norman. *Trends in American Electoral Behavior.* Itasca, Ill.: Peacock, 1983.
A very readable summary of electoral trends, including the decline of partisanship and of trust in the system.

The book makes use of current data but is not technical or difficult to understand. The first chapter summarizes very well the contemporary debate on stability or change in the American electorate.

Miller, Warren, and Levitin, Teresa. *Leadership and Change: Presidential Elections from 1952 to 1976.* Cambridge, Mass.: Winthrop, 1976.
A review of voting behavior from the 1950s to the 1970s. The book explains in great detail the impact of "new politics" of the 1960s on electoral behavior. The authors conclude that the impact of these new groups on the electorate has yet to be fully felt.

Nie, Norman, Verba, Sidney, and Petrocik, John R. *The Changing American Voter.* Cambridge, Mass.: Harvard University Press, 1979.
The new classic on voting behavior. The book reviews the change in voting behavior during the 1960s and 1970s. It finds that party identification has declined as an explanation and that issues have emerged as increasingly important.

Polsby, Nelson, and Wildavsky, Aaron. *Presidential Elections.* New York: Charles Scribner's Sons, 1984.
A basic and first-rate treatment of presidential elections, fully covering the process from securing the nomination to conducting the campaign. Not much on voting behavior.

Pomper, Gerald. *Voter's Choice: Varieties of American Electoral Behavior.* New York: Harper & Row, 1975.
A sophisticated study of voting behavior. Pomper looks at the changing motivation of the American voter and concludes that voters have become more concerned with issues than was previously the case.

Pomper, Gerald, and Lederman, Susan. *Elections in America,* 2nd edition. New York: Dodd, Mead, 1980.
A very good history of elections in America, covering such basic topics as the role of elections in a democracy and the right to vote. Gives a good overview of elections in America.

Rae, Douglas. *The Political Consequences of Electoral Laws.* New Haven, Conn.: Yale University Press, 1967.
One of the few books that look at the effects of election laws and the administration of elections. While sometimes complex, the book is a valuable resource for understanding how the conduct of elections shapes the electoral process.

The Presidency

Calling his administration "a new beginning," Ronald Reagan became the fortieth president of the United States. At the very moment the new president was speaking from the steps of the U.S. Capitol, fifty-two Americans held hostage in Iran were being released by their captors. Like his predecessor Jimmy Carter, who was weakened by the Iranian hostage crisis, Reagan made no call to greatness. Rather, he asked the citizenry to have patience and to make sacrifices in solving the problems confronting the nation. Inflation and unemployment shatter the lives of millions of Americans, Reagan said. Government cannot solve such problems; rather, "government is the problem." Thus the new president reminded Americans that the errors of the past two decades would not simply go away. However, Reagan remained firm in his optimism that answers were to be found. "I believe we the Americans of today are ready to act worthy of ourselves, ready to do what must be done to ensure happiness and liberty for ourselves, our children, and our children's children." The words of Ronald Reagan bear out the statement political scientist James Barber made regarding the presidency: "For better or for worse, the Presidency

Ronald Reagan takes the oath of office for his second term as the fortieth president of the United States.

Sun King Complex: *the term used by Louis Koenig to describe the American tendency to create for the president surroundings and resources fit for a king.*

remains the prime focus for our political sentiments and the prime source of guidance and inspiration for national politics. . . . If he is lucky and effective, he can call forth from the climate new energies, a new vision, a new way of working to suit a perennially new age."[1]

In the twentieth century, Americans came to see the presidency as the center—the source of public policy and a force for social change. Until 1964, Americans were confident that their president was the right person to lead the nation, that America was prospering, and that it was the president who possessed the knowledge and leadership to lead the nation toward greatness. But the abuses of presidential power in the following decade shook the confidence of the American people. Presidents Johnson and Nixon pushed presidential power to new limits. The public trust was abused and the office of the presidency was mired in illegality and cheap political retribution. Even popular Ronald Reagan, who used the Iranian hostage situation to defeat Jimmy Carter, became mired in his own Iranian scandal. Tales of secret arms to Iran, diversion of profits from those sales to aid Nicaraguan Contra rebels, and no one in the White House claiming knowledge or responsibility for the whole series of events, leave Americans wondering if presidential policies in the 1980s has improved substantially.

Presidential power had grown at the expense of traditional sources of authority: Congress, the bureaucracy, and public opinion. Since Franklin Roosevelt, the president has become our chief policymaker, "the hope of America."[2] The unique blending of foreign and domestic issues after the 1930s produced the unprecedented growth of presidential power. Arthur Schlesinger has observed that foreign policy put the president in command of the forces of war and peace, the decay of political parties left the president as the premier politician, and the efforts to regulate economic growth placed the president in charge of the economy. Hence, Schlesinger notes, "At this extraordinary historical moment, when foreign and domestic lines of force converged, much depended on whether the occupant of the White House was moved to ride the new tendencies of power or to resist them."[3]

We have created in the presidency what Louis Koenig labels a **Sun King complex.**[4] This is a monarchical tendency to create an office that serves the needs and desires of a single person. "Upon the President is lavished every facility to ease the travail of daily living and to assist his encounters with the 'great issues'."[5] We seek to provide for the president surroundings and resources fit for a king. And presidents bask in this sunlight of attention and power.

The Ascendancy of the Presidency

The excesses of presidential power brought many Americans to a profound distrust of executive authority and produced a sense of outrage against uncontrolled government power in general. Yet the presidency cannot be evaluated in the light of Vietnam and Watergate alone. As an institution, it has been growing in power almost since the Constitution was adopted.

Constitutional Dimensions

The framers of the Constitution were uncertain regarding the presidency. They would not have a monarchy, but the Articles of Confederation had proved the need for an executive. The problem confronting the framers was to establish an independent and viable executive capable of enforcing the laws and yet not so strong as to overpower the other branches of government.

The framers quickly settled on a single executive. Randolph had proposed a three-person executive council, but there was strong opposition. Elbridge Gerry felt that in military affairs a three-person executive would prove indecisive; James Wilson thought a plural executive would fail to provide "energy, dispatch, and responsibility to the office." The unity of a single executive would be the best safeguard against tyranny. The framers also rejected election by the legislature, although this proved more troublesome. Direct popular election by the people was unacceptable. The Virginia Plan provided that the president would be chosen by electors selected by Congress, thereby tying the election of the president to Congress and ensuring executive accountability. Some delegates proposed that Congress directly select the chief executive. Finally, the matter was turned over to a committee that proposed the system we currently have: election by electors equal to the number of senators and representatives and chosen by each state.

These two key convention decisions proved decisive to the establishment and growth of executive power. The decision not to have legislative elections gave the president a national constituency and endowed the chief executive with a status and role unrivaled by any other figure in government. The electoral college system has not prevented presidents from assuming the mantle of leadership or being the spokesmen for the nation. As E. S. Corwin noted, "The Constitution reflects the struggle between two conceptions of executive power: that it ought to be subordinate to the supreme legislative power, and that it ought to be, within general limits, autonomous and self-directing."[6]

The Constitution says little regarding executive authority. The power of the presidency is a rich blend of the written Constitution, custom, and person. Thomas Cronin's job description (Table 10.1) attempts to capture something of the complexity in the areas presidents must contend with as well as the types of activities they are called upon to perform. Presidents must move between areas and types of activity several times in one day— and do so with a clear mind and balanced judgment.

The powers and responsibilities of presidents have developed as they have interpreted and fashioned the apparatus of the executive to suit themselves and the needs of the nation. Yet we insist that this be a presi-

TABLE 10.1 The presidential job description

Types of activity	*The subpresidencies*		
	Foreign policy and national security (A)	*Aggregate economics* (B)	*Domestic policy and programs* (C)
Crisis management	Wartime leadership; missile crisis, 1962	Coping with recessions	Confronting coal strikes of 1978
Symbolic and morale-building leadership	Presidential state visit to Middle East or to China	Boosting confidence in the dollar	Visiting disaster victims and morale building among government workers
Priority setting and program design	Balancing pro-Israel policies with need for Arab oil	Choosing means of dealing with inflation, unemployment	Designing a new welfare program
Recruitment leadership (advisors, administrators, judges, ambassadors, etc.)	Selection of Secretary of Defense, U.N. Ambassador	Selection of Secretary of Treasury, Federal Reserve Board Governors	Nomination of federal judges
Legislative and political coalition building	Selling Panama or SALT treaties to Senate for approval	Lobbying for energy-legislation package	Winning public support for transportation deregulation
Program implementation and evaluation	Encouraging negotiations between Israel and Egypt	Implementing tax cuts or fuel rationing	Improving quality health care, welfare retraining programs
Oversight of government routines and establishment of an early-warning system for future problem areas	Overseeing U.S. bases abroad; ensuring that foreign-aid programs work effectively	Overseeing the IRS or the Small Business Administration	Overseeing National Science Foundation or Environmental Protection Agency

SOURCE: From Thomas E. Cronin, *The State of the Presidency*, 2nd ed., p. 155. Copyright © 1980 by Thomas E. Cronin. Reprinted by permission of Little, Brown, and Co.

dency within the Constitution, and constitutional provisions have helped to shape the presidency. These are the key provisions:

1. "The president shall be Commander in Chief of the Army and Navy of the United States. . . ." In foreign affairs, no phrase has aided the chief executive more. These words have become the basis for the president's war powers. This development would have astonished the framers, for they viewed the grant of authority as purely supervisory. But from Lincoln on, the role of commander in chief has grown. It was used by Roosevelt in World War II to set up executive agencies. Afterward, it justified rent and price controls when the veterans returned home. Several times presidents have moved, as commander in chief, to commit U.S. troops abroad to protect American lives and property. Eisenhower, for example, sent 14,000 troops into Lebanon in 1958 to forestall communist aggression; Gerald Ford committed U.S. Marines to free the merchant vessel *Mayaguez*, which had been captured in 1975 by the Cambodians; and

© *Chuck Ayers*, Akron Beacon Journal

Ronald Reagan sent U.S. Marines into Lebanon in 1982 as part of an international peace-keeping force for the Middle East. Reagan also used his power as commander in chief to send troops to Grenada in 1983 to protect U.S. medical students there as well as to prevent a communist regime from establishing itself and cementing friendly relations with Cuba. In 1986 Reagan again used this power to send warplanes into Libya to destroy terrorist camps and missile sites in retaliation for suspected Libyan acts of terrorism. Two undeclared wars, Korea and Vietnam, were results of presidents exercising their war powers as commander in chief. In both cases, Congress acknowledged the president's action as proper under his constitutional authority as commander in chief.

2. "He shall have Power, by and with the advice and consent of the Senate, to make treaties. . . ." In recent years, the treaty power, with the requirement of ratification by two-thirds of the Senate, has been supplanted by the use of **executive agreements** (see Table 10.2). Executive

Executive Agreements: *agreements made by the president that do not require Senate action but have the same legal standing as treaties.*

TABLE 10.2   Treaties and executive agreements, 1789 to 1980

Period	Treaties	Executive agreements	Totals
1789–1839	60	27	87
1839–1889	215	238	453
1889–1939	524	917	1,441
1940–1970	388	5,655	6,043
1971–1980	172	3,114	3,286
	1,359	9,951	11,310

SOURCE: *Guide to Congress*, 3rd ed. (Washington, D.C.: Congressional Quarterly Press, 1982), p. 291.

agreements do not require Senate action, but have the same legal standing as treaties. On different occasions Congress has moved, unsuccessfully, to limit the use of executive agreements. The Bricker Amendment in the 1950s would have eliminated the use of executive agreements as a substitute for treaties. In 1972 Congress passed the Case Act, which requires presidents to submit to Congress within sixty days any international agreement concluded with a foreign power. The act did not, however, limit such agreements.

3. "And he shall nominate, and by and with the advice and consent of the Senate, shall appoint Ambassadors, and other public ministers and consuls, judges of the Supreme Court, and all other officers of the United States . . ." The appointment power of the chief executive is a prerogative little challenged and interfered with. It is the president's primary means of establishing a functioning executive branch of government. The only limitation on the executive appointing power is Senate confirmation, and the great majority of presidential appointees are routinely accepted. One area of exception is judicial appointments, where senatorial courtesy functions. Senatorial courtesy gives senators a veto power over the appointment of judges in the senator's state. And in the case of Supreme Court appointments, judicial qualifications are scrutinized carefully.

The Courts have rejected any effort to restrict or interfere in the appointment power. In *Buckley* v. *Valeo* (1976), the Supreme Court rejected a provision for the Federal Election Commission that allowed congressional officers to appoint some members of the commission. Much earlier, in *Myers* v. *United States* (1926), the Court had rejected any connection between the advice-and-consent provisions for appointments and removal. The Court held that the Senate could not require presidents to consult the Senate on removing ministerial officers as part of the constitutional advice-and-consent function.

4. "He shall take care that the Laws be faithfully executed." Perhaps the broadest powers have been derived from this phrase. Not only does the phrase refer to the laws enacted by Congress, but as interpreted by the Supreme Court in *In re Neagle* (1890), it refers to "any obligation fairly and properly inferrible from [the Constitution], or any duty . . . to be derived from the general scope of . . . duties under the laws of the United States." This ruling was interpreted to mean not only enforcement of acts of Congress, but also enforcement of "rights, duties and obligations growing out of the Constitution itself, our international relations, and all the protection implied by the nature of the government under the Constitution."

Implied Powers: *the powers of the president that grow from the rights, duties, and obligations imposed on the president by the Constitution, the conduct of international relations, and the very nature of our government.*

Under the "implied-powers" authority, President Cleveland moved to end the long Pullman strike (1894) and President Truman seized the steel mills in 1952. The Supreme Court rejected Truman's act, ruling he had neither constitutional nor statutory authority for it. The president's **implied powers** once again came under question in the Pentagon Papers case of *New York Times* v. *United States* (1971). In that case the Court refused to grant the executive the authority to institute prior restraint on the press solely on the basis of inherent power in foreign affairs. It was willing to accept national security claims for confidentiality only if legislatively provided or if lack of confidentiality could be shown to cause "irreparable damage to our Nation or its people."

Presidential Immunity:
the protection of a president against any lawsuit for any official act performed while in office.

The president also enjoys absolute **immunity** from prosecution for any official act undertaken while in office. In *Nixon* v. *Fitzgerald* (1982), the Supreme Court said that a president is shielded from prosecution on acts within the "outer perimeter" of his official responsibilities.

The Growth of the Presidency

The Constitution alone does not explain the growth of the presidency; at best, it has accommodated change. The growth of the presidency must be accounted for by the changing nature of the union, the problems confronting the nation, and the nature of those occupying the office. Institution and individual have come together to magnify the powers of the modern presidency.

The institution of the presidency has greatly expanded over the years. When George Washington took office in 1789, there were four executive departments: state, war, treasury, and an attorney general. There were approximately 4 million Americans in the thirteen colonies to be governed. Today there are more than 4 million Americans on the executive payroll alone (2.9 million civilians and 2 million in the armed forces). The executive departments now number thirteen, with an additional host of boards, agencies, and commissions as well as an expanded Executive Office of the President. James Polk wrote in 1848, "I prefer to supervise the whole operations of the government myself." But by the twentieth century the president needed help. The Ninety-seventh Congress (1981–1982) alone passed 2,267 measures, which consumed, in the process, 52,679 pages in the *Congressional Record.* The president now oversees a federal budget that is almost a trillion dollars. Washington's first budget called for expending just over $84 million.

The growth of the institution of the presidency has occurred largely in direct response to issues. As the nation has grown and prospered, new, complex, and pressing issues have thrust the presidency into the forefront of leadership. War and foreign affairs most plainly have heightened the impact of the presidency. The realization, following World War II, that the globe had shrunk and that no country was immune to nuclear attack made it necessary for presidential power to grow. In foreign relations, the president is the central, dominant policymaker. In an age of computer-deployed multiple warheads (MIRVs) and guerrilla insurgencies, the chief executive has the prime responsibility for protecting the national security of the United States.

Social and economic problems have also broadened the scope and size of the presidency. Beginning with the New Deal, the presidency has become more and more involved in seeking solutions for social and economic problems. Congress has charged the president with maintaining

Over the years the presidency has come to include a wide variety of roles and responsibilities. *Clockwise from top:* Dwight D. Eisenhower, Theodore Roosevelt, Franklin D. Roosevelt, Jimmy Carter, and John F. Kennedy.

full employment. In 1970, Congress authorized the president to impose wage and price controls in order to stabilize the economy. Lyndon Johnson's Great Society sought massive social reordering of priorities through changed budgetary priorities. Presidential commissions now exist on civil rights and on the status of women. The executive branch has become a complex of agencies and advisors charged with fashioning alternatives for social and economic problems.

The mass media have also contributed to the expansion of presidential power. Owing both to their power to relay information instantaneously on foreign or domestic crises and to the potency of the presidency as the lone symbol of the nation's leadership, the media have focused on the presidency. Television and the newspapers cover the slightest move the president makes. Reporters travel with the president across the country and across the seas. To the American people, the president is news. This constant attention allows the president to help shape issues and moods. The less attention given to Congress, parties, and interest groups, the more the president can dominate the scene.

The third major factor contributing to the growth of the presidency has been personality. The powers of the presidency have been shaped and enlarged due to the nature of the men occupying the office. The particular stamp of individual personalities—how each has defined the task and confronted problems—has worked to enlarge the office.

Theodore Roosevelt at the turn of the century made the presidency a "bully pulpit," the object of attention for all within the political arena. His often-repeated view of executive authority, the **stewardship theory,** has become the standard for a strong executive. Roosevelt said:

Stewardship Presidency: *Theodore Roosevelt's view of executive authority, which became the standard for a strong executive. This theory affirmed the president's duty to do anything not illegal that the needs of the nation demanded.*

> My view was that every executive officer, and above all every executive officer in high position, was a steward of the people bound actively and affirmatively to do all he could for the people, and not to content himself with the negative merit of keeping his talents undamaged in a napkin. I declined to adopt the view that what was imperatively necessary for the nation could not be done by the President unless he could find some specific authorization to do it. *My belief was that it was not only his right but his duty to do anything that the needs of the nation demanded, unless such action was forbidden by the Constitution or by the laws.*[7]

Woodrow Wilson, a scholar and educator, dominated the second decade of the twentieth century. Wilson succeeded in getting Congress to pass the Clayton Antitrust Act and in creating the Federal Trade Commission and Federal Reserve System. In foreign affairs, Wilson was the architect of the League of Nations and a world figure. Said Wilson: "The President is at liberty, both in law and conscience, to be as big a man as he can." For greatness and the imaginative use of power, however, Franklin D. Roosevelt stands alone. Elected at the depth of the Depression, Roosevelt has become the yardstick for measuring presidential power.[8] His New Deal was a bold design for putting America back on its feet again. When Roosevelt faced opposition for his New Deal program, he took his appeal to the American people. His famous fireside chats rallied public support for his programs. Franklin Roosevelt is also responsible for helping "personalize" the presidency. During the war, Roosevelt kept morale high with his radio broadcasts. FDR was a skilled and astute politician who knew how to use the techniques of leadership and persuasion. John Kennedy also worked to personalize the presidency, and Lyndon Johnson sought to capture the spirit of the New Deal with his concept of the Great Society. Both saw the office as the seat of leadership and initiative.

Presidential Roles

Forces in the twentieth century have created for the president several roles that have given the chief executive "an awesome burden." And while these various roles and responsibilities cannot be neatly divided, since presidential activity is what Clinton Rossiter called a "seamless web," it is nonetheless useful to separate out the many and varied roles a president is asked to carry out.

Political and Popular Roles

A president comes to Washington a winner. The successful candidate has achieved an electoral victory, having received the votes of millions of Americans. This is taken by the incoming president as a mark of confidence from the people, the expression of a political mandate to govern the nation, and what Richard Pious called the "popular connection." "The President emphasizes a mandate based on an undifferentiated majority— no matter how narrow the victory." (Note in Table 10.3 the number of

TABLE 10.3   Presidents who governed without popular majorities

Years	President	Percentage of vote
1825–1829	Adams	30.5
1841–1845	Tyler	None
1845–1849	Polk	49.6
1849–1850	Taylor	47.3
1850–1853	Fillmore	None
1857–1861	Buchanan	45.3
1861–1865	Lincoln	39.8
1865–1869	Johnson	None
1877–1881	Hayes	48.0
1881	Garfield	48.3
1881–1885	Arthur	None
1885–1889	Cleveland	48.5
1889–1893	Harrison	47.9
1893–1897	Cleveland	46
1901–1905	Roosevelt	None
1913–1917	Wilson	41.8
1917–1921	Wilson	49.3
1923–1925	Coolidge	None
1945–1949	Truman	None
1949–1953	Truman	49.5
1961–1963	Kennedy	49.7
1963–1965	Johnson	None
1969–1973	Nixon	43.4
1974–1977	Ford	None

Fact File
Presidents and Vice-Presidents of the United States

President and political party	Born	Died	Age at inauguration	Native of	Elected from	Term of service	Vice-President
George Washington (F)	1732	1799	57	Va.	Va.	April 30, 1789–March 4, 1793	John Adams
George Washington (F)			61			March 4, 1793–March 4, 1797	John Adams
John Adams (F)	1735	1826	61	Mass.	Mass.	March 4, 1797–March 4, 1801	Thomas Jefferson
Thomas Jefferson (D-R)	1743	1826	57	Va.	Va.	March 4, 1801–March 4, 1805	Aaron Burr
Thomas Jefferson (D-R)			61			March 4, 1805–March 4, 1809	George Clinton
James Madison (D-R)	1751	1836	57	Va.	Va.	March 4, 1809–March 4, 1813	George Clinton
James Madison (D-R)			61			March 4, 1813–March 4, 1817	Elbridge Gerry
James Monroe (D-R)	1758	1831	58	Va.	Va.	March 4, 1817–March 4, 1821	Daniel D. Tompkins
James Monroe (D-R)			62			March 4, 1821–March 4, 1825	Daniel D. Tompkins
John Q. Adams (N-R)	1767	1848	57	Mass.	Mass.	March 4, 1825–March 4, 1829	John C. Calhoun
Andrew Jackson (D)	1767	1845	61	S.C.	Tenn.	March 4, 1829–March 4, 1833	John C. Calhoun
Andrew Jackson (D)			65			March 4, 1833–March 4, 1837	Martin Van Buren
Martin Van Buren (D)	1782	1862	54	N.Y.	N.Y.	March 4, 1837–March 4, 1841	Richard M. Johnson
W. H. Harrison (W)	1773	1841	68	Va.	Ohio	March 4, 1841–April 4, 1841	John Tyler
John Tyler (W)	1790	1862	51	Va.	Va.	April 6, 1841–March 4, 1845	
James K. Polk (D)	1795	1849	49	N.C.	Tenn.	March 4, 1845–March 4, 1849	George M. Dallas
Zachary Taylor (W)	1784	1850	64	Va.	La.	March 4, 1849–July 9, 1850	Millard Fillmore
Millard Fillmore (W)	1800	1874	50	N.Y.	N.Y.	July 10, 1850–March 4, 1853	
Franklin Pierce (D)	1804	1869	48	N.H.	N.H.	March 4, 1853–March 4, 1857	William R. King
James Buchanan (D)	1791	1868	65	Pa.	Pa.	March 4, 1857–March 4, 1861	John C. Breckinridge
Abraham Lincoln (R)	1809	1865	52	Ky.	Ill.	March 4, 1861–March 4, 1865	Hannibal Hamlin
Abraham Lincoln (R)			56			March 4, 1865–April 15, 1865	Andrew Johnson
Andrew Johnson (R)	1808	1875	56	N.C.	Tenn.	April 15, 1865–March 4, 1869	
Ulysses S. Grant (R)	1822	1885	46	Ohio	Ill.	March 4, 1869–March 4, 1873	Schuyler Colfax
Ulysses S. Grant (R)			50			March 4, 1873–March 4, 1877	Henry Wilson
Rutherford B. Hayes (R)	1822	1893	54	Ohio	Ohio	March 4, 1877–March 4, 1881	William A. Wheeler
James A. Garfield (R)	1831	1881	49	Ohio	Ohio	March 4, 1881–Sept. 19, 1881	Chester A. Arthur
Chester A. Arthur (R)	1830	1886	50	Vt.	N.Y.	Sept. 20, 1881–March 4, 1885	
Grover Cleveland (D)	1837	1908	47	N.J.	N.Y.	March 4, 1885–March 4, 1889	Thomas A. Hendricks
Benjamin Harrison (R)	1833	1901	55	Ohio	Ind.	March 4, 1889–March 4, 1893	Levi P. Morton

President and political party	Born	Died	Age at inauguration	Native of	Elected from	Term of service	Vice-President
Grover Cleveland (D)	1837	1908	55			March 4, 1893–March 4, 1897	Adlai E. Stevenson
William McKinley (R)	1843	1901	54	Ohio	Ohio	March 4, 1897–March 4, 1901	Garrett A. Hobart
William McKinley (R)			58			March 4, 1901–Sept. 14, 1901	Theodore Roosevelt
Theodore Roosevelt (R)	1858	1919	42	N.Y.	N.Y.	Sept. 14, 1901–March 4, 1905	
Theodore Roosevelt (R)			46			March 4, 1905–March 4, 1909	Charles W. Fairbanks
William H. Taft (R)	1857	1930	51	Ohio	Ohio	March 4, 1909–March 4, 1913	James S. Sherman
Woodrow Wilson (D)	1856	1924	56	Va.	N.J.	March 4, 1913–March 4, 1917	Thomas R. Marshall
Woodrow Wilson (D)			60			March 4, 1917–March 4, 1921	Thomas R. Marshall
Warren G. Harding (R)	1865	1923	55	Ohio	Ohio	March 4, 1921–Aug. 2, 1923	Calvin Coolidge
Calvin Coolidge (R)	1872	1933	51	Vt.	Mass.	Aug. 3, 1923–March 4, 1925	
Calvin Coolidge (R)			52			March 4, 1925–March 4, 1929	Charles G. Dawes
Herbert Hoover (R)	1874	1964	54	Iowa	Calif.	March 4, 1929–March 4, 1933	Charles Curtis
Franklin D. Roosevelt (D)	1882	1945	51	N.Y.	N.Y.	March 4, 1933–Jan. 20, 1937	John N. Garner
Franklin D. Roosevelt (D)			55			Jan. 20, 1937–Jan. 20, 1941	John N. Garner
Franklin D. Roosevelt (D)			59			Jan. 20, 1941–Jan. 20, 1945	Henry A. Wallace
Franklin D. Roosevelt (D)			63			Jan. 20, 1945–April 12, 1945	Harry S. Truman
Harry S. Truman (D)	1884	1972	60	Mo.	Mo.	April 12, 1945–Jan. 20, 1949	
Harry S. Truman (D)			64			Jan. 20, 1949–Jan. 20, 1953	Alben W. Barkley
Dwight D. Eisenhower (R)	1890	1969	62	Texas	N.Y.	Jan. 20, 1953–Jan. 20, 1957	Richard M. Nixon
Dwight D. Eisenhower (R)			66		Pa.	Jan. 20, 1957–Jan. 20, 1961	Richard M. Nixon
John F. Kennedy (D)	1917	1963	43	Mass.	Mass.	Jan. 20, 1961–Nov. 22, 1963	Lyndon B. Johnson
Lyndon B. Johnson (D)	1908	1973	55	Texas	Texas	Nov. 22, 1963–Jan. 20, 1965	
Lyndon B. Johnson (D)			56			Jan. 20, 1965–Jan. 20, 1969	Hubert H. Humphrey
Richard M. Nixon (R)	1913		56	Calif.	N.Y.	Jan. 20, 1969–Jan. 20, 1973	Spiro T. Agnew
Richard M. Nixon (R)			60		Calif.	Jan. 20, 1973–Aug. 9, 1974	Spiro T. Agnew 10-11-73 Gerald R. Ford 11-27-73
Gerald R. Ford (R)	1913		61	Neb.	Mich.	Aug. 9, 1974–Jan. 20, 1976	Nelson A. Rockefeller
James E. Carter (D)	1924		52	Ga.	Ga.	Jan. 20, 1976–Jan. 20, 1981	Walter F. Mondale
Ronald W. Reagan (R)	1911		69	Ill.	Calif.	Jan. 20, 1981–Jan. 20, 1985	George Bush
Ronald W. Reagan (R)			73			Jan. 20, 1985–	George Bush

Key to abbreviations: (D) Democrat, (D-R) Democrat-Republican, (F) Federalist, (N-R) National Republican, (R) Republican, (W) Whig.

SOURCE: Joseph Nathan Kane, *Facts About the President*, 3rd ed. (New York: H. W. Wilson Co., 1974).

TABLE 10.4   Rating the U.S. presidents

The five best	The five worst
Lincoln	Fillmore
Washington	Buchanan
Franklin D. Roosevelt	Pierce
Jefferson	Grant
Theodore Roosevelt	Harding

SOURCE: Arthur Schlesinger, Sr., "Our Presidents: A Rating by 75 Historians," *New York Times Magazine*, July 29, 1967, p. 12; Gary Maranell and Richard Dodder, "Political Orientation and Evaluation of Presidential Prestige: A Study of American Historians," *Social Science Quarterly* 51 (September 1970): 418; and U.S. Historical Society Survey 1977, reprinted in Thomas Cronin, *The State of the Presidency*, 2nd ed. (Boston: Little, Brown, 1980), pp. 387–388.

presidents who have governed without popular majorities.) "The 'voice of the people' may not have offered a mandate on issues in a clearcut campaign, but that does not prevent presidents from claiming to act in the name of the people."[9]

The popular role makes the president an instant superstar, who commands media attention and is looked to by the public for leadership. Whatever the president does is of concern to all Americans.

The presidential role of leader is most easily seen as *chief of state*. Here the president combines political leadership with the symbolic, and largely ceremonial, role of head of state. Unlike many countries, where political responsibilities are entrusted to a prime minister and the ceremonial tasks are handled by a monarch or a president, we expect our president to fulfill both functions, drawing no clear distinction between ceremonial and political power. It is precisely because the people view the president as head of state that they expect leadership and initiative. Table 10.4 lists a consensus of the best and worst presidents in U.S. history.

Presidents are the elected nominees of a political party, and are thus expected to play the role of *chief of their party*. As a politician, the president immediately has the advantage, or the disadvantage, of a partisan majority in Congress. Much of a president's legislative success depends on partisan ties. With the decline of the coattail effect, presidential campaigning for congressional candidates is less important than it once was. Nonetheless, congressional elections are frequently viewed as an expression of support for presidents and their policies. The decline of parties, however, has blurred the distinction between partisan and statesman.

Domestic Policy Roles

In part because of the popular role of leadership and partisan campaigning and in part because of the tide of rising expectations for domestic policy from the New Deal and Great Society, the president is the initiator of much domestic policy. The president sends up to Congress between one hundred and four hundred bills annually on domestic issues. Today, much of the initiative for domestic policy comes from the White House.

Practicing Politics:
What Happens When You Write to the President

Every piece of mail that comes into the White House is answered—not by the president himself, of course, for no one could read, much less answer, 40,000 to 70,000 letters a week. But every piece of mail is opened, sorted, and analyzed. Then, depending on the content, it is sent to the White House staff, the appropriate government agency, or the director of correspondence for a reply. Letters expressing general support or giving views and suggestions receive a reply from the director of correspondence. Those containing questions and problems are referred to the appropriate agency or department, and there is an internal followup system to make sure that someone having difficulty with, for example, social security checks receives a reply from the Social Security Administration.

Every week information gleaned from the letters is presented to the president and the senior White House staff in a statistical and narrative report summarizing the tone and content of the mail that week. The report is accompanied by a random sample of incoming letters to which the president replies personally. So your letter to the president is not just received and filed: you receive an answer, and what you have to say becomes part of the stream of information that keeps the president and the White House staff informed about what people want and what they are thinking.

Congratulations and many happy returns of the day. May you have a joyous celebration and all the best in the year to come. Our best wishes are with you for a very Happy Birthday. God bless you.

Nancy Reagan   Ronald Reagan

Presidents usually enter the White House with a bold design for new directions for America. They then seek to make good on their promises by submitting a legislative program to Congress. The congressional honeymoon generally lasts less than a year. The initially receptive legislature finds that separation of powers gives it ample opportunity to thwart the president's ability to be *chief legislator.* Says Louis Koenig: "Nowhere else in the Presidential enterprise is there found a greater gap between what the Chief Executive wants to do, what he promises to the electorate in his contest for the office, and what he can do in bringing Congress to enact the laws that alone can give effect to the party program of the previous campaign."[10]

Twentieth-century presidents have taken the lead in proposing legislation. The annual State of the Union message is an ideal way for a president to unveil his legislative program. But a president's ability to move Congress into action requires more than a program and the support of public opinion. Successful presidents find it necessary constantly to monitor proposals and consult with legislators (Figure 10.1). Ronald Reagan has proven adept in lobbying Congress for his proposals. In 1981 Reagan pushed through his economic proposal largely on the strength of his own personal efforts. He succeeded in getting cuts for social welfare programs, effecting a tax cut for individuals and businesses, and increasing defense appropriations. As with all presidents, however, Reagan's success with Congress has declined with his years in office.

In the role as legislative leader, a president soon discovers that in this area Congress is endowed with many powers: control of the purse strings, and of legislative calendars, filibusters, and so on, gives Congress

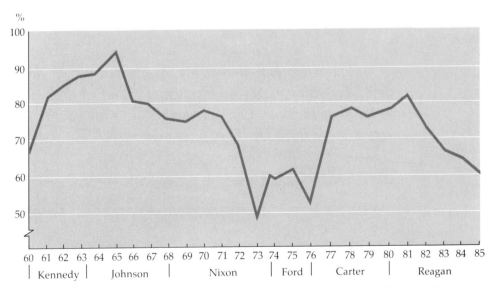

Figure 10.1 Presidential success on measures on which presidents took a position from 1960 to 1985

ample opportunity to deny presidents the laws they want.[11] In recent years, Republican chief executives have had to face Democratic majorities in Congress. But the president is not without legislative resources. The most obvious is the **veto**. The threat of a veto acts as a strong deterrent to the passage of legislation of which the president disapproves. It can also be used to effect compromise. The threat of a veto will often soften Congress and produce a law that has broad support.

After a bill is passed by Congress, the president has ten working days to sign or veto the bill; otherwise it becomes law without the presidential signature. The only exception is the **pocket veto**: if Congress adjourns before the ten-day period, the lack of presidential action effectively kills the bill. In the 1970s President Nixon sought to define the pocket veto to include recess as well as adjournment. The Constitution is not clear on this point, but court rulings restricted the pocket veto to formal adjournment of Congress, not a recess. In 1986 the Supreme Court agreed to hear a case designed to clarify the pocket veto. A court of appeals has ruled

Veto: *executive refusal to sign legislation approved by Congress, which effectively kills the bill.*

Pocket Veto: *a veto occurring when Congress adjourns within ten days after sending to the president a bill upon which he takes no action.*

TABLE 10.5   Presidential vetoes, 1789 to 1984

	Regular vetoes	Pocket vetoes	Total vetoes	Vetoes overridden
Washington	2	—	2	—
Madison	5	2	7	—
Monroe	1	—	1	—
Jackson	5	7	12	—
Tyler	6	3	9	1
Polk	2	1	3	—
Pierce	9	—	9	5
Buchanan	4	3	7	—
Lincoln	2	4	6	—
A. Johnson	21	8	29	15
Grant	45	49	94	4
Hayes	12	1	13	1
Arthur	4	8	12	1
Cleveland	304	109	413	2
Harrison	19	25	44	1
Cleveland	43	127	170	5
McKinley	6	36	42	—
T. Roosevelt	42	40	82	1
Taft	30	9	39	1
Wilson	33	11	44	6
Harding	5	1	6	—
Coolidge	20	30	50	4
Hoover	21	16	37	3
F. Roosevelt	372	261	633	9
Truman	180	70	250	12
Eisenhower	73	108	181	2
Kennedy	12	9	21	—
L. Johnson	16	14	30	—
Nixon	24	19	43	5
Ford	44	22	66	12
Carter	15	16	31	2
Reagan	31	8	39	4

SOURCE: *Statistical Abstract*, 1979; 1980–1984 data from *Congressional Quarterly, Weekly Report* (November 17, 1984): 2957.

that a president's holding of a bill for more than ten days is not a valid pocket veto even if Congress goes into intersession adjournment before the ten days expires. The appeals court also held that members of Congress have standing to bring suit to challenge the alleged unconstitutionality of the pocket veto.[12] Congress can override a veto by a two-thirds vote of both chambers. But as Table 10.5 illustrates, Congresses have had little success in overriding presidential vetoes.

Impoundment: *executive refusal to spend funds appropriated by Congress.*

Another power a president has in the legislative role is **impoundment,** a refusal to spend appropriated funds. Presidents have occasionally used impoundment as an **item veto.** Since presidents must veto entire legislative acts and cannot veto particular items or portions of laws, they have taken to impounding funds to reject those facets of the legislation they dislike. President Buchanan refused to spend appropriated money for post offices and other public buildings in 1857. Harry S. Truman impounded Air Force funds in 1949 as a means of an item veto, and Richard Nixon in 1972 and 1973 postponed several environmental and housing programs by impounding the appropriated money.[13] In the 1970s, Richard Nixon began a much broader use of impoundment. In fact, he used impoundment to change social policy when he proposed to abolish the Office of Economic Opportunity by refusing to spend the money appropriated for it. Although the Constitution does not require presidents to spend money, federal court decisions on impoundment have taken a narrow view and limited a president's authority to refuse to spend appropriated funds. In 1974 Congress passed the Budget and Impoundment Control Act, requiring a president to spend money appropriated by Congress. The status of the act was confused with the 1983 Court ruling that invalidates the legislative veto. It is unlikely that Congress can continue to compel a president to spend impounded funds.

Item Veto: *the power to disapprove of and block passage of specific parts of a bill. The president does not have this power.*

Executive Privilege: *the right of a president to withhold certain kinds of executive information from Congress or the public.*

The third power a president may exercise is **executive privilege.** Presidents have at times invoked the privilege of withholding information from Congress. Richard Nixon used this claim broadly to prevent subordinate officers from testifying before Congress. In defense of his position, Nixon cited historical precedent and the constitutional separation of powers. Congress, in turn, cited the need for information in legislating and inquiring after executive administration of congressional laws. At the height of Watergate, the case of executive privilege went before the Supreme Court. The Court recognized the constitutionality of executive privilege, in *U.S.* v. *Nixon,* but refused to accept a blanket claim for such privilege or a president's right to define its use.

Executive Power: *the blend of written constitutional provisions, custom, and person, that constitutes the power of the American presidency.*

Article II of the Constitution vests the **executive power** in a president of the United States and commands that the president "take care that the laws be faithfully executed." The Constitution does not say how the executive is to go about the task, but it anticipated the establishment of executive departments to assist the chief executive by allowing him to require the opinion "of the principal officer in each of the executive departments."

Although much administrative responsibility must be delegated to subordinates, the president is the one charged with final responsibility for the *administration of the laws*. The framers could not possibly have foreseen the enormous growth of government. The growth of the executive branch, in size and function, is unparalleled by the legislative and judicial branches. A vast and complex administrative structure assists the president in taking care that the laws are faithfully executed. There are now 2.9 million employees within executive agencies responsible for spending $1 trillion annually.

The executive branch is divided into thirteen executive departments headed by presidentially appointed secretaries. Departments are charged with implementing federal programs and with spending appropriated money for such programs. In addition to the cabinet-level departments, there are approximately sixty independent agencies that manage specific areas of concern. These independent agencies are housed within the executive branch but do not fall under the authority of any cabinet department; they are "independent" of executive agencies and are independent regulatory agencies. The president retains direct supervisory responsibility for the independent executive agencies; the regulatory agencies exercise their own quasi-executive and judicial powers under broad authority granted by Congress.

Since the tasks of supervision and control are so enormous, presidents have taken to establishing personal lines of information and supervision. In the past two decades, presidents have established personal presidential advisors and an Executive Office within the Office of the President in order to provide more direct and personal kinds of support for the task of managing the affairs of the nation. There has been a rapid growth in the Executive Office of the President. These officers are presidential appointees and have no responsibility other than serving the president.[14] Between 1954 and 1971 the number of presidential advisors grew from 25 to 45, the White House staff from 266 to 600, and the Executive Office staff from 1,175 to 5,395.[15] Since 1976, however, the Executive Office has been trimmed greatly. Reagan particularly has been a harsh critic of the size of government. As of 1985 the Executive Office of the President had 1,541 employees.

Since the New Deal, the president has assumed the major responsibility for *promoting economic growth*. Through the general powers to propose tax legislation and spend for the general welfare, the president has become the nation's chief economic manager. Legislation has laid economic management squarely at the feet of the president. In 1946, the Employment Act charged the president with maintaining the economy at full employment and submitting to Congress a report on the status of the economic health of the nation. The act empowered the president to control wages, prices, and rents in order to control the economy. This responsibility was extended in 1970 when Congress empowered President Nixon to freeze wages and prices to control inflation.

Much of the executive authority for managing the economy comes from the preparation of the budget. Ever since 1921, the president has had the responsibility for submitting an annual budget to Congress. This gives the president an opportunity to plan, fix priorities, and generally make fiscal policy. In the budget-preparation process, new programs may be proposed, domestic spending favored over military defense, or tax cuts initiated. The annual budget is viewed as a statement by the president of his priorities for the coming year.

In his administration Reagan found a new tool, the congressional budget process, to pass his spending cuts. Using a single budget-reconciliation resolution, Reagan and Republicans packaged $41 billion worth of cuts to more than eighty federal programs into a single act that mandated Congress to make the cuts in its programs. Budget reconciliation offers a president the potential to dictate budget levels for Congress.

The president has considerable help in managing the economy. The Office of Management and Budget (OMB) helps prepare the budget. All requests for funding are screened through OMB. This office also monitors the level of spending once the money has been appropriated by Congress. The chief advisors to the president on economic affairs are on his Council of Economic Advisors. They provide information and advice concerning inflation, government spending, and taxation. As of 1974, the Council on Wage and Price Stability monitors the health of the economy with respect to wages, costs, prices, and productivity, and it too is located within the Executive Office of the President.

In recent years, the rate of inflation coupled with high unemployment has resulted in a rather extensive presidential preoccupation with economic matters, and current problems indicate that this focus will continue.

Foreign Policy and the Military Role

No area of the presidential power is more direct and awesome than that affecting foreign affairs and the military. The president's responsibility in military and foreign policy matters has little challenge. From time to time Congress may check presidential initiative but it rarely, if ever, challenges the authority of the president to conduct foreign relations. It is in the area of foreign affairs that presidential leadership is at its height. The Constitution does not specifically grant the president power to conduct foreign relations, but "the President claims the silences of the Constitution. He finds a general 'power to conduct foreign relations' for the nation. Then he assumes that whatever has not been expressly assigned to Congress is to be exercised by the executive."[16]

Undoubtedly, the most awesome role for a president is that of *commander in chief* of the armed services. Sitting atop a nuclear arsenal, the president bears the burden for "pushing the button." Although the threat of nuclear warfare makes the role an "awesome burden," there is far more to it. Today the military is a fixed part of American government. More than 2 million Americans serve in the armed forces. In addition, the Defense Department and the branches of the service employ 1 million civilian employees. The military has a budget of more than $264 billion, one-quarter of the entire federal budget.

Donald Robinson has noted that two forces combined to make the role of commander in chief a prime area of responsibility: "The creation of a massive permanent military establishment, and the negotiation and ratification of a network of treaties, making explicit the responsibility of the United States for security around the world."[17] The president's responsibilities in deploying American troops and engaging in international negotiations make for a situation where Congress often has no alternative but to yield and support the president's actions. President Truman, as commander in chief, made the decision to drop the first atomic bomb in 1945. John F. Kennedy, after huddling with his advisors, blocked the ports of Cuba to Russian ships in 1962. Lyndon Johnson sent troops into Vietnam to support South Vietnam in 1965, Richard Nixon personally authorized the bombing of Cambodia in 1970, and Ronald Reagan authorized military assistance and advisors for El Salvador in 1982, invaded Grenada in 1983, and attacked Libyan terrorist bases in 1986.

Congress has the specific responsibility for declaring war. This has not deterred presidents, however, from making military commitments without congressional approval. In fact, Congress has generally supported presidential action to protect American interests around the globe. Vietnam, however, brought a reexamination of the president's war powers. Congress had passed the Gulf of Tonkin Resolution in 1964 supporting President Johnson's escalation of the war. Johnson, and President Nixon after him, argued that it was all the authorization they needed to take whatever steps they felt necessary to protect the national security of the United States. The secret bombings in Cambodia were more than Congress would tolerate. In 1973 it passed the War Powers Act, aimed at curbing unilateral presidential action. Passed over presidential veto, the act requires the president to inform Congress within forty-eight hours of committing any armed forces to combat abroad and further provides that such forces must be withdrawn in sixty days unless Congress authorizes their use. The status of the War Powers Act was called into question with the 1983 invalidation of the legislative veto. The Court specifically noted the act in its list of laws utilizing the veto. Presumably, Congress can no longer review a president's action and compel the alteration of that action.

Reagan's attack on Libya has aggravated the concern that led to the War Powers Act. Twice in less than a month Reagan employed military power against Libya, and neither time did he observe the provisions of the War Powers Act or seek wide advice or approval from Congress. Reagan asserted his exclusive power to act in "self-defense" against international terrorism. While both actions against Libya—moving into the Gulf of Sidra, which resulted in U.S. planes destroying several Libyan ships and missile sites, and the retaliatory strike against suspected terrorist camps for Libya's backing of acts of international terrorism—enjoyed widespread support in Congress, concern has surfaced that Reagan's actions violated the War Powers Act. The administration claims that certain forms of military response to terrorism are outside the provisions for consultation required by the act, but some members of Congress are not so sure. Senator Robert Byrd (D–W.Va.) has proposed an eighteen-member leadership committee, composed of veteran congressional leaders from both parties, to consult with the president prior to military action.

Whether the War Powers Act significantly redresses the balance of power remains to be seen. Generally presidents have enjoyed great public approval for their military actions. And until we seriously redefine America's role in world affairs, there appears to be little alternative to entrusting the president with broad war powers. As Clinton Rossiter observed, "We have placed a shocking amount of military power in the President's keeping, but where else, we may ask, could it possibly have been placed?"

The *diplomatic role* of the chief executive, an executive function from the start, has always been a source of strength and prestige for the president. Jefferson labeled the making of foreign policy "executive altogether," and Truman brashly declared, "I make American foreign policy." While the Constitution does not guarantee executive prerogative and occasionally requires the advice and consent of the Senate, presidents have generally been free to manage foreign affairs. In fact, commentators on the presidency have claimed there ought to be two presidents, one for domestic affairs and one for defense and foreign policy.[18] It is in the area of foreign affairs that presidents have enjoyed their greatest successes. And although many presidents began with high domestic priorities (Roosevelt and Johnson, for example), their greatest preoccupations were in foreign affairs. In fact, Wildavsky argues, "In the realm of foreign policy there has not been a single major issue on which Presidents, when they were serious and determined, have failed."[19]

The power of a president to act is constitutionally limited to appointing and receiving ambassadors and to making treaties with the advice and consent of the Senate. But today a president has the ability to commit Americans all across the globe. President Reagan made the Caribbean Basin Initiative to help "stabilize" the Caribbean and Central America. He declared the area of "vital interest" to the United States and stated that the administration would help the region resist leftist or communist movements by providing economic aid and military assistance. In 1986, he sought to pave the way to normalizing relations with Iran by secretly selling military weapons to Iran. He also hoped to use profits from those arms sales to support Contra rebels in Nicaragua when Congress had forbidden the President from providing military assistance in the Central American continent.

A network of information and advice coming from the State Department, the Pentagon, intelligence sources such as the CIA, as well as personal advisors for national security, affords the president knowledge that no other official has. And with the use of executive agreements instead of treaties, the president can enter into commitments that are not easily reversed.

The diplomatic role is most dramatically portrayed by the president's ability to engage the armed forces in war. We have had two "presidential wars" in the recent past: Korea and Vietnam. The president's power in foreign relations can be seen as well by the amount of time and energy presidents spend on this part of their job and the worldwide effect their actions have. Richard Nixon signaled a turn in American policy toward the Chinese Communists with his visit to Peking in 1971. Jimmy Carter's greatest achievement was his personal intervention to bring the Egyptian and Israeli leaders, Anwar Sadat and Menachem Begin, together for the summit at Camp David in 1978.

The Ultimate Responsibility: Nuclear Weapons and Foreign Policy

Americans live in a global community, and their political expectations are shaped as much by world affairs as by domestic events. Any realistic assessment of the U.S. government's ability to solve its problems must include foreign affairs and America's foreign policy. World affairs place many limitations upon American politics—some constitutional, some affecting the operation of the political process, some influencing the stability of the economy, some reflecting on Americans' image of themselves—all depending on circumstances over which we cannot exercise total control.

Americans firmly believe that the goals of American foreign policy are honorable, that the United States has been a responsible and even generous member of the global community. We have sought policies that remove foreign impediments to our policies and threats to our national security. Yet there remain serious limitations to America's ability to realize its policies, the most pressing problem being the proliferation of nuclear weapons.

The chief concern of every president is the security of the nation and the survival of its people. Everyone wants a world free of war and nuclear weapons, but presidents and the nation must deal with an imperfect world as they find it. And regrettable as it may be, today's world includes an arsenal of nuclear weapons.

Both the president and Congress are charged with providing for the common defense. Under the Constitution, Congress appropriates the money and legislates the size and nature of our military and its weapons. The president is commander in chief of the military, and so determines how military forces will be deployed to meet the challenges of a contemporary world. The president is the prime decision maker in foreign affairs, and nowhere is that responsibility more present—and more awe-

National Security Policy

The national security of the United States—the nation's physical well-being and the safety of its way of life—is the focus of two policy areas: foreign policy, whereby we conduct relations with other nations, and military policy, which revolves around the deployment of military forces and weapons.

The making of national security policy falls most heavily to the president, although both Congress and the executive branch maintain strong interests in foreign and military policies. But only the president can obtain and analyze the diverse sources of information needed, protect the confidentiality of that information, and act swiftly in cases of crisis.

In making national security policy, the president relies on a series of formal and informal advisors, which often creates a rivalry for power and influence between White House personnel and members of the State Department and Department of Defense. In foreign policy the two major groups of advisors are the National Security Council and the State Department. The National Security Council (NSC) has acquired great influence ever since the presidency of John F. Kennedy. Composed of the vice-president, secretary of state, secretary of defense, and other personnel designated by the president, the NSC has an expert staff directed by the special assistant for national security affairs. The special assistant has acquired considerable policy influence and advises the president directly on foreign policy. The staff analyzes policy alternatives and forecasts consequences for alternatives. The secretary of state and the career diplomats who make up the State Department are responsible for implementing the policies adopted by the president. Often their day-to-day operations expertise comes into conflict with the NSC and its more narrow purpose of advising the president.

For military policy a more integrated set of policy advisors exists: the branches of military service within the Department of Defense headed by the secretary of defense and the Joint Chiefs of Staff are statutory advisors to the National Security Council. Here the technical analysis of defense intelligence combines with NSC staff research to provide the president ready information on military activity around the globe.

The goals of American foreign policy are, broadly, four: (1) national security, (2) international peace and stability, (3) economic assistance, and (4) furthering United States interests globally. To this list President Carter added a fifth, protecting human rights.

Since World War II, the policy objective of national security has been preoccupied with communist containment. The Marshall Plan, NATO, military bases, and military activity—Korea, Vietnam, and to a lesser extent, Grenada and Nicaragua—were all part of a communist containment policy. In 1980 the Olympic boycott and cruise missiles were part of a containment policy.

From Richard Nixon through Jimmy Carter, the policy of the president was detente (negotiations to reduce tensions and increase trade and cultural exchanges) with Russia and China. The Strategic Arms Limitation Treaty (SALT) of 1972, designed to reduce the number of nuclear weapons and dependence on the military as a policy tool, was a result of the changed policy. Ronald Reagan has once again made communist containment the basis for his foreign policy. Most recently, Reagan has also had to contend with international terrorism as a threat to national security; one response was the attack on Libyan terrorist bases in 1986.

The second objective, international peace and stability, has meant, historically, support for the United Nations. It has also involved, more recently, the nuclear nonproliferation treaty (1968), the SALT treaty, and efforts to ratify SALT II. President Carter added a personal touch with the Camp David summit (1978), where he brought together Arab and Israeli leaders to secure a peaceful settlement in the Middle East.

Economic assistance has been tied to the first objective, national security, by providing economic aid to underdeveloped nations in order to gain their support and loyalty, thereby preventing the spread of communism. Foreign aid is the principal tool of economic assistance. More recently, since the formation of OPEC and the Arab embargo in 1973, the U.S. economic objective has been to maintain a balance of trade, keeping the balance of payments (income from exports less costs from import purchases) from becoming too great a drain on the economy. President Carter also resorted to an economic boycott to protest Iran's holding U.S. citizens hostage.

Human rights became a policy objective early in Carter's administration. He declared the protection of human rights in foreign countries to be an aim of U.S. foreign policy. Carter said that the United States would use its influence and resources to see that human rights were protected by other governments. The objective has proved difficult to implement, notably where other issues and policy objectives conflict, as with the Soviet Union. But with smaller, friendlier nations, such as South Korea and the Philippines, influence has been exerted to protect human rights.

President Reagan and Mikhail Gorbachev met at Geneva, Switzerland, for a summit conference in 1985.

some—than in the president's authority to "push the nuclear button" to launch a nuclear attack against an adversary.

Deterrence: *a means of reducing the risk of military attack by threatening massive nuclear retaliation in the event of such an attack.*

Ever since World War II the United States has maintained a strategic nuclear arsenal as a means of **deterrence.** Deterrence is designed to reduce the risk of military attack, although it cannot eliminate that risk. Deterrence is based on the threat of mutually assured destruction (MAD)—that is, that any nation attacking the U.S. will itself be destroyed in retaliation. Deterrence has been, in short, a strategy for dealing with the Soviet Union by threatening it with nuclear destruction in the event of an attack. Officially, the United States has said deterrence means the ability to retaliate against the Soviet Union so as to assure the destruction of one-fourth of its population and three-fourths of its industrial capacity.

The credibility of nuclear deterrence depends upon the ability and will to use the weapons in our arsenal. The will depends upon the foreign policy process—upon presidents conveying the message to the Soviets. The ability depends upon weapons capabilities—the number and size of the weapons and the ability to deliver them to a prearranged target. This strategy produces a heightened tension as the threat of war hangs over U.S.–Soviet foreign policy at every turn. Can the two superpowers reduce their threatening policies and engage in foreign relations without fear of nuclear war? This is the hope of the entire world.

The Arms Race

Cruise Missile: *an airplanelike, low-flying, terrain-guided missile that can be launched from virtually any platform—bomber, submarine, tactical aircraft, or ground vehicle.*

The current arms race has been going on for almost forty years. It is nearly impossible to keep score, yet keeping score is largely what the race is about. Three categories for scoring appear important: the kinds of strategic delivery systems, the number of nuclear warheads, and the explosive power of the warheads (typically expressed in megatons—millions of tons of TNT).

The United States has a "triad" of strategic weapons systems, including manned bombers, intercontinental ballistic missiles (ICBMs), and nuclear powered submarine-launched intermediate-range ballistic missiles (SLBMs). The mainstay of the strategic arsenal has been the manned bomber—the B-52. Produced between 1955 and 1968, the intercontinental bomber can carry a payload of eight short-range attack missiles (SRAMs), twelve cruise missiles (a pilotless missile that looks and flies like a jet plane), and four bombs—all with nuclear warheads.[20] The **cruise missile** is of more recent origin. Launched either from B-52s or submarines, the cruise missile has its own engine and guidance system to reach preprogrammed targets while flying at low altitudes. And because of the developing technology in cruise missiles and the advanced age of the B-52, presidents Carter and Reagan pushed development of a new supersonic manned bomber, the B-1. The B-1 flies at twice the speed of sound and is able to carry long-range cruise missiles. The price tag for one B-1 bomber is between $200 million and $500 million; it became operational in 1986.

The intercontinental ballistic missile has long been a source of competition with the Soviets. We now deploy some 1,050 ICBMs, the Soviets approximately 1,400. But at issue is the vulnerability of ICBMs to any first strike and their accuracy in delivering their payloads. The U.S. has generally emphasized the qualitative and technological aspects of ICBMs over the quantitative comparisons. Most U.S. ICBMs have multiple warheads—MIRVs (multiple independently targetable reentry vehicles). This allows one ICBM to fire three or more nuclear warheads at separate targets. One MIRVed Poseidon submarine missile can have fourteen separate warheads.

The U.S.'s newest entry in the ICBM arsenal is the MX missile. The MX is a MIRVed missile capable of carrying twelve warheads; it is more accurate than earlier ICBMs.

There has been controversy over the deployment of the MX missile. Not only is the lethal accuracy of the missile of concern to the Soviets, but the MX is to be deployed in hardened silos, making it a "hard target kill." In other words, in any nuclear exchange the Soviets would lose ground by having to use more warheads in an attack than the number of U.S. warheads destroyed. Remaining MX missiles would certainly hit strategic Soviet targets in retaliation. Critics see the MX missile as destabilizing in the quest to limit the nuclear arms race.

Embedded in the debate over deploying the MX missile is a call for a small ICBM or "Midgetman" missile. A small, single-warhead missile, the Midgetman is designed to slow down the arms race, a belated recognition that MIRVed missiles are destabilizing. Still, the Midgetman would be designed to destroy Soviet missile silos, having sufficient accuracy and yield "to put Soviet hardened military targets at risk."

Finally the United States has more than 640 SLBMs, submarine-launched ballistic missiles. The idea is simple but effective. Nuclear

Military weapons are a significant component of American foreign policy. *Above:* a camouflaged B-1 bomber, a prototype of the computerized war plane.

powered submarines can roam the oceans for weeks undetected, approach very near enemy targets, and launch a strike with little time for the enemy to respond. The first such type of submarine was the Polaris class. Still in operation, they are being replaced with the bigger Trident submarine, which carries more missiles. For its SLBM, the Navy has used the Poseidon, a MIRVed missile with up to fourteen warheads. Recently the Trident SLBM has been added to the arsenal for the Trident submarine. The Trident is a much longer-ranged missile with MIRVed warheads of great capacity.

The vulnerability of these missile-delivery systems is a controversial issue. The U.S. position is that the triad of delivery systems can withstand a first strike to such an extent that the U.S. retaliation, or **second strike,** can still be devastating. To ensure military survival in a first strike, new weapons and delivery systems are constantly under consideration. These efforts have led to cruise missiles, MIRVed warheads, and the MX missile.

President Reagan has offered the American people another defense, one that he claims would shield the country from the danger of a nuclear attack. In a speech in March 1983, Reagan proposed the **Strategic Defense Initiative** (SDI), commonly called Star Wars, in which scientists would devise methods of intercepting and destroying attacking missiles and their warheads in midflight. In essence, SDI proposes a two-layer defense: a boost-phase defense to attack Soviet missiles early in their flight, and a terminal defense to intercept warheads as they descend toward their targets at the ends of their trajectories.

The boost-phase defense is the most futuristic and technologically sophisticated. It would necessarily be based in space and depend upon satellites for surveillance. These very high-altitude satellites would monitor and track enemy missiles, relaying messages to other, lower-level satellites armed with "smart bullets." These battle-management satellites would carry tiny, highly computerized missiles that would track their targets using radar or heat waves, then attack the ICBMs either by colliding with them or by exploding nearby, releasing clouds of metal fragments to puncture the warheads and thereby disable their electronics. In another proposal, laser beams would melt the metal skin of missiles. Such laser beams could be projected from satellites, or they could be sent from the ground and reflected off aiming satellites.

The second layer of defense, or terminal defense, would be designed to attack warheads that managed to avoid the boost-phase defense. The warheads would be intercepted during their descent, but the interception would be designed to occur at a high altitude, well beyond the atmosphere, to protect the land below.

The SDI proposal is highly controversial. The cost is estimated at $60 billion; but this is only a guess, and some people place the cost billions of dollars higher. In addition, no one is even sure the concept will work. Some scientists think the technology is not capable of doing what is proposed; others argue that it cannot provide enough accuracy or security to justify the cost. Even a two-thirds or three-fourths success ratio would

Second Strike: *the ability to launch a sustained nuclear attack in retaliation to a nuclear attack, to strike back with nuclear weapons after an initial nuclear attack.*

Strategic Defense Initiative: *a proposal for high-technology outer space weapons to intercept and destroy nuclear warheads launched against the United States. Essentially defensive in nature, SDI would rely on satellites to provide a protective shield for the nation.*

leave the country vulnerable. Finally, other critics warn that SDI is but another round in the arms race, turning space into the next battlefield.

The sheer destructiveness of nuclear weapons can kill hundreds of millions of people, perhaps even end human life on the planet. The cost of the arms race spirals upward, each side trying to find new and more sophisticated ways to deliver the warheads. The result is a tension-filled world in which the wrong choice of words or mistaken intentions could end civilization. It seems clear, therefore, that the U.S. and U.S.S.R. must find ways to control nuclear weapons and live together.

A Collective Presidency

Collective Presidency: *the recognition that the presidency is an institution of several officials and offices, all in need of coordination. It recognizes that presidential responsibility is shared responsibility.*

A common thread running through all presidential power for the past fifty years has been the unmistakable existence of a **collective presidency.** No matter how strong or committed a president, institutional forces press in upon him. All presidents have sought to organize the presidency to expedite their will; all have found that the institution inhibited their doing what they wished to do. The tasks of the presidency far exceed the scope or ability of any single person.

The American people had deliberately designed ponderous machinery of separated but dependent power, making it difficult to make changes. Civil servants beyond the pale of presidential appointment, Congress and its slow, unwieldy committees, and federal judges all exist to check and restrain presidential will. Yet presidential responsibility has grown. World War II and the Cold War added new international responsibilities to the position of the chief executive just as fears of economic dislocation and inflation expanded the domestic role for the president. The economic and military positions of the United States in a global community are so powerful today that they require flexible and responsive instruments of government. These require in turn an energetic president with a comprehensive program to cope with today's problems. But this is not enough; there must be a will for collective responsibility.

Presidential power can be successfully exercised only when presidents are willing to reach out and coordinate the vast instruments of American government. A presidential program alone is not sufficient. There must also be the congressional support to carry through that program, which is possible only when there exist *real* (as opposed to *nominal*) congressional majorities, a condition obtained—and for a relatively short time at that— in the presidencies of Woodrow Wilson, Franklin D. Roosevelt, and Lyndon Johnson. Ronald Reagan, in his first two years in office, appeared to have created the same set of circumstances, though the trend of his policies was opposite to that of his predecessors. Presidents must also be managers, attending to the executive coordination and implementation of policy. Presidents need to designate program managers, at either the cabinet or White House level, to implement policy. They must delegate responsibility and control, because presidents have been notoriously poor managers; they were elected on their political skills, not their managerial abilities. But program management must have the support and concern of the president.

Far-reaching forces are fundamentally altering our government and society. The economy and employment are as much the result of foreign policy as they are of the workings of our industry. Defense spending affects domestic priorities as much as it does national security. We have expanded presidential power and responsibility to cope with the changes. The growth of the executive branch has occurred at all levels—the White House, cabinet departments, and civil service. Yet the changes far exceed the growth of presidential power. They demand great structural changes in government, changes we seem unable to make. The political climate has been altered in the past fifty years, as has been the responsibility for government, but there is little perception of the magnitude of the problem, let alone its solution. We continue to struggle for presidential leadership with a pieced-together presidency that can rise to challenges only in the most exceptional of circumstances, and only then with an acceptance of collective responsibility.

Redefining Presidential Power

Imperial Presidency: *the term used by Arthur Schlesinger, Jr., to describe the Nixon presidency and its lack of presidential accountability.*

The lack of presidential accountability led Arthur Schlesinger, Jr., to label the Nixon presidency the **"imperial presidency."**[21] It moved Richard Neustadt to call for the reestablishment of constraints in order to keep the president democratically rooted within the Constitution.[22] Citizens and political scientists alike are rethinking the idea of strong presidential power in the wake of the 1970s. Although some reforms would drastically limit or restructure the powers of the office, most serious proposals call for "shared powers." For the post-Watergate presidency, there is increased emphasis on sharing the establishment of priorities. Whether Congress or the president takes the initiative—and the likelihood remains great that the president will continue to exercise considerable initiative—there is little chance that the president will be able again to exert total dominance over public policy. Congress has now imposed many restraints. Yet the tools of presidential power remain substantial. Let us look at the organization of the presidency as it reflects the revised priorities of the post-Watergate era.

Executive Office of the President: *a part of the executive branch appointed to serve the president. It consists of agencies such as the Office of Management and Budget and the National Security Council.*

The Executive Office

As presidential functions and activities increased in the twentieth century, so did the staff serving the president within the **Executive Office of the President.** In 1939, when the Bureau of the Budget was transferred from the Department of Treasury to the president's Executive Office, it numbered under fifty. Today the number of budget examiners and managers approaches six hundred, and they have a staff of approximately five thousand employees. The growth of the presidential staff within the Executive Office led Tom Cronin to call the phenomenon the "swelling of the Presidency."[23]

The burdens on the presidency have brought a demand for swift and decisive action. Most presidents have felt constrained by cabinet secretaries and the bureaucracy. Secretaries are often appointed to appease particular interest groups and settle political debts; the bureaucracy often has a more limited and narrow focus. Hence presidents have preferred to go outside the regular administration for help and advice. The Executive Office staff serves at the pleasure of the president, and its members "speak the President's language."[24]

The executive establishment has grown at the expense of traditional sources of administrative policymaking—the cabinet and the bureaucracy. Under Nixon, presidential aides felt free to intrude into departmental affairs, to make decisions in the name of the president, and to recommend changes in staff or policy. They came to be known as the "palace guard," protecting and isolating the president from administrative and political officials. Said one then close to the presidency, "This represents the greatest of all barriers to Presidential access to reality."[25]

In 1977 President Carter reorganized the Executive Office, eliminating seven offices and cutting back the staff by a third. In all, Carter reduced the White House staff from 485 to 351 and eliminated another 250 positions from the Executive Office. Reagan too prefers a scaled-back Executive Office. In his administration the Executive Office numbers 1,540 employees, with the White House staff at 360.

Table 10.6 shows the offices that constitute the contemporary Executive Office of the President. The office can be broken down into six functional areas, reflecting the priorities of the contemporary presidency: (1) national security or foreign affairs, (2) domestic policy, (3) economic affairs, (4) administration or staff management, (5) congressional relations, and (6) public relations.

Most contemporary presidents, instead of utilizing the State Department and the advice of secretaries of state, have depended on the National Security Council (NSC) and the presidential assistant for national security affairs. Starting with Eisenhower, the NSC has played an inte-

TABLE 10.6   The reorganization of the Executive Office of the President, 1982

White House Office
Office of the Vice-President
Office of Management and Budget
Council of Environmental Quality
Council of Economic Advisors
Office of Science and Technology Policy
Office of U.S. Trade Representative
National Security Council
Office of Policy Development
Office of Administration

gral part in national defense policy. Kennedy used an executive committee of the NSC during the Cuban missile crisis, Henry Kissinger's influence in the Nixon administration as national security advisor was due to his dominance of the NSC, and Reagan used its members for his secret arms sales to Iran. As statutory members the National Security Council has the president, vice-president, secretary of state, and secretary of defense. Attached to it as advisors are the director of the Central Intelligence Agency and the chairman of the Joint Chiefs of Staff. Also included in its meetings is the assistant to the president for national security affairs.

In domestic policy there have been some changes. In 1970 Richard Nixon created a Domestic Council in the Executive Office. It was to be the domestic counterpart of the National Security Council in planning strategy and proposing public policy across a broad spectrum of issues. John Ehrlichman was the council's executive director and it included many cabinet officers, but it never seemed to do anything. It met only twice in 1973 and may have been, in part, a casualty of Watergate.[26] Carter abolished the Domestic Council in 1977 and replaced it with the Domestic Policy Staff (DPS). The DPS reported to the assistant to the president for domestic affairs and worked closely with departments and agencies in coordinating information before making recommendations to the president on domestic policy.

In 1981 President Reagan redesignated the DPS as the Office of Policy Development. Its functions changed very little. It continues to assist the president in the formation, coordination, and implementation of economic and domestic policy. In addition, it serves as the policy staff for the president's cabinet councils.

The Office of Management and Budget (OMB) and the Council of Economic Advisors are the Executive Office's main resources for economic policy. In President Carter's executive reorganization, three councils were dropped: the Economic Opportunity Council (its only function of preparing the catalog of domestic assistance had already been assumed by OMB), the Council on International Economic Policy, and the Energy Resources Council.

The Office of Management and Budget has become, since its creation by Richard Nixon in 1970, a major executive agency for fiscal and managerial control. The OMB, in fact, may well be the most powerful agency in government today. The main function of OMB is to assist the president in preparing the annual budget. David Stockman, Reagan's director of OMB until 1985, became Reagan's budget cutter, responsible for fashioning the budget to conform with "Reaganomics." All agency requests for appropriations must be cleared through OMB, and the office enforces presidential guidelines in the preparation of recommendations. OMB also acts as a clearinghouse for all proposed legislation from executive agencies; agencies submit proposals to OMB for the president's attention. Finally, OMB plays a major role in developing efficient and effective management techniques. It makes recommendations for implementing programs, reorganizing the administrative machinery, and reforming the federal bureaucracy.

The Council of Economic Advisors is the other main arm of the president in economic policy. Created after World War II, the council is composed of three members appointed by the president and confirmed by the Senate. This body maintains a small but highly technical and competent staff to analyze economic data and trends and to make economic forecasts. The major thrust of the council in recent years has been to advise the president on levels of unemployment, the rate of inflation, and levels of government spending. Of course, the principal weapon is the tax, and the council frequently advises the president on cutting or raising taxes to deal with the cost of living and employment.

President Carter created an Office of Central Administration to provide support for administrative services and to prevent unnecessary duplication and competition among staff. This move was a recognition that the Executive Office of the President had grown over the last few administrations and was now a permanent part of the government. In part, this move was a response to the isolation and autonomy of the presidential staff during the Nixon administration. The "palace guard" screened access to the president and moved in his name to implement presidential wishes when agencies balked or were slow to respond. But the move to create this office was also a recognition that any president's time must be managed carefully.

A fifth priority area in the Executive Office is congressional relations. The White House staff for congressional relations seeks to promote the policies supported by the president. Its activities are coordinated by an assistant to the president for congressional liaison, and rise and fall with the particular personal interest each president takes in legislation. White House aides seeking support for a president's policies must deal with congressional committees and their chairs, floor leaders and whips, bill sponsors, and other key figures. One former aide summed up the responsibilities: "We handled the agendas for the Congressional Committees, worked with leaders (like Rayburn and Mansfield), took head counts. We had to hire Congressional liaison people throughout the government, and we would have weekly meetings with them. Then, too, we also had to keep track of all the legislation—track it all down, keep big posters with all the relevant data. We had to work with some task-force people telling them the mood of Congress. We always had to know what was possible."[27]

Reagan's success with Congress can be traced not only to his personal involvement in lobbying but also to the creation of the Legislative Strategy Group within the White House. The Legislative Strategy Group revolves around White House assistants who map out strategy, coordinate work with the cabinet, and apply pressure on Congress to pass administration bills.

The final area of concern for the Executive Office falls into the general category of public relations. The president has a press secretary, and there is a special assistant to the president for media and public affairs and a deputy assistant for public liaison. But all presidential aides are concerned with the president's image and reputation. In the past few administrations, public relations has become a major operation. There are speech writers, media consultants, advance men, and information managers to control the flow of information from the White House. They seek to assess the impact of White House information on the media, the public, Congress, foreign leaders, popularity polls, executive agencies, and others. All recent presidents have been conscious of their reputations and have guarded their images with considerable care. This has led to the charge that presidents use their public relations staffs to manipulate public opinion. President Carter sought to soft-pedal the idea that a president can manipulate and control public opinion. For example, the Office of Telecommunications Policy, which was active under Richard Nixon, has been disbanded and many of its functions transferred to an office in the Department of Commerce.

The Cabinet

Cabinet: *collectively, the thirteen heads of the executive agencies together with the president and vice-president.*

Every president, beginning with George Washington, has had a **cabinet.** Today the cabinet includes the president, vice-president, the heads of the thirteen executive departments, and other executive branch officials to whom the president accords cabinet rank (see Table 10.7).

The rise of the White House staff in the Executive Office of the President has meant the decline of the cabinet as a policymaking group. Strong presidents want advice from those who "speak the president's language" and will not politically upstage them. The cabinet is not well suited to that role.

A number of criteria go into the selection of cabinet secretaries. First, these individuals are generally prominent politicians and statesmen who will lend credibility to a new administration. A president must also represent and balance as many interests as possible. Labor is concerned with

TABLE 10.7   The president's cabinet in order of formation

State	1789
Treasury	1789
Interior	1849
Justice	1870
Agriculture	1889
Commerce	1913
Labor	1913
Defense	1947
Health and Human Services[a]	1953
Housing and Urban Development	1965
Transportation	1966
Energy	1977
Education[a]	1979

[a]The Department of Education was separated and created from Health, Education and Welfare in 1979; HEW was then renamed Health and Human Services.

the appointment of the labor secretary; environmental groups are concerned with the appointment of an interior secretary. There are also other factors to balance: geographic representation, race, and sex. In short, presidents end up with a cabinet they can work with, but often prefer to work without. In recent years, Hess notes, the changes in campaigning, the financing of politics, and the diffusion of power in Congress lessen the traditional constraints on selecting the cabinet. "More than ever before they will be free to choose their department heads on the basis of ability."[28]

The president–cabinet relationship may be described as feudal. Each secretary has administrative responsibility for a department. Each department has its interests, including clientele groups, congressional committees, and political viewpoints. A secretary must balance these against the presidential perspective as it emerges from cabinet meetings. The result is, as Richard Fenno concludes, remarkable:

> One striking circumstance is the extent to which the cabinet concept breaks down in the course of the members' activities outside the cabinet meeting. . . . In the day-to-day work of the cabinet member, each man fends for himself without much consideration for cabinet unity. His survival, his support and his success do not depend on his fellow members.[29]

The Vice-President

"A damned peculiar situation to be in," said Spiro Agnew of the vice-presidency, "to have authority and a title and responsibility with no real power to do anything." All vice-presidents have complained that they have no place in the administration; they are outsiders looking in. The office of vice-president is a constitutional anomaly. Its only formal power is to preside over the Senate. Under the Twenty-fifth Amendment, the vice-president, with the concurrence of the cabinet or other body, may declare the president disabled and serve as acting president. If the president dies in office, resigns, or is impeached and removed from office, the vice-president becomes the president and serves for the remainder of the unexpired term of office.

Most presidents, having selected a running mate in the election, have stopped there. They have delegated little responsibility to vice-presidents for fear they might disrupt administration policy, or steal some thunder from the president. So vice-presidents languish with little to do. They are shunted off to chair advisory panels and eat chicken dinners at meetings presidents do not wish to attend. Nixon cautioned against turning the vice-president "into merely another bureaucrat—and a secretary of catch-all affairs at that."[30]

Traditionally, vice-presidents have been selected to "balance the ticket" in presidential elections. Lyndon Johnson, a southerner, provided geographical balance by naming Hubert Humphrey of Minnesota his vice-presidential nominee. Nixon selected Agnew to broaden his appeal with the eastern and southern border states. Carter, a southerner like Johnson, went to the North and nominated Walter Mondale, a liberal. Reagan, a conservative from the West, selected George Bush, a moderate from the important electoral state of Texas.

In some cases the choice of vice-presidential running mate can cause serious political difficulties. In 1972 George McGovern selected Thomas Eagleton of Missouri before it was learned that he had been under psychiatric treatment. In 1976 the conservative Ronald Reagan said that if he received the Republican nomination, his running mate would be a liberal senator from Pennsylvania, Richard Schweiker. This alarmed Reagan's conservative backers and brought charges that political expediency had overcome political commitment.

It is interesting to note that while vice-presidents have recently gained the presidency through death and resignation—Lyndon Johnson and Gerald Ford—few have been able to win the presidency on their own. Richard Nixon is the only recent example. The reasons for vice-presidents' failure to become president seem to be the public's desire for a change in party every so often and the lack of an active, visible role for vice-presidents to play in most administrations.

Recent presidents have undertaken to find more active roles and responsibilities for their vice-presidents. Lyndon Johnson used Humphrey as the promoter for the Great Society on Capitol Hill. Humphrey also acted as a liaison for urban affairs. Nixon was more inclined to put his vice-presidents, Agnew and Ford, in the front lines of political skirmishes. Each in his own way was a partisan campaigner toiling for the Nixon administration and candidates supporting the administration. Ross Baker labeled the use of Spiro Agnew the "Mario Puzo Theory of the Vice Presidency": "The President is the Godfather and the Vice President is his 'button man.' The Vice President is sent to knife, crush and garotte the opponents; after which the President turns up at the memorial services for the victim wearing a carnation."[31]

Joel Goldstein suggested that the model of Walter Mondale's vice-presidency offered some hope for the office. Recent vice-presidents are playing an expanded institutional role, including chairing commissions, acting as special envoys of the president, and serving as presidential advisors. Mondale assumed the latter role particularly: "The stature he achieved as an advisor was unprecedented for a Vice President. He helped choose cabinet members and influenced the appointment of several ranking figures. . . . He participated in most major decisions."[32]

George Bush, too, appears to have enjoyed an enlarged role within the Reagan administration. President Reagan has designated Vice-President Bush as chairman of two substantial presidential committees in his administration. Bush chairs the crisis management team within the National Security Council, which is to coordinate and control federal resources during periods of crisis. Bush also chairs the Task Force on

Regulatory Relief, the presidential commission to screen and approve government rules and regulations as an effort to cut down on governmental interference through unnecessary regulations. In addition, Bush has been used by Reagan as a liaison with Congress, working to secure support among Congress members for administration bills. But Vice-President Bush's most prominent role came with the attempted assassination of President Reagan. While no formal transfer of authority under the Twenty-fifth Amendment was deemed necessary, Reagan was unable to handle his work schedule for several weeks. Vice-President Bush assumed some of that workload, acting as the administration's spokesman and chairing executive meetings, including cabinet meetings.

The issue of the vice-presidency has become sensitive in the past two decades. President Kennedy was assassinated in office, and Ronald Reagan wounded by a would-be assassin. Two attempts were made on the life of President Ford as well, and two presidential candidates have been shot, and one killed, while campaigning for the presidency. One president, Richard Nixon, resigned from office rather than face the possibility of impeachment and removal. Thirteen vice-presidents have become president, six in this century. Many people therefore argue that we need strong, capable vice-presidents and a better process for selecting them. Both major parties have examined proposals for nominating a vice-president separately and taking control away from the presidential candidate. But nothing has happened yet. Some critics call for abolishing the office altogether. This appears unlikely; most Americans accept and approve of the office. The only other option is to provide some functions for the office, but there seems to be no way to do this without taking something away from the presidency. In Cronin's assessment:

> The verdict of history is harsh on the vice-presidency. The office has done only one thing well, solving our succession problem, and it is open to question whether it has done even that well enough. The vice-presidency in presidential government makes the presidency neither more manageable nor more democratic and accountable. Earl Warren cautioned that alternatives proposed in times of distrust and confusion are likely to develop more problems than they wish to solve.[33]

Goldstein proposes three modest reform possibilities. First, political parties could require presidential candidates to release a list of potential vice-presidential nominees. This would allow for public scrutiny and evaluation of the candidates. Second, parties could allow presidential nominees more time in selecting their choice for the number two post. This might encourage wider consultation and evaluation. Finally, vice-presidential nominees could be included in at least one presidential debate. Since the nominees now receive so little campaign attention, vice-presidential debates would give voters a greater chance to assess second candidates.[34]

Presidential Personality

By mid-twentieth century America came to view the presidency as a *heroic presidency*, celebrated for its competence and power as well as for its moral leadership. It was a reservoir of the "best and brightest" minds in the nation. The heroic presidency sought to merge the office, the powers, and the man into one; the ability to lead and the ability to exercise power were functions of personality. From this attempt Americans are coming to understand better the importance of personality—the presidential character—in presidential success and failure. We are learning that the way in which individual presidents perceive their roles and respond to crises can have direct effects on each of us.

Studies of presidential personality seek to explain the crisis of presidential leadership in terms of individual character. One major attempt is James David Barber's *The Presidential Character.*[35] Barber suggests that presidential character is the way presidents orient themselves toward their office and may be viewed as a function of their stance toward experience, their world view, and their style (Figure 10.2). These in turn interact with the situations presidents face—the climate of expectation and the power situations they must deal with. Barber contends that there are two dimensions to be looked at: the *degree of activity* presidents exert in performing their tasks and the *degree of enjoyment* they experience as a result of their activity. Barber pairs these two dimensions to develop a fourfold classification of presidential character:

Presidential Character: a study by James David Barber attempting to explain the crisis of presidential leadership in terms of individual character.

Active–Positive: extensive activity and the enjoyment of it; high self-esteem and success in relating to the environment.

Active–Negative: intense effort and low emotional reward for that effort; compulsive, ambitious and power seeking, but self-image is discontinuous and environment is seen as threatening.

Passive–Positive: compliant, cooperative, and agreeable rather than personally assertive; has an optimistic outlook and enjoys the routine of politics and popularity.

Passive–Negative: oriented toward dutiful service; limited activity; finds the office frustrating and escapes conflict by emphasizing procedural arrangements.

Says Barber: *"Active–positive* Presidents want most to achieve results. *Active–negatives* aim to get and keep power. *Passive–positives* are after love. *Passive–negatives* emphasize their civic virtue."[36]

The active–positive presidential character most closely fits the image of the strong, dominant leader. Franklin D. Roosevelt and John F. Kennedy are examples. However, Barber notes that some of our recent presidents, such as Lyndon Johnson and Richard Nixon, have been active–negative personalities. Such individuals may take driven, uncompromising stands owing to their perception of the environment as threatening. These ideas do much to explain the stubborn resistance of the Johnson administration to criticism of the escalation of the war in Vietnam. They also explain the "stonewalling" and "bunker mentality" of the Nixon administration at the height of the Watergate furor.

Recent presidents have not fit Barber's classification very well. Barber classified Jimmy Carter as active–positive. Yet, by 1980, Carter's presidency was marked by several disappointments and setbacks; few Americans felt the Carter administration a real success. Carter appears not to have experienced much of the joy associated with the combat of politics or its results. Barber, during the 1980 campaign, labeled Ronald Reagan as passive–positive.[37] However, the Reagan presidency more closely fits the active–positive model of presidential character. Reagan is known to be an optimist with extreme confidence in his policies and abilities. If a policy reflects the administration's basic principles, it will turn out all right.[38] With this confidence Reagan has forged boldly and dramatically ahead. His administration has been an active one. He has made deep cuts in social spending, pushed through a major tax cut, dramatically increased defense spending, and taken an aggressive anti-Soviet line. He has jumped into the congressional budget fracas, using the budget-reconciliation process of Congress to win his program-spending cuts. He is not known to back away from the heat of battle. He stood firm on the PATCO (Professional Air Traffic Controllers) strike. When striking air traffic controllers would not return to work, Reagan fired them, just as he promised he would do if they did not end the strike and return to work. Even when other nations refused to take action against Libya for its suspected support of terrorism, Reagan was willing to stand alone in the international arena and attack targets in Libya.

If there is any criticism of Ronald Reagan's personality, it is of his overoptimism and stubbornness regarding compromise. His faith in his principles, and in Reaganomics particularly, makes him intractable and liable

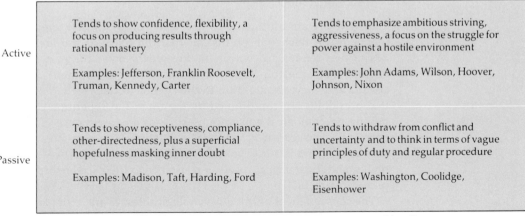

	Positive	Negative
Active	Tends to show confidence, flexibility, a focus on producing results through rational mastery Examples: Jefferson, Franklin Roosevelt, Truman, Kennedy, Carter	Tends to emphasize ambitious striving, aggressiveness, a focus on the struggle for power against a hostile environment Examples: John Adams, Wilson, Hoover, Johnson, Nixon
Passive	Tends to show receptiveness, compliance, other-directedness, plus a superficial hopefulness masking inner doubt Examples: Madison, Taft, Harding, Ford	Tends to withdraw from conflict and uncertainty and to think in terms of vague principles of duty and regular procedure Examples: Washington, Coolidge, Eisenhower

Energy levels in doing the job

Emotional attitudes toward the presidency

Figure 10.2   Different types of presidential characters

to take refuge in abstract doctrine or principle. This stubbornness can lead to impasse, particularly with Congress. Only with careful work can Reagan's advisors mollify the situation. He is more the salesman than the crafter of artful compromise. His optimism leads him to believe everything will work out for the best, and that the nation has mandated his program. This attitude apparently worked well, at least until 1986, when scandal hit the Reagan White House. The people have rated Reagan positively, even when troubled by his conservative philosophy, but the Iranian scandal caused them to reevaluate his personality, as Reagan was slow to recognize the extent of the problem within his White House.

The ideal president would be one who accepted a democratic style of authority and who exhibited the characteristics of flexibility, tolerance, openness, and persuasiveness. Such a person could accept the idea "that all major policy decisions would be taken openly as shared decisions across President and Congress and that decisions reached through open process of conflict, bargaining, and compromise are likely to be better in quality and more long lasting in their acceptance than those reached in secrecy."[39] We are not, Hargrove argues, yet able to build a comprehensive typology of presidential personalities, but we can note the harmful effects of *active-negatives* on the erosion of democratic norms of government, and we can see, in general, the criteria needed for a democratic style of authority. Hargrove identifies three requisite qualities:

1. An active, affirmative attitude toward themselves, their work, and life
2. Evidence that the individual can work in an immediate environment that reflects the norms of equality, respect for a diversity of views, and willingness to face unpleasant truths
3. Standard political skills to speak, to persuade, to maneuver and manipulate, to structure situations, and to secure agreement in the face of conflict[40]

If there are a multitude and complexity of issues that tempt our presidents, Bruce Buchanan points out that the office of president has self-destructive tendencies within it. Presidents must contend with forces beyond their control. Buchanan notes, "The environment delivers the agenda and compels attention to the agenda as delivered."[41] The result is that presidents are conditioned by the force and repetition of four compelling psychological encounters—*stress* as a consequence of crisis management, exposure to *deference* as a quality of face-to-face encounters, *dissonance* in translating political promises and preferences into public policy, and *frustration* at meeting resistance to their leadership and policy plans (Figure 10.3).[42]

The consequences of these psychological forces are to impair any president's ability to perform effectively and to place a premium on presidential personality. For, as Buchanan notes, the thrust of the exposures on presidents is to "(1) deplete their physical and emotional energy; (2) nur-

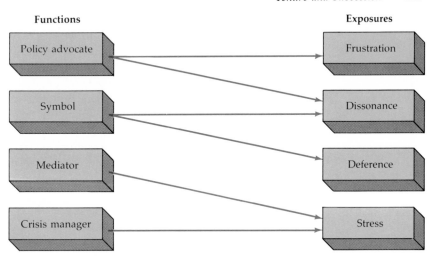

Figure 10.3   Functions of the presidency and resulting exposures

ture systematic distortions in the accuracy with which they perceive themselves and external events; (3) encourage the use of duplicity as an expedient political resource; and (4) erode any values or scruples that interfere with the preservation of presidential power."[43] It is, therefore, all the more necessary that we come to understand more fully presidential personality and to elect presidents who have a democratic style of authority.

Tenure and Succession

Tenure

A president, unlike a prime minister, is not selected by a legislature. The president derives the powers of the office from the Constitution; the Constitution also fixes the length of the term. This basic fact is the source of great presidential power: an American president is not obligated to the legislature for his office. **Tenure** of office is the source of power.

Tenure: the separate and independent election of the president to a specified term of office with the possibility of reelection to a second four-year term in office.

The Founding Fathers worried about the president's term of office and his eligibility for reelection. They wanted an independent executive, but not a dominant authority. The framers debated a term of seven years with no eligibility for reelection, then a term of six years, and finally the four-year term. The single, longer term of office appeared safest if Congress chose the president, as many delegates preferred. Once the electoral college was agreed upon, however, the limit on eligibility for reelection became superfluous, and the Founders quickly decided on a four-year term.

The two-term presidency soon became a tradition. The Founders were confident that George Washington would be the first president and would serve for the remainder of his years. At the end of his second term, however, Washington declined to be reelected: two terms had been enough. And for half a century, no succeeding president seriously challenged this tradition. Only one president, Franklin D. Roosevelt, served more than two terms, although several presidents in the latter half of the nineteenth century toyed with the prospect of a third term. In fact, in 1875 the possibility loomed large that Ulysses S. Grant would seek a third term. This moved the House of Representatives to pass a resolution suggesting that departure from the two-term tradition would be "unwise, unpatriotic and fraught with peril to our free institutions."[44]

In 1951, the Twenty-second Amendment to the Constitution did what the House of Representatives thought wise in 1875; it limited the presidency to two terms. No longer may a person be elected to the office of the president more than twice. And for those persons succeeding to the presidency during a term of office, such as Lyndon Johnson or Gerald Ford, no person "who has held the office of President, or acted as President, for more than two years of a term to which some other person was elected President shall be elected to the office of President more than once." Critics think the amendment unwise and undemocratic, arguing that it places too much restraint on executive authority and robs the country of good leadership. On the other side is the argument that a two-term limitation heightens and accelerates presidential power. Knowing that they have but eight years, presidents must move quickly and decisively to implement policy. Democratic representation is actually maximized by a president faced with a limited term.

Succession

Article II of the Constitution provides for the vice-president to succeed to the office of president in case the president is removed, dies, resigns, or becomes disabled. But the Constitution leaves it to Congress to provide for succession in the event that both president and vice-president are unable to discharge the duties of the office. Congress has three times enacted legislation for presidential succession. The last, in 1947, provides that in the event both president and vice-president are unable to discharge the duties of president, the office will devolve first on the Speaker of the House, then on the president pro tempore of the Senate, followed by the cabinet members in the order of their establishment. (The first law in 1792 was similar but placed the president pro tem of the Senate first in line; an 1886 law provided for cabinet succession, beginning with the secretary of state and continuing through the cabinet in order of establishment.) The Twenty-fifth Amendment, passed in 1967, sought to minimize the likelihood of such a double vacancy. It provides that the president, upon a vacancy in the office of the vice-president, nominates a vice-president who will take office upon confirmation by a majority vote of both houses of Congress.

The Twenty-fifth Amendment was used in 1973. Vice-President Agnew resigned after pleading guilty to charges of income tax evasion. President Nixon then nominated Gerald Ford, a popular legislative leader, to be vice-president. He was quickly confirmed. In 1974, President Nixon himself resigned rather than face impeachment proceedings. Ford assumed the presidency and again, under the Twenty-fifth Amendment, with the vice-presidency vacant, nominated Nelson Rockefeller as vice-president. With his confirmation, the nation had a president and vice-president who had both achieved their offices through the Twenty-fifth Amendment. Neither had been elected; there was no vote of the people and would not be until 1976.

Disability

The Twenty-fifth Amendment also makes provision for presidential disability. Several times in this century presidents have become disabled, but before the amendment was enacted there were no provisions for anyone else to assume the duties of the office. Woodrow Wilson was severely incapacitated by a stroke in 1919; Franklin Delano Roosevelt was confined to a wheelchair for the final days of his tenure as president; and President Eisenhower suffered several heart attacks while president. Public concern for the affairs of the office finally culminated in the passage of the Twenty-fifth Amendment.

This amendment allows presidents to declare their disability by so informing the president pro tempore of the Senate and the Speaker of the House. In such a case, the vice-president becomes the acting president. Presidents may resume their duties at any time by declaring to the same two officers of the Senate and House that they are able. The amendment also provides for a president to be declared disabled. The vice-president and a second body—a majority of the cabinet or other body as Congress may provide—may declare the president disabled and unable to discharge the duties of the office. The written declaration is transmitted to the president pro tempore of the Senate and the Speaker of the House, and the vice-president immediately assumes all the power and duties of the office as acting president. The president may resume office with a written declaration that no disability exists; unless the vice-president and the other body object, the president resumes full power and responsibility. If there is disagreement over a continuing disability, the Twenty-fifth Amendment states that Congress, by a two-thirds vote of both houses, shall determine who shall discharge the duties of the office of president—the president or the vice-president as acting president.

Ronald Reagan, once wounded in an attempted assassination and twice operated on for cancer, has refused to invoke the Twenty-fifth Amendment. Instead he directed, in a letter to Congress, that Vice-President Bush discharge the powers and duties of the office until he directed otherwise. Reagan claimed the Twenty-fifth Amendment did not apply to such brief and temporary periods of incapacity.

President Reagan did not invoke the Twenty-fifth Amendment during his bout with cancer; here, he looks fit after surgery.

TABLE 10.8   Presidents who have died while in office

William Henry Harrison	1841	
Zachary Taylor	1850	
Abraham Lincoln	1865	Assassination
James A. Garfield	1881	Assassination
William McKinley	1901	Assassination
Warren G. Harding	1923	
Franklin Delano Roosevelt	1945	
John F. Kennedy	1963	Assassination

Richard Nixon resigned from the presidency rather than face impeachment proceedings in the Senate.

Impeachment: *the constitutional provision for removing justices or a president from office. The House of Representatives is empowered to impeach (bring charges against), and the Senate, with the chief justice of the Supreme Court presiding, tries the case.*

Terminating Tenure

There are three ways a president's tenure may be terminated other than electoral defeat at the polls: death, resignation, and impeachment.

Death   Eight presidents have died in office—four of them victims of assassinations (Table 10.8).

Resignation   Only one president, Richard Nixon, has ever resigned from office, although Woodrow Wilson apparently seriously contemplated resigning. By resigning, Nixon was able to retain the benefits extended to all former presidents, namely pension, staff assistance, and secret service protection.

Impeachment   The nation has twice moved to remove a president by impeachment—Andrew Johnson in the wake of the Civil War and Richard Nixon for the abuses of Watergate.

The Constitution provides that a president may be removed from office for "treason, bribery, or other high crimes and misdemeanors." Under Article II, which lays out the criteria, the House of Representatives is empowered to impeach the president, and the Senate, with the chief justice of the Supreme Court presiding, removes him. A two-thirds vote of the Senate is necessary for conviction and removal from office. Technically, Andrew Johnson was impeached—the House of Representatives voted eleven articles of impeachment for trial in the Senate. But fortunately for Johnson, the Senate failed to convict by a single vote.

The hue and cry over Andrew Johnson was caused by his firing of his secretary of war, Edwin Stanton. This violated the Tenure of Office Act, which required that officers appointed with the advice and consent of the Senate be removed only with the consent of the Senate.[45] With Richard Nixon, impeachment centered directly on "high crimes and misdemeanors."[46]

President Nixon took the position that a president could be impeached only for specific, indictable criminal acts that were of a "very serious nature" and committed in his official capacity as president. This narrow definition, of course, overlooked the Andrew Johnson precedent, which had been blatantly political. Research suggested that political wrongdoing could be an impeachable offense. Ironically, Gerald Ford, vice-president under Nixon, was cited when, as a congressman, he said that

Agencies are sensitive to public opinion; bureaucrats are aware of the public mood and bewildered by it. Many agencies employ public information specialists to promote communication and good relations between the agency and the public. They know the decline in trust and confidence is affecting their ability to do their jobs well.

Interest Groups

Much of the apparent criticism of bureaucracy is rooted in the close affinity between agencies and the groups they serve. The public believes that special interest groups enjoy particular favor with government. Bureaucrats, however, understand that stable political power depends upon building and serving a constituent interest group.

Interest groups and bureaucratic agencies form strong alliances. Often an agency is created to serve a special constituency—the Department of Labor or the Environmental Protection Agency, for example. Interest groups prefer to present their problems to a specific agency charged with monitoring their interests. The sense of shared mutual interest between agency and interest group adds strong emotional and moral overtones to public policy. This was clearly the case when President Nixon sought to abolish the Office of Economic Opportunity by withholding funding for the agency. The agency saw itself as an advocate for disadvantaged groups, and it went to court to have the impounded funds released. Philip Selznick's classic study of the TVA revealed the extent to which a public agency would modify its original objectives in order to gain the support of interest groups in the area it served.[12] The TVA was willing to give up some autonomy in policymaking to buy the support of important local interests. In this way the agency gained an important lobby in support of its primary mission: expanding electric power in the Tennessee Valley.

The strongest alliance is at the middle level of the bureaucracy, where bureau chiefs dominate. Far enough removed from presidential politics, bureau chiefs bargain for political autonomy and power. They are long-term career administrators who develop keen perceptions of the politics within an agency, the groups with which they interact, and the strategic value of issues. Frequently it is to the administrator's advantage to form an alliance with **clientele groups.**[13] What has been called the **iron triangle** of politics—a three-sided symbiotic relationship of bureau chief, clientele group, and congressional committee or subcommittee—establishes a continual policy process with the bureaucracy at the heart of the decision-making process. There are advantages for the agency administrator, since "his organizational independence from both Congressional and Presidential directives is often directly related to his degree of dependence on the interest group clientele that benefits from his decisions. Clientele groups can also increase their bureau's clout with Congress, run interference with OMB for its policy interests, rally public opinion behind agency programs, and affect the chances for successful implementation of programs."[14]

The space shuttle *Challenger* was successfully launched in June, 1983. Among the crew was Sally Ride, the first American woman astronaut to work in space.

Iron Triangle: *a three-sided symbiotic relationship among bureau chiefs, clientele groups, and congressional committees and subcommittees. The iron triangle establishes a continual policy process with the bureaucracy at the heart of the decision-making process.*

Clientele Group: *the natural constituency or consumers of specific government services. The clientele relationship with bureaucratic agencies is a prime source of political power.*

Changing Consensus: Nuclear Power

For much of the twentieth century, Americans took the availability of energy for granted. The attitude of "use a lot, pay a little" prevailed. The people were told that electricity was dirt cheap; big cars with high horsepower were a sign of status. Depletion of natural resources was not a serious concern, nor was the prospect of a foreign embargo on oil. But with the 1970s those attitudes changed, and changed dramatically. Domestic production of oil and gas began to decline in the early 1970s; the 1973 OPEC embargo quadrupled the price of oil. Suddenly Americans realized their dependence on energy and that they would have to pay a more realistic price for it.

Nuclear power as a source of energy was not a serious concern until the 1973 oil embargo. Some had argued in 1954 for the public production of nuclear electricity, but the decision was to leave energy production to private industry. Nuclear power produced only a small fraction of our energy through 1970 (and for that matter, remains relatively unimportant compared to other energy sources).

Energy consumption by source (percent of total)

	1960	1970	1975	1980	1984
Petroleum	45.4	44.4	46.3	45.0	42.1
Natural gas	28.3	32.8	28.2	26.8	24.4
Coal	22.4	18.5	18.0	20.3	23.3
Nuclear power	—	0.3	2.7	3.6	4.7
Hydropower	3.9	4.1	4.5	4.1	5.2
Other	—	—	0.1	0.1	0.3

But since the Arab embargo elevated the cost of oil, utility firms have been looking more and more to nuclear power to produce electricity, and the concern over nuclear power has consequently grown. The number of nuclear power plants has risen dramatically since 1970, as has the amount of electricity generated by nuclear power plants. And with this increase in nuclear power generation comes a series of new and difficult questions, graphically dramatized in 1986 by the Soviet accident at Chernobyl.

	1965	1970	1975	1980	1984
Operable nuclear power plants	10	19	54	70	86
Percent of electricity generated	.4	1.4	9.0	11.0	13.6

The Chernobyl disaster realized the worst possibilities of nuclear power. The reactor core overheated, setting off a violent explosion that spewed radioactive material into the atmosphere. The intense heat of the fuel rods in the reactor core started a 4000°F fire that burned into the foundation of the reactor. Many feared a "China Syndrome," in which the core would burn through the reactor, into the ground, and deep into the earth, contaminating soil, water, and everything surrounding it. Fortunately this did not happen, but the possibility of catastrophe was all too real.

Could the same thing happen in the United States? Experts doubt it, but no one is sure. The U.S. has had four serious nuclear accidents, the worst of which occurred at Three Mile Island in Pennsylvania in March 1979. In that accident a valve malfunctioned and caused a partial core meltdown, allowing radioactive steam to escape into the atmosphere. Since then new safety procedures have been initiated, largely as a result of the TMI accident. But as the Nuclear Regulatory Commission noted, "In a population of 100 reactors, operating over a period of 20 years, the crude cumulative probability of a severe accident would be 45 percent."[15]

Another problem with nuclear power is disposal of radioactive nuclear wastes. No permanent disposal sites yet exist. The government is responsible for waste disposal, but has a poor record of waste management. There have been numerous leaks, causing soil and water contamination. The history of the problem is so colored that renewed efforts in the 1980s to find permanent waste disposal sites angered state and local political officials and citizens alike. They are skeptical that safe disposal techniques can be developed.

Finally, there is the question of cost. Nuclear power plants are expensive and are almost never constructed at the projected cost. The Department of Energy reported that costs for nuclear power plants were at least double those of preconstruction estimates at 77 percent of power plants, and at 28 percent of the power plants the real cost was four times the original estimate. These costs are passed on to consumers in the form of higher utility bills once the plants become operational. Many consumers and environmentalists wonder if this form of power is worth the risks and the money.

Failsafe nuclear energy is an unlikely prospect. What Americans must decide is how much energy they need, from what sources they want it, and how much they are willing to pay for it. Three Mile Island and Chernobyl teach us the danger of nuclear power, but they also provide opportunities to learn from our mistakes and make nuclear energy safer.

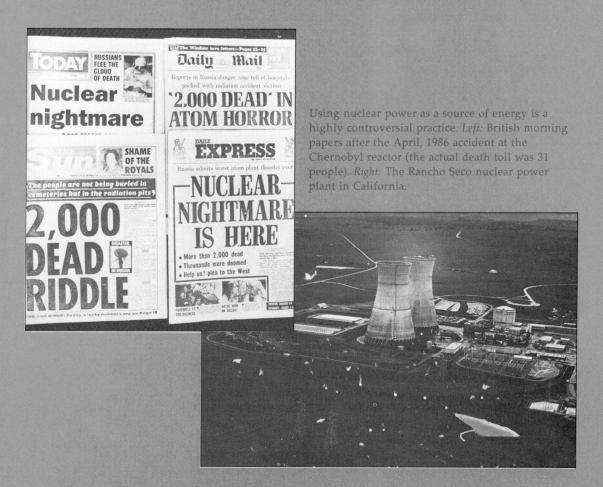

Using nuclear power as a source of energy is a highly controversial practice. *Left:* British morning papers after the April, 1986 accident at the Chernobyl reactor (the actual death toll was 31 people). *Right:* The Rancho Seco nuclear power plant in California.

In general, the clientele relationship with bureaucratic agencies is a prime source of access for interest groups. A bureau's clientele support can vary widely; not all bureaus have natural constituencies. Groups vary in size, cohesiveness, purpose, and popular support. The more a bureau builds political support among groups and maintains a favorable image within its clientele, the greater its political power will be.

Congress

Congress and the bureaucracy interact constantly (Figure 11.3): what Congress created, it feels free to review and oversee. Congress monitors implementation for several reasons: (1) it is congressional law that bureaucrats administer; (2) it is money appropriated by Congress that is spent; and (3) it is the representatives' constituents who are affected.

Agencies generally establish cordial relationships with congressional committees, particularly committee and subcommittee chairs. For exam-

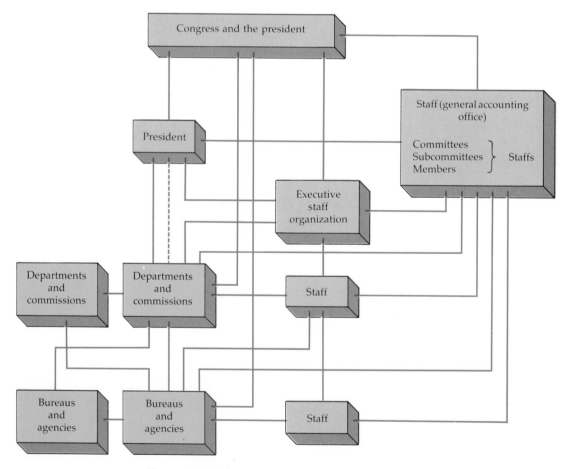

Figure 11.3   Administrative activity in Washington, D.C.

ple, for years branches of the military could count on southern Democrats holding powerful seats on appropriations and armed services committees to fund their budgets or restore money taken out by the administration. Cordial relationships are also important for representatives. Constituent service is a major element in survival, and this means going to the bureaucracy for help and answers. A prompt and satisfactory response is of value to the member of Congress.

A congressional presence in administration is also becoming more common. As more and more discretionary powers are delegated to the bureaucracy, congressional committees review and monitor the exercise of those powers. Oversight also provides evidence that Congress is "on the job," watching out for the taxpayer. Generally this is a mutually rewarding opportunity for both representative and administrator, as each seeks to extend his or her sphere of influence with the other.

This natural tendency to build reliable political support in Congress is most evident in the appropriations process. Agencies seek to maximize their budget requests. The stronger the relationship with Congress, the greater is the chance that agencies will get what they requested or, conversely, the smaller the cut. Agencies that produce tangible results—particularly when constituents benefit—have the strongest support with Congress and are more likely to be funded regardless of the president's budget. Congress frequently looks to agencies for support in congressional battles with the executive, and those agencies that provide support fare better at the hands of Congress than at those of OMB or the president.

The Executive Branch

The bureaucracy is part of the executive branch, although sometimes only nominally so; presidents exercise control over the bureaucracy only sporadically and then often with odd results. Presidents usually express frustration with their attempts to manage the bureaucracy and turn to other activities that are more pressing and more personally rewarding. But the attempts at control continue.

One major means of exercising control over the bureaucracy is executive reorganization. After World War II, the Hoover Commission on Organization of the Executive Branch recommended simplifying government and concentrating more power in central authority. President Nixon suggested a radical reorganization of cabinet-level departments to give him more control and provide for rational organization based on pressing problems. The proposal was a victim of Watergate. President Carter was also intent on reorganization. He streamlined the White House staff, made reforms in the civil service system, and added a department of education. President Reagan, for his part, has sought to eliminate two cabinet-level departments—education and energy—and to distribute their functions over other cabinet departments. Abolishing the Department of Energy has been a long-standing promise of President Reagan.

His intention is to put strategic petroleum reserves under the Interior Department and send DoE's lawyers over to the Justice Department.

The president's major resource in controlling the bureaucracy is the Office of Management and Budget. As noted in Chapter 10, this office is responsible for preparing the budget, monitoring spending, and recommending managerial efficiency. The president can tighten control by having OMB require agencies to submit budget requests for review. OMB then screens all requests before putting them together for the president to submit in the annual budget. Because of its ability to impose sanctions, OMB is a powerful tool for rewarding or punishing agencies for conforming or failing to conform to presidential directives.

The White House staff is a valuable asset for the president. It provides information unaffected by the politics and intrigues of agency affairs. But presidential staff may also meddle in agency affairs, as in the case of Watergate. On balance, however, the White House staff is an important

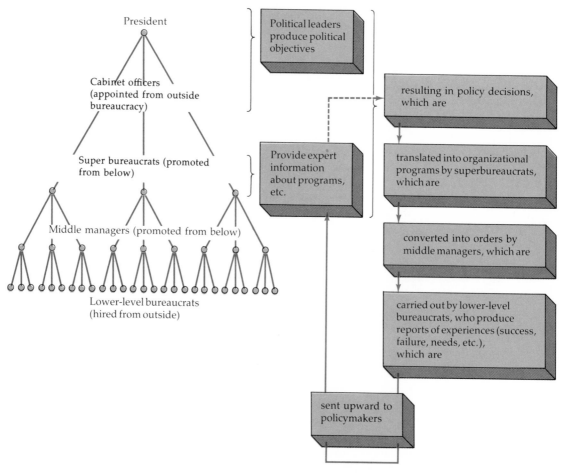

Figure 11.4 The flow of bureaucratic activity

source of information and ideas for any president seeking to move the bureaucracy.

Bureaucrats find little joy in presidential politics. Too often, presidents seek personal goals in administrative control and pay little attention to administrative procedures within agencies. Cabinet secretaries must balance presidential priorities and agency politics; they cannot advocate a departmental mission to a president whose priorities are turned in another direction, yet they must maintain morale and provide leadership. Agencies see top-level bureaucrats as unsympathetic and unknowledgeable about the problems of administration. Consequently, the bureaucrats turn to Congress, the interest group, or the public for support and rewards (Figure 11.4).

There are considerable restraints on presidential control. First, any president can devote only limited time to administration. Other roles with higher political priority demand attention. Moreover, most chief executives are not adept at management; they have neither a background nor an interest in administration. And a lack of information keeps the president and White House staff from exercising real control. The size and complexity of bureaucracy generally make adequate or timely information unavailable. Finally, the president must compete with other interested parties, Congress, and constituents for influence. These competitors can work to thwart presidential directives. Congress pulls the purse strings, and clients may rally public support and create a climate of expectations. This was the case with President Carter's civil service reorganization, when veterans groups resisted abolishing preferences for veterans in employment. As government becomes more complex and multifunctional with the inclusion of regulatory responsibilities, the decision-making power of the bureaucracy is increased. We turn now to a survey of important patterns in bureaucratic decision making: rule making, rule adjudication, law enforcement, implementation, and policy initiation.

Decision-Making Patterns

Rule Making

Rule Making: *the quasi-legislative function whereby bureaucratic rules have the force of law. Rule making is a prime responsibility of independent regulatory agencies.*

The addition of regulatory responsibility in the twentieth century greatly increased the bureaucracy's power of **rule making**—a quasi-legislative function yielding agency rules that have the force of law. Agency lawmaking spells out the public policy Congress has enacted in broad outline. Affected parties must be notified of possible rules, hearings must be held so the parties may voice their objections, and the final rules must be published in the *Federal Register*. At this writing, seventeen pages of agency rules are published each year for every page of statute law.[16] Critics contend that agency rule making has reversed the constitutional order of checks and balances. Congress is to legislate, the executive to veto and administer. Now, critics argue, Congress has deferred to the bureaucracy.

The Federal Register
All agencies, including the presidency, must give advance notice for all proposed rules and regulations or reorganization plans. These are printed in the *Federal Register,* which is therefore one of the most carefully read publications in Washington. Required to be printed in the *Federal Register* are the following: (1) presidential proclamations, executive orders and reorganization plans; (2) agency statements on their organization, authority, method of operation, and general policies; and (3) proposed rules and regulations and administrative orders from administrative agencies. The *Register* is published every working day by the U.S. government and totals approximately 60,000 pages annually.

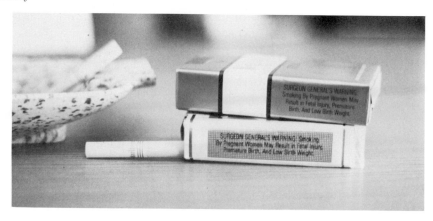

The rule-making responsibilities of bureaucratic agencies are typified by the surgeon general's warnings on all cigarette packages.

Rule making is a prime responsibility of independent regulatory agencies such as the ICC or FTC, but today all executive agencies make rules. Two examples will illustrate the importance of agency rule making. In 1964, after the surgeon general's report linked cancer to cigarette smoking, the Federal Trade Commission published rules requiring tobacco companies to warn consumers of the health hazards of smoking. The FTC proposed a limit on commercial advertising and a requirement that warning labels be placed on cigarette packages. The tobacco industry rallied and succeeded in lobbying Congress to modify and weaken the proposed rules, which went into effect in 1965. In 1974, the Office of Civil Rights of the Department of Health, Education and Welfare gave notice of proposed rules prohibiting sex discrimination in education for the Title IX provision of the 1972 Educational Amendments. The proposed regulations were to terminate federal financial assistance to educational institutions that discriminated on the basis of sex. The rules covered educational programs, housing, employment, admission, and athletics for elementary, secondary, and higher education. It was in college athletics that the greatest controversy emerged. The proposals required that women's teams would be funded on an equal-opportunity basis. Title IX rules are now law and facilitate greater educational opportunities for women.

Rule Adjudication:
the power of bureaucratic agencies to administer laws by charging persons or organizations suspected of violating rules. They can then apply administrative sanctions to persons or organizations found in violation.

Rule Adjudication

Despite the importance of bureaucratic rule making, many agencies spend a good deal of their efforts in adjudication of rules: agencies administer the laws by charging persons or organizations suspected of violating rules and can apply administrative sanctions to persons or organizations found in violation. Rules of procedure regarding notification, evidence, hearings, fairness, and so on must be followed, but unlike rule making, adjudication applies only to specific parties or classes of people;

it does not establish policy. A widespread practice in bureaucratic agencies, adjudication is a way of enforcing policy by demanding compliance.

The Food and Drug Administration frequently adjudicates when it declares drugs unsafe and bans them from the market. The case of the drug Laetrile is an example: the FDA demanded evidence of this drug's cancer-curing properties before allowing it on the market. The Social Security Administration adjudicates when it passes on disability-insurance eligibility. Adjudication is most controversial in the area of environmental protection. Industrial firms have been required by the EPA to install costly pollution-abatement devices or be fined. Proposed projects can be halted or held up until environmental impact statements are adjudicated; damming the Tennessee River, for example, was delayed due to the discovery of the impact the dam would have on one species of fish.

Law Enforcement

Law enforcement is nothing but the application of law to specific situations. Discretion is always involved: certain laws are more vigorously enforced than others. The applicability of one law over another must be judged in light of the particular situation. Bureaucratic agencies make decisions through selective law enforcement. Several federal agencies—such as the FBI; the Bureau of Alcohol, Tobacco, and Firearms; the Drug Enforcement Administration; and the Immigration and Naturalization Service—have direct law-enforcement responsibilities.

Implementation

Implementation: *the function of bureaucratic agencies involving attempts to put into practice the policies established through legislation or executive order.*

Frequently, when we think of bureaucratic activity, we think of policy implementation: agencies seeking to put into practice policies established through legislation or executive order. The impact of **implementation** can be seen, for example, in the Federal Reserve Board's changing the discount rate or altering the reserve requirement to keep down inflation, or when the Federal Communications Commission decides how many radio and television stations to license in a given city or area. Another good example of discretion in implementation was the Civil Service Commission's decision to force federal agencies to adopt goals and timetables for hiring minorities as a means of implementing the government policy of nondiscrimination and equal opportunity employment. In 1971, this practice amounted to a change in policy. Earlier, "benign" discrimination (the absence of minority employees or applicants) was permitted; now the Civil Service Commission was requiring affirmative action.

Incrementalism: *an approach to policy implementation that involves consideration of only a limited number of alternatives and making only incremental modifications of past government activities.*

One basic issue in policy implementation is whether administrators can use scientific management principles to provide a cost–benefit analysis of program effectiveness. Charles Lindblom has long argued that policymakers actually take an **incremental** approach to policy implementation; that is, bureaucratic momentum produces a sequential process whereby changes in policy occur in small or marginal amounts that do

*G*overnment policy in economic affairs has two principal objectives: (1) promoting, regulating, or controlling particular forms of economic activity; and (2) controlling levels of economic activity to maintain a healthy and stable economy. While debate continues over the level of government activity in the economy, events in the twentieth century have prompted a more favorable public attitude toward increased governmental activity in economics. First, the Great Depression brought massive unemployment and economic stress. Only extensive federal aid brought recovery to the economy. Second, World War II demanded full economic productivity, increased government spending, and, after the war, wage and price controls. Full postwar employment became a chief goal. Third, John Maynard Keynes's *General Theory of Employment, Interest, and Money* was a popular attack on free market economic thinking. He argued that the market was not self-regulating and that full employment and prosperity could require government deficit spending to prime economic growth.

Much of the first objective—promoting, regulating, and controlling economic activity—is designed to promote the free enterprise, market economy. The first legislation, the Sherman Antitrust Act of 1890, made it a crime to restrain trade or destroy competition in interstate commerce. This act was supplemented in 1914 by the Clayton Act, designed to ensure fair trade by preventing price fixing to eliminate competition. Also created that year was the Federal Trade Commission, an independent regulatory agency whose responsibility it was to maintain free economic competition. The government utilizes several means to promote competition and economic activity.* Government may employ direct subsidies to encourage business, as with the railroads in the nineteenth century and merchant-marine shipping in the twentieth. Promotion of business activity may also use tax policy such as exemptions,

deductions, credits, lower rates, or selective government expenditures. Other forms of promotion involve loans, public construction projects such as rivers, harbors, and airports, and technical information services.

Business regulation and control began with the Interstate Commerce Commission in 1887 and expanded broadly in the 1930s under the New Deal. Notably in the areas of minimum wages, food, health, and automobiles, regulatory responsibilities were added to department agencies. That is, industries had obligations and regulations on the way they conducted their business. The most recent regulatory additions are in environmental quality, pollution control, and occupational safety. In areas designated as public utilities, economic activity itself is controlled by government. Briefly, public utility regulation involves government sponsorship through licensure to operate, typically as a monopoly. Then a government regulatory commission is established to oversee and promulgate rules for the utility. Standards of service are erected, including the rates charged for service. The government commission also fixes the rate of profit the business may make.

The second broad objective is to maintain economic stability. Since World War II this has meant full employment and steady economic growth, which are achieved through three basic policies: fiscal, monetary, and income.

Fiscal policy involves the taxing and spending power of the federal government to influence economic activity. To stimulate or slow down the economy, government can vary the rate at which it raises or spends money. Government can hold spending constant and increase or decrease taxes or, conversely, may hold taxes constant and vary the level of spending—deficit spending. There are infinite combinations of both rates of taxing and of spending. The assumption is that more money in the economy stimulates economic activity.

Monetary policy falls under the direction of

the Federal Reserve Board and involves control of the supply of money and credit in the economy. Three basic tools are employed. First, the Federal Reserve Board buys and sells securities on the open market. Buying securities puts additional deposits in member banks, hence allowing them to make loans. Second, the Federal Reserve Board sets the discount rate, which is the interest rate charged by reserve banks to commercial banks borrowing money from them. Higher rates tighten credit and restrict the flow of money. The third tool is the reserve rate, which requires member banks to keep monetary reserves in ratio to their deposits. If the reserve rate is 20 percent, then banks must keep 20 percent of the total of loans in reserve in the bank.

Income policy is a more recent addition to government policy for economic stability, coming after World War II and resurfacing again in early 1971. Essentially, it involves setting wage and price guidelines in order to regulate inflation and economic growth. In 1971 President Nixon imposed mandatory wage and price controls. Ended in 1973, this was an unprecedented peacetime use of controls, which previously had been used only during wartime. President Carter opted for voluntary wage–price guidelines to keep down inflationary economic tendencies.

*J. Anderson, D. Brady, and C. Bullock, *Public Policy and Politics in America*, North Scituate, Mass.: Duxbury Press, 1978, pp. 201–204.

not disturb or reverse the direction of the initial decision implementing a policy.[17] The fact is that we have paid too little attention to implementation as a criterion in policy formulation. Two political scientists, for example, have traced the failure of the human resources training program in one city to inadequate attention given program implementation by Great Society architects in Washington, D.C., when the policy was designed.[18] Effort was made to involve community groups in the decision-making process on spending of federal funds for manpower training. Still, the legislation gave little thought to the "complexity of joint action"—how the groups would come together and agree on the distribution of funds. The result was to set community groups against one another, forcing delays and thereby disrupting program implementation.

Policy Initiation

Policy Initiation: *the suggestion of new policies and programs. It is usually filtered up through an agency to the department secretary and on to the president.*

The final area of decision making for the bureaucracy is policy initiation. Long accepted as part of bureaucratic responsibility, **policy initiation** is the suggesting of new policies and programs. In some ways the president and department secretaries depend on the agencies for recommendations for new policies or policy changes. Often the agency recommendations result from client requests or from promptings by Congress.

The military provides the clearest example of policy initiation; new weapons systems are frequently proposed by branches of the service. Congress often gets into the act because decisions on, say, MIRV missiles or manned bombers affect employment in the states and our defense posture with foreign nations. But other agencies also initiate policy. In 1976, for example, HEW began locating fathers of families on welfare (Aid to Families with Dependent Children). The goal was to force fathers to support their families, thereby reducing welfare costs. Something as major as America's new policy toward China can also result from bureaucratic initiatives. The policy obviously required presidential direction, but the State Department highlighted China's readiness to deal with America through such small initiatives as cultural exchanges, eased trade restrictions, and permits for scholarly and journalistic trips. Such State Department gestures gave Richard Nixon the opportunity to reopen talks with the Chinese and to travel to China. These initiatives, then, played a role in the normalization of relations that produced the new China policy.

Policy initiation can be threatening to agency heads, who are thereby placed in an exposed position and risk rebuke from the president and Congress. Often initiatives are undertaken in clientele-oriented agencies, where a strong constituency can be depended upon for support.

Patterns of Conflict

Bureaucracy is perceived as a monolithic structure, an impenetrable maze. Generalizations regarding bureaucracy and administration presume a unity of purpose and attitude that extends to all employees in all executive agencies. There is a certain anonymity and impersonalization to the federal government.

The picture from within the bureaucracy is markedly different. As in any complex modern organization, real people perform a wide variety of tasks. These people have numerous points of view that can and often do clash. For the serious student of bureaucracy, the stereotype vanishes when the attitudes and behavior of agency personnel are examined. A wide variety of attitudes and responses form patterns of conflict within the bureaucracy.

Democratic Values

We pay great attention to the democratic values of elected officials but very little to the values of the people who administer government programs. If bureaucracy is the fourth branch of government, and the one closest to the public through implementation, then its concern for and commitment to democratic values ought to be of primary concern. This is all the more important because career civil servants are neither elected nor removable by the electoral process.

Bob L. Wynia's study of federal bureaucrats' attitudes toward democracy[19] reached some striking conclusions (see Table 11.4). Surveying the democratic values of more than four hundred federal executives from fifty-two different federal agencies—their views regarding fairness and legal rights, free speech, equality, public interest, and influence—Wynia discovered 60 to 75 percent agreement on items pertaining to democracy. It is significant, however, that approximately one-quarter to one-third did *not* support basic constitutional protections (see Table 11.5). Said Wynia, "While the overall data lend support to the fact that there is extensive agreement with the democratic philosophy within the bureauc-

TABLE 11.4   Bureaucracy agreement with the democratic philosophy

Item	Percentage of bureaucrats who agree with item
There are times when it almost seems better for the people to take the law into their own hands rather than wait for the machinery of government to act.	32
We might as well make up our minds that in order to make the world free a lot of innocent people will have to suffer.	31
We have to teach children that all men are created equal but almost everyone knows that some are better than others.	38
To bring about great changes for the benefit of mankind often requires cruelty and even ruthlessness.	27
The true American way of life is disappearing so fast that we may have to use force to save it.	19

TABLE 11.5　Bureaucratic agreement with application of democratic values

| | | Percentage of agrees | | | | | | | | | |
| | | Agency | | | Years of education | | | Years in service | | | |
Item	Average	Social	Dept. of Defense	Other	0–12	13–15	16+	1–5	6–15	16–25	26+
When the country is in great danger, we may have to force people to testify against themselves even if it violates their rights.	24.6	25.3	30.9	20.4	25.6	26.3	22.5	15.2	23.3	24.6	28.8
Any person who hides behind the laws when he is questioned about his activities doesn't deserve much consideration.	24.8	19.0	29.3	24.4	41.0	26.6	19.1	12.1	16.5	24.6	37.5
We have to teach children that all men are created equal, but almost everyone knows that some are better than others.		34.6	43.9	34.7							
Just as is true of fine race horses, some breeds of people are just naturally better than others.		19.5	28.5	17.3							
Regardless of what some people say, there are certain races in the world that just won't mix with Americans.		13.3	26.0	13.8							

SOURCE: Bob Wynia, "Federal Bureaucrats' Attitudes Toward a Democratic Ideology." Reprinted from *Public Administration Review* 34 (March/April 1974). Copyright © 1974 by the American Society for Public Administration, 1225 Connecticut Ave., N.W., Washington, D.C. All rights reserved.

racy, there are many areas of grave and undisputed disagreement on specific applications of democratic principles."[20] When Wynia compared agencies, education of bureaucrats, and years of service, a different picture emerged. Defense agencies tended to draw more "undemocratic types," individuals inclined toward the use of force and toward justifying unfairness in the name of some greater purpose. These people scored lowest on equality: "Defense agency executives, for whatever reasons, consistently demonstrate attitudes of an antidemocratic nature, whenever the issue of racial or social equality is raised."[21]

Years in service and years of education also seemed to be critical variables in attitude determination and change. Wynia discovered that the less education federal executives had, the more antidemocratic were their attitudes. Formal education apparently is positively correlated with acceptance of basic political and constitutional values of human equality, freedom of speech, and a democratic decision-making process. Also, the longer one had spent in federal service, the lower was the acceptance of a democratic ideology. It is disturbing to note that the "bureaucratic environment" is not conducive to democratic values. The longer one serves in federal agencies, the more one's democratic commitment is eroded.

The results of Wynia's study are not altogether encouraging. If we say that bureaucrats have a major responsibility regarding public policy, then their commitment to democratic values is of some importance. They keep the system going, and they are responsible for keeping it open, responsive to needs, and sensitive to the public.

Change of Administration

Every four to eight years there is a change in administration. New programs are introduced; priorities change. Elected presidents and political appointees have only a limited time in which to implement their policies. They must contend with a career civil service that is not always loyal or sympathetic to a new administration. Richard Nixon took office in 1969 after a decade of Democratic administrations. His administration reflected a high level of mistrust of the career bureaucracy; in short, he and his staff felt that the career civil service was stacked against the administration. A manual for political appointees in the Nixon administration stated, "Because of the rape of the career service by the Kennedy and Johnson Administration . . . this Administration has been left a legacy of finding disloyalty and obstruction at high levels while those incumbents rest comfortably on career civil service status."[22]

Do new administrations face a hostile environment? an unsympathetic and disloyal bureaucracy? Two political scientists set out to discover whether Richard Nixon's feeling was warranted. In general, they found that it was. A disproportionate number of Democrats filled key domestic agencies (HEW, HUD, and OEO) and directed social services toward partisan constituencies. Moreover, the beliefs of personnel within such agencies were in conflict with the policies of the incoming Nixon administration. Stated Aberbach and Rockman,

> Our findings document a career bureaucracy with very little Republican representation but even more pointedly portray a social service bureaucracy dominated by administrators ideologically hostile to many of the directions pursued by the Nixon Administration in the realm of social policy. Democratic administrators in the social service agencies were the most hostile to these directions, but even Republican administrators in these same agencies . . . held attitudes that were not wholly sympathetic to the social service retrenchments sought by the Nixon Administration.[23]

Presidential policies are aimed at short-term political goals; bureaucracies are relatively immune from such time pressures. A time lag also thwarts any new administration; it takes a while to change top personnel and get new policies going. And of course any expectation of retrenchment and cost cutting will meet with bureaucratic resistance.

Reform and Responsibility

At this point, there is a consensus that the bureaucracy needs reform. Conservatives and liberals alike agree that there is too much government.

Presidents have found their goals resisted by an unsympathetic bureaucracy, and citizens feel intimidated by the host of incomprehensible rules and regulations costing them tax dollars. Reforming the bureaucracy is a high priority in American politics. Recent presidents have been active in suggesting reform measures, thus contributing to the changing climate of attitudes toward the bureaucracy. Richard Nixon reformed the old Bureau of the Budget into the Office of Management and Budget; he created the Domestic Council, by which the White House staff could plan and coordinate domestic policy in the same way in which national security policy was coordinated. Jimmy Carter added two cabinet departments, energy and education, and pushed through civil service reform. Ronald Reagan too pledged reorganization by scaling back on the size of the bureaucracy as well as simplifying procedures and requiring less paperwork.

Responsible Bureaucrats

Since the 1960s many new social regulatory agencies have been established. This has created new rules and regulations as well as reporting requirements and paperwork. Critics charge that bureaucrats in such agencies take a hostile, adversarial attitude toward the industries they regulate. The result has been not only more government but different government as well. This picture, however, is not very accurate, according to Stanley Rothman and S. Robert Lichter. They did a survey of 200 top-level administrators from both "established traditional agencies" (departments of commerce, agriculture, and the treasury, and the Bureau of Prisons in the Department of Justice) and "activist agencies" (Environmental Protection Agency, Federal Trade Commission, Action, Consumer Product Safety Commission, Equal Employment Opportunity Commission, Food and Drug Administration, Department of Health and Human Services, Department of Housing and Urban Development, and the Justice Department's Civil Rights Division).[24] They found little evidence to support charges of a hostile bureaucracy, and concluded that "senior civil servants as a whole are indeed somewhat more liberal than most Americans. However, they are considerably less disaffected from traditional American values than their conservative critics contend. Moreover, while key bureaucrats in the activist agencies are somewhat more liberal than those in the traditional agencies, the differences are not large enough to explain the 'adversarial' behavior of which businessmen complain."[25] On most issues senior administrators were more liberal than the general public, activist bureaucrats to a greater degree than traditional bureaucrats (63 percent to 48 percent for traditional bureaucrats; approximately 21 percent of the general public have liberal attitudes). The bureaucrats tended to vote Democratic more frequently than the general public. They also expressed deep and fundamental commitment to the political system. They support private enterprise and believe it to be basically fair; they are not hostile to efforts at deregulation. On almost all questions, bureaucrats were considerably more supportive of American society than are leading journalists, public interest group activists, or the Hollywood elite. Concluded Rothman and Lichter, "They [bureaucrats] come across to us as liberal and reformist, but not alienated from American society and not particularly hostile to business. In general, they describe themselves as desiring to improve the system rather than to change it in fundamental ways."[26]

Civil Service Reform

Civil service reform was Carter's most significant bureaucratic reform. Passed by Congress in October 1978, the Civil Service Reform Act became law with Carter's signature. According to its provisions, the Civil Service Commission was abolished and replaced with two new agencies: the Office of Personnel Management (OPM) and a Merit Systems Protection Board (MSPB), which became the new board of appeals for employee grievances.

The thrust of the reform is to evaluate bureaucrats and reward them for their productivity. Managers and supervisors at GS 13 through GS 15 levels are no longer given automatic pay increases each year; rather, merit pay is offered these employees based upon an evaluation of their performance. (Table 11.6 presents federal salary levels.) The system is designed to stimulate better performance and greatly increase the ability

TABLE 11.6   Federal salary levels

GS 1	$ 9,339–11,686
GS 2	10,501–13,216
GS 3	11,458–14,896
GS 4	12,862–16,723
GS 5	14,390–18,710
GS 6	16,040–20,855
GS 7	17,824–23,170
GS 8	19,740–25,662
GS 9	21,804–28,347
GS 10	24,011–31,211
GS 11	26,381–34,292
GS 12	31,619–41,105
GS 13	37,599–48,876
GS 14	44,430–57,759
GS 15	52,262–67,940
GS 16	61,296
GS 17	71,804[a]
GS 18	84,157[a]
Executive Schedule	
ES 1	$61,296
ES 2	63,764
ES 3	66,232
ES 4	68,700
ES 5	70,500
ES 6	72,300

[a]Limited to $68,700, rate for level 4 of Executive Schedule.
SOURCE: Office of Personnel Management, Salary Table No. 70, December 1984.

of cabinet secretaries and other political appointees to manage their agencies by putting together a management team from the top grades of career civil servants.

Senior Executive Service: *a cadre of senior, experienced bureaucrats who form management teams and move among agencies to help administer difficult programs.*

The reform created a new **Senior Executive Service,** which Jule Sugarman, vice-chairman of the Civil Service Commission, claims is composed of "the most experienced people in government, and collectively they make 90 percent of the decisions in the executive branch—maybe more."[27] This cadre of 9,200 top federal executives can be moved in and out of agencies as "management teams." They are evaluated annually by administrators and can be demoted in grade with no appeal if their performance is unsatisfactory. SES employees are ineligible for automatic, annual pay raises, but are rewarded by a bonus system for high performance on the job.

Critics of the reform fear political intrusion and partisan politics—exactly what the civil service was designed to avoid. They fear that management teams will become political units formed to implement presidential policies.

Rational Decision Making

Although reorganization has been a favored technique for reforming the bureaucracy, in recent years numerous other techniques have been developed to permit more intelligent decisions and the assessment of agency performance. Often referred to as rational decision making, these approaches attempt to make greater use of quantitative data to break out of the incremental mold of decision making. Such techniques borrow heavily from private industry practices. By using system and cost–benefit analysis, it is expected that more efficient management of agency resources will heighten rational control over public policy and increase economy in government. The goal of rational decision making is to make it possible to arrive at decisions on the basis of hard, scientific data analysis rather than on hunches formed out of past experience.

The new methods were first introduced into the federal government by Defense Secretary Robert McNamara in 1961. In an effort to systematize military decision making in the Pentagon, McNamara inaugurated new management tools utilizing computers and quantifiable objectives. The goal was to gain control over the vast sums of money being expended to achieve national defense objectives. The new techniques culminated in a comprehensive budget process called **Planning, Programming, Budgeting System (PPBS).** This process required defense agencies to identify their policy objectives, design programs and alternatives to meet those objectives, and measure the costs for the resources needed. The use of quantified data would allow policymakers to achieve objectives at the lowest cost. The results were less than encouraging. Most federal agencies were not equipped to measure the "cost effectiveness" of policies. They lacked personnel skilled in the technique. Agencies were also threatened by the perceived control over agency budgets. A mass of

Planning, Programming, Budgeting System (PPBS): *a comprehensive budget process that requires federal departments to define their goals precisely and to measure the costs and benefits of alternative programs to achieve those goals.*

Practicing Politics: How to Gain Access to Government

The federal bureaucracy is huge and sometimes impossible to penetrate. Here are three sources, found in your local or university library, that can help you begin if you have a problem or want to influence the decisions of an agency.

1. *The Encyclopedia of U.S. Government Benefits* (Union City, N.J.: W. H. Wise, 1971, 1978) tells you how to get small business loans, home mortgages, scholarships, farm loans, veterans' benefits, grants, surplus products, government publications, and valuable free information.

2. Ralph Nader's Center for the Study of Responsive Law has produced a manual for citizen access to federal agencies called *Working on the System* (published by Basic Books). It is organized by federal agency and gives information sources, agency activities, rules of the game, and how to gain access and participate.

3. *Protecting Your Right to Privacy: A Digest of Systems of Records, Agency Rules, and Research Aids* (New York: Basic Books, 1974) has been published by the government to help implement the Privacy Act passed in December 1974. It tells you how to find out what, if any, information an agency has about you, who else has regular access, how to have errors corrected, and how to get a copy of your records.

Don't forget your representatives in Congress! Congressional offices are prepared to aid constituents with problems in the bureaucracy. Casework on behalf of constituents is a major function of congressional staff, and they are good at it. They *do* help citizens who have problems with the government. You can also approach one of the many organizations devoted to monitoring government in the public interest. Ralph Nader has founded a number of these: Center for the Study of Responsive Law, PO Box 19367, Washington, D.C. 20036; Congress Watch, 215 Pennsylvania Ave. SE, Washington, D.C. 20003; and Public Citizen, 2000 P Street NW, Washington, D.C. 20036. Also, Common Cause is a national citizens' lobby formed to make government more accountable (2030 M Street NW, Washington, D.C. 20036), and the Center for Federal Policy Review monitors congressional committees and makes committee members' actions known to their constituents (1509 Sixteenth Street NW, Washington, D.C. 20036).

Some of these are membership organizations, some handle cases, some are solely sources of information. Check your community as well; there may be local organizations or groups engaged in lobbying or watchdog activities that could provide you with advice and help.

Management by Objectives (MBO): *a management system that requires agencies to identify short- and long-term objectives and then establish techniques to monitor the achievement of those objectives.*

paperwork resulted, yet efficiency did not improve. PPBS was finally abandoned by the federal government in 1971.[28]

Richard Nixon replaced PPBS with a less threatening management system, **Management by Objectives (MBO).** Under MBO, agencies were required to identify short- and long-term objectives and then establish techniques to monitor the achievement of those objectives. Agencies were asked to develop "milestones," actions that aided in realizing the specified objectives. The intent was to disassociate MBO from resource allocation, and to eliminate any perceived threat to the budget resources of an agency in order to allow agencies to evaluate the achievement of their stated goals.

The implementation of MBO was greeted with mixed reactions. Some agencies, such as the State Department, found the identification of quantifiable objectives and milestones difficult. Bureau chiefs and line managers felt MBO was an effort on the part of the president to control agencies or to criticize agency performance by means of a performance audit. Moreover, President Nixon took little interest in the implementation of MBO, and the Office of Management and Budget never became a serious proponent of it. The chief beneficiaries of MBO appear to have been political appointees in departments—secretaries and undersecretaries: "The MBO system provides the secretary with information about the programs for which he is responsible. . . . The MBO system establishes routine reporting mechanisms about major departmental concerns. These objectives are then regularly and consistently monitored in management conferences."[29]

Zero Based Budgeting (ZBB): *an approach to budgetary decision making in which each agency must justify all its programs and resources annually. Each agency starts its budget at zero.*

The more recent technique, advocated by President Carter, was **Zero Based Budgeting (ZBB).** Zero Based Budgeting put every agency in the position of justifying its programs and resources annually. As the term implies, each agency starts its budget at zero. Agencies place programs in priority order and provide detailed information justifying the resources needed to operate them annually. Each agency and department then submits a list of programs in priority ranking to the president via the Office of Management and Budget. In this way priorities and resource costs can be quickly compared and weak programs easily weeded out. Costly but low-priority programs can be targeted and resources shifted to more urgent areas. Critics argue that ZBB raises bureaucratic anxiety. Any program receiving a low priority is destined to be eliminated, so the tendency is for agencies to protect their resources and give all programs a high priority. Items given low priority are often those that are favorites of Congress, the agencies knowing full well that Congress will not allow the administration to eliminate them. Supporters of ZBB argue that it is a means of restoring efficiency and economy to government. One author, examining the creation of government organizations between 1923 and 1973, discovered that of 175 organizations existing in 1923, no fewer than 148 were still alive in 1973. In the meantime, no fewer than 246 new agencies had been created, for a 1973 total of 394.[30]

There is no question that these techniques can generate great quantities of information that serve to clarify program operation and alternatives. But they cannot provide answers for policy choices that are fundamentally political. The problems of national health care, welfare for dependent children, parity prices for farmers, and clean water remain essentially political in nature. No amount of quantitative information can make these hard choices for our representative public officials.

Responsible Bureaucracy

Running the government is big business. The administrative apparatus has now become a symbol for corruption and inefficiency, but it was not always so. This is what Kenneth J. Meier had to say in 1979:

> In the United States we are fortunate because the federal bureaucracy is much better than we deserve. Combining the value dimensions of responsiveness and competence, the American federal bureaucracy is clearly the best in the world. No other national bureaucracy has won as many Nobel prizes, and no other bureaucracy responds to as wide an array of interests. These benefits of bureaucracy have come despite numerous obstacles posed by the American people.[31]

But the federal bureaucracy's responsible behavior in the past is no assurance that it will always perform responsibly. The bureaucracy is an independent force within American government. It defies control by any

"Then it's agreed. The problem's not *our* fault, because the country's run by *low*-level bureaucrats."

Drawing by Dana Fradon; © 1981 The New Yorker Magazine, Inc.

of the branches of government, including the executive. If the bureaucracy has performed competently and responsively, it is not because constitutional checks limit its activities. In an age when regulation, specialization, and complex information are needed, the constitutional branches of government alone cannot meet the challenges government faces. Yet bureaucracy has not escaped the constitutional checks-and-balances system of a democratic political order.

It is precisely because agency administration is a political process that bureaucracy is of interest to Congress, the president, courts, and interest groups. It must compete for power with these other policymakers and share its power with them for the successful implementation of public policy. Congress, the president, and the interest groups "check" the bureaucracy because it is an integral part of our politics. They understand that the bureaucracy is not neutral, but subject to political demands from many sources across our political process. This constant tugging and pulling on the bureaucracy may very well ensure its continuing accountability in American government.

The 1980s continue to pose new problems. Bureaucracy is becoming more important, not less. Demands for energy conservation, consumer protection, public interest representation, and public order can be met only through the effective administration of programs. The bureaucracy has forever altered the tripartite constitutional separation of powers. Yet bureaucracy is a constitutional mechanism of government; it conforms to the spirit and law of the Constitution. There may be reason to fear the growth of bureaucratic government and doubt the ability of a bureaucracy to meet the challenges held by the last years of the twentieth century, but there is no reason to fear that the bureaucracy will not operate within constitutional, democratic limits.

Summary

1. The bureaucracy stands at the center of American government, carrying out the programs enacted by Congress and the president. It receives the brunt of criticism for the cost and inefficiency in government, yet without bureaucrats government service would come to an abrupt halt. Bureaucracy is indispensable to modern government.

2. There is no neat organization for the bureaucracy, nor is the president at the head as chief manager. Rather, in addition to thirteen cabinet departments, there are independent executive agencies, regulatory agencies, and government corporations. The Executive Office of the President, assisting the president in executive functions, is itself a bureaucracy. Presidents have been notoriously bad managers, little involved with the routine of administration.

3. The stereotype of the anonymous bureaucrat as a neutral administrator impartially following directives is largely a myth. The bureaucracy is enmeshed in the political process. Bureaucratic agencies respond as

much to congressional committees and interest groups as to presidential policies. Agencies have points of view, little altered by presidential politics during an administration no matter how intent a president is on change.

4. The bureaucracy affords considerable political insulation. Recent presidents have sought reform and reorganization to alter the decision-making patterns of bureaucrats and to make the bureaucracy more manageable. Rational decision-making proposals as well as civil service reforms have proved less than successful to date, but reform will continue.

5. Responsible bureaucracy remains the goal of American government. Despite criticism, Americans have been fortunate in the quality of federal administrators. New regulations and problem areas will make the bureaucracy more, not less, important in the future.

Research Projects

1. *Bureaucratic agencies*   How many federal bureaucratic agencies are there in your city and what do they do? Make a list of local federal agencies and what they do. Get the list by looking under United States Government in the telephone book. To find what they do, look in the *U.S. Government Manual* or the *Washington Information Directory* published by the Congressional Quarterly Press. If you are still not sure what a local agency is responsible for, call it and ask.

2. *What is a bureaucracy?*   This chapter covered the nature of a bureaucracy and the procedures by which it operates. How common is the bureaucratic apparatus in other organizations? Look at your school or a local corporation and examine the way in which it compares and contrasts with the public bureaucracy.

3. *Federal employment*   Are you interested in a career with the federal government? What is the civil service? Investigate the procedures and requirements for applying for a job with the civil service of the national government. Make a list of possible jobs, their entry requirements, and the type of examinations required. There is a federal network on job information called the Federal Job Information Center; it is available through the Office of Personnel Management (they have a toll-free number). Among the several available guides to civil service work are ARCO, *Civil Service Handbook, Complete Guide to U.S. Civil Service Jobs,* and *Pace.*

4. *Regulatory agencies*   Examine the powers and responsibilities of an independent regulatory agency. Again, the *U.S. Government Manual* and the *Federal Regulatory Directory* published by the Congressional Quarterly Press are good sources. Is there an office of the agency in your state or city? Write a brief essay on the major problems or criticisms leveled against that agency. For this you will have to review back issues of newspapers, magazines, the *Congressional Quarterly,* or *National Journal.* Use the *Reader's Guide to Periodic Literature* and newspaper indexes to facilitate your research.

Notes

1. Subcommittee on Intergovernmental Relations of the Committee on Government Operations, *Confidence and Concern: Citizens View American Government* (Washington, D.C.: Government Printing Office, 1973), p. 310.
2. *National Journal* (September 30, 1978): 1540.
3. H. H. Gerth and C. Wright Mills, *From Max Weber: Essays in Sociology* (New York: Oxford University Press, 1946), pp. 214 and 232.
4. *National Journal* (September 30, 1978): 1540–1541.
5. See Ralph P. Hummell, *The Bureaucratic Experience* (New York: St. Martin's Press, 1977).
6. Peter Drucker, *The Age of Discontinuity* (New York: Harper & Row, 1969), p. 220.
7. See James Q. Wilson, "The Rise of the Bureaucratic State," *Public Interest* 41 (Fall 1975) for a clear statement of the bureaucratic problem.
8. Wilson, "The Rise of the Bureaucratic State," p. 96.
9. *National Journal* (November 10, 1981): 1824.
10. Robert L. Kahn et al. "Americans Love Their Bureaucrats," *Psychology Today* (June 1975): 70.
11. Daniel Katz, Barbara A. Gutek, Robert L. Kahn, Eugenia Barton, *Bureaucratic Encounters* (Ann Arbor, Mich.: Institute for Social Research, 1975), pp. 185–186.
12. Philip Selznick, *TVA and the Grass Roots* (Berkeley, Calif.: University of California Press, 1949).
13. See J. Lieper Freeman, *The Political Process: Executive Bureau—Legislative Committee Relations* (New York: Random House, 1965).
14. Carol Greenwald, *Group Power* (New York: Praeger, 1977), p. 226.
15. *U.S. News and World Report* (May 12, 1986): 22.
16. Kenneth J. Meier, *Politics and the Bureaucracy* (North Scituate, Mass.: Duxbury Press, 1979), p. 75.
17. Charles F. Lindblom, *The Policy-Making Process* (Englewood Cliffs, N.J.: Prentice-Hall, 1980).
18. Jeffrey L. Pressman and Aaron Wildavsky, *Implementation* (Berkeley, Calif.: University of California Press, 1973).
19. Bob L. Wynia, "Federal Bureaucrats' Attitudes Toward a Democratic Ideology," *Public Administration Review* 34 (March/April 1974): 156–162.
20. Ibid., p. 158.
21. Ibid., p. 161.
22. Cited by Joel D. Aberbach and Bert Rockman, "Clashing Beliefs within the Executive Branch: The Nixon Administration Bureaucracy," *American Political Science Review* 70 (June 1976): 457.
23. Ibid., pp. 466–467.
24. Stanley Rothman and S. Robert Lichter, "How Liberal Are Bureaucrats?" *Regulation* (November/December 1983): 16.
25. Ibid., p. 17.
26. Ibid., p. 21.
27. *National Journal* (September 30, 1978): 1543.
28. See Allen Schick, "A Death in the Bureaucracy: The Demise of Federal PPB," *Public Administration Review* 33 (March/April 1973): 146–156.
29. Richard Rose, *Managing Presidential Objectives* (New York: Free Press, 1976), p. 120.
30. Herbert Kaufman, *Are Government Organizations Immortal?* (Washington, D.C.: The Brookings Institution, 1976), p. 35.
31. Meier, *Politics and the Bureaucracy*, p. 204.

Bibliography

Downs, Anthony. *Inside Bureaucracy.* Boston: Little, Brown, 1967.
    An explanation of bureaucratic behavior. Fairly comprehensive and complex in its treatment, the book explains how bureaucracies and bureaucrats work.
Fritschler, A. Lee. *Smoking and Politics: Policy-Making and the Federal Bureaucracy.* Englewood Cliffs, N.J.: Prentice-Hall, 1983.
    An examination of the federal bureaucracy through a study of the cigarette warning label issue. Much of the book examines policymaking within the agency and the pressures the agency was subjected to.
Kaufman, Herbert. *Are Government Organizations Immortal?* Washington, D.C.: The Brookings Institution, 1976.
    Bureaucratic agencies, like old soldiers, never die. Kaufman provides data and discussion on what happens to public agencies once created. It seems few are ever buried.
Lindblom, Charles E. *The Policy-Making Process.* Englewood Cliffs, N.J.: Prentice-Hall, 1980.
    A brief book that attempts to cover the topics involved with public policymaking. Lindblom's argument is that public policy ends up being incremental because of the complex environment in which it is made.
Meier, Kenneth J. *Politics and the Bureaucracy.* North Scituate, Mass.: Duxbury Press, 1979.
    A brief text on the bureaucracy that examines the relationship of the bureaucracy and political institutions. There is a discussion of the interaction of bureaucrats with interest groups and political parties.
Rourke, Francis. *Bureaucratic Power in National Politics.* Boston: Little, Brown, 1986.
    A collection of essays on the bureaucracy and bureaucratic power in American government. Some of the useful areas covered are constituencies, expertise, and popular control of bureaucracies.
Seidman, Harold. *Politics, Position, and Power: The Dynamics of Federal Organization.* New York: Oxford University Press, 1980.
    An insider's view of the political world of the bureauc-

racy. Seidman has considerable insight into the struggles of agencies with Congress, the president, and other bureaucratic agencies.

Wildavsky, Aaron. *The Politics of the Budgetary Process.* Boston: Little, Brown, 1983.
A standard work on the budgetary process of the federal government. Wildavsky stresses the political and incremental nature of the process.

Woll, Peter. *American Bureaucracy.* New York: W. W. Norton, 1977.
A basic, readable text on the bureaucracy. Woll gives needed attention to administrative law and the courts. He also covers the bureaucracy's relations with Congress and the presidency.

Congress

The more things change, the more they stay the same. This traditional saying might well be applied to Congress. In 1987 the 100th Congress convened—200 years of continuous lawmaking by one of the most unique legislatures in the world. The members of Congress taking the oath of office for the centennial Congress were, however, part of an institution that has changed a great deal from the Congress of only a few decades earlier.

The 1980s have presented Congress with distinct challenges. The landslide victories of Ronald Reagan provided Congress with a popular chief executive and a changed mandate. Republican control of the Senate created divided congressional government for only the third time in the twentieth century. The membership of Congress also changed greatly: only 53 percent of the present membership were part of the Ninety-seventh Congress in 1981. Congress, then, is seeking to establish continuity and to recover a mandate in the aftermath of two decades of reform.

Throughout the 1970s Congress struggled with reform, hoping to revive its power in the wake of Vietnam and Watergate. Congressional change took place in response to both external forces in the political process and internal demands to alter the legislative process. With presidents dominating the exercise of political power, Congress passed the War Powers Act in 1974 to restrain executive control of foreign policy and created impoundment controls to limit the president's refusal to spend appropriated funds. Congress also implemented a new budget process and budget office to compete with the president in budgetary affairs. Congress members found independent sources of election funds from political action committees, which fostered a spirit of independence and individualism. Internally, Congress members rebelled against the seniority system, rejecting several veteran House chairpersons in the early 1970s. Subcommittees were created to give less senior members more authority to shape policy. A subcommittee bill of rights guaranteed autonomy, staff, and chair selection to subcommittee members. Leadership was revitalized and given increased powers, including control over the powerful House Rules Committee. In all, the reforms of the 1970s produced a very different Congress in the 1980s.

The era of congressional reform is over. The changes it brought have been institutionalized; a few have been modified, but almost none have been rejected. In their wake Congress seeks to act on those reforms to become once again a major force in shaping public policy. But the period of postreform transition also involves substantial risk. Reagan's popular support, coupled with a strong economy and adventurism in foreign affairs, has kept Congress on the defensive. PAC funding and committee reforms have driven decentralization tendencies within Congress. These have inhibited Congress's ability to work as a cohesive institution and to form a partnership with the president. The remainder of the 1980s will tell the story for Congress—of its successful resurgence of power or of opportunity lost.

Congressional Power

Changes in the wake of the Vietnam War and Watergate again made Congress a contender in public policymaking. The War Powers Act, the Budget and Impoundment Control Act, oversight, and the Budget Office are all designed to enhance Congress's control over the priorities of American public policy. Although the Court decision overturning the legislative veto undermines those acts, the decision left Congress ample opportunity to influence national priorities. Within Congress, redistribution and widening of power have occurred; no longer can a few powerful figures dominate. A shift of power from committees to subcommittees and the election of committee chairs have had a tremendous effect on the status and influence of individual legislators. Finally, the scandals and ethics violations that plagued Congress resulted in new and more stringent regulations on representatives' outside activities. Codes of ethics

Changing Consensus: TV Coverage of Congress

"Not a pretty thing to watch," said Senator J. Bennett Johnston (D–La.), but television coverage of the United States Senate nevertheless began in June 1986. The vote of the Senate to allow live radio and television broadcasts of floor debates on a trial basis for two months came after 15 years of discussion and debate and six years of television coverage in the House of Representatives. "The public will never understand why it's important to this institution and to the nation for the Senate to play the role of the saucer where the political passions of the nation are cooled," remarked Johnston.

The House of Representatives has had gavel-to-gavel television coverage since March 1979. The House had experimented with closed-circuit telecasts to Capitol Hill offices for two years prior. The experiment was labeled a success, and the House recommended complete coverage. That coverage commenced in 1979 on the Cable-Satellite Public Affairs Network (**C-SPAN**) and was made available to commercial cable systems. The House retains control over the operation, and the cameras are fixed so as to show only members at the podium. The House wanted to avoid cameras scanning an empty chamber or showing members of Congress reading newspapers or huddled in conversation while debate was proceeding.

The Senate had been reluctant to follow suit. Many senators remembered the live TV coverage of Vice-President Nelson Rockefeller's swearing-in ceremony, during which the lights and equipment made for cramped quarters and a very warm chamber. In 1975 Republican senators asked for live broadcast coverage of the debate over the disputed 1974 New Hampshire Senate election. Many senators, however, thought television coverage would merely embarrass senators and cause further partisan rankling. The Senate was not going to be given over to "media-provoked theatrics."

But the Senate has reluctantly followed the lead of the House; on June 1, 1986, gavel-to-gavel broadcasts of Senate proceedings were broadcast on C-SPAN. As in the House, Senate cameras are fixed on the Speaker and the presiding officer; cameras can pan the chamber only during a roll-call vote. Coverage is prohibited during closed sessions and during quorum calls, which are frequently used to stall while senators confer to line up votes. The experiment proved a success, as the Senate voted in 1986 to make television coverage permanent.

Does televising Congress alter its performance? Most think not. Senator Byrd of West Virginia, then Senate minority leader, said televising the Senate means taking "a giant step toward helping our citizens understand the decisions that impact on their daily lives." Majority leader Dole hoped live television coverage would force the Senate to streamline its procedures. Still, some reason that representatives and senators will play to the cameras, making partisan and dramatic speeches for the TV audience, and not for their congressional colleagues.

There has been some of that. In 1979 upstart Republicans in the House took advantage of the daily opening period in the House, during which members were allowed to give one-minute speeches. They used the television time to attack President Carter and administration

© Dan Hofoss, Canada/ROTHCO

policies. The speeches so annoyed Democratic House leaders that for a brief time they moved the one-minute speeches to the end of the day's business. In 1984 GOP Representative Newt Gingrich used the one-minute period to attack Democrats, many by name, as being soft on communism. He began to read a lengthy document into the record before the live television cameras. So angered was Speaker Tip O'Neill that he ordered cameras to pan the House, showing Gingrich and his colleagues railing at an empty chamber.

The Senate too worries over partisan use of television. Senators are free to videotape their speeches and use them for publicity with tele-vision stations back home. Whether this will lead to grandstanding theatrics remains to be seen. "Statesmanship is all too scarce a commodity as it is now," said Senator Russell Long (D–La.); "it will be even more scarce with television."

But times have changed. The American public wants to know and understand the congressional process. At this point it is too early to tell whether the glare of television will affect the pace of deliberation or the temperament of decisions. But then, Congress is not the same institution it was two decades ago; deliberation and decision must face the sunshine of an inquiring populace.

C-SPAN: *Cable-Satellite Public Affairs Network made available to commercial cable systems over which televised proceedings of the House of Representatives and Senate are broadcast.*

and conflict of interest are now taken seriously. New limitations have been set on congressional use of the franking (free mailing) privilege; outside sources of income have been severely restricted; and new quarterly spending reports are required for staff salaries, travel, postage, and office funds. Congress has been cleaning its own house.

Yet will reform alter Congress? The role of Congress in the democratic political process depends on its ability to resume a major role within a constitutionally divided system of government. Congressional reform must speak to the ability of Congress to fulfill certain roles if the vitality of democracy is to be realized.

The primary function of Congress is *legislation*. Most of the controversy over Congress has been about its ability to legislate, to be innovative and creative in meeting the needs of a changing and complex environment. Critics charge that Congress has abdicated its legislative role to the chief executive. Yet no other body has a more elaborate set of procedures or rules designed to facilitate deliberation. The entire congressional process is designed to facilitate a deliberated judgment. If properly exercised, the lawmaking function should lead to effective public policy.

Second, Congress performs a unique *representational* role. The decentralized structure of congressional committees acknowledges a multiplicity of interests deserving access to the decision-making process. Congress affords legitimate interests an opportunity to help shape public policy. Effective interest representation can result in broad consensus legislation directed toward shared goals.

Third, Congress gives the public a direct link with government through *constituency service*. Unlike the other branches, Congress has individual legislators representing specific constituents. Constituency service affords the citizen an opportunity for personal attention in a large, complex political process.

These primary goals are complemented by several other important functions. Increasingly today Congress assumes the function of *administrative oversight* in monitoring the executive performance. This role has been heightened by the growth of presidential power since the New Deal and dramatized by events such as Vietnam and Watergate. Another function emerging in importance is that of *informing* the public. Through the use of committee investigations, Congress has informed and even generated public opinion on several important matters of public policy. The Senate Select Committee on Campaign Practices (Ervin Committee) first revealed the breadth and depth of Watergate; Congress kept pressing President Reagan for answers to the Iran arms sales scandal, culminating finally in a special prosecutor being named; congressional committees investigating nutrition, aging, and the environment have revealed to Americans the problems of hunger and malnutrition, growing old and retirement, and pollution.

Appropriations: *a congressional act authorizing public funds for specific governmental purposes. All agencies of government must come to Congress annually to have their operating budgets renewed.*

Next, control of the purse strings gives Congress a marked advantage in **appropriations.** The fact is that all agencies of government must come before Congress annually to have their operating budgets renewed. Frequently Congress can use the role of appropriations to investigate or check executive power. Finally, Congress performs any number of lesser functions as a *check and balance* to the other branches of government. Regarding the executive branch, Congress confirms major executive appointments, ratifies treaties, determines presidential disability, and votes impeachment. Regarding the judiciary, Congress creates judgeships, establishes legal procedures for the courts, and establishes law and its violations. And with the bureaucracy, Congress is involved with reorganization, clearance for administrative rules, and policymaking.

These are all significant roles for Congress. But reform cannot make Congress into something it is not or was not intended to be:

> Congress is not now and never has been well designed to create its own agenda and then to act on it in a coordinated way to produce a unified domestic and/or foreign policy program. It is particularly well structured to react to many publics (including other governmental institutions) and, in reacting, to criticize, refine, promote alternative proposals, bargain and compromise. Reforms directed away from these strengths are unlikely to improve Congress or, in fact, to be taken seriously for very long.[1]

The Legislators

The typical image of members of Congress is one of aging politicians waiting for the seniority system to endow them with power. But that stereotyped view is incorrect. Senility is not a fault of the contemporary Congress; the average age for representatives has been dropping over the past twenty years. In 1979 the average age went below fifty (49.5) for the first time since World War II, and for two Congresses in a row (the Ninety-fifth and Ninety-sixth) no members of the House of Representatives were over eighty years of age.

The Constitution says little about the qualifications for a member of Congress: the only restrictions are age and residency. Members of the House of Representatives must be at least twenty-five years of age and residents of the state from which elected (although the representative need not reside in the district from which elected), and must have been citizens of the United States for seven years. Senators must have attained the age of thirty, been citizens for nine years, and be residents of the state electing them. Generally, members have considerable prior political experience; they do not reflect the population as a whole. Legislators have been, and continue to be, predominantly male, white, Protestant, professional, and middle-aged (Table 12.1).

Blue-Collar Caucus: *a caucus representing working-class occupations, formed in 1977 by fourteen members of the House of Representatives.*

A legal background has traditionally been the most popular route to Congress. In 1979, however, the figures showed the lowest percentage of law degrees in Congress since record keeping began. Fewer than half the members of the House of Representatives for the One-hundredth Congress had law degrees. This marked a dramatic decline since 1977 in the

Joseph McCarthy
A Republican senator from Wisconsin from 1947 to 1957, Senator McCarthy contributed to the alarm over alleged communist agents in the U.S. government in the 1950s. McCarthy used his chairmanship of the Senate Permanent Investigations Subcommittee to probe communist infiltration and influence within the State Department, Voice of America, and the U.S. Army. His zeal for exposing Communists and communist sympathizers, often based on unsubstantiated evidence or rumor, became known as McCarthyism. The nation became keenly aware of McCarthy's investigations in the summer of 1954 during hearings about alleged Communists in the Army. For 35 days and 187 television hours, some 20 million Americans watched the conflict between McCarthy and the U.S. Army. In the end, the Senate censured McCarthy for his conduct and the Red Scare began to subside.

TABLE 12.1   Background characteristics of the One-hundredth Congress, 1985–1989

	House	Senate
Party		
Democrats	258	55
Republicans	177	45
Sex		
Male	412	98
Female	23	2
Age		
Oldest	86	85
Youngest	29	38
Average	50.7	54.4
Minorities		
Black	23	0
Oriental	10	2
Hispanic	12	0
Religion		
Protestant	266	69
Roman Catholic	123	19
Jewish	29	8
Mormon	8	3
Other	9	1
Profession[a]		
Lawyers	184	62
Business/bankers	142	28
Educators	38	12
Farmers	20	5
Journalists	20	8
Public service/politics	94	20
Professional athletes	5	1

[a]Some legislators listed more than one occupation.

number of lawyers in the House. As a result of the changing composition, fourteen members of the House in 1977 formed a **blue-collar caucus,** representing working-class occupations. Hardly a potent force, its members nonetheless represent a challenge to the traditional image of members of Congress.

Religious affiliations too have shifted. Protestants still predominate, but they have been losing strength since the 1960s to Jews and Roman Catholics. Catholics represented 20 percent of the membership in the House in 1961, and now make up 29 percent. In 1961 there were eleven Jewish members of the House; today there are twenty-nine. The Senate's population of Jewish members grew from one to eight during the same period.

Tenure and Careerism

As we have already seen, incumbency is a great advantage in running for public office. A majority of the congressional electoral contests are not close; two-thirds to three-fourths are noncompetitive (with the winning candidate receiving more than 55 percent of the popular vote; Figure

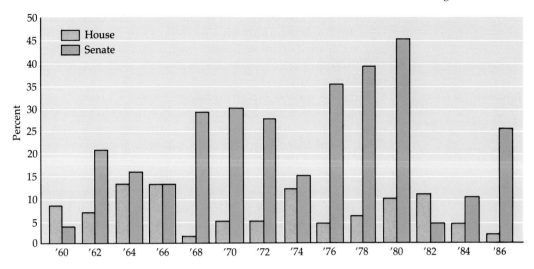

Figure 12.1 Percent of incumbents seeking reelection who lost

12.1). We call these *safe seats.* It is principally incumbents who win big and enjoy the safe seats. In what David Mayhew entitled the "case of the vanishing marginals," he discovered that the number of incumbent representatives running in the marginal zone (40 to 59.5 percent of popular vote) had roughly halved in the sixteen-year period from 1956 to 1972.[2] For some reason, it has become considerably easier for incumbent members to poll three-fifths of the vote in November.

Careerism: *the tendency for a legislative politician to build a professional career by running for and holding public office.*

This ease of electoral success has helped develop a pattern of **careerism** in Congress. Throughout the twentieth century, the average number of years in office has increased. By the mid-1960s the average House member had been in office for eleven years, or nearly six terms; the average Senator for twelve years, or two terms; and the percentage of new members entering Congress declined to less than 17 percent of the total body. Congress had become an attractive career. By the election of 1979, however, things had changed again. By the Ninety-sixth Congress, 68 percent

TABLE 12.2 Congressional turnover: freshmen elected to Congress, 1970–1986

	House			Senate		
	Dem.	*GOP*	*Total*	*Dem.*	*GOP*	*Total*
1970	33	23	56	5	5 + 1 (Ind.)[a]	11
1972	27	42	69	8	5	13
1974	76	16	92	9	2	11
1976	47	20	67	10	8	18
1978	41	36	77	9	11	20
1980	22	52	74	2	16	18
1982	57	24	81	2	3	5
1984	12	32	44	5	2	7
1986	27	23	50	11	2	13

[a]One independent was elected who chose to caucus with the GOP.

of the House and 60 percent of the Senate had been elected in 1970 or later. In the One-hundredth Congress, 49 percent of the House and 37 percent of the Senate had been elected in 1981 or after. In all, as Table 12.2 illustrates, 215 House members and 37 senators had been in office less than seven years.

Turnover: *the rapid change in congressional membership such that the average length of time in office is declining.*

There are several explanations for this rapid **turnover** and for the declining careerism. Reapportionment after the 1970 and 1980 censuses altered constituencies as population shifts continued; the Twenty-sixth Amendment added several million eighteen- to twenty-one-year-old voters to the rolls. But the two main factors appear to be the retirement of veteran representatives and the electoral defeat of members of Congress in the late 1970s and early 1980s. During the 1970s, many members who came to Congress after the New Deal or World War II were in their late sixties and seventies. Rather than face stiff challenges, they opted for retirement. The large freshman class elected in 1974 probably reflected the Watergate backlash and the growing public mood of distrust. Republican members of Congress were particularly hurt by electoral defeat in 1974.

The Republican victories in 1980 turned a number of Congress members out of office, this time many of them Democrats. While Republican turnover has been almost twice that for Democrats in the past two decades—59.3 percent to 35.8 percent—change is in the offing. The 1980s are likely to see higher levels of voluntary retirements for Democrats as well as stiffer electoral competition. The emergence of conservatism in the South means more GOP success there. There no longer exists a solid South for Democrats. The percentage of House Democrats from the South averaged 42 percent in the 1950s, 35 percent in the 1960s, and had further slipped to 28 percent by 1975. In the 1980s, the figure has hovered around 32 percent.

The Legislative Environment

The legislative environment for a member of Congress is composed of two worlds. First there is Washington, D.C., and the world of government officials. Then there is the home constituency, where members of Congress must inform and serve the public with an eye to reelection.

Demands on a legislator's time are tremendous; representatives are on the go at a frantic pace. Congress is in session nearly year-round, and between sessions there are committee hearings, committee reports, party caucuses, office work to do, letters to answer, executive officials to listen to, constituents to see, speeches to make, and trips back home. Some years ago Congressman Clem Miller of California described his typical day. It went as follows:

6:45 A.M.   Rise, read *Washington Post.*
8:00 A.M.   Breakfast with the British ambassador.
8:30 A.M.   Look over mail, dictate replies to important inquiries.

9:00 A.M.	Office appointment with business lobbyist to discuss trade legislation.
10:00 A.M.	Subcommittee hearings on depressed-area bill.
12:00 noon	Attend debate on House floor.
1:00 P.M.	Lunch in office. Read state and local newspapers.
2:00 P.M.	Meeting with Harvard economist John Kenneth Galbraith to discuss tight money and economic policy.
2:45 P.M.	Listen to debate on floor of Congress.
3:30 P.M.	Meeting with a member of the House Appropriations Committee on public works in home district.
5:00 P.M.	Sign letters dictated in morning. Go over afternoon mail. Meet with constituents.
6:15 P.M.	Leave for home.
7:15 P.M.	Eat dinner.
8:00 P.M.	Read another newspaper from home district. Go through reports, speeches, and magazines. File material for future speeches.
11:00 P.M.	Read chapter from book.
11:45 P.M.	To sleep.[3]

It is not unusual for a member's average day to be twelve hours long.

Members must keep in touch with their constituencies. It is not enough to answer mail or read local newspapers or deal with constituent problems; members must return to their home constituencies frequently. Re-election is a high priority, and physical presence in the state or district is important. The average representative will make 35 trips home a year and spend an average of 138 days (counting recesses) in the home district.[4]

Pay and Perquisites

By some standards, members of Congress are well paid. Salaries have risen steadily in the post-World War II years; in 1985 senators and representatives were paid $75,100. But even these salaries are frequently viewed as low compared to those in private industry. Because the salaries are often inadequate for members to maintain two residences, travel frequently, and live modestly in Washington, most representatives have supplemented their incomes with money from outside sources—speaking fees and consulting, for example. This has raised serious questions of conflict of interest and resulted, in 1979, in a House rule limiting outside income. The House set the limit at 30 percent of salary. The Senate reluctantly followed suit in 1984 but raised its limit to 40 percent of salary in 1985. For senators, outside speaking fees and honorariums are easy to come by; House members seldom reach the 30 percent level. In 1985 only seventy-two House members reportedly earned more than $20,000 in outside income. The Senate is more resistant to outside income limitations because larger constituencies, travel schedules, and public demands place greater financial demands on senators. The 40 percent limit permits senators to earn $30,000 in outside income.

TABLE 12.3   Congressional allowances, 1985[a]

	House	Senate
Salary	$75,100[b]	$75,100[b]
Washington office		
Clerk-hire	$379,480	$668,504–1,343,218[c]
Committee legislative assistants	—[e]	$207,342
Interns	$1,840	—
General office expenses	$47,300	$36,000–156,000[c]
Telephone/telegraph	15,000 long-distance minutes to district	—[d]
Stationery	—[d]	1.4–25 million pieces[c]
Office space	2–3 room suites	5–8 room suites
Furnishings	—[d]	—[d]
Equipment	Provided	Provided
District/state offices		
Rental	2,500 sq. ft.	4,800–8,000 sq. ft.
Furnishings/equipment	$35,000	$22,550–31,350[c]
Mobile office	—	One
Communications		
Automated correspondence	—[d]	Provided by Senate computer center
Audio/video recordings; photography	—[d]	—[d]
Travel	Formula (min. $6,200; max. approx. $67,200)	—[d]

[a]In some cases no dollar value is given because of the difficulty in determining the range of reimbursed costs—for example, in travel or telephone reimbursements. Most of the 1985 allowances are transferable from one account to another.

[b]Salary established Jan. 1, 1985; leaders' salaries are higher.

[c]Senators are allowed expenses based on a sliding scale linked to the state's population.

[d]Expenses are covered through the general office expenses line item. In most cases supplies and equipment are charged at rates well below retail levels.

[e]Provided for members of Appropriations, Budget, and Rules committees.

SOURCE: Roger Davidson and Walter Oleszek, *Congress and Its Members*, 2nd ed. (Washington, D.C.: Congressional Quarterly Press, 1985).

Perquisites: *allowances for travel, postage, and hiring of staff employees that supplement a legislator's salary.*

Salaries are supplemented by liberal privileges for travel, postage, and the hiring of staff employees, benefits called **perquisites.** Table 12.3 illustrates these congressional allowances. Perquisites have also been a source of trouble for members recently. Frequent trips at taxpayers' expense and the use of free mailing privileges and office staff funds for reelection activities have caused the public, and Congress, to look carefully at the privileges and their use. House members are allowed thirty-three free round trips home each year; senators receive from forty to forty-four such free trips, depending on the size of the state. Each member of Congress is given a stationery and supplies allotment, telephone allowances, free mailing privileges, and office allowance. All these congressional perquisites have risen significantly in the previous decade. The average allowance in perquisites for a representative is nearly $500,000 a year and is almost $1 million a year for a senator.

Legislative Roles

The need to keep up in two worlds puts inordinate demands on the time and resources of representatives. How they respond to the demands and how they spend their time and resources determine the kinds of legislators they will be. Legislators differ widely in how they spend their time and therefore in the legislative roles they perform.

Members must orient themselves to the work routine of Congress. Thousands of bills and resolutions come before Congress—in committees, before party caucuses, and for floor votes. Different members see their purpose in Congress in different ways. There are the "ritualists," who devote themselves to legislative work—committee hearings, learning rules and procedures, and following the progress of legislation. There are "tribunes," who see their role as expressing popular feeling and supporting popular causes. They are the showhorses of Congress; the ritualists are the workhorses. Others view themselves as "brokers"; they facilitate compromise and arbitrate disputes.

In making decisions, representatives respond to differing constituencies. Not all members pay equal heed to their home constituency. Some, the "trustees," see themselves as free agents, able to decide what a district or the nation needs. Legislators who see the job as speaking for the district or state that elected them are "delegates." A delegate would put aside a personal judgment for what constituents thought best. A "politico" would be more inclined to seek political constituencies, and would concentrate on the political party or caucus within Congress. Politicos combine the trustee and delegate roles. One study of House members found 28 percent of representatives identifying with the trustee role, 23 percent with the delegate role, and a near majority, 46 percent, claiming to be politicos.[5]

Home Style: *the manner in which legislators explain their Washington activity to their constituents.*

Home style[6] expresses the manner in which legislators project themselves to their home states and districts. Members are concerned about their constituencies; they care about getting reelected. Hence they spend much of their time and resources cultivating their constituencies. Richard Fenno measures home style along three dimensions. The first is the allocation of personal and office resources. How much of the scarcest resource—time—the legislator spends in the district helps show the degree of attention paid to constituents. The other valuable resource is the representative's staff. The greater the number of staff members and the larger the amount of their time that goes to constituents, the more focus is on constituents. The second ingredient of home style is "presentation of self," the face-to-face contact the legislator has with constituents in explaining and justifying issues and votes. Members return home in order to seek or maintain political support. Finally, Fenno chooses the representative's explanation of his or her Washington activity to illustrate home style. All members relate relevant issues and concerns to district constituencies and explain their activities on those issues. All claim to be hard-working, diligent supporters of constituent interests. What was surprising, Fenno decided in his study, was the extent to which they all "ran against" Congress: "differentiating himself or herself from the others in Congress, attacking Congress as an institution, and portraying himself or herself as a fighter against its manifest shortcomings."[7]

Some commentators suggest that these legislative roles can be related back to a single goal—getting reelected. In what David R. Mayhew called the "electoral connection," he argued: "Congressmen are interested in those activities which get them reelected, indeed, interested in nothing else."[8] Mayhew found it useful to view congressional behavior from the vantage point of its serving members' electoral needs. Richard Fenno describes reelection as one of a legislator's three primary goals, the other two being influence within Congress and making good public policy.[9] Whether or not election plays this pervasive a role, the continuing need to go before the people every two or six years is of major importance in the life of a member. "You should say 'perennial' election rather than 'biennial,'" said one former congressman, "it is with us every day."[10]

Organization and Power in Congress

Congress is composed of two separate and distinct houses. There is a Senate, made up of 100 senators, two from each state; terms in this house are for six years with one-third up for election every two years. The House of Representatives has 435 members, all elected every two years from single-member districts. Each house is responsible for its own organization and operation and each sets its own rules, selects committee members, and acts on legislation. Table 12.4 summarizes the major differences between the House and the Senate. All legislation must run the obstacle course of each house, either of which has the power to stop action. Yet legislation is a shared function, a power of the whole Congress.

The Founding Fathers had a special concern for legislative power. "In republican government," stated James Madison, "the legislative authority necessarily predominates." The framers had every intention of ensuring that Congress would dominate policymaking. They took great care in Article I of the Constitution (half of the entire Constitution) to delineate

TABLE 12.4   Major differences between the House and Senate

House	Senate
Larger (435)	Smaller (100)
Shorter term of office (2 years)	Longer term of office (6 years)
More procedural restraints on members	Fewer procedural restraints on members
Narrower constituency	Broader, more varied, constituency
Policy specialists	Policy generalists
Less press and media coverage	More press and media coverage
Power less evenly distributed	Power more evenly distributed
Less prestigious	More prestigious
More expeditious in floor debate	Less expeditious in floor debate
Less reliance on staff	More reliance on staff

SOURCE: Walter J. Oleszek, *Congressional Procedures and the Policy Process*, 2nd ed. (Washington, D.C.: Congressional Quarterly Press, 1984), p. 22.

the specific grants of power given this new bicameral legislature. Congress was endowed with a considerable range of fundamental authority:

1. To levy and collect taxes, duties, imports, and excises
2. To regulate foreign and interstate commerce
3. To coin money and regulate its value
4. To establish post offices
5. To create inferior courts
6. To declare war
7. To provide for an army and navy
8. To make laws necessary and proper for executing its enumerated powers

The Constitution confers some additional responsibilities on the Senate:

1. To confirm major executive appointments
2. To ratify treaties
3. To try all impeachments

The House has an additional responsibility: to originate all revenue bills (but the Senate must approve all bills and is free to amend any revenue bill).

Apparently, the framers' special concern for legislative power meant that all legislation was to be expressed through the formal, bicameral process of enacting legislation—at least so declared the Supreme Court in 1983 when it struck down the legislative veto as unconstitutional.

Legislative Veto: *congressional approval of executive agency rules and regulations prior to their implementation. The Supreme Court ruled the legislative veto unconstitutional in 1983.*

The **legislative veto** was a process whereby Congress approved or vetoed rules and regulations enacted by executive agencies to implement congressional legislation. Since 1932 Congress had employed the veto to allow one or both houses of Congress the power to approve or disapprove executive action. It had become an increasingly popular device in recent years. Often Congress could not legislate the specifics of policy, yet Congress could retain control over the shape and direction of law by reviewing agency rules to enforce the laws passed by Congress. It also afforded Congress a means to review the activities of the executive branch and to respond to the public clamor against federal rules and regulations. By 1983 there were 196 laws containing more than 295 legislative veto provisions—163 of those provisions enacted in the last decade.

In what may well be one of the Court's most historic twentieth-century decisions, *Immigration and Naturalization Service* v. *Chadha* (1983), the Supreme Court declared the use of the legislative veto, by one house or both houses of Congress, unconstitutional. It violated the requirements of Article I of the Constitution as well as the separation of powers doctrine.[11]

Mr. Chief Justice Burger, writing for a 7–2 majority, said the Founding Fathers never intended to give Congress that kind of power. "It emerges clearly that the prescription for legislative action in Article I, Section 7 represents the framers' decision that the legislative power of the Federal government be exercised in accord with a single, firmly wrought and exhaustively considered, procedure." This meant legislation must pass both houses of Congress—the bicameral requirement—and be presented for the president's signature or veto—the presentment requirement. In this manner legislative power would be exercised only after full study and debate in separate sittings, and the executive would be protected from Congress just as the whole people would be protected from improvident laws. "We see therefore that the framers were acutely conscious that the bicameral requirement and the presentment clauses would serve essential Constitutional functions."

The legislative veto thus violated the legislative process required in Article I of the Constitution. It further violated the principle of separation of powers and the checks and balances. By allowing one house of Congress to overturn executive agency action, in this case refusing to accept the Immigration Department's order granting resident alien status to Jugdish Rai Chadha, Congress had exercised a veto and altered the legal rights, duties, and relations of persons, including the attorney general, executive branch employees, and Mr. Chadha, all people outside the legislative branch. Thus, Chief Justice Burger concluded, "to preserve those checks and balances, and maintain the separation of powers, the carefully defined limits on the power of each branch must not be eroded. To accomplish what has been attempted by one house of Congress in this case requires action in conformity with the express procedures of the Constitution's prescription for legislative action: passage by a majority of both houses and presentment to the president."

Congress has responded to the *Chadha* decision. It continues to introduce bills containing provisions for the legislative veto, although in slightly different forms. The most common method proposed by Congress is the joint resolution. This is a bicameral process subject to presidential veto; hence it appears in compliance with the requirements set by the Supreme Court. But other forms also are being used. Prevalent among these are committee vetoes over the reprogramming or use of appropriated funds. Apparently Congress believes that the appropriations process is not vulnerable to the logic of *Chadha*. This is an area in which Congress has held wide sway and been afforded considerable latitude. Administrators are reluctant to challenge the actions of appropriations committees. Nonetheless such vetoes are committee vetoes, and committee action, in the normal process of legislation, requires further action. Whether appropriations committees alone can bar the use of funds for a specified purpose remains to be seen. Another approach is to place time-period provisions in one-house or two-house vetoes. Such vetoes place time restrictions that either prevent action or require that action be taken by a specified date. The Justice Department has stated that time-period provisions in legislative vetoes stand the test of *Chadha*. Congress used the two-house veto by creating a waiting period for arms sales as a means of control.

Practicing Politics:
How to Learn about Your Congressional Representatives

1. Ask your local or university librarian for the current *Congressional Directory.*
2. Locate your district in the map section.
3. See the biographical section, arranged by state and district, for brief biographical sketches of your senators and representatives, including the electoral history of each and a description of the boundaries of your district.
4. The alphabetical list will show home address, office address, and phone number in Washington.
5. The individual index lists the committees on which senators and representatives serve; check the committee entries to find out what the committees do and where and when they meet.

6. To find your representatives' voting record on important issues, check the *Congressional Quarterly Almanac,* which abstracts voting records from the *Congressional Record.*
7. You may wish to know more about your representatives' positions on important issues. Several groups rate members of Congress on their voting records, for example:
   - Americans for Democratic Action (liberal)
   - Americans for Constitutional Action (conservative)
   - AFL-CIO (labor)
   - National Chamber of Commerce (business)
   - Environmental Action (environment)

The president addresses a joint session of Congress after a summit conference.

The legislative veto is apparently not about to disappear. Congress continues to approve bills containing provisions for the legislative veto. In the years since *Chadha* some thirty such vetoes have been included in a dozen bills passed by Congress. It has been at issue in some of Congress's hottest questions: Stinger missile sales in the Middle East, production of MX missiles, and military aid to El Salvador.[12] Still, its use is sporadic and ad hoc, and Congress has reached no consensus on its merits or its future. In all likelihood, the fate of the legislative veto remains with the Court.

Congress was intended to have major responsibility for policymaking. Yet in our post-Watergate environment there has been much concern that Congress has abdicated its responsibilities in legislation. Not so, says Lewis A. Froman, Jr.: "The United States Congress is probably more powerful as a legislative body vis-a-vis the executive than in any other legislative body in the world. . . . In no other country has the legislature so much capacity for acting independently and for thwarting the will of the executive as in the United States."[13]

The Leadership

Party leadership exerts considerable influence on the legislative process. In 1977, both houses chose new majority party leaders: Thomas P. (Tip) O'Neill, Jr., as Speaker of the House, and Robert C. Byrd as majority leader of the Senate. In 1987 both houses once again chose new leaders.

Joseph G. Cannon
"Uncle Joe" Cannon was Speaker of the House from 1903 to 1911. He was responsible for enlarging and strengthening the office of Speaker. Cannon became Speaker at age 67, and was then the oldest representative with the longest service ever to become Speaker. "Cannonism," a conservative Republicanism out of touch with the progressive mood of the Theodore Roosevelt presidency, became symbolic of the obstructive use of the Speaker's powers to block legislation. Growing opposition to Cannon's powers culminated in 1911 when a Democratic majority replaced him as Speaker. He stayed in Congress until 1923, having served forty-six years in Congress.

Texas Democrat Jim Wright succeeded Thomas "Tip" O'Neill as Speaker of the House in 1986.

Jim Wright of Texas moved up from majority leader to Speaker of the House with the retirement of Tip O'Neill. The Democrats regained control of the Senate and Robert C. Byrd again became majority leader, replacing Robert Dole, who had led the Republican majority in the Senate. Both men sought to revive the powers of leadership after a decade of decline.

Speaker of the House: *the leader of the majority party and the presiding officer in the House of Representatives.*

The office of **Speaker of the House,** the chamber's presiding officer and the majority party's leader, has had a history of strong-willed, dominant occupants. The office has thus become a powerful political post. Between 1890 and 1910, "Czar" Reed and "Uncle Joe" Cannon exercised considerable power in support of the Republican majorities in the House. During the 1940s and 1950s, Sam Rayburn exercised much the same power for the Democrats, bargaining with individuals and applying the rules from the Speaker's chair. But with John McCormack in the 1960s and Carl Albert from 1971 to 1977, the power of the Speaker ebbed. Neither was aggressive, and when faced with party disunity, neither liked to make arbitrary rulings. Remarked Albert, "I don't want to do anything to offend anyone. I want to be remembered as a Congressman's Speaker, well liked by his colleagues, from whom I am able to get the most cooperation without too much arm-twisting." Tip O'Neill had other aspirations. An activist and partisan who left legislative details to assistants, O'Neill used the powers of his office to get his way. As a partisan, O'Neill led the Democratic congressional charge against Ronald Reagan's economic policies. Jim Wright of Texas comes to the speaker's table with a different style and a different philosophy. Unlike O'Neill, who was uncomfortable as a spokesman, Wright is known as an orator with a flair for the dramatic. Speaker Wright also is a master of the legislative process. He meticulously watches legislative issues, becoming personally involved in the details of issues and the legislative process. Wright became speaker after twenty-three years in the House; the last 10 of them as majority leader.

The powers of the Speaker of the House are primarily those of personal influence developed through years of service in the House and in lesser leadership posts. The Speaker must be a master of the rules. The Speaker's primary duties are presiding over the House, interpreting the rules and deciding points of order, referring bills and resolutions to committees, scheduling legislation for floor action, and appointing House members of joint and conference committees.

Majority Floor Leader of the Senate: *the leader of the majority party and the ranking official in the Senate.*

The Senate has no formal post comparable to that of the Speaker of the House. The Constitution makes the vice-president the presiding officer in the Senate. When the vice-president is not in attendance, the president pro tempore presides. Neither officer has any real political power to compare with that of the Speaker. The real leadership in the Senate is exercised by the **majority floor leader.** The Senate leadership, too, changed with the election of Robert C. Byrd in 1977 as majority leader. And with Republican control in 1981 the GOP selected Howard Baker, followed by Robert Dole in 1984. Democratic control once again in 1987 brought back

Robert C. Byrd as majority leader. Elected by the party caucus in the Senate, the majority leader guides party legislation through the Senate. For fifteen years prior to Byrd, the majority leader was Mike Mansfield, a quiet, scholarly Democrat from Montana. Unlike his predecessor, Lyndon Johnson, who was flamboyant and domineering, Mansfield preferred the quiet and dignity of a low profile.[14] Said Mansfield, "I don't collect any IOU's. I don't do any special favors. I try to treat all Senators alike." Byrd, like his predecessors, was a long-time senator. He had faithfully served his party in the Senate and had occupied lesser leadership posts before being elected majority leader in 1977. His style was more like Mansfield's in that he was quiet and unassuming, but he was intent on leading. Byrd developed a complete mastery of Senate rules and used the prerogative of first recognition to control the agenda in the Senate.

Robert Dole was an activist, no-nonsense majority leader. He was personally involved with the affairs of the Senate, keeping most of the meetings under his own direction. His main tactic was to call groups of senators into his office for meetings—lots of meetings. In this way he was able to mediate conflict and keep the Senate moving. Unlike his predecessor Howard Baker, who projected a more relaxed manner, Dole was more the taskmaster, keeping the Senate in session long hours to find solutions for problems.

The Senate is a much more informal body than the House, which is highly structured and governed by formal rules. The speaker may interpret the rules but there is little occasion to suspend them. In the Senate, Byrd proceeds most of the time on the basis of **unanimous consent** (one objection can stop a debate or delay a decision). There is little need or occasion to apply formal rules. Byrd defined the role of the majority leader this way: "He facilitates, he constructs, he programs, he schedules, he takes an active part in the development of legislation, he steps in at crucial moments on the floor, offers amendments, speaks on behalf of legislation, and helps to shape the outcome of the legislation."

The power of the majority leader is based on the ability to build and maintain a loose alliance of senators to pass or defeat legislation coming before the chamber. The major weapon of the majority leader is influence over the scheduling of action. In the Senate, the majority leader is the ranking official. Neither the president of the Senate nor its president pro tempore holds such rank. The majority leader also helps formulate the party's legislative program and priorities, nominating members to party committees, suggesting assignments for standing committees, and appointing task forces to study and recommend legislation on a wide variety of subjects.

The positions of leadership in the House and Senate are so important that an institutional structure assists the Speaker and majority leader (Figure 12.2). The leadership structure in the two chambers is essentially the same. Each chamber has a majority and minority floor leader (in addition to the Speaker of the House), assistant floor leaders (called **whips**), several assistants, and a variety of party organizations responsible for for-

Unanimous Consent: *the Senate procedure used to call up a bill from the calendar.*

Whips: *assistant floor leaders who assist the majority and minority leaders in carrying out the party's legislative program.*

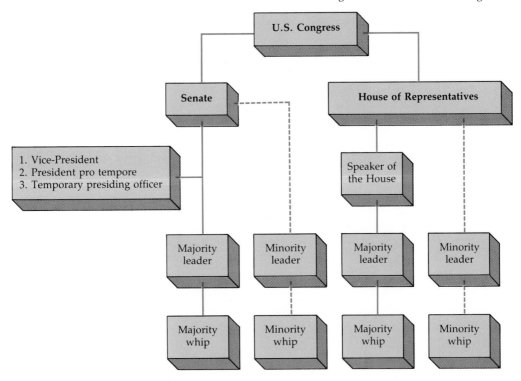

Figure 12.2 Congressional leadership

mulating the legislative program, steering it through the chamber, and making committee assignments. (Figure 12.3 gives a historical view of congressional majority from 1900 to 1985.)

The majority leader in the House of Representatives is the lieutenant for the Speaker and stands to become Speaker should the present one resign or retire. The evolutionary progression to leadership posts in Congress has the earmarkings of an automatic procedure. Whips become majority leaders, who, in turn, are selected as Speakers. Majority leaders work to shape and direct party strategy. They have a major responsibility for scheduling legislation and keeping the party together on issues dividing the chamber. Their specific functions are to formulate the party's legislative program, steer the program through the House, monitor committee action on important bills, and schedule appropriate action on matters of legislation.

The minority leaders' duties are much the same except that they cannot schedule legislation or depend on the support of a majority. Yet minority leaders act as party leaders for their party in the House or Senate. In the Senate they are consulted by the majority leader on scheduling of items of business and, if the party occupies the White House, act as the president's spokesperson in the chamber. The greatest function the minority leaders serve, however, is summarizing minority-party criticism of the

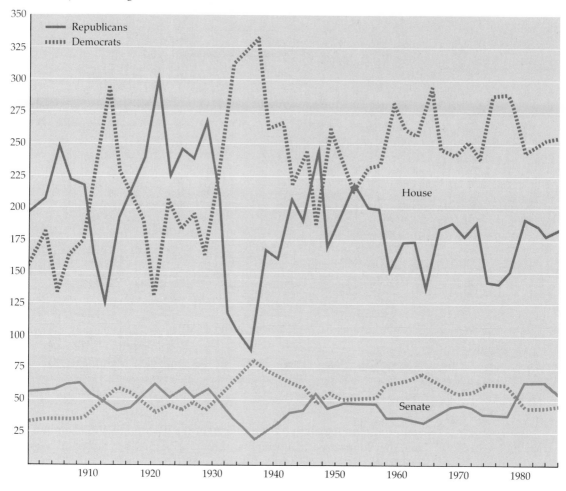

Figure 12.3 The congressional majority: 1900–1985

majority party's legislative performance. But because minority leaders usually end up on the losing side of the aisle, they are more likely to retire voluntarily or be defeated at the polls.[15] As of 1967, only two of twelve majority leaders had retired or been defeated. But of thirteen minority leaders over time, five voluntarily retired and three were defeated in reelection bids.

Both parties designate whips to assist the majority and minority leaders in carrying out the party's legislative program. In recent years the House Democrats' whip organization has consisted of a chief whip elected by the party caucus and twenty-two assistant whips selected on a regional basis by the state party delegations. In the Ninety-ninth Congress, the House Republicans had a chief whip, four regional whips, and fifteen area whips. The selections are made by the party conference. In the Senate the organization is much the same, although smaller, and the degree of success in the Senate is much smaller as well. Senate whips have periodically defied party leadership; senators, in general, have been less amenable to whip pressure to support party preferences.

The prime function of the whip organization is to assist the floor leaders and ensure membership attendance for key action and voting. In a chamber as large as the House of Representatives, it is a major task to keep track of members and ensure their presence on the floor for important votes. In addition to this strategic function, whips are also vital in transmitting information between party leadership and members. The "whip's package" contains a summary of key legislation and what it would do. It also contains a review of the status of all bills, where they are in the process, and when action will be taken. The whip's office also writes speeches and provides information to legislators. Whips are instrumental in counting noses for the leadership on close votes and applying some pressure to keep the party majority intact. Said one congressman: "The key to effective whip action is timing. The Whip is on the floor surveying the scene and weighing alternatives. . . . If he puts out a call too soon, too urgently, many members will assemble, take a quick look, and then begin to fade until there is a critical deficiency when the vote is taken."[16]

The Party Caucus

Party committees are established by both parties in both houses to establish legislative priorities and programs, elect leaders, and approve committee assignments.

Caucus: *the organization that includes all party members in that chamber of Congress. There are four caucuses: Senate Democrats, Senate Republicans, House Democrats, and House Republicans.*

The party conference, or **caucus,** consists of all party members in the chamber. Each party has made periodic use of the conference, but it rarely functions as a deliberative body. In the Senate particularly, the caucus has ratified legislative programs and approved party leaders, but has not commanded obedience through binding decisions. The Democratic conference meets only a few times a year. The Republican conference meets regularly, frequently weekly, although its actions are not binding for Senate Republicans. In the House, however, the Democratic caucus has become the vehicle for change and reform.

Beginning in the 1960s, newer liberal House Democrats began trying to revitalize the caucus, their aim being to attack the arbitrary power of conservative committee chairs and the seniority system. They formed a group known as the Democratic Study Group in 1959 and by 1970 had succeeded in securing regular monthly meetings of the Democratic caucus. They tried unsuccessfully to unseat John McCormack as Speaker in 1970. By 1973, these more liberal members had sufficient strength to alter the automatic selection of committee chairs based on seniority. The caucus requires a secret-ballot election for the selection of committee chairs. This resulted in 1975 in the unseating of three long-time committee chairs: Wright Patman (Tex.) of the Banking Committee, F. Edward Hebert (La.) of the Armed Services Committee, and W. R. Poage (Tex.) of the Agriculture Committee. The caucus also opened bill-drafting sessions to the public, created a Steering and Policy Committee under the party leadership to set party and legislative priorities, and gave to this new committee the responsibility for making committee assignments (taking it away from the Ways and Means Committee).

The wave of reform, and with it the use of the caucus, has subsided somewhat since the Ninety-fourth Congress. But to prove the issue was not dead, House Democrats in 1985 jolted seniority once again. They unseated Armed Services Committee Chairman Melvin Price (D–Ill.) and replaced him with Les Aspin (D–Wis.), the seventh-ranking Democrat on the committee. It had been a decade since House Democrats challenged committee chairs and denied seniority, and this was the first time Democrats had dropped so far down the seniority ladder to pick a successor to a chair. In a secret ballot, the Democratic caucus voted to unseat Price, who was considered too frail to lead the important committee. Aspin's nomination came from the caucus floor, because more senior committee members commanded little support in the caucus.

The Republican majority in the Senate did bolster the Senate Republican Conference. The conference has expanded its operations, principally with a media operation to publicize the views and accomplishments of GOP senators. With a Republican in the White House and a majority in the Senate, the conference felt a renewed sense of purpose and opportunity.

The only organization in Congress is party organization. Party leadership provides a measure of coherence and integration to what is otherwise a decentralized process. These qualities help shape the environment in which legislators seek to make public policy.

Committee Assignments

Committee on Committees: *groups of veteran Congress members selected by each party in both houses of Congress to make their party's appointments to congressional committees.*

In the House of Representatives, up until the twentieth century, committee assignments were made by the Speaker. Since then, the parties have delegated that responsibility to a special party committee on committees (Table 12.5). The Republican **Committee on Committees** is composed of a representative from each state with GOP membership, usually the senior member, and is chaired by the House GOP leader. Assignments must be approved by the Republican conference. The Democrats, beginning in 1974, transferred the assignment power out of the Ways and Means Committee to the newly formed Policy and Steering Committee as a part of the reform drive of the Ninety-fourth Congress to wrest power from senior members of Congress. The twenty-four-person Policy and Steering Committee is composed of House party leaders, twelve regionally elected members, and nine members appointed by the Speaker. The steering committee's decisions are subject to ratification by the Democratic caucus.

Richard Fenno's study of committee assignments identified three goals that help to explain which committees members seek.[17] Committee assignments may be viewed in terms of career and legislative goals. First, assignment to a committee can enhance chances of reelection. Some com-

TABLE 12.5   Selecting committee members

Members of Congress stay on the same committee from one Congress to another. As a rule, Congress members remain on the same committee throughout their careers. They are ranked by seniority on their committees. New members request committee assignment, and veteran ones may ask for a transfer to another committee if there is a vacancy. But new committee members, even senior Congress members new to a committee, are ranked at the bottom in committee seniority.

House Democrats
Nominations are made by the Steering and Policy Committee, an arm of the leadership. All nominations are subject to caucus approval. An exception applies to Democratic members of the Rules Committee, where the Speaker is given power to nominate all party members of the Rules Committee, again subject to ratification by the caucus.

House Republicans
The GOP Committee on Committees is composed of one representative from every state having Republican representation in the House. The committee is subdivided into an executive committee of approximately fifteen members who cast as many votes as there are Republican members in their state delegations. This is called weighted voting. The nominations are submitted to the full Committee on Committees for approval. The House Republican Conference does not vote on all committee nominations; however, it does vote on the ranking Republican members of each committee.

Senate Democrats
Democratic nominations are made by the Democratic Steering Committee, headed by the party leader, who appoints the other Steering Committee members. The nominations are approved by the Democratic caucus.

Senate Republicans
The Republican Committee on Committees, appointed by the chairman of the Republican conference (caucus), draws up the list of nominations. The Republican conference does not vote on the committee's nominations.

SOURCE: *Guide to Congress*, 3rd ed. (Washington, D.C.: Congressional Quarterly Press, 1982), p. 459.

---

mittees, such as Agriculture, Post Office and Civil Service, and Interior, provide a representative with an opportunity to perform constituency service and thereby increase his or her stock with voters. Second, a committee assignment is a means of maximizing influence over public policy in a given area. Committees such as Education, Foreign Affairs, and Judiciary provide real opportunities for a member to help shape and direct public policy. Third, some committees are highly valued because they provide a means for representatives to maximize their influence within the House or Senate. Because such committees are critical to the operation of Congress, they afford committee members an opportunity to exercise influence over the whole Congress. Some examples are Senate Finance and House Ways and Means (taxes), Appropriations (spending) and House Rules Committee (scheduling).

Since some committees are more desirable than others, competition for seats is keen. Because motivations for seeking a committee may differ, the House of Representatives has classified its committees as *exclusive, semiexclusive,* or *nonexclusive.* Members assigned to an exclusive committee serve only on that committee and on no other standing committee. The **exclusive committees** are Appropriations, Ways and Means, and Rules. Members assigned to semiexclusive committees, which are the major policy-area committees that authorize programs, may be assigned to non-

Exclusive Committee: *the designation given to the Appropriations, Ways and Means, and Rules committees of the House of Representatives. Members assigned to an exclusive committee serve on only that committee and no other standing committee.*

exclusive committees. The nonexclusive committees are viewed as the least attractive, and there are no restrictions on assignments.

The inclination in the past had been for members to gravitate from the nonexclusive to the more exclusive committees as vacancies occurred. New members seeking first committee assignments were rewarded on the basis of their need for reelection help or their ideological stance. Transfer requests were judged on regional balance, party loyalty, and ideological commitment. A recent study of committee assignments in the House concluded, however, that "freshman representatives who came to the House in recent years were reasonably successful in securing desirable committee assignments, and that most of those who were not so fortunate during the first term transferred to preferred committees during the second or third term."[18] Irwin Gertzog calls this the "routinization of committee assignments." Almost all House members were appointed to committees they most preferred by their fifth year in office (two-thirds were granted that preference at once in their first term), and there was little variation in success between Republicans and Democrats.

In 1983, Representative Phil Gramm, a Democrat who was instrumental in helping Republicans in the House enact many of President Reagan's economic programs during the Ninety-seventh Congress, was removed from his committee seat on the House Budget Committee by the Democrats. In turn, Representative Gramm resigned from Congress and then ran as a Republican in the special Texas congressional election to fill his own vacancy. He won. Thereupon he rejoined the Ninety-eighth Congress, and the GOP promptly awarded him a committee seat on the House Budget Committee—as a Republican. In 1984 Gramm ran for and was elected to the U.S. Senate as a Republican.

Seniority

Seniority System: *the practice of ranking congressional committee members, by party, according to years of continuous service on a committee.*

One of the major motivations for securing the preferred committee assignment early is seniority. The **seniority system** is the practice, in the Senate and the House, of ranking committee members, by party, according to years of continuous service on a committee. The ranking majority-party member—that is, the majority-party member with the longest consecutive service on the committee—is automatically designated chair of the committee. New members of the committee are added, by party, to the bottom of the list. As vacancies occur, members move up the seniority ladder. When the chair becomes vacant, the next most senior majority-party member steps up. Note that seniority specifies *consecutive* service. If a member is defeated and then reelected later, or transfers committees, that person is placed at the bottom of the seniority list.

Seniority encourages a member to make Congress and a committee a career; it discourages committee hopping. Seniority also aids in reinforcing the congressional norms of specialization and institutional loyalty. It provides a measure of stability and continuity in the congressional process. But seniority is also one of the most heavily criticized aspects of

Congress. The Ralph Nader task force on Congress called seniority "antiquated," a Darwinian "survival of the survivors."[19] Others have labeled it the bastion of old men, a "senility system" rewarding those who wait out their terms of office in order to accrue the seniority necessary to affirm their power. The chief argument against seniority is that power is not bestowed on the ablest or most effective, but only on those who stay the longest. In the past, seniority rewarded conservative southern Democrats with safe seats. These representatives were the beneficiaries of the seniority system, though they were unrepresentative of a changing America. The committee chairs used their independent power bases to thwart party programs or presidential initiatives in social welfare, civil rights, and foreign affairs.

By 1970 seniority was under full attack. The House, in the Legislative Reorganization Act of 1970, provided that seniority need not be the sole consideration for the selection of committee chairs, but the measure was defeated. Representative Schwengel (R–Iowa) offered a motion providing majority election of chairs by committee vote from the three most senior majority party members, but this motion too went down to defeat. However, the 1970 Congress did create a committee, headed by Julia Butler Hansen (D–Wash.) to study reform of seniority. In 1973 House Democrats approved the Hansen Committee recommendations requiring a caucus vote approving committee chairs. Under the Hansen rule, 20 percent of the party membership could request a secret ballot on committee chairs. The revolt had begun. Although no chairs were rejected in 1973, when Congress convened in 1975 the House Democratic caucus voted to unseat F. Edward Hebert as chair of the Armed Services Committee, W. R. Poage as chair of the Agriculture Committee, and Wright Patman as chair of the Banking Committee. Dissatisfaction with a fourth chair, Wilbur Mills of the powerful Ways and Means Committee, caused the caucus to enlarge that committee by almost 50 percent and remove from it to a newly formed Steering Committee the responsibility for committee assignments. (Mills's personal life had achieved notoriety with a series of bizarre incidents including association with a Washington, D.C., striptease dancer who jumped from Mills's car into the water of the Tidal Basin when the car was stopped by police for speeding.) A decade later, the reforms permitted Democrats to remove Melvin Price as chair of the Armed Services Committee. As further evidence of House dissatisfaction with seniority, the caucus limited the chair power over subcommittees. A committee caucus would select subcommittee chairs, not the committee chair. A plan was adopted whereby senior committee members could choose two of their current subcommittee positions. Once they had chosen, the more junior members would have free rein to pick the remaining subcommittee slots. Also passed was the "subcommittee Bill of Rights," which forced chairs to respect subcommittee jurisdiction and resources.

Dissatisfaction with seniority had moved Congress to reform, aided, no doubt, by the election to the House of seventy-five new members in 1974. The moves against seniority, however, reflected a growing trend within

Congress. Times had changed since World War II, when safe, conservative southern Democrats occupied the seats of power in Congress; the South had become increasingly competitive, while northern safe seats had increased. As a percentage of overall Democratic membership in Congress, southern power had declined dramatically. The overall percentage of southern representation in the House and Senate went from 49 percent of the 1947 Senate to only 27 percent in the 1979 Senate, and in the House the figures showed a decline from 55 percent in 1947 to 27 percent in 1979. That general decline was also reflected in the southerners' diminishing share of committee and subcommittee posts.

The balance of power in Congress has been shifting. There is less tolerance for the "let them wait" attitude. Seniority is less persuasive today than it once was, but it has not been abandoned. One can assume that as northern liberals continue to climb the seniority ladder, challenges to seniority may decrease. The reforms have had two obvious effects. First, House and Senate committee assignments are more democratic—that is, committee chairs and subcommittee posts more broadly reflect the membership. Second, the routinization of committee assignment puts almost everyone where he or she wants to be, with caucus decision making ensuring sensitivity to party and member needs on the part of chairs. But the democratization of committees has further decentralized legislative decision making. There are more subcommittees than ever and their jurisdictions and their independence from the committee and its chair are guaranteed. This places an added burden on party leadership to coordinate and schedule and to provide the integration necessary to produce timely and meaningful public policy.

The President and Congress

There is an old story that when a Tammany politician was faced with President Grover Cleveland's opposition to a bill on constitutional grounds, the politician responded by saying, "What's the Constitution between friends?"[20]

What is the Constitution between friends? Each branch of government is endowed with an array of powers, each branch of government is separate, and yet together the branches are to produce legislation and public policy that benefit the nation. A tension runs through presidential-congressional relations. In part, the Founding Fathers deliberately arranged it that way by creating separate branches of government and by providing for checks and balances. But the strain results more from political motives and the quest for power than from the structure of the government. Political fortunes rise and fall; disagreements over domain are inevitable.

The tension between a president and Congress may be healthy. It prevents the accumulation of too much power in one branch of government and checks the potential for abuse of power. But the American people also find it frustrating. Presidential–congressional relations seem to border on stalemate. Each side seems more intent on making its claims, on "posturing" on issues, than in producing harmonious legislation. Jimmy Carter entered the White House with Democratic majorities in both houses, yet he was continually frustrated by his relations with Congress. The election of Ronald Reagan in 1980 with a GOP majority in the Senate presented a split-party government, yet Reagan found initial success with Congress. Parties, issues, and personalities dominate the presidential-congressional arena.

Jimmy Carter's difficulty with Congress, in spite of the large Democratic majorities in Congress, resulted in part from his campaign stance as an outsider and his announced intention to sweep clean old-style politics. Undoubtedly these factors did not endear him to Capitol Hill regulars. His Georgia colleagues were not schooled in the ways of Washington and preferred to avoid the political power brokers of Washington. But Carter was not a good salesman, and his lack of popularity with the American people hurt his ability to sell his legislative program. Also, he made a series of mistakes, failing to consult adequately with members of Congress and introducing bills that did not have the support of key figures. Carter's congressional liaison team was inexperienced and lacked contacts on the Hill, and its style did not invite confidence. Unreturned telephone calls, a lack of attention to congressional requests, and a paucity of White House invitations reinforced poor first impressions. More seriously, Carter's timing in handling legislation left many Congress members embarrassed or in an awkward position with constituents. The harmony and trust pledged by Carter did not materialize in his four-year term of office.

Ronald Reagan has proven more successful. In 1981 he was able to push through almost all his economic proposals—to reduce federal spending, cut taxes, and reduce federal regulations—in good part owing to his personal efforts. Reagan campaigned on these themes, declared himself committed to their success, and personally lobbied for legislation to implement them. His personal popularity and involvement aided his victories in these areas. Also assisting his success has been the Legislative Strategy Group, a White House "think tank" of presidential advisors working to pass the Reagan program. The Legislative Strategy Group carefully chooses its issues and knows when to compromise. It is a loose association of top White House advisors with close ties to both the president and Congress. The group has successfully pressed the president to moderate many of his heavier "supply-side" economic policies.

The Competitive Sharing of Power

The Constitution endows both the Congress and the president with ample powers with which to contend in the arena of public policy. But while formal powers explain part of the sharing of authority, much more depends on the personalities and wills involved. A wide variety of circumstances intrude to determine the balance of power between Congress and the president.

Shifts in power between the institutions of governance have been common. Scholars are fond of referring to eras of "congressional government" and "presidential government." In recent decades we have seen periods of imperialized presidential power (Nixon administration) and congressional resurgence (Carter years). The 1980s have witnessed two vital institutions each staking their claim to legitimate areas of decision making. There are several explanations for this.

First, congressional reforms of the 1970s energized Congress and equipped it with the leadership and direction needed to contend with presidential leadership and dominance. In particular, the centralization of leadership in the House, coupled with attacks on seniority, gave that chamber a renewed sense of purpose and power. For example, the new Congressional Budget Office and the War Powers Act were designed to rein in an independent chief executive.

Second, the agenda shift to economic and budget issues in the 1980s pitted the two institutions against each other in an arena where both felt at home. Here a popular president pressed a new mandate. Ronald Reagan personally lobbied for reductions in social spending, tax cuts, and renewed defense appropriations, which he believed were mandated by the people in his election victories. He did not hesitate to go to the public to pressure Congress to enact his economic proposals. But budgets and economic policies are familiar turf for Congress. The budget with its spending prerogatives is particularly closely guarded by Congress. The result has been a series of victories and defeats for both sides, depending on their skill at mobilizing resources and the impact of outside events.

A third explanation is the change of personnel in each institution. Congress became more susceptible to Reagan's lobbying effort in 1981 with a GOP Senate and many southern Democrats sympathetic to Reagan's message. The 1982 election and larger Democratic majorities in the Ninety-eighth Congress fortified the will of the House to resist the president more often. The personnel in the White House also changed. Chief of Staff James Baker moved over to become treasury secretary, and Deputy Chief of Staff Michael Deaver resigned, as have a number of White House and cabinet secretaries. All of these affect presidential–congressional relations and the administration's ability to work with Congress.

A final reason for swings in the pendulum between Congress and the president is changing events and attitudes. Reagan took office in 1981 amid double-digit inflation and high unemployment. The consensus was that the economy was in shambles and that drastic action had to be taken. Later, with inflation curbed and slow but steady economic growth, budget cuts and tax reform seemed less urgent. International events—for example, terrorism—easily intrude to create new crises and divert attention. Presidents have more success when public attention and sentiment are with them. A changed public agenda alters chances for success. Congress is normally slower to respond to these changes, but the basis of its powers remains.

Arthur Schlesinger, Jr., once wrote, "The relationship between the Congress and the presidency has been one of the abiding mysteries of the American system of government."[21] And so it shall remain.

The Legislative Process

The process of making legislation is basic to our political system, yet it is a process that is confusing and poorly understood by most Americans. No institution in America receives more attention than Congress; it conducts its business in full view of the public and, starting in 1979, before the television cameras. Yet the public often finds Congress undemocratic and slow to respond to public needs.

The legislative process has grown in size and complexity over the years, and understanding Congress is no easy task. Twenty thousand bills and resolutions are introduced every two years; two thousand committee reports are filed. The work load of Congress has doubled in the past two decades. The First Congress, in 1789, saw only 142 bills introduced and 85 committee reports filed. Today Congress is in session for almost two-thirds of the year, meeting for nearly nine thousand hours. The increased demands on Congress are due in great measure to the increased complexity and scope of government. Competing demands for resources in the public forum keep Congress deliberative and slow to act.

The federal government requires such extensive paperwork that in one year this many additional employees were hired to process the material.

The legislative process is decentralized. Each bill and resolution must pass both chambers. No bill becomes law without a cumulative number of deliberate affirmative actions; one negative action in either chamber can kill a bill. Of the twenty thousand bills introduced every two years, the vast majority die in committee for lack of action. For example, in 1985, 8,400 measures were introduced into Congress, and that year Congress passed 1,200 bills. In fact, no legislation has a serious chance of success without the backing of party leaders or key legislators in the legislative process. The adoption process is much the same in both chambers of Congress (Figure 12.4).

Every bill must be introduced in the House or Senate by a member of the chamber. Once a bill is introduced into Congress it is sent to committee. The committee then decides whether or not to consider further action. Usually a subcommittee will hold hearings and do the "mark up" of the bill. Once the bill has been marked up, or amended, the full committee votes and makes a recommendation to the full chamber. If the full body, after debating the bill, approves, the bill is sent to the other house and the process begins all over again. If the two chambers approve the bill, but with differences, a conference committee is created to work out a compromise.

Fact File
Résumé of Congressional Activity of the Ninety-Eighth Congress

	First session January 3 through November 18, 1983			Second session January 23 through October 12, 1984		
	Senate	House	Total	Senate	House	Total
Days in session	150	146	—	131	120	—
Time in session	1,010 hrs., 47'	851 hrs., 45'	—	940 hrs., 28'	852 hrs., 59'	—
Congressional Record						
Pages of proceedings	17,224	10,665	27,889	14,650	12,293	26,896
Extensions of remarks	—	—	5,985	—	—	4,580
Public bills enacted into law	101	114	215	166	242	408
Private bills enacted into law	—	6	6	17	29	46
Bills in conference	3	2	5	5	6	11
Bills through conference	4	29	33	22	30	52
Measures passed, total	596	611	1,207	726	737	1,463
Senate bills	170	70	—	159	128	—
House bills	99	234	—	240	323	—
Senate joint resolutions	89	46	—	90	67	—
House joint resolutions	34	49	—	55	61	—
Senate concurrent resolutions	25	16	—	24	18	—
House concurrent resolutions	15	31	—	40	42	—
Simple resolutions	164	165	—	118	125	—
Measures reported, total	570[a]	497[a]	1,067	568[a]	482[a]	1,050
Senate bills	270	23	—	230	26	—
House bills	44	327	—	80	335	—
Senate joint resolutions	87	—	—	99	2	—
House joint resolutions	9	9	—	16	12	—
Senate concurrent resolutions	19	3	—	17	—	—
House concurrent resolutions	2	7	—	4	2	—
Simple resolutions	139	132	—	122	105	—
Special reports	25	54	—	11	45	—
Conference reports	4	33	—	—	53	—
Measures pending on calendar	155	105	—	221	122	—
Measures introduced, total	2,795	5,642	8,437	1,302	2,462	3,764
Bills	2,198	4,580	—	897	1,862	—
Joint resolutions	209	440	—	150	223	—
Concurrent resolutions	86	237	—	69	142	—
Simple resolutions	302	385	—	186	235	—
Quorum calls	18	35	—	19	55	—
Yea-and-nay votes	381	297	—	292	227	—
Recorded votes	—	201	—	—	181	—
Bills vetoed	3	4	7	8	9	17
Vetoes overridden	1	1	—	1	1	—

[a]These figures on measures reported include all placed on calendar or acted on by Senate even if there was no accompanying report. In the Senate 344 reports were filed during the first session and 320 in the second session; the House filed 588 in the first session and 580 in the second session.

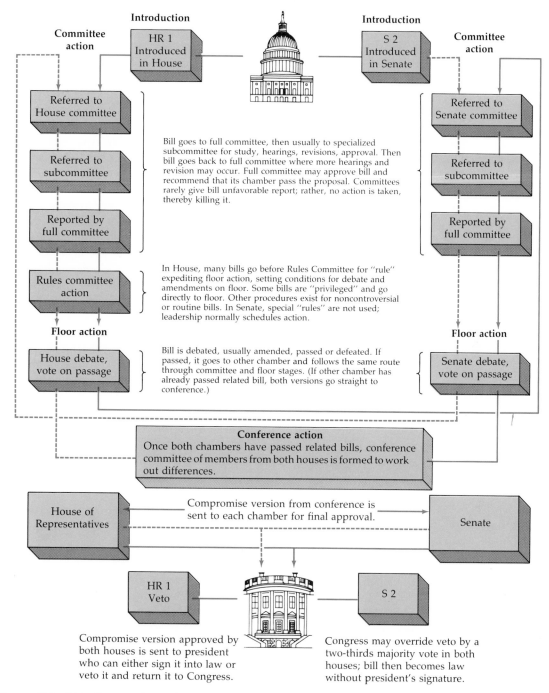

Introduction
HR 1
Introduced
in House

Committee action

Referred to
House committee

Referred to
subcommittee

Reported by
full committee

Bill goes to full committee, then usually to specialized subcommittee for study, hearings, revisions, approval. Then bill goes back to full committee where more hearings and revision may occur. Full committee may approve bill and recommend that its chamber pass the proposal. Committees rarely give bill unfavorable report; rather, no action is taken, thereby killing it.

Rules committee
action

In House, many bills go before Rules Committee for "rule" expediting floor action, setting conditions for debate and amendments on floor. Some bills are "privileged" and go directly to floor. Other procedures exist for noncontroversial or routine bills. In Senate, special "rules" are not used; leadership normally schedules action.

Floor action

House debate,
vote on passage

Bill is debated, usually amended, passed or defeated. If passed, it goes to other chamber and follows the same route through committee and floor stages. (If other chamber has already passed related bill, both versions go straight to conference.)

Introduction
S 2
Introduced
in Senate

Committee action

Referred to
Senate committee

Referred to
subcommittee

Reported by
full committee

Floor action

Senate debate,
vote on passage

Conference action
Once both chambers have passed related bills, conference committee of members from both houses is formed to work out differences.

House of
Representatives

Compromise version from conference is sent to each chamber for final approval.

Senate

HR 1
Veto

S 2

Compromise version approved by both houses is sent to president who can either sign it into law or veto it and return it to Congress.

Congress may override veto by a two-thirds majority vote in both houses; bill then becomes law without president's signature.

Figure 12.4 This diagram shows the most typical way in which proposed legislation is enacted into law. There are more complicated routes and simpler routes, and most bills fall by the wayside and never become law. Each of the two hypothetical bills, House bill No. 1 (HR 1, solid line) and Senate bill No. 2 (S 2, dotted line) must be passed by both houses of Congress in identical form before it can become law. In reality, most legislation begins as similar proposals in both houses.

Introducing a Bill

A bill is first drafted in proper form and placed in the "hopper," a box on the clerk's desk. The bill is numbered and labeled with the sponsor's name and then sent to the Government Printing Office, where sufficient copies for study are printed. Bills introduced into the House are prefixed with an HR and bills in the Senate with an S. This format is used whether it is a public bill, resolution, or private legislation. **Resolutions,** subject to the same procedure as other bills, are used for the internal business of either chamber or for expressing the sense of the House or Senate and are passed by that chamber only. Concurrent resolutions can affect the internal affairs of Congress, express the opinion of Congress, and require the approval of both the House and Senate. They are not sent to the president for signature, nor do they have the force of law. A joint resolution, passed by both chambers, has the force of law and requires the same procedure as bills. Bills introduced into Congress can be either *public* or *private*. A private bill deals with individual matters such as claims against the government, immigration, and land titles. Public bills deal with general categories of people on general questions and become public laws if approved by Congress and signed by the president.

Resolution: *a bill concerned with the internal business of either the House of Representatives or the Senate and passed by that chamber only.*

The first reading of a bill constitutes its referral to committee, normally a perfunctory task. The presiding officer usually follows the wishes of the bill's sponsor in referring the bill to committee, although tradition and rules govern the procedure. Presiding officers have a measure of discretion. In cases of new programs or where bills involve overlapping jurisdiction, the presiding officer may select the committee for referral. This happened in 1963, when the civil rights bill was sent to the Senate Commerce Committee instead of the southern-dominated Judiciary Committee. The presiding officer may also split a bill, referring parts of it to different committees.

Committee Action

What happens next is critical to the life or death of a bill. Less than 10 percent of bills referred to committee are ever reported out to the entire house by the committee. Often called "little legislatures," committees are the heart and soul of the legislative process, where the legislative work is done. Many say that floor debate is for show and that committee action shapes the direction of Congress. Clearly the size of Congress, the number of bills it handles, and time constraints preclude much meaningful floor action, especially in the House of Representatives. Congress depends on its committees to get most of the work done. There are 22 standing committees in the House of Representatives, 16 in the Senate (see Table 12.6 for both houses), and 245 subcommittees in Congress.

Committee members and staff normally have a high degree of expertise in the subject matter within the committee's jurisdiction. The committee makes several decisions with regard to proposed legislation. The first is whether to take up the bill in the first place. A committee actually

TABLE 12.6   House and Senate committees of the One-hundredth Congress

	Chairs and states
Senate committees	
Agriculture, Nutrition and Forestry	Patrick J. Leahy, Vt.
Appropriations	John C. Stennis, Miss.
Armed Services	Sam Nunn, Ga.
Banking, Housing and Urban Affairs	William Proxmire, Wis.
Budget	Lawton Chiles, Fla.
Commerce, Science and Transportation	Ernest F. Hollings, S.C.
Energy and Natural Resources	J. Bennett Johnston, La.
Environment and Public Works	Quentin Burdick, N.D.
Finance	Lloyd Bensten, Tex.
Foreign Relations	Clairborne Pell, R.I.
Governmental Affairs	John Glenn, Oh.
Judiciary	Joseph R. Biden, Jr., Del.
Labor and Human Resources	Edward M. Kennedy, Mass.
Rules and Administration	Wendell H. Ford, Ky.
Select Ethics	Howell Heflin, Ala.
Select Intelligence	David L. Boren, Ok.
Small Business	Dale Bumpers, Ark.
Special Aging	John Melcher, Mont.
Veterans' Affairs	Alan Cranston, Calif.
House committees	
Agriculture	E. dela Garza, Tex.
Appropriations	Jamie Whitten, Miss.
Armed Services	Les Aspin, Wis.
Banking, Finance and Urban Affairs	Fernand J. St. Germain, R.I.
Budget	James R. Jones, Okla.
District of Columbia	Ronald V. Dellums, Calif.
Education and Labor	Carl D. Perkins, Ky.
Energy and Commerce	John D. Dingell, Mich.
Foreign Affairs	Clement J. Zablocki, Wis.
Government Operations	Jack Brooks, Tex.
House Administration	Augustus F. Hawkins, Calif.
Interior and Insular Affairs	Morris K. Udall, Ariz.
Judiciary	Peter W. Rodino, N.J.
Merchant Marine and Fisheries	Walter B. Jones, N.C.
Post Office and Civil Service	William D. Ford, Mich.
Public Works and Transportation	James J. Howard, N.J.
Rules	Claude Pepper, Fla.
Science and Technology	Robert A. Roe, N.J.
Select Aging	Edward Roybal, Calif.
Select Children, Youth, and Families	George Miller, Calif.
Select Intelligence	Lee Hamilton, Ind.
Select Narcotics Abuse and Control	Charles Rangel, N.Y.
Small Business	John J. LaFace, N.Y.
Standards of Official Conduct	Louis Stokes, Ohio
Veterans' Affairs	G. V. Montgomery, Miss.
Ways and Means	Dan Rostenkowski, Ill.

Discharge Petition: *a petition to withdraw a bill from a House committee. It must be signed by a majority of House members.*

considers only a small fraction of the bills referred to it. Failure to consider a bill usually kills it. A bill can also be withdrawn from committee in the House through a **discharge petition,** a petition signed by a majority of the House membership. In the Senate, adoption of a special resolution is necessary. In both houses, such attempts rarely succeed. The other committee options are to adopt the bill, amend it somewhat, or rewrite it entirely.

In the past, committee chairs exercised considerable discretionary power over what bills their committees would consider. They still have some power over the workload and set the tone for the committee, but the reforms of the 1970s considerably moderated their power over bills. The 1960s were known as an era of committee government; the 1970s, an era of subcommittee government. Between 1971 and 1975, the growing Democratic caucus in the House of Representatives moved to curb the authority of committee chairs and to increase the number and autonomy of subcommittees. By 1975, subcommittees and subcommittee chairs had come to dominate the legislative process. The power of committee chairs was pared in several ways:

1. No House member could hold more than one subcommittee chair (reform adopted in 1971). This reform prevented committee chairs from chairing all subcommittees themselves and opened up opportunities for less senior committee members. In fact, it gave sixteen Democrats elected since 1958 their first subcommittee chairs on such key committees as Judiciary; Foreign Affairs; and Banking, Currency, and Housing.

2. All committees with twenty or more members were required to establish four or more subcommittees (1974). Aimed at the Ways and Means Committee, which had never used subcommittees, this action set a precedent and institutionalized subcommittee government.

Subcommittee Bill of Rights: *a measure passed in the Ninety-fourth Congress that forced committee chairs to respect subcommittee jurisdictions and resources.*

3. A **subcommittee Bill of Rights** established rules for the protection of subcommittees (1973). Caucuses of Democratic committee members were given the authority to select subcommittee chairs, establish subcommittee jurisdictions, set party ratios, and provide adequate budgets for subcommittees. Committee chairs were required to submit bills to subcommittees within two weeks. No longer could a chair kill the bill through delay.

4. Subcommittee chairs and the ranking minority members could hire one staff person each to work directly with them on subcommittee business (1975). This strengthened the resources of subcommittees.

5. Senior Democrats were restricted to membership on two or fewer subcommittees (1974). Again the Democratic caucus sought to curb the power of seniority, because conservatives were dominating the subcommittees. This measure was aimed primarily at the House Appropriations Committee. The result of the revolt in the House strengthened the jurisdiction and autonomy of subcommittees. Their work load increased, more hearings were held, and subcommittees began steering bills onto the floor of the House.

In 1977, the Senate also undertook reorganization of its committees. In the new system, no senator can hold more than three committee or subcommittee chairs. The reform also reduced the total number of standing committees. The Senate has begun to use subcommittees more frequently but has never been overwhelmed with the spirit of reform. The number of Senate subcommittees has increased in the 1980s. In 1977, nearly 80 percent of senators had between six and eight subcommittee assignments.

By 1983 even those figures were being stretched; the number of senators with more than eight subcommittee assignments in 1983 had tripled.[22]

In the House, it is the subcommittee that normally schedules hearings on bills and invites testimony, thus creating a public record for the legislation. As a way of gathering information, holding congressional hearings is a poor procedure; very few minds are changed as a result. At hearings, attendance is haphazard, testimony is frequently prepared and read, and questions are often silly. But these hearings afford interested groups and citizens an opportunity to express their opinions. Committee hearings may also be used to mold public opinion on major topics of concern to Congress. In recent years such members of Congress as Senator George McGovern have used committee hearings to focus public attention on the problems of malnutrition and hunger in America. Hearings can also become the launching pad for a national career or a reelection bid.

Most hearings are held in open session; both houses have adopted **sunshine rules** that require open hearings. The House in 1973 and the Senate two years later required all committee meetings to be open to the public unless a majority of the members on a roll-call vote close the meeting. Under the rule, a vote to close a meeting can be taken only if public disclosure violates rules or "endangers national security." After conducting public hearings, the subcommittee, or sometimes the full committee, meets to mark up the bill. In the **mark-up** session the committee drafts the bill in the form it wants. Each line is amended or rewritten. Committee members debate, compromise, take a final vote, and write a report explaining their actions. Under the 1974 reforms, mark-up sessions are open to the public.

The full committee receives the marked-up bill from the subcommittee or does the mark-up itself and then votes on the bill. It may ratify the subcommittee draft and order the bill reported to the full chamber. Occasionally full committees may report out a bill unfavorably, though it is simpler not to report out such a bill. Often the full committee will consider amendments, frequently from minority members, and then must approve, alter, or reject these amendments before the bill can be put to a final vote. The committee reports the bill to the full chamber for final disposition. A report of the committee, justifying its actions, accompanies the bill. Dissenting committee members may submit a minority report urging that the reported bill be defeated.

After a bill is reported out of committee, it is placed on a calendar in the House or Senate. All bills are placed on the calendar in chronological order as they are reported to the chamber. Rarely, however, are bills called up for floor action in that order.

House Floor Action

The House of Representatives has five legislative calendars to sort out legislative business: *Union* (for revenue and spending bills), *House* (for public, controversial bills), *Consent* (for noncontroversial bills), *Private* (for private relief for individual citizens), and *Discharge* (for petitions to discharge bills from committees). The Union calendar is a privileged calendar, meaning that action may be taken without using the Rules Committee when items are placed on it. A few other items are also privileged: conference committee reports, Budget Committee reports, and vetoed bills. These are also considered by the House as they are reported to it. Special days of the month are set aside for consideration of the Consent, Private, and Discharge calendars.

The House Rules Committee   Since the calendar system sorts out legislation in the House, with the bulk of controversial issues placed on the House calendar, the House of Representatives needs "rules" to govern floor action on legislation. The House has empowered its **Rules Committee** to establish such rules.

Rules Committee: *the House committee empowered to establish rules governing floor consideration of legislation.*

As a practical matter, few controversial bills ever reach the floor of the House without a "rule" from the Rules Committee. A rule may be requested by the chair of the committee reporting the bill. That request is considered by the Rules Committee. The granting of a special rule sets the date, time, and limits for debate on a bill and in effect removes the bill from the House calendar. The Rules Committee can prohibit amendments from being offered (a *closed rule*) or grant an *open rule*, which permits amendments from the floor. The Rules Committee can also decide whether points of order can be waived for portions of the bill.

The scheduling of legislation makes Rules a powerful House committee, the gatekeeper for floor action in the House. By failing to grant a special rule to a bill, the Rules Committee can effectively kill legislation. The threat of withholding a rule has often been enough to make a committee delete provisions objectionable to the Rules Committee.

Owing to its power, the Rules Committee has been a source of controversy. In the early 1960s conservative southerners led by Rules Chair Howard Smith of Virginia effectively prevented civil rights bills from passing Congress by refusing a rule for such bills. In 1973 reform-minded Democrats allowed House Democrats to refer Ways and Means legislation to the Democratic caucus to instruct the Rules Committee to write an open rule. In 1975 the reform was extended to require all Ways and Means revenue bills to receive a rule prior to floor action. Further efforts at reform in 1975 gave the Speaker of the House power to name all Democratic members of the Rules Committee, subject to ratification by the caucus. Said Bruce Oppenheimer: "By gaining full control over the recruitment of Democratic members to the committee and by filling vacancies carefully, the Speaker has turned the [Rules] committee into an arm of the leadership. It can now be relied on to be a traffic cop that serves the leadership instead of one that serves the chairman of the committee."[23]

There are ways of avoiding the Rules Committee, but they are cumbersome and seldom successful. A piece of legislation can be brought to the floor through a suspension of the rules, through a discharge petition, or

Calendar Wednesday:
a method of avoiding the House Rules Committee by allowing committee chairs, in alphabetical order of committees, to call up any bills from the House or the Union calendars on Wednesdays.

on **calendar Wednesday.** Suspension of the rules requires a two-thirds vote of those present; the discharge petition takes a majority of House members' signatures; and calendar Wednesday allows committee chairs, in alphabetical order of committees, to call up any of their bills from the House or the Union calendars on Wednesdays. None of these measures is used very often.

Senate Floor Action

The Senate, being the smaller body, has only two calendars, the *Executive Calendar,* for treaties and nominations, and the *Calendar of Business,* to which all other legislation is assigned. A bill is brought to the Senate either by a call of the calendar or by unanimous consent to take a bill out of calendar order. The Senate has no elaborate rules or procedures for bringing a bill to the floor and no rules committee.

Under Senate rules, any senator at almost any time may ask to bring a bill to the floor. Such a motion is debatable, however, and even subject to filibuster; hence, such motions are rarely used. More often, the majority leader requests unanimous consent of the Senate to remove bills from the Calendar of Business. The practice is for the majority leader, with the aid of the party Policy Committee and the minority party leader, to schedule debate on agreed-upon legislation by asking the Senate for unanimous consent. This process accommodates individual senators and ensures that important legislation reaches the floor. Majority leader Byrd uses unanimous consent extensively. With it he controlls the pace both of the Senate and of pending legislation.

Final Floor Action

Citizens frequently travel to Washington to see Congress in action. Sitting high in the gallery, they expect to hear a spirited debate. Most come away disappointed. Attendance on the floor of Congress is often sparse, action predetermined, and voting routine. Often individual members read remarks into the *Congressional Record,* the daily journal of legislative business, while other members go about the routine of congressional life. By the time an issue reaches the floor, controversial territory has already been well covered. Committee hearings, the Rules Committee, and consultation with majority and minority leaders provide a relatively clear sense of the issues and their direction. Floor debate, then, is often for show. On some issues, of course, floor debate is critical, amendments may be offered, and the final outcome is in doubt. Here supporters and opponents marshal their forces, and whips round up members for quorum calls. But these are infrequent moments of high drama.

Floor Manager: *the congressional member responsible for directing the floor action on a bill. Usually the bill's subcommittee chair or a senior committee member acts as floor manager.*

The floor action on a bill is directed by the bill's **floor manager,** typically the bill's subcommittee chair or a senior committee member. The ranking minority member on the committee normally leads any opposition to the legislation. Debate in the House is governed by the rule granted from the Rules Committee. When the House debates, the amount of time is determined by the special rule. If there is no rule, each member is allocated one hour for debate. Since the latter is unwieldy, the House may move into a committee of the whole and apportion debate equally between proponents and opponents. Since 1973 the House has used electronic devices to record instantly the votes of members. Members may vote yea (yes), nay (no), or present (abstain). Results are displayed on a large board in the front of the House, where all members can see the results at once.

In the Senate, debate is more commonplace. There are no restrictions on time. Of course, the privilege of unlimited debate can be used to delay legislative action. The **filibuster,** extended debate intended to prevent a vote, has been used on occasion to prevent a majority from passing legislation. **Cloture** can be invoked to close debate, but this requires a three-fifths vote of the Senate and rarely succeeds.

Filibuster: *extended debate by a single senator, or a group of senators, used to prevent a vote on a piece of legislation.*

Cloture: *a Senate procedure invoked to close debate. It requires a three-fifths vote of the Senate.*

Voting in the Senate is by voice vote, division (standing), or roll call. The Senate has no electronic equipment. It uses only one method on any given issue. Roll calls are frequent and easily obtained (on request of one-fifth of those present).

Action in the Second Chamber   Once a bill has passed one house, it must be transmitted to the other house for action, and the process begins all over again.

A House-passed bill in the Senate is most commonly referred to committee for consideration. On a few occasions the bill may be placed directly on the Senate calendar. A Senate-passed bill received by the House must be referred to committee for action.

The normal procedure for considering legislation is followed. The second chamber's committee schedules hearings and receives amendments offered in committee or from the floor. In the House, a rule from the Rules Committee is likely to be necessary; then follows floor debate and action. If the bill passes both houses with no changes, which is unlikely, it is sent to the president. However, in all likelihood the second chamber will have made changes in the bill. The bill is then sent back to the chamber of origin, which may accept the second chamber's amendments or request a conference.

Conference Committee   Because most controversial legislation results in conflicts between the House and Senate, it is often necessary to call a conference. Senator Bennett Clark of Missouri once suggested that "all bills and resolutions shall be read twice and, without debate, referred to conference." He was, of course, referring to the crucial role **conference committees** play in the final shape of legislation. Often called the "third house" of Congress, conference committees seek to resolve differences between House and Senate versions of a bill. They have the power to rewrite legislation.

Conference Committee: *a congressional committee formed to draft a compromise bill when different versions of a similar bill have been passed by the House and Senate.*

Either chamber can request a conference, but both chambers must agree to it. The presiding officers appoint members to a joint House–

Senate conference committee. The presiding officers, by tradition, consult with the chairs of the respective committees that considered the bill, then appoint between three and twenty members from their house. Typically there will be three to six House members and five to ten Senate members (the Senate routinely sends larger groups than the House). The majority comes from the party in the majority in that chamber. The delegation votes as a unit according to how the majority of that delegation feels. Seniority influences the selection of members. The chairs of the committees and the ranking minority members are usually selected, along with senior committee members. Almost always, members are selected from the standing committee that considered or marked up the bill. The House requires the Speaker to appoint a majority of members "who generally supported the House position as determined by the Speaker."

The conference committee has wide latitude. Until 1974, conference sessions were secret and no records were kept. Recent reforms require conference hearings to be open to the public unless a majority of either delegation votes to close them. When the conference committee arrives at an agreement, the bill is reported out to both houses for final disposition. Conference reports are privileged items and do not need to be placed on a calendar or receive a rule. They can and do interrupt most other legislative business. The final bill, as reported by the conference committee, however, may only be approved or rejected; it cannot be amended. On occasion a bill will be remanded back to conference committee, but the final House and Senate action is an all-or-nothing proposition.

The Final Step   Should a bill survive the process in both houses, it is then sent to the White House to await final action by the president.

The president has ten days in which to act, and three alternatives. He may sign the bill, thereby indicating approval; in this case the bill becomes law. If the president does not approve of the legislation, he may veto the bill and return it to Congress with a message outlining his objections. If Congress takes no further action, the bill dies. Congress can override the president's veto with a two-thirds vote of those present in both houses. Such action may come at any time during the session after a veto; if the override is successful, the bill becomes law.

The third option for the president is to do nothing. If after ten days the president has not acted, the bill becomes law without his signature. A president may wish to do this for bills he does not strongly support but does not wish to veto. The only exception to a bill becoming a law in ten days without the president's signature is when Congress adjourns before the ten days expire. In this case, we say the bill has been pocket vetoed.

Bills passed by Congress and signed by the president to become law are given a numerical designation. There are two series of numbers, one for private law and one for public law. An example of a private law number is Private Law 99-153 (the one hundred fifty-third private law passed by the Ninety-ninth Congress); Public Law 218 passed in the Ninety-ninth Congress would be designated PL 99-218.

Congressional Staff

The increasing work load of Congress and the increasing complexity of legislation have naturally led to a growth in congressional staff. Both the staffs for individual representatives and those for committees have increased markedly (Figure 12.5).

Personal staff perform a variety of tasks for the representative. The administrative assistant supervises the overall operation of the member's office and is the legislator's right arm. In general, staff answer mail, solve constituent problems, and keep the representative informed. Staff also research bills, attend committee hearings, and draft reports and speeches.

The rapid expansion of committee staffs reflects the decentralization of Congress. Subcommittee government and the right of majority and minority members of committees to have separate staffs are also part of this trend. Committee staffs are instrumental in drafting legislation, conducting investigations, and writing legislative reports. Fox and Hammond's survey indicated that committee staff spent most of their time supplying information, doing legislative research and bill drafting, and engaging in investigations and bureaucratic oversight.[24] Committee staff also work closely with executive agency officials and interest group representatives.

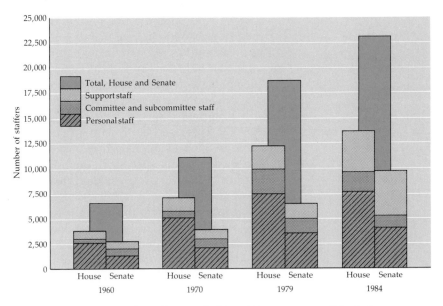

Figure 12.5 Where Hill staffers work. Note: The support staff includes employees in offices such as the House clerk, Capitol architect, and sergeants at arms.

They are an important source of contact for both the executive branch and for lobbyists.

Congress has come to depend on staff. Remarked Senator Clark (D–Iowa), "There is no question of our enormous dependency and their influence. In all legislation, they're the ones that lay out the options."[25]

Support Agencies

Besides increasing its staff, Congress has also expanded and upgraded its support agencies, particularly two old agencies, the General Accounting Office (GAO) and the Congressional Research Service (CRS) of the Library of Congress. Congress has also established two new agencies: the Office of Technology Assessment and the Congressional Budget Office.

The General Accounting Office has recently coordinated its activities with those of Congress, though technically it is an independent agency. Its main responsibility is to conduct independent audits of executive agencies, but it also gives legal advice to agencies, reviews management practices, and handles claims and debts against the federal government. The GAO responds to requests from congressional offices and congressional committees. In recent years, the GAO has aided Congress in the performance of its oversight function.

The Congressional Research Service (CRS) handles legislative requests for information on topics of concern for individual members and congressional committees. The service receives more than 430,000 requests annually and requires a staff of 850 to field all the requests. Many of the daily requests from representatives concern requests from constituents for information, but the CRS has the capacity to provide detailed information on a vast array of complex issues. It does not conduct investigations, but relies on published materials that it pulls together for a legislator or committee. The CRS seeks to be politically neutral and does not advocate policy positions.

The Office of Technology Assessment (OTA) was created in 1972 to "provide early indications of the probable beneficial and adverse impacts of the applications of technology." This body is governed by a board of six senators and six representatives, divided equally by party. The office has established seven areas for concentration: energy, food, health, materials, oceans, transportation, and world trade. With only 139 permanent employees, most of OTA's work is accomplished through contracted projects. OTA hires approximately two thousand outside experts each year to research projects in the seven areas of concentration.

The most recent creation of Congress, in 1974, is the Congressional Budget Office (CBO), designed to generate fiscal analysis in order to rival the president's Office of Management and Budget. The 225 staff members make economic forecasts, summarize cost projections for proposed legislation, and alert Congress to budget targets. The CBO works closely with the newly created House and Senate Budget Committees, and with the Appropriations and Ways and Means Committees. It aids in implementing the new congressional budget procedure.

Legislative Decision Making

The major function of the legislature is lawmaking. The legislative process affords several opportunities for members of Congress to help shape public policies. How they decide what they will do is of considerable importance. What are the factors that influence members' decision making? We will look at a few: the voters, the members' policy position, and their colleagues.

The Voters

Many commentators explain congressional behavior by members' need to be reelected. A good deal of members' Washington behavior depends on their perception of their constituencies and how constituents view them. Those who win by close margins pay particularly close attention to the voters in their constituencies.[26] Even those with large margins at the polls are likely to claim that they achieve those margins by paying attention to needs of and issues important to the voters.[27] David Mayhew contends that the single-minded focus on reelection explains the activities and goals of Congress.[28] Whether or not reelection is a pervasive motive, representatives feel constrained to explain their activities to their constituents.

Policy Positions

Representatives do not come to Washington without having taken any stands on issues. They have basic, fundamental beliefs that shape their attitude toward legislation. They may be liberal, conservative, or moderate, and they may oppose greater federal spending or look favorably on domestic welfare programs, but most surely they have some personal policy preference.

Aage Clausen studied voting patterns and concluded that members typically vote according to their previously stated position on policies.[29] Most Republicans cluster with other Republicans in opposition to Democrats. Members will vote with the policy of their party about two-thirds of the time. Although such policy voting was stronger in the nineteenth century, it became more predominant again in the mid-1970s than it was in the years after World War II. Typically, policy differences are more evident over domestic, welfare, and government-management issues than over foreign affairs or civil liberty issues.

Colleagues

With the intense demands on a representative's time and the vast array of legislation, individuals cannot keep informed on every piece of legislation. They must depend on certain colleagues. Most members develop trusted relationships with a few others, often those whose thinking is similar to theirs. From these trusted colleagues, they receive "cues" for voting. The cue giver may be a respected member of a committee or a senior member of the state delegation. "[This] makes it possible for the ordinary Congressman both to vote in a reasonably rational fashion and to do so on the basis of exceedingly little information."[30]

State delegations form particularly important groups of colleagues in the House of Representatives. Numerous commentators have examined state delegations and found them cohesive bodies in which members rely heavily upon one another for information.[31] Such information networks make the job of a representative far less hectic.

Other Internal Influences

Several informal groups exist in Congress, predominantly in the House, that perform largely social and informational functions. The freshmen Democrats in the Ninety-fourth Congress (1975–1976), for instance, formed a group and even had their own whip organization. This group sought to promote unity on a number of issues. And from the late 1950s on, House members began to form groups designed to bargain with party leaders, committees, and other groups in the House to influence and shape legislative policy. (See Table 12.7.)

The oldest and most influential such group is the Democratic Study Group. Formed in 1957 by liberal House Democrats, this group has evolved into a loose alliance of more than 220 House members. Members pay dues and fund activities out of their staff allowances. Presently the study group employs a staff of about twenty-five, elects a chair, and has a whip system. Group members form task forces and issue reports on various subjects relevant to legislation. They also put out a weekly *Legislative Report*, which summarizes legislative activity for the upcoming week, as well as "fact sheets," which analyze bills of major importance. The group was instrumental in the House reforms in the mid-1970s. Members vote together on roll-call votes; they form a very cohesive group.[32]

Liberal Republican House members have also formed a policy group. Known as the Wednesday Group, it was formed in 1963 and meets weekly on Wednesdays. Relatively small (it grew from fourteen members in 1963–1964 to thirty-six in 1976), the group has a small staff and produces issue papers on matters of common concern. Because of its small size, it possesses little power and bargaining advantage with Republican leadership in the House. More recently, conservatives in the House have organized. In 1973 conservative Republicans formed the Republican Study Committee. This group has grown to 130 members, and its activity is limited to publishing fact sheets for members. Conservative Democrats banded together in 1972 to form the Democratic Research Organization. With about one hundred members in 1984, the organization seeks to counterbalance the liberal Democratic Study Group. It produces legislative fact sheets and sponsors speakers to explain conservative positions. In the late 1970s and the 1980s new conservative Democratic members to

TABLE 12.7 Informal congressional groups, 1984[a]

House of Representatives	Senate	Bicameral
Democratic Budget Study Group (60) Calif. Democratic Congressional Delegation (28) Congressional Populist Caucus (15) Conservative Democratic Forum ("Boll Weevils") (38) Democratic Study Group (228) House Democratic Research Organization (100) Ninety-fifth Democratic Caucus (35) Ninety-sixth Democratic Caucus (20) Ninety-seventh Democratic Caucus (24) Ninety-eighth Democratic Caucus (52) Populist Caucus (14) United Democrats of Congress (125) **Republican** Conservative Opportunity Society House Republican Study Committee (130) House Wednesday Group (32) Ninety-fifth Republican Club (14) Northeast–Midwest Republican Coalition ("Gypsy Moths") Republican Freshman Class of the 96th, 97th, 98th Congresses The '92 Group **Bipartisan** Ad Hoc Congressional Committee on Irish Affairs (110) Conference of Great Lakes Congressmen (100) Congressional Agricultural Forum Congressional Arts Caucus (186) Congressional Automotive Caucus (53) Congressional Black Caucus (21) Congressional Border Caucus (12)	**Democratic** Moderate/Conservative Senate Democrats (15) **Republican** Senate Steering Committee Senate Wednesday Group **Bipartisan** Border Caucus Northeast–Midwest Senate Coalition (40) Senate Caucus on the Family (31) Senate Children's Caucus Senate Coal Caucus (39) Senate Drug Enforcement Caucus (44) Senate Footwear Caucus Senate Steel Caucus (46) Senate Wine Caucus	Ad Hoc Congressional Committee on the Baltic States and the Ukraine (75) Arms Control and Foreign Policy Caucus (129) Coalition for Peace through Strength (232) Congressional Alcohol Fuels Caucus (90) Congressional Caucus for Science and Technology (15) Congressional Caucus for Women's Issues (129) Congressional Clearinghouse on the Future (84) Congressional Coalition for Soviet Jews Congressional Crime Caucus (180) Congressional Jewelry Manufacturing Coalition Congressional Leaders United for a Balanced Budget (67) Congressional Senior Citizens Caucus Congressional Wood Energy Caucus Environmental and Energy Study Conference (377) Friends of Ireland (80) Long Island Congressional Caucus Military Reform Caucus National Water Alliance New York State Congressional Delegation (36) Non-Nuclear Proliferation Task Force Pacific Northwest Trade Task Force Pennsylvania Congressional Delegation (27) Pro-Life Caucus (60) Renewable Energy Congressional Staff Group (50)

House of Representatives	Senate	Bicameral
Congressional Caucus for Science and Technology (15)		San Diego Congressional Delegation
Congressional Coal Group (55)		Senate/House Ad Hoc Monitoring Group on
Congressional Emergency Housing Caucus		Southern Africa (53)
Congressional Hispanic Caucus (11)		Vietnam Veterans in Congress (38)
Congressional Human Rights Caucus (150)		
Congressional Metropolitan Area Caucus (8)		
Congressional Mushroom Caucus (60)		
Congressional Port Caucus (150)		
Congressional Rural Caucus (100)		
Congressional Space Caucus (161)		
Congressional Steel Caucus (120)		
Congressional Sunbelt Council		
Congressional Territorial Caucus (4)		
Congressional Textile Caucus (42)		
Congressional Travel and Tourism Caucus (154)		
Export Task Force (102)		
Federal Government Service Task Force (38)		
House Caucus on North American Trade		
House Fair Employment Practices Committee		
House Footwear Caucus		
Local Government Caucus (22)		
New England Congressional Caucus (24)		
Northeast-Midwest Congressional Coalition (196)		
Pennsylvania Congressional Delegation Steering		
Committee (5)		
Task Force on Devaluation of the Peso		
Task Force on Industrial Innovation and Productivity		
Tennessee Valley Authority Caucus (23)		

[a]Numbers of members, where available, in parentheses. Also includes two groups organized in early 1985, The '92 Group and the Coalition for Soviet Jews. SOURCE: Roger H. Davidson and Walter J. Oleszek. *Congress and Its Members*, 2nd ed. (Washington, D.C.: Congressional Quarterly Press, 1985), pp. 364–365.

509

Boll Weevils: *conservative southern Democratic members of Congress who defected from their party to support President Reagan's economic policies in Congress.*

Congress formed the Conservative Democratic Forum. Made up of the so-called **Boll Weevils,** who supported Reagan's economic proposals, this group is balanced in the House by moderate Republicans, the Gypsy Moths, who oppose some of Reagan's proposals.

The 1970s also saw the formation of *issue groups*. There are at least three dozen such groups in Congress. The oldest, formed in the mid-1960s, was the Members of Congress for Peace. Made up of "doves" on Vietnam, this group included both Republicans and Democrats, representatives and senators.

Today there are caucuses on almost every major topic before Congress. The Environmental and Energy caucus provides information on environmental and energy issues for more than 370 House members and senators. The caucus provides weekly bulletins and occasional briefings for members. There is also a Congressional Rural Caucus with 100 members, dealing with rural development. The Congressional Caucus for Women's Issues, with 129 members, draws attention to issues of particular concern

The Black Caucus consists of senators and representatives, and is a respected advocate for black Americans within Congress.

to women and produces a weekly newsletter. More recent additions include Vietnam Veterans in Congress and the Senate/House Ad Hoc Monitoring Group on Southern Africa.

Ethnic-group organizations have also emerged within Congress. The Congressional Hispanic Caucus was formed in 1976. Another organization is an older, more recognized force in the House: the Congressional Black Caucus. Formed in 1971, as of 1983 it had twenty-one members. It focuses attention on leading issues of concern to blacks.

The Budget Process

Controlling the purse strings, Congress is intended to have ascendancy in money matters. Yet Congress has struggled with appropriations as a means of control, having twice in the last decade made major revisions in the way it decides how to spend money. The first major initiative—the 1974 Budget and Impoundment Control Act—gave Congress a better perspective on the federal budget. The act required Congress to set annual tax and spending levels, thereby assuring congressional control over spending levels and the size of the deficit. The act also created a Congressional Budget Office (CBO) to provide a congressional counterforce to the president's Office of Management and Budget. But this act proved unsuccessful in limiting spending or controlling deficits, so Congress in 1985 made another bold move, passing mandated across-the-board cuts for five years to reduce the level of the deficit. The Balanced Budget and Emergency Deficit Control Act of 1985 forced Congress collectively to do what it had heretofore been unable to do through the budget and appropriations process: cut spending.

The 1974 budget process was based on two congressional actions—two concurrent resolutions (a concurrent resolution is used to regulate the internal affairs of Congress). This process was subsequently modified by the 1985 act.

Under the 1974 act Congress adopted a tentative budget by May 15 of the year. This was the First Concurrent Resolution adopted by both houses of Congress. After reviewing the president's budget, hearing the advice of the Congressional Budget Office, and eliciting the recommendations of their own Budget Committees, the House and the Senate outlined a tentative budget projecting income and revenue outlays. Overall targets were set for spending in nineteen areas—defense, health, energy, agriculture, income security, and so on. The tentative budget included any projected changes in tax revenues or in the level of the public debt. Once this budget was adopted, the appropriation committees went to work. The second concurrent resolution was then adopted by September 15, just prior to the start of the new fiscal year. This was the final budget, which established the spending limits finally agreed upon once the houses of Congress had worked with the target levels specified in the first resolution.

Reconciliation: *a part of the congressional budget process whereby the final budget resolution setting spending limits can be adjusted to meet new congressional decisions on appropriations.*

But congressional decisions did not always fit the final budget-resolution totals. Hence the Budget Act provided for a process known as **reconciliation,** authorizing the Budget Committee to report a new resolution specifying the amounts by which appropriations were to change. Included were the budget authority (the authority to incur obligations), spending authority (spending authorized outside the appropriations process), revenue laws, and public debt level.[33] All these changes were grouped together in one reconciliation bill and reported to the floor. The reconciliation bill directed affected committees to make adjustments in their funding recommendations and to report the adjusted bill to the Budget Committee.

While the 1974 Budget Act was designed to give Congress a "handle" on the budget and to limit federal spending, political pressure usually prevailed. During much of the late 1970s Congress set targets sufficiently high to accommodate new programs and new spending. This seemed reasonable, since the economy's recovery was slow in the aftermath of the Vietnam War. As a result, spending commitments grew, as did the federal deficit and inflation. By 1980 the public felt spending was out of control. It elected Ronald Reagan to limit federal spending and curb inflation. At this time, the congressional budget process had come to seem a meaningless exercise. The spending targets were not guiding Congress, and final action was being put off until after the election. Congress had fallen behind the Budget Act's timetable, and deficit levels had had to be revised upward in 1979 and 1980. There were inaccuracies in economic projection, often CBO and congressional estimates for economic recovery differed widely from White House projections, and by 1981 the Budget Act and reconciliation were in disarray. Finally, the budget was six months late.

But Ronald Reagan and the Republican Budget Committee changed all that, moving without precedent in 1981 to use budget reconciliation to push through Congress $41.4 billion worth of spending cuts for more than eighty programs. With OMB Director David Stockman supplying the cuts and Senate Budget Committee Chairman Pete Domenici (R–N.M.) designing the use of reconciliation, all budget cuts were put into one budget-reconciliation resolution that prevented committees or factions from holding onto pet programs. The strategy worked. Congress passed the most extensive round of budget cuts in its history. The resolution trimmed fiscal 1982 spending by nearly $35.2 billion and made reductions totaling $130.6 billion in fiscal 1981–1984.[34]

The budget process became even more complicated in 1985 when Congress took a historic step by committing itself to five years of mandatory deficit reductions, setting for itself the goal of a balanced budget by 1990. The law, called the Balanced Budget and Emergency Deficit Control Act of 1985, is better known as **Gramm-Rudman-Hollings,** after the measure's three sponsors in the Senate. The law mandates across-the-board cuts in nearly all federal programs by a uniform percentage to achieve specified deficit levels if regular budget and appropriations actions fail to

Gramm-Rudman-Hollings: *a congressional act mandating deficit reduction by automatic, across-the-board cuts in spending for five years to eliminate budget deficits.*

TABLE 12.8 Congressional budget timetable

	1974 act	1985 act
President submits budget	15 days after Congress convenes	First Monday after January 3
Congressional Budget Office submits budget estimates to budget committees	April 1	February 15
Committees submit program cost estimates to budget committees	March 15	February 25
First concurrent resolution	April 15	—
Congressional action on budget resolution	—	April 15
Congress acts on all appropriations bills	Seventh day after Labor Day	June 10
Second concurrent resolution	September 15	—
Congress completes action on reconciliation bill	September 25	June 15
Spending and revenue projection with deficit level by CBO and OMB	—	August 15
GAO sequester order with automatic spending cuts	—	August 20
President issues sequester order	—	September 1
Sequester order takes effect	—	October 1
Fiscal year begins	October 1	October 1

achieve those deficit goals. The General Accounting Office and Congressional Budget Office are to report on the status of deficit targets and to prepare a "sequester" order requiring automatic spending cuts should regular congressional action not fall within those deficit reduction targets. Table 12.8 shows the 1974 budget process and the changes made to it by the 1985 Gramm-Rudman-Hollings Act.

The bill is a radical revision of budgetary procedures. If normal legislative budgeting fails to reduce the deficit, automatic spending cuts go into effect. The budget-balancing bill's sponsors—Phil Gramm (R–Tex.), Warren B. Rudman (R–N.H.), and Ernest F. Hollings (D–S.C.)—call it "a bad idea whose time has come." The major provisions of the budget plan are as follows:

- Federal budgets with deficits not exceeding
    $171.9 billion in 1986
    $144 billion in 1987
    $108 billion in 1988
    $72 billion in 1989
    $36 billion in 1990
    $0 in fiscal 1991
- Across-the-board cuts by a uniform percentage to achieve deficit targets if regular budget and appropriations actions fail to meet the deficit goals
- Cuts equally divided between defense and nondefense areas
- Exemptions from automatic cuts include:
    Social security
    Interest on the federal debt
    Veterans' pensions
    Medicaid
    AFDC

WIC (food program for women and children)
Supplemental security income
Food stamps

The bill authorizes the General Accounting Office and Congressional Budget Office to monitor the progress of Congress in meeting the deficit reduction targets. If by August 15 the deficit levels are not being reached through budget and appropriations action, the GAO will prepare automatic spending cuts through a sequester order. In this way the budget timetable is altered. Congress is to take action on regular appropriation bills by the end of June and the new fiscal year begins October 1. Between that time the GAO sequester order is issued and takes effect. Gramm-Rudman-Hollings modifies the budget process as follows:

Action on regular appropriation bills	June 30
"Snapshot" of economic indicators, spending and revenue summaries, and projected deficit by CBO and OMB	August 15
GAO prepares sequester order making automatic spending cuts	August 20
GAO forwards deficit and sequester report to president	August 25
President issues sequester order	September 1
Sequester order takes effect	October 1
Fiscal year begins	October 1

This provision to permit the General Accounting Office to make the automatic across-the-board cuts has proved troublesome. On the same day on which President Reagan signed the bill into law, Representative Mike Synar (D–Okla.) went to court claiming the automatic cuts were unconstitutional. Congress had anticipated such a challenge and had written a fallback provision into the law. Should the automatic cuts be declared unconstitutional, the GAO's sequester order would be given to both chambers of Congress for their approval, then presented to the president for action. But the fallback option strikes at the heart of the statute—the threat of automatic cuts if Congress cannot make the budgetary and appropriations decisions in the normal course of legislation. Congress in the past has not been able to make such decisions.

The Supreme Court did declare the automatic cuts by the comptroller general unconstitutional. In *U.S.* v. *Synar* the Supreme Court declared that this provision of the Gramm-Rudman-Hollings deficit reduction act violated the Constitution's separation of powers by encroaching on the president's authority to execute the laws.[35] The provision was invalidated because it gave the comptroller general, who is subject to removal by Congress, the executive power to estimate, allocate, and order the spending cuts needed to meet deficit targets set by law.

The Court reasoned the comptroller general was an officer of the legislative branch; he is removable only at the initiative of Congress. And since Congress retains removal power over the comptroller general, "he may not be entrusted with executive powers." The Court thus concluded "that Congress cannot reserve for itself the power of removal of an officer charged with the execution of the laws except by impeachment. To permit the execution of the laws to be vested in an officer answerable only to Congress would, in practical terms, reserve in Congress control over the execution of the laws."

In making its decision the Supreme Court saw a parallel with the legislative veto ruled unconstitutional in *Chadha.* Permitting the comptroller general, an officer controlled by Congress, to execute the law was tantamount to a congressional veto. "Congress could simply remove, or threaten to remove, an officer for executing the law in any fashion found to be unsatisfactory to Congress. This kind of congressional control over the execution of the laws, *Chadha* makes clear, is constitutionally impermissible." It was precisely this congressional intrusion into the execution of the law that violated the separation of powers of the Constitution.

The bill's sponsors—Gramm, Rudman, and Hollings—offered an amendment to the law struck down by the Supreme Court, substituting the Office of Management and Budget for the comptroller general. Under the revision the automatic mechanism works the same way, except that now determination of the deficit size and the need for automatic cuts are in the hands of the Office of Management and Budget, a part of the Executive Office under the president.

Under the revised format, the deficit is still estimated by the Congressional Budget Office and the Office of Management and Budget. But now the estimates are only reviewed by the comptroller general, who in turn forwards them to the Office of Management and Budget for final determination of deficit size and the need for a sequester order. The Office of Management and Budget of course remains bound to the details of the law from Congress that specifies allowable deficit size and how any cuts should be made once the deficit has been determined.

Congressional Power: Separate but Equal?

The decade of the 1970s brought changing expectations to what Congress could and should accomplish. Congress played an important part in shaping governmental response to the decade of change. First there was congressional reform: the legislature sought to make its lawmaking capacity more democratic and responsive to the changing environment. A second series of changes occurred in congressional power, largely in the aftermath of Vietnam and Watergate, as Congress sought to redress the balance of power between itself and the president.

The Trend to Reform

The first set of changes was somewhat contradictory: there was both decentralization and centralization of power in the hands of party leadership. The reforms for decentralization occurred early in the decade, occasioned largely by the influx of new members into the House of Representatives. The move toward centralization followed these changes and sought to integrate them to make Congress more responsive.

The decentralization of Congress was the result of two distinct yet related reforms: the rise of subcommittee government and the attack on committee chairs and their source of power, seniority. The growth of subcommittees came as a direct result of the recognition of the increasing complexity of legislation and the need for greater specialization. The work load simply became too great for a committee to handle. This development was coupled with an influx of new members—80 percent of the House had been elected since 1967—who were impatient with seniority and committee chairs. Subcommittee government bolsters the forces of decentralization because it fragments control over legislation.

The reforms creating subcommittees were reinforced by the attacks on seniority and committee chairs. As subcommittee autonomy was established, the power of committee chairs was eroded. Conversely, as committee chairs were being challenged, subcommittees inherited decision-making powers. The ad hoc revolts were led by the revitalized liberal caucus in the House. The requirement that committee chairs be subject to secret ballot by party caucus reflected the unwillingness of these junior representatives to erode completely the position of committee chair, though they still refused to be tied to seniority. The rejection of three southern committee chairs in 1975 was evidence of the power change in Congress. Yet committee chairs were not without influence. The effort had been to make chairs more solicitous of the committee and party membership that can deprive them of their seats. By depriving chairs of some of their resources these changes made the position of chair less valuable and seniority a smaller factor in achieving it. In order to prevent abuse of power, chairs still controlled the agenda and set the tone, but now within an environment of sensitivity to members' needs and goals.

The second series of reforms sought to revitalize party government in Congress and to provide a new set of roles and powers for the party leadership in the House and Senate. In a very real sense, the party caucuses and the power of the leadership became centralizing forces in shaping and influencing decision making in Congress. The emergence of the party caucus served to legitimize the reform proposals and became the seedbed of renewed activism. By altering the procedure for the selection of committee chairs, the caucus sought to create responsiveness within the House. The creation of the Steering and Policy Committee put committee membership in the control of the party leadership and made it possible for the caucus to influence policy by placing members on committees.

The caucus has been particularly active in restoring trust and confidence to Congress. When scandal broke out over misuse by Wayne Hays (D–Ohio) of his staff allowance and fringe benefits, including a secretary who served primarily as his mistress, the House Democratic caucus made it clear that it intended to remove Hays from his influential committees. In 1985 the caucus rejected eighty-year-old Melvin Price as chair of the House Armed Services Committee. It wanted a younger, more articulate spokesman for defense policy. The Armed Services chairmanship is the Democrats' most visible forum for addressing military policy and defense spending. The caucus also has led the fight to place limits on outside income as well as to require disclosure of such income.

The strengthening of the caucus meant a renewed strengthening of party leadership posts. Traditionally powerful offices, in the 1960s these positions had become weak. The House and Senate were willing to strengthen the positions of party leaders in the 1970s for several reasons. First, the positions were occupied by relatively compliant individuals, Carl Albert in the House and Mike Mansfield in the Senate, who did not oppose reform. Second, there was a divided government. The Democrats held a substantial majority in both the House and Senate, and the White House was occupied by a Republican, at least until 1976. Strong leadership could provide a congressional counterweight to the chief executive. Third, the thrust of reform necessitated protection against disorganization and incoherent policy. The renewal of the caucus afforded an opportunity to enhance leadership authority in tandem with the party caucus.

The increase in power for party leadership came with the 1973 attack on Wilbur Mills and the Ways and Means Committee. The Policy and Steering Committee was created to develop party strategy. By 1975, the committee also selected committee members. This twenty-four-person committee was dominated by the party leadership: the Speaker, majority leader, chief whip, chief deputy whip, three deputy whips, and four members appointed by the Speaker were all members. The power of the party leadership to dominate floor proceedings was also strengthened. In the House, the Speaker's power to refer bills was increased. In the Senate, the majority leader's ability to schedule and control floor debate was the result of reform. With these changes also came a strengthened whip system. The resources and staff for the whip's office were increased. The new Congressional Budget Office also provided the leadership with information and resources with which to coordinate decision making.

Congressional Power

The second trend in Congress since the 1970s has been a renewed sense of congressional power. Congress has made an effort to restore its authority vis-a-vis the executive and to participate more fully as an equal partner in policymaking.

The trend began in 1973 with the Senate Select Committee's hearings into campaign abuses that led to Watergate and subsequently to the impeachment hearings in the House Judiciary Committee. At this time Congress began to look anew at the executive branch and at the use of executive authority. The impeachment proceedings reestablished a sense of authority and challenge to the executive. The House Judiciary Committee

Social Welfare Policy

The welfare state, as we refer collectively to our social welfare policies, is a development of the twentieth century. Programs have frequently had presidential sponsorship, but Congress has also taken liberal responsibility for creating welfare programs or altering them to meet constituent and interest-group demands. Social welfare has increasingly become the responsibility of the federal government.

Welfare programs date back to 1935, when Aid to Families with Dependent Children (AFDC) was enacted by Congress. Essentially, welfare provides direct cash assistance to needy people who can establish eligibility. AFDC provides support to children without adequate parental support. In twenty-six states aid is also provided to children in families in which fathers are unemployed. Benefits are paid to families on the basis of income and number of dependents. As income rises, benefits are reduced. Critics charge that this system reduces the incentive to work. The largest category of recipients are female, and half are black. In 1984 there were 11 million AFDC recipients costing the federal government $16 billion.

The other major welfare program is the distribution of food stamps. Started as a modest form of nutritional support in 1962, the program today is a $13.3 billion component of the welfare system, serving some 20 million people. The food stamp program provides coupons (food stamps) to be used in lieu of cash to purchase food (excluding such items as liquor, cigarettes, and cleaning supplies). The program is administered by the Department of Agriculture. Again there is an eligibility requirement, but critics charge that enforcement is minimal, since striking workers and middle-class families have little trouble signing up under the program.

Social welfare programs have changed measurably for those who are employed. Under the New Deal, social security and unemployment compensation were enacted to prevent economic catastrophe, basically as public insurance programs whereby individuals and employers contribute to a trust fund. There is no need criterion for participation in these programs as these are prevention programs to ensure recipients a source of income during periods of unemployment or retirement. While the programs have proved popular, social security has become controversial in recent years as the fund has become actuarially unsound. The number of contributors has been declining relative to the increase in beneficiaries. Large increases in social security taxes have been necessary to keep the program solvent.

A major change occurred with the war on poverty. The New Deal programs were preventive or alleviative, but the war on poverty was curative, seeking to slow the cycle of poverty by providing training and jobs. In the mid-1960s youth programs such as Head Start, Neighborhood Youth Corps, and Job Corps attempted to remove children from poverty environments with enrichment programs and employment training, and adult programs such as the Manpower Development and Training Act sought to give job training. In 1973 Congress added the Comprehensive Employment and Training Act (CETA). CETA created public service jobs for the unemployed and unskilled by making available federal funds to local governments and private groups. CETA expired in 1982. In its place Congress passed a more limited $4.6 billion job plan focusing on public works projects, general construction, and water projects designed to create some 400,000 new full-time jobs. The money would be distributed directly to states and localities using a formula that targeted the areas of most need based on unemployment.

Medical care policy is a newer element of social welfare policy. Passed by Congress in 1965, the two medical programs are Medicare and

Medicaid. Medicare provides limited hospitalization or nursing home care for retired persons receiving social security benefits; it is funded from an additional payroll tax collected with the social security tax. Participants must enroll in this voluntary program and pay a small monthly fee. Participants must also pay the first $50 for medical services and 20 percent of the cost thereafter. Medicaid acts more like welfare, in that free medical care is provided for categoric groups such as AFDC families and states are reimbursed for up to 83 percent of the cost for medical treatment for the poor.

States may choose not to participate, but Reagan has proposed making Medicaid part of his new federalism "swap," thereby making the program fully the responsibility of the national government.

Since Medicare and Medicaid are limited in scope and some 20 million Americans lack health insurance, the question of national health insurance has become a policy issue. Several bills have been introduced in Congress but none has passed. Most proposals call for payroll taxes to be shared by employees and employers, usually with employers paying the larger share.

A final area of social welfare policy is housing. Originally begun in 1937, housing programs meant grants for the construction of public housing. This served a twofold purpose: reduction of substandard housing and support for the construction industry.* Communities were given money to construct low-cost rental housing. In urban areas this meant high-rise public housing projects. In the 1960s, as part of the war on poverty, housing programs turned toward subsidized loans to private groups to build and renovate housing, thereby giving the private sector a larger voice in housing programs. In 1968 a rent-supplement program was started to aid tenants who paid 25 percent of their income for rent. Today rent subsidies are

the backbone of the housing program. Many critics charge that housing is the weak link in the social welfare policy in the United States.

*J. Anderson, D. Brady, and C. Bullock, *Public Policy and Politics in America* (North Scituate, Mass.: Duxbury Press, 1978), p. 115.

"You should live quite well for six months out of the year, Mr. Figby."

GRIN AND BEAR IT By Lichty & Wagner © Field Enterprises, Inc. 1983. By Permission of News America Syndicate.

refused to be rushed, yet moved with reason and determination in voting impeachment.

In foreign policy, Congress was responding to Vietnam and Cambodia. It enacted the War Powers Act in 1973, which limited the length of time for which the president could commit armed forces in any emergency to ninety days. Within ninety days, Congress, by concurrent resolution not subject to presidential veto, would be allowed to direct the president to disengage such armed forces. The act also directed the president to consult the Congress "in every possible instance" before introducing forces into combat. By declaring the legislative veto unconstitutional, the Supreme Court has affected the War Powers Act. It is now unclear how Congress will respond to executive action in committing U.S. troops. But it does seem clear that Congress cannot exercise a veto, requiring the president to rescind an action.

In 1974 Congress took similar action on the domestic front with the Congressional Budget and Impoundment Control Act. The nonspending of appropriated funds as a discretionary power of the president was curtailed. Under the act, the president is obligated to report to Congress any impoundment of appropriated funds. Either chamber, by a resolution, could direct the president to spend any funds temporarily set aside. Should the impoundment be intended as permanent, the action would be void unless agreed to by both chambers within forty-five days. This act, too, was affected by the 1983 Supreme Court decision declaring the legislative veto unconstitutional. It is unlikely that Congress can any longer compel the executive to spend impounded funds, because the means for such action was a House or Senate resolution, exactly the kind of one-House veto specifically struck down by the Court in the *Chadha* case. The 1974 act also created a new budgeting procedure and a Congressional Budget Office. The law gives Congress the resources to combat presidential resources in fiscal and budgetary affairs.

Oversight: *the continuous supervision over the programs and agencies administering congressional legislation.*

Finally, Congress has become increasingly active in **oversight** activities. Through a broad range of devices—committee investigations, confirmation hearings, budget hearings, legislative clearance—congressional oversight of the executive has increased. A 1974 reform in the House required each committee to create an oversight subcommittee or to designate one subcommittee as an oversight committee. In 1977 the Senate reaffirmed its intent to engage in comprehensive oversight. Such devices as sunset legislation, which fix a time for programs to expire, and zero based budgeting are further evidence of the seriousness with which Congress intends to examine the operation of the executive branch of government.

Congressional Responsiveness

There is striking evidence that Congress has been responsive to the changes in societal demands over the last few decades. For example, marked changes have taken place in five areas of public policy: government management of the economy and national resources, social welfare, civil liberties, agricultural assistance, and international involvement. Aage Clausen and Carl Van Horn's study of political upheaval and congressional voting[36] found that policy positions in Congress, as analyzed through roll-call votes, had changed markedly on civil liberties and government-management issues and that two new issues had emerged: the relatively narrow question of agricultural subsidies and the more fundamental issue of national security. On government-management issues there was a depolarization of parties, and the change in positions on civil rights indicated a lessening of support and increasing similarity in the positions of southern Democrats and Republicans. Said Clausen and Van Horn:

> We have found considerable evidence of responsiveness to new conditions and new demands. One form of response has been change in policy positions occurring when continuing members reacted to the disturbing developments in the 1960s and 1970s. . . . Another form of responsiveness evidenced by Congress was the emergence of two new policy dimensions.[37]

Barbara Deckard has argued that these changes in policy positions are the result of a changed agenda for Congress, that although there has been a general decline in party voting, the nature of roll-call voting patterns has changed as the issues have changed.[38] In social welfare a decline has occurred in housing programs, social security, and minimum-wage issues, and these subjects have been replaced by votes on aid to the poor. For civil rights, the roll call shifted from civil rights for blacks, notably voting rights, to questions on the sale of housing, punishing student protestors, and Washington, D.C. home rule.

The 1980s also spawned a mandate for policy change. High inflation made economic policy the center of the political agenda. Reagan's landslide victory in 1980 was interpreted by many—southern Democrats and Republicans alike—as a mandate for his policies. Reagan forces were quick to exploit this perception by pressing for a changed direction in economic policy and defense spending. Congress did respond, passing in 1981 and 1982 the tax cuts and reductions in social programs proposed by Reagan; they also voted the substantial increases in defense spending requested by the president. And while the success rate of the early years has faded somewhat—the House no longer focuses almost exclusively on Reagan's economic and defense proposals—the agenda established by Ronald Reagan and the election of 1980 continue to dominate congressional business. The decisions cannot be classified as incremental.

Congress is not perfect, and at times it is slow to respond. But as E. E. Schattschneider said long ago regarding American government, "the struggle for democracy is still going on." We should view Congress as neither unequal nor undemocratic; rather, Congress is a complex, changing organization wrestling with a changing environment.

Summary

1. Congress struggled with reform throughout the 1970s and now seeks to reassert itself vis-a-vis the executive and to strengthen its internal procedures for doing business.

2. Members of Congress perform many roles. They are provided with considerable resources and staff to assist in these roles. Owing to the multiple obligations placed on Congress, the legislative environment is demanding and time consuming. Members of Congress must balance the demands of Capitol Hill with those of the home constituency and reelection.

3. Congress is a decentralized institution in which much of the work is done in committees and subcommittees. Party leadership seeks to provide cohesion and direction to this process; both forces have been strengthened by reform. Subcommittees have been increased and strengthened in power. Committee chairs have been weakened by revitalization of the party caucus, and party leaders have a freer hand in scheduling legislation.

4. The legislative process is complex and burdensome. Reforms of the 1970s alleviated some obstacles such as seniority, Rules Committee, and the Senate filibuster. Yet the process remains serial and labors under a heavy load of bills and resolutions.

5. The congressional budget process both frustrates and empowers Congress. Inability to limit spending produced an ineffectual budget process; the automatic deficit reduction plan renewed Congress's effort to control the federal budget. Budgeting remains a major preoccupation of Congress.

6. Today Congress enjoys a renewed sense of power. The major questions facing Congress are legislation and representation. Critics wonder if Congress can ever recapture major policy initiative from the executive branch. Supporters stress the democratic character of Congress giving it the ability to represent multiple and diverse interests in society.

Research Projects

1. *Writing members of Congress* Write your congressional representative a letter on an issue before Congress in which you have an interest. You can find out the name and address of your representative from the *Congressional Directory* or Congressional Quarterly's *Washington Information Directory*. Does he or she have a local or regional office in your area? Finally, study the response you get. If several students in class write, compare the results for form and content. Do you think the responses are prepared responses?

2. *Committee assignments*   Determine the committee assignments for your representative and two senators. You should look for the following information:

- Committee and subcommittee membership
- Seniority on those committees
- Chairs of committees and/or subcommittees

The best sources for this information are the *Congressional Directory* and *Congressional Quarterly, Weekly Report;* they describe the organization of Congress every two years. Useful material may also be found in *Almanac of American Politics.*

3. *Roll-call votes*   Select an issue on which the Senate and/or House of Representatives took a roll-call vote. Analyze the vote, looking for levels of support by party and region, breakdown of liberals versus conservatives, and state delegation. Most editions of *Congressional Quarterly, Weekly Report* will have listings for important roll-call votes. They will also contain periodic discussions on voting by party, region, ideology, and so on. Look in the indexes to find these.

4. *Congressional district*   How well do congressional representatives reflect the values of their districts? Make a list of senators and representatives from your state or describe their history in a district. Develop a set of characteristics from their socioeconomic background: age at election, sex, occupation, race and ethnic origins, and income. These data can be obtained from *Congressional Directories* and the *Almanac of American Politics.* Using census data (the best source is *Congressional District Data Book,* published by the Bureau of the Census), compare these characteristics with the dominant characteristics of the district in terms of percentage of people in age, income, occupation, and so on. Is there a similarity between district and representative?

Notes

1. Charles O. Jones, "Will Reform Change Congress?" in Lawrence C. Dodd and Bruce I. Oppenheimer, eds., *Congress Reconsidered,* 3rd ed. (Washington, D.C.: Congressional Quarterly Press, 1985), p. 250.
2. David R. Mayhew, "Congressional Elections: The Case of the Vanishing Marginals," *Polity* 6 (Spring 1974): 295–317.
3. Clem Miller, *Member of the House: Letters of a Congressman* (New York: Charles Scribner & Sons, 1962), p. 66.
4. Richard F. Fenno, Jr., "U.S. House Members in Their Constituencies," *American Political Science Review* 71 (September 1977): 890–897.
5. Roger H. Davidson, *The Role of the Congressman* (New York: Pegasus, 1969), pp. 117–119.
6. This expression is taken from a book by that title; see Richard F. Fenno, Jr., *Home Style: House Members in Their Districts* (Boston: Little, Brown, 1978).
7. Ibid., p. 167.
8. David R. Mayhew, *Congress: The Electoral Connection* (New Haven, Conn.: Yale University Press, 1974).
9. Richard F. Fenno, Jr., *Congressmen in Committees* (Boston: Little, Brown, 1973), p. 1.
10. Charles L. Clapp, *The Congressman: His Work as He Sees It* (Washington, D.C.: The Brookings Institution, 1963), p. 330.
11. *Immigration and Naturalization Service* v. *Chadha* 462 U.S. 919 (1983).
12. Joseph Cooper, "The Legislative Veto in the 1980s," in Lawrence Dodd and Bruce Oppenheimer, eds., *Congress Reconsidered,* 3rd ed. (Washington, D.C.: Congressional Quarterly Press, 1985), p. 385.
13. Lewis A. Froman, Jr., *The Congressional Process: Strategies, Rules, and Procedures* (Boston: Little, Brown, 1967), p. 3.
14. Robert Peabody, *Leadership in Congress* (Boston: Little, Brown, 1976), p. 340.

15. Randall Ripley, *Party Leadership in the House of Representatives* (Washington, D.C.: The Brookings Institution, 1967).

16. Miller, *Member of the House*, p. 53.

17. Fenno, *Congressmen in Committees.*

18. Irwin Gertzog, "The Routinization of Committee Assignments in the U.S. House of Representatives," *American Journal of Political Science* 20 (November 1976): 698.

19. Mark Green and others, *Who Runs Congress* (New York: Bantam Books, 1972), p. 58.

20. Louis Fisher, *The Constitution Between Friends* (New York: St. Martin's Press, 1978), p. v.

21. Arthur M. Schlesinger, Jr., and Alfred de Grazia, *Congress and the Presidency: Their Role in Modern Times* (Washington, D.C.: American Enterprise Institute, 1967), p. 1.

22. Christopher J. Deering and Steven S. Smith, "Subcommittees in Congress," in Lawrence C. Dodd and Bruce I. Oppenheimer, eds., *Congress Reconsidered*, 3rd ed. (Washington, D.C.: Congressional Quarterly Press, 1985), p. 191.

23. Bruce I. Oppenheimer, "The Rules Committee: New Arm of Leadership in a Decentralized House," in Lawrence C. Dodd and Bruce I. Oppenheimer, eds., *Congress Reconsidered*, 3rd ed. (Washington, D.C.: Congressional Quarterly Press, 1985), pp. 113–114.

24. Harrison Fox and Susan Webb Hammond, *Congressional Staffs* (New York: Free Press, 1977), p. 119.

25. Ibid., p. viii.

26. It was interesting, however, that Richard Fenno could find no connection between electoral margin and attentiveness to the district—trips home or staff resources directed to the district. See Richard F. Fenno,

Jr., "U.S. House Members in Their Constituencies," *American Political Science Review* 71 (September 1977).

27. John W. Kingdon, *Congressmen's Voting Decisions* (New York: Harper & Row, 1973), p. 31.

28. Mayhew, *Congress: The Electoral Connection.*

29. Aage R. Clausen, *How Congressmen Decide: A Policy Focus* (New York: St. Martin's Press, 1973), p. 213.

30. Donald R. Matthews and James A. Stimson, *Yeas and Nays: Normal Decision Making in the U.S. House of Representatives* (New York: Wiley, 1975), p. 45.

31. See John Kessel, "The Washington Congressional Delegation," *Midwest Journal of Political Science* 8 (February 1964); and Barbara Deckard, "State Party Delegations in the U.S. House of Representatives: A Comparative Study of Group Cohesion," *The Journal of Politics* 34 (February 1972).

32. Arthur G. Stevens, Jr., Arthur H. Miller and Thomas E. Mann, "Mobilization of Liberal Strength in the House, 1955–1970: The Democratic Study Group," *American Political Science Review* 68 (June 1974).

33. Allen Schick, *Reconciliation and the Congressional Budget Process* (Washington: American Enterprise Institute, 1981), p. 4.

34. *Congressional Quarterly, Weekly Report* (August 15, 1981): 1464.

35. *U.S.* v. *Synar,* _____ U.S. _____ (1986).

36. Aage R. Clausen and Carl E. Van Horn, "The Congressional Response to a Decade of Change, 1963–1972," *Journal of Politics* 39 (August 1977).

37. Ibid., p. 665.

38. Barbara Deckard, "Political Upheaval and Congressional Voting: The Effects of the 1960's on Voting Patterns in the House of Representatives," *Journal of Politics* 38 (May 1976).

Bibliography

Clapp, Charles. *The Congressman: His Work as He Sees It.* New York: The Brookings Institution, 1963.
Somewhat dated, the book provides a description of congressional life based upon interviews with congressional representatives. Gives good and readable coverage to congressional relations, dealings with interest groups and constituents.

Davidson, Roger, and Oleszek, Walter J. *Congress and Its Members*, 2nd ed. Washington, D.C.: Congressional Quarterly Press, 1985.
A detailed and comprehensive description of the two worlds of Congress—the individual politicians who constitute its membership and the institution, with its process and procedures. The authors devote considerable attention to policymaking and change within Congress over the years.

Dodd, Lawrence C., and Oppenheimer, Bruce I., eds. *Congress Reconsidered*, 3rd ed. Washington, D.C.: Congressional Quarterly Press, 1985.
Essays on Congress as it has changed in the 1970s. The first essays give an excellent overview while later articles cover specific facets of Congress and its activity with other units of government.

Fenno, Richard F., Jr. *Congressmen in Committees*. Boston: Little, Brown, 1973.
The best work on the behavior of congressional representatives in committee. Provides a good discussion of values and approaches used by different committees to meet their and their members' objectives.

Fenno, Richard F., Jr. *Home Style: House Members in Their Districts*. Boston: Little, Brown, 1978.
Fenno traveled with several congresspeople when they returned to their home districts. The book is Fenno's account of how representatives related their activity to their home constituents.

Fox, Harrison, and Hammond, Susan Webb. *Congressional Staffs*. New York: Free Press, 1977.
The only work that covers congressional staffs in detail. Based on surveys and interviews of staff, the volume is a wealth of information and data on the impact of congressional staffs on the legislative environment.

Froman, Lewis A., Jr. *The Congressional Process: Strategies, Rules, and Procedures*. Boston: Little, Brown, 1967.
The most basic and thorough treatment of the rules and procedures of Congress and how they are used. While

dated, the book is still basic to understanding the operation of Congress.

Hinckley, Barbara. *Stability and Change in Congress,* 3rd ed. New York: Harper & Row, 1983.
A brief and readable overview of Congress. Hinckley gives a nice discussion of the forces of stability and how the roles and norms in Congress mutually reinforce each other to maintain that stability.

Matthews, Donald R. *U.S. Senators and Their World.* New York: Vintage Press, 1960.
Still the best work describing the U.S. Senate and its members. While largely dated, the work provides insight on the life and activity of U.S. senators that remains valid.

Mayhew, David R. *Congress: The Electoral Connection.* New Haven, Conn.: Yale University Press, 1974.
Mayhew argues that the driving force to congressional activity is the never-ending quest for reelection. Much of what Congress does and what congresspeople do must be so understood, he claims.

Miller, Clem. *Member of the House: Letters of a Congressman.* New York: Scribners, 1962.
An amusing and illustrative collection of letters written some time ago by Representative Clem Miller to his constituents. The letters provide useful insight into how Congress operates and what legislators do.

Oleszek, Walter. *Congressional Procedures and the Policy Process,* 2nd ed. Washington, D.C.: Congressional Quarterly Press, 1983.
A newer account of congressional rules and procedures and how they affect the business of Congress. Oleszek has written a readable and nontechnical book and has included the recent changes and reforms in congressional procedures.

Peabody, Robert. *Leadership in Congress.* Boston: Little, Brown, 1976.
The most thorough study of congressional leadership.

Peabody focuses on the individuals and their careers, selection, and relations with each other. The book covers the stability and succession of leadership since the 1950s.

Redman, Eric. *The Dance of Legislation.* New York: Simon and Schuster, 1973.
A study of the legislative process, particularly in the Senate. Redman served on the staff of a senator and here gives a lively account of all the political maneuvering and infighting as a bill goes through the Senate.

Ripley, Randall. *Congress: Process and Policy,* 3rd ed. New York: W. W. Norton, 1983.
A textbook on Congress by a respected authority. The book provides excellent coverage of elections, committees, leadership, and presidential relations, and describes a typology for policymaking roles.

Schick, Allen. *Reconciliation and the Congressional Budget Process.* Washington, D.C.: American Enterprise Institute, 1981.
The foremost student of the congressional budget process examining budget reconciliation in a brief but useful work. Schick argues that reconciliation could have far-reaching effects on the budgetary process.

Sinclair, Barbara. *Majority Leadership in the U.S. House.* Baltimore: Johns Hopkins University Press, 1983.
An overview of party leadership in the House, the book focuses on how leadership puts together winning coalitions. The book also contrasts present leadership activities and styles with those of the 1970s.

Smith, Steven, and Deering, Christopher. *Committees in Congress.* Washington, D.C.: Congressional Quarterly Press, 1984.
A fresh examination of the importance of committees in Congress. The book looks at committees after the period of reform in the 1970s, noting how the activities of committees and the personal goals of committee members have changed as a result.

The Judiciary

An independent judiciary is one of the basic ingredients of a democratic society. A free people leans heavily upon the judiciary for protection, and this gives the courts great power and responsibility. But this same responsibility subjects judges to certain legal, political, social, and ideological restraints. Judges are inevitably drawn into political contests when broad issues of social policy call for the reallocation of resources, and they have the capacity to do great good or great evil, depending upon how they use their power and how it is controlled.[1]

The Framework of Judicial Power

Clearly the most dramatic source of the Supreme Court's power is judicial review, the power of the Court to make authoritative interpretations of federal and state laws and political actions in relation to the United States Constitution. From *Marbury* v. *Madison*, which established the precedent for judicial review, down through *U.S.* v. *Nixon,* the Supreme Court has indefatigably defended "the province and duty of the judicial department to say what the law is."

Judicial Review

The framers gave the courts no express power of judicial review, although there is some evidence that they considered it and that some at least approved of it. This power was added by the Court in *Marbury* v. *Madison* in 1803. In 1800 Thomas Jefferson was elected to the presidency; the Federalist era was over. John Adams and the Federalists did not take the defeat well. A lame-duck Congress that did not adjourn until March 1801 created several new federal judgeships, and Adams eagerly filled them with loyal Federalists. One such appointment, justice of the peace for the District of Columbia, went to William Marbury. Working right up to the change of office on March 3, Adams signed the appointments and turned them over to his secretary of state, John Marshall, to seal and deliver. Not all, however, could be delivered by the next day, and the new president had no intention of filling the posts with Federalists. Jefferson ordered his secretary of state, James Madison, not to deliver the seventeen remaining undelivered appointments.

Writ of Mandamus: *a judicial order directing a public official to behave in a particular manner or to perform a specific duty.*

Marbury sued to recover his appointment. Under Article 13 of the Judiciary Act of 1789, the Supreme Court had been given original jurisdiction to issue **writs of mandamus.** Such a writ directs a public official to act in a certain way or to perform a particular duty. Delivery of a properly authorized and approved judicial appointment was suitable matter for a writ of mandamus. Marbury sued Secretary of State Madison for delivery of the justice of the peace appointment for the District of Columbia, and the case came before the Supreme Court on original jurisdiction.

Jefferson had said plainly he would not have the appointment delivered. Could the Court compel Jefferson to comply? That is, could the Court interfere with the executive? The Supreme Court issued its opinion on February 24, 1803. Speaking for the Court, Chief Justice John Marshall, himself a lame-duck appointee to the Supreme Court by John Adams, reasoned that the appointment was proper and that Marbury was entitled to the commission. Marshall also held that a writ of mandamus was the proper judicial remedy when a public official failed to perform a ministerial function. But, he concluded, the Supreme Court could not issue such a writ. Article 13 of the Judiciary Act of 1789 enlarged the original jurisdiction of the Supreme Court in Article III of the Constitution. This was contrary to the Constitution, for the Supreme Court had original jurisdiction only in cases affecting an ambassador or a foreign minister, or in which a state is a party. Marbury was none of these. The case was dismissed.

What Marshall had done was to avoid direct confrontation with President Jefferson. Marbury did not get his post, but Marshall made it clear

Judicial Review: *the power of the courts to interpret the Constitution, keeping all laws and actions of public officials consistent with the language and meaning of the Constitution. While not specifically provided for, the power of judicial review was assumed to the courts in the 1803 decision of* Marbury v. Madison.

John Marshall
Marshall, a fervent Federalist from Virginia, was the fourth chief justice of the Supreme Court, serving from 1801–1835. He served in the revolutionary army, was elected to Congress in 1799, and was chosen secretary of state by President Adams in 1800. When the position of chief justice of the Supreme Court became vacant in 1801, Adams appointed Marshall to the office. While the election of 1800 marked the end of the era of Federalist domination in politics, Marshall continued to extend Federalist policies from the high court for thirty-four years.

that Marbury had been entitled to the appointment. Marshall then went on to declare that the courts have the power of **judicial review,** the power to make authoritative interpretations of the Constitution.

> It is emphatically the province and duty of the judicial department to say what the law is. Those who apply the rule to particular cases, must of necessity expound and interpret that rule. If two laws conflict with each other, the courts must decide on the operation of each.[2]

Today we can fully appreciate the magnitude of this power of the courts. The president and the Court had disagreed on an interpretation of the Constitution, and the Court clearly declared that judges—not the executive—are to interpret the law: "If two laws conflict with each other, the courts must decide on the operation of each." Marshall had been shrewd: in a masterpiece of judicial reasoning, he had disarmed a potential constitutional crisis of the first magnitude, thus maintaining the integrity, and the power, of the judiciary.

The need for judicial interpretation is enhanced by the general and brief language employed by the Constitution. Some of the most important sections of the Constitution refer to "foreign and interstate commerce," "equal protection," "due process," and "the executive power." Nowhere are these phrases defined, so their edification rests less on the meaning of the words themselves than on the policy preferences of the nine judges occupying the Supreme Court bench at any given time.

Judicial interpretation, however, is not restricted to constitutional interpretations. Statutory interpretations are equally necessary. Courts are called on to interpret the meaning and extent of authorizing authority for a good many laws, from the president's use of war powers to economic regulations and rent and price controls. The judiciary, with its appellate process leading to the Supreme Court, which makes the final judicial determination of the meaning of law, interprets the language and intent of such laws. This is perhaps inevitable, because general laws must be applied to specific circumstances, and because Congress was tentative in defining the scope of law, leaving it to the courts to resolve the dilemma.

A second source of power is the Court's prestige. The Supreme Court enjoys a moderately high reputation in the minds of the public. This base of public support plays a large role in maintaining the Court's ability to render decisions and obtain compliance.

Since the Court's power is exercised through actual legal suits involving two or more aggrieved parties in real controversies, another source of judicial power is legitimation of action; that is, through the settlement of a case, one side is interpreted as having acted properly or interpreted the law correctly. In the 1952 *Steel Seizure* case, President Truman was declared to have overstepped his authority and was required to return the steel mills to private ownership. And even though Richard Nixon had to turn over his tapes, the Court did agree to the constitutional doctrine of executive privilege—the first time a court had formally acknowledged the principle. In a sense, the Court thereby legitimized executive privilege for future presidents.

In a democracy there are many modes of legitimizing activity, not the least of which is the ballot box. The lawsuit is another. By declaring one course of action legitimate and another unconstitutional, the Court plays a significant part in the legitimation of activity and the peaceful resolution of conflict in a free society.

In *U.S. v. Nixon*, the Supreme Court made it clear that no one—not even the president of the United States—is above the law. On this historic commitment to the rule of law rests "the very integrity of the judicial system and public confidence in the system."[3]

Respect for the law is a fundamental principle of democratic government; we recognize it as binding on governors and governed alike. Such respect is essential to the equitable and just operation of popular government. Law represents the efforts of a community to establish rules of conduct. Law is an evolutionary, changing process; it is adjusted as the needs of the community change. Laws are enacted by political representatives of the people, codified into statutes, and called statutory law; or they evolve out of judicial solutions to disputes, when unwritten legal customs and traditions are applied to render justice, as in common law and equity.

Common Law

Stare Decisis: a Latin phrase meaning "to adhere to the decision." This principle of looking to past decisions, and the reasoning in previous similar cases, is often used by judges in deciding cases.

Common law is judge-made law. Its roots go back to the eleventh century in England. Judges, seeking settlement for disputes, applied prevailing customs to make decisions. Common law is based on precedent; it is a storehouse of custom and principles that informs and binds present decisions. The common law grew through the application of *stare decisis*, which means "to adhere to the decision." Judges look to past decisions, and the reasoning in previous similar cases, to aid in making a decision in the case presently before the bench. As a supplement to common law, Anglo-American law developed the principle of **equity.** Sometimes called the "conscience" of the law, equity is also based on stare decisis and is judge-made law. It allows the judge to take action where there is no law. Equity begins where the law ends; equity allows a judge to issue a decree to prevent future wrongs, usually in the form of a writ—an injunction or restraining order—to afford relief that otherwise would be unobtainable. Some states have separate courts of equity; the federal government does not.

Equity: a legal principle of fairness that allows judges to provide for preventive measures and legal remedies where there is no applicable law.

Statutory Law

Statutory Law: the laws, called statutes, passed by legislative bodies.

The laws passed by legislative bodies are called statutes and are collectively known as **statutory law.** They spell out in writing, and often in great detail, the intent of the law, to whom the law applies, and the penalties to be assessed when the law is violated. The law is codified, written, and classified by subject matter. The United States Code is the national government's codification of existing statutory law.

When we think of statutory law, we generally distinguish between two types: private law and public law. **Private law,** often called civil law, regulates the relationships between private citizens in such areas as marriage, divorce, wills, deeds and contracts. Although the state is involved in applying and enforcing the statutes, it is neither the subject of the right nor the object of the obligation. Legal regulations and obligations that apply to public officials, in their capacity as public officials, are known as **public law.** The public law is concerned with the definition, regulation, and enforcement of rights and obligations where the state is the subject of the right or the object of the obligation. It regulates the public order, and includes the criminal law. Public law applies to all people in the nation, and regulates activity between citizens and government and between branches of the government. The sources of public law are the Constitution, legislative statutes, and administrative regulations. One great branch of public law is constitutional law. The Constitution is the source by which all other law is judged. Constitutional law, however, includes not only the document itself but all the interpretations of it rendered by the courts. The authoritative interpretation comes from decisions of the United States Supreme Court. Of all public law, the most rapidly expanding area is administrative law. With the vast delegation of rule-making power to agencies of administration in recent decades, judges are frequently asked to review the propriety of those rules and regulations and to determine whether fair procedures were followed in their promulgation and application.

Law, then, is the cornerstone of American democracy, the wellspring for a government of law, not persons. It is our nature to turn political issues into legal ones. This is what Alexis de Tocqueville observed a century and a half ago, when he said: "Scarcely any political question arises in the United States that is not resolved, sooner or later, into a judicial question."[4]

Private Law: *statutory law regulating the relationships between private citizens in such areas as marriage, divorce, wills, deeds, and contracts.*

Public Law: *legal regulations and obligations that apply to public officials, in their capacity as public officials. The public law is concerned with the definition, regulation and enforcement of rights and obligations where the state is the subject of the right or the object of the obligation.*

Judicial Power

What do courts do? Article III, Section 2 of the Constitution defines the jurisdiction of the federal judiciary, using the words "cases and controversies," which we have since interpreted to mean actual disputes capable of settlement by judicial means. But Section 2 gives only a brief indication of the scope of judicial activity. A more complete answer is found in the courts' jurisdictional power. Courts, in the American system, perform three functions: they administer law, resolve conflicts, and make policy.[5]

Administration of the Laws

The judicial process is viewed as a neutral arena where two contending parties argue their differences to establish the culpability of one or the

Adversarial Process:
the judicial process whereby two contending parties argue their differences in order to establish the culpability of one or the other of them.

other. In other words, the judicial process is an **adversarial process** to determine the guilt or innocence of the contending parties. Each side argues its side as hard and as best it can; from this presentation of evidence the court is supposedly able to discover the truth. Law has defined certain acts to be crimes and fixed certain punishments. The court seeks to establish, as a neutral arbitrator, that wrong was done, and then to administer the law and apply the penalty to the wrongdoer. But the court does not *define* the law; it seeks only to establish the facts in order to determine whether the law has been violated.

Conflict Resolution

Because conflicts arise in every society, there needs to be a way to resolve disputes peacefully. In American society, courts perform this function. The conflict may be between private individuals, or it may involve government itself. Conflict resolution takes place within carefully crafted guidelines. Courts will hear only cases and controversies that are **justiciable,** actual disputes that may be settled by legal methods available to the court. Courts insist that there be a case or controversy—a real conflict with injured parties directly affected by the outcome. They will not, for example, entertain "political questions."

Justiciable Disputes:
actual disputes that may be settled by legal methods available to the court. Courts will hear only the cases and controversies that are justiciable.

The courts provide three services for the resolution of conflicts. First, there is the set of procedures and remedies that we call *due process.* Second, judicial settlement provides legitimation. The court resolves that the neighbor owns the land and the fence is permissible, and it rules that the president's claim of executive privilege must give way to the need for evidence in a criminal prosecution. The court puts a seal of approval on one course of action or another, or one interpretation of power over another. The third service in resolving conflict is the grant of governmental power to enforce a decision. The citizen may get a restraining order preventing a neighbor from tearing down the backyard fence, or the landlord may secure an eviction notice for a tenant who has not paid rent. This is no different from the district court's issuing a subpoena to President Nixon ordering him to deliver the tapes to the Watergate special prosecutor.

Policymaking

In administering and applying the laws, the court necessarily is drawn into policymaking. There is a maze of legal rules, contending legislative and executive rules, and constitutional principles to sort through. In finding which rules and procedures to apply to the specific case or controversy before it, the court makes policy. When judges resolve conflict, they legitimize action and create precedent.

Policymaking is unique to the American judicial system. We have placed in our courts, the "least dangerous branch" of government, the power to make authoritative interpretations on matters of public policy. Because we have a hierarchical structure, in which appellate courts re-

Energy and Environmental Policy

*B*y the late 1970s Americans were keenly aware of the need for comprehensive energy and environmental policies. The 1973 OPEC embargo, electrical brownouts, and high gas and heating fuel bills led to America's realization that it was experiencing an energy crisis. Fossil fuels were being depleted, and America was dependent upon imported oil. Nuclear power raised serious questions for safety, as the Three Mile Island accident reminded people. The disposal of nuclear waste raised environmental concerns. Other forms of energy development were either commercially unfeasible or caused environmental problems.

Traditional energy policy has focused on public utility regulation as a means to control production. Government policy has been designed to prevent overproduction of energy in order to stabilize the industry. Government sought to provide for the unlimited consumption of cheap energy and at the same time to guarantee industry a fair rate of profit. Participants in energy policy were limited to the producer groups—oil, coal, natural gas, and nuclear power manufacturers—relevant government agencies, and a few representatives and senators from producer states. Producer groups tended to dominate the policy agenda. But with the emergence of the energy crisis, both the issues and the participants in energy policy changed. New groups were politicized into energy policies, consumer and environmental groups became active, western states' congressional representatives took a more collective interest, and two new government agencies were established—the cabinet-level Department of Energy and the Environmental Protection Agency.

The reality of the energy crisis forced public recognition of United States dependence on limited fossil fuels and imported oil. As a result the old energy policy of limited production and cheap energy began yielding to new energy policies. Three approaches for solving the nation's energy crisis began to emerge: technological-scientific, economic, and political.*

The technological-scientific approach seeks to utilize scientific research and technological applications to increase present energy supplies and create new sources of energy. It looks to past success in technological applications (such as outer space) to increase efficiency and make practical solar, geothermal, wind, and synthetic energy sources. The economic solution demands a better allocation of energy supplies either by a free-market mechanism or by government taxation to regulate consumption and revenues generated by the sale of energy. The political solution attempts to find a balance between consumer and producer interests. It tries to maintain supplies at an affordable price while still maintaining producer profitability, keeping both in balance.

These three approaches have produced a changed energy policy, employing in various combinations the three approaches for solving the present energy crisis. The new energy policy lacks comprehensiveness, but its structure is evident:

1. *All-out production* By abandoning the policy of limited production and cheap supplies, government has encouraged producers to expand production and pass the increased costs on to consumers as necessary. Industry is also encouraged to develop marginal sources of energy—strip mining and shale oil—and to explore new sources of fossil fuels—offshore drilling and natural gas deposits. The policy places a premium on the technological-scientific approach to energy but also requires economic support to make the undertaking economically profitable for producers.

2. *Energy independence* This policy employs both the technological-scientific and political approaches. It urges conservation techniques

by industries and consumers in the use of petroleum while promoting the use of plentiful domestic supplies—coal and nuclear power. The long-term solution depends on the development of such alternative sources of energy as solar, geothermal, wind, and synthetic fuels.

3. *Environmental protection* The development of energy in either of the two previous policies must acknowledge concern for the environment. A major regulating responsibility of government is the protection of environmental quality. Energy production will be required to protect and to follow closer regulations for nuclear power safety and waste disposal, strip mining of coal, offshore drilling, and pollution.

With increasing frequency, courts have become an avenue for promoting environmental protection. Several environmental groups have already gone to the courts seeking injunctions or restraints. Such groups include the Sierra Club, Environmental Action, Natural Resources Defense Council, Environmental Defense Fund, and public interest lawyers, to name a few.

*J. Anderson, D. Brady, and C. Bullock, *Public Policy and Politics in America*, North Scituate, Mass.: Duxbury Press, 1978, pp. 39–40.

Acid rain, which is eroding this statue *(left)*, and the damage to the landscape caused by the Alaska pipeline *(right)*, are among the many environmental issues that arouse widespread concern.

view the decisions of lower courts and the Supreme Court is at the apex of the hierarchy, it is appellate courts, especially the Supreme Court, that are most concerned with matters of public policy. But all courts make policy. There are several reasons for this judicial role in policymaking in the American system:

1. The fundamental law, the Constitution, has been altered little since 1787, yet American society has changed drastically. So the Constitution must be adapted to a changing world.
2. Americans traditionally distrust excessive government, and therefore use the courts to maintain individual liberties.
3. American federalism does not distinguish clearly between the powers state governments may exercise exclusively and the powers they share with the national government. The result has been a flood of litigation in which courts, and ultimately the Supreme Court, have ruled on a case-by-case basis.
4. The judiciary is the arbiter in the system of separation of powers.
5. The power of judicial review provides a means for authoritative interpretation of the law.

Policymaking is most typically exercised through judicial review. Courts historically have engaged in policymaking, but some observers argue that the courts are currently practicing an unprecedented activism. Indeed, there is some evidence to suggest that this view is correct.

The Supreme Court, for example, has played a very active policymaking role in the past few decades. Though much of the activism centered on civil rights issues in the 1950s and 1960s, during the twenty-five year period from 1960 to 1985 the Court struck down 45 federal laws and 405 state and local laws—one-third of all the laws that have been declared unconstitutional in the Court's history.[6]

In addition to their expansion of civil liberties, the courts have been active in many other areas. In 1982, for example, the Supreme Court rejected the bankruptcy court system that had been in effect since 1978. In 1983 the Court struck down the legislative veto used by Congress to check the executive branch. And in 1985 the Court gave Congress almost unlimited powers in regulating interstate commerce. These decisions typify the pattern of involvement in policy by the courts in recent years, which is surely without precedent.

How can this surge of policymaking be explained? Lawrence Baum offers several explanations.[7] First, he contends that the strong liberalism of many appellate courts dictates that they assert themselves to move the law in a liberal direction. This explanation alone, of course, is incomplete, because the more conservative judiciary of recent years should have moderated this activism. A second reason advanced by Baum is the growth of government at all levels. As government policy touches more people in more ways and more deeply than in the past, it is to be expected that more questions of the legal validity of government action arise. Third is the growth of interest-group litigation, much of it intended to secure activist policies. Such organizations as the NAACP Legal Defense Fund, the American Civil Liberties Union, and the Public Interest Research Group have frequently challenged government policy. They often provide opportunities for an activist court to impose new legal rules. Finally, Baum identifies momentum as the fourth factor. Policy activism leads to more activism. When one reform is made it becomes easier to convince federal judges to make further reforms. Furthermore, an activist decision-altering policy may well require futher policy alterations to fill in gaps and implement the original decision. The *Roe* v. *Wade* abortion decision and the *Miranda* decision on police interrogation are cases in point.

The courthouse represents justice and the peaceful resolution of conflict.

Jurisdiction and Standing

Judges cannot initiate action; they can only respond to cases brought by others. Nor are courts free to respond to all suits brought before them. Two further conditions must be met: the court must have jurisdiction, and the party bringing action must have standing to sue.

Jurisdiction: *the authority of a court to hear and decide an issue brought before it.*

Jurisdiction   **Jurisdiction** is the authority of a court to hear and decide an issue brought before it. In the broadest sense, federal jurisdiction is outlined in Article III of the Constitution. No court can determine for itself its jurisdiction; that is established by the Constitution and law. Only the Supreme Court has power over its appellate jurisdiction. All other courts must receive all cases brought before them when they have jurisdiction.

We can distinguish three kinds of jurisdiction: subject matter, geographic, and hierarchical. Subject-matter jurisdiction deals with the nature of the issues brought before the courts. Geographic jurisdiction defines the area in which a court hears cases, while hierarchical jurisdiction defines the level of the court as a trial court or as an appeals court, hence the common designation as "lower" and "higher" courts. The federal judiciary has general jurisdiction as outlined in the Constitution and law and special jurisdiction on subject matters defined for it by law. The major federal courts (district courts, courts of appeal, and the Supreme Court) have general jurisdiction. There are also courts with special subject-matter jurisdiction: the U.S. Claims Court, the court of international trade, and the tax court. States frequently divide subject-matter jurisdiction even further, into separate civil and criminal courts, and these may be further subdivided so that some courts hear only minor (misdemeanor) criminal cases or specific civil cases. Whatever the subject-matter jurisdiction of a court, it may hear cases only when one of the parties or the issue being litigated is located within the geographical area for which the court has responsibility. The federal courts use states as the geographical area for which the court has responsibility. The ninety-four federal district courts are divided into jurisdictional areas within a state. In addition, we distinguish between original jurisdiction and cases heard on appeal (appellate jurisdiction). Trial courts with subject-matter jurisdiction try cases (original jurisdiction). On the federal level, these are the district courts. If there is a question over law or fact in rendering the decision, the case may be reheard, or appealed to an appellate court that has jurisdiction to review the case. These are the courts of appeal and the Supreme Court.

Standing: *the interest a person has in the judicial resolution of a conflict. In recent years, the doctrine of standing has been liberalized, thereby permitting a wider range of people to challenge government or corporate interests in court.*

Standing   The other limitation to court power in hearing cases is the **standing** a person has to seek judicial redress. Standing is defined as the interest a person has in the judicial resolution of the conflict. Whereas in jurisdiction the court has no discretion, it does have some discretion in interpreting standing. In recent years, the Supreme Court and Congress have greatly liberalized the doctrine of standing, thereby widening the range of persons permitted to challenge government or corporate interests in the courts.[8]

For standing in the federal courts, a party may file suit where there is a **case or controversy.** All cases are controversies, but some controversies are not cases. For standing, courts require a real dispute between contending parties whose interests are directly at stake. There can be no friendly suits, cases dreamed up or feigned to render a desirable verdict. Nor can the federal courts render advisory opinions.

Standing requires legal injury. It is not enough that two parties have a conflict. The conflict must pertain to something that is legally defined, either public or private. A public injury involves the commission of a crime. A private injury is referred to as a **tort.** The determination of standing may also depend on the finality of action. Courts will not entertain suits unless all nonjudicial remedies have been exhausted first. The issue must be "ripe"; that is, all administrative remedies must have been explored before suit is filed. But with the press of certain social issues, normal bureaucratic delays, and agency caution, courts sometimes do not insist on exhaustive nonjudicial remedies before they admit some parties to standing.[9]

There can be no standing when an issue is a political question. But what exactly is a political question? There is no clear answer. Any issue is deemed political if the court decides the matter is better resolved by some other agency or branch of government. The Supreme Court has ruled that the determination of a republican form of government in a state is a political question.[10] So too, apparently, is the authority to decide whether a state has ratified a constitutional amendment.[11] What once was a political question, however, need not remain a political question forever. A classic example is legislative reapportionment. Once it was held to be a political question, but in 1962 the Supreme Court ruled that federal courts have jurisdiction and that reapportionment is a justiciable issue. The result was the one person–one vote principle laid down by the Supreme Court in 1964.

"Cases and Controversies": *the phrase used in Article III of the Constitution to define the jurisdiction of the federal judiciary. This phrase has been interpreted to mean actual disputes capable of settlement by judicial means.*

Tort: *a private injury or wrongful act for which a civil action can be brought.*

The American Court System

The United States is a federal system, so it has a dual court system. The two court systems, national and state courts, exist side by side but remain largely separate in jurisdiction. The federal courts have no jurisdiction or control over state courts, except when the Constitution or federal law becomes an issue in a state court. Otherwise, state-court jurisdiction is fixed by state constitutions and federal-court jurisdiction by the national Constitution.

The United States Constitution established only one court, the Supreme Court, and empowered Congress to create inferior courts (Figure 13.1). The first Congress established the pattern, never seriously disturbed, of creating districts for courts of original jurisdiction and combining those districts into regions for appellate courts. Thus, the hierarchical pattern of the federal judiciary consists of district courts, courts of appeals, and one Supreme Court. There are also special courts and administrative law judges.

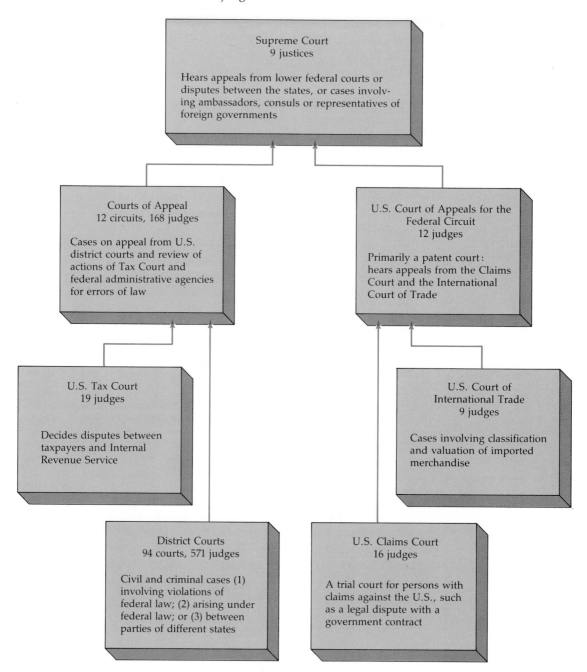

Figure 13.1 Organization of the federal courts

District Courts

United States District Courts are courts of original jurisdiction for the federal judiciary. There are ninety-four district courts, with at least one in each state; larger states have several district courts. From one to twenty-seven judges are assigned within each district to hear cases. At present, there are just over 570 permanent federal district-court judgeships in the United States. All are appointed by the president of the United States and confirmed by the Senate. And, like all federal judges, district-court judges hold office for life or good behavior.

Grand Jury: *a jury used by trial courts to investigate accusations against persons charged with crime and indict them for trial.*

Petit Jury: *a jury used to weigh evidence and decide the issues of a trial in court.*

District courts are trial courts. They hear almost all the civil and criminal cases arising under federal jurisdiction on original jurisdiction. As trial courts, district courts are the only federal courts to regularly employ **grand** (indicting) and **petit** (trial) **juries.** They do so in about half the cases they hear. District courts are also required to enforce as well as review administrative orders from executive agencies. Well over three-fourths of the cases filed in district courts are noncriminal. In 1984, 640,688 cases were filed in district courts: 261,485 civil cases, 34,928 criminal cases, and 344,275 bankruptcy cases.[12] Only a small percentage of these cases are trial cases: 14,374 civil cases (5 percent) and 6,456 criminal cases (18 percent) were tried before a jury. There has been an explosion in the work load of the district courts, and indeed of the entire judiciary. The result is delay: the time interval between the filing of a case and its coming to trial ranged from four to thirty-nine months in 1959; from four to forty-nine months in 1965; and from one to fifty-two months in 1972–1973.[13]

Because of work load, judges are provided with an array of assistants, all appointed by the judges themselves. There are court reporters, stenographers, clerks and bailiffs, and, since 1971, court administrators who relieve the chief judges of administrative and management responsibilities. Most important are the United States magistrates. Magistrates, appointed by district-court judges for eight-year terms, handle the preliminary steps in the pretrial phase of a case. They can issue arrest warrants, hear evidence to bind an accused over for grand jury indictment, set bail, and try cases for minor federal offenses (with up to six months imprisonment and/or $500 fines).

A majority of district-court decisions are final. If there is an appeal, in rare instances a decision may be appealed directly to the Supreme Court. The great bulk of district decisions, however, go to the next highest level in the federal hierarchy, the courts of appeal.

Bankruptcy Courts   Congress passed Bankruptcy Amendments of 1984 creating bankruptcy courts as adjuncts to federal district courts. Until 1984 bankruptcy proceedings were in a state of confusion. In 1978 Congress created separate bankruptcy courts and bankruptcy judges, which were given a variety of responsibilities relating to bankruptcy. But in June 1982 the Supreme Court ruled that the 1978 act was unconstitutional because it gave bankruptcy judges too much authority over nonbankruptcy issues. At the same time the high court said bankruptcy judges were not sufficiently independent from the other branches of government (Congress could reduce their salaries during their tenure in office).[14] From 1982 until 1984, therefore, bankruptcy proceedings were handled by the U.S. Judicial Conference, which had had responsibility for bankruptcies prior to 1978.

The 1984 amendments created a new bankruptcy law and court structure. Provisions of the amendments include:

Jurisdiction: All bankruptcy cases are assigned to U.S. district courts, which will have original jurisdiction over all such proceedings. All separate bankruptcy referees are abolished. Clear-cut bankruptcy cases may be assigned to a bankruptcy judge by the district court.

Judges: 232 bankruptcy judges were created as Article III justices and assigned to the 94 federal judicial districts. Bankruptcy judges are to be appointed for fourteen-year terms by federal appeals courts.

Suits: Companies using bankruptcy to invalidate labor contracts must seek court approval, and only after making a proposal to the union and seeking to negotiate changes in the labor contract.

By this legislation, bankruptcy judges would be created and assigned to district courts, but they would be appointed by courts of appeal rather than district court judges. Their decisions could be appealed to the district court or to a panel of bankruptcy judges.

The bankruptcy work load has become simply enormous in the 1980s, with 344,000 bankruptcy proceedings in 1984 alone. There is a need to keep these proceedings as much as possible from clogging up district court business and calendars. Yet the bankruptcy judges want recognition as full judges. This brings them into conflict with other federal judges, who do not want their own status diminished. Feelings run deep on this issue, and no quick resolution appears likely.

Courts of Appeal

Appellate Courts: *intermediate courts and the supreme courts in the state and federal court systems that have jurisdiction to review a case.*

Courts of appeal serve as the major **appellate courts** (those hearing cases that have been tried before in lower, or inferior, courts) in the federal judicial system. They review civil and criminal decisions appealed from federal district courts. Additionally, courts of appeal have the responsibility for enforcing and reviewing the activities of executive agencies endowed with quasi-judicial functions such as the Interstate Commerce Commission, the Federal Communications Commission, and the National Labor Relations Board. In 1984 the records show that 29,651 cases were filed with the courts of appeal: 4,881 criminal cases, 6,259 civil cases, 15,466 private civil cases, and 3,045 administrative appeals.[15] Approximately 90 percent of the cases end at this level; only a small fraction are appealed to the Supreme Court.

There are thirteen federal courts of appeal: eleven regional circuits (until 1948 the courts of appeal were known as circuit courts), a twelfth

TABLE 13.1   U.S. courts of appeal

First Circuit:	Maine, Massachusetts, New Hampshire, Rhode Island, Puerto Rico
Second Circuit:	Connecticut, New York, Vermont
Third Circuit:	Delaware, New Jersey, Pennsylvania, Virgin Islands
Fourth Circuit:	Maryland, North Carolina, South Carolina, Virginia, West Virginia
Fifth Circuit:	Louisiana, Mississippi, Texas
Sixth Circuit:	Kentucky, Michigan, Ohio, Tennessee
Seventh Circuit:	Illinois, Indiana, Wisconsin
Eighth Circuit:	Arkansas, Iowa, Minnesota, Missouri, Nebraska, North Dakota, South Dakota
Ninth Circuit:	Arizona, California, Idaho, Montana, Nevada, Oregon, Washington, Hawaii, Alaska, Guam
Tenth Circuit:	Colorado, Kansas, New Mexico, Utah, Oklahoma, Wyoming
Eleventh Circuit:	Alabama, Florida, Georgia
	Court of Appeals for the District of Columbia
	U.S. Court of Appeals for Federal Circuit

circuit, known as the Court of Appeals for the District of Columbia, and a U.S. Court of Appeals for the Federal Circuit, which is a court that primarily hears patent cases (see Table 13.1). The latter is the only appeals court with subject-matter jurisdiction; all other appeals courts have geographical jurisdictions.

From four to twenty-eight judges are assigned to each circuit. Because a court of appeals is an appellate court, cases are heard by three- to nine-judge panels. The judges may sit *en banc*—that is, the entire panel of judges for the court may sit to hear the case—but most often courts of appeal work in three-judge panels because of the increased work load. They work from the case record of the trial court, and only the more significant cases are scheduled for oral arguments. The remainder are judged solely on the basis of briefs and documents submitted to supplement the lower court record. New evidence may not be admitted in appellate proceedings; these courts work from the record established by the trial court of original jurisdiction.

The Supreme Court

The Supreme Court is the national symbol of justice. There exists no higher court. At times there have been as few as five justices (1789) and as many as ten (1863), but the number has been fixed at nine by Congress ever since the time of President Grant in 1869. The Court is composed of eight associate justices and a chief justice.

The Supreme Court has both original and appellate jurisdiction, although its original jurisdiction is rarely exercised. Technically, the Constitution gives the Supreme Court original jurisdiction in four areas: (1) cases between the United States and one of the fifty states; (2) cases between two or more states; (3) cases involving foreign ambassadors, and other foreign public ministers and consuls; and (4) cases begun by a state against citizens of another state or aliens, or against a foreign country.[16] Congress has extended concurrent original jurisdiction to the federal dis-

TABLE 13.2   Cases filed with the U.S. Supreme Court

	1960	1965	1970	1975	1980	1985
Original	0	8	20	14	24	15
Appellate	1,940	2,766	4,192	4,747	5,120	4,991

SOURCE: *Statistical Abstract*, 1981 and 1986; U.S. Bureau of the Census, *Historical Statistics, Colonial Times to 1970*, 1975.

trict courts for area (3) and most cases in areas (1) and (4). The only real original jurisdiction exercised by the Supreme Court is in a case or controversy between two or more states. The Court has exercised this jurisdiction only 155 times since its first term back in 1789.

The principal work of the Supreme Court is *appellate* (see Table 13.2). As an appellate court, it serves as the final arbitrator in disputes and as the final interpreter of law, including the Constitution of the United States. As an appellate court, the Supreme Court traditionally controls its own docket. Cases may come before the Court on a **writ of appeal,** as a matter of right. This happens when a state supreme court has declared a federal law or treaty unconstitutional, or upheld a state law that conflicts substantially with a federal law or treaty. It also happens when a federal court declares a federal law or treaty unconstitutional in a case in which the United States is a party to the suit. In these cases there is a statutory right of appeal to the Supreme Court. The Court, however, exercises considerable discretion in its "review." Unless a substantial federal question is involved, the Court may reject the appeal. On balance, 85 to 90 percent of such appeals are rejected, and the remaining cases constitute only about 10 percent of the Court's work load. All other cases reaching the Supreme Court come by invitation of the Court. There exists no right of appeal to the Supreme Court. Litigants, however, have the privilege of petitioning the Court to review a case. This is a **writ of certiorari,** meaning literally "making more certain." Of the cases the Supreme Court hears, 90 percent come on grants of writs of certiorari, and these are primarily issues to review the record from courts of appeal. Four justices must approve before a writ of certiorari can be issued.

Writ of Appeal: *the basis for a case to come to the Supreme Court as a matter of right. The Court must consider such writs because they involve a substantial federal question.*

Writ of Certiorari: *a writ that declares the Supreme Court's intention to review a case from a lower court.*

Special Courts

In addition to the courts created under Article III of the Constitution, Congress has established special courts, commonly known as *legislative courts* because they were created under Article I, the legislative article. Congress has altered the status of such courts from time to time. There used to be a customs court and a court of claims. The customs court has become the International Court of Trade, and the court of claims was abolished in 1982 with the establishment of the new U.S. Court of Appeals for the Federal Circuit and a claims court that is a trial court hearing cases of persons with claims against the United States. The former court of claims and patent-appeals cases are heard by the Court of Appeals for the Federal Circuit. This new court of appeals handles the patent cases and appeals from the new claims court.

The difference between constitutional and special courts is that the special courts possess nonjudicial functions. They were created to aid Congress in the administration of specific statutes. Nonetheless, their judgments are as legal and authoritative as those of any constitutional court. Judges in the special courts have been granted the same tenure—life or good behavior—as in the constitutional courts.

The United States Claims Court This is a new trial-level court replacing the U.S. Court of Claims. It hears cases involving claims against the United States, such as legal disputes over contracts with the government. Sixteen judges are assigned to the claims court.

The United States Court of International Trade With nine judges, this customs court is the largest of the special courts. It has jurisdiction to review rulings and appraisals on imports by the collectors of customs, the "dumping" of exports by foreign countries, and decisions by the secretaries of Commerce and Labor for assistance under the Trade Act of 1974. Its decisions may be appealed to the Court of Appeals for the Federal Circuit.

The United States Court of Military Appeals More properly called a legislative court, this body of three civilian judges applies military law. It is the "civilian supreme court of the military," meaning it offers service personnel a genuine appellate court to interpret and apply military law. This court, at its discretion, reviews courts-martial involving bad conduct discharges and prison sentences of more than one year. It must review courts-martial of generals and admirals, cases in which the death penalty was decreed, and cases certified for review by the judge advocate general.

The United States Tax Court Technically not part of the judiciary, this court is an adjunct of the executive branch, a quasi-administrative agency with independent status in the Internal Revenue Service. Yet its nineteen judges, appointed by the president for twelve-year terms, carry the official designation of judge. The tax court reviews IRS deficiency assessments of income, gift, self-employment, and excess profit taxes that have been challenged by the taxpayer. The commissioner of Internal Revenue is always the defendant in such cases.

Administrative Law Judges

Sometimes called the "hidden judiciary," administrative law judges now outnumber district and appeals court judges sitting on the federal bench. In 1947 there were 197 administrative law judges; in 1979, there were 1,072. Table 13.3 lists the major agency administrative law judges and their primary activities. Appeals of the rules and regulations promulgated by administrative agencies go to administrative law judges. These

TABLE 13.3 Administrative law judges and their functions

Agency	Prime function	Number of judges
Agriculture Department	Disciplinary proceedings against stockyard owners, produce dealers, brokers and commission merchants	5
Bureau of Alcohol, Tobacco and Firearms, Treasury Department	Permits to import, sell or distill alcoholic beverages	1
Civil Aeronautics Board	Airline route and rate applications, foreign permits and mergers	17
Coast Guard, Transportation Department	Misconduct, negligence and incompetence; narcotics cases	16
Commodity Futures Trading Commission	Suspension or revocation of broker registration	4
Consumer Product Safety Commission	Violations of laws protecting the public from hazardous products	1
Drug Enforcement Administration, Treasury Department	Suspension or revocation of controlled substance registration	1
Environmental Protection Agency	Permits to discharge pollutants into navigable waters; pesticide registration	6
Federal Communications Commission	Licensing of radio, TV, cable and common carriers	14
Federal Energy Regulatory Commission	Natural gas pipeline construction, abandonment, curtailment and rates; electric rates	23
Federal Labor Relations Authority	Federal employee labor relations	4
Federal Maritime Commission	Investigation and suspension of proposed rates; complaint proceedings for reparations	7
Federal Mine Safety and Health Review Commission	Violations of miner health and safety	12
Federal Trade Commission	False or misleading advertising; restraint of trade	12
Food and Drug Administration, Department of Health and Human Services	New drug applications; food standards, color additives	1
Housing and Urban Development Department	Lack of full disclosure in interstate land sales	1
Interior Department	Coal mine health and safety violations, mining claims and grazing rights	8
International Trade Commission	Import law violations	2
Interstate Commerce Commission	Complaints, investigations and applications in the regulation of railroads, motor carriers and water carriers	61
Labor Department	Unfair labor practices; longshoremen compensation claims and rates in government contracts	49
Maritime Administration, Commerce Department	Merchant marine operating differential subsidies; adequacy of U.S. flag service	3
Merit Systems Protection Board	Appeals from disciplinary proceedings against employees of the federal government	1
National Labor Relations Board	Unfair labor practices cases	98
National Transportation Safety Board	Challenges to denial, suspension or revocation of Federal Aviation Administration certification	6
Nuclear Regulatory Commission	Construction permit safety reviews	1
Occupational Safety and Health Review Commission	Employer health and safety violations	47
Postal Rate Commission	Changes in mail classification and rates	1
Postal Service	False representation to obtain money through the mail; second class mail privileges	2
Securities and Exchange Commission	Denial, suspension or revocation of broker-dealer and investment advisor registration	8
Social Security Administration, Department of Health and Human Services	Disability insurance and black lung benefits	660
	Total	1,072

SOURCE: Administrative Conference of the United States, January 1979. Reprinted in *National Journal* (July 28, 1979).

judges review the substance of agency rules, the procedures under which the rules were promulgated, and the fairness with which they are applied. The judges hold hearings, establish a record, and recommend action to agencies or commissions. Decisions can be appealed to the federal courts.

Slightly more than half of the administrative law judges work for one agency, the Social Security Administration, hearing disability cases. Judges are appointed by the agency for which they work. The Office of Personnel Management examines and interviews candidates, and sends the top candidates to the agency for final selection. Administrative law judges have life tenure. President Carter unsuccessfully recommended that administration of the judges be shifted from the Office of Personnel

"I've simply redesigned the blindfold, that's all."
© *Dennis Renault,* Sacramento Bee, *Cal./ROTHCO*

Management to the Administrative Conference of the United States, that terms of office be limited to seven years, and that reapportionment be dependent on the conference finding judges "affirmatively well qualified."

Judicial Administration

Former Chief Justice Warren Burger, an outspoken critic of judicial administration, urged modernization of the federal court system. President Carter, too, proposed reform. Over the years, Congress has aided the process of judicial administration by establishing the Judicial Conference of the United States and the Administrative Office of the United States Courts.

The Judicial Conference, presided over by the chief justice of the United States Supreme Court, consists of the chief judge from each of the courts of appeals and one district court judge from each of the twelve circuits. Its function is "to submit to Congress an annual report of the proceedings of the Judicial Conference and its recommendation for legislation." Through the use of committees, the conference studies procedures for the federal courts and formulates recommendations for use by the courts. These recommendations automatically become effective unless rejected by Congress within ninety days. The Administrative Office of the United States Courts handles much of the day-to-day routine for the federal judiciary. It prepares the budgets for the courts, examines dockets, procures supplies, and keeps records.

Judges and Judicial Selection

Senatorial Courtesy: *the right of a senator to veto lower judicial appointments in the senator's state. In practice, this means that the president consults the senator's recommendation prior to making such judicial appointments.*

Blue Slip: *the Senate procedure for exercising senatorial courtesy. So named because the Senate Judiciary Committee stationery is blue, a negative review or even nonreturn of the committee request by the senator of the nominee's state results in nonconsideration of the candidate.*

Unlike members of Congress or the president and unlike most state judges, who are elected by the people, federal judges are appointed. The Constitution places in the hands of the president, with the advice and consent of the Senate, the selection of all federal judges.

The Selection Process

The Senate's role in the selection of federal judges is jealously guarded. The practice of **senatorial courtesy** gives a senator veto power over judicial appointments in his or her state, provided the senator is of the same party as the president. The Senate Judiciary Committee sends a **blue slip** to the home-state senator asking for an evaluation of the nominee. If the letter is not returned, or if it is returned with an objection, the nominee is not even considered. Presidential nominations come before the president upon the recommendation from the attorney general's office, which actively recruits and screens potential nominees to balance the president's interests against judicial qualifications, regional balance, and interest-group support for any nominee.

Since the Truman administration an increasingly important factor has been the evaluation of judicial nominees made by the American Bar Association's (ABA) twelve-member Committee on the Federal Judiciary. Over the years this committee has come to have an important, influential voice in nominating federal judges, at least below the level of the Supreme Court. President Carter sought to broaden the evaluation process beyond the Senate and the ABA by establishing, through executive order, citizen nominating commissions in the states. Senators must consult these private citizen groups in evaluating judicial qualifications. The order carries no enforcement mechanism, however, so Carter's proposal struck an accommodationist balance between his personal belief and the harsh reality of senatorial politics.

There is ample evidence that candidates campaign for the federal bench. Interest groups increasingly feel they have a right to make their thoughts known. Judges on the court also campaign. The chief justice of the Supreme Court may consult with the president on proposed nominees. The impact of a letter from a Supreme Court justice cannot be dismissed. The selection of federal judges is, and remains, a political process. Presidents are keenly aware that the people they place in the federal judiciary, through their decisions, help make public policy.

The Characteristics of Federal Judges

The characteristics of federal judges reflect the considerations that go into the appointment process: political party, ideology, and prior experience.

Political Party   Party affiliation has always been an important consideration in the selection of federal judges; presidents rarely choose judges from the opposite party (Table 13.4). They acknowledge this, but when pressed to divide judgeships between the parties, President Kennedy responded, "I would hope that the *paramount* consideration in the appointment of a judge would not be his political party but his qualifications. . . ."[17]

TABLE 13.4 Partisan affiliation of newly appointed federal circuit and district judges, 1933–1984

President (party) years	Democrat	Republican	Percent same as president's party
Roosevelt (D), 1933–1945	188	6	97%
Truman (D), 1945–1953	116	9	93
Eisenhower (R), 1953–1961	9	165	95
Kennedy (D), 1961–1963	111	11	91
Johnson (D), 1963–1969	159	9	95
Nixon (R), 1969–1974	15	192	93
Ford (R), 1974–1977	12	52	81
Carter (D), 1977–1980	233	25	90
Reagan (R), 1981–1984	4	156	98

SOURCE: *Congressional Quarterly, Weekly Report* (November 19, 1977): 2444. Data for Carter and Reagan from Sheldon Goldman, "Reaganizing the Judiciary," *Judicature* (April/May 1985): 313.

Ideology   As important as party is finding a person with the right kind of judicial philosophy. Lincoln expressed this view with his appointment of Salmon P. Chase as Chief Justice in 1864: "We wish for a Chief Justice who will sustain what has been done in regard to emancipation and the legal tenders." Eisenhower bitterly complained that his biggest mistake as president was to appoint Earl Warren, who as chief justice became the symbol of a liberal, activist court. Richard Nixon pledged to appoint a law-and-order judiciary, and his 207 appointments, including four Supreme Court justices, have had a profound impact on public policy.

The question of ideology is important because judges serve for life; their influence can extend long beyond the tenure of the appointing president. Presidents seek to assess past career performance, public controversies, political activities, as well as recommendations from trusted advisors. One study concluded that presidents are generally successful in appointing judges who conform to their expectations about three-fourths of the time.[18] Conversely, judges contemplating retirement often do so with an eye to the White House. Chief Justice Taft refused to retire in 1929. "I must stay on the Court," he stated, "in order to prevent the Bolsheviks from getting control." Justice Douglas tried, unsuccessfully, to delay retirement until a Democrat replaced Gerald Ford as president. Jus-

THE NEW 5-4 LOOK

Hy Rosen—Albany Times-Union, N.Y.

tices Brennan and Marshall contemplated retirement but were unwilling to give President Reagan the opportunity to make more appointments.

The Reagan administration has been particularly intent on appointing judges with an ideologically conservative philosophy. The 1984 GOP platform made the point: "In his second term, President Reagan will continue to appoint Supreme Court and other federal judges who share our commitment to judicial restraint." And indications are that Ronald Reagan has done just that. The Reagan administration has created an appointment structure to ensure that conservative judges are identified, screened, and appointed to the federal bench. The administration appears well satisfied with the results. "There is fragmentary evidence that has begun to emerge [however] that suggests that the Reagan Administration on the whole is satisfied. For example, a study by the Center for Judicial Studies of every decision published by every Reagan appointee serving during the first two years of Reagan's first term concluded that the overwhelming majority of appointees demonstrated judicial restraint along the lines favored by the Administration."[19]

Prior Experience The basic prerequisite for judicial appointment is the law degree. Many judges have no or limited prior judicial experience; most, however, have public experience. Since judicial appointments are political appointments, federal judges normally have distinguished themselves in political careers. Approximately one-third of the district court judges served previously as state judges; three in five judges on the court of appeals came with judicial experience, largely as federal district court judges. Carter's record for nominations was somewhat better: 45 percent of his district court and appellate court nominations had prior judicial experience.[20] Of the 102 individual justices appointed as of 1974 to the Supreme Court, 42 had no judicial experience at all, and only 20 percent had ten or more years of previous judicial experience. In fact, many of the eminent names on the roll of Supreme Court justices are persons with no prior judicial experience.

Presidents and Judicial Selection All presidents intend to shape the judiciary through their appointments to the federal bench, especially to the Supreme Court. But because all federal judges have life tenure, different presidents have different opportunities to make such appointments. (See Table 13.5.) Presidents Carter and Reagan were both given unique opportunities to influence and shape the federal judiciary.

Because Congress in 1978 created the largest number of new federal court judgeships ever by a single act of Congress, Jimmy Carter had the unique opportunity of filling 117 new district court judgeships and 35 new positions added to the court of appeals. Ronald Reagan, too, has been given ample opportunity to appoint federal judges. In his first term alone he made 160 appointments to the federal bench. In addition, the new bankruptcy law will afford Reagan opportunity to appoint at least another 100 federal judges, as the act created anew 61 district court judges and 24 appellate judges.

TABLE 13.5   Judicial appointments

	White		Black		Hispanic		Asian		Male		Female	
	U.S. Court of Appeals *Ethnic background*								Sex			
Johnson	95.0%	(38)	5.0%	(2)	—		—		97.5%	(39)	2.5%	(1)
Nixon	97.8	(44)	—		—		2.2%	(1)	100.0	(45)	—	
Ford	100.0	(12)	—		—		—		100.0	(12)	—	
Carter	78.6	(44)	16.9	(9)	3.6	(2)	1.8	(1)	80.4	(45)	19.6	(11)
Reagan (first term)	93.5	(29)	3.2	(1)	3.2	(1)	—		96.8	(30)	3.2	(1)
	U.S. District Court											
Johnson	93.4%	(114)	4.1%	(5)	2.5%	(3)	—		98.4%	(120)	1.6%	(2)
Nixon	95.5	(171)	3.4	(6)	1.1	(2)	—		99.4	(178)	0.6	(1)
Ford	88.5	(46)	5.8	(3)	1.9	(1)	3.9	(2)	98.1	(51)	1.9	(1)
Carter	78.7	(159)	13.9	(28)	6.9	(14)	0.5	(1)	85.6	(173)	14.4	(29)
Reagan (first term)	93.0	(120)	0.8	(1)	5.4	(7)	0.8	(1)	90.7	(117)	9.3	(12)

SOURCE: Sheldon Goldman, "Reaganizing the Judiciary," *Judicature* 68 (April/May 1985).

Sandra Day O'Connor Justice O'Connor, the first woman to serve on the Supreme Court, was appointed an associate justice of the Supreme Court in 1981 by President Reagan. She is a graduate of Stanford Law School and was a superior court judge and an appeals court judge in Arizona prior to her nomination to the high court.

The two presidents approached judicial selection quite differently. Under Carter, merit selection of judges was a guiding force, and he was also publicly committed to enlarging the numbers of blacks, women, and Hispanics on the federal judiciary. By the time he left office in 1980, he had appointed 40 women, 37 blacks, and 16 Hispanics to the courts—more than any other president.[21] The principal vehicle for merit appointment of judges was the establishment of "merit nominating commissions" in several of the states. By executive order, Carter created panels composed of lawyers and lay members to recommend candidates for the federal bench. At the district court level, these nominating commissions worked through U.S. senators in the states. By one count, in 1979 and 1980, two-thirds of Carter's district court nominations came through these commissions.[22]

The Reagan administration has approached judicial appointments quite differently. President Reagan promised judges who would restore "traditional family values and the sanctity of innocent human life." This is a promise he has kept, along with his pledge to appoint less active federal judges.

Reagan began his presidency with a surprise Supreme Court nomination, that of Sandra Day O'Connor. She became the first woman to sit on the high court. While the appointment presumably pleased feminists and women's groups, Justice O'Connor has proven to be no liberal, activist judge. When Warren Burger resigned in 1986, Reagan had a second opportunity to make a Supreme Court nomination. He chose Associate Justice William Rehnquist for the position of chief justice and then selected Antonin Scalia, an appeals judge from the Court of Appeals, District of Columbia, for the position vacated by Mr. Justice Rehnquist. This action achieved a twofold goal for President Reagan: first, younger justices ap-

William H. Rehnquist
William H. Rehnquist replaced Warren Burger as Chief Justice of the Supreme Court in 1986. Rehnquist is only the fourth associate justice to become chief in the Court's history. Rehnquist was first appointed to the Supreme Court in 1971, by Richard Nixon. Born in Milwaukee, Wisconsin, he received his law degree from Stanford University Law School, where he was a classmate of Sandra Day O'Connor, Reagan's first appointee to the Supreme Court. Rehnquist practiced law in Arizona before going to Washington in 1969 as assistant attorney general in the Nixon administration. He was serving in that office when Nixon appointed him to the Court. Rehnquist is a strong advocate of judicial restraint and he believes in allowing elected officials wide latitude in making public policy. As an associate justice he was the Court's most frequent dissenter.

pointed to the Court—Rehnquist assumed the key position of Chief Justice at age 62, and the new justice, Antonin Scalia, was 51 at appointment; second, conservative justices on the Court. Rehnquist had been the acknowledged leader and most consistent conservative on the Burger Court. Antonin Scalia was noted for his conservative appeals court decisions. Both colleagues and critics describe him as a brilliant and exceptionally well-qualified jurist who also is known for his judicial restraint and conservative judicial philosophy.

This approach to judicial selection typifies the Reagan administration. Reagan's appointments to life-tenure positions on the federal bench—district court and appeals courts—have been well-qualified persons who share the president's conservative ideology.

To obtain this sort of judge, President Reagan abandoned the merit nominating commissions and instead used a President's Committee on Federal Judicial Selection. This is a nine-member committee operating from within the White House, where high-level staff play an active role in screening and recommending judges, thus institutionalizing and formalizing the White House's role in judicial selection. Concludes political scientist Sheldon Goldman, "Legislative, patronage, political, and policy considerations are considered to an extent never before so systematically taken into account. This has assured policy coordination between the White House and the Justice Department, as well as White House staff supervision of judicial appointments."[23]

The Justice Department continues to review and recommend names to the president, but the process is coordinated with the President's Committee on Judicial Selection. Indeed, Reagan has transferred this responsibility from the deputy attorney general's office to the Office of Legal Policy in the Justice Department, whose head is a member of the President's Committee on Judicial Selection. In addition, the President's personnel office conducts its own investigation of prospective nominees independent of the Justice Department. The result has been the kind of judiciary Ronald Reagan wants. "It is perhaps not an overstatement to observe that the formal mechanism of the Committee has resulted in the most consistent ideological or policy-orientation screening of judicial candidates since the first term of Franklin Roosevelt."[23]

When compared to Carter's and previous administrations, nearly all Reagan administration appointments bear the president's stamp: white, male, and conservative. There have been only 7 percent blacks and other minority appointees to district court judgeships; 10 percent have been women. To positions on the courts of appeal there have been only two (6 percent) minority appointments and only one woman (3 percent). Many of the gains made by the Carter administration in appointing minorities and women have been lost as the Reagan administration searched for true ideologically conservative judges.

Among judicial appointments, selection of Supreme Court justices is the crown jewel. Their appointment takes on special significance, because most presidents see their selection as a unique opportunity to influence

Name	State	Date of birth	Nominated by	To replace	Date of appointment	Confirmation or other action[a]	Date resigned	Date of death	Years service
John Jay	N.Y.	12/12/1745	Washington		9/24/1789	9/26/1789	6/29/1795	5/17/1829	6
John Rutledge	S.C.	1739	Washington		9/24/1789	9/26/1789	3/5/1791	6/21/1800	1
William Cushing	Mass.	3/1/1732	Washington		9/24/1789	9/26/1789		9/13/1810	21
Robert H. Harrison	Md.	1745	Washington		9/24/1789	9/26/1789 (D)		4/20/1790	
James Wilson	Pa.	9/14/1742	Washington		9/24/1789	9/26/1789		8/21/1798	9
John Blair	Va.	1732	Washington		9/24/1789	9/26/1789	1/27/1796	8/31/1800	6
James Iredell	N.C.	10/5/1751	Washington	Harrison	2/8/1790	2/10/1790		10/20/1799	9
Thomas Johnson	Md.	11/4/1732	Washington	Rutledge	11/1/1791	11/7/1791	3/4/1793	10/26/1819	1
William Paterson	N.J.	12/24/1745	Washington	Johnson	2/27/1793	2/28/1793 (W)		9/9/1806	13
William Paterson[c]			Washington	Johnson	3/4/1793	3/4/1793			
John Rutledge[b]			Washington	Jay	7/1/1795	12/15/1795 (R, 10–14)			
William Cushing[b]			Washington	Jay	1/26/1796	1/27/1796 (D)			
Samuel Chase	Md.	4/17/1741	Washington	Blair	1/26/1796	1/27/1796		6/19/1811	15
Oliver Ellsworth	Conn.	4/29/1745	Washington	Jay	3/3/1796	3/4/1796 (21–1)	9/30/1800	11/26/1807	4
Bushrod Washington	Va.	6/5/1762	Adams	Wilson	12/19/1798	12/20/1798		11/26/1829	31
Alfred Moore	N.C.	5/21/1755	Adams	Iredell	12/6/1799	12/10/1799	1/26/1804	10/15/1810	4
John Jay[b]			Adams	Ellsworth	12/18/1800	12/19/1800 (D)			
John Marshall	Va.	9/24/1755	Adams	Ellsworth	1/20/1801	1/27/1801		7/6/1835	34
William Johnson	S.C.	12/27/1771	Jefferson	Moore	3/22/1804	3/24/1804		8/4/1834	30
H. Brockholst Livingston	N.Y.	11/25/1757	Jefferson	Paterson	12/13/1806	12/17/1806		3/18/1823	16
Thomas Todd	Ky.	1/23/1765	Jefferson	New seat	2/28/1807	3/3/1807		2/7/1826	19
Levi Lincoln	Mass.	5/15/1749	Madison	Cushing	1/2/1811	1/3/1811 (D)		4/14/1820	
Alexander Wolcott	Conn.	9/15/1758	Madison	Cushing	2/4/1811	2/13/1811 (R, 9–24)		6/26/1828	
John Quincy Adams	Mass.	7/11/1767	Madison	Cushing	2/21/1811	2/22/1811 (D)		2/23/1848	
Joseph Story	Mass.	9/18/1779	Madison	Cushing	11/15/1811	11/18/1811		9/10/1845	34
Gabriel Duvall	Md.	12/6/1752	Madison	Chase	11/15/1811	11/18/1811	1/10/1835	3/6/1844	23
Smith Thompson	N.Y.	1/17/1768	Monroe	Livingston	12/8/1823	12/19/1823		12/18/1843	20
Robert Trimble	Ky.	11/17/1776	J. Q. Adams	Todd	4/11/1826	5/9/1826 (27–5)		8/25/1828	2
John J. Crittenden	Ky.	9/10/1787	J. Q. Adams	Trimble	12/17/1828	2/12/1829 (P)		7/26/1863	
John McLean	Ohio	3/11/1785	Jackson	Trimble	3/6/1829	3/7/1829		4/4/1861	32
Henry Baldwin	Pa.	1/14/1780	Jackson	Washington	1/4/1830	1/6/1830 (41–2)		4/21/1844	14
James M. Wayne	Ga.	1790	Jackson	Johnson	1/7/1835	1/9/1835		7/5/1867	32
Roger B. Taney	Md.	3/17/1777	Jackson	Duvall	1/15/1835	3/3/1835 (P)		10/12/1864	28
Roger B. Taney[c]			Jackson	Marshall	12/28/1835	3/15/1836 (29–15)			
Philip P. Barbour	Va.	5/25/1783	Jackson	Duvall	12/28/1835	3/15/1836 (30–11)		2/25/1841	5
William Smith	Ala.	1762	Jackson	New seat	3/3/1837	3/8/1837 (23–18) (D)		6/10/1840	
John Catron	Tenn.	1786	Jackson	New seat	3/3/1837	3/8/1837 (28–15)		5/30/1865	28

Name	State	Date of birth	Nominated by	To replace	Date of appointment	Confirmation or other action[a]	Date resigned	Date of death	Years service
John McKinley	Ala.	5/1/1780	Van Buren	New seat	9/18/1837	9/25/1837		7/19/1852	15
Peter V. Daniel	Va.	4/24/1784	Van Buren	Barbour	2/26/1841	3/2/1841 (22–5)		5/31/1860	19
John C. Spencer	N.Y.	1/8/1788	Tyler	Thompson	1/9/1844	1/31/1844 (R, 21–26)		5/18/1855	
Reuben H. Walworth	N.Y.	10/26/1788	Tyler	Thompson	3/13/1844	6/17/1844 (W)		11/27/1867	
Edward King[c]	Pa.	1/31/1794	Tyler	Baldwin	6/5/1844	6/15/1844 (P)			
Edward King[c]			Tyler	Baldwin	12/4/1844	2/7/1845 (W)	11/28/1872	5/8/1873	27
Samuel Nelson	N.Y.	11/10/1792	Tyler	Thompson	2/4/1845	2/14/1845		12/13/1873	
John M. Read	Pa.	2/21/1797	Tyler	Baldwin	2/7/1845	No action		11/29/1874	
George W. Woodward	Pa.	3/26/1809	Polk	Baldwin	12/23/1845	1/22/1846 (R, 20–29)		5/10/1875	
Levi Woodbury	N.H.	12/22/1789	Polk	Story	12/23/1845	1/3/1846		9/4/1851	5
Robert C. Grier	Pa.	3/5/1794	Polk	Baldwin	8/3/1846	8/4/1846	1/31/1870	9/26/1870	23
Benjamin R. Curtis	Mass.	11/4/1809	Fillmore	Woodbury	12/11/1851	12/29/1851	9/30/1857	9/15/1874	5
Edward A. Bradford	La.	9/27/1813	Fillmore	McKinley	8/16/1852	No action		11/22/1872	
George E. Badger	N.C.	4/13/1795	Fillmore	McKinley	1/10/1853	2/11/1853 (P)		5/11/1866	
William C. Micou	La.	1806	Fillmore	McKinley	2/24/1853	No action		4/16/1854	
John A. Campbell	Ala.	6/24/1811	Pierce	McKinley	3/22/1853	3/25/1853	4/26/1861	3/13/1889	8
Nathan Clifford	Maine	8/18/1803	Buchanan	Curtis	12/9/1857	1/12/1858 (26–23)		7/25/1881	23
Jeremiah S. Black	Pa.	1/10/1810	Buchanan	Daniel	2/5/1861	2/21/1861 (R, 25–26)		8/19/1883	
Noah H. Swayne	Ohio	12/7/1804	Lincoln	McLean	1/21/1862	1/24/1862 (38–1)	1/24/1881	6/8/1884	19
Samuel F. Miller	Iowa	4/5/1816	Lincoln	Daniel	7/16/1862	7/16/1862		10/13/1890	28
David Davis	Ill.	3/9/1815	Lincoln	Campbell	12/1/1862	12/8/1862	3/7/1877	6/26/1886	14
Stephen J. Field	Calif.	11/4/1816	Lincoln	New seat	3/6/1863	3/10/1863	12/1/1897	4/9/1899	34
Salmon P. Chase	Ohio	1/13/1808	Lincoln	Taney	12/6/1864	12/6/1864		5/7/1873	8
Henry Stanbery	Ohio	2/20/1803	Johnson	Catron	4/16/1866	No action		6/26/1881	
Ebenezer R. Hoar	Mass.	2/21/1816	Grant	New seat	12/15/1869	2/3/1870 (R, 24–33)		1/31/1895	
Edwin M. Stanton	Pa.	12/19/1814	Grant	Grier	12/20/1869	12/20/1869 (46–11)		12/24/1869	
William Strong	Pa.	5/6/1808	Grant	Grier	2/7/1870	2/18/1870	12/14/1880	8/19/1895	10
Joseph P. Bradley	N.J.	3/14/1813	Grant	New seat	2/7/1870	3/21/1870 (46–9)		1/22/1892	21
Ward Hunt	N.Y.	6/14/1810	Grant	Nelson	12/3/1872	12/11/1872	1/7/1882	3/24/1886	9
George H. Williams	Ore.	3/23/1823	Grant	Chase	12/1/1873	1/8/1874 (W)		4/4/1910	
Caleb Cushing	Mass.	1/17/1800	Grant	Chase	1/9/1874	1/13/1874 (W)		1/2/1879	
Morrison R. Waite	Ohio	11/29/1816	Grant	Chase	1/19/1874	1/21/1874 (63–0)		3/23/1888	14
John M. Harlan	Ky.	6/1/1833	Hayes	Davis	10/17/1877	11/29/1877		10/14/1911	34
William B. Woods	Ga.	8/3/1824	Hayes	Strong	12/15/1880	12/21/1880 (39–8)		5/14/1887	6
Stanley Matthews	Ohio	7/21/1824	Hayes	Swayne	1/26/1881	No action			
Stanley Matthews[c]			Garfield	Swayne	3/14/1881	5/12/1881 (24–23)		3/22/1889	7

Fact File

Supreme Court Nominations, 1789–1986 continued

Name	State	Date of birth	Nominated by	To replace	Date of appointment	Confirmation or other action[a]	Date resigned	Date of death	Years service
Horace Gray	Mass.	3/24/1828	Arthur	Clifford	12/19/1881	12/20/1881 (51–5)	7/9/1902	9/15/1902	20
Roscoe Conkling	N.Y.	10/30/1829	Arthur	Hunt	2/24/1882	3/2/1882 (39–12)(D)		4/18/1888	
Samuel Blatchford	N.Y.	3/9/1820	Arthur	Hunt	3/13/1882	3/27/1882		7/7/1893	11
Lucius Q. C. Lamar	Miss.	9/17/1825	Cleveland	Woods	12/6/1887	1/16/1888 (32–28)		1/23/1893	5
Melville W. Fuller[c]	Ill.	2/11/1833	Cleveland	Waite	4/30/1888	7/20/1888 (41–20)		7/4/1910	22
David J. Brewer	Kan.	1/20/1837	Harrison	Matthews	12/4/1889	12/18/1889 (53–11)		3/28/1910	20
Henry B. Brown	Mich.	3/2/1836	Harrison	Miller	12/23/1890	12/29/1890	5/28/1906	9/4/1913	15
George Shiras Jr.	Pa.	1/26/1832	Harrison	Bradley	7/19/1892	7/26/1892	2/23/1903	8/2/1924	10
Howell E. Jackson	Tenn.	4/8/1832	Harrison	Lamar	2/2/1893	2/18/1893		8/8/1895	2
William B. Hornblower	N.Y.	5/13/1851	Cleveland	Blatchford	9/19/1893	1/15/1894 (R, 24–30)		6/16/1914	
Wheeler H. Peckham	N.Y.	1/1/1833	Cleveland	Blatchford	1/22/1894	2/16/1894 (R, 32–41)		9/27/1905	
Edward D. White	La.	11/3/1845	Cleveland	Blatchford	2/19/1894	2/19/1894		5/19/1921	17
Rufus W. Peckham	N.Y.	11/8/1838	Cleveland	Jackson	12/3/1895	12/9/1895		10/24/1909	13
Joseph McKenna	Calif.	8/10/1843	McKinley	Field	12/16/1897	1/21/1898	1/5/1925	11/21/1926	26
Oliver W. Holmes	Mass.	3/8/1841	Roosevelt	Gray	12/2/1902	12/4/1902	1/12/1932	3/6/1935	29
William R. Day	Ohio	4/17/1849	Roosevelt	Shiras	2/19/1903	2/23/1903	11/13/1922	7/9/1923	19
William H. Moody	Mass.	12/23/1853	Roosevelt	Brown	12/3/1906	12/12/1906	11/20/1910	7/2/1917	3
Horace H. Lurton	Tenn.	2/26/1844	Taft	Peckham	12/13/1909	12/20/1909		7/12/1914	4
Edward D. White[b]			Taft	Fuller	12/12/1910	12/12/1910			10[b]
Charles E. Hughes	N.Y.	4/11/1862	Taft	Brewer	4/25/1910	5/2/1910	6/10/1916	8/27/1948	6
Willis Van Devanter	Wyo.	4/17/1859	Taft	Moody	12/12/1910	12/15/1910	6/2/1937	2/8/1941	26
Joseph R. Lamar	Ga.	10/14/1857	Taft	White	12/12/1910	12/15/1910		1/2/1916	5
Mahlon Pitney	N.J.	2/5/1858	Taft	Harlan	2/19/1912	3/13/1912 (50–26)	12/31/1922	12/9/1924	10
James C. McReynolds	Tenn.	2/3/1862	Wilson	Lurton	8/19/1914	8/29/1914 (44–6)	1/31/1941	8/24/1946	26
Louis D. Brandeis	Mass.	11/13/1856	Wilson	Lamar	1/28/1916	6/1/1916 (47–22)	2/13/1939	10/5/1941	22
John H. Clarke	Ohio	9/18/1857	Wilson	Hughes	7/14/1916	7/24/1916	7/18/1922	3/22/1945	6
William H. Taft	Ohio	9/15/1857	Harding	White	6/30/1921	6/30/1921	2/3/1930	3/8/1930	8
George Sutherland	Utah	3/25/1862	Harding	Clarke	9/5/1922	9/5/1922	1/17/1938	7/18/1942	15
Pierce Butler	Minn.	3/17/1866	Harding	Day	11/23/1922	12/21/1922 (61–8)		11/16/1939	17
Edward T. Sanford	Tenn.	7/23/1865	Harding	Pitney	1/24/1923	1/29/1923		3/8/1930	7
Harlan F. Stone	N.Y.	10/11/1872	Coolidge	McKenna	1/5/1925	2/5/1925 (71–6)		4/22/1946	16
Charles E. Hughes[b]			Hoover	Taft	2/3/1930	2/13/1930 (52–26)	7/1/1941		11[b]
John J. Parker	N.C.	11/20/1885	Hoover	Sanford	3/21/1930	5/7/1930 (R, 39–41)		3/17/1958	
Owen J. Roberts	Pa.	5/2/1875	Hoover	Sanford	5/9/1930	5/20/1930	7/31/1945	5/17/1955	15
Benjamin N. Cardozo	N.Y.	5/24/1870	Hoover	Holmes	2/15/1932	2/24/1932		7/9/1938	6

Name	State	Date of birth	Nominated by	To replace	Date of appointment	Confirmation or other action[a]	Date resigned	Date of death	Years service
Hugo L. Black	Ala.	2/27/1886	Roosevelt	Van Devanter	8/12/1937	8/17/1937 (63–16)	9/17/1971	10/25/1971	34
Stanley F. Reed	Ky.	12/31/1884	Roosevelt	Sutherland	1/15/1938	1/25/1938	2/26/1957		19
Felix Frankfurter	Mass.	11/15/1882	Roosevelt	Cardozo	1/5/1939	1/17/1939	8/28/1962	2/22/1965	23
William O. Douglas	Conn.	10/16/1898	Roosevelt	Brandeis	3/20/1939	4/4/1939 (62–4)	11/12/1975	1/19/1980	36
Frank Murphy	Mich.	4/13/1890	Roosevelt	Butler	1/4/1940	1/15/1940		7/19/1949	9
Harlan F. Stone[b]			Roosevelt	Hughes	6/12/1941	6/27/1941			5[b]
James F. Byrnes	S.C.	5/2/1879	Roosevelt	McReynolds	6/12/1941	6/12/1941	10/3/1942	4/9/1972	1
Robert H. Jackson	N.Y.	2/13/1892	Roosevelt	Stone	6/12/1941	7/7/1941		10/9/1954	13
Wiley B. Rutledge	Iowa	7/20/1894	Roosevelt	Byrnes	1/11/1943	2/8/1943		9/10/1949	6
Harold H. Burton	Ohio	6/22/1888	Truman	Roberts	9/19/1945	9/19/1945	10/13/1958	10/28/1964	13
Fred M. Vinson	Ky.	1/22/1890	Truman	Stone	6/6/1946	6/20/1946		9/8/1953	7
Tom C. Clark	Texas	9/23/1899	Truman	Murphy	8/2/1949	8/18/1949 (73–8)	6/12/1967	6/13/1977	18
Sherman Minton	Ind.	10/20/1890	Truman	Rutledge	9/15/1949	10/4/1949 (48–16)	10/15/1956	4/9/1965	7
Earl Warren	Calif.	3/19/1891	Eisenhower	Vinson	9/30/1953	3/1/1954	6/23/1969	6/9/1974	15
John M. Harlan	N.Y.	5/20/1899	Eisenhower	Jackson	1/10/1955	3/16/1955 (71–11)	9/23/1971	12/29/1971	16
William J. Brennan, Jr.	N.J.	4/25/1906	Eisenhower	Minton	1/14/1957	3/19/1957			
Charles E. Whittaker	Mo.	2/22/1901	Eisenhower	Reed	3/2/1957	3/19/1957	4/1/1962	11/26/1973	5
Potter Stewart	Ohio	1/23/1915	Eisenhower	Burton	1/17/1959	5/5/1959 (70–17)	7/3/1981		22
Byron R. White	Colo.	6/8/1917	Kennedy	Whittaker	3/30/1962	4/11/1962			
Arthur J. Goldberg	Ill.	8/8/1908	Kennedy	Frankfurter	8/29/1962	9/25/1962	7/25/1965		3
Abe Fortas	Tenn.	6/19/1910	Johnson	Goldberg	7/28/1965	8/11/1965 (69–11)	5/14/1969		4
Thurgood Marshall	N.Y.	6/2/1908	Johnson	Clark	6/13/1967	8/30/1967			
Abe Fortas[b]			Johnson	Warren	6/26/1968	10/4/1968 (W)			
Homer Thornberry	Texas	1/9/1909	Johnson	Fortas	6/26/1968	No action			
Warren E. Burger	Minn.	9/17/1907	Nixon	Warren	5/21/1969	6/9/1969 (74–3)	7/10/1986		17
Clement Haynsworth, Jr.	S.C.	10/30/1912	Nixon	Fortas	8/18/1969	11/21/1969 (R, 45–55)			
G. Harrold Carswell	Fla.	12/22/1919	Nixon	Fortas	1/19/1970	4/8/1970 (R, 45–51)			
Harry A. Blackmun	Minn.	11/12/1908	Nixon	Fortas	4/14/1970	5/12/1970 (94–0)			
Lewis F. Powell, Jr.	Va.	9/19/1907	Nixon	Black	10/21/1971	12/6/1971 (89–1)			
William H. Rehnquist	Ariz.	10/1/1924	Nixon	Harlan	10/21/1971	12/10/1971 (68–26)			14
John Paul Stevens	Ill.	4/20/1920	Ford	Douglas	11/28/1975	12/17/1975 (98–0)			
Sandra Day O'Connor	Ariz.	3/26/1930	Reagan	Stewart	7/7/1981	9/21/1981 (99–0)			
William Rehnquist[b]			Reagan	Burger	6/17/1986	9/17/1986 (65–33)			
Antonin Scalia	N.J.	3/11/36	Reagan	Rehnquist	6/17/1986	9/17/1986 (98–0)			

Boldface = Chief Justice; Italics = did not serve; D = Declined; W = Withdrawn; P = Postponed; R = Rejected
[a] Where no note is listed, confirmation is unrecorded.
[b] Earlier court service. See above.
[c] Earlier nomination not confirmed. See above.
SOURCE: *Guide to the U.S. Supreme Court* (Congressional Quarterly Press, 1979), pp. 946–948.

TABLE 13.6   Age of Supreme Court justices

Justice	Age as of January 1987	President making appointment
William Brennan	80	Eisenhower
Lewis Powell	79	Nixon
Thurgood Marshall	78	Johnson
Harry Blackmun	78	Nixon
Byron White	69	Kennedy
John Stevens	66	Ford
William Rehnquist	62	Nixon
Sandra Day O'Connor	56	Reagan
Antonin Scalia	51	Reagan

public policy in America. Franklin Roosevelt appointed nine justices in his thirteen years; Eisenhower made five appointments in his eight years. Richard Nixon made four appointments in his six years in office; three of those four appointments are part of the contemporary Supreme Court. So it was with great expectation that Ronald Reagan approached his second term and the opportunity of making more Supreme Court appointments.

Of the present Supreme Court, four of the justices are over 75 years of age. Several justices have expressed a desire to retire soon, due either to the heavy work load of the Court or to ill health (see Table 13.6). The resignation of Chief Justice Burger and appointment of Antonin Scalia affords Ronald Reagan the further opportunity to influence the federal judiciary, leaving a lasting impact on the Supreme Court rivaling that of Franklin Roosevelt or Richard Nixon.

The Supreme Court

The Supreme Court is more than a legal institution. It serves as our national symbol of justice and functions to resolve questions of national policy. As was the case in *U.S.* v. *Nixon* and again in *California Regents* v. *Bakke,* the Court has been called on to make difficult and profoundly consequential decisions. "To consider the Supreme Court of the United States as strictly a legal institution is to underestimate its significance in the American political system," said Robert A. Dahl, "for it is also a political institution, an institution, that is to say, for questions of national policy."[25]

Politics, Policy, and Public Opinion

The past three decades have witnessed a considerable expansion of judicial activity in the United States. The scope of judicial policy making has broadened. While judges continue to hear cases long a part of their judical work load, their activity has expanded into areas once thought unfit for adjudication: welfare administration, prison life, educational policies, road and bridge building, automotive safety standards, and nat-

Practicing Politics: Serving on a Jury

*S*ome of the regulations for jury service vary from place to place, but everywhere in the United States jury service is the legal duty of a citizen. Your notice to serve is issued in the form of a legal summons; it is not a request, and failure to answer is punishable under the law. Here is how the system generally works.

1. An office of the court designated to handle jurors obtains lists of the names of those residing within a certain area. Voter registration lists are used everywhere; some places also use motor vehicle registration and license lists, data from the Internal Revenue Service, and even names from public utility or telephone company billings.

2. All those who appear on these various lists are sent questionnaires to determine whether they are qualified to be jurors. (A juror, for example, must be a citizen of the United States.)

3. The names of those selected as qualified are printed on slips of paper, and the slips placed in a drum. Selection of those to be summoned is done by drawing randomly from the drum, as in a lottery.

4. The selected persons are sent summonses to appear for jury duty on a certain date. By law, the summons must be answered and the person must serve, but there are, of course, exemptions: a registered nurse, a doctor in private practice, a lawyer, the sole proprietor of a business, and certain other categories of people may appear before a judge, present their reasons for not wishing to serve, and be exempted.

5. A trial juror serves at least two weeks (longer if he or she is chosen to serve on the jury for a lengthy trial). A grand juror (a person chosen to sit on a jury that hears charges to determine whether or not a case should go to trial) must serve at least twenty days.

6. Jurors are paid a daily stipend for serving; the amount varies from locality to locality, but it is usually a token and does not equal the person's regular salary.

7. Being chosen for jury service does not automatically mean that you will be part of a trial. You go to the courthouse each morning, and as cases come up on the calendar, you may be chosen to be among those questioned by the lawyers for each side. Even if you are chosen, you may or may not be selected as a juror. Lawyers, who have the right to reject prospective jurors, are of course looking for people they think will render a fair judgment in their particular case.

8. If you are selected, you may be part of the judicial process in anything from a minor traffic accident to a sensational murder, and once on the jury, you serve until the case has been disposed of, whether it is two weeks or a month.

ural resource management.[26] The courts are now actively involved in making social policy.

The development of judicial activism extends back to the Warren Court and the 1954 school-desegregation cases, which signaled a willingness on the part of the courts to test the conventional boundaries of judicial action. Social groups frustrated by the political process now saw the opportunity to use litigation to achieve their goals.

Historically, we might have expected the period of judicial activism to be followed by a period of quietism. This was true in the wake of *Dred Scott* (1857), and in the activities of the Court after overturning New Deal legislation in the 1930s. The Supreme Court has no independent means to enforce its decrees. It must follow the dictates of public opinion, and the president is more in touch with the public than the Court. So a period of activism is usually followed by one of restraint as the president, through the appointive process, redresses the balance. This is the assumed check on judicial power: a Court that goes too far is replaced, through judicial appointment, with a more passive set of justices.

Yet this has not happened in the wake of the Warren Court. The Burger Court, in the main, maintained the policy of judicial activism, continuing to make social policy that altered American life. It was the Burger Court in 1971 that ordered busing of schoolchildren to overcome segregation in urban cities; the *Roe* v. *Wade* decision permitting abortions was a statement affecting the essence of human rights; and the *Bakke* decision illustrated just how strongly the Court intended to further affirmative action programs. We are in a period of institutionalized activism: "The power of the Court has been exercised so often and so successfully over the last 20 years, and the ability to restrict or control it by either new legislation, Constitutional amendments, or new appointments has met with such uniform failure, that the Court, and the subordinate courts, are now seen as forces of nature, difficult to predict and impossible to control."[27]

Institutionalized Activism

Judicial Activism: *a judicial style that involves a willingness on the part of the courts to test conventional boundaries of judicial action, playing an active role in shaping public policy.*

Judicial activism (the tendency of courts, or, more properly, of individual judges, to read the law and to decide cases on the basis of their own values and interpretation of the law) is now an institutionalized feature of the Supreme Court. In the absence of legislative remedies, the Court has shown a propensity to "take the heat" and involve itself in social policy. Often Congress has built into its programs the opportunity for social groups to seek judicial relief if policies are promulgated without their being consulted or have a negative impact on them. But much of the activity has occurred independently of Congress and the bureaucracy. Courts have ordered special education for disturbed, retarded, or hyperactive students. Courts have struck down residency requirements for eligibility for welfare payments and have established comprehensive programs of care and treatment for the mentally ill in hospitals. And they

In many cities neighborhood legal-aid clinics advise and assist citizens who are unable to afford legal counsel.

have done all this by using the traditional judicial powers; these decisions were extensions of regular activities, not departures.

New Areas of Adjudication   One cause of institutionalized activism is the emergence of new areas of adjudication. For example, housing and welfare rights are the result of litigation, prompted to some degree by congressional legislation. Courts have ordered building programs and decreed that states must "adequately fund" such institutions as mental hospitals and education. In the area of personal freedom, the courts have ruled on marital and cohabitation rights as well as abortion. They have awarded alimony to fathers because of the wife's ability to pay. Courts have equalized school expenditures for teachers' salaries, decreed that bilingual education be provided for Mexican-American children, and suspended the use of National Teacher Examinations by school boards. Courts have required the Farmers Home Administration to restore a disaster-loan program, stopped the Forest Service from cutting timber, and directed the Army Corps of Engineers to maintain the nation's non-navigable waterways.[28]

New Litigants with Standing to Sue   The thrust of the Court into new areas of social policy is, in part, a result of the Court's willingness to broaden standing to initiate litigation to include private litigants and to permit class action suits. In the early 1960s, only one such private center, the NAACP Legal Defense Fund, was granted standing. Beginning with the Great Society and the Economic Opportunity Act, however, several poverty law centers were created. As a result of the NAACP precedent, there was a rash of litigation in almost every conceivable area of social policy: welfare, housing, health, education, and penology. New clients—Mexican-American and Indian groups, mental health patients, prisoners, welfare recipients, and women's organizations—found the law a potentially quick and effective means to social change.

The Supreme Court in Action

The Supreme Court's term runs from the first Monday in October through the end of June. The Court must narrow down the 5,000 cases filed annually to a manageable number for the term (see Table 13.7). The first month or so is spent deliberating over which cases the Court will take. The rest of the term, normally through April, is spent calling for briefs and listening to oral arguments. In May and June the Court renders its verdicts and releases opinions explaining the basis for its decisions.

Dockets: *the calendars used by the Supreme Court to schedule business in order to dispose of cases filed with the Court.*

Filing on the Docket

To handle the requests for consideration of cases, the Supreme Court has established three calendars of business to act upon cases, called **dockets.**

Changing Consensus: Judicial Restraint

When Ronald Reagan became president he pledged to appoint to the federal judiciary judges who would practice judicial restraint. To the Reagan administration, however, judicial restraint means something different from its common legal usage.

The president believes the courts should have a much more limited role in American governance; he feels that judges must cut back on their role in setting social policy. However, President Reagan's beliefs in this area are closely tied to his conservative social agenda. Observed Philip Kurland of the University of Chicago Law School, "Judges are being appointed in the expectation that they will rewrite laws and the Constitution to the administration's liking. Reagan's judges are activists in support of conservative dogma."

To the Reagan administration and conservatives, judicial restraint is a bold effort to remove authority from the courts and rebalance the Constitution's separated powers. Older limits of restraint are often breached in their struggle to remake the law. To permit legalized prayer in school, for example, Reagan personnel are prepared to overturn forty-year-old precedents. Said Assistant Attorney General William Bradford Reynolds, "Our position is the Supreme Court must be crafted in such a way as to make abundantly clear that we view and *Engel* [court decisions on prayer in school] as wrong and unworthy of respect." The same attitude is taken toward abortion, affirmative action, and the rights of the accused. Thus, for example, Attorney General Edwin Meese publicly called for the repeal of *Miranda* rights, suggesting that anyone arrested for a crime must be guilty unless innocence can be proven.

While the overturn of precedent is not, in inself, a violation of judicial restraint, the approach taken by the Reagan administration departs dramatically from traditional understanding. The administration would, over-night, wash away decisions it believes wrong. There would be no gradual laying of legal foundations; precedent would not be allowed to guide the decisions in these new cases.

This revision in judicial restraint is counter to the common understanding of judicial restraint in constitutional history. Because the Court has the power of judicial rule, to make authoritative decisions on fundamental principles of American governance, that power must be exercised with the greatest respect—and caution. It may be used to facilitate changed attitudes, allowing a majority to govern, or it may become a check and balance to protect individuals and principles from the majority. To ease the tension between individual protection and majoritarian governance, judges have generally observed the practice of judicial restraint. "There is not under our Constitution a judicial remedy for every political mischief, for every undesirable exercise of legislative power," wrote Felix Frankfurter, a long-time Supreme Court justice and a practitioner of judicial restraint. "The Framers carefully and with deliberate forethought refused so to enthrone the judiciary."

In this tradition, judicial restraint meant the Supreme Court and other federal courts should defer to the judgments of democratically elected bodies wherever possible. Exercising passive virtues, the courts should decide no case unnecessarily. When they do rule, it should be on the narrowest possible grounds, and they should avoid constitutional issues whenever possible. When rendering verdicts, judges should avoid rash decisions, keep to the law, and follow the precedent of previous cases. Judges should narrowly interpret the law, including previous cases, and the Constitution so as not to disturb the continuity of public policy. In this tradition, judicial restraint has been an instrument of gradualism, protecting the authority of judges in a careful, gradual evolution of the law. This is judicial conservatism, not ideological conservatism.

Supporters of judicial restraint objected to much of what occurred in the 1950s and 1960s in the Warren Court, when the courts became an instrument of social change. The Reagan administration wants to change much of the policy that resulted from that period of judicial activism, but it is not willing to allow the time or gradualism that judicial restraint calls for. It is result oriented and is prepared to find judges who are willing to be activists in the name of judicial restraint. But this form of judicial restraint would represent a changed consensus from the traditional constitutional meaning of the term.

TABLE 13.7   Disposition of cases before the Supreme Court, 1982–1985

	Original	Appelate	
		In forma pauperis	*Paid*
1982–1983			
Acted on during term	3	2,013	2,297
Granted review on merit	—	10	169
1983–1984			
Acted on during term	7	1,992	2,220
Granted review on merit	—	9	140
1984–1985			
Acted on during term	8	2,087	2,253
Granted review on merit	—	18	167

SOURCE: Office of the Supreme Court.

In Forma Pauperis: requests made by indigent appellants using relaxed standards of the Supreme Court to ask for a review of their cases.

All requests are assigned to one of the three: the *original* docket contains all cases filed for decision under the Court's original jurisdiction; the *appellate* docket contains all the formal appeals from lower court decisions. There are strict rules for filing certiorari writs; in addition, all writs of appeal are put here. The *miscellaneous* docket contains all the petitions filed *in forma pauperis* (in the manner of a pauper). There is a growing trend for jailhouse lawyers and indigent appellants to use the relaxed standards of the Court to ask for a review of their cases. Requests are often handwritten or typed single-page arguments prepared and researched by the petitioner, using jail libraries and word-of-mouth advice.

Several times during the term, the justices meet to consider the requests. They discuss and vote on which petitions should be granted. If any four justices approve a petition, it is accepted. Fewer than one in ten cases is accepted for formal legal action. Figure 13.2 illustrates how a case gets to the Supreme Court.

However, acceptance for review by the Supreme Court does not necessarily mean further briefs or oral argument. Many cases are summarily decided—that is, they are decided upon the basis of the information submitted with the request. In 1984–1985, only 175 (3.5 percent) of the 5,006 cases on the docket were accepted for argument; the remainder were dismissed, denied, summarily decided, or carried over (73 or 1.5 percent were by summary judgment; 4,003 or 80 percent were denied or dismissed).[29]

Oral Argument

The Court listens to oral arguments in the first two weeks of each month. The Court spends the last two weeks behind closed doors discussing the merits of the case and writing opinions.

Brief: a lengthy written document citing law and precedent, used in court by counsel.

Before the oral presentation, the lawyers for the contending sides submit **briefs:** lengthy written documents citing law and precedent supporting their positions. Forty copies are required! The contending party has

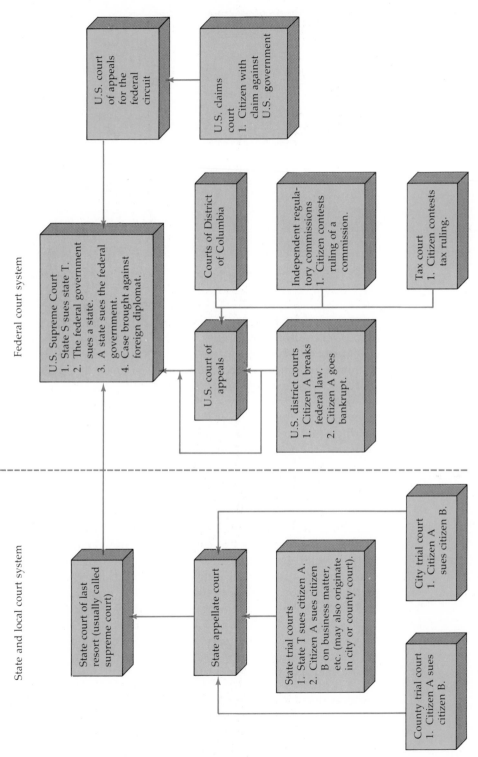

Figure 13.2   How cases go through the state and local court systems and the federal court systems to get to the Supreme Court

Federal court system

State and local court system

U.S. court of appeals for the federal circuit

U.S. claims court
1. Citizen with claim against U.S. government

Courts of District of Columbia

Independent regulatory commissions
1. Citizen contests ruling of a commission.

Tax court
1. Citizen contests tax ruling.

U.S. Supreme Court
1. State S sues state T.
2. The federal government sues a state.
3. A state sues the federal government.
4. Case brought against foreign diplomat.

U.S. court of appeals

U.S. district courts
1. Citizen A breaks federal law.
2. Citizen A goes bankrupt.

State court of last resort (usually called supreme court)

State appellate court

State trial courts
1. State T sues citizen A.
2. Citizen A sues citizen B on business matter, etc. (may also originate in city or county court).

City trial court
1. Citizen A sues citizen B.

County trial court
1. Citizen A sues citizen B.

President Reagan, former Chief Justice Burger, and members of the United States Supreme Court.

Amicus Curiae: "friend of the court" briefs submitted by interested parties at the invitation of the Court.

forty-five days to submit a brief; the answering party, thirty days thereafter. The Court may also invite parties who have an interest in the outcome to prepare *amicus curiae*, or "friend of the court" briefs. Important cases draw numerous amicus curiae briefs; the 1954 *Brown* case had fifty, and *Bakke* drew fifty-seven such briefs.

At 10 A.M. on the designated day, oral arguments are heard. The black-robed justices file into the marble chamber from behind the velvet curtain. Led by the Chief Justice, the justices sit in order of seniority, faced by the tables for the counselors. Time for oral arguments is strictly limited and enforced. Each side is allotted one hour, sometimes only a half-hour. Two lights on the lectern inform counsel of time remaining. When a white light flashes, five minutes remain; a red light flashes when time has expired, and the counsel must stop immediately.

Oral argument is informal. Reading from the brief is frowned on; Rule 44 of the Court states that "the Court looks with disfavor on any oral argument that is read from a prepared text." The justices frequently interrupt with questions. In one case several years ago, the justices interrupted counsel eighty-four times during two hours of oral argument. In the *Bakke* case, Archibald Cox, representing the Regents of the University of California, was asked the meaning of benchmark ratings, why Asian-Americans were included in the special admissions program, and the relevance of Title VI of the Civil Rights Act. For his part, Reynold Colvin, Mr. Bakke's attorney, got this question from Mr. Justice Powell:

The University doesn't deny or dispute the basic facts. We are here . . . primarily to hear a Constitutional argument . . . I would like help, I really would, on the Constitutional issues. Would you address that?[30]

Whether oral argument sways the outcome of a case is questionable. Nonetheless, it may have a dramatic impact on the issues before the Court. Justice John Harlan thought oral argument critical; he said oral argument "may in many cases make the difference between winning and losing, no matter how good the briefs are.[31]

Solicitor General: *the third highest ranking official in the Justice Department. When the United States is a party to a case before the Supreme Court, the solicitor general acts as the lawyer for the government.*

When the United States is a party to a case before the Supreme Court, the lawyer for the government is the **solicitor general** of the United States, the third highest ranking official in the Justice Department. The solicitor general oversees all federal appeals in the courts and approves all appeals to the Supreme Court. Archibald Cox, who defended the University of California, Davis, in *Bakke* and who was the first special prosecutor in Watergate, was solicitor general in the Kennedy administration. Before Thurgood Marshall was appointed to the Supreme Court, he served as solicitor general for Lyndon Johnson.

Conference

Friday is conference day. Approximately thirty times a session, the justices are summoned by a buzzer at 10 A.M. on Fridays. They meet in private to consider requests for petitions and to discuss cases just argued before the Court. Seated around a large U-shaped table, the justices hear the chief justice outline the facts and explain his view of how the case should be decided. Each justice, in terms of seniority, is then expected to present his or her opinion on the case. When all opinions and arguments have been voiced, a vote is taken. Each justice votes in reverse order of seniority, with the chief justice voting last, and the case is decided.

Opinion of the Court: *the majority opinion of the Court that represents the official reasoning of the Court in rendering its decision.*

Concurring Opinion: *a judicial statement explaining a justice's separate reasoning for voting with the majority.*

Dissenting Opinion: *a judicial statement explaining the minority justices' reasoning for questioning the majority verdict.*

Chief Justices play a special, significant role in these conferences. As chair of the conference, they have ample opportunity to influence its agenda. Since they lead the discussion, they can present the facts and precedents that govern much of the discussion. As moderators, they "make peace" among the several justices. And finally, by voting last the Chief Justice may cast the deciding vote on a controversial case. The Court is noted for its five-to-four rulings. On appeal, the decision most frequently is either to affirm a lower court ruling or to reverse that ruling. The reasons for that decision are stated in the **opinion of the Court,** the official basis for the Court's ruling in a case. Justices who voted with the majority but have different reasons for so voting may write a separate **concurring opinion.** Justices in the opposing minority can write **dissenting opinions.**

Opinion Writing

Per Curium Opinion: *a short, unsigned judicial statement of a decision of the Supreme Court, used for relatively simple cases that command a strong majority.*

The opinion is the core of the policymaking role of the Supreme Court. It is the means by which the Court announces its decisions and justifies its reasoning to the world. Through its opinions, the Supreme Court lays down principles that govern future courts and, inevitably, the nation.

If a case is relatively simple and commands a strong majority, the decision may be announced in a *per curium* **opinion.** Such an opinion is short

SUPREME COURT

"I feel ornery today—Let's declare unconstitutional something that everybody likes!"
© *Artemus Cole/ROTHCO*

and unsigned; it simply announces the decision and the facts in the decision. Most cases selected by the Supreme Court, however, require a lengthy, signed opinion.

If the Chief Justice voted in the majority, he or she can write the opinion or assign it to one of the other justices in the majority. If the Chief Justice is not among the majority, the opinion-writing task falls to the senior justice in the majority. The selection of the opinion writer is crucial, as the task of building a majority consensus is difficult. The justice assigned the task of writing the opinion first writes a draft that is circulated to the other members of the Court. The majority members may suggest revisions, and the writer tries to accommodate their suggestions. At this juncture, the other justices either commit themselves to the opinion or write concurring or dissenting opinions. In the famous *Bakke* case, there was a total of six opinions for the Court.

Plural Decisions:
decisions made by the Supreme Court in which no one line of reasoning can command a majority. These decisions find three or four judges taking one position, one or two justices concurring in part and dissenting in part, and three or four judges dissenting. Thus, a majority is formed only to render decisions.

Plural Decisions The justices on the present Supreme Court have served together for many years, with the exception of Antonin Scalia, appointed in 1986. But serving together has not brought the justices closer together on issues. In recent years under Warren Burger the Court experienced more **plural decisions**—decisions on which fewer than five justices agreed—than at any prior time in the history of the Supreme Court.[32] In 1980–1981 there were six such plural decisions; three more were made in 1981–1982. In the 1984–1985 term the Court rendered ten plural decisions. The cases decided in this way have been among the most controversial and important faced by the Supreme Court, involving, for example, public financing of private schools, reverse discrimination and racial quotas, and sex discrimination. What makes the plural-

decisions issue important is that the Court has a role beyond resolving individual disputes. "More than a mere agreement on the result is needed; without a majority rationale for the result, the Supreme Court abdicates its responsibility to the institutions and parties depending on it for direction. Each plurality decision thus represents a failure to fulfill the Court's obligations."[33]

Marshalling the Court

Decision making in the Supreme Court does not just happen. It is the result of a complex, and often intimately personal, relationship among nine justices.[34] Justices bargain intently with one another to secure a desired point of law or the needed votes to produce a majority. Agreements and majorities are not automatic, nor do they happen with the voting at the culmination of the conference. Each justice is a distinct personality, intelligent and learned in the law. A justice considers ways to "capture" another justice's vote. "A Justice would have to consider the tactics open to him to carry out his efforts to persuade on the merits of his policy choice, to capitalize on personal regard, to bargain, to threaten, and if possible, to have a voice in the selection of new personnel."[35]

In order to produce a majority on the high court, justices form blocs and devise strategies to trade on the judicial philosophy and professional reputation of other justices. Sections of opinions are written to accommodate judicial positions; drafts of opinions are rewritten to keep a wavering justice from voting with the opposition. Murphy notes that the justices trade on personal regard to win votes, that they selectively vote or withhold votes to gain support, that they volunteer to draft opinions in hopes of soothing differences of opinion, that they bargain with philosophy and points of law, and that they co-opt new members to become part of voting blocs in the Court.[36]

Woodward and Armstrong's *The Brethren* describes this intensely political atmosphere of judicial decision making. Votes are often switched on important and sensitive cases. Furthermore, the Chief Justice, who votes last and often reserves voting, can command a majority and assign the opinion, thereby influencing the breadth of judicial policymaking.

Compliance

For all the weight and power attached to Supreme Court decisions, the Court faces important problems in assuring compliance. The Court depends on the interpretation and action of other political institutions and policymakers for compliance. It is by no means automatic—or swift.

In its decisions, the Court is speaking to lower federal courts, state courts, and other political institutions, requiring or forbidding some particular activity, and these institutions and individuals may see or interpret the Court's decisions in different ways. In 1954, reaction to the desegregation decision caused one federal judge to disqualify himself from subsequent desegregation litigation because he opposed the decision. Another federal judge went further; he refused to implement the ruling and declared, "I believe that it will be seen that the Supreme Court based its decision on no law but rather on what the Court regarded as more authoritative, more psychological knowledge."[37]

This does not mean that federal courts can or do disregard Supreme Court decisions. By and large there is compliance. Attorneys can appeal, as happened in the example cited above in the desegregation case. The appellate courts overturned the lower court, and compliance with the Supreme Court was effected. In the case of police interrogations and *Miranda* rights, courts will utilize the exclusionary rule and throw out tainted evidence illegally obtained in violation of the guidelines set forth in *Miranda*. Public officials are harder to control, and yet by and large they comply. Richard Nixon publicly stated he would only obey a "definitive decision" regarding release of the Watergate tapes. When the eight to zero verdict in *U.S.* v. *Nixon* was handed down, he complied.

Limitations on Judicial Power

For all its power and prestige, the Supreme Court faces the very basic limitation of having to wait for suits to be brought to it. There must be a real case or controversy that is capable of judicial settlement. And there are the numerous "technical" checks that limit judicial power: jurisdiction, standing, a justiciable question, and the rule of precedent.

The Court is also limited by other institutions and courts. It is influenced by Congress and the president as well as by lower court interpretations of its decisions.

Congress has control of the appellate jurisdiction of the Supreme Court as well as its size. From time to time, it may take issues from the Court's jurisdiction. It may deny funding for the enforcement of decisions it does not like. Congress tried several times to prevent funding for busing to integrate school districts, and there have been attempts to eliminate public funds to pay for legal abortions. Congress always possesses the power to initiate a constitutional amendment to overturn a Court decision. The Sixteenth Amendment for the personal income tax is one example of congressional response to the Court's declaring a law unconstitutional.

The president and the executive branch also limit the Court. The president's appointment power has already been noted. The matter of bringing suit in the first place rests with the solicitor general and the Department of Justice. Whether a decision is appealed and ultimately reaches the Supreme Court depends, in part, on the Justice Department's decision. And enforcement of Court decisions depends on the executive branch. The president may press for enforcement vigorously or reluctantly, or not at all. When the Court rendered the *Brown* decision in 1954, it was President Eisenhower who sent in the federal marshals to desegregate the Little Rock, Arkansas high school.

Finally there is the limitation judges place upon themselves. Known as **judicial self-restraint,** this doctrine holds that judges should refrain from imposing their own values and policy preferences and decide a case on its merit and according to established legal precedent. For the most part, the justices exercise their authority with great caution and with careful attention to the weight of legal precedent. They understand that they cannot create solutions to the political controversies that divide a nation, no matter how actively they engage in policymaking.

Courts are limited institutions of power. They are part of the checks-and-balances process of our governmental scheme, and the constraints on them are severe. Ultimately, the judiciary needs the concurrence of Congress, the president, and the bureaucracy. The ultimate shaping of public policy cannot proceed in a vacuum. For better or worse, the continued existence and strength of democracy rest on our tripartite governmental system. Democracy and the values of freedom and equality are not the sole province of the courts, but are ultimately the responsibility of each and every citizen.

The ability of the courts to provide social policy guidance in a period of change is all the more critical when other institutions are groping for direction and purpose; and the Court has responded to this challenge. The danger comes when we expect too strong a response too quickly. What the Court has been doing is not likely to change drastically. We are likely to see further convergence among policymaking institutions, including the Court. Groups are likely to continue to appeal to the courts for social justice. And the courts will probably throw the questions back to the traditional policy institutions, Congress and the president, perhaps with recommendations for action.

Judicial Self-Restraint: *a judicial doctrine that holds that judges should restrain from imposing their own values and policy preferences and should decide a case on its merit according to established legal precedent.*

Summary

1. American democracy is premised on the notion of a government of law, not persons. To the courts fall the prime responsibility of maintaining the rule of law. Judges administer the law, both civil and criminal. They are also charged to interpret administrative rules and regulations as well as the Constitution itself.

2. Judicial power extends far beyond the neutral arena to resolve conflict; courts are actively involved in politics and create policy. There are, however, several legal-technical questions of jurisdiction that serve to restrict the consideration of cases. This allows the courts to avoid many cases and thereby preserve their reputation as neutral arbitrators.

3. The American court system is a dual-court system. National and state courts exist side by side but have separate jurisdictions. Federal courts include district courts, courts of appeals, and one Supreme Court. In addition there are several special courts.

4. All federal judges are appointed by the president of the United States. Political party and judicial philosophy are important criteria in the selection of federal judges.

5. The Supreme Court occupies a very special role in American politics. It derives its most important power from its political pronouncements and interpretations of the constitutional powers of other political institutions. The Supreme Court acts as the guardian of the Constitution.

6. Judicial activism has become a permanent feature of the Supreme Court, indeed of all courts. Able to control the cases it hears, the Supreme Court selects only the most important cases that affect American political and social life. The process of arriving at decisions by the Supreme Court is complex and intensely personal among the nine individual justices.

Research Projects

1. *Supreme Court justices*   Write a biography of a Supreme Court justice. Among other things you will want to note:

• Education and legal training
• Judicial experience
• Political reputation and activity
• Appointment to the Court
• Record while on the Court
• Judicial philosophy

Several good biographies exist on the more eminent justices who have served on the high court over the years. Also consult the major decisions the justice wrote while a member of the Court.

2. *Blocs on the Court*   The Court has been noted for its five to four decisions. Pick one or two years and look at the major decisions of the Court for that year. List the judges who were in the majority and those in the minority. Can you find any pattern of justices consistently voting together? Are there "swing" justices? "Swing" justices vote sometimes with more liberal judges and on other cases vote with conservative judges. The best resource for this project is the *United States Reports,* which reports all decisions of the Supreme Court and lists the cases and each justice's votes. Decisions are classified as to whether they were majority, concurring, or dissenting opinions.

3. *Judicial Procedures*   Go to a federal or local court in your area and observe the proceedings. Are these trials, arraignments, bail hearings? You may need a good law dictionary to understand what is going on. Make a list of the activities and the procedures employed, paying attention to two aspects: (1) the judicial activity taking place that is not trial proceedings; and (2) the many legal procedures involved in the law. When you are done, review the activities and procedures to see if you understand them and why they went together as they did.

Notes

1. This section borrows from Walter F. Murphy's discussion of the framework of judicial power, *Elements of Judicial Strategy* (Chicago: University of Chicago Press, 1964), pp. 12–18.
2. *Marbury* v. *Madison,* 1 Cranch 137 (1803).
3. *U.S.* v. *Nixon,* 418 U.S. 683 (1974).
4. Alexis de Tocqueville, Phillips Bradley, ed. *Democracy in America* (New York: Alfred A. Knopf, 1944), p. 280.
5. David W. Rhode and Harold J. Spaeth, *Supreme Court Decision Making* (San Francisco: W. H. Freeman, 1976), p. 2. This section relies heavily on the discussions in Rhode and Spaeth.
6. Lawrence Baum, *American Courts: Process and Policy* (Boston: Houghton Mifflin, 1986), p. 300.
7. Ibid., pp. 300–301.
8. Karen Orren, "Standing to Sue, Interest Group Conflict in the Federal Courts," *American Political Science Review* 70 (September 1976): 723–741.
9. *Dombrowski* v. *Pfister,* 380 U.S. 479 (1965).
10. *Luther* v. *Borden,* 7 Howard 1 (1849).
11. *Coleman* v. *Miller,* 307 U.S. 433 (1939).
12. U.S. Bureau of the Census, *Statistical Abstract,* 1981, pp. 186 and 539.
13. Henry J. Abraham, *The Judicial Process,* 5th ed. (New York: Oxford University Press, 1986), p. 159.
14. *Northern Pipeline Co.* v. *Marathon Pipeline,* 458 U.S. 50 (1982).
15. U.S. Bureau of the Census, *Statistical Abstract,* 1981, p. 185.
16. Abraham, *The Judicial Process,* p. 171.
17. *New York Times* (August 31, 1960), cited in Harold Chase, *Federal Judges: The Appointing Process* (Minneapolis, Minn.: University of Minnesota Press, 1972).
18. Robert Scigliano, *The Supreme Court and the Presidency* (New York: Free Press, 1971), p. 146.
19. Sheldon Goldman, "Reaganizing the Judiciary: The First-Term Appointments," *Judicature* 68 (April/May 1985): 327.
20. *Congressional Quarterly, Weekly Report* (October 27, 1979): 2419.
21. *Congressional Quarterly, Weekly Report* (December 8, 1984): 3075.
22. Baum, *American Courts,* p. 114.
23. Goldman, "Reaganizing the Judiciary," p. 315.
24. Ibid.
25. Robert A. Dahl, "Decision Making in a Democracy: The Role of the Supreme Court as an Internal Policy Maker," *Journal of Public Law* 6 (1958): 279.
26. See Donald L. Horowitz, *The Courts and Social Policy* (Washington, D.C.: The Brookings Institution, 1977), p. 4.
27. Nathan Glazer, "Toward an Imperial Judiciary," *Public Interest* 41 (Fall 1975): 110.
28. Horowitz, *The Courts and Social Policy,* pp. 4–5.
29. Rhode and Spaeth, *Supreme Court Decision Making,* p. 59.
30. Cited in Allan P. Sindler, *Bakke, De Funis, and Minority Admissions* (New York: Longmans, 1978), p. 257.
31. Cited in Rhode and Spaeth, *Supreme Court Decision Making,* p. 60.
32. "Plurality Decisions and Judicial Decisionmaking," *Harvard Law Review* 94 (March 1981): 1127.
33. Ibid., p. 1128.
34. For a behind-the-scenes glimpse at the personal nature of Supreme Court proceedings, see Bob Woodward and Scott Armstrong's *The Brethren* (New York: Simon and Schuster, 1979).
35. Murphy, *Elements of Judicial Strategy,* p. 43.
36. Ibid., Chapter 3.
37. Cited in Abraham, *The Judicial Process,* p. 224.

Bibliography

Abraham, Henry. *The Judicial Process,* 5th ed. New York: Oxford University Press, 1986.
An excellent book and the standard for examining the organization and function of the federal judiciary. The book contains considerable information and provides an overview of law and the courts.

Abraham, Henry. *Justices and Presidents: A Political History of Appointments to the Supreme Court.* New York: Oxford University Press, 1985.
A study of the selection, nomination, and appointment of each of the justices to the Supreme Court. The book also includes a good deal of useful information about the Court itself.

Baum, Lawrence. *American Courts: Process and Policy.* Boston: Houghton Mifflin, 1986.
A very good survey of American courts—national and states—that addresses a wide range of judicial activities. From court organization to judicial selection and court functioning, the book examines the operation of and problems within the American court system. A major concern of the book is the role of courts in making policy.

Baum, Lawrence. *The Supreme Court.* Washington, D.C.: Congressional Quarterly Press, 1985.
A book that focuses on the Supreme Court as a political institution. Baum examines the operation of the Court and how its behavior is affected by politics and political institutions. There is a good discussion of how cases reach the Supreme Court and how the justices reach a verdict.

Berger, Raoul. *Government by Judiciary: The Transformation of the Fourteenth Amendment.* Cambridge, Mass.: Harvard University Press, 1975.
An historical and scholarly analysis of the origin and transformation of the Fourteenth Amendment. It is Berger's contention that modern jurists have misinterpreted and misused the amendment.

Chase, Harold. *Federal Judges: The Appointing Process.* Minneapolis, Minn.: University of Minnesota Press, 1972.
The basic work on the process and politics of appointing federal judges. This examination of the prerogative of the president contains considerable historical information and much detail from the Kennedy administration.

Cox, Archibald. *The Role of the Supreme Court in American Government.* New York: Oxford University Press, 1976.
A very brief but insightful discussion of the role of the Supreme Court in modern political events. Cox reacts with some sympathy to the active role of the Court in deciding matters of social policy.

Horowitz, Donald L. *The Courts and Social Policy.* Washington, D.C.: The Brookings Institution, 1977.
A basic work illustrating the active role courts have come to play in determining matters of social welfare. Sometimes technical and often critical, Horowitz provides an essential understanding of what has happened with the courts and social policy.

Jacob, Herbert. *Justice in America.* Boston: Little, Brown, 1984.
A fairly brief but concise book that looks at the role of law and the courts in the political process. Gives a good overview of the functions, participants, and structure of American courts.

Krislov, Samuel. *The Supreme Court in the Political Process.* New York: Macmillan, 1965.
A fine overview of the Supreme Court as it has affected the political process. Krislov makes the case that the Court is enmeshed in politics, discussing judicial appointments, the Court's agenda, and decision making.

Murphy, Walter F. *Elements of Judicial Strategy.* Chicago: University of Chicago Press, 1964.
Probably the best and most comprehensive effort to examine how Supreme Court justices reach a verdict. Murphy examines the behavior of judges in seeking to influence one another.

Murphy, Walter, and Pritchett, Herman. *Courts, Judges, and Politics.* New York: Random House, 1986.
An extensive effort covering the full range of legal politics. The book is a collection of essays and court opinions covering the role of courts and judges in the American political process.

Rhode, David W., and Spaeth, Harold J. *Supreme Court Decision Making.* San Francisco: W. H. Freeman, 1976.
An empirical study of decision making in the Supreme Court. In a sometimes technical work, the authors seek to examine the variables of decision making—goals, rules, and situations. The book contains good discussions of judicial activity and the Supreme Court.

Scigliano, Robert. *The Supreme Court and the Presidency.* New York: Free Press, 1971.
Examines the historical relationships between the president and the Supreme Court. Gives a good account of how presidents have tried to influence the Court, including an extensive coverage of judicial appointments.

Woodward, Bob, and Armstrong, Scott. *The Brethren.* New York: Simon and Schuster, 1979.
A journalistic behind-the-scenes look at the operation of the Supreme Court. Gives an intimate and personal portrayal of the personalities and interactions between the several justices.

The Future of American Politics

America is rapidly leaving the twentieth century. In but a decade, a period encompassing one of the greatest social and political transformations of all time will have become history. The United States has changed from a somewhat isolated, sparsely populated and geographically concentrated, rural country into a mobile, urban nation leading the world in economic productivity and military power, the focus of world attention. More pragmatic than ideological, Americans have fashioned a political process admirably suited to accommodate the changes that have taken place; now they seem to be redirecting their future once again.

This change in public purpose may be as significant as that brought about by the New Deal of 1932. The election of Ronald Reagan in 1980 signaled a rejection of the liberal policies and steadily increasing role of government that had characterized the previous fifty years. Reagan's vision for the transformation of America includes less government and more private enterprise, and he seeks to lead America into the twenty-first century with that new agenda.

The Revolution of Changing Expectations

As the 1970s drew to a close, two-thirds of the American people felt that the United States was in deep trouble. Long lines at the gas pumps convinced Americans that the energy shortage was real. Inflation eroded earning power, and people complained that they could not keep ahead of it. Scandal and influence peddling had eroded the optimism and self-confidence of Americans and their trust in the political system, leaving a fearful mixture of gloom and personal protectionism. The taxpayer revolt emphasized government's inability to limit spending. Old solutions no longer seemed to work; the political system seemed to have failed.

Ronald Reagan came to the presidency with a clear vision of what had to change. He set for himself, and the American people, the objectives of reducing the size of the federal government, restoring economic prosperity, and increasing national security. It was a conservative philosophy that attracted new and different constituencies and repudiated much of the old liberal philosophy of the New Deal. Part of the vision included a rekindled dedication to traditional values of family and country. But in his first administration, Reagan concentrated on economic and budgetary objectives.

All presidents pledge support to God and country, but what is distinctive about the Reagan vision is his framework for this support. Reagan fundamentally believes in a more limited role for government, that economic and social prosperity emerge from personal liberty, not from government programs. Yet he also believes that national security and traditional family values require an alert government that actively promotes these values. The result of this requirement seems often to be expanded government activity. "It is a consistent philosophy, given its premises: that economic growth will flow from the inherent entrepreneurial spirit and enterprise of the American people; that social problems can be largely solved by church, family, and neighborhood; that freedom is our greatest national asset; and that its protection requires, above all, military strength."[1]

But the translation of this vision into effective governance has proved difficult and its successes have been less than clear-cut. Having given the American people a clear picture of changing expectations in the 1980s, Reagan needed a program to achieve those objectives. The early priorities were clear: tax cuts took precedence over balancing the budget, military buildup was more important than reducing federal spending, and slowing inflation was a higher priority than unemployment and the recession. But these priorities have become less urgent and their validity less clear in Reagan's second term.

To accomplish his objectives, Ronald Reagan had to compromise his vision, to sacrifice the singular clarity of his message for political results. Indeed, the focus on short-run political success has raised doubts about the seriousness of the government's efforts to balance the budget and

Practicing Politics: Working for the Environment

*M*any national groups now lobby in Washington and across the country for environmental causes. Here are some of the larger and more active ones; write or call for information about activities and membership.

- Environmental Action, 1346 Connecticut Avenue NW, Washington, D.C. 20036
- Environmental Defense Fund, 1040 Park Avenue, New York, NY 10016
- Friends of the Earth, 145 Sansome Street, San Francisco, CA 94111
- National Audubon Society, 950 Third Avenue, New York, NY 10022
- National Parks and Conservation Association, 1701 Eighteenth Street NW, Washington, D.C. 20009
- National Wildlife Federation, 1412 Sixteenth Street NW, Washington, D.C. 20036
- Natural Resources Defense Council, 22 East 42nd Street, New York, NY 10168
- Sierra Club, 530 Bush Street, San Francisco, CA 94108
- Wilderness Society, 1901 Pennsylvania Avenue NW, Washington, D.C. 20006

The issue of hazardous waste disposal raises difficult political questions, illustrating the conflict between economic and social values.

equitably raise revenues. No long-term, broad political coalitions have emerged to replace the shattered political alignments of the 1970s. The Reagan administration's success has been personal, achieved through heavy-handed concentration of power in the White House at the expense of traditional avenues of governance.

Indications are that expectations have changed in response to the Reagan vision. The Reagan administration has restored public confidence and trust in political institutions and public officials, and there has been a shift toward conservatism in social issues and political ideology, especially among college-age youth. Many Americans today feel that federal spending is still too high and that government deficits hurt the nation. Yet a deep faith in the welfare state remains. Americans find government a comfort and necessity in resolving virtually all their major problems.

If the welfare state promised more than it was able to deliver, it was not without some achievements. The twentieth-century transformation in social, economic, and political power was due in no small measure to welfare politics. A vast array of benefits has been delivered to wide assortments of constituencies, guided by a faith that Americans could improve their world, at home and abroad. The evidence may be that the welfare state has run its course or is flawed, but as Palmer and Sawhill conclude:

> Ronald Reagan's brand of conservativism has similar flaws. His faith, of course, is in unfettered private initiative. Government is the problem and not the solution. However, across-the-board reductions in taxes, domestic spending, and regulations also turn out to have rather anemic effects. If government is not always the solution, neither is it always the problem. Moreover, the process of shrinking government has simply substituted one set of beneficiaries for another. Indeed, changes in social priorities and in the distribution of well-being over the past few years have turned out to be precisely what a constituency-based theory of government would have predicted.[2]

Americans have traditionally held freedom and equality as operative ideals, and these expectations continue. The press for equality is legitimate, but what was once thought of in largely economic terms has broadened. We now speak of social and political equality, and we demand that government provide all these equalities for everyone. Here we face the ultimate problem as America enters its third century: Can the nation face and solve its problems, and solve them in terms of a democratic political process that many increasingly see as a luxury?

A Second Republic

Theodore Lowi has labeled modern America a Second Republic because of the changes produced by liberal democratic practices:

During the decade of the 1960's the United States had a crisis of public authority and died. A Second Republic was left standing in its place. We had held no constituent assembly and had written no second Constitution. Yet at some point, beginning in the 1930's and culminating in the 1960's, cumulative changes in national power, national institutions, and in ideology altered our relationship to the Constitution of 1787, making the Second Republic a reality, not a metaphor.[3]

This Second Republic began in earnest during the New Deal, which signaled the growth of government, in both size and function. But most noteworthy were the changed functions of the federal government. Subsidy policies continued, but increasingly the government was adopting entirely new functions, particularly those of regulation and redistribution, and these increasingly brought together the citizen and the coercive power of government. The institutionalization of the Second Republic occurred in the 1960s, when the national government first monopolized various areas of private activity. Major changes included economic stabilization and wage–price controls, housing and poverty programs, and many of the Great Society programs. Following monopolization, programs were authorized and administrative agencies organized, without legal guidelines, so that the broad areas monopolized by the government could be returned piece by piece as privileges to specific individuals or groups.[4] Or as Lowi puts it, "socialism for the organized, capitalism for the unorganized."

There were several ways in which the federal government carried out this monopolization. There was direct financial domination, as in outer space, highways, and hospitals, where private resources could not compete with the infusion of tax dollars. A second method was to preempt activity through licensing, as in communications, corporate mergers, or wage increases, where activity required permission by the federal government. Finally, the federal government monopolized activity by underwriting risk, thereby guaranteeing activity and established interests. This was the case with the loan to the Lockheed Corporation in 1971 and the bank bailout of Continental Illinois in 1984. All this was done, Lowi says, "in the name of maintaining public order and avoiding disequilibrium."[5] And so the state grew and the promise of liberal democracy was maintained. But the costs were great. The result of these policies has been, Lowi maintains, to place America in a state of "permanent receivership." Permanent receivership refers to the contemporary method of maintaining social order during a crisis involving the bankruptcy of an individual or enterprise by maintaining the assets in their prebankrupt form and never disposing of them at all, regardless of inequities, inefficiencies, or the cost of maintenance.[6] Permanent receivership assures stability, but only for established groups and organizations. Policies are discretionary, the work of bargaining for privilege between established

One of the most basic issues of public policy is who governs. Political scientists are very divided on who, in practice, exercises control over decisions of public policy. They have developed macropolitical approaches to explain political phenomena and control of the policy process: institutional democracy, elitism, interest-group pluralism, and systems analysis.

The *institutional democracy* explanation is the classical view of power in the policy process. Policy is formulated and adopted by governmental institutions—that is, by legislatures, executives, courts, and bureaucracies. These institutional policymakers represent the people either individually or collectively through the representative institutions of interest groups and political parties. Elections are the means of legitimating one set of policymakers over another. The people hold power and collectively exercise influence over the policymakers.

While institutional democracy is concerned with formal organizations, legal powers, and procedural process, it does not slight the political realities of power or the informal interaction of participants in the government. Rather, it insists that for policies to be binding, the formal, legal institutions must adopt them. Policies are legitimate because of the democratic context of policy formulation, both the open context for agenda setting and the control people exercise over official policymakers.

In the perspective of *elitism*, public policy is considered to reflect the values and choices of a governing elite that is likely neither to be composed of the officially elected representatives nor to reflect the values of the people at large. The core of elitism says that public policy is made by a very few people, who possess power because of their position and influence in society. Public officials and government agencies implement the policies established by the elite. The people have little influence and less control over the elite's formulation of policy.

Policy serves the needs of the elite, not necessarily that of the public welfare, although this cannot be capriciously ignored by the elite.

In *interest-group pluralism* public policy is seen as an equilibrium reached between elite dominance of policy formulation and democratic control of policymakers. From this perspective, policy is the result of interaction among politically active interest groups. Policy in any given instance is the result of the dominance of one group or a number of groups; as new groups enter the political arena or as the other groups gain or lose influence, policy shifts to reflect the changed pattern of influence. The same array of groups is not involved in all issues; hence group activity and influence vary with groups' interest and effort to influence policy in a given issue. Government strives to moderate the struggle and responds to the dominant pull of group interests.

The interest-group approach assumes that interest-group elites compete for policy influence. Individuals may influence policy to the extent that they participate in political group affairs, but the struggle for policy takes place between elite representatives of interest groups. At this level there is little individual activity or influence.

Systems analysis attempts to establish public policy as a political response resulting from demands made in the environment. The political system is made up of identifiable and interrelated institutions and activities that make authoritative decisions. The political system receives inputs from the environment, these being either demands on the system or supports for it. The resulting policies, or outputs, constitute the authoritative decisions. These resultant outputs then become the substance for new inputs.

The value of systems analysis is that it can relate a wide range of complex data to public policy. It is not limited to political, economic, or even cultural variables. It further illustrates the dynamic nature of the policy process as formulated policies become the agenda (inputs) for policy adopted in the future. Systems analysis, however, is limited by its very general and abstract nature. It specifies neither how policy is made nor who makes it. Rather, it provides a framework for the integration of divergent variables.

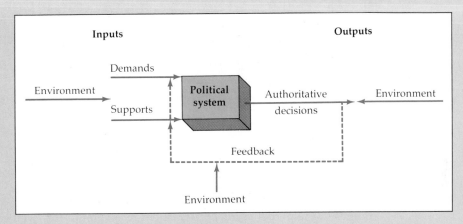

Lee Iacocca, chairman of Chrysler Corporation, repays a government loan seven years ahead of schedule.

interests. The perpetuation of permanent receivership may well mean the end of capitalism, because it uses economic resources to shore up political and social values; the goal is to maintain the process. There are no ends or direction; maintaining the process is the end.

The American citizen today stands directly before government, unbuffered by the insulation once afforded by political parties and traditional alliances. The instruments of political power have been exposed to the people. Our philosophy of democracy encourages citizens to use those instruments, and Americans are doing so in increasing numbers. The 1980s offered a new opportunity for exercising the historic and honored principles of liberal democracy. The question is whether such renewal will reestablish a national vitality and dedication providing national purpose and pride, or whether democracy will further fracture our political and social fabric by advancing self-interest. The future will prove either how great democracy is for inspiring dedicated self-government or how petty it can become.

Era of Reassessment

Americans came out of World War II attempting to reconstruct order and stability in their lives, both abroad and at home. It was a time to consolidate gains and to distribute the benefits of the most advanced, prosperous nation on earth. It was an era when presidential power expanded, Congress settled into routine, and distributive policymaking dominated.[7] But as we have discussed, events of the 1960s and 1970s fundamentally altered that political scene. Our economic base has shifted from industrial mass production to a postindustrial service economy. World affairs have moved us into a global community where international relations and domestic policies intersect. And we face a crisis in legitimacy, in which political institutions become intractable and consensus impossible because of the fracturing of interests within and without the institutions.

Postindustrial Society

The dominant political struggle of industrial America—the political and social class struggle over taxes or jobs—has given way to a situation in which a growing portion of society is concerned with interdependent, collective well-being. The economy based on mass production, capital, raw material, and raw labor has been displaced by technology and service delivery. Hence, industrial assembly-line jobs have become vulnerable to increased education and technology, relocation of work sites, more leisure-time pursuits, and government intervention.

The postindustrial, service economy is closely associated with government policy. First, there are millions of Americans directly dependent on the government for income maintenance. These are people who are beyond their working years (social security) or temporarily dislocated from the job market (unemployment compensation), or whose situation makes employment impossible (welfare). Second, the changed economy creates demands for guarantees—entitlements by government—that ensure people the right to qualify for the new jobs. This may be in the form of student loans to provide the education needed in high technology jobs or it may come in moving allowances on tax returns designed to assist persons who relocate for employment reasons.

The final consequence is more government regulation of public and private service delivery. It has become the responsibility of the government to maintain full employment and a healthy economy. For workers to be employed in a service economy, people must have jobs and income levels high enough to purchase the services. And as we reach this level of affluence, people demand protection—protection for their income but also for their life-style. There are increased demands to maintain the quality of life—clean air, safe streets, recreational opportunities, and the like. This quality-of-life issue is a growing concern. It presses government into service. People who have aspired for years to a better life are reluctant to abandon what they have acquired or to settle for inferior goods and services. They expect government to help protect that life-style through regulation and protection.

The demand for a quality of life imposes some economic costs. It can interfere with economic productivity and growth. Environmental opposition to offshore oil drilling and demands for wilderness protection do impact the production and cost of energy. Air pollution abatement devices and catalytic converters on cars add to the cost of products. These tangible economic costs must be weighed in light of the less tangible, but no less real, benefits from clean air and wilderness beauty.

Nowhere is this dilemma more evident than with hazardous waste and nuclear power. No one wants to live near a waste dump site or within range of nuclear fallout from a nuclear power reactor accident. Yet where is an energized, active nation of 235 million persons going to get the goods and services it needs to satisfy its voracious appetite? Without electricity there are no video games or home computers. Government policy will have to deal with hazardous waste and nuclear power as more and more citizens become concerned about these questions that threaten their quality of life.

Global Affairs

Americans live in a global community. Americans' expectations toward politics are shaped as much by world affairs as by domestic events. Any realistic assessment of the ability of the government of the United States to solve its problems must include foreign affairs and America's conduct in foreign policy. World affairs place many limitations upon American politics—some constitutional, some affecting the operation of the political process, some shaking the stability of the economy, some reflecting on Americans' self-image—all depending on circumstances over which we cannot exercise total control. The most recent example is international terrorism, as Americans have become the victims of random violence by an international community opposed to U.S. policies.

Despite many political differences, Americans believe the goals of U.S. foreign policy are honorable, that the country has formulated its policies

Terrorism challenges the basic assumptions and security of a free democratic people.

in the best interests of the free world. Yet the nation must contend with considerable foreign resistance to its foreign policy. The guarantee of national security is not an easy task. There are many complex contemporary problems that beset American foreign policy, the most important of which are the proliferation of nuclear weapons, undue dependence on foreign oil, and the military–industrial complex.

Issues once thought to be matters of international politics—outside the arena of domestic politics and largely bipartisan—generate political controversy and activate public opinion, interest groups, and other branches of government. Traditional foreign policy featured an aggressive, leading executive supported by Congress and a unified public, with interest groups and other concerned participants keeping a fair distance lest they be charged with harming the national interest. Recent events have made that approach unrealistic. Possibly as a consequence of the changing expectations of the Vietnam–Watergate era or simply because of the global press of mutual interdependence, we are experiencing what some observers have called **intermestic politics.** By telescoping the words *international* and *domestic* to create *intermestic*, we define the issues of the foreign policy process to be the same as those in the domestic arena.[8] Larger numbers of persons become involved in the process—congressional committees, courts, interest groups, protest movements, public opinion; issues cannot be neatly classified as foreign or domestic. As Haitian refugees landed on U.S. shores, they were detained at centers. Some took jobs, others went on welfare. Courts ordered that the children of illegal immigrants receive a free public education. Conversely, domestic policies on energy conservation, civil defense, and automobile loans affect our position in international relations. As a result of intermestic politics, John Spanier writes,

> The larger number of actors, the important stakes that key legislators and lobbyists will now perceive in foreign policy—ranging from billions of dollars in profit in resources and food to such noneconomic stakes as concern for the environment, human dignity and social justice—will make it far harder to arrive at policy decisions.[9]

The arms race and nuclear disarmament are the next great social issues facing the American people. Just as civil rights in the 1950s and the Vietnam War in the 1960s and early 1970s moved the conscience of the nation, so will nuclear disarmament in the 1980s.

Much of the debate focuses on the nuclear freeze movement, which originated in the House of Representatives in 1979. It was a nonbinding resolution calling on the president to seek a "mutual and verifiable freeze" on the testing, production, and deployment of additional nuclear weapons. In March 1982, Senators Kennedy and Hatfield introduced their freeze resolution, calling for a complete halt to the arms race and a "mutual and verifiable freeze on the testing, production, and future deployment of nuclear warheads, missiles, and other delivery systems."

Intermestic Politics: *a growing awareness of the interrelationship between international affairs and domestic politics. International events affect domestic priorities just as domestic affairs influence international relations. The two words are combined to suggest this close relationship.*

Both the United States and the Soviet Union sense the mood favoring arms reduction. In his 1985 summit with Mikhail Gorbachev, President Reagan called for early progress on arms reduction agreements; both sides pledged a 50 percent reduction in nuclear weapons, although the two countries were far apart in defining what kinds of weapons would be covered by such a cut. There is growing sentiment, in and out of government, that the arms race has gone too far. But the summit conference also illustrates how difficult it is for nations to agree to limit the arms race.

Crisis in Legitimacy[10]

The election of Ronald Reagan in 1980 suggested a crisis in legitimation for the policies that have been in place since the New Deal. Reagan does not believe in the welfare state. He has sought policies that reduce social welfare programs and has cut government spending in those areas. He has called for a new federal–state partnership, with states assuming much of the responsibility for social, educational, and welfare programs. Reagan places unwavering faith in capitalism, in the ability of private enterprise, freed from government regulation and interference, to create jobs and maintain a healthy, prosperous economy. His philosophy of economics and government is contrary to the weight of public policy in this country for the past half-century.

The policies of the previous era did not bring us solutions. The realization of the postindustrial society brought us instead scarce resources, dependence on foreign nations for our own well-being, and a further separation of Americans into interest groups bent on their own self-protection. These events have challenged our faith in representative government and weakened popular support for government. They have made it harder for coalitions and consensus to emerge from our separated political institutions. They have even weakened support for the constitutional fabric that holds our society together. Reagan touched a sympathetic chord when he said, "Government is not the solution, it is the problem."

When there is a reduced capacity to govern, individuals and groups rush forward to protect their status. A new environment for public policy is created. The nation faces a series of complex and seemingly insoluble problems—redistribution of economic resources with a stable, non-growth economy; substantive justice for those persons, often of minority status, for whom the American dream has not materialized; economic and national security in a world of expanding foreign resources and foreign goods; modernization of our military defense capacity at a time when domestic social programs require substantial financial outlays.[11] But solutions are not in sight. Government is organized to respond to demands for distributive choices that require only incremental changes in public policy. Today the changes require "comprehensive, innovative, and re-distributive policy actions."[12] This incapacity to govern—both in its policies and in the organization of government—points to a crisis in legitimacy in national government.

What we may be witnessing, according to Lawrence Dodd, is the self-destruction of the Madisonian system of government. Madison had held that the preservation of a republic, and hence liberty, depended on the ability of a nation's representative institutions to accommodate several interests. The more interests that were represented, the less likely it would be that any one interest could impose its view on a majority. Said Madison, "Extend the sphere and you take in a greater variety of parties and interests; you make it less probable that a majority of the whole will have a common motive to invade the rights of other citizens." Yet this seems not to be the case. Members of society have come to seek representation of their concerns and redress of their grievances. There is nothing evil or sinister in this; it is their constitutional right. But Congress has found it convenient and rewarding to facilitate the representation of special interests. Its organization is particularly conducive to this approach. In this way interests have become entrenched and seemingly immovable. Presidential power, too, has expanded greatly in providing economic stability and international security. Yet the growth of power has often been personalized, based on a particular coalition. Presidents have made precious little effort to form a national consensus, or even a presidency coordinated within its own administration or with Congress.

With these changes of the past few decades, and with the presidency of Ronald Reagan, we experienced an era of reassessment. There are a host of questions that confront our government—economic and social policies, federal–state relations, social justice, presidential–legislative cooperation, bureaucratic intervention, and military power in a free society. How do we face these issues in a postindustrial society and yet maintain representative institutions? This is the question that confronts us now and that could lead to the end of representative government.

The Future

There have never been any easy answers or simple solutions for America's problems. Decision making is necessarily confounded by our historic commitment to the values of liberal democracy. Yet the politics of that order is being attacked. Emerging conservative values and different political interests once again change expectations. Our political institutions struggle to maintain their representative character.

The basic values of democracy—equality, freedom, and individualism—seem more remote today than at any time in our history. The expanded role of government has made the individual into a dependent. With its budget of almost one trillion dollars and increased activity in myriad areas, the government has left little opportunity for individual

self-reliance. Individual freedom and equality depend, in greater and greater degree, upon what government does and does not do.

With the press of issues over which individuals exercise little control—inflation, oil prices, and terrorism, for example—citizens turn to government for help. They seek personal security and protection, asking government to protect that which individuals and families have achieved. Issues have therefore become more important, resulting in single-issue politics. This development has placed increased demands upon government, demands that conflict and increasingly strain the social fabric. As a consequence, traditional loyalties and patterns of behavior have begun to disappear, yet no new coalitions or political alignments have emerged to replace them.

In this climate of changing expectations, the institutions of government—president, Congress, and courts—seek to renew and redefine their representational role in a democracy. Higher levels of trust and confidence have infused these institutions with renewed hope after a lengthy period of decline. Congress struggles to redress the balance of power by both managing the massive federal deficit and dealing with the altered agenda of President Reagan. Presidential power has continued to expand and now must be limited without losing its vitality. Courts find the law called upon to settle increasing numbers of political disputes. With expectations changing, constituencies also change. As government attempts to respond, greater contests than ever will occur among governmental institutions over policies and legitimacy in representing the new priorities of the people.

In the coming decade the greatest test for democracy will come from the institutions that now shroud themselves in abstractions without any serious commitment to or conformity with the operative ideals of democratic government. It falls to the citizens to decide whether the principles of democracy are worth preserving. Much of what government does will be justified as compatible with democracy, if only to preserve the present. But only if the citizens decide that national purpose is worth the struggle can democracy remain a viable form of social organization capable of transcending individual differences.

Notes

1. John L. Palmer and Isabel V. Sawhill, *The Reagan Record* (Cambridge, Mass.: Ballinger, 1984), p. 2.
2. Ibid., p. 32.
3. Theodore J. Lowi, *The End of Liberalism*, 2nd ed. (New York: W. W. Norton, 1979), p. 271.
4. Ibid., p. 278.
5. Ibid.
6. Ibid., p. 279.
7. Lawrence C. Dodd, "Congress, the Constitution, and the Crisis of Legitimacy," in Lawrence Dodd and Bruce Oppenheimer, eds., *Congress Reconsidered*, 2nd ed. (Washington, D.C.: Congressional Quarterly Press, 1981), p. 400.
8. John Spanier, *Games Nations Play*, 3rd ed. (New York: Holt, Rinehart & Winston/Praeger, 1978), p. 495.
9. Ibid.
10. In this section I have relied extensively on Lawrence Dodd. See his *Congress Reconsidered*, especially pp. 414–418.
11. Ibid., p. 414.
12. Ibid.

Appendix A
Annotated Declaration of Independence

(as it reads in the parchment copy)

The Unanimous Declaration of the Thirteen United States of America

Purpose

When in the Course of human events, it becomes necessary for one people to dissolve the political bands, which have connected them with another, and to assume among the powers of the earth, the separate and equal station to which the Laws of Nature and of Nature's God entitle them, a decent respect to the opinions of mankind requires that they should declare the causes which impel *Philosophy of government* them to the separation.—We hold these truths to be self-evident, that all men are created equal, that they are endowed by their Creator with certain unalienable *natural rights* Rights, that among these are Life, Liberty and the pursuit of Happiness.—That to *contract* secure these rights, Governments are instituted among Men, deriving their just powers from the consent of the governed,—That whenever any Form of Government *rebellion* ment becomes destructive of these ends, it is the Right of the People to alter or to abolish it, and to institute new Government, laying its foundation on such principles and organizing its powers in such form, as to them shall seem most likely to effect their Safety and Happiness. Prudence, indeed, will dictate that Govern-*Cause not entered into lightly* ments long established should not be changed for light and transient causes; and accordingly all experience hath shewn, that mankind are more disposed to suffer, while evils are sufferable, than to right themselves by abolishing the forms to *rules of contract broken* which they are accustomed. But when a long train of abuses and usurpations, pursuing invariably the same Object evinces a design to reduce them under absolute Despotism, it is their right, it is their duty, to throw off such Government, and to provide new Guards for their future security.—Such has been the patient *patient suffering* sufferance of these Colonies; and such is now the necessity which constrains them to alter their former Systems of Government. The history of the present King of Great Britain is a history of repeated injuries and usurpations, all having in direct object the establishment of an absolute Tyranny over these States. To prove this, *The Bill of Particulars* let Facts be submitted to a candid world.—He has refused his Assent to Laws, the *violated self-government* most wholesome and necessary for the public good.—He has forbidden his Gov-*through legislative* ernors to pass Laws of immediate and pressing importance, unless suspended in *assemblies* their operation till his Assent should be obtained; and when so suspended, he has

587

utterly neglected to attend to them.—He has refused to pass other Laws for the accommodation of large districts of people, unless those people would relinquish the right of Representation in the Legislature, a right inestimable to them and formidable to tyrants only.—He has called together legislative bodies at places unusual, uncomfortable, and distant from the depository of their public Records, for the sole purpose of fatiguing them into compliance with his measures.—He has dissolved Representative Houses repeatedly, for opposing with manly firmness his invasions on the rights of the people.—He has refused for a long time, after such dissolutions, to cause others to be elected; whereby the Legislative powers, incapable of Annihilation, have returned to the People at large for their exercise; the State remaining in the meantime exposed to all the dangers of invasion from without, and convulsions within.—He has endeavoured to prevent the population of these States; for that purpose obstructing the Laws for Naturalization of Foreigners; refusing to pass others to encourage their migrations hither, *destroyed separation of* and raising the conditions of new Appropriations of Lands.—He has obstructed *powers* the Administration of Justice, by refusing his Assent to Laws for establishing Judiciary powers.—He has made Judges dependent on his Will alone, for the tenure of their offices, and the amount and payment of their salaries.—He has erected a multitude of New Offices, and sent hither swarms of Officers to harass our people, and eat out their substance.—He has kept among us, in times of peace, Standing Armies without the Consent of our legislatures.—He has affected to render the Military independent of and superior to the Civil Power.—He has combined with others to subject us to jurisdiction foreign to our constitution, and unacknowledged by our laws; giving his Assent to their Acts of pretended Legislation.—For quartering large bodies of armed troops among us:—For protecting them, by a mock Trial, from punishment for any Murders which they should commit on the Inhabitants of these States:—For cutting off our Trade with all parts of the world:—For imposing Taxes on us without our Consent:—For depriving us in many cases, of the benefits of Trial by Jury:—For transporting us beyond Seas to be tried for pretended offenses:—For abolishing the free System of English Laws in a neighboring Province, establishing therein an Arbitrary government, and enlarging its Boundaries so as to render it at once an example and fit instrument for introducing the same absolute rule into these Colonies:—For taking away our Charters, abolishing our most valuable Laws, and altering fundamentally the Forms of our Governments:—For suspending our own Legislatures, and declaring themselves invested with power to legislate for us in all cases *tyranny* whatsoever.—He has abdicated Government here, by declaring us out of his Protection and waging War against us.—He has plundered our seas, ravaged our Coasts, burnt our towns, and destroyed the lives of our people.—He is at this time transporting large Armies of foreign Mercenaries to compleat the works of death, desolation and tyranny, already begun with circumstances of Cruelty & perfidy scarcely parralleled in the most barbarous ages, and totally unworthy the Head of a civilized nation.—He has constrained our fellow Citizens taken Captive on the high Seas to bear Arms against their Country, to become the executioners of their *British lawlessness* friends and Brethren, or to fall themselves by their Hands.—He has excited domestic insurrections amongst us, and has endeavoured to bring on the inhabitants of our frontiers, the merciless Indian Savages, whose known rule of warfare, is an undistinguished destruction of all ages, sexes and conditions. In every stage of these Oppressions We have Petitioned for Redress in the most humble terms: Our repeated Petitions have been answered only by repeated injury. A Prince whose character is thus marked by every act which may define a Tyrant, is unfit to be the ruler of a free people. Nor have We been wanting in attentions to our British brethren. We have warned them from time to time of attempts by their legislature to extend an unwarrantable jurisdiction over us. We have reminded them of the circumstances of our emigration and settlement here. We have appealed to their native justice and magnanimity, and we have conjured them by the ties of our common kindred to disavow these usurpations, which would inevitably interrupt our connections and correspondence. They too have been deaf to the voice of justice and of consanguinity. We must, therefore, acquiesce in the necessity, which denounces our Separation, and hold them, as we hold the rest of mankind, Enemies in War, in Peace Friends.—

Declaration of separation   We, therefore, the Representatives of the United States of America, in General Congress, Assembled, appealing to the Supreme Judge of the world for the rectitude of our intentions do, in the Name, and by Authority of the good People of these Colonies, solemnly publish and declare, That these United Colonies are, and of Right ought to be Free and Independent States; that they are Absolved from all Allegiance to the British Crown, and that all political connection between them and the State of Great Britain, is and ought to be totally dissolved: and that as Free and Independent States, they have full Power to levy War, conclude Peace, contract Alliances, establish Commerce, and to do all other Acts and Things which Independent States may of right do.—And for the support of this Declaration, with a firm reliance on the protection of divine Providence, we mutually pledge to each other our Lives, our Fortunes and our sacred Honor.

Signatures

John Hancock.	Fran^s Lewis.
Samuel Chase.	Lewis Morris.
Wm Paca.	Richd Stockton.
Tho. Stone.	Jno Witherspoon.
Charles Carroll of Carrollton.	Fra. Hopkinson.
George Wythe.	John Hart.
Richard Henry Lee.	Abra Clark.
Th Jefferson.	Josiah Bartlett.
Benj^a Harrison.	Wm Whipple.
Tho. Nelson jr.	Saml Adams.
Francis Lightfoot Lee.	John Adams.
Carter Braxton.	Robt Treat Paine.
Robt Morris.	Elbridge Gerry.
Benjamin Rush.	Step Hopkins.
Benj^a Franklin.	William Ellery.
John Morton.	Roger Sherman.
Geo Clymer.	Saml Huntington.
Ja Smith.	Wm Williams.
Geo. Taylor.	Oliver Wolcott.
James Wilson.	Matthew Thornton.
Geo. Ross.	Wm Hooper.
Caesar Rodney.	Joseph Hewes.
Geo Read.	John Penn.
Tho M: Kean.	Edward Rutledge.
Wm Floyd.	Tho Heyward Junr
Phil. Livingston.	Thomas Lynch Junr
Arthur Middleton.	Lyman Hall.
Button Gwinnett.	Geo Walton.

Appendix B
Annotated Constitution of the U.S.

Preamble

WE THE PEOPLE of the United States, in Order to form a more perfect Union, establish Justice, insure domestic Tranquility, provide for the common defence, promote the general Welfare, and secure the Blessings of Liberty to ourselves and our Posterity, do ordain and establish this Constitution for the United States of America.

Article. I.

Bicameral congress

Section. 1. All legislative Powers herein granted shall be vested in a Congress of the United States, which shall consist of a Senate and House of Representatives.

Election to House of Representatives

Section. 2. [1]The House of Representatives shall be composed of Members chosen every second Year by the People of the several States and the Electors in each State shall have the Qualifications requisite for Electors of the most numerous Branch of the State Legislature.

qualifications

[2]No person shall be a Representative who shall not have attained to the Age of twenty five Years, and been seven Years a Citizen of the United States, and who shall not, when elected, be an Inhabitant of that State in which he shall be chosen.

apportionment of seats

[3][Representatives and direct Taxes shall be apportioned among the several States which may be included within this Union, according to their respective Numbers, which shall be determined by adding to the whole Number of free Persons, including those bound to Service for a Term of Years, and excluding Indians not taxed, three fifths of all other Persons.]* The actual Enumeration shall be made within three Years after the first Meeting of the Congress of the United States, and within every subsequent Term of ten Years, in such Manner as they shall by Law direct. The Number of Representatives shall not exceed one for every thirty Thousand, but each State shall have at Least one Representative; and

NOTE. This text of the Constitution follows the engrossed copy signed by Washington and the deputies from twelve states. The superior number preceding each paragraph designates the number of the clause; it was not in the original.

*The words within brackets were changed by Section 2 of the Fourteenth Amendment.

until such enumeration shall be made, the State of New Hampshire shall be entitled to chuse three, Massachusetts eight, Rhode-Island and Providence Plantations one, Connecticut five, New-York six, New Jersey four, Pennsylvania eight, Delaware one, Maryland six, Virginia ten, North Carolina five, South Carolina five, and Georgia three.

⁴When vacancies happen in the Representation from any State, the Executive Authority thereof shall issue Writs of Election to fill such Vacancies.

power of impeachment ⁵The House of Representatives shall chuse their Speaker and other Officers; and shall have the sole Power of Impeachment.

Election to the Senate **Section. 3.**   ¹The Senate of the United States shall be composed of two Senators from each State, [chosen by the Legislature thereof,]* for six Years; and each Senator shall have one Vote.

apportionment of seats ²Immediately after they shall be assembled in Consequence of the first Election, they shall be divided as equally as may be into three Classes. The Seats of the Senators of the first Class shall be vacated at the Expiration of the second Year, of the second Class at the Expiration of the fourth Year, and of the third Class at the Expiration of the sixth Year, so that one third may be chosen every second Year; [and if Vacancies happen by Resignation, or otherwise, during the Recess of the Legislature of any State, the Executive thereof may make temporary Appointments until the next Meeting of the Legislature, which shall then fill such Vacancies].**

qualifications ³No Person shall be a Senator who shall not have attained to the Age of thirty Years, and been nine Years a Citizen of the United States, and who shall not, when elected, be an Inhabitant of that State for which he shall be chosen.

⁴The Vice President of the United States shall be President of the Senate, but shall have no Vote, unless they be equally divided.

⁵The Senate shall chuse their other Officers, and also a President pro tempore, in the Absence of the Vice President, or when he shall exercise the Office of President of the United States.

power to try impeachments ⁶The Senate shall have the sole Power to try all Impeachments. When sitting for the Purpose, they shall be on Oath or Affirmation. When the President of the United States is tried, the Chief Justice shall preside: And no Person shall be convicted without the Concurrence of two thirds of the Members present.

⁷Judgment in Cases of Impeachment shall not extend further than to removal from Office, and disqualification to hold and enjoy any Office of honor, Trust or Profit under the United States: but the Party convicted shall nevertheless be liable and subject to Indictment, Trial, Judgment and Punishment, according to Law.

States prescribe elections **Section. 4.**   ¹The Times, Places and Manner of holding Elections for Senators and Representatives, shall be prescribed in each State by the Legislature thereof; but the Congress may at any time by Law make or alter such Regulations, except as to the Places of chusing Senators.

²The Congress shall assemble at least once in every Year, and such Meeting shall [be on the first Monday in December,]*** unless they shall by Law appoint a different day.

---

*The words within brackets were changed by Section 1 of the Seventeenth Amendment.
**The words within brackets were changed by Section 2 of the Seventeenth Amendment.
***The words within brackets were changed by Section 2 of the Twentieth Amendment.

Rules of organization

Section. 5. ¹Each House shall be the Judge of the Elections, Returns and Qualifications of its own Members, and a Majority of each shall constitute a Quorum to do Business; but a smaller Number may adjourn from day to day, and may be authorized to compel the Attendance of absent Members, in such Manner, and under such Penalties as each House may provide.

²Each House may determine the Rules of its Proceedings, punish its Members for disorderly Behaviour, and, with the Concurrence of two thirds, expel a Member.

³Each House shall keep a Journal of its Proceedings, and from time to time publish the same, excepting such Parts as may in their Judgment require Secrecy; and the Yeas and Nays of the Members of either House on any question shall, at the Desire of one fifth of those Present, be entered on the Journal.

⁴Neither House, during the Session of Congress, shall, without the Consent of the other, adjourn for more than three days, nor to any other Place than that in which the two Houses shall be sitting.

Compensation, privileges, and immunities for members of Congress

Section. 6. ¹The Senators and Representatives shall receive a Compensation for their Services, to be ascertained by Law, and paid out of the Treasury of the United States. They shall in all Cases, except Treason, Felony and Breach of Peace, be privileged from Arrest during their Attendance at the Session of their respective Houses, and in going to and returning from the same; and for any Speech or Debate in either House, they shall not be questioned in any other Place.

no appointive office while serving in Congress

²No Senator or Representative shall, during the Time for which he was elected, be appointed to any civil Office under the Authority of the United States, which shall have been created, or the Emoluments whereof shall have been encreased during such time; and no Person holding any Office under the United States, shall be a Member of either House during his Continuance in Office.

Revenue bills originate in House of Representatives

Section. 7. ¹All Bills for raising Revenue shall originate in the House of Representatives; but the Senate may propose or concur with Amendments as on other Bills.

Veto and procedure for veto override

²Every Bill which shall have passed the House of Representatives and the Senate, shall, before it become a Law, be presented to the President of the United States; If he approve he shall sign it, but if not he shall return it, with his Objections to that House in which it shall have originated, who shall enter the Objections at large on their Journal, and proceed to reconsider it. If after such Reconsideration two thirds of that House shall agree to pass the Bill, it shall be sent, together with the Objections, to the other House, by which it shall likewise be reconsidered, and if approved by two thirds of that House, it shall become a Law. But in all such Cases the Votes of both Houses shall be determined by Yeas and Nays, and the Names of the Persons voting for and against the Bill shall be entered on the Journal of each House respectively. If any Bill shall not be returned by the President within ten Days (Sundays excepted) after it shall have been presented to him, the Same shall be a Law, in like Manner as if he had

pocket veto

signed it, unless the Congress by their Adjournment prevent its Return, in which Case it shall not be a Law.

Presidential approval

³Every Order, Resolution, or Vote to which the Concurrence of the Senate and House of Representatives may be necessary (except on a question of Adjournment) shall be presented to the President of the United States; and before the Same shall take Effect, shall be approved by him, or being disapproved by him, shall be repassed by two thirds of the Senate and House of Representatives, according to the Rules and Limitations prescribed in the Case of a Bill.

Powers of Congress

Section. 8. [1]The Congress shall have Power To lay and collect Taxes, Duties, Imposts and Excises, to pay the Debts and provide for the common Defence and general Welfare of the United States; but all Duties, Imposts and Excises shall be uniform throughout the United States;

taxes

borrow money

[2]To borrow Money on the credit of the United States;

regulate commerce

[3]To regulate Commerce with foreign Nations, and among the several States, and with the Indian Tribes;

naturalization and bankruptcies

[4]To establish an uniform Rule of Naturalization, and uniform Laws on the subject of Bankruptcies throughout the United States;

coin money

[5]To coin Money, regulate the Value thereof, and of foreign Coin, and fix the Standard of Weights and Measures;

punish counterfeiting

[6]To provide for the Punishment of counterfeiting the Securities and current Coin of the United States;

establish post offices

[7]To establish Post Offices and post Roads;

secure patents

[8]To promote the Progress of Science and useful Arts, by securing for limited Times to Authors and Inventors the exclusive Right to their respective Writings and Discoveries;

create inferior courts

[9]To constitute Tribunals inferior to the supreme Court;

define piracy

[10]To define and punish Piracies and Felonies committed on the high Seas, and Offences against the Law of Nations;

declare war

[11]To declare War, grant Letters of Marque and Reprisal, and make Rules concerning Captures on Land and Water;

raise an army and navy

[12]To raise and support Armies, but no Appropriation of Money to that Use shall be for a longer Term than two Years;

[13]To provide and maintain a Navy;

[14]To make Rules for the Government and Regulation of the land and naval Forces;

nationalize the militia

[15]To provide for calling forth the Militia to execute the Laws of the Union, suppress Insurrections and repel Invasions;

[16]To provide for organizing, arming, and disciplining, the Militia, and for governing such Part of them as may be employed in the Service of the United States, reserving to the States respectively, the Appointment of the Officers, and the Authority of training the Militia according to the discipline prescribed by Congress;

exercise authority for District of Columbia

[17]To exercise exclusive Legislation in all Cases whatsoever, over such District (not exceeding ten Miles square) as may, by Cession of particular States, and the Acceptance of Congress, become the Seat of the Government of the United States, and to exercise like Authority over all Places purchased by the Consent of the Legislature of the State in which the Same shall be, for the Erection of Forts, Magazines, Arsenals, dock-Yards, and other needful Buildings;—And

the necessary and proper clause

[18]To make all Laws which shall be necessary and proper for carrying into Execution the foregoing Powers, and all other Powers vested by this Constitution in the Government of the United States, or in any Department or Officer thereof.

Prohibition of powers to Congress

Section. 9. [1]The Migration or Importation of such Persons as any of the States now existing shall think proper to admit, shall not be prohibited by the Congress prior to the Year one thousand eight hundred and eight, but a Tax or duty may be imposed on such Importation, not exceeding ten dollars for each Person.

no slave trade

no suspension of writ of habeas corpus

[2]The Privilege of the Writ of Habeas Corpus shall not be suspended, unless when in Cases of Rebellion or Invasion the public Safety may require it.

no bill of attainder or
ex post facto

no direct tax

no state tariff

no state preference

no unauthorized
expenditure of money

no titles of nobility

³No Bill of Attainder or ex post facto Law shall be passed.

⁴No Capitation, or other direct, Tax shall be laid, unless in Proportion to the Census or Enumeration herein before directed to be taken.*

⁵No Tax or Duty shall be laid on Articles exported from any State.

⁶No Preference shall be given by any Regulation of Commerce or Revenue to the Ports of one State over those of another: nor shall Vessels bound to, or from, one State, be obliged to enter, clear, or pay Duties in another.

⁷No Money shall be drawn from the Treasury, but in Consequence of Appropriations made by Law; and a regular Statement and Account of the Receipts and Expenditures of all public Money shall be published from time to time.

⁸No Title of Nobility shall be granted by the United States: And no Person holding any Office of Profit or Trust under them, shall, without the Consent of the Congress, accept any present, Emolument, of Office, or Title, of any kind whatever, from any King, Prince, or foreign State.

Prohibition of powers to
the states

no treaties, coin money,
bill of attainder,
title of nobility

no duties on imports
or exports

no foreign or interstate
compacts, no declaration
of war

Section. 10. ¹No State shall enter into any Treaty, Alliance, or Confederation; grant Letters of Marque and Reprisal; coin Money; emit Bills of Credit; make any Thing but gold and silver Coin a Tender in Payment of Debts; pass any Bill of Attainder, ex post facto Law, or Law impairing the Obligation of Contracts, or grant any Title of Nobility.

²No State shall, without the Consent of the Congress, lay any Imposts or Duties on Imports or Exports, except what may be absolutely necessary for executing its inspection Laws: and the net Produce of all Duties and Imposts, laid by any State on Imports or Exports, shall be for the Use of the Treasury of the United States; and all such Laws shall be subject to the Revision and Controul of the Congress.

³No State shall, without the Consent of Congress, lay any Duty of Tonnage, keep Troops, or Ships of War in time of Peace, enter into any Agreement or Compact with another State, or with a foreign Power, or engage in War, unless actually invaded, or in such imminent Danger as will not admit of delay.

Article. II.

Executive power in single
president

term
electoral college

Section. 1. ¹The executive Power shall be vested in a President of the United States of America. He shall hold his Office during the Term of four Years, and, together with the Vice President, chosen for the same Term, be elected, as follows

²Each State shall appoint, in such Manner as the Legislature thereof may direct, a Number of Electors, equal to the whole Number of Senators and Representatives to which the State may be entitled in the Congress: but no Senator or Representative, or Person holding an Office of Trust or Profit under the United States, shall be appointed an Elector.

[The Electors shall meet in their respective States, and vote by Ballot for two Persons, of whom one at least shall not be an Inhabitant of the same State with themselves. And they shall make a List of all the Persons voted for, and of the Number of Votes for each; which List they shall sign and certify, and transmit sealed to the Seat of the Government of the United States, directed to the President of the Senate. The President of the Senate shall, in the Presence of the Senate

*See also the Sixteenth Amendment.

and House of Representatives, open all the Certificates, and the Votes shall then be counted. The Person having the greatest Number of Votes shall be the President, if such Number be a Majority of the whole Number of Electors appointed; and if there be more than one who have such Majority, and have an equal Number of Votes, then the House of Representatives shall immediately chuse by Ballot one of them for President; and if no Person have a Majority, then from the five highest on the List the said House shall in like Manner chuse the President. But in chusing the President, the Votes shall be taken by States, the Representation from each State having one Vote; A quorum for this Purpose shall consist of a Member or Members from two thirds of the States, and a Majority of all the States shall be necessary to a Choice. In every Case, after the Choice of the President, the Person having the greatest Number of Votes of the Electors shall be the Vice President. But if there should remain two or more who have equal Votes, the Senate shall chuse from them by Ballot the Vice President.]*

³The Congress may determine the Time of chusing the Electors, and the Day on which they shall give their Votes; which Day shall be the same throughout the United States.

qualifications

⁴No Person except a natural born Citizen, or a Citizen of the United States, at the time of the Adoption of this Constitution, shall be eligible to the Office of President; neither shall any Person be eligible to that Office who shall not have attained to the Age of thirty five Years, and been fourteen Years a Resident within the United States.

succession

⁵In Case of the Removal of the President from Office, or of his Death, Resignation, or Inability to discharge the Powers and Duties of the said Office,** the Same shall devolve on the Vice President, and the Congress may by Law provide for the Case of Removal, Death, Resignation or Inability, both of the President and Vice President, declaring what Officer shall then act as President, and such Officer shall act accordingly, until the Disability be removed, or a President shall be elected.

⁶The President shall, at stated Times, receive for his Services, a Compensation, which shall neither be encreased nor diminished during the Period for which he shall have been elected, and he shall not receive within that Period any other Emolument from the United States, or any of them.

oath

⁷Before he enter on the Execution of his Office, he shall take the following Oath or Affirmation:—"I do solemnly swear (or affirm) that I will faithfully execute the Office of the President of the United States, and will to the best of my Ability, preserve, protect and defend the Constitution of the United States."

*Power of the president
as commander in chief*

Section. 2. ¹The President shall be Commander in Chief of the Army and Navy of the United States, and of the Militia of the several States, when called into the actual Service of the United States; he may require the Opinion, in writing, of the principal Officer in each of the executive Departments, upon any Subject relating to the Duties of their respective Offices, and he shall have Power to grant Reprieves and Pardons for Offences against the United States, except in Cases of Impeachment.

pardons and reprieves

treaties and appointments

²He shall have Power, by and with the Advice and Consent of the Senate, to make Treaties, provided two thirds of the Senators present concur; and he shall nominate, and by and with the Advice and Consent of the Senate, shall appoint

*This paragraph has been superseded by the Twelfth Amendment.
**This provision has been affected by the Twenty-fifth Amendment.

Ambassadors, other public Ministers and Consuls, Judges of the supreme Court, and all other Officers of the United States, whose Appointments are not herein otherwise provided for, and which shall be established by Law: but the Congress may by Law vest the Appointment of such inferior Officers, as they think proper, in the President alone, in the Courts of Law, or in the Heads of Departments.

³The President shall have Power to fill up all Vacancies that may happen during the Recess of the Senate, by granting Commissions which shall expire at the End of their next Session.

Legislative responsibilities

Section. 3.   He shall from time to time give to the Congress Information of the State of the Union, and recommend to their Consideration such Measures as he shall judge necessary and expedient; he may, on extraordinary Occasions, convene both Houses, or either of them, and in Case of Disagreement between them, with Respect to the Time of Adjournment, he may adjourn them to such Time as he shall think proper; he shall receive Ambassadors and other public Ministers; he shall take Care that the Laws be faithfully executed, and shall Commission all the Officers of the United States.

Impeachable offenses

Section. 4.   The President, Vice President and all civil Officers of the United States, shall be removed from Office on Impeachment for, and Conviction of, Treason, Bribery, or other high Crimes and Misdemeanors.

Article. III.

Federal courts

Section. 1.   The judicial Power of the United States, shall be vested in one supreme Court, and in such inferior Courts as the Congress may from time to time ordain and establish. The Judges, both of the supreme and inferior Courts, shall hold their Offices during good Behaviour, and shall, at stated Times, receive for their Services, a Compensation, which shall not be diminished during their Continuance in Office.

Jurisdiction of courts

Section. 2.   ¹The judicial Power shall extend to all Cases, in Law and Equity, arising under this Constitution, the Laws of the United States, and Treaties made, or which shall be made, under their Authority;—to all Cases affecting Ambassadors, other public Ministers and Consuls;—to all Cases of admiralty and maritime Jurisdiction;—to Controversies to which the United States shall be a Party;—to Controversies between two or more States;—between a State and Citizens of another State;*—between Citizens of different States,—between Citizens of the same State claiming Lands under Grants of different States, and between a State, or the Citizens thereof, and foreign States, Citizens or Subjects.

original and appellate jurisdiction of Supreme Court

²In all Cases affecting Ambassadors, other public Ministers and Consuls, and those in which a State shall be Party, the supreme Court shall have original Jurisdiction. In all the other Cases before mentioned, the supreme Court shall have appellate Jurisdiction, both as to Law and Fact, with such Exceptions, and under such Regulations as the Congress shall make.

jury trial

³The Trial of all Crimes, except in Cases of Impeachment, shall be by Jury; and such Trial shall be held in the State where the said Crimes shall have been com-

*This clause has been affected by the Eleventh Amendment.

mitted; but when not committed within any State, the Trial shall be at such Place or Places as the Congress may by Law have directed.

Section. 3.   ¹Treason against the United States, shall consist only in levying War against them, or in adhering to their Enemies, giving them Aid and Comfort. No Person shall be convicted of Treason unless on the Testimony of two Witnesses to the same overt Act, or on Confession in open Court.

²The Congress shall have Power to declare the Punishment of Treason, but no Attainder of Treason shall work Corruption of Blood, or Forfeiture except during the Life of the Person attainted.

Article. IV.

Full faith and credit

Section. 1.   Full Faith and Credit shall be given in each State to the public Acts, Records, and judicial Proceedings of every other State. And the Congress may by general Laws prescribe the Manner in which such Acts, Records and Proceedings shall be proved, and the Effect thereof.

Privileges and immunities

Section. 2.   ¹The Citizens of each State shall be entitled to all Privileges and Immunities of Citizens in the several States.

Extradition

²A Person charged in any State with Treason, Felony, or other Crime, who shall flee from Justice, and be found in another State, shall on Demand of the executive Authority of the State from which he fled, be delivered up, to be removed to the State having Jurisdiction of the Crime.

³[No Person held to Service or Labour in one State, under the Laws thereof, escaping into another, shall, in Consequence of any Law or Regulation therein, be discharged from such Service or Labour, but shall be delivered up on Claim of the Party to whom such Service or Labour may be due.]*

Admission of new states

Section. 3.   ¹New States may be admitted by the Congress into this Union; but no new State shall be formed or erected within the Jurisdiction of any other State; nor any State be formed by the Junction of two or more States, or Parts of States, without the Consent of the Legislatures of the States concerned as well as of the Congress.

governing territories

²The Congress shall have Power to dispose of and make all needful Rules and Regulations, respecting the Territory or other Property belonging to the United States; and nothing in this Constitution shall be so construed as to Prejudice any Claims of the United States, or of any particular State.

Republican form of government

Protect from domestic violence

Section. 4.   The United States shall guarantee to every State in this Union a Republican Form of Government, and shall protect each of them against Invasion; and on Application of the Legislature, or of the Executive (when the Legislature cannot be convened) against domestic Violence.

Article. V.

Amending the Constitution

The Congress, whenever two thirds of both Houses shall deem it necessary, shall propose Amendments to this Constitution, or, on the Application of the Legisla-

---

*This paragraph has been superseded by the Thirteenth Amendment.

tures of two thirds of the several States, shall call a Convention for proposing Amendments, which, in either Case, shall be valid to all Intents and Purposes, as Part of this Constitution, when ratified by the Legislatures of three fourths of the several States, or by Conventions in three fourths thereof, as the one or the other Mode of Ratification may be proposed by the Congress; Provided [that no Amendment which may be made prior to the Year One thousand eight hundred and eight shall in any Manner affect the first and fourth Clauses in the Ninth Section of the first Article; and]* that no State, without its Consent, shall be deprived of its equal Suffrage in the Senate.

Article. VI.

Confederate debts valid

¹All Debts contracted and Engagements entered into, before the Adoption of this Constitution, shall be as valid against the United States under this Constitution, as under the Confederation.

Federal supremacy

²This Constitution, and the Laws of the United States which shall be made in Pursuance thereof; and all Treaties made, or which shall be made, under the Authority of the United States, shall be the supreme Law of the Land; and the Judges in every State shall be bound thereby, any Thing in the Constitution or Laws of any State to the Contrary notwithstanding.

No religious tests

³The Senators and Representatives before mentioned, and the Members of the several State legislatures, and all executive and judicial Officers, both of the United States and of the several States, shall be bound by Oath or Affirmation, to support this Constitution; but no religious Test shall ever be required as a Qualification to any Office or public Trust under the United States.

Article. VII.

Ratification of Constitution

The Ratification of the Conventions of nine States, shall be sufficient for the Establishment of this Constitution between the States so ratifying the Same.

Done in Convention by the Unanimous Consent of the States present the Seventeenth Day of September in the Year of our Lord one thousand seven hundred and Eighty seven and of the Independence of the United States of America the Twelfth. IN WITNESS whereof We have hereunto subscribed our Names.

GΩ WASHINGTON—
Presid'. and deputy from Virginia.

[*Signed also by the deputies of twelve States.*]

New Hampshire. John Langdon, Nicholas Gilman.

Massachusetts. Nathaniel Gorham, Rufus King.

Connecticut. Wm. Saml. Johnson, Roger Sherman.

New York. Alexander Hamilton.

New Jersey. Wil: Livingston, Wm. Paterson, David Brearley, Jona: Dayton.

*Obsolete.

Pennsylvania. B Franklin, Thomas Mifflin, Rob¹ Morris, Geo. Clymer, Thos. FitzSimons, Jared Ingersoll, James Wilson, Gouv Morris.

Delaware. Geo: Read, Gunning Bedford, jun, John Dickinson, Richard Bassett, Jaco: Broom.

Maryland. James McHenry, Dan of S¹ Thos. Jenifer, Dan¹ Carroll.

Virginia. John Blair, James Madison Jr.

North Carolina. Wm. Blount, Rich'd Dobbs Spaight, Hu Williamson.

South Carolina. J. Rutledge, Charles Cotesworth Pinckney, Charles Pinckney, Pierce Butler.

Georgia. William Few, Abr Baldwin. Attest: William Jackson, *Secretary.*

[*The Constitution was adopted by a convention of the States on September 17, 1787, and was subsequently ratified by the several States on the following dates: Delaware, December 7, 1787; Pennsylvania, December 12, 1787; New Jersey, December 18, 1787; Georgia, January 2, 1788; Connecticut, January 9, 1788; Massachusetts, February 6, 1788; Maryland, April 28, 1788; South Carolina, May 23, 1788; New Hampshire, June 21, 1788.*
Ratification was completed on June 21, 1788.
The Constitution was subsequently ratified by Virginia, June 25, 1788; New York, July 26, 1788; North Carolina, November 21, 1789; Rhode Island, May 29, 1790; and Vermont, January 10, 1791.]

Articles in Addition to, and Amendment of, the Constitution of the United States of America, Proposed by Congress, and Ratified by the Legislatures of the Several States Pursuant to the Fifth Article of the Original Constitution

Article [I]*

Freedom of religion, speech, press, and assembly

Congress shall make no law respecting an establishment of religion, or prohibiting the free exercise thereof; or abridging the freedom of speech, or of the press; or the right of the people peaceably to assemble, and to petition the Government for a redress of grievances.

Article [II]

Right to bear arms

A well regulated Militia, being necessary to the security of a free State, the right of the people to keep and bear Arms, shall not be infringed.

Article [III]

Quartering troops

No Soldier shall, in time of peace be quartered in any house, without the consent of the Owner, nor in time of war, but in a manner to be prescribed by law.

*Only the Thirteenth, Fourteenth, Fifteenth, and Sixteenth articles of amendment had numbers assigned to them at the time of ratification.

Article [IV]

Unreasonable searches and seizures

The right of the people to be secure in their persons, houses, papers, and effects, against unreasonable searches and seizures, shall not be violated, and no Warrants shall issue, but upon probable cause, supported by Oath or affirmation, and particularly describing the place to be searched, and the persons or things to be seized.

Article [V]

Grand jury, double jeopardy, self-incrimination

No person shall be held to answer for a capital, or otherwise infamous crime, unless on a presentment of indictment of a Grand Jury, except in cases arising in the land or naval forces, or in the Militia, when in actual service in time of War or public danger; nor shall any person be subject for the same offence to be twice put in jeopardy of life or limb; nor shall be compelled in any criminal case to be a witness against himself, nor be deprived of life, liberty, or property, without due process of law; nor shall private property be taken for public use without just compensation.

Article [VI]

Jury trial, know charges, confront witness, and counsel

In all criminal prosecutions the accused shall enjoy the right to a speedy and public trial, by an impartial jury of the State and district wherein the crime shall have been committed, which district shall have been previously ascertained by law, and to be informed of the nature and cause of the accusation; to be confronted with the witnesses against him; to have compulsory process for obtaining Witnesses in his favor, and to have the assistance of counsel for his defense.

Article [VII]

Jury trial in civil cases

In Suits at common law, where the value in controversy shall exceed twenty dollars, the right of trial by jury shall be preserved, and no fact tried by a jury, shall be otherwise reexamined in any Court of the United States, than according to the rules of the common law.

Article [VIII]

Excessive bail and cruel and unusual punishment

Excessive bail shall not be required, nor excessive fines imposed, nor cruel and unusual punishments inflicted.

Article [IX]

Unenumerated rights protected

The enumeration in the Constitution, of certain rights, shall not be construed to deny or disparage others retained by the people.

Article [X]

Reserved powers

The powers not delegated to the United States by the Constitution, nor prohibited by it to the States, are reserved to the States respectively, or to the people.

[*The first ten amendments to the Constitution, and two others that failed of ratification, were proposed by the Congress on September 25, 1789. They were ratified by the following states, and the notifications of the ratification by the governors thereof were successively communicated by the president to the Congress: New Jersey, November 20, 1789; Maryland, December 19, 1789; North Carolina, December 22, 1789; South Carolina, January 19, 1790; New Hampshire, January 25, 1790; Delaware, January 28, 1790; New York, February 24, 1790; Pennsylvania, March 10, 1790; Rhode Island, June 7, 1790; Vermont, November 3, 1791; and Virginia, December 15, 1791.*

Ratification was completed on December 15, 1791.

The amendments were subsequently ratified by Massachusetts, March 2, 1939; Georgia, March 18, 1939; and Connecticut, April 19, 1939.]

Article [XI]

Federal court jurisdiction limited

The Judicial power of the United States shall not be construed to extend to any suit in law or equity, commenced or prosecuted against one of the United States by Citizens of another State, or by Citizens or Subjects of any Foreign State.

[The Eleventh Amendment to the Constitution was proposed by the Congress on March 4, 1794. It was declared, in a message from the president to Congress, dated January 8, 1798 to have been ratified by the legislatures of twelve of the fifteen states. The dates of ratification were: New York, March 27, 1794; Rhode Island, March 31, 1794; Connecticut, May 8, 1794; New Hampshire, June 16, 1794; Massachusetts, June 26, 1794; Vermont, between October 9, 1794 and November 9, 1794; Virginia, November 18, 1794; Georgia, November 29, 1794; Kentucky, December 7, 1794; Maryland, December 26, 1794; Delaware, January 23, 1795; North Carolina, February 7, 1795.

Ratification was completed on February 7, 1795.

The amendment was subsequently ratified by South Carolina on December 4, 1797. New Jersey and Pennsylvania did not take action on the amendment.]

Article [XII]

Electoral college revised

separate balloting

The electors shall meet in their respective states and vote by ballot for President and Vice-President, one of whom, at least, shall not be an inhabitant of the same state with themselves; they shall name in their ballots the person voted for as President, and in distinct ballots the person voted for as Vice-President, and they shall make distinct lists of all persons voted for as President, and of all persons voted for as Vice-President, and of the number of votes for each, which lists they shall sign and certify, and transmit sealed to the seat of the government of the United States, directed to the President of the Senate;—The President of the Senate shall, in the presence of the Senate and House of Representatives, open all the certificates and the votes shall then be counted;—the Person having the greatest number of votes for President, shall be the President, if such number be a major-

House selects from top three for president

ity of the whole number of Electors appointed; and if no person have such majority, then from the persons having the highest numbers not exceeding three on the list of those voted for as President, the House of Representatives shall choose immediately, by ballot, the President. But in choosing the President, the votes shall be taken by states, the representation from each state having one vote; a quorum for this purpose shall consist of a member or members from two-thirds of the states, and a majority of all the states shall be necessary to a choice. [And if the House of Representatives shall not choose a President whenever the right of choice shall devolve upon them, before the fourth day of March next following, then the Vice-President shall act as President, as in the case of the death or other constitutional disability of the President.]* The person having the greatest number of votes as Vice-President, shall be the Vice-President, if such number be a majority of the whole number of Electors appointed, and if no person have a majority, then from the two highest numbers on the list, the Senate shall choose the Vice-President; a quorum for the purpose shall consist of two-thirds of the whole number of Senators, and a majority of the whole number shall be necessary to a choice. But no person constitutionally ineligible to the office of President shall be eligible to that of Vice-President of the United States.

Senate chooses vice-president from top two

[*The Twelfth Amendment to the Constitution was proposed by the Congress on December 9, 1803. It was declared, in a proclamation of the secretary of state, dated September 25, 1804, to have been ratified by the legislatures of thirteen of the seventeen states. The dates of ratification were: Vermont, October 28, 1803; North Carolina, December 21, 1803; Maryland, December 24, 1803; Kentucky, December 27, 1803; Ohio, December 30, 1803; Pennsylvania, January 5, 1804; Virginia, February 3, 1804; New York, February 10, 1804; New Jersey, February 22, 1804; Rhode Island, March 12, 1804; South Carolina, May 15, 1804; Georgia, May 19, 1804; New Hampshire, June 15, 1804.*

Ratification was completed on June 15, 1804.

The amendment was subsequently ratified by Tennessee, July 27, 1804.

The amendment was rejected by Delaware, January 18, 1804; Massachusetts, February 3, 1804; Connecticut, at its session begun May 10, 1804.]

Article [XIII]

Prohibition of slavery

Section 1. Neither slavery nor involuntary servitude, except as a punishment for crime whereof the party shall have been duly convicted, shall exist within the United States, or any place subject to their jurisdiction.

Section 2. Congress shall have power to enforce this article by appropriate legislation.

[*The Thirteenth Amendment to the Constitution was proposed by the Congress on January 31, 1865. It was declared, in a proclamation of the secretary of state, dated December 18, 1865, to have been ratified by the legislatures of twenty-seven of the thirty-six states. The dates of ratification were: Illinois, February 1, 1865; Rhode Island, February 2, 1865; Michigan, February 2, 1865; Maryland, February 3, 1865; New York, February 3, 1865; Pennsylvania, February 3, 1865; West Virginia, February 3, 1865; Missouri, February 6, 1865; Maine, February 7, 1865; Kansas, February 7, 1865; Massachusetts, February 7, 1865; Virginia, February 9, 1865; Ohio, February 10, 1865; Indiana, February 13, 1865; Nevada, February 16, 1865; Louisiana, February 17, 1865; Minnesota, February 23, 1865; Wisconsin, February 24, 1865; Vermont, March 9, 1865; Tennessee, April 7, 1865; Arkansas, April 14, 1865; Connecticut, May 4, 1865; New Hampshire, July 1, 1865; South Carolina, November 13, 1865; Alabama, December 2, 1865; North Carolina, December 4, 1865; Georgia, December 6, 1865.*

Ratification was completed on December 6, 1865.

The amendment was subsequently ratified by Oregon, December 8, 1865; California, December 19, 1865; Florida, December 28, 1865 (Florida again ratified on June 9, 1868, upon its adoption of a new constitution); Iowa, January 15, 1866; New Jersey, January 23,

---

*The words in brackets have been superseded by Section 3 of the Twentieth Amendment.

1866 (after having rejected the amendment on March 16, 1865); Texas, February 18, 1870; Delaware, February 12, 1901 (after having rejected the amendment on February 8, 1865).

The amendment was rejected by Kentucky, February 24, 1865, and by Mississippi, December 4, 1865.]

Article [XIV]

Citizenship—U.S. and state

Section 1. All persons born or naturalized in the United States, and subject to the jurisdiction thereof, are citizens of the United States and of the State wherein they reside. No State shall make or enforce any law which shall abridge the privileges or immunities of citizens of the United States; nor shall any State deprive any person of life, liberty, or property, without due process of law; nor deny to any person within its jurisdiction the equal protection of the laws.

due process
equal protection

Reduced representation for abridging vote

Section 2. Representatives shall be apportioned among the several States according to their respective numbers, counting the whole number of persons in each State, excluding Indians not taxed. But when the right to vote at any election for the choice of electors for President and Vice President of the United States, Representatives in Congress, the Executive and Judicial officers of a State, or the members of the Legislature thereof, is denied to any of the male inhabitants of such State, being twenty-one years of age,* and citizens of the United States, or in any way abridged, except for participation in rebellion, or other crime, the basis of representation therein shall be reduced in the proportion which the number of such male citizens shall bear to the whole number of male citizens twenty-one years of age in such State.

Confederate officials denied federal office

Section 3. No person shall be a Senator or Representative in Congress, or elector of President and Vice President, or hold any office, civil or military, under the United States, or under any State, who, having previously taken an oath, as a member of Congress, or as an officer of the United States, or as a member of any State legislature, or as an executive or judicial officer of any State, to support the Constitution of the United States, shall have engaged in insurrection or rebellion against the same, or given aid or comfort to the enemies thereof. But Congress may by a vote of two-thirds of each House, remove such disability.

Confederate debts invalid

Section 4. The validity of the public debt of the United States, authorized by law, including debts incurred for payment of pensions and bounties for services in suppressing insurrection or rebellion, shall not be questioned. But neither the United States nor any State shall assume or pay any debt or obligation incurred in aid of insurrection or rebellion against the United States, or any claim for the loss of emancipation of any slave; but all such debts, obligations and claims shall be held illegal and void.

Section 5. The Congress shall have power to enforce, by appropriate legislation, the provisions of this article.

[The Fourteenth Amendment to the Constitution was proposed by the Congress on June 13, 1866. It was declared, in a certificate by the secretary of state dated July 28, 1868, to have been ratified by the legislatures of twenty-eight of the thirty-seven states. The dates of ratification were: Connecticut, June 25, 1866; New Hampshire, July 6, 1866; Tennessee, July 19, 1866; New Jersey, September 11, 1866 (subsequently the legislature rescinded its

*See the Twenty-sixth Amendment.

ratification, and on March 5, 1868, readopted its resolution of rescission over the Governor's veto); Oregon, September 19, 1866 (and rescinded its ratification on October 15, 1868); Vermont, October 30, 1866; Ohio, January 4, 1867 (and rescinded its ratification on January 15, 1868); New York, January 10, 1867; Kansas, January 11, 1867; Illinois, January 15, 1867; West Virginia, January 16, 1867; Michigan, January 16, 1867; Minnesota, January 16, 1867; Maine, January 19, 1867; Nevada, January 22, 1867; Indiana, January 23, 1867; Missouri, January 25, 1867; Rhode Island, February 7, 1867; Wisconsin, February 7, 1867; Pennsylvania, February 12, 1867; Massachusetts, March 20, 1867; Nebraska, June 15, 1867; Iowa, March 16, 1868; Arkansas, April 6, 1868; Florida, June 9, 1868; North Carolina, July 4, 1868 (after having rejected it on December 14, 1866); Louisiana, July 9, 1868 (after having rejected it on February 6, 1867); South Carolina, July 9, 1868 (after having rejected it on December 20, 1866).

Ratification was completed on July 9, 1868.*

The amendment was subsequently ratified by Alabama, July 13, 1868; Georgia, July 21, 1868 (after having rejected it on November 9, 1866); Virginia, October 8, 1869 (after having rejected it on January 9, 1867); Mississippi, January 17, 1870; Texas, February 18, 1870 (after having rejected it on October 27, 1866); Delaware, February 12, 1901 (after having rejected it on February 8, 1867); Maryland, April 4, 1959 (after having rejected it on March 23, 1867); California, May 6, 1959.]

Article [XV]

Suffrage for freed slaves

Section 1. The right of citizens of the United States to vote shall not be denied or abridged by the United States or by any State on account of race, color, or previous condition of servitude.

Section 2. The Congress shall have power to enforce this article by appropriate legislation.

[The Fifteenth Amendment to the Constitution was proposed by the Congress on February 26, 1869. It was declared, in a proclamation of the secretary of state, dated March 30, 1870, to have been ratified by the legislatures of twenty-nine of the thirty-seven states. The dates of ratification were: Nevada, March 1, 1869; West Virginia, March 3, 1869; Illinois, March 5, 1869; Louisiana, March 5, 1869; North Carolina, March 5, 1869; Michigan, March 8, 1869; Wisconsin, March 9, 1869; Maine, March 11, 1869; Massachusetts, March 12, 1869; Arkansas, March 15, 1869; South Carolina, March 15, 1869; Pennsylvania, March 25, 1869; New York, April 14, 1869 (and the legislature of the same state passed a resolution January 5, 1870, to withdraw its consent to it, which action it rescinded on March 30, 1970); Indiana, May 14, 1869; Connecticut, May 19, 1869; Florida, June 14, 1869; New Hampshire, July 1, 1869; Virginia, October 8, 1869; Vermont, October 20, 1869; Missouri, January 7, 1870; Minnesota, January 13, 1870; Mississippi, January 17, 1870; Rhode Island, January 18, 1870; Kansas, January 19, 1870; Ohio, January 27, 1870 (after having rejected it on April 30, 1869); Georgia, February 2, 1870; Iowa, February 3, 1870.

Ratification was completed on February 3, 1870, unless the withdrawal of ratification by New York was effective; in which event ratification was completed on February 17, 1870, when Nebraska ratified.

---

*The certificate of the secretary of state, dated July 20, 1868, was based upon the assumption of invalidity of the rescission of ratification by Ohio and New Jersey. The following day, the Congress adopted a joint resolution declaring the amendment a part of the Constitution. The secretary of state issued a proclamation of ratification without reservation.

The amendment was subsequently ratified by Texas, February 18, 1870; New Jersey, February 15, 1871 (after having rejected it on February 7, 1870); Delaware, February 12, 1901 (after having rejected it on March 18, 1869); Oregon, February 24, 1959; California, April 3, 1962 (after having rejected it on January 28, 1870).]

Article [XVI]

Income tax

The Congress shall have power to lay and collect taxes on incomes, from whatever source derived, without apportionment among the several States, and without regard to any census or enumeration.

[The Sixteenth Amendment to the Constitution was proposed by the Congress on July 12, 1909. It was declared, in a proclamation of the secretary of state, dated February 25, 1913, to have been ratified by thirty-six of the forty-eight states. The dates of ratification were: Alabama, August 10, 1909; Kentucky, February 8, 1910; South Carolina, February 19, 1910; Illinois, March 1, 1910; Mississippi, March 7, 1910; Oklahoma, March 10, 1910; Maryland, April 8, 1910; Georgia, August 3, 1910; Texas, August 16, 1910; Ohio, January 19, 1911; Idaho, January 20, 1911; Oregon, January 23, 1911; Washington, January 26, 1911; Montana, January 30, 1911; Indiana, January 30, 1911; California, January 31, 1911; Nevada, January 31, 1911; South Dakota, February 3, 1911; Nebraska, February 9, 1911; North Carolina, February 11, 1911; Colorado, February 15, 1911; North Dakota, February 17, 1911; Kansas, February 18, 1911; Michigan, February 23, 1911; Iowa, February 24, 1911; Missouri, March 16, 1911; Maine, March 31, 1911; Tennessee, April 7, 1911; Arkansas, April 22, 1911 (after having rejected it earlier); Wisconsin, May 26, 1911; New York, July 12, 1911; Arizona, April 6, 1912; Louisiana, June 28, 1912; Minnesota, July 11, 1912; West Virginia, January 31, 1913; New Mexico, February 3, 1913.
Ratification was completed on February 3, 1913.
The amendment was subsequently ratified by Massachusetts, March 4, 1913; New Hampshire, March 7, 1913 (after having rejected it on March 2, 1911).
The amendment was rejected by Connecticut, Rhode Island, and Utah.]

Article [XVII]

Direct election of senators

The Senate of the United States shall be composed of two Senators from each State, elected by the people thereof, for six years; and each Senator shall have one vote. The electors in each State shall have the qualifications requisite for electors of the most numerous branch of the State legislatures.

When vacancies happen in the representation of any State in the Senate, the executive authority of such State shall issue writs of election to fill such vacancies: *Provided,* That the legislature of any State may empower the executive thereof to make temporary appointments until the people fill the vacancies by election as the legislature may direct.

This amendment shall not be so construed as to affect the election or term of any Senator chosen before it becomes valid as part of the Constitution.

[The Seventeenth Amendment to the Constitution was proposed by the Congress on May 13, 1912. It was declared, in a proclamation by the secretary of state, dated May 31, 1913, to have been ratified by the legislatures of thirty-six of the forty-eight states. The dates of ratification were: Massachusetts, May 22, 1912; Arizona, June 3, 1912; Minnesota, June 10, 1912; New York, January 15, 1913; Kansas, January 17, 1913; Oregon, January 23, 1913; North Carolina, January 25, 1913; California, January 28, 1913; Michigan, January 28, 1913; Iowa, January 30, 1913; Montana, January 30, 1913; Idaho, Janu-

ary 31, 1913; West Virginia, February 4, 1913; Colorado, February 5, 1913; Nevada, February 6, 1913; Texas, February 7, 1913; Washington, February 7, 1913; Wyoming, February 8, 1913; Arkansas, February 11, 1913; Maine, February 11, 1913; Illinois, February 13, 1913; North Dakota, February 14, 1913; Wisconsin, February 18, 1913; Indiana, February 19, 1913; New Hampshire, February 19, 1913; Vermont, February 19, 1913; South Dakota, February 19, 1913; Oklahoma, February 24, 1913; Ohio, February 25, 1913; Missouri, March 7, 1913; New Mexico, March 13, 1913; Nebraska, March 14, 1913; New Jersey, March 17, 1913; Tennessee, April 1, 1913; Pennsylvania, April 2, 1913; Connecticut, April 8, 1913.

Ratification was completed on April 8, 1913.

The amendment was subsequently ratified by Louisiana, June 11, 1914.

The amendment was rejected by Utah on February 26, 1913.]

Article [XVIII]

Prohibition of alcohol

[Section 1. After one year from the ratification of this article the manufacture, sale, or transportation of intoxicating liquors within, the importation thereof into, or the exportation thereof from the United States and all territory subject to the jurisdiction thereof for beverage purposes is hereby prohibited.

[Section 2. The Congress and the several States shall have concurrent power to enforce this article by appropriate legislation.

[Section 3. This article shall be inoperative unless it shall have been ratified as an amendment to the Constitution by the legislatures of the several States, as provided in the Constitution, within seven years from the date of the submission hereof to the States by the Congress.]*

[The Eighteenth Amendment to the Constitution was proposed by the Congress on December 18, 1917. It was declared, in a proclamation by the acting secretary of state, dated January 29, 1919, to have been ratified by the legislatures of thirty-six of the forty-eight states. The dates of ratification were: Mississippi, January 8, 1918; Virginia, January 11, 1918; Kentucky, January 14, 1918; North Dakota, January 25, 1918; South Carolina, January 29, 1918; Maryland, February 13, 1918; Montana, February 19, 1918; Texas, March 4, 1918; Delaware, March 18, 1918; South Dakota, March 20, 1918; Massachusetts, April 2, 1918; Arizona, May 24, 1918; Georgia, June 26, 1918; Louisiana, August 3, 1918; Florida, December 3, 1918; Michigan, January 2, 1919; Ohio, January 7, 1919; Oklahoma, January 7, 1919; Idaho, January 8, 1919; Maine, January 8, 1919; West Virginia, January 9, 1919; California, January 13, 1919; Tennessee, January 13, 1919; Washington, January 13, 1919; Arkansas, January 14, 1919; Kansas, January 14, 1919; Alabama, January 15, 1919; Colorado, January 15, 1919; Iowa, January 15, 1919; New Hampshire, January 15, 1919; Oregon, January 15, 1919; Nebraska, January 16, 1919; North Carolina, January 16, 1919; Utah, January 16, 1919; Missouri, January 16, 1919; Wyoming, January 16, 1919.

Ratification was completed on January 16, 1919.

The amendment was subsequently ratified by Minnesota on January 17, 1917; Wisconsin, January 17, 1919; New Mexico, January 20, 1919; Nevada, January 21, 1919; New York, January 29, 1919; Vermont, January 29, 1919; Pennsylvania, February 25, 1919; Connecticut, May 6, 1919; and New Jersey, March 9, 1922.

The amendment was rejected by Rhode Island.]

*Repealed by Section 1 of the Twenty-first Amendment.

Article [XIX]

Women's suffrage

The right of citizens of the United States to vote shall not be denied or abridged by the United States or by any State on account of sex.

Congress shall have power to enforce this article by appropriate legislation.

[*The Nineteenth Amendment to the Constitution was proposed by the Congress on June 4, 1919. It was declared, in a certificate by the secretary of state, dated August 26, 1920, to have been ratified by the legislatures of thirty-six of the forty-eight states. The dates of ratification were: Illinois, June 10, 1919 (and that State readopted its resolution of ratification June 17, 1919); Michigan, June 10, 1919; Wisconsin, June 10, 1919; Kansas, June 16, 1919; New York, June 16, 1919; Ohio, June 16, 1919; Pennsylvania, June 24, 1919; Massachusetts, June 25, 1919; Texas, June 28, 1919; Iowa, July 2, 1919; Missouri, July 3, 1919; Arkansas, July 28, 1919; Montana, August 2, 1919; Nebraska, August 2, 1919; Minnesota, September 8, 1919; New Hampshire, September 10, 1919; Utah, October 2, 1919; California, November 1, 1919; Maine, November 5, 1919; North Dakota, December 1, 1919; South Dakota, December 4, 1919; Colorado, December 15, 1919; Kentucky, January 6, 1920; Rhode Island, January 6, 1920; Oregon, January 13, 1920; Indiana, January 16, 1920; Wyoming, January 27, 1920; Nevada, February 7, 1920; New Jersey, February 9, 1920; Idaho, February 11, 1920; Arizona, February 12, 1920; New Mexico, February 21, 1920; Oklahoma, February 28, 1920; West Virginia, March 10, 1920; Washington, March 22, 1920; Tennessee, August 18, 1920.*

Ratification was completed on August 20, 1920.

The amendment was subsequently ratified by Connecticut on September 14, 1920 (and that State reaffirmed on September 21, 1920); Vermont, February 8, 1921; Maryland, March 29, 1941 (after having rejected it on February 24, 1920; ratification certified on February 25, 1958); Alabama, September 8, 1953 (after that State had rejected it on September 22, 1919); Virginia, February 21, 1952 (after rejecting it on February 12, 1920); Florida, May 13, 1969; Louisiana, June 11, 1970 (after having rejected it on July 1, 1920); Georgia, February 20, 1970 (after rejecting on July 24, 1919); North Carolina, May 6, 1971.

The amendment was rejected by South Carolina, January 28, 1920; Mississippi, March 29, 1920; Delaware, June 2, 1920.]

Article [XX]

Terms of office changed to January

Section 1.   The terms of the President and Vice President shall end at noon on the 20th day of January, and the terms of Senators and Representatives at noon on the 3rd day of January, of the years in which terms would have ended if this article had not been ratified; and the terms of their successors shall then begin.

Section 2.   The Congress shall assemble at least once in every year, and such meeting shall begin at noon on the 3rd day of January, unless they shall by law appoint a different day.

Emergency succession to presidency

Section 3.   If, at the time fixed for the beginning of the term of the President, the President elect shall have died, the Vice President elect shall become President. If a President shall not have been chosen before the time fixed for the beginning of his term, or if the President elect shall have failed to qualify, then the Vice President elect shall act as President until a President shall have qualified; and the Congress may by law provide for the case wherein neither a President elect nor a Vice President elect shall have qualified, declaring who shall then act as President, or the manner in which one who is to act shall be selected, and such person shall act accordingly until a President or Vice President shall have qualified.

Section 4.   The Congress may by law provide for the case of the death of any of the persons from whom the House of Representatives may choose a President whenever the right of choice shall have devolved upon them, and for the case of the death of any of the persons from whom the Senate may choose a Vice President whenever the right of choice shall have devolved upon them.

Section 5.   Sections 1 and 2 shall take effect on the 15th day of October following the ratification of this article.

Section 6.   This article shall be inoperative unless it shall have been ratified as an amendment to the Constitution by the legislatures of three-fourths of the several States within seven years from the date of its submission.

[*The Twentieth Amendment to the Constitution was proposed by the Congress on March 2, 1932. It was declared, in a certificate by the secretary of state, dated February 6, 1933, to have been ratified by the legislatures of thirty-six of the forty-eight states. The dates of ratification were: Virginia, March 4, 1932; New York, March 11, 1932; Mississippi, March 16, 1932; Arkansas, March 17, 1932; Kentucky, March 17, 1932; New Jersey, March 21, 1932; South Carolina, March 25, 1932; Michigan, March 31, 1932; Maine, April 1, 1932; Rhode Island, April 14, 1932; Illinois, April 21, 1932; Louisiana, June 22, 1932; West Virginia, July 30, 1932; Pennsylvania, August 11, 1932; Indiana, August 15, 1932; Texas, September 7, 1932; Alabama, September 13, 1932; California, January 4, 1933; North Carolina, January 5, 1933; North Dakota, January 9, 1933; Minnesota, January 12, 1933; Arizona, January 13, 1933; Montana, January 13, 1933; Nebraska, January 13, 1933; Oklahoma, January 13, 1933; Kansas, January 16, 1933; Oregon, January 16, 1933; Delaware, January 19, 1933; Washington, January 19, 1933; Wyoming, January 19, 1933; Iowa, January 20, 1933; South Dakota, January 20, 1933; Tennessee, January 20, 1933; Idaho, January 21, 1933; New Mexico, January 21, 1933; Georgia, January 23, 1933; Missouri, January 23, 1933; Ohio, January 23, 1933; Utah, January 23, 1933.*

Ratification was completed on January 23, 1933.

The amendment was subsequently ratified by Massachusetts on January 24, 1933; Wisconsin, January 24, 1933; Colorado, January 24, 1933; Nevada, January 26, 1933; Connecticut, January 27, 1933; New Hampshire, January 31, 1933; Vermont, February 2, 1933; Maryland, March 24, 1933; Florida, April 26, 1933.]

Article [XXI]

Repeal of prohibition

Section 1.   The eighteenth article of amendment to the Constitution of the United States is hereby repealed.

Section 2.   The transportation or importation into any State, Territory, or possession of the United States for delivery or use therein of intoxicating liquors, in violation of the laws thereof, is hereby prohibited.

Section 3.   This article shall be inoperative unless it shall have been ratified as an amendment to the Constitution by conventions in the several States, as provided in the Constitution, within seven years from the date of the submission hereof to the States by the Congress.

[*The Twenty-first Amendment to the Constitution was proposed by the Congress on February 20, 1933. It was declared, in a certificate of the acting secretary of state, dated*

December 5, 1933, to have been ratified by conventions in thirty-six of the forty-eight states. The dates of ratification were: Michigan, April 10, 1933; Wisconsin, April 25, 1933; Rhode Island, May 8, 1933; Wyoming, May 25, 1933; New Jersey, June 1, 1933; Delaware, June 24, 1933; Indiana, June 26, 1933; Massachusetts, June 26, 1933; New York, June 27, 1933; Illinois, July 10, 1933; Iowa, July 10, 1933; Connecticut, July 11, 1933; New Hampshire, July 11, 1933; California, July 24, 1933; West Virginia, July 25, 1933; Arkansas, August 1, 1933; Oregon, August 7, 1933; Alabama, August 8, 1933; Tennessee, August 11, 1933; Missouri, August 29, 1933; Arizona, September 5, 1933; Nevada, September 5, 1933; Vermont, September 23, 1933; Colorado, September 26, 1933; Washington, October 3, 1933; Minnesota, October 10, 1933; Idaho, October 17, 1933; Maryland, October 18, 1933; Virginia, October 25, 1933; New Mexico, November 2, 1933; Florida, November 14, 1933; Texas, November 24, 1933; Kentucky, November 27, 1933; Ohio, December 5, 1933; Pennsylvania, December 5, 1933; Utah, December 5, 1933.

Ratification was completed on December 5, 1933.

The amendment was subsequently ratified by Maine, on December 6, 1933, and by Montana, on August 6, 1934.

The amendment was rejected by South Carolina, on December 4, 1933.]

Article [XXII]

President limited to two terms

Section 1.   No person shall be elected to the office of the President more than twice, and no person who has held the office of President, or acted as President, for more than two years of a term to which some other person was elected President shall be elected to the office of the President more than once. But this Article shall not apply to any person holding the office of President when this Article was proposed by the Congress, and shall not prevent any person who may be holding the office of President, or acting as President, during the term within which this Article becomes operative from holding the office of President or acting as President during the remainder of such term.

Section 2.   This article shall be inoperative unless it shall have been ratified as an amendment to the Constitution by the legislatures of three-fourths of the several States within seven years from the date of its submission to the States by the Congress.

[The Twenty-second Amendment to the Constitution was proposed by the Congress on March 21, 1947. It was declared, in a certificate by the administrator of general services, dated March 3, 1951, to have been ratified by the legislatures of thirty-six of the forty-eight states. The dates of ratification were: Maine, March 31, 1947; Michigan, March 31, 1947; Iowa, April 1, 1947; Kansas, April 1, 1947; New Hampshire, April 1, 1947; Delaware, April 2, 1947; Illinois, April 3, 1947; Oregon, April 3, 1947; Colorado, April 12, 1947; California, April 15, 1947; New Jersey, April 15, 1947; Vermont, April 15, 1947; Ohio, April 16, 1947; Wisconsin, April 16, 1947; Pennsylvania, April 29, 1947; Connecticut, May 21, 1947; Missouri, May 22, 1947; Nebraska, May 23, 1947; Virginia, January 28, 1948; Mississippi, February 12, 1948; New York, March 9, 1948; South Dakota, January 21, 1949; North Dakota, February 25, 1949; Louisiana, May 17, 1950; Montana, January 25, 1951; Indiana, January 29, 1951; Idaho, January 30, 1951; New Mexico, February 12, 1951; Wyoming, February 12, 1951; Arkansas, February 15, 1951; Georgia, February 17, 1951; Tennessee, February 20, 1951; Texas, February 22, 1951; Nevada, February 26, 1951; Utah, February 26, 1951; Minnesota, February 27, 1951.

Ratification was completed on February 27, 1951.

The amendment was subsequently ratified by North Carolina on February 28, 1951; South Carolina, March 13, 1951; Maryland, March 14, 1951; Florida, April 16, 1951; Alabama, May 4, 1951.

The amendment was rejected by Oklahoma in June 1947, and Massachusetts on June 9, 1949.]

Article [XXIII]

Electoral vote for District of Columbia

Section 1. The District constituting the seat of Government of the United States shall appoint in such manner as the Congress may direct:

A number of electors of President and Vice President equal to the whole number of Senators and Representatives in Congress to which the District would be entitled if it were a State, but in no event more than the least populous State; they shall be in addition to those appointed by the States, but they shall be considered, for the purposes of the election of President and Vice President, to be electors appointed by a State; and they shall meet in the District and perform such duties as provided by the twelfth article of amendment.

Section 2. The Congress shall have power to enforce this article by appropriate legislation.

[*The Twenty-third Amendment to the Constitution was proposed by the Congress on June 17, 1960. It was declared, in a certificate by the administrator of general services, to have been ratified by thirty-eight of the fifty states. The dates of ratification were: Hawaii, June 23, 1960 (and that state made a technical correction to its resolution on June 30, 1960); Massachusetts, August 22, 1960; New Jersey, December 19, 1960; New York, January 17, 1961; California, January 19, 1961; Oregon, January 27, 1961; Maryland, January 30, 1961; Idaho, January 31, 1961; Maine, January 31, 1961; Minnesota, January 31, 1961; New Mexico, February 1, 1961; Nevada, February 2, 1961; Montana, February 6, 1961; South Dakota, February 6, 1961; Colorado, February 8, 1961; Washington, February 9, 1961; West Virginia, February 9, 1961; Alaska, February 10, 1961; Wyoming, February 13, 1961; Delaware, February 20, 1961; Utah, February 21, 1961; Wisconsin, February 21, 1961; Pennsylvania, February 28, 1961; Indiana, March 3, 1961; North Dakota, March 3, 1961; Tennessee, March 6, 1961; Michigan, March 8, 1961; Connecticut, March 9, 1961; Arizona, March 10, 1961; Illinois, March 14, 1961; Nebraska, March 15, 1961; Vermont, March 15, 1961; Iowa, March 16, 1961; Missouri, March 20, 1961; Oklahoma, March 21, 1961; Rhode Island, March 22, 1961; Kansas, March 29, 1961; Ohio, March 29, 1961.*

Ratification was completed on March 29, 1961.

The amendment was subsequently ratified by New Hampshire on March 30, 1961 (when that state annulled and then repeated its ratification of March 29, 1961).

The amendment was rejected by Arkansas on January 24, 1961.]

Article [XXIV]

Prohibits poll tax

Section 1. The right of citizens of the United States to vote in any primary or other election for President or Vice President, for electors for President or Vice President, or for Senator or Representative in Congress, shall not be denied or abridged by the United States or any State by reason of failure to pay any poll tax or other tax.

Section 2. The Congress shall have power to enforce this article by appropriate legislation.

[*The Twenty-fourth Amendment to the Constitution was proposed by the Congress on August 27, 1962. It was declared, in a certificate of the administrator of general services, dated February 4, 1964, to have been ratified by the legislatures of thirty-eight of the fifty states. The dates of ratification were: Illinois, November 14, 1962; New Jersey, December 3, 1962; Oregon, January 25, 1963; Montana, January 28, 1963; West Virginia, February 1, 1963; New York, February 4, 1963; Maryland, February 6, 1963; California, February 7, 1963; Alaska, February 11, 1963; Rhode Island, February 14, 1963; Indiana, February 19, 1963; Utah, February 20, 1963; Michigan, February 20, 1963; Colorado, February 21, 1963; Ohio, February 27, 1963; Minnesota, February 27, 1963; New Mexico, March 5, 1963; Hawaii, March 6, 1963; North Dakota, March 7, 1963; Idaho, March 8, 1963; Washington, March 14, 1963; Vermont, March 15, 1963; Nevada, March 19, 1963; Connecticut, March 20, 1963; Tennessee, March 21, 1963; Pennsylvania, March 25, 1963; Wisconsin, March 26, 1963; Kansas, March 28, 1963; Massachusetts, March 28, 1963; Nebraska, April 4, 1963; Florida, April 18, 1963; Iowa, April 24, 1963; Delaware, May 1, 1963; Missouri, May 13, 1963; New Hampshire, June 12, 1963; Kentucky, June 27, 1963; Maine, January 16, 1964; South Dakota, January 23, 1964.*

Ratification was completed on January 23, 1964.

The amendment was rejected by Mississippi on December 20, 1962.]

Article [XXV]

Presidential succession and disability

Section 1.   In case of the removal of the President from office or of his death or resignation, the Vice President shall become President.

Section 2.   Whenever there is a vacancy in the office of the Vice President, the President shall nominate a Vice President who shall take office upon confirmation by a majority vote of both Houses of Congress.

declaration of disability

Section 3.   Whenever the President transmits to the President pro tempore of the Senate and the Speaker of the House of Representatives his written declaration that he is unable to discharge the powers and duties of his office, and until he transmits to them a written declaration to the contrary, such powers and duties shall be discharged by the Vice President as Acting President.

Section 4.   Whenever the Vice President and a majority of either the principal officers of the executive departments or of such other body as Congress may by law provide, transmit to the President pro tempore of the Senate and the Speaker of the House of Representatives their written declaration that the President is unable to discharge the powers and duties of this office, the Vice President shall immediately assume the powers and duties of the office as Acting President.

Thereafter, when the President transmits to the President pro tempore of the Senate and the Speaker of the House of Representatives his written declaration that no inability exists, he shall resume the powers and duties of his office unless the Vice President and a majority of either the principal officers of the executive department or of such other body as Congress may by law provide, transmit within four days to the President pro tempore of the Senate and the Speaker of the House of Representatives their written declaration that the President is unable to discharge the powers and duties of his office. Thereupon Congress shall decide the issue, assembling within forty-eight hours for that purpose if not in session. If the Congress, within twenty-one days after receipt of the latter written declaration, or, if Congress is not in session, within twenty-one days after Congress is required to assemble, determines by two-thirds vote of both Houses that the President is unable to discharge the powers and duties of his office, the Vice

President shall continue to discharge the same as Acting President; otherwise, the President shall resume the powers and duties of his office.

[*The Twenty-fifth Amendment to the Constitution was proposed by the Congress on July 6, 1965. It was declared, in a certificate of the administrator of general services, dated February 23, 1967, to have been ratified by the legislatures of thirty-nine of the fifty states. The dates of ratification were: Nebraska, July 12, 1965; Wisconsin, July 13, 1965; Oklahoma, July 16, 1965; Massachusetts, August 9, 1965; Pennsylvania, August 18, 1965; Kentucky, September 15, 1965; Arizona, September 22, 1965; Michigan, October 5, 1965; Indiana, October 20, 1965; California, October 21, 1965; Arkansas, November 4, 1965; New Jersey, November 29, 1965; Delaware, December 7, 1965; Utah, January 17, 1966; West Virginia, January 20, 1966; Maine, January 24, 1966; Rhode Island, January 28, 1966; Colorado, February 3, 1966; New Mexico, February 3, 1966; Kansas, February 8, 1966; Vermont, February 10, 1966; Alaska, February 18, 1966; Idaho, March 2, 1966; Hawaii, March 3, 1966; Virginia, March 8, 1966; Mississippi, March 10, 1966; New York, March 14, 1966; Maryland, March 23, 1966; Missouri, March 30, 1966; New Hampshire, June 13, 1966; Louisiana, July 5, 1966; Tennessee, January 12, 1967; Wyoming, January 25, 1967; Washington, January 26, 1967; Iowa, January 26, 1967; Oregon, February 2, 1967; Minnesota, February 10, 1967; Nevada, February 10, 1967.*

Ratification was completed on February 10, 1967.

The amendment was subsequently ratified by Connecticut, February 14, 1967; Montana, February 15, 1967; South Dakota, March 6, 1967; Ohio, March 7, 1967; Alabama, March 14, 1967; North Carolina, March 22, 1967; Illinois, March 22, 1967; Texas, April 25, 1967; Florida, May 25, 1967.]

Article [XXVI]

Voting age lowered to eighteen

Section 1. The right of citizens of the United States, who are eighteen years of age or older, to vote shall not be denied or abridged by the United States or by any State on account of age.

Section 2. The Congress shall have power to enforce this article by appropriate legislation.

[*The Twenty-sixth Amendment to the Constitution was proposed by the Congress on March 23, 1971. It was declared, in a certificate of the administrator of general services, dated July 5, 1971, to have been ratified by the legislatures of thirty-nine of the fifty states. The dates of ratification were: Connecticut, March 23, 1971; Delaware, March 23, 1971; Minnesota, March 23, 1971; Tennessee, March 23, 1971; Washington, March 23, 1971; Hawaii, March 24, 1971; Massachusetts, March 24, 1971; Montana, March 29, 1971; Arkansas, March 30, 1971; Idaho, March 30, 1971; Iowa, March 30, 1971; Nebraska, April 2, 1971; New Jersey, April 3, 1971; Kansas, April 7, 1971; Michigan, April 7, 1971; Alaska, April 8, 1971; Maryland, April 8, 1971; Indiana, April 8, 1971; Maine, April 9, 1971; Vermont, April 16, 1971; Louisiana, April 17, 1971; California, April 19, 1971; Colorado, April 27, 1971; Pennsylvania, April 27, 1971; Texas, April 27, 1971; South Carolina, April 28, 1971; West Virginia, April 28, 1971; New Hampshire, May 13, 1971; Arizona, May 14, 1971; Rhode Island, May 27, 1971; New York, June 2, 1971; Oregon, June 4, 1971; Missouri, June 14, 1971; Wisconsin, June 22, 1971; Illinois, June 29, 1971; Alabama, June 30, 1971; Ohio, June 30, 1971; North Carolina, July 1, 1971; Oklahoma, July 1, 1971.*

Ratification was completed on July 1, 1971.

The amendment was subsequently ratified by Virginia, July 8, 1971; Wyoming, July 8, 1971; Georgia, October 4, 1971.]

■ *Proposed Amendment*

[*The amendment proposing that the District of Columbia be treated as a state for purposes of congressional representation and election of president and vice president was proposed by the Ninety-fifth Congress. It passed the House on March 2, 1978, and the Senate on August 22, 1978.*]

Article

Proposed amendment extending full representation to District of Columbia

Section 1.   For purposes of representation in the Congress, election of the President and Vice President, and article V of this Constitution, the District constituting the seat of government of the United States shall be treated as though it were a State.

Section 2.   The exercise of the rights and powers conferred under this article shall be by the people of the District constituting the seat of government, and as shall be provided by the Congress.

Section 3.   The twenty-third article of amendment to the Constitution of the United States is hereby repealed.

Section 4.   This article shall be inoperative, unless it shall have been ratified as an amendment to the Constitution by the legislatures of three-fourths of the several States within seven years from the date of its submission.

■ *Proposed Amendment*

[*The amendment relative to equal rights for men and women was proposed by the Ninety-second Congress. It passed the House on October 12, 1971 and the Senate on March 22, 1972. The ratification deadline expired June 30, 1982. A new amendment has been introduced into Congress.*]

Article

Proposed amendment prohibiting discrimination based on sex

Section 1.   Equality of rights under the law shall not be denied or abridged by the United States or by any State on account of sex.

Section 2.   The Congress shall have the power to enforce, by appropriate legislation, the provisions of this article.

Section 3.   This amendment shall take effect two years after the date of ratification.

Glossary

ABSCAM: ABSCAM was an FBI undercover investigation begun in 1978 to lure people involved in organized crime into selling stolen securities and art objects. FBI agents posed as representatives of Arab businessmen and sheiks (hence Arab Scam or ABSCAM). Eight congressmen were approached and asked to use their positions to help Arabs to conclude real estate deals or to obtain such things as U.S. residency and gambling licenses. These deals were tape recorded and videotaped. Ultimately, six members of the House and one senator were convicted of accepting bribes. Many people considered FBI tactics to be a form of entrapment. A 1983 congressional act would allow "sting" operations only when "reasonable suspicion of criminal conduct" exists.

access: the contact with public officials that forms the basis for lobbying activity. Access depends on reaching key decision makers at key points in the political process.

adversarial process: the judicial process whereby two contending parties argue their differences in order to establish the culpability of one or the other of them.

affirmative action: the policy of providing special assistance to minorities in an effort to equalize results in areas such as education and employment.

agenda setting: the identification of important issues. The media perform what is called the agenda-setting function.

amicus curiae: "friend of the court" briefs submitted by interested parties at the invitation of the court.

anti-Federalists: opponents of the Constitution drafted in 1789. They favored local government and a weak central government.

appellate courts: intermediate courts and the supreme courts in the state and federal court systems that have jurisdiction to review a case.

appropriations: a congressional act authorizing public funds for specific governmental purposes. All agencies of government must come to Congress annually to have their operating budgets renewed.

arms race: the development of new and more deadly military weapons, particularly nuclear weapons, to achieve military superiority over other countries, especially the Soviet Union.

Articles of Confederation: adopted in 1777, the articles served as the United States constitution until replaced by the present Constitution. As a form of government, the articles granted more power to the individual states than to the national government.

badge of slavery: private acts of racial discrimination that violate the Thirteenth Amendment.

bad-tendency test: a test established by the Supreme Court in 1925 to deal with the prohibition of speech threatening the overthrow of the government.

balancing doctrine: the Court-held view that the individual's right to liberty must be balanced against the needs of public order and safety.

bandwagon effect: the tendency of people to vote for the apparent winning candidate. The reporting of election results from the East coast before polls close in the West influences voters to vote for the candidate reported to be winning in the East. This is a controversial practice.

bill of attainder: a law declaring a particular individual guilty of a crime and naming the punishment without benefit of trial.

Bill of Rights: the first ten amendments to the Constitution. They specify the rights of individuals and the limitations of the national government.

blanket primary: a form of direct primary in which the voter is given both party ballots and can vote back and forth between the parties in choosing nominees for public office.

block grant: a form of federal aid to state and local governments for broadly defined purposes within which local officials have discretion over the specific programs to be operated.

blue-collar caucus: a caucus representing working-class occupations, formed in 1977 by fourteen members of the House of Representatives.

blue slip: the Senate procedure for exercising senatorial courtesy. So named because the Senate Judiciary Committee stationery is blue, a negative review or even non-return of the committee request by the senator of the nominee's state results in nonconsideration of the candidate.

Boll Weevils: conservative southern Democratic members of Congress who defected from their party to support President Reagan's economic policies in Congress.

brief: a lengthy written document citing law and precedent, used in court by counsel.

Brown v. Board of Education of Topeka: the 1954 Supreme Court decision that declared laws requiring segregation of schools to be unconstitutional.

bureau: a subdivision of a bureaucratic department.

busing: a court-ordered remedy to overcome intentional discrimination against racial minorities. Students are transported out of their neighborhoods to schools some distance from home, if necessary, to break the pattern of segregation.

cabinet: collectively, the thirteen heads of the executive agencies together with the president and vice-president.

calendar Wednesday: a method of avoiding the House Rules Committee by allowing committee chairs, in alphabetical order of committees, to call up any bills from the House or the Union calendars on Wednesdays.

capital punishment: the use of the death penalty as a form of criminal punishment.

careerism: the tendency for a legislative politician to build a professional career by running for and holding public office.

"cases and controversies": the phrase used in Article III of the Constitution to define the jurisdiction of the federal judiciary. This phrase has been interpreted to mean actual disputes capable of settlement by judicial means.

categorical grant: a system of national aid to state and local government for a specific purpose, allowing the recipient little discretion in use of the money.

caucus: the organization that includes all party members in that chamber of Congress. There are four caucuses: Senate Democrats, Senate Republicans, House Democrats, and House Republicans.

checks and balances: a system by which each branch of government exercises a check on the actions of the other branches of government.

child-benefit theory: a Court-held position that state aid for parochial education does not violate the establishment clause when the principal benefit is to the child.

civil law: private or statutory law regulating the relationships between private citizens.

civil liberties: basic rights and freedoms outside the control of the federal government.

civil service: the government employment system based on merit and the premise that similar employees performing like functions should be treated and paid the same.

class action suit: a lawsuit brought by a group of persons with a common legal concern who are willing to share the costs of bringing suit.

clear-and-present-danger test: the test proposed by Supreme Court Justice Holmes for determining when government had the right to restrict free speech. Only when speech provoked a "clear and present danger" were restrictions permissible.

clientele group: the natural constituency or consumers of specific government services. The clientele relationship with bureaucratic agencies is a prime source of political power.

closed primary: a form of direct primary in which voters must make a prior declaration of party affiliation in order to vote in the party's primary.

closed rule: a provision made by the House Rules Committee that prohibits amendments from being offered from the floor.

cloture: a Senate procedure invoked to close debate. It requires a three-fifths vote of the Senate.

coattail effect: the power of a presidential candidate to attract voters so that congressional candidates of the same party are elected to office.

collective presidency: the recognition that the presidency is an institution of several officials and offices, all in need of coordination, and that presidential responsibility is shared responsibility.

commerce clause: the power granted Congress in Article I, Section 8 of the Constitution to "regulate commerce with foreign nations and among the several states." The clause has been interpreted so as to give Congress broad authority over a variety of activities affecting the several states.

commercial speech: protection of legal advertising from government regulation as a First Amendment form of free speech.

Committee on Committees: groups of veteran Congress members selected by each party in both houses of Congress to make their party's appointments to congressional committees.

common law: a system of judge-made law based on custom and precedent.

commonwealth: a system in which parts of a constitution are independent of each other and each class of interests in society is separate and independent in its political authority and function.

community standards: the court test to determine obscenity. Each community must determine for itself its standard for judging obscenity.

compact colonies: colonies that based their organization on ideas borrowed from religious theory. Government was created out of consent of the governed.

comparable worth: an attempt to provide equal pay for equal work for women by comparing the skills and tasks required for every job. Dissimilar jobs requiring equivalent skills or efforts would have the same pay.

compensation: government programs to aid victims who have suffered loss or injury as a result of a crime.

concurrent powers: powers exercised by both national and state governments, such as the power to levy taxes or regulate commerce.

concurring opinion: a judicial statement explaining a justice's separate reasoning for voting with the majority.

confederation: a system of government in which legal authority is held by constituent governments that, in turn, may choose to create and delegate authority to a central government. This was the type of government system created by the Articles of Confederation.

conference committee: a congressional committee formed to draft a compromise bill when different versions of a similar bill have been passed by the House and Senate.

consent of the governed: the belief that political power originates with the popular approval of the people.

constitutionalism: the principle of granting and limiting political authority under a written or unwritten covenant (constitution).

contract: the idea that government represents a convenant between those who govern and those who are governed. Government power needs the consent of the governed to be legitimate.

cooperative federalism: an interpretation of federalism that emerged in the 1930s. This interpretation is characterized by a sharing of governmental powers for the purpose of joint problem solving.

core voters: individuals who vote in almost all elections, presidential and off year. Core voters are more likely to hold strong partisan loyalties.

countercyclical revenue sharing: an emergency federal grant program to provide an anti-recessional financial boost to areas facing severe economic and fiscal problems.

creative federalism: a form of cooperative federalism extending federal grants-in-aid beyond general governments to special districts and private organizations.

critical realignment: a long-term change in party identification with a relocation of groups across party lines.

cruel and unusual punishment: a phrase used in the Eighth Amendment provision intended to regulate the manner and severity of criminal punishment.

cruise missile: an airplanelike, low-flying, terrain-guided missile that can be launched from virtually any platform—bomber, submarine, tactical aircraft, or ground vehicle.

C-SPAN: Cable-Satellite Public Affairs Network made available to commercial cable systems; televised proceedings of the House of Representatives and Senate are broadcast over this network.

deadly force: use of all necessary force, including shooting to kill, to effect an arrest.

dealignment: the decline of political party loyalty, leading to the ultimate destruction of the party system. Party preference is replaced with political independence.

democracy: rule by the people.

department: the major functional division within the bureaucracy by which the executive branch of government administers the laws and carries out the programs established by Congress.

deregulation: frees private industry from federal government rules and regulations. This is a basic tenet of the Reagan administration.

desegregation: abolishing the practice of racial segregation.

deterrence: a means of reducing the risk of military attack by threatening massive nuclear retaliation in the event of such an attack.

direct primary: popular elections used to determine party nominees for public office and to select state and national convention delegates and party officers.

discharge petition: a petition to withdraw a bill from a House committee. It must be signed by a majority of House members.

dissenting opinion: a judicial statement explaining the minority justices' reasoning for questioning the majority verdict.

dockets: the calendars used by the Supreme Court to schedule business in order to dispose of cases filed with the Court.

doctrinal party: a minor political party that professes a particular doctrine and nominates candidates to the presidency over several elections.

dual federalism: a nineteenth-century concept of government recognizing a duality of power between national and state governments, each having a distinct sphere of authority and jurisdiction.

due process: legal, constitutional protections of personal rights and liberties.

elastic clause: the clause in the Constitution that gives Congress the power to make all laws "necessary and proper" to execute enumerated powers. This clause allows for the existence of implied powers.

electoral college: the group of electors, appointed by the states, who select the president. To be elected president, a candidate must receive a majority of electoral votes.

elite opinion: the opinions of political leaders and media representatives.

enabling act: an act of Congress allowing the people of a territory to draft a constitution, preparing the way for statehood.

entitlement programs: programs that guarantee financial benefits to individuals by virtue of their age, income, or employment status.

enumerated powers: the powers of the national government specifically provided for and listed in the Constitution.

Equal Employment Opportunity Commission: the federal agency charged with initiating and investigating charges of job discrimination against private and public employers.

equal protection: the phrase in the Fourteenth Amendment that has been the basis for overturning laws that seek to unreasonably classify people on the basis of race.

Equal Rights Amendment: a proposed constitutional amendment, recently before the states for ratification, that would prohibit sex-based classifications. It was not ratified but has been reintroduced.

equity: a legal principle of fairness that allows judges to provide for preventive measures and legal remedies where there is no applicable law.

establishment clause: the part of the First Amendment that prohibits the federal government or any state from setting up a church, passing laws to aid any religion, or preferring one religion over another.

Everson v. Board of Education: the 1947 Supreme Court decision establishing the "wall of separation" doctrine.

ex post facto laws: laws that impose punishment for an act that was not a crime when it was committed.

exclusionary rule: the court device of excluding from a trial evidence that was obtained as a result of an illegal search and seizure.

exclusive committee: the designation given to the Appropriations, Ways and Means, and Rules committees of the House of Representatives. Members assigned to an exclusive committee serve on only that committee and no other standing committee.

executive agreements: agreements made by the president that do not require Senate action but have the same legal standing as treaties.

Executive Office of the President: a part of the executive branch appointed to serve the president. It consists of agencies such as the Office of Management and Budget and the National Security Council.

executive power: the blend of written constitutional provisions, custom, and person, that constitutes the power of the American presidency.

executive privilege: the power of a president to withhold information from Congress and the public.

extradition: a constitutional provision whereby a state shall surrender a fugitive to the state within whose jurisdiction the crime was committed.

fairness doctrine: a requirement by the Federal Communications Commission that radio and television broadcasters provide time for replies in case of personal attack and political editorial.

Federal Election Commission: a bipartisan commission that has the responsibility to enforce campaign finance laws and to administer public financing of presidential elections. The six-member commission is appointed by the president and confirmed by the Senate.

federalism: a system of government based on a constitutional separation of powers between a national government and component states.

The Federalist: a series of articles by Alexander Hamilton, James Madison, and John Jay providing a statement of the principles behind the proposed Constitution and urging its adoption.

Federalists: eighteenth-century Americans who supported a strong central government and favored ratification of the Constitution.

filibuster: extended debate by a single senator, or a group of senators, used to prevent a vote on a piece of legislation.

fiscal federalism: shared responsibility between the national and state (and local) governments for taxing and spending policies.

floor manager: the congressional member responsible for directing the floor action on a bill. Usually the bill's subcommittee chair or a senior committee member acts as floor manager.

Freedom of Information Act: passed in 1974, the FOIA makes available to citizens, upon request, all documents and records of the federal government and its agencies, except in some sensitive areas such as national security and law enforcement.

free-exercise clause: the part of the First Amendment that protects the right of individuals to worship as they choose.

Frost Belt: the area of the nation comprising the urban Northeast, factory regions of the Midwest, and the Northwest, known for its depressed economic climate and its political liberalism.

full faith and credit clause: a clause in Article IV of the Constitution requiring states to accept the laws, records, and court decisions (in noncriminal cases) of other states.

fundamental liberties: individual rights so basic to liberty and justice that they need not be enumerated in order to be protected.

fungibility: the ability to use revenue-sharing money in place of local tax receipts.

gag rule: court orders restricting the printing of information about criminal proceedings in cases where publication might violate the rights of a defendant or prejudice a prospective jury.

gatekeepers: media personnel who make the decisions on what information is used as news in the media.

gender gap: the tendency for men and women to vote differently in presidential elections. This tendency has increased in the 1980s.

generation gap: the tendency of voters under 30 years of age to vote differently from older voters.

gerrymandering: the drawing of electoral districts so as to disadvantage a political group at the polls; often results in oddly shaped districts.

Gibbons v. *Ogden:* the 1824 Supreme Court decision expanding national authority in interstate commerce.

Gitlow v. *New York:* the 1925 Supreme Court decision that for the first time held that a provision of the Bill of Rights could not be impaired by states any more than it could be by the national government.

Gramm-Rudman-Hollings: a congressional act mandating deficit reduction by automatic, across-the-board cuts in spending for five years to eliminate budget deficits.

grand jury: a jury used by trial courts to investigate accusations against persons charged with crime and indict them for trial.

grant-in-aid: a form of money payment from the national (or state) government to state (or local) governments for specified programs, under whatever conditions the granting authority wishes to impose.

Great Compromise: the compromise at the Constitutional Convention that resulted in a two-chamber Congress, with Senate membership based on equality of the states and membership in the House of Representatives based on population. Also known as the Connecticut Compromise.

Great Society: President Lyndon Johnson's program designed to end poverty and racial injustice through governmental social engineering.

Griswold v. *Connecticut:* the 1965 Supreme Court decision recognizing the right to privacy as a constitutionally protected freedom.

Gulf of Tonkin Resolution: the 1964 act of Congress authorizing the president to send troops to protect any area seeking American help "in defense of its freedom." This power was used by the Johnson administration to escalate and sustain the war effort in Vietnam.

Gypsy Moths: moderate northeastern and midwestern Republican members of Congress who seek to lessen the impact of President Reagan's economic policies on their states.

hierarchical authority: a principle of organizational authority in which direction and orders come from the top down, in a pyramidal design.

home style: the manner in which legislators explain their Washington activity to their constituents.

horizontal federalism: the federal relationship between states, including the obligations imposed by Article IV of the Constitution.

impeachment: the constitutional provision for removing justices or a president from office. The House of Representatives is empowered to impeach (bring charges against), and the Senate, with the chief justice of the Supreme Court presiding, tries the case.

imperial presidency: the term used by Arthur Schlesinger, Jr., to describe the Nixon presidency and its lack of presidential accountability.

implementation: the function of bureaucratic agencies involving attempts to put into practice the policies established through legislation or executive order.

implied consent: a law in several states that says that by holding a driver's license, a person also has given consent to a blood-alcohol test if stopped on suspicion of driving while intoxicated.

implied powers: the powers of the national government that can be inferred from enumerated powers.

impoundment: executive refusal to spend funds appropriated by Congress.

in forma pauperis: requests made by indigent appellants using relaxed standards of the Supreme Court to ask for a review of their cases.

income protection: government payments that guarantee financial benefits to individuals by virtue of their age, income, or employment status.

incrementalism: an approach to policy implementation that involves consideration of only a limited number of alternatives and making only incremental modifications of past government activities.

incumbency: public officials in office running for reelection. Incumbents often attract voters because of their office and greater name recognition.

inherent powers: powers of the national government that flow not from the Constitution but from the fact that it exists as a government, such as the power to conduct foreign relations.

intensity: the strength of the political opinions held by a given individual.

interest group: a group of individuals who band together seeking the support and resources of others to achieve common goals. When the goal becomes to pressure government to enhance the group's objectives, it becomes a political pressure group.

intermestic politics: a growing awareness of the interrelationship between international affairs and domestic politics. International events affect domestic priorities just as domestic affairs influence international relations. The two words are combined to suggest this close relationship.

interstate compacts: legal and binding agreements between states made with the consent of Congress.

iron triangle: a three-sided symbiotic relationship among bureau chiefs, clientele groups, and congressional committees and subcommittees. The iron triangle establishes a continual policy process with the bureaucracy at the heart of the decision-making process.

isolationism: a theory of foreign policy that opposes international alliances, foreign aid, or trade with communist nations.

issue groups: interest groups that are formed in direct response to a specific public controversy. For example, the Right to Life Association was founded in response to the controversy over the 1973 Supreme Court decision permitting abortions.

issue voting: a growing tendency on the part of voters to take clear positions on issues and to cast their ballots on the basis of issues, instead of party identification or group affiliation.

item veto: the power to disapprove of and block passage of specific parts of a bill. The president does not have this power.

Jim Crow: a term used to refer to racial discrimination or segregation.

job specialization: the organizational principle that attempts to match competent people with a task required by the organization. Each task must be identified along with the necessary skills before an individual is recruited.

joint-stock colonies: colonies founded as commercial ventures by English trading companies.

judicial activism: a judicial style that involves a willingness on the part of the courts to test conventional boundaries of judicial action, playing an active role in shaping public policy.

judicial review: the power of the courts to interpret the Constitution, keeping all laws and actions of public officials consistent with the language and meaning of the Constitution. While not specifically provided for, the power of judicial review was assumed to the courts in the 1803 decision of *Marbury v. Madison*.

judicial self-restraint: a judicial doctrine that holds that judges should restrain from imposing their own values and policy preferences and should decide a case on its merit and according to established legal precedent.

jurisdiction: the authority of a court to hear and decide an issue brought before it.

justiciable disputes: actual disputes that may be settled by legal methods available to the court. Courts will hear only the cases and controversies that are justiciable.

Keynesian economics: the theory that government spending should be used to regulate the economy.

Koreagate: a congressional scandal of the late 1960s and early 1970s involving the testimony of Korean businessman Tongsun Park that he bribed congressmen for their continued support of U.S. economic and military aid to Korea.

legislative veto: congressional approval of executive agency rules and regulations prior to their implementation. The Supreme Court ruled the legislative veto unconstitutional in 1983.

libel: written or spoken statements, known to be false, that defame a person's character or reputation.

Liberty Federation: The renamed moral majority, combined with some other fundamentalist religious groups. It is headed by evangelist minister Rev. Jerry Falwell.

lobbying: a form of communication whereby an interest group interacts with public officials for the purpose of influencing decision making.

loophole or winner-take-all primary: presidential primaries in which the winning candidate receives all the state's convention delegates, regardless of how slim the margin of victory.

The Magna Carta: an English document, signed in 1215, affirming that the power of the king was not absolute.

majority floor leader of the Senate: the leader of the majority party and the ranking official in the Senate.

majority opinion: the judicial statement supporting a decision made by a majority of the justices. If the chief justice voted in the majority, he can write the opinion or assign it to one of the other justices in the majority.

majority rule: the principle of democracy that holds that the greatest number of citizens should have their way, as in elections or in choosing policy.

Management by Objectives (MBO): a management system that requires agencies to identify short- and long-term objectives and then establish techniques to monitor the achievement of those objectives.

mark-up: the committee draft of a bill. Each line is amended or rewritten in the form the committee or subcommittee chooses.

McCarran Act: a 1950 act of Congress that required Communists and communist organizations to register with the Subversive Activities Control Board.

McCulloch v. Maryland: the 1819 Supreme Court decision affirming that Congress had certain implied powers in addition to those specifically enumerated in the Constitution. This set the stage for expansion of national authority.

midterm referendum: the term referring to the off-year, or midterm, congressional election that constitutes a referendum on the president's performance over the previous two years.

Miranda v. Arizona: the Supreme Court decision that detailed the principles governing police interrogation.

Moral Majority: a conservative, Christian political interest group founded by evangelist Jerry Falwell. It has backed political candidates and campaigned for Christian issues in elections. Renamed Liberty Federation in 1986.

Mutually Assured Destruction: the policy of nuclear deterrence that assures massive nuclear retaliation for any first use of nuclear weapons in a military attack against the United States.

national committee: the national party organization responsible for setting up the process for the national nominating convention.

natural rights: inherent, inalienable human rights, such as life, liberty, and property.

new federalism: Ronald Reagan's proposal of returning social and economic programs from the federal government to the states.

New Jersey Plan: a plan submitted to the Constitutional Convention that differed little from the Articles of Confederation. It called for a plural executive with limited authority and equal representation in Congress for each state regardless of population.

no-preference position: the doctrine that holds that government may support religion but cannot show any preference to one religion over another.

normal vote: electoral behavior based on stable patterns of partisan loyalty and group affiliation, which are adjusted for short-term variations. The normal vote examines partisan tendencies within socioeconomic groupings to make predictions.

nuclear freeze: a nonbinding congressional resolution calling on the United States and the Soviet Union to freeze production, testing, and deployment of nuclear weapons.

objective influence: the ability of an interest group to make good its demands upon government through direct personal contact with political officials.

obscenity: a lewd or indecent publication expressing or presenting something offensive that appeals to the prurient interest.

occupational groups: a classification of interest groups by occupation. This typical categorization of interest groups is dominated by business and labor groups.

office block (Massachusetts) ballot: a form of ballot that lists candidates by the office sought. Party affiliation is noted after the candidate, but straight party voting is difficult.

open primary: a form of political election in which any qualified voter may participate simply by showing up at the polls. No statement of party support is required; the voter is merely asked to choose one party ballot or the other.

operational liberals: persons indicating approval for specific programs involving government policy and power, such as compulsory medical insurance and low-rent housing.

opinion of the Court: the majority opinion of the Court that represents the official reasoning of the Court in rendering its decision.

overlapping membership: the tendency for individuals to belong to more than one interest group. These memberships may be "crosscutting" and lead to a conflict in views and activities.

oversight: the continuous supervision over the programs and agencies administering congressional legislation.

party caucus: the party conference, consisting of all party members in the legislative chamber.

party column (Indiana) ballot: a form of ballot that lists candidates by parties in straight columns.

party identification: citizen loyalty to one of the two political parties. Partisan attachment begins early in life and is an enduring feature of American politics. In recent years, party identification has been on the decline.

Pendleton Act: the 1883 act of Congress creating the civil service system.

penumbras: zones of privacy emanating from several provisions in the Bill of Rights, particularly the First Amendment. Penumbras were used by the Supreme Court as the basis for its 1965 recognition of the right to privacy as a constitutionally protected freedom.

per curium opinion: a short, unsigned judicial statement of a decision of the Supreme Court, used for relatively simple cases that command a strong majority.

peripheral voters: individuals who come out only because of presidential elections and normally do not vote in off-year elections.

perquisites: allowances for travel, postage, and hiring of staff employees that supplement a legislator's salary.

petit jury: a jury used to weigh evidence and decide the issues of a trial in court.

plain view evidence: evidence of a crime uncovered as a result of legitimate search for evidence for an unrelated crime. Courts allow such evidence to be admitted in a trial even though it was not the product of a search warrant.

Planning, Programming, Budgeting System (PPBS): a comprehensive budget process that requires federal departments to define their goals precisely and to measure the costs and benefits of alternative programs to achieve those goals.

platform: the document, written at the national convention, that specifies a party's position on issues.

Plessy v. Ferguson: the 1896 Supreme Court decision establishing the separate-but-equal doctrine.

plural decisions: decisions made by the Supreme Court in which no one line of reasoning can command a majority. These decisions find three or four judges taking one position, one or two justices concurring in part and dissenting in part, and three or four judges dissenting. Thus, a majority is formed only to render decisions.

plurality: the largest number of voters.

pocket veto: a veto occurring when Congress adjourns within ten days after sending to the president a bill upon which he takes no action.

Policy and Steering Committee: a 24-person committee composed of House Democratic leaders. Its primary function is to recommend positions on legislation and assign House Democrats to committees.

policy initiation: the suggestion of new policies and programs. It is usually filtered up through an agency to the department secretary and on to the president.

political action committees (PACs): a legal method for labor unions, professional associations, corporations, or other organizations to solicit funds to be spent for political purposes.

political amateurs: individuals who are politically motivated by issues or attachment to a candidate, not by party loyalty.

political efficacy: an individual's attitude about his or her effectiveness in influencing the government.

political speech: political advertising and campaigning are forms of free speech covered under the First Amendment. Political speech is basic to the democratic process.

Posse Comitatus: meaning "power of the country," an ultraconservative political group, primarily in the Midwest, that believes in no government above the county level. The group also believes in vigilante justice and common law.

postindustrial society: a mature economy based on technology and service delivery. It is heavily dependent on government fiscal and regulatory policies.

Presidential Character: a study by James David Barber attempting to explain the crisis of presidential leadership in terms of individual character.

presidential immunity: the protection of a president against any lawsuit for any official act performed while in office.

prior restraint: the power of government to require approval before information can be communicated. In most instances, prior restraint is prohibited under the First Amendment.

private law: statutory law regulating the relationships between private citizens in such areas as marriage, divorce, wills, deeds, and contracts.

privatization: selling to private enterprise of any number of government functions as a way to reduce the scope and cost of government.

privileges and immunities: a clause in Article IV of the Constitution extending to citizens of other states the full protection of state law, access to state courts, and nondiscriminatory treatment.

probable cause: the basis upon which a search warrant is issued and, thus, a necessary condition for police searches.

procedural democracy: the process whereby citizens confer legitimacy on public officials. Procedural democracy stresses the importance of the mechanisms for popular government, in particular, the electoral system.

procedural due process: the aspect of due process that refers to the fairness with which laws are enforced.

proprietary colonies: land grants in America to friends of the Crown, bestowing on the proprietor virtually sole power over the territory.

public interest groups: interest groups that claim to seek goals that will benefit society in general rather than narrow, special interests.

public law: legal regulations and obligations that apply to public officials, in their capacity as public officials. The public law is concerned with the definition, regulation, and enforcement of rights and obligations where the state is the subject of the right or the object of the obligation.

quota sample: a method used in opinion polling in which members of various groups are surveyed in proportion to their percentage in the population as a whole.

random sample: a method used in opinion polling in which people surveyed are selected completely by chance.

Reaganomics: the term applied to Reagan's economic philosophy of reduced federal spending and tax cuts to enhance private economic activity.

realignment: the alteration of political party loyalty by large numbers of persons for an extended period of time. Party preference changes such that the minority party becomes the preferred and dominant party.

reapportionment: the mandatory redrawing by state legislatures of congressional and state legislative boundaries every ten years, after the decennial census.

reconciliation: a part of the congressional budget process whereby the final budget resolution setting spending limits can be adjusted to meet new congressional decisions on appropriations.

Reed v. Reed: the 1971 Supreme Court decision that for the first time offered equal protection guarantees against sex discrimination, under the Fourteenth Amendment.

registration: the physical act of establishing legal qualification to vote. To be eligible to vote a citizen must meet minimum age and residency requirements.

regulatory agency: a government agency specifically designed to regulate some sector of national life while remaining outside executive and congressional control.

representative democracy: a government in which the people select representatives to make and enforce laws on their behalf.

republic: a form of government in which people do not govern directly but consent to representatives who make and administer laws for the people.

republicanism: a system of mixed government intended to prevent people from having either an interest in subverting, or a power to subvert, the government.

reserved powers: the term used in reference to state powers. The Tenth Amendment reserved for the states all

Credits

Figures

Chapter One **8,** Figure 1-1 from Warren Miller, Arthur Miller, and Edward Schneider, *American National Election Studies Data Sourcebook*, Cambridge, Mass.: Harvard University Press, 1980. Data for 1980 and 1984 from ICPSR National Election Studies Center for Political Studies. **9,** Figure 1-2 from *Public Opinion*, April/May 1985, p. 39.1 **16,** Figure 1-3 from *Statistical Abstract*, 1981. **17,** Figure 1-4 from *Statistical Abstract*, 1985. **18,** Figure 1-5 from U.S. Bureau of the Census, *Pocket Book Data*, 1976; 1980 data, Bureau of the Census. **19,** Figure 1-6 from *Money Income and Poverty Status of Families and Persons in the United States: 1984*, Bureau of the Census. **20,** Figure 1-7 from *Statistical Abstract*, 1981; the data for the 1980s are from Bureau of Labor Statistics, *CPI Detailed Report*, and *Employment and Earnings*. **22,** Figure 1-8 from *Federal Budget*, Office of Management and Budget, 1987. **23,** Figure 1-9 from *Statistical Abstract*, 1981; and *Federal Budget*, Office of Management and Budget, 1987. **24,** Figure 1-10 from *Statistical Abstract*, 1962 and 1981; data for 1985 from *Federal Budget*, Office of Management and Budget, 1987. **28,** Figure 1-11 from Gallup Polls. **31,** Figure 1-12 from *U.S. Government Manual*, 1985–1986, Office of the Federal Register.

Chapter Three **101,** Figure 3-2 from *Statistical Abstract*, 1981.

Chapter Nine **337,** Figure 9-10 data compiled from returns reported in *Congressional Quarterly*, 1950–1984.

Chapter Eleven **425,** Figure 11-1 from *The American Electorate: Attitudes and Action*, by Bruce A. Campbell. Copyright © 1979 by Holt, Rinehart & Winston. Reprinted by permission of Holt, Rinehart & Winston. **442,** Figure 11-3 from *Democracy in the Administrative State*, by Emmette S. Redford. Copyright © 1969 by Oxford University Press, Inc. Reprinted by permission. **448,** Figure 11-4 from David V. Edwards, *The American Political Experience: An Introduction to Government*, © 1979, p. 217. Reprinted by permission of Prentice-Hall, Inc., Englewood Cliffs, N.J.

Photos

Chapter One **3:** (top) Claude Johner, Gamma/Liaison; (middle) Owen Franken, SYGMA; (bottom) Gamma/Liaison; **4:** (left) Elizabeth Hamlin, Stock Boston, Inc.; (right) UPI/Bettmann Newsphotos; **10:** Peter Menzel, Stock Boston, Inc.; **14:** Bruce Kliewe, Jeroboam, Inc.; **15:** (top) AP/Wide World Photos, Inc.; (bottom) Allan Tannenbaum, SYGMA; **17:** Elizabeth Crews, Stock Boston, Inc.; **20:** © Alon Reininger 1984, Woodfin Camp & Associates.

Chapter Two **39:** (both) Library of Congress; **42:** Culver Pictures; **43:** The Granger Collection; **46:** Library of Congress; **57:** (top) Library of Congress; (bottom) Brown Brothers; **61:** AP/Wide World Photos, Inc; **68:** (left) Brown Brothers; (right) Jean-Louis Atlan, SYGMA; **71:** Nixon Library; **75:** A. Brucelle, SYGMA; **76:** Michael Grecco, Stock Boston, Inc.

Chapter Three **83 & 85:** Wide World Photos, Inc.; **87:** © Douglas Kirkland 1984, Woodfin Camp & Associates; **98:** Chris Reeberg, DPI, Inc.; **100:** Frank Siteman, Stock Boston, Inc.; **103:** © Alon Reininger 1984, Woodfin Camp & Associates; **109:** United States Army.

Chapter Four **120:** Bonnie Hawthorne; **127 & 129:** AP/Wide World Photos, Inc.; **130:** (margin) Library of Congress; (left) Baughman, SYGMA; (right) Owen Franken, Stock Boston, Inc.; **132:** © Jim Anderson 1982, Stock Boston, Inc.; **136:** Michelle Bogre, Black Star, Inc.; **138:** UPI/Bettmann Newsphotos; **141:** Matt Mahurin, TIME Magazine, Inc.; **142:** © Dan Budnik 1983, Woodfin Camp & Associates; **143:** AP/Wide World Photos, Inc.; **145:** © John Lei, OPI.

Chapter Five **162:** (top left) UPI/Bettmann Newsphotos; (top right) AP/Wide World Photos, Inc.; (middle both) UPI/Bettmann Newsphotos; (center) © James Karalas, DPI; (bottom) Barbara Alper, Stock Boston, Inc.; **163:** Topeka Capital Journal; **169:** Barbara Alper, Stock Boston, Inc.; **172:** AP/Wide World Photos, Inc.; **176:** © Tyrone Hall, Stock Boston, Inc.; **178:** United States Marine Corps; **181:** © Charles Gupton, Stock Boston, Inc.; **183:** © Olivier

Rebbot, Woodfin Camp & Associates; **186:** Cary Wolinsky, Stock Boston, Inc.; **197:** AP/Wide World Photos, Inc.; **198:** (top left) SYGMA; (top right) Ellis Herwig, Stock Boston, Inc.; (bottom) Elizabeth Hamlin, Stock Boston, Inc.

Chapter Six   212: Jean-Louis Atlan, SYGMA; **215:** AP/Wide World Photos, Inc.; **220:** John Running, Stock Boston, Inc.; **224:** (left) AP/Wide World Photos, Inc.; (right) Bernard Bisson, SYGMA; **225:** (left) Kyriasis, SYGMA; (right) AP/Wide World Photos, Inc.; **227:** Atlan, SYGMA; **235:** T. C. Fitzgerald, The Picture Cube; **238:** UPI/Bettmann Newsphotos; **242:** Office of Assemblyman Sam Farr.

Chapter Seven   251: Judy S. Gelles, Stock Boston, Inc.; **255:** (left) UPI/Bettmann Newsphotos; (right) Judy Sloan, Gamma/Liaison; **257, 258, 261, & 270:** AP/Wide World Photos, Inc.

Chapter Eight   286: Diego Goldberg, SYGMA; **288:** (left) Brown Brothers; (right) Owen Franken, Stock Boston, Inc.; **295:** (left) Owen Franken, Stock Boston, Inc.; (right) Michael Haymen, Stock Boston, Inc.; **298:** AP/Wide World Photos, Inc.; **303:** UPI/Bettmann Newsphotos; **307:** (left) Randy Taylor, SYGMA; (right) © Bill Stanton, Magnum; (bottom) AP/Wide World Photos, Inc.

Chapter Nine   318: Historical Pictures Service; **319:** Owen Franken, Stock Boston, Inc.; **325:** Diego Goldberg, SYGMA; **336:** AP/Wide World Photos, Inc.; **344:** (top both) AP/Wide World Photos, Inc.; (middle left) Ira Wyman, SYGMA; (middle center) UPI/Bettmann Newsphotos; (middle right) David Burnett, Woodfin Camp & Associates; (bottom left) AP/Wide World Photos, Inc.; (bottom right) © John Crispin 1984, Woodfin Camp & Associates;

351: George Bellrose, Stock Boston, Inc.; **369:** Owen Franken, Stock Boston, Inc.

Chapter Ten   376: © Shelly Katz 1981, Black Star; **382:** (top) John Zimmerman, Black Star; (middle left) UPI/Bettmann Newsphotos; (middle right) Library of Congress; (bottom left) The Carter Library; (bottom right) The Granger Collection; **387:** The White House; **397:** A. Nogues, SYGMA; **399:** (both) AP/Wide World Photos, Inc.; **416:** (top) AP/Wide World Photos, Inc.; (bottom) J. P. Laffont, SYGMA; **418:** Library of Congress.

Chapter Eleven   426: (left) Library of Congress; (right) Michael Weisbrot, Stock Boston, Inc.; **433:** (top) The Granger Collection; (bottom) Stacy Pick 1984, Stock Boston, Inc.; **438:** Library of Congress; **439:** R. Taylor, SYGMA; **441:** (left) AP/Wide World Photos, Inc.; (right) Evan Johnson, Jeroboam, Inc.; **447 & 457:** Judy K. Blamer, Brooks/Cole.

Chapter Twelve   470: UPI/Bettmann Newsphotos; **479:** Judy Sloan, Gamma/Liasion; **480:** UPI/Bettmann Newsphotos; **482:** Historical Pictures; **493:** © John Marmaras, Woodfin Camp & Associates; **510:** Fred Ward, Black Star.

Chapter Thirteen   528: AP/Wide World Photos, Inc.; **533:** (left) AP/Wide World Photos, Inc.; (right) American Petroleum Institute; **535:** Library of Congress; **550:** AP/Wide World Photos, Inc.; **551:** Dennis Brack, Black Star; **559:** Daniel S. Brady, Stock Boston, Inc.; **564:** The White House; **567:** Yochi R. Okamoto, Photo Researchers, Inc.

Chapter Fourteen   577: Owen Franken, SYGMA; **580:** AP/Wide World Photos, Inc.; **582:** Suzanne Mulhauser, SYGMA; **586:** AP/Wide World Photos, Inc.

Index